People
in the News
1996

Also by David Brownstone and Irene Franck

Timelines of the 20th Century
Timelines of War: A Chronology of Warfare from 100,000 BC to the Present
Timelines of the Arts and Literature
Women's World: A Timeline of Women in History
Dictionary of 20th Century History
20th Century Culture: A Dictionary of the Arts and Literature of Our Time
Parent's Desk Reference
Women's Desk Reference
The Green Encyclopedia
Island of Hope, Island of Tears: The Great Migration Through Ellis Island
  to America Told by Those Who Made the Passage
The Silk Road: A History
To the Ends of the Earth: The Great Travel and Trade Routes of Human History
Work Throughout History series
America's Ethnic Heritage series
Historic Places of Early America
Natural Wonders of America
Great Historic Places of America
On the Tip of Your Tongue: The Word / Name / Place Finder
Where to Find Business Information

People in the News 1996

David Brownstone

Irene Franck

MACMILLAN LIBRARY REFERENCE USA
Simon & Schuster Macmillan
NEW YORK
Prentice Hall International
LONDON   MEXICO CITY   NEW DELHI   SINGAPORE   SYDNEY   TORONTO

Acknowledgments for illustrative materials are on pp. 427–429, which shall be considered a continuation of the copyright page.

Macmillan Library Reference USA
Simon & Schuster Macmillan
1633 Broadway
New York, NY 10019

Library of Congress Catalog Card Number: 91-14962

Printed in the United States of America

Printing number

1   2   3   4   5   6   7   8   9   10

ISSN: 1062-2713
ISBN: 0-02-860279-X

Library of Congress Cataloging-in-Publication Data

The Library of Congress has catalogued the first edition of this serial as follows:

Brownstone, David M.
   People in the news / David Brownstone and Irene Franck.
    p. cm.
   Includes bibliographical references and index.
   Summary: Presents clear, up-to-date biographical information on a wide selection of the most newsworthy people in the world.
   ISBN 0-02-897073-X (1991 Edition)
   1. Celebrities—Biography—Juvenile literature.   2. Biography—20th century—Juvenile literature. [1. Celebrities. 2. Biography.] I. Franck, Irene M.   II. Title.
CT120.B76   1991   91-14962
920—dc20   CIP

The paper used in this publication meets the minimum requirements of American National Standard for Information Sciences—Permanence of Paper of Printed Library Materials, ANSI Z39.48-1984 ∞ ™

Contents

Preface

As in previous editions of *People in the News*, we have in this sixth edition developed current profiles of a wide selection of the world's most newsworthy people—the presidents, prime ministers, generals, musicians, film stars, directors, scientists, doctors, sports notables, business leaders, spies, criminals, victims, writers, judges, and the rest who are the main stuff of day-to-day reportage on screen and radio, and in print throughout the year. People are selected for inclusion on the basis of their current activities and importance, not on their past achievements or celebrity status alone. The profile for each person first stresses 1995 activities, giving an up-to-date précis of the major events of the year for that person, then presents a concise biography, and finally offers a further reading list, for readers who want to dig deeper into the person's current and past history. Each obituary offers a capsule overview of the person's life, also with a further reading list.

Each volume of *People in the News* covers approximately 500 living and currently active people and 200 obituaries. Because newsmaking activities come and go, and fame can be fleeting, some people appear only once, and others drop in and out of the series, while new people arrive to take their places. Each edition has somewhat different emphases, depending on current events. The current "Republican revolution" in the U.S. Congress and the start of the campaign for the Republican presidential nomination has dictated a substantial complement of politicians in this edition. As usual, we have included people involved in several high-profile criminal cases, not just the O. J. Simpson trial but also John Salvi III, Colin Ferguson, Omar Abdel Rahman, and key figures relating to the April 1995 Oklahoma City bombing. Also as usual, we have included a mix of new celebrities, such as songwriter-singer-producer Babyface (Kenny Edmonds), basketball star Grant Hill, singer Sheryl Crow, author Carol Shields, actor Hugh Grant, and astronaut Norman Thagard, and established figures whose activites have brought them back into the news, such as author William Burroughs, singer-actress Julie Andrews, evangelist Billy Graham, singer Joni Mitchell, Olympic-gold-medalist diver Greg Louganis, Apollo 13 astronaut Jim Lovell, World Series MVP pitcher Tom Glavine, and neurologist-author Oliver Sacks. Figures newly emerged on the political and social scene are also included, such as new

NAACP head (and former U.S. Congressman) Kweisi Mfume, AFL-CIO leader John Sweeney, and Lonnie Bristow, the first African-American president of the American Medical Association.

One noteworthy aspect of this edition, and a sign of the times, is that of the 200 obituaries, six were for people over 100 years old: director George Abbott, public relations luminary Edward Bernays, musical theater star Dorothy Dickson, political matriarch Rose Fitzgerald Kennedy, journalist-writer George Seldes, and best-selling author Bessie Delany; several others were just months short of their centenaries. By contrast, at least two obituaries were of young people whose lives have been cut short by AIDS: rap star Eazy-E (Eric Wright) and writer Paul Monette.

Because of our focus on currently active people and on their most recent newsworthy activities, approximately 75-80 percent of the material in each edition of *People in the News* is completely new, even though many of the people in any single edition will have been profiled in one or more previous editions. That will remain so, given the nature of the work, because for each person material from previous years is condensed and merged into the background biographies, leaving room for coverage of their current activities, which usually forms the largest portion of the entry. Entries on living people are current to the end of 1995, and sometimes a bit later. Suggestions for further reading have also been updated, with newer bibliographic citations added and older ones dropped. Note that for people with massive bibliographies, such as Bill Clinton, we include periodical references only for 1995; readers seeking older material can check previous editions.

Each edition of *People in the News* is organized alphabetically, and so is self-indexed. However, as in the second and subsequent editions, we have also included a cumulative alphabetical index and a cumulative occupational index, which cover the first six editions of *People in the News*. These make it possible for readers to quickly and easily reach the whole set of people who appeared in any edition of *People in the News*. In response to several requests, beginning with the fifth edition, we added to the index an asterisk next to those entries where a photograph of the person appears; this feature covers all six editions and should be especially helpful to students who need to locate photographs of people for reports.

Our thanks once again to Philip Friedman, former president and publisher of Macmillan Reference; his assistant, Emily Skolnik; our new editor, Catherine Carter; managing editor Andrew Ambraziejus; copyeditors Sabrina Bowers and Michael Burke; and cover designer Mike McIver who have all, once again, so capably seen this book through the publishing process. Our thanks also to our expert photo researchers, visual resources consultants Susan Hormuth and Rudi Schreiber, and to Mary Racette for her invaluable assistance in organizing the research materials and bibliographies. We also again thank the staff of the Chappaqua Library: Director Mark Hasskarl; the expert reference staff, including Martha Alcott, Teresa Bueti, Maryanne Eaton, Sue Farber, Carolyn Jones, Jane Peyraud, Paula Peyraud, and Carolyn Reznick; and the circulation staff, including Marilyn Coleman and Jane McKean—and their colleagues throughout the northeastern library network, who have as always been so helpful in fulfilling our research needs. And finally thanks to the other librarians who have written to us with helpful comments about *People in the News* and suggestions for ways to make it even better.

David Brownstone
Irene Franck
Chappaqua, New York

Abbott, George Francis (1887–1995)

Celebrated producer, director, playwright, and actor George Abbott, who died at the age of 107, made his Broadway acting debut in 1913, in *The Misleading Lady*. He emerged as a leading playwright in the 1920s, his breakthrough coming with *Broadway* (1926), coauthored with Philip Dunning, which Abbott also directed. In the same year, he directed *Chicago*, and in 1927 directed Helen Hayes in *Coquette*.

In a career that spanned 81 years, Abbott became a legendary figure, writing and in some instances directing and producing such works as *Three Men on a Horse* (1935), *Where's Charley* (1948), *The Pajama Game* (1954), *Damn Yankees* (1955), and *Fiorello* (1959). Among the other plays he directed were *Jumbo* (1935), *On Your Toes* (1936), *The Boys From Syracuse* (1938), *Pal Joey* (1940), and *On the Town* (1944). He also wrote, directed, or produced almost a score of films, from the late 1920s through the film versions of *The Pajama Game* (1957) and *Damn Yankees* (1958). Abbott continued working into his eleventh decade; in 1994, he was actively associated with a revival of *Damn Yankees*. He was survived by his third wife, Joy. (d. Miami; January 31, 1995)

FURTHER READING

"Mister Broadway." JACK KROLL. *Newsweek*, Feb. 13, 1995.
"Exit the master. . . ." *People*, Feb. 13, 1995.
Obituary. *Independent*, Feb. 2, 1995.
Obituary. *Times* (of London), Feb. 2, 1995.
Obituary. *New York Times*, Feb. 2, 1995.
Obituary. *Variety*, Feb. 2, 1995.

Abdelgani, Amir: See Abdel Rahman, Omar.

Abdelghani, Fadil: See Abdel Rahman, Omar.

Abdel Rahman, Omar (1938–) On October 1, 1995, after a trial that had begun with jury selections on January 9, Sheik Omar Abdel Rahman and nine other defendants were convicted by a federal jury of having conspired to commit a series of assassinations and bombings of major buildings in New York City. Some of the actions that were part of the alleged conspiracy: the 1993 World Trade Center bombing, an aborted bombing of the United Nations, and the 1990 murder of Rabbi Meir Kahane, as well as a considerable range of other terrorist plans, including the projected assassination of Egyptian president Hosni Mubarak. The trial was part of the series of investigations and trials stemming from the massive World Trade Center bombing, which killed six people, injured at least 1,000, and caused enormous damage, but Abdel Rahman and the other defendants were not accused or convicted of specific involvement in that bombing. The convictions, somewhat unusual in that they were based largely on a post–Civil War seditious conspiracy law, were to be appealed by the defense.

On January 16, 1996, federal District Court judge Michael B. Mukasey sentenced Abdel Rahman to life imprisonment and nine codefendants to long prison terms. Defendant **El Sayyid A. Nosair** (1957–), a Jersey City maintenance worker, was convicted on a wide range of charges, including the 1990 murder of Rabbi Meir Kahane; he was sentenced to life imprisonment. He and his cousin, defendant **Ibraham A. Elgabrony** (El-Gabrowny; 1952–), were found not guilty of one aspect of the bombing conspiracy. Brooklyn resident Elgabrony, convicted on many other charges, received a 57-year prison sentence.

Four defendants received 35-year sentences: **Victor Alvarez** (1967–), a Puerto Rican-born Jersey City stock clerk; **Tarig Elhassan** (1956–), a Sudanese-born Manhattan handyman, painter, and former cab driver; **Clement Hampton-El** (1939–), a Brooklyn hospital lab technician who had fought in Afghanistan; and **Mohammed Saleh** (1957–), a Palestinian from Jordan who owned a Yonkers gas station. **Fares Khallafalla** (1963–), a Sudanese-born Jersey City resident, and **Amir Abdelgani** (1961–), a Sudanese-born Jersey City cab driver, received 30-year sentences. Abdelgani's cousin, **Fadil Abdelghani** (1963–), a Brooklyn resident, received a 25-year sentence.

Egyptian Islamic fundamentalist cleric Omar Abdel Rahman, blind since childhood, began his long career as an antigovernment activist in the late 1960s. Arrested several times by Egypt's Nasser and Sadat governments, he was believed to have been a leading influence in the terrorist Islamic Jihad, though his exact status vis-à-vis that organization and other terrorist groups has never been clear. He fled Egypt in 1976, returning in 1980. In 1981, he was charged with complicity in the assassination of President Anwar Sadat but was acquitted in 1984, held under house arrest, and then allowed to travel abroad. He arrived in the United States in 1990 and was accused of complicity but not indicted in connection with the 1990 murder of Rabbi Meir Kahane. He was also involved in a series of government hearings as to his immigration and possible asylum status through 1992, while at the same time building a following at Jersey City's Magjid-al-Salaam mosque. Abdel Rahman attended the Cairo University theology school and Cairo's Al Azhar University. He is reportedly married, with ten children.

FURTHER READING

"Defending Islam. . . ." WILLIAM DOWELL. *Time*, Oct. 9, 1995.
Two Seconds Under the World. JIM DWYER. Crown, 1994.
"Scouring the Koran. . . ." JEFFERY L. SHELER. *U.S. News & World Report*, Aug. 16, 1993.
"How the Sheik got in." JAY PETERZELL. *Time*, May 24, 1993.
"The trail of the sheikh. . . ." MARY ANNE WEAVER. *New Yorker*, Apr. 12, 1993
"Bloody Sheikh. . . ." JUDITH MILLER. *New Republic*, Mar. 29, 1993.
"Sheik Omar speaks out." "A voice of holy war." JILL SMOLOWE. *Time*, Mar. 15, 1993.

Abdul, Paula (1962–) Singer, dancer, and choreographer Paula Abdul was once again a highly visible recording artist in 1995, as her first album in four years, *Head Over Heels*, headed for the upper ranges of the charts, with such songs as "My Love Is For Real," "Crazy Cool," "Ain't Never Gonna Give You Up," "Love Don't Come Easy," and "Sexy Thoughts." "My Love Is For Real," the first single drawn from the album, featured an Arab-world style and quickly became a hit in radio airplay, landing on the Billboard top 40 soon after its release. It was followed by a second hit, the popular dance-style single "Crazy Cool," and then by the pop-funk single "Ain't Never Gonna Give You Up," with Abdul singing opposite Color Me Badd. By year's end, the album was clearly headed for its first million sales.

Abdul had recently come through a difficult period that included a highly publicized marriage and divorce from actor Emilio Estevez and a successful fight against bulimia, which included a stay in a psychiatric clinic. She had also finally won a lawsuit in which another singer charged that her voice had been used without permission in a previous Abdul album. Abdul's hit 1995 album and singles represented a major career turnaround.

Of Syrian, Brazilian, and French-Canadian descent, California-born Abdul studied tap and jazz dancing as a child, performing summers in a traveling group. She began her work as a choreographer during her six-year engagement as one of the Laker Girls, cheerleaders at the Los Angeles Lakers basketball games. In 1984, she also began to choreograph for Michael Jackson and his brothers, then for Janet Jackson and other entertainment figures, including the Pointer Sisters, Eddie Murphy in *Coming to America*, and Tracey Ullman. She won an Emmy for her choreography of the "Tracey Ullman Show." In 1988, her career took an entirely new turn, as her first album, *Forever Your Girl*, hit the top of the best-seller charts with such hits as "Straight Up," "(It's Just) The Way That You Love Me," "Knocked Out," "Forever Your Girl," "Cold-Hearted," and "Opposites Attract." "Straight Up" was named the most performed song of 1989 by ASCAP (American Society of Composers, Authors and Publishers). Abdul also won a 1990 Emmy for her choreography of the American Music Awards. Her second hit album was *Shut Up and Dance (The Dance Mixes)* (1990), and her third was *Spellbound* (1991). She has also appeared in several videos, among them her music video *Under My Spell* (1993), filmed in Japan during her 1992 Asian tour. She attended California State University.

FURTHER READING

"Straight up. . . ." STEVE POND. *Us*, July 1995.
"A brave new song. . . ." KAREN S. SCHNEIDER. *People*, June 19, 1995.
Paula Abdul: Straight Up. M. THOMAS FORD. Dillon/Macmillan, 1992.
"Abdul, Paula." *Current Biography*, Sept. 1991.
Magic of Paula Abdul: Straight Up to Spellbound. DEVRA NEWBERGER. Scholastic, 1991.

Abdul-Jabbar, Kareem (Lew [Lewis Ferdinand] Alcindor; 1947–) The all-time leading scorer in National Basketball Association history, Kareem Abdul-Jabbar was inducted into the Basketball Hall of Fame in 1995, selected (to no one's surprise) in his first year of eligibility. Although he retired from the NBA after the 1988–89 season, he has hardly retired. He has various business, television, and movie interests, primarily in Los Angeles, his longtime home. He also continues to play basketball, leading a team of players on international exhibition tours. In 1995, it became the first team in 24 years to defeat the celebrated Harlem Globetrotters, ending their 8,829-game winning streak—actually defeating the Globetrotters twice in an 11-game series that was part of a European tour.

New York-born Lew Alcindor attended St. Jude grammar school and Power Memorial High School, where he immediately became a basketball star, and then the University of California at Los Angeles, receiving his B.S. in 1969. He played in only six losing games in high school (record: 95-6) and two in college (109–2), leading the UCLA team to three NCAA championships (1967–69). He was named the NCAA Tournament's most outstanding player and a member of the *Sporting News* All-America first team all three college championship years. He was also twice named *Sporting News* college player of the year (1967; 1969), and capped his career with the Naismith Award (1969). Converting to Islam in 1971, he changed his name to Kareem Abdul-Jabbar.

Turning professional, Abdul-Jabbar joined the Milwaukee Bucks (1969–75), was elected Rookie of the Year (1970), and won the NBA championship in 1971. He was then traded to the Los Angeles Lakers (1975–89), where, teamed with Earvin (Magic) Johnson, he won five more NBA championships (1980; 1982; 1985; 1987–88). He was twice named MVP of the NBA Finals (1971; 1985) and six times named the league's MVP (1971–72; 1974; 1976–77; 1980). In his two decades of professional play, he set records for seasons played (20), games played (1,560), minutes played (57,446), points scored (38,387), field goals attempted (28,307), field goals made (15,837), shots blocked (3,189), personal fouls (4,657), and All-Star games played (18; he was not selected in 1978, and was selected but did not play in 1973). Abdul-Jabbar published *Giant Steps: The Autobiography of Kareem Abdul-*

Jabbar (1983), written with Peter Knobler, and *Kareem* (1990), a diary covering his final NBA year, with Mignon McCarthy. He has also appeared as a guest star on numerous television shows and movies, including *The Fish That Saved Pittsburgh* (1979), *Airplane* (1980), and *Fletch* (1985). His marriage to Habiba Abdul-Jabbar (Janice Brown) ended in divorce; he has four children.

FURTHER READING

"Kareem Abdul-Jabbar." KENNETH SHOULER. *Sport,* Nov. 1995.
Kareem Abdul-Jabbar: Basketball Great. R. THOMAS COBOURN. Chelsea House, 1995.
Kareem Abdul-Jabbar. HELEN A. BORRELLO. Chelsea House, 1994.
American Jihad. STEVEN BARBOZA. Doubleday, 1994.
Kareem Abdul-Jabbar. WILLIAM R. SANFORD and CARL R. GREEN. Silver Burdett, 1993.
"Abdul-Jabbar's. . . ." MICHAEL FLEMING. *Variety,* May 4, 1992.
Kareem Abdul-Jabbar: Basketball Great. JACOB MARGOLIES. Watts, 1992.

Abu-Jamal, Mumia (1954–) On the night of December 9, 1981, at the corner of 13th and Locust Streets in downtown Philadelphia, White police officer Daniel Faulkner was shot and killed while on duty. Officer Faulkner had stopped African-American motorist

William Cook for a traffic infraction, and a dispute followed. Cook's brother, African-American journalist Mumia Abu-Jamal (then Wesley Cook), who was moonlighting as a cab driver, was passing by, saw the altercation, and stopped to intervene. He had a gun. What happened after that generated an explosively controversial murder case and an international campaign.

In 1982 Abu-Jamal was tried and convicted of the murder of Officer Faulkner, and sentenced to death by presiding judge Albert F. Sabo. Abu-Jamal then spent more than 13 years on Death Row, through a long series of unsuccessful appeals during which an increasingly wide and bitter controversy grew. Supporters of his conviction and death sentence maintained that the evidence of his guilt was overwhelming, that he had received a fair trial before a racially mixed jury, and that he had availed himself of a very long appeals process. His supporters maintained that he was innocent, charging that the evidence was tainted, the trial marred by police and judicial misconduct, his court-appointed defense crippled by incompetence and lack of funds, and that two African-Americans on the jury were too few for a fair trial.

Abu-Jamal was scheduled to be executed on August 17, 1995. But his lawyers instituted a last-ditch proceeding, demanding a new trial and producing a new witness who claimed that he had been on the scene 13 years before and that Abu-Jamal was innocent. Simultaneously, a wide range of celebrities issued an international appeal on his behalf. Judge Sabo, who presided over the new trial proceeding, issued an indefinite stay of execution on August 7. On September 15, he refused to grant a new trial.

Further appeals were expected, which might take several more years to complete. The controversy continued.

Abu-Jamal continued to write and publish while in prison, and in 1995 published the essay collection *Live From Death Row*.

Mumia Abu-Jamal was at the age of 15 a founding member of the Philadelphia chapter of the Black Panther Party, and continued to be an activist for African-Americans in the Philadelphia area in the years that followed, and a leading critic of the city's police force. He became a journalist and talk show host, and is a past president of the Philadelphia chapter of the National Association of Black Journalists.

FURTHER READING

"Death watch." JOE DAVIDSON. *Emerge,* Nov. 1995.
"Defense mechanism:. . ." GEORGE MANNES.
   Entertainment, Aug. 11, 1995.
"Book by. . . ." CALVIN REID. *Publishers Weekly,* May
   1, 1995.

Agassi, Andre Kirk (1970–) In early
1995, tennis great Andre Agassi continued the
strong play that had won him the 1994 U.S.
Open, in an astonishing comeback from a weak
1993 season and early 1994 wrist surgery. He
began 1995 ranked number two behind Pete
Sampras, whom he defeated in the finals of the
Australian Open. In April, he passed Sampras to
take the number one ranking. However, Agassi
lost the other 1995 Grand Slams, falling to Yevgeny Kafelnikov in the quarterfinals of the
French Open, to Boris Becker in the semifinals
of Wimbledon, and to Sampras in the finals of
the U.S. Open. Even so, by August he had racked
up a career record of seven tournaments wins.
But in September, during Davis Cup play,
Agassi was forced to the sidelines with a chest
muscle injury. He then had to sit out the rest of
the year, losing his number one ranking to Sampras in November. The strong but friendly rivalry between them was used in a television
commercial that showed them setting up a net
and playing on a Manhattan street.

Born in Las Vegas, Nevada, Agassi's early
career was marked by impatience, loss of concentration, and unforced errors. Though his
unconventional dress and personal style have
bothered some tennis purists, he has captured
crowds of all ages. After an early win at Itapa-
rica in 1987, he posted six wins in 1988. A leaner
1989 followed, with only a win at Orlando, where
he won again in 1991. He had four more wins in
1990, including the ATP Tour World Championship, and another in 1991, before his first Grand
Slam win in 1992 at Wimbledon.

FURTHER READING

"Sampras or. . . ." PETER DE JONGE. *New York Times
   Magazine,* Aug. 27, 1995.
"Educating Andre." MARTHA SHERRILL. *Esquire,* May
   1995.
"Crossfire! . . ." DAVID HIGDON. *Tennis,* May 1995.
Andre Agassi. RICHARD RAMBECK. *Childs World,* 1995.
"Taking care. . . ." DAVID HINGDON. *Tennis,* Dec. 1994.

*Agassi: The Fall and Rise of the Enfant Terrible of
   Tennis.* ROBERT PHILIP. Trafalgar, 1993.
"Agassi and ecstasy." CURRY KIRKPATRICK. *Sports
   Illustrated,* July 13, 1992.
"Agassi. . . ." RONALD ATKIN. *Observer,* July 12, 1992.

Aikman, Troy Kenneth (1966–) After
two consecutive Super Bowl championships,
Dallas Cowboys quarterback Troy Aikman entered 1995 looking for a third. It was not to be. In
mid-January, in the National Football Conference championships, the Dallas Cowboys were
demolished by the San Francisco 49ers, falling
behind by 21–0 early in the first quarter. Though
the Cowboys rallied to a final 38–28, the loss—
including three interceptions by Aikman—was
devastating. It was Aikman's first post-season
loss.

At the start of the 1995 season, the Cowboys
were focused on getting past the defending
champion 49ers for another run at the Super
Bowl. The 49ers had other ideas, and in mid-
November handed the Cowboys another devastating defeat. The Dallas team already had
injuries to key players, including a knee injury
to Aikman, which kept him out of several games.
From that point on, the Cowboys' play became
inconsistent and tempers frayed; even Aikman
was seen criticizing his teammates and coaches—indirectly, if not directly. Part of the problem was injuries and changes on the offensive
line, so Aikman no longer had the protection
needed for accurate passing; other teams increasingly saw Aikman as vulnerable. Even so,
the team ended the season with a 12–4 record,
second in the league behind Kansas City (13–3),
but first in the NFC. It remained to be seen
whether Aikman would be successful in rallying
his teammates for the post-season Super Bowl
drive.

Aikman himself was named to the Pro Bowl
behind rising quarterback Brett Favre. He
ended the 1995 regular season with a 64.8 percent completion rate (280 of 432 attempts) and
had produced 16 touchdowns, with 7 interceptions; his season rating was 93.6, which ranked
in third place among the league's quarterbacks.
In 1995, Aikman also published the autobiographical book *Things Change.*

Born in California, and raised there and in
Oklahoma, Aikman graduated from Henryetta
High School in Oklahoma and spent two years at

Oklahoma University before transferring to UCLA. There he led his team to wins at the 1988 Aloha Bowl, when he was named collegiate All-American, and the 1989 Cotton Bowl. His 64.8 percent completion record, for 5,298 yards and 41 touchdowns, with only 17 interceptions, made him the third-highest-rated passer ever in NCAA history. He was the top pick of the 1989 NFL college draft, selected by the Dallas Cowboys (1989–), which he led to two successive Super Bowl championships. He holds the career Super Bowl record for highest pass completion percentage (71.9) and the post-season career record for pass completion percentage (68.9), average gain (8.56 yards), and longest pass completion (94 yards). Aikman has been named to the Pro Bowl five times (1991–95), but he could not play in 1993 and 1995 due to injury. In 1993, he published *Reaching for the Stars*, coauthored with Roger Staubach and Jeanne T. Warren.

FURTHER READING

"Aikman." ED WERDER. *Sport,* July 1995.

"Aikman, Troy." *Current Biography,* May 1995.

Troy Aikman: All-American Quarterback. R. CONRAD STEIN. Childrens, 1995.

Sports Great Troy Aikman. GLEN MACNOW. Enslow, 1995.

Troy Aikman. CARL R. GREEN. Macmillan, 1994.

Troy Aikman, Quick-Draw Quarterback. JOEL DIPPOLD. Lerner, 1994.

"A rude awakening. . . ." PAUL ATTNER. *Sporting News,* Nov. 15, 1993.

"Troy's triumph." PAT JORDAN. *Playboy,* Oct. 1993.

Albright, Madeleine Korbel (1937–)

Reflecting her long and expert focus on Eastern European affairs, U.S. Ambassador to the United Nations Madeleine Albright continued to exert substantial influence on U.S. policy on the Bosnian War during 1995. As the UN ground peace-keeping mission in Bosnia foundered, she was an increasingly effective advocate in the UN and the Clinton administration of the air war and of the force-fed negotiation policies, which the United States eventually pushed through all the way to the U.S.-sponsored Dayton peace negotiations and subsequent peace treaty. At the UN, she was also chief American advocate of the whole range of Clinton administration policies, perhaps most notably as a strong proponent of continuing strong UN sanctions against Iraq, and in the fostering of the Middle East peace process.

Albright led the official U.S. delegation to the Fourth United Nations Conference on Women, held in Beijing (Sept. 4–15), strongly defending the U.S. decision to attend the conference despite China's poor human rights record, contending that the conference would spotlight that record very effectively. On the same grounds, she strongly defended First Lady Hillary Rodham Clinton's decision to attend the conference, and applauded her September 5 speech to the conference, which was highly critical of China's forced family planning policies, and of the kind of "son preference" that results in the murders of large numbers of female babies in several countries, by implication including China. On September 6, Albright addressed the conference in much the same way, adding that a White House Council on Women was to be formed, along with other actions aimed at furthering American women's rights.

Albright received her 1959 B.A. from Wellesley College; she also attended the Johns Hopkins School of Advanced International Studies (1962–63), and earned her M.A. and Ph.D. at Columbia University's Department of Public Law and Government. In 1976, she began her Washington career as a staff assistant to Senator Edmund Muskie, and from 1978 worked on the White House National Security Council staff. She was Research Professor of International Affairs and Director of Women in Foreign Service at Georgetown University's School of Foreign Service (1982–92), and president of the Center of National Policy (1989–92), as well as a foreign policy adviser in the Mondale, Dukakis, and Clinton presidential campaigns. She became U.S. Ambassador to the United Nations in 1993. Her books include *The Role of the Press in Political Change: Czechoslovakia 1968* (1976) and *Poland: The Role of the Press in Political Change* (1983). Albright is divorced and has three daughters.

FURTHER READING

"Why women's rights . . ." CINDI LEIVE. *Glamour,* Oct. 1995.

"Albright, Madeleine Korbel." *Current Biography,* May 1995.

"Clinton's gung-ho. . . ." RICHARD Z. CHESNOFF. *U.S. News & World Report,* Feb. 13, 1995.

U. N. Ambassador: A Behind-the-Scenes Look at

Madeleine Albright's World. ROBERT MAASS. Walker, 1995.

"Albright's mission. . . ." JACOB HEILBRUNN. *New Republic*, Aug. 22, 1994.

Alda, Alan (1936–)

In the film comedy *Canadian Bacon*, stage and screen star Alan Alda played a contemporary American president with a reputation for seeking peace and a pronounced tendency to say or do anything at all that would win him popularity with the voters—a resonant political comedy subject at a time of enormous popular disillusionment with politics and politicians. The late John Candy co-starred as Sheriff Bud Boomer, in a cast that included Rhea Perlman as Deputy Honey, Kevin Pollak as Stuart Smiley, and Rip Torn as General Dick Panzer. The film, written and directed by Michael Moore, was well received at the 1995 Cannes Film Festival, but received mixed reviews at its later New York opening.

Forthcoming for Alda were starring roles opposite Ben Stiller, Patricia Arquette, Mary Tyler Moore, and Lily Tomlin in the film *Flirting with Disaster*, written and directed by David O. Russell; and in a 1995 as-yet-untitled film written and directed by Woody Allen, in a cast that included Julia Roberts, Tim Roth, Judy Davis, Bette Midler, and Drew Barrymore.

New York-born Alda, the son of actor Robert Alda, appeared on the New York stage from the late 1950s in such plays as *Purlie Victorious* (1961), *The Owl and the Pussycat* (1964), and *The Apple Tree* (1966). He became a television star in the 1970s in *The Glass House* (1972), and then as Korean War surgeon Benjamin Franklin "Hawkeye" Pierce in the long-running series "M*A*S*H" (1972–83). He has also starred in such films as *The Moonshine War* (1970), *California Suite* (1978), *Same Time Next Year* (1978), and *The Seduction of Joe Tynan* (1979), and appeared in many other films, including *Crimes and Misdemeanors* (1989; he won the Directors Guild of America's best supporting actor award), *Whispers in the Dark* (1992), *Manhattan Murder Mystery* (1993), *And the Band Played On* (1993), and *White Mile* (1994). Alda wrote, directed, and starred in the films *The Four Seasons* (1981), *Sweet Liberty* (1986), and *Betsy's Wedding* (1989). He scored a 1992 Broadway stage success in *Jake's Women*.

Alda attended Fordham University. In 1957,

he married Arlene Weiss, with whom he wrote *The Last Days of M*A*S*H* (1984); they have three children.

FURTHER READING

"Alan Alda." JAMES BRADY. *Parade,* Dec. 31, 1995.
"Memories of M*A*S*H." CRAIG TOMASHOFF. *People,* Nov. 25, 1991.

Alexander, Jane (Jane Quigley; 1939–)

Celebrated actress and National Endowment for the Arts (NEA) head Jane Alexander spent much of 1995 resisting those who wanted to destroy the NEA—or to cut its funds so deeply as to accomplish much the same thing. The Christian Coalition's "Contract for the American Family" called for outright abolition of the NEA and the National Endowment for the Humanities (NEH). It found support in Congress, where many Republicans and several Republican presidential candidates called either for dismantling the NEA or for quickly ending its funding, some charging that the NEA fosters "pornography" and is "left-wing-oriented." In late June, early in the long federal budget fight, the Republican-dominated Congress voted to "phase out" NEA funding, the House over a two-year period, the Senate over a five-year period. Intensive lobbying by NEA supporters, including many stage, screen, and music stars, who went directly to Washington to buttonhole legislators, failed to shake Republican resolve.

On June 4, at the annual Tony Award ceremony, the NEA—and, by extension, Jane Alexander—won a special Tony for its outstanding contribution to the theater. The NEA's "seed money" grants to hundreds of small, struggling arts groups had long been recognized as making a vital contribution to the development of the arts.

At year's end, the budget fight continued, and future of the NEA and of Alexander's leadership role in developing her country's arts was very much in question. What was never in question, however, was that a decision to return to performance would be welcomed by theater-lovers the world over.

Alexander played in regional theater in the mid-1960s. She emerged as a major dramatic actress on Broadway in 1968, in her Tony-winning role opposite James Earl Jones in *The Great*

White Hope. Some of her most notable stage roles were in *6 Rms Riv Vu* (1972), *Find Your Way Home* (1974), *The Heiress* (1976), *First Monday in October* (1978), *Hedda Gabler* (1981), *Old Times* (1984), *Night of the Iguana* (1988), *Shadowlands* (1990), and *The Sisters Rosenzweig* (1993). On screen, she was nominated for a best actress Oscar for the film version of *The Great White Hope* (1970), and she also appeared in such films as *All the President's Men* (1976), *Kramer vs. Kramer* (1979), *Testament* (1983), and *Glory* (1989). She has also made several telefilms, most notably *Eleanor and Franklin* (1976) as a classic Eleanor Roosevelt, *Playing for Time* (1980), *Calamity Jane* (1984), and *A Marriage: Georgia O'Keeffe and Alfred Stieglitz* (1991). She put her acting career on hold in 1993, accepting President Bill Clinton's nomination to head the somewhat battered National Endowment for the Arts. She was overwhelmingly confirmed by the Senate, and set about the task of simultaneously restoring the NEA's prestige and resisting very aggressive conservative attacks on the institution.

Alexander attended Sarah Lawrence College and the University of Edinburgh. Previously divorced, she married Edwin Sherin in 1975, and has one child.

FURTHER READING

"Jane's addiction. . . ." DANTE RAMOS. *New Republic,* Jan. 9, 1995.
"Jane Alexander." MELISSA HARRIS. *Interview,* July 1994.
"See Jane run the NEA." CHRIS BULL. *Advocate,* Feb. 22, 1994.

Alexander, Lamar

(Andrew Lamar Alexander, Jr.; 1940–) Former U.S. Secretary of Education Lamar Alexander began to try to build a "national" political image during 1994, and formally entered the race for the 1996 Republican presidential nomination on February 28, 1995. At a press conference in Marysville, Tennessee, his hometown, he billed himself as a shirt-sleeves conservative populist and struck the themes that he would attempt to carry through the campaign. Among these were abolition of the federal Department of Education, which he had headed (1991–93), and the dismantling of a very wide range of other federal programs. Seeking to ride the wave of public disenchantment with the federal government, he attempted to position himself as a Tennessee country candidate, and attacked other Republican candidates Bob Dole and Phil Gramm as Washington "insiders" who were part of the problem.

Alexander's candidacy drew only modest support, although it was greatly helped by his success in fundraising. By mid-April, he had raised more than $5 million dollars and spent more than $2 million. In June, he began campaign advertising in New Hampshire, and he placed fourth in the August Iowa straw poll. Although he received 22 percent of the votes in the November Florida Republican straw poll, it was clear that his campaign had by no means "taken off," and that the early-1996 primaries would determine his future as a candidate.

With several others, Alexander coedited the 1995 book *The New Promise of American Life.*

Tennessee-born Alexander received his 1962 B.A. from Vanderbilt University and his 1965 LL.D. from New York University. He began his career as an assistant to U.S. Senator Howard S. Baker (1967–69), and briefly worked in the White House as a Congressional liaison aide (1969). He practiced law in Tennessee during the 1970s, made an unsuccessful gubernatorial run (1974), and won next time around, serving as state governor (1979–87). He also served a term as chairman of the National Governors Association (1985–86), and as president of the University of Tennessee (1988–1990) before becoming U.S. Secretary of Education for two years during the Bush adminstration. Alexander has published *Steps Along the Way: A Governor's Scrapbook* (1986) and *Six Months Off: An American Family's Australian Adventure* (1988). He and his wife, Honey Alexander, have four children.

FURTHER READING

"Bill? Phil? Bob? . . ." WILLIAM F. BUCKLEY, JR. *National Review,* June 26, 1995.
"The rich rise . . ." DOUG IRELAND. *Nation,* Apr. 17, 1995.
"Dressing down . . ." STEPHEN GOODE. *Insight on the News,* Apr. 3, 1995.
"Tennessee Waltz. . . ." DAN GOODGAME. *Time,* Mar. 13, 1995.
"Taking it to the top." JOE AGRON. *American School & University,* Sept. 1992.

"Lamar Alexander and. . . ." GEORGE R. KAPLAN. *Phi Delta Kappan*, June 1992.

"Lamar's choice." WILLIAM McGURN. *National Review*, May 25, 1992.

"Alexander the Great?" JON STEWART. *Parenting*, May 1992.

"Lamar Alexander's. . . ." SUSAN CHIRA. *New York Times Magazine*, Nov. 24, 1991.

"Alexander, Andrew Lamar, Jr." *Current Biography*, July 1991.

Alfven, Hannes Olof Gosta (1908–95)

Celebrated Swedish physicist Hannes Alfven earned his Ph.D. in physics at the University of Uppsala in 1934, and from 1940 taught at Stockholm's Royal Institute of Techology. He later also taught at the University of California at San Diego. During the 1930s, Alfven began to make major contributions to modern physics, especially in magnetohydrodynamics (MHD), the study of plasmas and the movement of electrically conducting fluids within magnetic fields. The conducting waves so created came to be called Alfven waves. Despite early ridicule by his peers, the validity of his work was later established, and Alfven won a 1970 Nobel Prize in physics for his work. Building on that work, Alfven made major contributions to the study of "solar winds," the plasma emitted by the sun, and in the study of sunspots. His theories as to the nature of interstellar matter proved central to much work that followed. Alfven, an early advocate of nuclear power, became one of the first to warn of the creation of massive amounts of nuclear waste that would present extraordinarily difficult disposal problems, a warning borne out by later worldwide experience. He also opposed the developing nuclear arms race, and was active in the antinuclear Pugwash movement. In addition to his specialist monographs, he published the general books *Worlds-Antiworlds: Antimatter in Cosmology* (1966), *Atom, Man, and the Universe: The Long Chain of Complications* (1969), and *Living on the Third Planet* (1972; written with Kertsin Alfven). He was survived by five children. (d. Djurshohm, Sweden; April 2, 1995)

FURTHER READING

Obituary. *Times* (of London), Apr. 27, 1995.
Obituary. *Independent*, Apr. 14, 1995.
Obituary. *New York Times*, Apr. 5, 1995.

Allen, Gay Wilson (1903–95)

North Carolina–born teacher and writer Gay Allen was a leading authority on poet Walt Whitman. Allen received his 1926 A.B. and his 1928 M.A. from Duke University, and his 1934 Ph.D. from the University of Wisconsin. He taught English at Lake Erie College (1929–31) and Shurtleff College (1934–35), before settling down as an English professor at Ohio State University (1935–46) and New York University (1946–69). Allen was a prolific author, most notably of several books on Whitman, among them *The Walt Whitman Handbook* (1946; new ed. 1975), the critically acclaimed *The Solitary Singer: A Critical Biography of Walt Whitman* (1955), *Walt Whitman as Man, Poet, and Legend* (1961), and *The Collected Works of Walt Whitman* (as editor). Among his other works were *William James: A Biography* (1967) and *Waldo Emerson: A Biography* (1981). He was survived by a sister. (d. Raleigh, North Carolina; August 6, 1995)

FURTHER READING

Obituary. *New York Times*, Aug. 8, 1995.

Allen, Marcus (1960–)

Running back Marcus Allen continued to put distance between himself and his former team, the Los Angeles (now, again, Oakland) Raiders. He has made it clear that if he goes into football's Hall of Fame it will be as a member of the Kansas City Chiefs. That the question is not if, but when, was demonstrated once again in 1995—ironically in a December 3, 1995 game against the Raiders—when Allen became the first person in National Football League history to reach 10,000 rushing yards and 5,000 receiving yards in his professional career. In that same game, Allen tied Walter Payton for third place on the all-time list for most career touchdowns, with 125.

Not coincidentally, that game gave the Chiefs the best won-lost record in the AFC for the second time in three seasons. That surprised many because after the retirement of quarterback Joe Montana the team had been expected to finish in fourth or fifth place. At year's end, the Chiefs had a league-leading 13–3 record, giving them home-field advantage throughout the playoffs; however, their drive toward the Super Bowl was ended with an early January 1996 loss to the Indianapolis Colts.

For the regular season, Allen led the team in rushing with 890 yards on 207 attempts, for an average of 4.3 yards; his 210 receiving yards gave him a total of 1,100 yards from scrimmage.

Born in San Diego, Allen graduated from Lincoln High School in San Diego and attended the University of Southern California, taking USC's football team to four bowls, including two Rose Bowls, and winning football's prestigious Heisman Trophy as top college player (1981) and numerous other awards. Turning professional, he joined the Los Angeles Raiders (1982–93) and was named *Sporting News* Rookie of the Year (1982). He would become the Raiders' all-time rushing leader, with 8,545 yards, as well as 3,928 receiving yards. In 1984, when the Raiders won the Super Bowl, he was named the game's Most Valuable Player, gaining a then-record total of 191 yards and scoring two rushing touchdowns (a still-standing shared record), one a 74-yard run from scrimmage, also still an NFL record. In his best year, 1985, Allen led the NFL with 1,759 rushing yards; gained 2,314 combined yards (rushing and receiving), also an NFL record; scored 14 touchdowns; and was named the NFL's Most Valuable Player, also setting an NFL record by gaining over 100 yards in 11 consecutive games over the 1985–86 seasons.

However, Allen became engaged in a contract dispute with Raiders owner Al Davis in 1989, the split between the two widening after Allen joined the football player's free agency suit in 1991. Allen was relegated to the sidelines, in the 1992 season as third-string running back. On becoming a free agent, he joined the Kansas City Chiefs (1993–), in his first season there scoring a league-leading 12 touchdowns (10 rushing; 2 receiving), including three in one game, and being named to the Pro Bowl for the sixth time (1982; 1984–87; 1993; he did not play in 1986 due to injury). His brother, Damon Allen, is quarterback of the Edmonton Eskimos of the Canadian Football League.

FURTHER READING

"Marcus Allen. . . ." Dan Dieffenbach. *Sport,* Oct. 1994.

"Rush job. . . ." Rick Weinberg. *Sport,* Aug. 1991.

"Allen tackles. . . ." Chris Mortensen. *Sporting News,* July 22, 1991.

Allen, Tim (Tim Allen Dick; 1953–) Tim Allen was at the top of the heap in 1995. His 1994 book *Don't Stand Too Close to a Naked Man* had spent 17 weeks on the *Publishers Weekly* hardcover best-seller list, and in 1995 was released as a best-selling paperback. His Christmas 1994 film *The Santa Clause* was one of the season's most popular films. Meanwhile, "Home Improvement," the comedy television series on which he stars as the Tool Man, with Patricia Richardson, was in its fourth season and remained one of television's leading series. Indeed, in the first week of December 1994, all three were in the top spots on their respective charts. For his work in *The Santa Clause,* Allen was named best male newcomer (theatrical) at the June 1995 Blockbuster Entertainment Awards, and for "Home Improvement," he won the Golden Globe award as best actor in a television musical or comedy series. At the People's Choice Awards in March, he was named both best actor in a comedy motion picture and favorite male television performer, though surprisingly he received no Emmy nominations. "Home Improvement" was not quite so successful in the new 1995–96 season, partly because new episodes were competing directly with reruns of earlier ones on other television channels.

Late 1995 saw the opening of the Disney computer-animated film *Toy Story,* in which Allen starred as the voice of toy astronaut Buzz Lightyear, along with the voices of Tom Hanks, Don Rickles, and others. Also new for 1995 was a hammer partly designed by Allen, which may be the beginning of a Tim Allen line of tools and gadgets, with profits to go to charity (like Paul Newman's food products). At year's end, Allen was nominated for another Golden Globe award as best actor in a musical or comedy series. Forthcoming were another book and a role in the film *Indian in the City*.

Denver-born Allen attended Central Michigan University and received his B.A. in television production from Western Michigan University in 1976. On graduating, he worked in a sporting goods store, moving to the store's advertising agency. He made his first public appearance in 1979 at Detroit's Comedy Castle; then, after some months of imprisonment for selling cocaine, he built a career as a stand-up comedian, working live and in radio, television, and film, including commercials. He first came to wide attention on cable, notably with his Showtime specials *Men Are Pigs* (1990) and *Tim Allen Rewires America* (1991), winning an ACE award in 1991. Working with cocreator Matt Williams from Allen's own idea, he then developed the television series "Home Improvement" (1991–), as star, cowriter, and coproducer. The series gained strength throughout the early 1990s, emerging as a top hit in the 1993–94 season. He is married to Laura Allen; they have one daughter.

FURTHER READING

"Tim Allen. . . ." BILL STADIEM. *Cosmopolitan,* Sept. 1995.

"Allen, Tim." *Current Biography,* May 1995.

"When Camille met Tim." CAMILLE PAGLIA. *Esquire,* Feb. 1995.

Tim Allen Laid Bare: Unauthorized. MICHAEL ARKUSH. Avon, 1995.

"Tim Allen." *People,* Dec. 26, 1994.

"Tim at the top. . . ." RICHARD ZOGLIN. *Time,* Dec. 12, 1994.

"Sleighing 'em. . . ." TIM APPELO. *Entertainment,* Nov. 18, 1994.

"Home for. . . ." RUSSELL MILLER. *Ladies Home Journal*, Dec. 1993.

"Tim Allen." *Playboy,* Feb. 1993.

Allen, Woody (Allen Stewart Konigsberg; 1935–) During 1995, Allen's peers continued to honor him. He received a Golden Lion lifetime achievement award at the Venice Film Festival; he and Douglas McGrath received a best original screenplay Oscar nomination for *Bullets Over Broadway*.

Allen wrote, directed, and starred in his Manhattan-set comedy film *Mighty Aphrodite*, opposite Mira Sorvino as the Greek prostitute who turns out to be the mother of his adopted child, and whose life he redirects into paths more acceptable to him. Helena Bonham Carter played his wife; the cast also included Michael Rapaport, Claire Bloom, F. Murray Abraham, and Olympia Dukakis.

Allen also wrote the one-act play *Central Park West*, directed by Michael Blakemore and starring Debra Monk, Linda Lavin, Gerry Becker, Paul Guilfoyle, and Tari T. Signor, about an older man who leaves his wife for a younger woman. Allen was also slated to write and direct an as-yet-untitled film; its cast included Julia Roberts, Tim Roth, Judy Davis, Alan Alda, Bette Midler, and Drew Barrymore.

On the personal side, the New York State Court of appeals dismissed Allen's appeal to reverse a lower court decision awarding custody of Moses, Dylan, and Satchel Farrow to Mia Farrow.

A New Yorker, Allen emerged as a leading television comedy writer in the late 1950s, and during the 1960s also worked in cabaret and theater, beginning a long series of hit films as the writer and star of *What's New Pussycat?* (1965). He then became one of the leading filmmakers of his time, with such films as his Oscar-winning *Annie Hall* (1977), *Manhattan* (1979), *Hannah and Her Sisters* (1984), *Crimes and Misdemeanors* (1989), *Scenes from a Mall* (1991), *Shadows and Fog* (1992), *Husbands and Wives* (1992), *Manhattan Murder Mystery* (1993), and *Bullets over Broadway* (1994).

Allen attended City College and New York University. Formerly married to Louise Lasser, Allen had a long-term relationship with Farrow (1980–92); though they never married, they had three children: their biological son Satchel, an adopted daughter Dylan, and an adopted son Moses. Their breakup and subsequent bitter custody suit was complicated by disclosure of Allen's affair with Farrow's 21-year-old adopted daughter, Soon-Yi Farrow Previn, which continued into 1995.

FURTHER READING

"King of comedy." STUART JEFFRIES. *Guardian,* Apr. 10, 1995.

Woody, Mia, and Soon-Yi. DAVID W. FELDER. Felder Books, 1995.

Perspectives on Woody Allen. RENE CURRY. Twayne, 1995.

Woody Allen: Profane and Sacred. RICHARD A. BLAKE. Scarecrow, 1995.

Woody Allen at Work: The Photographs of Brian Hamill. CHARLES CHAMPLIN. Abrams, 1995.

"If you knew. . . ." DOUGLAS MCGRATH. *New York*, Oct. 17, 1994.

" 'So, you're. . . .' " BILL ZEHME. *Esquire*, Oct. 1994.

Woody Allen on Woody Allen. STIG BJORKMAN, ed. Grove-Atlantic, 1994.

Mia and Woody: Love, Betrayal and Heartbreak. KRISTI GROTEKE. Carx & Graf, 1994.

"All stick, no shtick." JOHN EPHLAND. *Down Beat*, Oct. 1993.

"Woody Allen. . . ." ANTHONY DeCURTIS. *Rolling Stone*, Sept. 16, 1993.

The Films of Woody Allen. SAM B. GIRGUS. Cambridge University Press, 1993.

"Bananas. . . ." ROGER ROSENBLATT. *New Republic*, Sept. 21, 1992.

" 'But she's not. . . .' " JACK KROLL. *Newsweek*, Aug. 31, 1992.

" 'The heart wants. . . .' " WALTER ISAACSON. *Time*, Aug. 31, 1992.

"Woody and Mia. . . ." ERIC LAX. *New York Times Magazine*, Feb. 24, 1991.

Woody Allen: A Biography. ERIC LAX. Knopf, 1991.

Woody Allen Encyclopedia. MARK A. ALTMAN. Movie Publications, 1991.

Woody Allen: His Films and Career. DOUGLAS BRODE. Carol, 1991.

Allende, Isabel

Allende, Isabel (1942–   ) Isabel Allende's new book for 1995 was an extremely personal one, named after her daughter Paula, who in December 1991 was diagnosed with the rare hereditary metabolic disorder porphyria (the same disease that maddened and eventually killed England's King George III) and soon fell into a coma, eventually dying in December 1992. Written during that year-long coma, as Allende sat by her daughter's bedside, *Paula* takes the form of a personal and family autobiography. In passionate communication with her comatose daughter, and in a tone of celebration and finally farewell, Isabel Allende reminisces about the recent generations of her family as they worked out their lives over four continents, including the career of her uncle, Chilean President Salvador Allende, who was assassinated in 1973. This was not the first time she had taken this approach to writing. Her first novel, *The House of Spirits*, actually began as a letter to her grandfather as he lay dying. In this and many of her other

works, she strongly conveys the notion that spirits from the past remain present in our daily lives, an approach sometimes called "magical realism."

Born in Peru to a Chilean family, Allende was raised in Chile, Bolivia, Europe, and the Middle East, following family diplomatic postings; she herself began working for a branch of the United Nations at age 17. Married at 19 to Miguel Frias, she had two children, and worked as a journalist beginning in 1967. Forced to leave Peru after the 1973 military coup, Allende lived with her family in exile in Venezuela, continuing work as a journalist, in print and on television. Her career as a novelist began in 1982 with the publication of *The House of Spirits*, a much praised multigenerational family chronicle set in Chile (basis for the 1993 film), and continued with *Of Love and Shadows* (1984), *Eva Luna* (1989), and *The Infinite Plan* (1993); other works included the short story collection *The Stories of Eva Luna* (1990) and the children's story *La Gorda de Porcelana* (1984). Later divorced, Allende married San Francisco attorney William Gordon in 1988.

FURTHER READING

"Isabel Allende's. . . ." ROSA PINOL. *World Press Review*, Apr. 1995

"Isabel Allende." BOB BALDOCK and DENNIS BERNSTEIN. *Mother Jones*, Sept.–Oct. 1994.

"Lady of the spirits." MARJORIE ROSEN and NANCY MATSUMOTO. *People*, May 2, 1994.

"Latin lady of letters. . . ." SYLVIE DRAKE. *Variety,*
Mar. 28, 1994.

"Keeper of. . . ." KATE KELLAWAY. *Observer*, Mar. 7,
1993.

"The shaman. . . ." MARILYN BERLIN SNELL. *New
Perspectives Quarterly*, Winter 1991.

Critical Approaches to Isabel Allende's Novels. SONIA
R. ROJAS and EDNA A. REHBEIN. P. Lang, 1991.

*Beyond the Border: A New Age in Latin American
Women's Fiction.* NORA ERRO-PERALTA and CARIDAD
SILVA-NUNEZ, eds. Cleis, 1991.

Alvarez, Victor: See Abdel Rahman, Omar.

Amir, Yigal: See Rabin, Yitzhak.

Amis, Kingsley (1922–95)

London-born Kingsley Amis, a leadng satirist, was recognized as one of Britain's prototypical "angry young men" of the 1950s with publication of his first novel, *Lucky Jim* (1954), a bitterly comic attack on the British academic establishment, his own setting at the time. After World War II military service, he had attended Oxford University, then became a lecturerer at Swansea University (1949–59) and later a fellow at Cambridge University's Peterhouse College (1961–63). Amis went on to write a score of novels, among them *That Uncertain Feeling* (1955), *I Like It Here* (1958), *Take a Girl Like You* (1960), *One Fat Englishman* (1963), *Ending Up* (1974), *Jake's Thing* (1978), *The Green Man* (1969; basis of the 1990 telefilm), *The Riverside Murders* (1973), *Stanley and the Women* (1984), *The Old Devils* (1986; he won the Booker Prize), *The Russian Girl* (1994), and *The Biographer's Moustache* (1995). He also published the poetry collections *A Case of Samples* (1956) and *Collected Poems 1944–1979*, as well short stories and a wide range of essays. At least in his public utterances, Amis became a notably bitter social conservative in his later years. His autobiography was *Memoirs* (1991). He was twice married and divorced, to Hilary Anne Bardwell and to the novelist Elizabeth Jane Howard. He was survived by three children, one of them the writer Martin Amis. (d. London; October 22, 1995)

FURTHER READING

"The irritable young man. . . ." PAUL GRAY. *Time,*
Nov. 6, 1995.

"Kingsley's ransom." JAMES WOLCOTT. *New Yorker,*
Oct. 30, 1995.

Obituary. *Independent,* Oct. 23, 1995.

Obituary. *Times* (of London), Oct. 23, 1995

Obituary. *New York Times*, Oct. 23, 1995.

"Curmudgeons never. . . ." JOANNA COLES. *Guardian,*
Aug. 26, 1995.

Understanding Kingsley Amis. MERRITT MOSELEY.
University of South Carolina Press, 1993.

The Anti-Egoist: Kingsley Amis, Man of Letters.
PAUL FUSSELL. Oxford University Press, 1994.

Kingsley Amis: Modern Novelist. DALE SALWAK. B&N
Imports, 1992.

"A character. . . ." ERIC FELTEN. *Insight on the News,*
Sept. 30, 1991.

" 'I'm a great man. . . .' " *Economist,* Mar. 9, 1991.

Kingsley Amis: In Life and Letters. DALE SALWAK, ed.
St. Martin's, 1991.

Amis, Martin Louis (1949–)

In January 1995, Britain's literary world buzzed at Martin Amis demanding (through his new American agent) and receiving more than a million dollars for his forthcoming novel. Multimillion-dollar advances are rare in Britain, and Amis was widely criticized in the media for unseemly greed. When the novel, *The Information*, was actually published, it became a number one bestseller in Britain and also won considerable critical praise for its satirical view of competition between two longtime "friends" in the literary world, dark with jealousy and revenge. In fact, it was so well received that when the book was not shortlisted for Britain's prestigious Booker Prize, the fact was treated as front-page news in no less than the London *Times*. *The Information* also garnered generally favorable reviews in the United States. Also in 1995, Amis's *Visiting Mrs. Nabokov and Other Excursions*, a 1994 collection of sketches and essays, was reprinted in paperback.

On the personal side, Amis lost his father, the British novelist Kingsley Amis.

Educated at Exeter College, Oxford, Martin Amis has made his substantial reputation as an angry young satirist, who focuses on what he perceives as the decline and fast-approaching end of British society and the poisoning of the environment. Among his other works are *The Rachel Papers* (1973), which won the Somerset

Maugham writing award, *Dead Babies* (1975), *Success* (1978), *Other People* (1981), *Money* (1984), *The Moronic Inferno* (1986), *London Fields* (1989; U.S., 1990), and *Time's Arrow, or, the Nature of the Offense* (1992). Amis married Antonia Phillips in 1984; they had two sons, before divorcing a decade later.

FURTHER READING

"The prose and cons. . . ." GRAHAM FULLER. *Interview,* May 1995.
"Famous Amis." MICHAEL SHNAYERSON. *Vanity Fair,* May 1995.
Understanding Martin Amis. JAMES DIEDRICK. University of South Carolina Press, 1995.
Bomb: Interviews. BETSY SUSSLER, ed. City Lights, 1992.
"Britain's mavericks." ANTHONY DECURTIS. *Harper's Bazaar,* Nov. 1991.

Anaya, Rudolfo (1937–) America's best-known Chicano author, Rudolfo Anaya published a new novel in 1995: *Zia Summer*. It is the second of what is envisioned as a quartet of the seasons. The first was *Alburquerque* (using the original spelling of the city's name), focusing on a young barrio boxer seeking to find his identity as a Chicano. Unusual for Anaya, *Zia Summer* is a murder mystery; Zia is the Pueblo symbol for the sun, and provides clues to the solution of the mystery confronting Albuquerque private detective Sonny Baca, which involves a

cousin's murder, nuclear waste disposal, and eco-terrorism. The third novel of the quartet, *Rio Grande Fall*, was scheduled for 1996 publication and will again feature Baca.

Also in 1995, *The Anaya Reader*, an anthology of his writings, was published, as was one of Anaya's early children's stories, *The Farolitos of Christmas. Jalamanta: A Message from the Desert* was scheduled for publication in 1996.

New Mexico–born Anaya is a leading writer of the American Southwest whose work reflects an absorption in his Hispanic heritage. His very well received first novel, a classic coming-of-age work, was *Bless Me, Ultima* (1972). Later novels include *Heart of Aztlan* (1976) and *Tortuga* (1979), which won the American Book Award of the Before Columbus Society. He has also published volumes of short stories and poetry, including the short-story collection *The Silence of the Llano* (1982), and a travel journal, *A Chicano in China* (1986); written several plays, screenplays, and nonfiction works, including *The Adventures of Juan Chicaspatas* (1984) and *Lord of the Dawn: The Legend of Quetzalcoatl* (coauthored with David Johnson; 1987); and edited (and sometimes translated) several anthologies, including the periodical *Blue Mesa Review*. Anaya received his 1963 B.A. and his 1968 M.A. from the University of New Mexico at Albuquerque, and his 1984 Ph.D. from Crest College. He taught in the New Mexico public school system (1963–70) and at the University of New Mexico at Albuquerque (1974–93), specializing in Chicano literature and creative writing. He married Patricia Lawless, also a writer, in 1966.

FURTHER READING

"Rudolfo Anaya. . . ." WILLIAM CLARK. *Publishers Weekly,* June 5, 1995.
Rudolfo A. Anaya: Focus on Criticism. CESAR A. GONZALEZ, ed. Lalo, 1991.

Andrews, Julie (Julia Elizabeth Welles; 1935–) One of the most extraordinary careers in the history of the musical theater blossomed once again in 1995. After touring the country in the show for much of the year, Julie Andrews opened on Broadway in a stage musical version of her 1982 hit film musical *Victor/Victoria*, again playing Victoria Grant, a starving Depression-era English singer who becomes a star in Paris cabaret while masquerading as a man who masquerades as a woman. Her husband, Blake Edwards, who had directed the film, wrote the book and directed the musical, with music by Henry Mancini and lyrics by Leslie Bricusse. Tony Roberts as Carroll Todd (the Robert Preston film role), Michael Nouri as King Marchan (the James Garner role), and Rachel Todd as Norma Cassidy (the Lesley Ann Warren role) co-starred. Andrews was once again a star on Broadway, her musical a major hit. On her Broadway opening night, October 25, National Public Television's Great Performances series broadcast the biofilm *Julie Andrews: Back on Broadway*.

Andrews, the child of a British theater family, began her nearly five-decades-long singing career at the age of 12, in the *Starlight Roof* revue. She emerged as a star in the Broadway production of *The Boy Friend* (1954), became a major figure in the musical theater for her creation of the Eliza Doolittle role in *My Fair Lady* (1956), and then created Guinevere in the musical *Camelot* (1960). Passed over for the Doolittle role in the film version, she instead made her film debut in the title role of *Mary Poppins* (1964), a worldwide hit musical, winning a Best Actress Academy Award in the role. In 1965, she scored another triumph as Maria von Trapp in *The Sound of Music*, an Oscar-winning worldwide hit. Her films also included *The Americanization of Emily* (1964), *Torn Curtain* (1966), *Hawaii* (1966), *Thoroughly Modern Millie* (1967), *Star!* (1968), *Darling Lili* (1970), *The Tamarind Seed* (1974), *10* (1980), *Little Miss Marker* (1980), *S. O. B.* (1981), *The Man Who Loved Women* (1983), *That's Life* (1986), *Duet For One* (1986), and *A Fine Romance* (1992). She has also starred in several television specials and won an Emmy Award as host of "The Julie Andrews Hour" (1972–1973). Previously divorced, she married director Blake Edwards in 1969; she has one daughter.

FURTHER READING

"Return of. . . ." PHILIP WEISS. *New York Times Magazine,* Oct. 1, 1995.
"Victor/victorious." JONATHAN VAN METER. *Vanity Fair,* Oct. 1995.
"My fair Victor/Victoria. . . ." JOHN GRUEN. *Dance Magazine,* Sept. 1995.
"The thrills are alive." ADAM SWEETING. *Guardian,* Nov. 24, 1994.
"Andrews, Julie." *Current Biography,* Apr. 1994.

Andrews, Maxene (1916–95) Minneapolis-born singer Maxene Andrews, with her sisters LaVerne (1915–67) and Patty (1920–), organized the extraordinarily popular singing trio the Andrews Sisters in 1932. They became an enormous hit with their rendition of "Bei Mir Bist Du Schon" (1937), which became their signature song, and went on to become one of the most popular groups of the late 1930s and 1940s, ultimately selling more than 50 million copies of their many hits, among them "The Beer Barrel Polka," "The Pennsylvania Polka," "The Strip Polka," "Beat Me Daddy, Eight to the Bar," "The Boogie Woogie Boogie Boy" (introduced by them in the film *Buck Privates*, one of more than a score of their films), "Don't Sit Under the Apple Tree," and "Rum and Coca-Cola." Their act, overtaken by changes in musical styles and beset by personal disagreements, broke up in the early 1950s; though later reunited, they were not again a very popular group. Her later career was largely as a soloist in cabaret and as an actress and singer in stage musicals. With Bill Gilbert, she wrote *Over Here, Over There: The Andrews Sisters and the USO Stars in World War II* (1993). She was survived by her sister Patty, a daughter, a son, an adopted daughter, and a foster son. (d. Hyannis, Massachusetts; October 21, 1995)

FURTHER READING

Obituary. *Independent,* Oct. 28, 1995.
Obituary. *New York Times,* Oct. 23, 1995.
Obituary. *Variety,* Oct. 23, 1995
"Sister." *New Yorker,* Nov. 11, 1991.

Anfinsen, Christian Boehmer (1916–95) Pennsylvania-born Christian Anfinsen, a leading biochemist, received his 1937 B.A. from Swarthmore College, his 1939 M.A. from the University of Pennsylvania, and his 1943 Ph.D. from Harvard University. During the balance of World War II he worked with the U.S. Office of Research and Development. He held several teaching positions before joining the National Institutes of Health in 1950, and headed the chemical biology laboratory of that organization (1963–82), later becoming a professor of biology at Johns Hopkins University. He was also long associated with Israel's Weizmann Institute of Sciences, was a prolific author in his field, and served on the editorial boards of publications in his field. His most notable work was in molecular structure, with particular emphasis on the structure and folding patterns of proteins. For his body of work in that area, he shared the 1973 Nobel Prize for chemistry. Anfinsen was survived by his wife, Libby Shulman Anfinsen, three daughters, four sons, and a sister. (d. Randallstown, Maryland; May 15, 1995)

FURTHER READING

Obituary. *Times* (London), May 29, 1995.
Obituary. *Independent*, May 24, 1995.
Obituary. *New York Times*, May 16, 1995.

Arafat, Yasir (Yasser Arafat; 1929–) On September 24, 1995, Palestine Liberation Organization (PLO) leader Yasir Arafat, now also leader of the Palestine National Authority (PNA), scored yet another triumph. After more than a year of on-and-off negotiations, he and Israeli Foreign Minister Shimon Peres initialed a detailed agreement providing for greatly increased Palestinian home rule on the West Bank and in the Gaza Strip, areas occupied by Israel in 1967, after the Six-Day War (Third Arab-Israeli War). The agreement provided for a phased withdrawal of Israeli troops from most Palestinian cities and towns, with a small force left to guard Israeli settlers in Hebron, leaving Israeli troops still in control of much of the countryside; a phased release of most Palestinian prisoners; internationally supervised free elections; and protection of access to certain Jewish and Muslim sacred places. After ratification by a bitterly divided Israeli parliament, Arafat and Israeli Prime Minister Yitzhak Rabin signed the agreement in a formal White House ceremony attended by President Clinton, Egypt's President Hosni Mubarak, and Jordan's King Hussein.

Arafat still faced violent opposition to the peace process from the Islamic fundamentalist Hamas organization and from some organizations on the left, sometimes in tacit alliance with hard-line right-wing Israeli nationalists. While condemning Hamas terrorism, Arafat continued to call for Israeli withdrawal from Jerusalem, a demand flatly rejected by the Israelis, and for further extension of PNA authority. Yet even though facing many challenges, Arafat was very firmly set as the leader of the emerging Pales-

tinian state, and even the November 4 assassination of Israeli Prime Minister Yitzhak Rabin did not derail the peace process or diminish Arafat's leadership role.

Jerusalem-born Arafat was a founder of Al Fatah (1956) and of its guerrilla army (1959). He has headed the PLO and been the top leader of the Palestinian national movement since 1969. He suffered major personal defeats when his forces were expelled from Jordan (1970–71) and Lebanon (1983). In the mid-1980s, he moved toward negotiation and publicly renounced terrorism, and seemed for a time all but overwhelmed by the more extreme terrorist elements within his own movement. In late 1988, he forced the Palestine National Council and the PLO to accept key United Nations resolutions 242 and 338. On November 15, 1988, he issued a Palestinian declaration of independence, and in the years that followed more than 50 countries recognized the Palestinian state.

Arafat backed Saddam Hussein against his Arab allies in the Persian Gulf War and subsequently lost much of the PLO's funding and his main military base at Sidon to Syrian-backed Lebanese army forces; by 1992 he had seemed to lose much of his support within the PLO. But he made an extraordinary comeback: On September 13, 1993, he and Israeli Prime Minister Yitzhak Rabin shook hands on the White House lawn, approving the historic declaration of principles that had a few minutes earlier been signed by their respective ministers, Mahmoud Abbas and Shimon Peres, which established a basis for Palestinian self-rule, beginning in the Gaza Strip and Jericho.

On July 1, 1994, Arafat ended his 27-year exile from Palestine, and on July 5 was sworn in as the head of the PNA. He then named a cabinet and began the difficult task of developing a new government and introducing PLO armed forces as Palestinian police. Arafat, Rabin, and Peres were awarded the 1994 Nobel Peace Prize for their roles in the Middle East peace process.

Arafat attended Cairo University and was an engineer before becoming a full-time political leader. He married Suha Tawil in 1992; they have a daughter.

FURTHER READING

" 'We became more than friends.' " SCOTT MACLEOD. *Time*, Nov. 20, 1995.
"The survivor." ISABEL KERSHNER. *World Press Review*, Sept. 1995.

Yasir Arafat: The Battle for Peace in Palestine.
ELIZABETH FERBER. Millbrook, 1995.
The Mystery of Arafat. DANNY RUBINSTEIN. Steerforth
Press, 1995.
"Arafat, Yasir." *Current Biography*, Nov. 1994.
"Arafat. . . ." LISA BEYER. *Time*, May 16, 1994.
"Arafat in the storm." T. D. ALLMAN. *Vanity Fair*,
May 1994.
" 'I am paying. . . .' " LALLY WEYMOUTH and
CHRISTOPHER DICKEY. *Newsweek*, Mar. 14, 1994.
"Yitzhak Rabin and Yasser Arafat." NANCY GIBBS.
"To conquer the past." LANCE MORROW. *Time*, Jan.
3, 1994. (Men of the Year: The Peacemakers)
Arafat: A Biography. ANDREW GOWERS and TONY
WALKER. Interlink, 1994.
*Behind the Myth: Yasser Arafat and the Palestinian
Revolution.* ANDREW GOWERS and TONY WALKER.
Interlink, 1992.
Arafat and the Palestine Liberation Organization.
DIANA REISCHE. Watts, 1991.

Aramony, William (1927–) On April 3,

1995, a federal court jury in Alexandria, Virginia
found former United Way president William
Aramony guilty on 25 counts of conspiracy, mail
and wire fraud, false income tax returns filing,
and stolen property transactions. He had
been accused of illegally taking more than $1.2
million from United Way for a variety of personal uses and had resigned his presidency in
1992. Two of his associates, Thomas J. Merlo
and Stephen J. Paulachak, were found guilty on
multiple related counts. The case was one of the
most spectacular to involve a major charitable
organization, and United Way contributions
were greatly affected when the scandal came to
light. On June 23, Aramony was sentenced to a
seven-year prison term, and his associates to
lesser prison terms. All announced that they
planned to appeal the verdict.

Connecticut-born Aramony attended Clark
University. He received his 1951 M.A. in social
work from Boston College. After a period of military service (1951–53), he swiftly became a
leading social service executive. He was executive director of United Community Service in Columbia, South Carolina (1958–61), and in St.
Joseph County, Indiana (1961–64). He moved
up to become executive vice-president of the
United Fund of Dade County, Florida (1964–70),
and from 1970 until his fall was the much-
honored president of United Way International.
Aramony published *United Way: The Next Hundred Years* (1987). He is married to Bebe Ann
Nojeim; they have three children.

FURTHER READING

*The United Way Scandal: An Insider's Account of
What Went Wrong and Why.* JOHN S. GLASER.
Wiley, 1993.
"Charity case. . . ." JOSEPH FINDER. *New Republic*,
May 4, 1992.
"It works. . . ." ALICIA MUNDY. *Regardie's Magazine*,
Feb.–Mar. 1992.

Aristide, Jean-Bertrand (1953–) In

his first full year back in office, Haiti's President
Jean-Bertrand Aristide continued to be by far
his country's most popular politician, who had
largely fulfilled his promise to disband the
former military and make Haiti a less dangerous
place to live. Although at least a score of probable political assassinations were reported in
1995, Haiti's level of violence was far lower than
it had been during the previous military dictatorship. However, Aristide had by late 1995 made
very little progress in solving or even seriously
addressing Haiti's massive economic problems.
Haiti was still the poorest country in the Western
Hemisphere, jobs were scarce to nonexistent, and
in those circumstances the future of Haitian democracy was uncertain, although the December
presidential elections were conducted without serious incident. Aristide repeatedly pledged to
step down on completion of his term in February
1996, and did not stand for reelection. United Nations troop withdrawals were scheduled for 1996;
whether Haiti would then see right-wing resurgence was a matter of conjecture, as was Aristide's future course of action.

Aristide also published the 1995 book *Peace,
Justice and Power: My Return to Haiti, the
United States and the New World Order*.

Haitian-born Aristide, an orphan, was raised
by the Catholic Salesian order, was ordained a
Catholic priest in 1982, and soon became a leading and much admired worker among the poor in
his very poor country. At the same time, he became a leader in the fight against Haitian dictator François "Papa Doc" Duvalier and the Tonton
Macoutes, and for Haitian democracy, surviving
several attempts on his life. One of the young
priests who brought liberation theology to Latin
America, he was a source of great discomfort to
conservative Catholic leaders and was expelled

from the Salesian order in 1986. In 1987, a massive popular street protest stopped Church hierarchy attempts to transfer Aristide out of Haiti.

On December 17, 1990, Aristide was elected president of Haiti, in his country's first democratic election. He was deposed by an army coup in September 1991 and fled abroad, while the military tightened its hold on the country, embarking on a long reign of terror. Meanwhile, as in earlier times of trouble, a new exodus of the "boat people," illegal immigrants trying to reach the United States, began. In 1993, with international sanctions in force, Haiti's military rulers reneged on an agreement to step down from power, and a United Nations blockade of the island was imposed. Aristide returned to Haiti on October 15, 1994, following the September 18 agreement that provided for the peaceful takeover of the country by American armed forces and the agreement of generals Raoul Cedras and Philippe Biamby to resign from government and leave the country.

Among Aristide's other books are *In the Parish of the Poor: Writings from Haiti* (1990) and *Aristide: An Autobiography* (1992).

FURTHER READING

"Aristide to go. . . ." ARTHUR JONES. *National Catholic Reporter,* Dec. 29, 1995.
"After the Yanks have gone." MAGGIE O'KANE. *Guardian,* Feb. 18, 1995.
"Remembrance, not vengeance." Oct. 17, 1994. "The once and future president." Sept. 26, 1994. AMY WILENTZ. *Time.*
"Our man in Haiti." RUSSELL WATSON. *Newsweek,* Sept. 26, 1994.
"Jean-Bertrand Aristide. . . ." CATHERINE S. MANEGOLD. *New York Times Magazine,* May 1, 1994.
"Haiti and. . . ." ANTHONY P. MAINGOT. *Current History,* Feb. 1992.
"The oppositionist. . . ." AMY WILENTZ. *New Republic,* Oct. 28, 1991.
"Interview with. . . ." BISHOP EMERSON J. MOORE. *America,* Oct. 12, 1991.
"President Jean Bertrand Aristide." ANNE-CHRISTINE D'ADESKY. *Interview,* Oct. 1991.
"Aristide, Jean-Bertrand." *Current Biography,* May 1991.

Armey, Dick (Richard Keith Armey; 1940–) In his first year as House of Representatives majority leader, ultraconservative Texas Republican Dick Armey, in very close alliance

with House Speaker Newt Gingrich, went forward with the program outlined in their 1994 book *Contract with America: The Bold Plan.* Armey, Gingrich, and their followers were able to get much, though not all, of their program through the Republican-dominated House of Representatives, much less of it through the more cautious Republican-dominated Senate—and did not have the votes to routinely override Presidential vetos, as the year-end budget crisis illuminated very clearly. Armey's repeatedly expressed goals included the balanced budget amendment, killed by the Senate; the term limits bills, killed by the House; the school prayer amendment, which had no chance of passage; the destruction of the Social Security system, which was not formally proposed; and the outlawing of abortion, which did not occur and remained a major issue in American society. He and Gingrich did ultimately succeed in cutting federal expenditures on many social service programs, in shifting considerable federal social service funds to the states, and in cutting some current and future federal expenditures.

Always sharply abrasive, Armey figured in a major and very self-damaging incident on January 27, when in a weekly briefing to radio broadcasters, he referred to Massachusetts Democratic Representative Barney Frank, one of three openly homosexual members of Congress, as "Barney Fag." Armey was immediately attacked for his comment on the floor of the House and throughout the country, with many calling it an act of "hate speech" and "bigotry." Armey denied any such intention, and in a letter to the *New York Times* called the words a verbal "stumble"; a lead editorial in the *Times* had called his words "bigotry aforethought."

Armey published the 1995 book *The Freedom Revolution: The New House Majority Leader Tells Why Big Government Failed, Why Freedom Works and How We Will Rebuild America: A Strategy for the Rebirth of Freedom.*

North Dakota–born Armey received his 1963 B.A. from North Dakota's Jamestown College, his 1964 M.A. from the University of North Dakota, and his 1968 Ph.D. from the University of Oklahoma. Before entering poltics, he taught economics at the University of Montana (1964–65), West Texas State University (1967–68), Austin College (1968–72), and North Texas State University (1972–83). He was elected to the House from Texas's 26th Congressional District in 1984, and vaulted over many far more senior Republicans to become House Republican Conference chairperson in 1992. After the Republican victory in the 1994 congressional elections, he became the incoming majority leader of the House of Representatives. Armey wrote *Price-Theory: A Policy-Welfare Approach* (1977) and with others coauthored *Champions of Freedom, Vol. 14: The Privatization Revolution* (1989). He is married to Susan Byrd; they have four children.

FURTHER READING

"Dick Armey. . . ." PAUL BURKA. *Texas Monthly,* Sept. 1995.
"Armey, Richard K." *Current Biography,* June 1995.
"A think tank. . . ." GLORIA BORGER. *U.S. News & World Report*, Dec. 12, 1994.
"Newt's battle-ready Armey." HILARY HYLTON. *Time,* Nov. 28, 1994.

Arnold, Roseanne: See Roseanne.

Arnold, Tom (1959–) Actor Tom Arnold's major film lead of the year was to have been as the head of a very stupid family in *The Stupids*, directed by John Landis and based on the Henry Allard books. Made in 1995 and scheduled for December release, the film's opening was delayed until 1996. In 1995, Arnold costarred in a sleeper, the very popular film comedy *Nine Months*, opposite Hugh Grant as a yuppie, child-averse child psychiatrist and Julianne Moore as Grant's pregnant wife; Robin Williams, Joan Cusack, and Jeff Goldblum costarred; Chris Columbus wrote and directed.

Forthcoming were starring roles in the films *Carpool*, directed by Arthur Hiller and costarring David Paymer; *Big Bully*, directed by Steve Miner; and *Highway Patrol*.

On the personal side, Arnold married 22-year-old Julie Lynne Champnella in July.

Born in Ottumwa, Iowa, Arnold attended Indian Hills Community College there, and began his career in 1979, as a standup comedian in cabaret in Minneapolis. He joined the "Roseanne" show as a writer and co-producer in 1988; he and Roseanne at the same time developed a highly publicized relationship. They married in 1990 and divorced in 1994. They costarred in the situation comedy "BackField in Motion" (1991) and the television film *The Man Who Loved Elvis* (1992). Arnold starred in the title role of the television series "The Jackie Thomas Show" (1992–93). His other films include *Hero* (1992), *Undercover Blues* (1993), and *True Lies* (1994).

FURTHER READING

"20 questions. . . ." DAVID RENSIN. *Playboy,* June 1995.
"Tom in the eye. . . ." LISA SCHWARZBAUM. *Entertainment*, Aug. 5, 1994.
"Clash of the titans." MICHAEL A. LIPTON. *People,* May 2, 1994.
"Strange bedfellows." FRANK SWERTLOW. *Redbook,* June 1993.
"Roseanne & Tom Arnold." *Playboy,* June 1993.
"Two against. . . ." TOM GLIATTO. *People,* Mar. 29, 1993.
"Hog wild. . . ." JIM SCHMALTZ. *Advocate,* Mar. 9, 1993.
"Tom Arnold . . ." MARK MORRISON. *Us,* Feb. 1993.
"Tom Arnold. . . ." MICHAEL ANGELI. *Esquire,* Apr. 1992.

Asahara, Shoko (Chizuo Matsumoto; 1955–) On March 20, 1995, terrorists using the nerve gas sarin made several simultaneous attacks on the Tokyo subway sytem; coming at rush hour, the deadly gas killed 11 people and injured more than 5,000, many very seriously. On April 19, a phosgene gas attack injured more

than 300 at the main Yokohoma railway station. Several other less damaging attacks were also reported during the spring of 1995.

Police atttention immediately focused on the Aum Shinriko religious movement, led by Shoko Asahara, who had prophesied massive deaths due to gas attacks. Aum Shinriko, which claimed a worldwide membership of 30,000, had previously been accused of poison gas production, though no formal legal charges had been made. Massive police raids in the weeks that followed found many tons of chemicals that could be used to produce sarin and other poison gases, as well as large quantities of gas masks. Asahara went into hiding after the Tokyo attack; he and many of his followers were arrested on May 16, during a massive police raid on his headquarters at Kamikuishiki

Born in a rural town on the island of Kyushu, Asahara moved to Tokyo after graduating from high school. He worked as an acupuncturist and ran a folk medicine store for some years, then in 1984 founded the Aum company, which established a yoga school and health food store. In 1987, he founded the Aum Shinriko religious movement, which quickly became a very successful cult, attracting large numbers of people seeking a wholly absorbing new spiritual lifestyle. Asahara and his associates made heavy use of computers and stressed pseudoscience, while at the same time pursuing such standard cult practices as brainwashing through malnutrition, isolation, and repetition. They also demanded large sums of money from their recruits. Asahara had in recent years complained of failing health, and along with this had taken an increasingly dark view of the future of humanity. Among his works published in English are *Supreme Initiation* (1988) and *Maha Yana Sutra* (1989).

FURTHER READING

"Japan's mad messiah. . . ." RICHARD JEROME. *People,* June 12, 1995.
"Shoko Asahara. . . ." JAMES WALSH. "Prophet of poison." DAVID VAN BIEMA. *Time,* Apr. 3, 1995.

Aspin, Les (Leslie Aspin, Jr.; 1938–95) Milwaukee-born Les Aspin, an economist and Democratic politician, earned his 1960 B.A. from Yale, his 1962 M.A. from Oxford University, and his 1965 Ph.D. from the Massachusetts Institute of Technology. He taught economics at Marquette University (1962–65). Turning to politics, he was elected to Congress from Wisconsin in 1970 as an anti–Vietnam War liberal. Joining the Armed Services Committee, he quickly became a Congressional antiwar leader, and simultaneously a leading critic of the military on a very wide range of issues. He became increasingly influential on military matters, and in 1985 became chairman of the powerful House Armed Services Committee. At the same time, he moved toward more conservative positions in many areas, and urged his party to do the same. Aspin was at first cautious about U.S. involvement in the Persian Gulf, but later fully supported the 1991 Persian Gulf War. He was highly critical of Bush administration military policies after that war. Hoping to create a "peace dividend," he called for far greater military spending cuts than those proposed by the Pentagon. During the 1992 presidential campaign, he and Senator Sam Nunn served as key military affairs advisors to candidate Bill Clinton.

In December 1992 Aspin was appointed Secretary of Defense for the incoming Clinton administration. During his very difficult time in office, he encountered several major problems, beginning with the military's successful resistance to President Clinton's attempt to end the armed forces ban on gays. There were also difficult budget fights. Most damaging was Aspin's refusal to supply requested tanks to field commanders in Somalia, just before a firefight that cost the lives of 19 lightly armed American soldiers, for which Aspin publicly apologized. Aspin was the first Cabinet-level casualty of the Clinton administration, resigning on December 15, 1993. He left no survivors. (d. Washington, D.C.; May 21, 1995)

FURTHER READING

"Summing up." KEN ADELMAN. *Washingtonian,* July 1995.
"Les was more.. . . ." *New Republic,* June 12, 1995.
"A 'whiz kid'. . . ." WARD JUST. *Newsweek,* June 5, 1995.
Obituary. *Independent,* May 23, 1995.
Obituary. *Times* (of London), May 23, 1995.
Obituary. *New York Times,* May 22, 1995.
The Secretary of Defense Through Les Aspin. BOB ITALIA. Abdo & Daughters, 1993.
"The Aspin papers. . . ." MORTON KONDRACKE. *New Republic,* Apr. 27, 1992.

Assad, Hafez al- (1928–) Syrian President Hafez al-Assad settled into a newly cordial post–Gulf War relationship with the United States during 1995, with repeated gestures toward conclusion of his long negotiations with Israel over the future of the Golan Heights, which Israel occupied after the 1967 Six-Day War (Third Arab-Israeli War). But despite two meetings with U.S. President Bill Clinton in 1994, and repeated "shuttle diplomacy" visits between the two sides by U.S. Secretary of State Warren Christopher in 1995, no agreement was reached. There were, however, repeated public statements of good will by both sides, and repeated reports of an imminent breakthrough. At year's end, Syrian-Israeli peace talks began in Washington.

Meanwhile, Assad continued to focus on the ever-shifting mosaic of Middle East and Muslim world power relations—perhaps most notably the volatile situation in neighboring Iraq and the continuing rise of armed revolutionary fundamentalism in many countries. During 1995, Assad played a major role in securing a Saudi Arabian-Yemeni agreement on longstanding border disputes.

Assad began his political and military career as a Baath party activist and air force officer. He became an air force general after the 1963 Baathist coup, and air force commander in chief and minister of defense in 1966. He took power in 1970 and was named president of Syria in 1971. During the Cold War, he was closely allied with, and his armed forces were supplied by, the Soviet Union. His forces were badly defeated by Israel in the fourth Arab-Israeli (Yom Kippur) war of 1973.

During the Iran-Iraq war of the 1980s, he supported Iran against Iraq, a longtime enemy. During the early 1990s, he completed the process of turning Lebanon into a Syrian protectorate, while seeking U.S. help in securing the return of the Israeli-occupied Golan Heights and somewhat lessening Syrian support for anti-Israeli Hezbollah forces in southern Lebanon. During the Persian Gulf War, he supported the anti-Iraq coalition, and after the war courted the United States, as his former Soviet supporters and suppliers had vanished.

Born in Qirdaha, Assad attended Syria's Air Force College, graduating as an air lieutenant in 1955 and then taking other military training. He is married and has a daughter and three surviving sons. His oldest son and political heir, Major Basil al-Assad, head of his father's personal security forces, died in a 1994 traffic accident.

FURTHER READING

"Hope is as scarce. . . ." RAYMOND A. SCHROTH. *National Catholic Reporter*, Sept. 3, 1993.
"Hafez Assad. . . ." *Time*, Nov. 30, 1992.
"Syria's game. . . ." JUDITH MILLER. *New York Times Magazine*, Jan. 26, 1992.

Atanasoff, John Vincent (1903–95) Electrical engineer, physicist, and mathematician John Vincent Atanasoff, with Clifford E. Berry, built the world's first fully electronic computer, the ABC Computer (Atanasoff-Berry Computer). After receiving his 1930 doctorate in physics from the University of Wisconsin, Atanasoff taught at Iowa State University. It was there that he and graduate student Berry built their computer (1939–42). In 1941 he showed the computer to John Mauchly, one of the creators of the ENIAC computer; heavily funded by the federal government during World War II, the ENIAC was completed by 1945, and was for decades thought to have been the first electronic computer. Atanasoff and Berry obtained no patents for their work and were not credited until 1973, when the ENIAC patent was voided by a federal judge during a lawsuit over disputed royalties. Atanasoff's later career included World War II work with the federal Naval Ordnance Laboratory, postwar work on nuclear weapons, and his founding of the Ordnance Engineering Company. He continued to work with computers throughout his career. He was survived by his second wife, Lura Meeks Atanasoff, two daughters, and a son. (d. Frederick, Maryland; June 15, 1995)

FURTHER READING

Obituary. *Independent,* June 26, 1995.
Obituary. *New York Times,* June 17, 1995.

Atwood, Margaret (1939–) Fans of Canadian writer Margaret Atwood were rewarded with not one or two, but three books in 1995. Surprisingly, none were novels. Midyear saw *Morning in the Burning House*, her first poetry collection since 1987's *Selected Poems II*. This

Margaret Atwood: Writing and Subjectivity. COLIN NICHOLSON, ed. St. Martin's, 1994.
Writers & Company. ELEANOR WACHTEL. Knopf, 1993.
"Margaret Atwood. . . ." CLAUDIA DREIFUS. *Progressive,* Mar. 1992.
Margaret Atwood: Conversations. EARL G. INGERSOLL, ed. Ontario Review Press, 1991.
Margaret Atwood: A Reference Guide. JUDITH McCOMBS and CAROLE L. PALMER. G.K. Hall, 1991.

Aung San Suu Kyi (1945–) On July 10, 1995, Nobel laureate and world human rights leader Aung San Suu Kyi was unconditionally released from house arrest by the military government of Myanmar (Burma). She had been held for almost six years, while a worldwide protest movement demanded her release. Only a month before, at their annual meeting, the heads of the Group of Seven industrialized nations had strongly urged her release. During her long imprisonment, Aung San had maintained the support of the vast majority of Myanmarese; her imprisonment had also impeded Myanmar in its drive toward economic expansion, which required greater entry into world markets and access to international investment funds. On her release, Aung San quickly entered into talks aimed at freeing the hundreds of political prisoners still held by the military government, and simultaneously moved to rebuild the nation's democratic political movement.

Aung San took a very notably conciliatory attitude toward Myanmar's military in the months that followed her release, calling for talks aimed at a peaceful transition to democracy, leniency in prosecution of crimes committed by the military, and a possible place for the military leaders in a future democratic state. On November 29, however, she announced that the National League for Democracy, which she headed, would boycott the constitutional convention set up by the military without the participation of her party; as the military began to make threatening gestures, a major confrontation seemed possible.

Rangoon-born Aung San Suu Kyi is the daughter of Aung San (1914–47), the founder of modern Burma (now Myanmar), who became Burma's first prime minister in 1947 and was assassinated on July 19, 1947. She left Burma in 1960, when her mother became Burmese ambassador to India; she was educated in India and at Oxford University, and married archaeologist Michael Aris in 1972; they have two sons. She

was followed by *Strange Things: Fictions of the Malevolent North in Canadian Literature,* from three lectures on Canadian themes and writers. She also published a new children's book, *Princess Prunella and the Purple Peanut,* a parody of fairy tale classics such as "The Princess and the Pea," with illustrations by Maryann Kovalski. Another book, *Good Bones and Simple Murders,* a collection of tales and sketches, had been published in December 1994. Atwood also coedited (with Robert Weaver) the *New Oxford Book of Canadian Short Stories* (2nd ed.) and contributed a piece to *Women on Hunting,* edited by Pam Houston. A new novel was scheduled for 1996 publication.

Educated at the University of Toronto and Harvard University, Atwood is a versatile poet, novelist, short story writer, essayist, and editor, whose other works include *The Edible Woman* (1969), *Surfacing* (1973), *Life Before Man* (1979), *Murder in the Dark* (1983), *The Handmaid's Tale* (1986, basis for the 1990 film), *Cat's Eye* (1989), *Wilderness Tips* (1991), *The Robber Bride* (1993), and a children's environmental work, *For the Birds.* She is married to Graeme Gibson; they have one child.

FURTHER READING

Women Who Write II. LUCINDA SMITH. Simon & Schuster, 1994.
Who's Writing This?: Notations on the Authorial I, with Self-Portraits. DANIEL HALPERN, ed. Ecco, 1994.

returned to Burma in 1988 to nurse her sick mother, who died later that year, and soon became a leader of the democratic opposition, heading the nonviolent National League for Democracy. In 1988 she was placed under house arrest and forbidden to run for office and, after the brief democratic government was overthrown in August 1988, stayed on in house arrest to lead the democratic opposition. Her party swept the May 1990 democratic elections, which the military refused to honor, instead tightening its control of the country and making her imprisonment even more difficult. Her books include *Aung San of Burma: A Biographical Portrait by His Daughter* (1984) and the essay collection *Freedom from Fear* (1992).

FURTHER READING

"The lady triumphs." EDWARD KLEIN. *Vanity Fair,* Oct. 1995.

"Dark victory." BARBARA BRADLEY. *Vogue,* Oct. 1995.

"Glass rods. . . ." *Economist,* July 22, 1995.

Prisoner for Peace: Aung San Suu Kyi and Burma's Struggle for Democracy. JOHN PARENTEAU. M. Reynolds, 1994.

"Extraordinary people." HERBERT BUCHSBAUM. *Scholastic Update,* Dec. 3, 1993.

"Burma's Gandhi." DAVID S. TOOLAN. *America,* Feb. 8, 1992.

"Aung San Suu Kyi." *Current Biography,* Feb. 1992.

B

Babyface (Kenneth Edmonds; 1958–)
Singer, songwriter, and producer Kenneth
"Babyface" Edmonds was greatly honored by his
peers in 1995. He received five Grammy nominations; two of them became Grammy Awards—
for best male rhythm and blues performance of
the song "When Can I See You," and for writing
the song "I'll Make Love to You," the Boyz II
Men hit.

Babyface was for the fourth time named songwriter of the year by the Broadcast Music Institute (BMI). Tony Braxton's recording of his song
"Breathe Again" was BMI's most performed song
of the year; it was one of seven 1995 Babyface
BMI award-winners. He was also named American Music Awards top soul and rhythm and
blues artist of the year.

Sure to garner a good many future awards was
his soundtrack album for the film *Waiting to Exhale*, starring Whitney Houston; containing fifteen of his new songs, among them "Exhale
(Shoop Shoop)," performed by Houston, Toni
Braxton, Aretha Franklin, Brandy, Mary J.
Blige, Faith Evans, and several other major
woman singers, it went right to the top of the
charts. Babyface also continued to be a prolific
record producer; among his 1995 productions
was the album *Reflections*, featuring the work of
the group After 7, which included his brothers,
Melvin and Kevon Edmonds.

Indianapolis-born Edmonds emerged as a
leading figure in the late 1980s, after playing in
bands and beginning his songwriting and producing collaboration with Antonio "L.A." Reid.
In 1987, he and Reid founded the LaFace record
company, working with such artists as Whitney
Houston, Boyz II Men, Bobby Brown, Toni Braxton, and Paula Abdul. As a performer, his singles include the albums *Lovers* (1989), *Tender
Lover*, and *For the Cool in You* (1993). He also
co-wrote the soundtrack of the film *Boomerang*
(1993). His second wife is Tracey Edmonds.

FURTHER READING

"Babyface boom. . . ." JEREMY HELLIGAR. *People,* Feb.
   27, 1995.
"Babyface shows. . . ." LAURA B. RANDOLPH. *Ebony,*
   July 1994.
"Babyface talks. . . ." *Jet,* Mar. 14, 1994.

Bacon, Kevin (1958–) Emerging film star Kevin Bacon played a major role in a very major film in 1995, as astronaut Jack Swigert opposite Tom Hanks and Bill Paxton as astronauts Jim Lovell and Fred Haise in *Apollo 13,* directed by Ron Howard; Gary Sinise, Ed Harris, Kathleen Quinlan, and Jean Speegle Howard co-starred. Based on the autobiographical book *Lost Moon,* by Lovell and Jeffrey Kluger, the film tells the story of the Apollo 13 moon flight, in which the American spaceship *Odyssey* came very close to landing on the moon, but was forced to abort the mission after an on-board explosion caused the main spacecraft to lose oxygen and power; the astronauts took refuge in their exploration craft, the *Aquarius,* and ultimately piloted the craft safely back to Earth. The acclaimed film and its stars were widely regarded as Academy Award contenders.

Bacon also starred as Henry Young, a convicted murderer and inhumanly treated prisoner in the film *Murder in the First,* directed by Marc Rocco and co-starring Christian Slater and Gary Oldman. In a considerable change of pace, Bacon also starred as the voice of the half-dog, half-wolf title character of the animated Alaskan action film *Balto,* co-starring Bob Hoskins as the voice of the snow goose Boris; Bridget Fonda as the voice of the husky, Jenna; Jim Cummings as the voice of the dog, Steele; and Phil Collins as the voices of the polar bears Muk and Luk; Simon Wells directed.

Forthcoming was a starring role in the film *Sleepers,* written, directed, and produced by Barry Levinson, and co-starring Robert De Niro, Brad Pitt, and Jason Patric.

Philadelphia-born Bacon made his Hollywood screen and New York stage debuts in 1978, in the film *National Lampoon's Animal House* and the off-Broadway play *Getting Out.* He won an off-Broadway Obie Award for his role in the play *Forty Deuce* (1981) and made his Broadway debut in *Slab Boys* (1983).

Further films included *Starting Over* (1979), *Friday the 13th* (1980), *Only When I Laugh* (1981), *Diner* (1982), *Footloose* (1984), *Quicksilver* (1985), *White Water Summer* (1987), *Planes, Trains and Automobiles* (1988), *She's Having a Baby* (1988), *The Big Picture* (1989), *Flatliners* (1990), *He Said/She Said* (1991), *JFK* (1992), *A Few Good Men* (1992), *The River Wild* (1994), and *The Air Up There* (1994). He has also appeared in several television films and many series episodes. He is married to actress Kyra Sedgwick; they have two children.

FURTHER READING

"25 helpings of. . . ." RAY ROGERS. *Interview,* Oct. 1994.
"Totally candid. . . ." CHRIS CHASE. *Cosmopolitan,* Sept. 1994.

Baldwin, Alec (Alexander Rae Baldwin, 3rd; 1958–) Stage and screen star Alec Baldwin re-created his 1992 stage role as Stanley Kowalski in a 1995 television production of Ten-

Alec Baldwin (right) and Penelope Ann Miller.

nessee Williams' classic play *A Streetcar Named Desire*, opposite Jessica Lange as Blanche DuBois, John Goodman as Mitch, and Diane Lane as Stella Kowalski. Glenn Jordan produced and directed the very well received television film. Baldwin was nominated for a Golden Globe award as best actor in a miniseries or telefilm for the role.

Baldwin also co-starred as the narrator of the film *Two Bits*, set in Depression-era Philadelphia. Al Pacino starred as Grandpa, a wise, dying old man who passes his insights on to his 12-year-old grandson, played by Jerry Barrone; Baldwin plays the grandson as an adult, telling the story decades later. Mary Elizabeth Mastrantonio co-starred as the boy's mother. The film was directed by James Foley and written by Joseph Stefano.

Forthcoming were starring roles opposite Demi Moore in the film *The Juror*, directed by Brian Gibson and written by Ted Tally; and in the film *Incognito*, directed by Peter Weller and co-starring Patsy Pollack. Still forthcoming was a starring role in *Heaven's Prisoners*, directed by Phil Joanou, with a cast that included Mary Stuart Masterson, Teri Hatcher, Kelly Lynch, and Eric Roberts.

Long Island–born Baldwin starred in the television series "Knots Landing," and in the New York theater in such plays as *Serious Money* and *Prelude to a Kiss* (for which he won an Obie award), and in his Tony-nominated role as Stanley Kowalski in the 1992 Broadway revival of *A Streetcar Named Desire*. He became a film star in the late 1980s, in such films as *She's Having a Baby* (1988), *Beetlejuice* (1988), *Married to the Mob* (1988), *Talk Radio* (1988), and *Working Girl* (1988), making his major breakthrough in *The Hunt for Red October* (1990). His other films include *Miami Blues* (1990), *Alice* (1990), *The Marrying Man* (1991), *Glengarry Glen Ross* (1992), *Prelude to a Kiss* (1992), *Malice* (1993), *Sliver* (1993), *The Getaway* (1994), and *The Shadow* (1994).

Baldwin attended George Washington University (1976–79), and studied theater at New York University and the Lee Strasberg Institute (1979–80). He and actress Kim Basinger married in 1993. Three younger brothers—Daniel, William, and Stephen—are also actors.

FURTHER READING

" 'My work came first. . . .' " DOTSON RADER. *Parade*, July 3, 1994.
"Kim and Alec." STEVE POND. *Us*, Mar. 1994.
"Alec Baldwin. . . ." IVAN SOLOTAROFF. *Esquire*, Feb. 1994.
"Baldwin, Alec." *Current Biography*, July 1992.

Ballantine, Ian Keith (1916–95) New York City–born Ian Ballantine attended Columbia University and the London School of Economics. While in London in the late 1930s, he became associated with Allen Lane of the pioneering paperback publisher Penguin Books. On their return to the United States in 1939, Ballantine and his wife and partner, Betty, established the New York office of Penguin Books. They left Penguin in 1945 to found Bantam Books as a pioneering, highly successful reprint house, publishing inexpensive paperback editions of popular books, mixing classics and the mystery and western genres. In 1952, they founded the equally successful Ballantine Books, changing their focus from reprints to original publications, and working largely in the mystery, western, science fiction, and fantasy genres, though also publishing more general fiction and nonfiction. They also pioneered in the simultaneous hardcover and softcover publication of some books. After selling Ballantine Books to Random House in 1974, they rejoined Bantam Books, also developing Rufus Publications, in which they worked as publishers and editors. He was survived by his wife, a son, and a brother. (d. Barryville, New York; Mar. 9, 1995)

FURTHER READING

Obituary. *New York Times*, Mar. 16, 1995.
Obituary. *Times* (of London), Mar. 15, 1995.
Obituary. *Independent,* Mar. 14, 1995.

Barkley, Charles Wade (1963–) In the 1994–95 season, basketball star Charles Barkley still led his Phoenix Suns team in minutes played, rebounds, and points, and remained the seventh-leading active scorer in the league, averaging 23.3 points per game. But it was, again, not good enough to take them to a long sought National Basketball Association championship. Again, it was the Houston Rockets who barred the way, knocking off Phoenix in the Western Conference semifinals in a hard-fought seven-game series. Phoenix won the first two games, but the defending champion Rockets came back in the third game to rout Phoenix, holding Barkley to a career-low five points. In the seventh and final game, which Phoenix lost by just one point, Barkley had 18 points and 23 rebounds, even though he was hobbled by a leg injury. After that loss, he again said he would probably retire, and later underwent arthroscopic surgery to repair torn cartilage in his left knee.

But in late September, Barkley announced that he would return, partly because Phoenix made some trades to make the team more competitive. Though he said his knee was rehabilitated and his back felt fine, he sat out much of the preseason. Other teammates had injuries, too, and at year's end the Suns had a surprisingly poor record of 13–14. Barkley himself was seventh in the league in scoring, averaging 23.5 points a game, and fourth in rebounding, with 11.5. It remained to be seen if Barkley (and his teammates) could regain their health and regroup to become contenders.

In February 1995, Barkley had been one of two starting forwards on the Western Conference team in the All-Star game; during All-Star weekend, he was roasted by Billy Crystal at a charity dinner.

Born in Leeds, Alabama, Barkley emerged as a nationally recognized player at Auburn University (1981–84). Although often overweight and at odds with his coaching staff, he was a strong scorer and the leading rebounder in the Southeastern Conference. He was a first-round choice in the NBA draft after his junior year, going to the Philadelphia 76ers (1984–92). He became one of the league's leading rebounders and scorers, and a perennial All-Star forward, on the second team (1986–87), then on the starting team (1988–92 for the East; 1993 and 1995 for the West). He was named Most Valuable Player in the 1991 All-Star game; in 1994, he was the leading vote-getter, but was unable to play because of injury. He was also part of the gold-medal-winning "Dream Team" at the 1992 Barcelona Olympics.

Barkley joined the Phoenix Suns (1992–). In his first season there he was named the NBA's MVP, posted the league's best record, and won the Western Conference championship, but lost to Michael Jordan and the Chicago Bulls in the NBA finals. The always quotable Barkley published an autobiography, *Outrageous* (1992), written with Roy Johnson, Jr., and *Sir Charles: The Wit and Wisdom of Charles Barkley* (1994), written with Rick Reilly. Barkley and his wife, Maureen Barkley, have a daughter.

FURTHER READING

"The many faces of. . . ." "Barkley. . . ." DARRYL
    HOWERTON. "Things you never knew about. . . ."
    WILLIAM LADSON. "Favorite Sun. . . ." BARRY M.
    BLOOM. "Charles in charge." CAM BENTY. *Sport,*
    June 1995.
"Barkley's last shot." FRANK DEFORD. *Vanity Fair,*
    Feb. 1995.
The Phoenix Suns and Charles Barkley. MIKE
    TULEMELLO. Longstreet, 1995.
"Meaty beaty. . . ." PETER RICHMOND. *GQ,* Nov. 1994.

Somebody's Gotta Be Me: The Wide World of the One and Only Charles Barkley. DAVID CASSTEVENS. Andrews & McMeel, 1994

Sport Shots: Charles Barkley. CHIP LOVITT. Scholastic, 1994.

"Who are you. . . ." VERN E. SMITH and ARIC PRESS. *Newsweek,* May 24, 1993.

"Chuck." MARK JACOBSON. *Esquire,* May 1993.

"Charles Barkley." TOM BOSWELL. *Playboy,* May 1993.

"Prodigal Sun. . . ." WILLIAM PLUMMER. *People,* Feb. 22, 1993.

"Hot head." Nov. 9, 1992. "Charles Barkley." Mar. 9, 1992. RICK REILLY. *Sports Illustrated.*

Sports Great Charles Barkley. GLEN MACNOW. Enslow, 1992.

"Barkley, Charles." *Current Biography,* Oct. 1991.

"Headstrong." JEFF COPLON. *New York Times Magazine,* Mar. 17, 1991.

Barr, Roseanne: See Roseanne.

Barry, Dave (ca. 1947–)

Unlike Dave Barry's previous books, which were collections of his newspaper pieces, his 1995 offering was written specifically for book publication. *Dave Barry's Complete Guide to Guys: A Fairly Short Book* plumbs the shallows of the question "What is a guy?". Though reviewers frequently praised his sophomoric humor, some suggested that it was better suited to the short doses of his columns. The book itself was published in time for Father's Day, with Barry going on a ten-city two-week publicity tour. It was also released in audiobook form and on CD, with John Ritter reading and an introduction read by Barry.

Born in Armonk, New York, Barry received his B.A. from Haverford College. He began his career in journalism as a reporter and editor for the West Chester, Pennsylvania, *Daily Local News* (1971–75), and later worked for the Associated Press out of Philadelphia (1975–83). He moved to Miami as a columnist for the *Miami Herald* (1983–), winning a writing award from the Society of Newspaper Editors (1987) and a Pulitzer Prize for commentary (1988). He emerged a widely read author in the early 1980s, with books such as *Taming of the Screw: Several Million Homeowner's Problems Sidestepped* (1983), *Babies and Other Hazards of Sex* (1984), *Dave Barry's Bad Habits: A One Hundred Percent Fact-Free Book* (1985; 1993), *Stay Fit and Healthy Until You're Dead* (1985), *Dave Barry's Guide to Marriage and/or Sex* (1987), *Claw Your Way to the Top* (1987), *Dave Barry's Greatest Hits* (1988), *Homes and Other Black Holes: The Happy Homeowner's Guide* (1988), *Dave Barry Slept Here: A Sort of History of the United States* (1989), *Dave Barry Turns 40* (1990), *Dave Barry Talks Back* (1991), *Dave Barry's Only Travel Guide You'll Ever Need* (1991), *Dave Barry Does Japan* (1992), and *Dave Barry Is Not Making This Up* (1994). Barry achieved new celebrity with the television series "Dave's World" (1993–), starring Harry Anderson playing Barry. He and his second wife, Beth (Elizabeth) Barry, an editor of the *Miami Herald*'s Sunday magazine, have one son. They were in the process of divorcing in 1995.

FURTHER READING

" 'All I think. . . .' " GLENN GARVIN. *Reason,* Dec. 1994.

"Sharp sting. . . ." SIMON HOGGART. *Observer,* May 2, 1993.

Barry, Marion Shepilov, Jr. (1936–)

Washington mayor Marion Barry, who had made an extraordinary comeback in winning the 1994 election despite his earlier prison term for cocaine possession, encountered a fiscal crisis in 1995. Barry had asked Congress to provide large funds for the insolvent city, projecting a $722 million deficit in 1995, half again as much as the $490 million deficit projected by former mayor

Sharon Pratt Dixon Kelly. At the same time, he had refused to cut expenditures. The city's power to borrow was essentially gone, its bond ratings so low that huge interest rates would be necessary if it were to go into the bond market. Congress responded to the fiscal crisis by appointing a new financial control board, headed by former Federal Reserve Board governor Andrew Brimmer, with powers so broad as to give it effective control over the city's finances and major aspects of its administration. Barry continued on as mayor, but with much power diminished.

On the personal side, Barry had a successful operation for prostate cancer.

Mississippi-born Barry was active in the civil rights movement of the 1960s and moved into Washington, D.C. politics in the early 1970s, as a member of the school board and then in 1976 of the city council. He began his long, highly controversial tenure as mayor of Washington in 1979. He was convicted on one misdemeanor count of cocaine possession in 1990, and served a six-month federal prison term. Then, stressing his African-American heritage and announcing that he had given up drink and drugs, he re-emerged as a power in city politics. In 1994, he won the Washington Democratic mayoralty primary and then went on to win a fourth term as mayor.

Barry's 1958 B.S. was from Lemoyne College and his 1960 M.S. was from Fisk University. He and his third wife, Effi Barry, separated in 1990 and were later divorced; they had one child. He married Cora Masters, a teacher, in 1994; she has two daughters from a previous marriage.

FURTHER READING

"Marion Barry. . . ." JEFFREY GOLDBERG. *New York Times Magazine,* Oct. 29, 1995.
"Born again." BILL GIFFORD. *New Republic,* Sept. 19, 1994.
"Marion Barry's. . . ." PAUL RUFFINS. *Nation,* Sept. 5, 1994.

Barrymore, Drew (1975–) Moving toward top roles in what could become another extraordinary Barrymore career, Drew Barrymore in 1995 starred opposite Chris O'Donnell in the well-received film *Mad Love.* She played a manic-depressive "wild" young woman, he a sober young man in love, who gives everything up

to free her from a mental hospital and run away with her in an odyssey that soon goes outside the law. Antonia Bird directed.

Barrymore also starred in the film *Boys on the Side* as Holly, a troubled young woman who becomes one of a group of three women traveling together across the country; they ultimately find themselves living together as an extended family. Whoopi Goldberg and Mary-Louise Parker costarred; Herbert Ross wrote and directed. Barrymore also played a strong supporting role in the hit sequel *Batman Forever,* directed by Joel Schumacher and starring Val Kilmer, Nicole Kidman, Tommy Lee Jones, and Jim Carrey.

Forthcoming were starring film roles in Marshall Herskovitz's *The Honest Courtesan, Frigid and Impotent,* and a forthcoming Woody Allen movie.

Bearer of a great name in the American theatre, Barrymore is the daughter of John Barrymore, Jr. and Jaid Barrymore, and the granddaughter of legendary actor John Barrymore (John Sidney Blythe; 1882–1942), who was the brother of Ethel and Lionel Barrymore and the son of Georgianna Drew Barrymore and Maurice Barrymore. Drew Barrymore made her film debut as a child in *Altered States* (1980), and appeared in *E.T: The Extra-Terrestrial* (1982), *Irreconcilable Differences* (1984), *Firestarter* (1984), and *Cat's Eye* (1985), as well as several television films. She soon encountered substance abuse problems, which cut her early career short. Barrymore resumed her career in her late teens, then quickly moving into starring roles. Among her feature films were *Far From Home* (1989), *Poison Ivy* (1992), *Guncrazy* (1993), and *Bad Girls* (1994); her television film roles included *Beyond Control: The Amy Fisher Story* (1993). At age 14, she published the autobiography *Little Girl Lost* (1990). Barrymore married Welshman Jeremy Thomas in 1994.

FURTHER READING

"Drew Barrymore. . . ." CHRIS MUNDY. *Rolling Stone,* June 15, 1995.
"The Drew that grew." INGRID SISCHY. *Interview,* May 1995.
"Xpansive Drew." RICKI LAKE. *Interview,* Oct. 1994.
"Tough stuff." TRISH DEITCH ROHRER. *Us,* May 1994.
"Love at first light." SUSAN SCHINDEHETTE and TODD GOLD. *People,* Apr. 11, 1994.
"Drew Barrymore is." *Esquire,* Feb. 1994.
"Crazy for Drew." ELLEN VON UNWERTH and DAVID HANDELMAN. *Vogue,* June 1993.
"Drew Barrymore. . . ." MARTHA FRANKEL. *Cosmopolitan,* May 1993.
"Good bad girl." BERNARD WEINRAUB. *Guardian,* Mar. 19, 1993.
"Drew Barrymore." KEVIN KOFFLER. *Seventeen,* Jan. 1992.

Bates, Kathy (1948–   ) In 1995, stage and screen star Kathy Bates played the title role as the housekeeper accused of murder in the film *Dolores Claiborne*, adapted for film by Tony Gilroy from the Stephen King novel and directed by Taylor Hackford; the cast included Jennifer Jason Leigh as her daughter, Christopher Plummer, and Judy Parfitt. Bates also starred as the mother opposite George C. Scott as the grandfather and Charley Talbert as the teenage title character in the coming-of-age film *Angus,* directed by Patrick Read Johnson.

On television, Bates costarred as a homeless neighborhood woman in the television film *The West Side Waltz,* written and directed for television by Ernest Thompson, based on his play, and costarring Shirley MacLaine, Liza Minnelli, Jennifer Grey, and Robert Pastorelli. She directed and starred in a segment of the television film *Talking With,* part of the "Great Performances" series.

Forthcoming were starring roles in the film *Diabolique,* opposite Sharon Stone, Chazz Palminteri, and Isabelle Adjani, and directed by Jeremiah Chechick; opposite Emilio Estevez and Martin Sheen in the film *The War at Home;* and in the film *To Gillian, on her 37th Birthday,* directed by Michael Pressman and costarring Michelle Pfeiffer, Clair Danes, and Peter Gallagher.

Memphis-born Bates began her acting career in New York in 1970, often working in children's and regional theater, with occasional small film roles, as in Milos Forman's *Taking Off* (1971) and Dustin Hoffman's *Straight Time* (1978), and guest spots on television series and telefilms. Her first lead was in the off-Broadway play *Vanities* (1976), and she originated the role of Lenny McGrath in Beth Henley's Pulitzer Prize–winning play *Crimes of the Heart* (1979). Her breakout stage role was as the suicidal Jessie Cates in Marsha Norman's Pulitzer Prize–winning '*Night Mother* (1983), for which she won the Outer Critics Circle Award and a Tony nomination. This was followed by a string of leading stage roles, including *Come Back to the Five and Dime, Jimmy Dean, Jimmy Dean* (1982) and *Frankie and Johnny in the Claire de Lune* (1987), for which she won an Obie Award.

After her 1985 move to Los Angeles, she began to play supporting roles on film, as in *Arthur 2: On the Rocks* (1988) and *Dick Tracy* (1990). She won a best actress Oscar for *Misery* (1990), and also starred in *At Play in the Fields of the Lord* (1991), *Fried Green Tomatoes* (1991), *The Road to Mecca* (1992), *Shadows and Fog* (1992), *Prelude to a Kiss* (1992), *Used People* (1992), *A Home of Our Own* (1993), *Curse of the Starving Class* (1994), and *North* (1994). Bates graduated from Southern Methodist University in Dallas. She married actor Tony Campisi in 1991.

FURTHER READING

"Kathy Bates. . . ." MELANIE BERGER. *Ladies Home Journal*, Jan. 1993.
"Kathy Bates. . . ." WAYNE MILLER. *First for Women*, June 8, 1992.
"Kathy Bates. . . ." BROOK HERSEY. *Glamour*, Feb. 1992.
"Bates, Kathy." *Current Biography*, Sept. 1991.
"Kathy Bates." MICHAEL LASSELL and TIMOTHY GREENFIELD-SANDERS. *Interview*, Aug. 1991.
" 'I never was. . . .' " DAVID SACKS. *New York Times Magazine*, Jan. 27, 1991.

Bazargan, Mehdi (1907–95)

Tehran-born Mehdi Bazargan, an engineer, educator, and politician, studied engineering in Paris in the 1930s, then returned to Iran to teach at Tehran University, where he ultimately chaired the engineering faculty. During the early post–World War II period, he became a leader of the opposition to the Shah and in 1951 joined the National Front government of Mohammed Mossadeq as head of the nationalized National Iranian Oil Company. He went underground after the army revolt of August 1953 toppled Mossadeq's government. He cofounded the National Resistance Movement in 1961 and was imprisoned by the Shah's government several times.

Bazargan was a prominent supporter of Ayatollah Ruhollah Khomeini in the late 1970s and became prime minister of Khomeini's new government on February 11, 1989. He resigned on November 6, 1989, at odds with Khomeini over the seizure of the American embassy in Tehran, and went over into opposition of Khomeini's increasingly tyrannical government. Bazargan continued to serve in the parliament until 1984; his Iranian Freedom Movement was the only legal opposition until it, too, was outlawed in 1990. Among his works published in English are *Work and Islam* and *The Inevitable Victory* (both 1979). He was survived by his wife, Malak, three daughters, and two sons. (d. Zurich, Switzerland; January 20, 1995)

FURTHER READING

Obituary. *Independent*, Jan. 21, 1995.
Obituary. *Times* (of London), Jan. 21, 1995.
Obituary. *New York Times*, Jan. 21, 1995.

Begelman, David (1922–95)

New York City–born David Begelman, a longtime entertainment industry executive, was at the center of a notable Hollywood scandal in 1978. He was forced to step down as president of Columbia Pictures after he had pleaded no contest to the crime of forging three checks totaling $40,000. One of the checks, for $10,000, was a false expense check to actor Cliff Robertson, who never received the money and blew the whistle on Begelman when the phantom check caused him tax problems. In a distasteful Hollywood twist publicized by author David McClintock in his book *Indecent Disclosure* (1982), Begelman was quickly reinstated in his job, while Robertson was blacklisted by Hollywood for many years, suffering massive career damage.

Begelman's career began with an 11-year stay at the Music Corporation of America (1948–60). He then cofounded the Creative Management Associates agency, which he left to become president of Columbia Pictures (1973–76). He turned ailing Columbia around, producing several commercial hits. Begelman stayed at Columbia as an independent producer until 1980, then left to become president of MGM, where much of what his company produced failed in the film marketplace. He lasted at MGM only until 1982, then left to form his own production company, Gladden. In 1994, Gladden production company was forced to declare bankruptcy after four entertainment unions charged Begelman with failing to pay more than $4 million in residuals to their members. His money troubles multiplying, Begelman committed suicide. He was survived by his third wife, Annabelle, a daughter, a sister, and a brother. (d. Los Angeles; August 8, 1995)

FURTHER READING

"Final exposure." DAVID McCLINTICK. *Vanity Fair*, Nov. 1995.
"The man who. . . ." PETER BART. *Variety*, Aug. 14, 1995.
Obituary. *Times* (of London), Aug. 12, 1995.
Obituary. *Independent*, Aug. 11, 1995.
Obituary. *New York Times*, Aug. 9, 1995.
Obituary. *Variety*, Aug. 9, 1995

Belle, Albert Jojuan (Joey Belle; 1966–)

Cleveland Indians outfielder Albert Belle was the American League's home run leader in 1995, with 50, and was tied with Edgar Martinez for

most doubles, with 51. He therefore became the first major league player ever to have 50 or more home runs and doubles in the same season, even though it had been shortened by a strike, and the only active player ever to have 30 or more home runs in four straight seasons. Belle's 17 home runs in September tied a record for that month set by Babe Ruth in 1927. His 31 homers in August and September set a new record for a two-month period; Babe Ruth and Roger Maris had had 28. Belle also led the league in slugging percentage, with .690; tied Martinez for the league lead in runs scored, with 121; and tied with Mo Vaughn for most runs batted in, with 126. He was also eighth in the league in batting average, with .317, and tied for seventh in total hits, with 173. Belle was the starting left-fielder in the American League line-up for the All-Star game.

However, in postseason play Belle went into a slump. In the American League championship series against the Seattle Mariners, though the Indians won, Belle had only 4 hits for 18 times at bat, for a batting average of .222, and scored only one run, a homer. Little better in the World Series, he had four hits for 17 times at bat, for an average of .235, and drove in four runs. One of his two home runs came off Atlanta's ace pitcher, Greg Maddux, early in game 5, but Cleveland ultimately lost in six games.

Belle narrowly lost to Mo Vaughn as the American League's Most Valuable Player. Some suggest that Belle would have won if not for his notoriously surly personal style, which has frequently involved abuse of sports reporters, most notably a profanity-laden tirade against NBC television reporter Hannah Storm during the 1995 World Series. (Belle later apologized.) On Halloween, when some teenagers threw eggs at Belle's house, Belle allegedly tried to run them down in his car, and was charged with a misdemeanor: willful or wanton disregard of safety.

Born in Shreveport, Louisiana, Belle graduated from Huntington High School there, then spent three years at Louisiana State University (1985–87), where he set numerous university records. Selected by the Cleveland Indians in the 1987 free agent draft, he played in the minor leagues (1987–89), at Kinston, Waterloo, and Canton-Akron, before coming to the majors with the Indians (1989–90; 1991); he went back to the minors (1990; 1991) with Colorado Springs and Canton-Akron, before coming into the majors for good (1992–   ). He led the American League in runs batted in, with 129 (1993), and in total bases, with 294 (1994); and was named to the American League All-Star team three times (1993–95).

FURTHER READING

"Belle epoque." BRUCE SCHOENFELD. *Sporting News*, July 4, 1994.

Bening, Annette (1958–   ) Actress Annette Bening starred opposite Michael Douglas in the 1995 film comedy *The American President*, directed and produced by Rob Reiner. Bening played environmentalist lobbyist Sydney Wade, who, to the horror of the White House staff, falls into an innocent love affair with Michael Shepherd, (played by Douglas), a liberal, decent human being and widower who is also a very popular President about to run for a second term. Despite frantic staff efforts, their affair supplies the opposition with a very juicy scandal, exploited to the hilt by villainous Senator Bob Rumson, played by Richard Dreyfuss. Martin Sheen, Michael J. Fox, Anne Deavere Smith, David Paymer, and Samantha Mathis costarred. Bening was nominated for a Golden Globe award as best actor in a musical or comedy.

In a wholly different vein, Bening starred as powerful and effective Queen Elizabeth in a very well received film adaptation of Shakespeare's

Richard III, opposite Ian McKellen in the title role; McKellen cowrote the screenplay with director Richard Loncraine. The classic work was reinterpreted as a murder-laden 1930s gangster film, set in English high society. Costarring were Jim Broadbent as Buckingham, Robert Downey, Jr. as Rivers, Nigel Hawthorne, Kristin Scott, Maggie Smith, and John Wood.

Kansas-born Bening was raised in San Diego and attended San Diego's Mesa College and San Francisco State University. She spent five years at San Francisco's American Conservatory Theatre (ACT)—first as student, then company member—and a season at the Denver Theater Center, before coming to New York. Winning the lead in Tina Howe's *Coastal Disturbances*, she garnered a 1987 Tony nomination on its move to Broadway. She had brief roles in John Hughes' film *The Great Outdoors* (1988) and on Broadway in Michael Weller's *Spoils of War* (1988) before being signed for her breakthrough role in *Valmont* (1988), then going on to star in *The Grifters* (1990), *Regarding Henry* (1991), *Guilty by Suspicion* (1991), *Bugsy Siegel* (1991), and *Love Affair* (1994). Formerly married to actor Steve White, Bening married actor Warren Beatty in 1992; they have a daugter and a son.

FURTHER READING

"The lady vanquishes." JESSE KORNBLUTH. *Town & Country*, Dec. 1995.
"Love story." DOMINICK DUNNE. *Vanity Fair*, Sept. 1994.

"Annette Bening. . . ." *Cosmopolitan*, Dec. 1991.
"Regarding Annette." CHRISTOPHER CONNELLY and TIMOTHY WHITE. *Premiere*, July 1991.
"Annette Bening." GRAHAM FULLER. *Interview*, May 1991.

Bennett, Alan (1934–) Fresh out of university in 1960, Alan Bennett became celebrated as one of the quartet of actor-writers who created the enormously popular satirical revue *Beyond the Fringe*, his cohorts being Peter Cook, Jonathan Miller, and Dudley Moore. Though Bennett continues to be seen ocasionally as an actor, it is as a deft and sensitive writer, primarily of plays and scripts, that he has come to be best known. In 1995, American Bennett aficianados had a rare treat, a new book: *Writing Home*. The collection of reviews, essays, sketches, and diary excerpts had already been a best-seller in England, and was warmly received in America, where Bennett toured in August. Particularly praised was "The Lady in the Van," Bennett's portrait of Miss Shepherd, a homeless woman who lived in squalid vans, one of which Bennett allowed her to park in his yard for 17 years, until she died in 1989. At home in Britain, Bennett hosted a Christmas Day television special "The Abbey," on the cathedral at Westminster. Bennett the actor was also heard, if not seen, as reader on the BBC Radio dramatization of A. A. Milne's *Winnie the Pooh* and *The House at Pooh Corner*, released on audiocasette late in 1995.

A native of Leeds, in northern England, Bennett was educated at Leeds Modern School and Exeter College, Oxford University. He was briefly junior lecturer in modern history at Magdalen College, Oxford (1960–62), while beginning his career as a playwright and actor in *Beyond the Fringe*, originally in Edinburgh (1960), then with great success in London (1961) and New York (1962). Among his other plays are *Getting On* (1971), *Habeas Corpus* (1973), *The Old Country* (1977), *Enjoy* (1980), *Kafka's Dick* (1986), *Single Spies* (1988), *The Madness of George III* (1991; basis of the 1994 film), and his adaptation of *The Wind in the Willows* (1990). His filmscripts include *A Private Function* (1984) and *Prick Up Your Ears* (1987). Bennett has also written numerous scripts for television films and series, such as "On the Margin" (1966), *A Day Out* (1972), *Sunset Across the Bay* (1975), *An Englishman Abroad* (1982), *The Insurance*

Man (1986), *102 Boulevard Haussman* (1991), and "Talking Heads" (1992), a notable series of monologues that won Britain's Olivier Award. Bennett's other published works include *Objects of Affection* (1982) and *The Writer in Disguise* (1985).

FURTHER READING

"The poet of. . . ." STEPHEN SCHIFF. *New Yorker,* Sept. 6, 1993.
"King of the hill." GEORGINA HOWELL. *Vogue,* Sept. 1993.

Bennett, Charles (1899–95) British screenwriter and playwright Charles Bennett began his seven-decades-long writing career in the 1920s. His debut film was Alfred Hitchcock's and Britain's first talking film—the thriller *Blackmail* (1929), adapted for screen by Bennett from his own play. Bennett went on to write or co-write more than 50 films and later a wide range of television series episodes. His Hitchcock film screenplays included *The Man Who Knew Too Much* (1934) and *The Thirty-Nine Steps* (1935), both made in Britain; and, after his 1937 emigration to Hollywood, the American-made films *Foreign Correspondent* (1940) and *Saboteur* (1942; uncredited). Among his other films were *Secret Agent* (1936), *King Solomon's Mines* (1937), *The Young in Heart* (1938), *Balalaika* (1939), *Reap the Wild Wind* (1942), *Forever and a Day* (1943), *The Story of Dr. Wassell* (1944), *Unconquered* (1947), *Madness of the Heart* (1949; he wrote and directed), *The Green Glove* (1952), *No Escape* (1953; he wrote and directed), *The Big Circus* (1959), *The Lost World* (1960), and *Voyage to the Bottom of the Sea* (1961). He was survived by a son. (d. Hollywood, California; June 15, 1995)

FURTHER READING

Obituary. *Independent,* June 22, 1995.
Obituary. *Variety,* June 16, 1995.
"The scripted life. . . ." JOHN HISCOCK. *California,* June 1991.

Bennett, John Coleman (1902–95) Ontario-born Congregational minister John Coleman Bennett received his 1924 B.A. from Williams College and did graduate work at Ox-

ford University and the Union Theological Seminary. He held several teaching posts in theology in the 1930s and early 1940s, and joined the Union Theological Seminary in 1943, later becoming its dean of faculty (1955–64) and president (1964–70). Bennett was one of the leading Protestant ministers of his day, deeply and very visibly committed to the ecumenical movement in Christianity and to several major social and political positions identified as liberal causes, among them pre–World War II antifascism, civil rights, women's rights, equality of economic opportunity, opposition to the Vietnam War, and nuclear disarmament. With Reinhold Neibuhr, he was a cofounder of the periodical *Christianity in Crisis.* Among his many books were *Social Salvation* (1935), *Christian Ethics and Social Policy* (1946), *Christianity and Communism* (1947), *Christians and the State* (1958), *Nuclear Weapons and the Conflict of Conscience* (1962), *Christian Social Ethics in a Changing World* (1966), *Foreign Policy in Christian Perspective* (1968), and *The Radical Imperative* (1975). He was survived by a daughter and two sons. (d. Claremont, California; April 27, 1995)

FURTHER READING

"Ethical engagement." LEON HOWELL. *The Christian Century,* May 24, 1995.
Obituary. *New York Times,* May 2, 1995.

Bennett, Tony (Anthony Dominick Benedetto; 1926–) Celebrated jazz and pop singer Tony Bennett was highly honored by his peers in 1995. His album *MTV Unplugged,* produced by David Kahne, won a Grammy Award as best album of the year, and he won a Grammy for best traditional pop vocal performance. He and k. d. lang had also been nominated for a Grammy for best pop vocal collaboration for "Funny How Time Slips Away," a track from the album *Rhythm, Country & Blues.*

In 1995, Bennett issued the "theme" album *Here's to the Ladies,* in which he paid tribute to many classic women pop and jazz singers by singing 18 songs associated with them; among the singers so honored were Ella Fitzgerald, Judy Garland, Barbra Streisand, Billie Holiday, and Lena Horne. He also somewhat confusingly appeared in a television concert film titled *Here's to the Ladies,* which bore no relation to the al-

two-volume *Tony Bennett/Jazz* (1987), *Bennett and Berlin* (1988), *Astoria: Portrait of the Artist* (1990), the four-CD retrospective *Forty Years: The Artistry of Tony Bennett* (1991), *Perfectly Frank* (1992; a tribute to Frank Sinatra), *Steppin' Out* (1993; a tribute to Fred Astaire), and *MTV Unplugged*, the classic jazz fruit of his extraordinarily popular appearance on MTV's "Unplugged" show in May 1994, which marked the beginning of his love affair with the younger generation.

Bennett is also an accomplished and exhibited painter. He was twice married, to Patricia Beech (1952–71) and Sandra Grant (1971–84), and had two children from each marriage. Danny Bennett, a son from his first marriage, is his personal manager.

FURTHER READING

"Bennett, Tony." *Current Biography,* June 1995.
"He keeps coming. . . ." ALAN EBERT. *Good Housekeeping,* Apr. 1995.
"Tony Bennett. . . ." ROBERT SULLIVAN and JOE McNALLY. *Life,* Feb. 1995.
"Talking with Tony." PATRICK PERRY. *Saturday Evening Post,* Jan.–Feb. 1995.
Tony Bennett: Steppin' Out. Warner Brothers, 1993.

bum, but rather was the tape of a live Hollywood benefit on behalf of Columbia University's addiction and drug abuse center, attended by President Clinton and other notables; its music consisted largely of a series of duets by Bennett and such woman headliners as Mary-Chapin Carpenter, Liza Minnelli, Roseanne, and Brandy. He also appeared in the live concert video *A Special Evening With Tony Bennett*, shot at New York's Bottom Line, singing many standards, including his signature song "I Left My Heart in San Francisco." Bennett continued to tour widely, at his normal 200-shows-a-year pace.

One of Bennett's paintings, *Brotherhood*, was used as a design for a special 50th anniversary stamp for the United Nations in June 1995.

Born in New York City, Bennett was discovered in talent shows (as Joe Bari); after World War II service, he studied at the American Theatre Wing school. His breakthrough songs were the number one hits "Because of You" and "Cold, Cold Heart" (both 1951), and "Rags to Riches" (1953). The most notable of his other top-40 hits was his signature song "I Left My Heart in San Francisco" (1962), which won Grammys as best solo vocal and best record of the year. In the next decade, Bennett recorded 25 albums, but as popular audiences turned toward rock, Bennett turned toward jazz. From 1972, he dropped out of major-label recording, but kept on singing and touring, even starting his own small label, Improv. Among his most recent recordings are the

Bennett, William John (1943–) He has been a Secretary of Education, head of federal antidrug initiatives, and even a presidential hopeful, but in recent years William J. Bennett has been best known as a best-selling author. It all started with *The Book of Virtues: A Treasury of Great Moral Stories* in 1993, a collection of readings espousing "family values," which at the end of 1995 was still on *Publishers Weekly*'s religion best-seller list and had more than 2.5 million copies in print. But 1995 saw three new best-selling Bennett books, all—like the original—consisting of readings organized around themes such as self-discipline, courage, compassion, responsibility, honesty, loyalty, friendship, perseverance, and faith. The first two were *The Children's Book of Virtues*, designed for preschool through grade three, and *The Book of Virtues for Young People: A Treasury of Great Moral Stories*, for children in middle school. The third, for adults, was *The Moral Compass: Stories for a Life's Journey*, a massive compilation of stories, poems, and essays. It was released in audiobook form simultaneously with the hardcover book, read by Bennett and others. PBS was preparing

an animated television series, "Adventures from *The Book of Virtues*," to be hosted by Bennett, scheduled for fall 1996.

Bennett continued to be a voice on the political scene. In July 1995, early in the campaign for the presidential nomination, he notably accused contender Pat Buchanan of "flirting" with fascism, and urged Republicans to reject Buchanan and his views. Bennett heads a political advocacy group called Empower America.

Brooklyn-born Bennett's 1965 B.A. was from Williams College, and his 1971 J.D. from Harvard Law School. He was assistant to the president of Boston University (1972–76), executive director (1976–79) and then president (1979–81) of the National Humanities Center of North Carolina, and also a professor at North Carolina State University (1979–81), before being named president of the National Endowment for the Humanities in North Carolina (1981–85). He then became a highly controversial U.S. Secretary of Education in the second Reagan administration (1985–88). Originally a Democrat, Bennett joined the Republican Party in 1986. He then practiced law in Washington until his appointment as director of the U.S. Office of National Drug Control Policy of the Bush administration (1989–90). He resigned in 1990 to become head of the Republican Party, but then withdrew, citing economic reasons; many had criticized his outspoken, often abrasive politically conservative style. He then became associated with the DC-based conservative think tank Empower America and worked as senior editor at the *National Review*. Among his other publications is *The De-Valuing of America: The Fight for Our Culture and Our Children* (1992). Bennett married Mary Elayne Glover in 1982; they have two children.

FURTHER READING

"William J. Bennett." PETER ROSS RANGE. *Modern Maturity,* Mar.–Apr. 1995.
"The fabulous Bennett boys." FRANK DEFORD. *Vanity Fair,* Aug. 1994.
"Virtue man." MICHAEL CROMARTIE. *Christianity Today,* Sept. 13, 1993.
"A far different Bill. . . ." MICHAEL RUST. *Insight on the News,* May 31, 1993.

Berenger, Tom (1950–) Film star Tom Berenger starred opposite Barbara Hershey in the 1995 film *Last of the Dogmen*, written and directed by Tab Murphy; the film was about law-

men pursuing escaped prisoners in Montana, who with the help of anthropologist Hershey ultimately find their way to a mythical Cheyenne village hidden for a century.

Berenger also coproduced and starred in the television film *The Avenging Angel*, directed by Craig R. Baxley, and costarring Charlton Heston as Mormon leader Brigham Young, James Coburn, and Fay Masterson. Berenger played one of the Mormon Danites (Avenging Angels), armed guards assigned to protection duties.

Forthcoming were starring roles in the action film *The Substitute*, directed by Robert Mandel and costarring Diane Venora, Ernie Hudson, Richard Brooks, and William Forsyth; and in Salome Breziner's film *An Occasional Hell*.

Chicago-born Berenger began his career on stage, appearing in several off-Broadway productions in the early 1970s; he also appeared in the daytime soap "One Life to Live." He made his film debut in *Beyond the Door* (1975). He emerged as a star in his breakthrough film *The Big Chill* (1983), then starred in such films as *Platoon* (1986; he received an Oscar nomination), *Someone to Watch Over Me* (1987), *Born on the Fourth of July* (1989), *At Play in the Fields of the Lord* (1991), *Sliver* (1993), *Sniper* (1993), *Chasers* (1994), and *Major League II* (1994). He also starred in several television films. Berenger attended the University of Missouri.

FURTHER READING

"Terrific good old boy. . . ." SUSAN SPILLMAN. *Cosmopolitan,* Nov. 1991.

Bergman, Ingmar (1918–) Celebrated

Swedish director and writer Ingmar Bergman continued to create masterworks as he approached his eighth decade, among them the two Royal Dramatic Theatre of Sweden productions he brought to the Brooklyn Academy of Music in 1995—Shakespeare's *The Winter's Tale* and Yukio Mishima's *Madame De Sade*. Bibi Andersson, who starred in several of his classic films, led a *Winter's Tale* cast that included Borje Ahlstedt, Pernilla August, Kristina Tornqvist, and Krister Henriksson, while Stina Ekblad played Madame De Sade. A major New York retrospective of Bergman's whole body of work accompanied the two plays. Much-honored Bergman was also the second winner of the Dorothy and Lillian Gish prize for artistic contribution.

Bergman is a central figure in world film history and at the same time a major figure in the Swedish theater. From the mid-1950s, he created a series of tremendously influential film masterworks, including such classics as *Smiles of a Summer Night* (1955), *Wild Strawberries* (1957), *The Magician* (1958), *The Virgin Spring* (1960), *Through a Glass Darkly* (1961), *Scenes from a Marriage* (1974), *After the Rehearsal* (1984), and *The Best Intentions* (1989). He also wrote the screenplay, based on his own novel, for the autobiographical film *Sunday's Children* (1992), directed by his son Daniel Bergman. In 1990, he received the D. W. Griffith award of the Directors Guild of America, for lifetime contribution to film. He has published the autobiographies *The Magic Lantern* (1987) and *Images: My Life in Film* (1994).

Bergman attended Stockholm University. He has been married six times, and has eight children. His sister Margareta Bergman is a novelist.

FURTHER READING

Ingmar Bergman: An Artist's Journey. ROGER W. OLIVER, ed. Arcade, 1995.
Between Stage and Screen: Ingmar Bergman Directs. EGIL TORNQVIST. IBD Ltd., 1995.
The Rite of Redemption: An Interpretation of the Films of Ingmar Bergman, rev. ed. ARTHUR GIBSON. E. Mellen, 1995.
Film and Stage Work of Ingmar Bergman. ROBERT E. LONG. Abrams, 1994.
Ingmar Bergman: The Art of Confession. HUBERT I. COHEN. Macmillan, 1993.
"Ingmar Bergman." JOHN CLARK. *Premiere*, Sept. 1992.
Ingmar Bergman: A Critical Biography, rev. ed. PETER COWIE. Limelight, 1992.

Berlusconi, Silvio (1936–) Financier,

industrialist, and politician Silvio Berlusconi, who had been forced to step down as Italian prime minister in December 1994 because of charges that he was involved in corruption, spent much of 1995 pressing hard, but unsuccessfully, for early national elections. Still heading a coalition that included his own Forza Italia party, he steadfastly denied all charges of corruption, calling them merely a plot to rob Italian voters of the new leadership they had demanded by voting the ruling Christian Democrats out of power. At first he disclaimed any intention to hold the prime minister's post again, giving up his caretaker's role when interim prime minister Alberto Dini took office in mid-January 1995. On June 12, however, Berlusconi announced that he would be a candidate for the prime minister's office. But new elections seemed even further away when the Milanese judiciary announced on October 14 that he must stand trial on the corruption charges in January 1996.

Milan-born Berlusconi emerged as Italy's foremost communications industry magnate during the 1980s, and as a leading financier through his control of the Fininvest conglomerate. Beginning with real estate developments in the Milan area, he became the owner of a financial, industrial, and communications empire that included a virtual monopoly of Italian private television broadcasting, the Cinema 5 movie theater chain, Estudios Roma, the La Standa department store chain, and the Milan AC football club. His Alliance for Freedom coalition, which included his own Forza Italia, the neofascist National Alliance, the Northern League, and two small centrist parties, won the March 1995 parliamentary elections, and he took office as prime minister in May, riding a wave of anticorruption sentiment in his scandal-ridden country. But Berlusconi lost public confidence after he was accused of involvement in the bribery of government tax inspectors. Facing a vote of no confidence that he could not have survived, he resigned on December 22, taking a caretaker's role until a new government was formed.

A lawyer, Berlusconi studied at Milan Catholic National University. His second wife is actress Veronica Lario; they have three children. He also has two children from his first marriage.

FURTHER READING

"Arrivederci Berlusconi?" JUDY BACHRACH. *Vanity Fair*, Jan. 1995.

"Phony Berlusconi. . . ." MARK LILLA. *New Republic*, Sept. 12, 1994.

"Berlusconi, Silvio." *Current Biography*, Aug. 1994.

"The white stallion of TV." VITTORIO ZUCCONI. *New Perspectives Quarterly*, Summer 1994.

"Berlusconi. . . ." DANIEL SINGER. *New Statesman & Society*, May 20, 1994.

"Enter Berlusconi. . . ." SCOTT STEELE. *Maclean's*, Apr. 11, 1994.

"Italy's miracle man." *Economist*, Apr. 2, 1994.

Bernays, Edward (1891–1995)

Vienna-born Edward Bernays, a nephew of Sigmund Freud, emigrated to the United States with his family in 1892, settling in New York City, where he began his public relations career as a publicity agent in the theater before World War I. After military service as a public relations officer, he and Doris E. Fleishman, later his wife, became pioneering public relations consultants, based in New York. During the 1920s, Bernays emerged as one of the leading public relations professionals of his era, working for a wide range of corporate clients, very notably including the American Tobacco Company, for which he developed a highly successful campaign to make women's smoking in public socially acceptable. Later in his life, he was to become an antismoking activist. His major clients also included such companies as General Motors, Proctor and Gamble, General Electric, and Time, Inc. Bernays, who later deplored the state of his profession, unsuccessfully urged the licensing of public relations professionals. He published several books on his craft, the most recent being *The Later Years: Public Relations Insights, 1956–1986* (1986). He was survived by two daughters. (d. Cambridge, Massachusetts; March 9, 1995)

FURTHER READING

Obituary. *Independent*, Mar. 22, 1995.

Obituary. *Times* (of London), Mar. 13, 1995.

Obituary. *New York Times*, Mar. 10, 1995.

"Ya gotta have hype!" LOU HARRY. *Philadelphia Magazine*, Apr. 1991.

Bhutto, Benazir (1943–)

One of the world's leading women, Pakistan's Prime Minister Benazir Bhutto played a major role at the United Nations Fourth World Conference on Women, at Beijing (Sept. 4–15, 1995). On the opening day she delivered a powerful speech that focused on the worldwide abuse of women and female children, especially on the "son preference" that in many countries, including the host country, China, results in massive abortions of female fetuses and, all too often, in the murder of female babies.

At home, Bhutto in 1995 continued her working alliance with Pakistan's army and landowning elites, with them facing a major and growing challenge from Islamic fundamentalists and supporters of the Pakistani-assisted insurgent movements in Kashmir and other areas of northern India, where near-civil war raged. In several areas of Pakistan, and especially in Karachi in the summer and fall, Mohajir Quami Movement guerrillas launched armed attacks that required major police and military responses. In mid-October, the Bhutto government arrested at least 40 serving military officers accused of plotting an antigovernment coup.

Abroad, the Bhutto government continued to aid Muslim insurgents in Kashmir and other parts of northern India, as it had since the 1947 partition of India into two countries, Pakistan and India. It also admitted for the first time that it had developed some nuclear weapons capability, and refused to disarm, unless India also did so. Pakistan also continued to aid some Afghan factions in the continuing Afghan Civil War, though formally denying that aid. Bhutto's government also continued to aid Bosnian Muslim fighting forces, and specifically declined to honor the Western arms embargo against the Bosnian Muslims.

Bhutto also campaigned with partial success to lift the American embargo on military supplies and foreign aid to Pakistan, imposed in 1990 when she refused to stop seeking nuclear weapons capability. She hosted First Lady Hillary Rodham Clinton in Pakistan in late March, and visited U.S. President Bill Clinton in early April, calling for delivery of $1 billion in already purchased U.S. armaments or the return of $650 million already paid for them. U.S. economic aid was restored by the Senate in September, and lifting of the arms embargo was in prospect.

Bhutto's father, Zulfikar Ali Bhutto, had been Pakistan's prime minister (1972–77); he was executed in 1979 by Mohammed Zia Ul-Haq's military government. After the coup that deposed him, Benazir Bhutto and her mother were under house arrest in Pakistan (1977–84). She left Pakistan in 1984, returned for the funeral of a brother in 1985, and was rearrested and expelled from her country. She returned again in 1986, as head of the Pakistan People's Party, and led the opposition to the government.

After the death of Zia Ul-Haq in an August 1988 plane crash, Bhutto was elected prime minister of Pakistan in the free election of December 2, 1988. In office, she faced increasing opposition from the Pakistani army and fundamentalist religious leaders. On August 6, 1990, she was removed from office by president Ishaq Khan, acting with the support of the military; she was charged with corruption, her husband and many supporters were arrested, and she was forbidden to leave the country. She and her party were defeated in the October 1990 elections, which she called fraud-ridden. They made an extraordinary comeback in the October 1993 general elections, winning a plurality, and she became the head of a coalition government, now apparently in alliance with Pakistan's military and landholding elites, formerly her bitter opponents.

Bhutto attended Harvard University and Lady Margaret Hall, Oxford University. In 1989, she published *Daughter of Destiny: An Autobiography*. She married Asif Ali Zardari in 1987; they have three children.

FURTHER READING

Women in World Politics: An Introduction. FRANCINE D'AMICO and PETER R. BECKMAN. Greenwood, 1995.
"Benazir Bhutto." CLAUDIA DREIFUS. *New York Times Magazine*, May 15, 1994.
"Bhutto's fateful moment." MARY ANNE WEAVER. *New Yorker*, Oct. 4, 1993.
Benazir Bhutto. DIANE SANSEVERE-DREHER. Bantam, 1991.

Bingham, Mary Caperton (1904–95)

Richmond-born editor, newspaper executive, and philanthropist Mary Bingham received her 1928 B.S. at Radcliffe College, and was a Charles Eliot Norton Fellow at the American School of Classical Studies at Athens in 1929. In 1931, she married Barry Bingham, heir to the Louisville-based Bingham newspaper chain. The Binghams raised five children together (two predeceased her), and at the same time worked together in developing the family's massive media interests, centered on the *Louisville Courier-Journal*, one of the country's great newspapers. Mary Bingham was a very active vice president and director of the *Courier-Journal* and several other family holdings, and was editor of the *Courier-Journal*'s "World of Books" column (1943–67). She was also a prominent philanthropist, with particular attention to the Actor's Theater of Louisville and other cultural institutions, and to environmental causes. She was survived by two daughters and a son. (d. Louisville, Kentucky; April 18, 1995)

FURTHER READING

"Remembering. . . ." PHILIP HAMBURGER. *New Yorker*, May 22, 1995.
Obituary. *New York Times*, Apr. 20, 1995.

Blaine, Vivian (Vivian Stapleton; 1921–95)

Newark, New Jersey–born Vivian Blaine, a singer and actress, began her career as a child, singing in cabaret, and became a touring band singer in the late 1930s. She began her film career as a contract player with 20th Century Fox in 1941, played in several supporting roles in film musicals during the early 1940s, and moved into musical leads in 1944, in *Greenwich Village* and *Something for the Boys*. Among her other 1940s films were *Nob Hill* (1945), *State Fair* (1945), and *Three Little Girls in Blue* (1946). In 1950, she appeared in the role for which she became best known by far, that of night club singer Adelaide in the hit Broadway musical *Guys and Dolls*, opposite Sam Levenson as Nathan Detroit, Robert Alda as Sky Masterson, and Isabel Bigley as Sister Sarah. She re-created the role in the 1955 film version, opposite Frank Sinatra as Detroit, Marlon Brando, and Jean Simmons, and re-created it again in a 1966 stage revival of the work. Her later career included stage, screen, and television appearances. She was married and divorced three times; there were no survivors. (d. New York City; December 9, 1995)

FURTHER READING

Obituary. *Variety*, Dec. 15, 1995
Obituary. *New York Times*, Dec. 14, 1995.

Blair, Tony (Anthony Charles Lynton Blair; 1953–) Labour Party leader Tony Blair was able to position himself as a centrist in British politics during 1995, greatly enhancing his

chances of defeating prime minister John Major or any other visible Conservative Party candidate in the next general elections. In October 1994, his attempt to abolish Labour's formal commitment to public ownership of industry—clause four of the party's charter—had failed. On March 13, 1995, he tried again, and won over the party's leadership, with ratification coming at a special party conference in April. In one blow, he had changed his party's formal socialist commitment over to a far more popular liberal democratic commitment—although to the great discomfort of the Left in his party. He followed up by securing a commitment to cut the impact of union leadership block voting within the party. In domestic politics, Blair also continued to lead Labour's attack on Conservative economic policies, while in foreign affairs he led the attack on the increasingly unpopular Conservative support of the European Union, and especially the projected European Monetary Union. Blair also led attempts to build an alliance between Labour and the Liberal Democrats.

A barrister, Tony Blair graduated from Fettes College, Edinburgh, and St. John's College, Oxford. He was elected to Parliament from Sedgefield in 1983, and from 1984 served in several Labour shadow cabinet positions, as "shadow home secretary"—Labour spokesperson on matters within the home secretary's jurisdiction—from 1992. On July 21, 1994, he succeeded recently deceased John Smith as leader of the Labour Party. He is married to lawyer Cherie Booth; they have a daughter and two sons.

FURTHER READING

"Vanity Blair. . . ." ANDREW MARR. *New Republic,* Dec. 18, 1995.
"Son of Margaret?" STUART HALL. *New Statesman & Society,* Oct. 6, 1995.
"Beyond the vision." HUGO YOUNG. *Guardian,* Oct. 2, 1995.
"Action man." DAVE HILL. *New Statesman & Society,* Sept. 29, 1995.
"The Blair effect in Britain." NORMAN GELB. *The New Leader,* May 8, 1995.
"Mining the middle. . . ." NORMAN GELB. *New Leader,* Aug. 15, 1994.
"The heir apparent. . . ." BRUCE WALLACE. *Maclean's,* July 25, 1994.
"Blair necessities." GEOFF MULGAN et al. *New Statesman & Society,* July 22, 1994.
"The British Clinton?" TARIQ ALI. *New Statesman & Society,* May 20, 1994.

Bolt, Robert (1924–95)

Bolt, Robert (1924–95) Manchester-born playwright, screenwriter, and director Robert Bolt saw military service during World War II and became a teacher after his graduation from Manchester University in 1949. He began his writing career with several radio plays, and emerged as a playwright in the late 1950s with *The Critic and the Heart* (1957), and his first major success, the comedy *The Flowering Cherry* (1957), a hit in London and New York. He became a major figure in the English-speaking theater with his play *A Man For All Seasons* (1960), which starred Paul Scofield as Sir Thomas More in London and New York, where it won five Tony awards. Among his best known other plays are *The Tiger and the Horse* (1960), *Gentle Jack* (1963), and *Vivat! Vivat Regina* (1970). He was also a major screenwriter, whose best known works included *Lawrence of Arabia* (1962), for which he received his first Oscar nomination; *Dr. Zhivago* (1965), for which he won his first Oscar; and his adaptation of his own *A Man For All Seasons* (1966), for which he won his second Oscar, the film winning six Oscars in all, including best picture. His other screenplays included *Ryan's Daughter* (1980) and *The Mission* (1986). He also directed several films. He was survived by his wife, the actress Sarah Miles, a daughter, and two sons. (d. Petersfield, Hampshire, England; February 20, 1995)

FURTHER READING

Obituary. *Independent,* Feb. 23, 1995.
Obituary. *Times* (of London), Feb. 23, 1995.
Obituary. *New York Times,* Feb. 23, 1995.
Obituary. *Variety,* Feb. 22, 1995.

Bolton, Michael (1953–)

Bolton, Michael (1953–) Singer, songwriter, and guitarist Michael Bolton was again honored by his peers in 1995. At the 22nd annual American Music Awards, he was named top male pop/rock artist of the year and top adult contemporary artist of the year. He also received a best pop vocal performance Grammy nomination for "Said I Loved You . . . But I Lied."

In 1995, Bolton issued the well-received album *Michael Bolton Greatest Hits 1985–1995,* which included such Bolton standards as "Said I Loved You . . . But I Lied," and "Soul Provider," but also contained five new songs, among them "Can I Touch You . . . There?" and "A Love So

"Michael Bolton. . . ." Dave DiMartino. *Entertainment Weekly*, Oct. 23, 1992.

Beautiful." Both of the latter songs were released as singles, with "Can I Touch You?" moving toward the top range of the charts.

Bolton continued to work with his Michael Bolton Foundation to assist poor and abused women and children. He also joined hundreds of other artists to lobby Congress on behalf of funds for the threatened National Endowment for the Arts.

Bolton began his career in the late 1960s, while still a teenager in New Haven, Connecticut. He emerged as a leading lyricist in the mid-1980s, as cowriter of "How Am I Supposed To Live Without You" (1983), and as a popular singer in 1987, singing his own "That's What Love Is All About." His albums include *The Hunger* (1987), *Soul Provider* (1989; he won a Grammy for best male vocal), *Time, Love and Tenderness* (1991), *Timeless (The Classics)* (1992), and *The Only One* (1994). He was formerly married, and has three children.

FURTHER READING

"Bolton, Michael." *Current Biography*, Aug. 1993.

"Michael Bolton. . . ." Laura Morice. *McCall's*, Aug. 1993.

"Michael Bolton." Laura Morice. *Us*, Feb. 1993.

"Nine million. . . ." Michael Angeli. *Esquire*, Jan. 1993.

Michael Bolton: Time, Love, and Tenderness. Lee Randall. Simon & Schuster, 1993.

"The power source. . . ." Steve Dougherty. *People*, Dec. 7, 1992.

Bonior, David Edward (1945–) Michigan Democratic Representative David Bonior, the House of Representatives minority whip, emerged in 1995 as the day-to-day leader of the Democratic liberal and moderate attack on the new House Republican majority, especially singling out for attack its ultraconservative leader, House Speaker Newt Gingrich. Throughout the year, he demanded House Ethics Committee action on a wide range of ethics charges involving Gingrich, placing great emphasis on the $4.5 million book advance from Rupert Murdoch's HarperCollins publishing company, later foregone by Gingrich after great pressure. Bonior and others coupled the advance to alleged links between Murdoch and Gingrich regarding matters before Congress and federal regulators, and raised several other ethical questions, as well. Bonior's main work in the House, however, was not a personal attack on Gingrich, but rather the development of a series of defensive actions aimed at slowing down and in many instances stopping the adoption of Gingrich's "Contract with America," which Bonior and other Democrats, led by President Bill Clinton, labeled "extremism." Some of the conservative Republican proposals found their way into law in 1995; many did not; most remained to be decided in 1996. Bonior was expected to continue playing the same role on the way to their resolution by the 1996 presidential elections.

Detroit-born Bonior began his political career in 1972, soon after completing four years in the air force. He served in the Michigan House of Representatives (1973–77) and then began his long congressional career (1977–). A liberal from a politically diverse district with many blue-collar workers, he was a leading opponent of aid to the Nicaraguan Contras, was during the 1980s an advocate of stimulating the Middle East peace process by pushing the parties toward the negotiating table, and crossed party lines to oppose the North American Free Trade Agreement (NAFTA), believing that it threatened the jobs of many in his district. He won the position of Democratic House majority whip in 1991, the third position after the Speaker and majority leader. After the Republican victory in the 1994 congressional elections, he defeated conservative Charles Stenholm 145–60 to win the position of minority whip, the second Democratic House position behind minority leader Richard A. Gephardt.

Bonior received his 1967 B.A. from the University of Iowa and his M.A. in history from Chapman College in California. He coauthored *The Vietnam Veteran: A History of Neglect* (1984). He has two children.

FURTHER READING

"Hail to the chiefs. . . ." *Economist*, Dec. 10, 1994.

Bon Jovi, Jon (John Bongiovi; 1962–   ) Singer and songwriter Jon Bon Jovi, the leading figure in the rock group Bon Jovi, had an extraordinarily successful 1995. The group's late-1994 album *Crossroad* stayed near the top of the charts for several months early in the year, reportedly selling more than 13 million copies worldwide through May 1995, while its top single "Always" rose to the fourth position on *Billboard*'s Hot 100 chart. Bon Jovi's worldwide tour in support of the album brought massive crowds; in Jakarta, Indonesia, fans rioted in a crowded stadium.

June saw issuance of the very well-received new Bon Jovi pop/rock album *These Days*, with such immediately popular songs as the title track, "Something For The Pain," "This Ain't A Love Song," and "Lie To Me." The album quickly became a best-seller, hitting a million U.S. sales by late July. "This Ain't" and "Something" were also issued as singles and both quickly became hits.

Extending his career on a different front, Jon Bon Jovi made his film debut as a romantic interest opposite Elizabeth Perkins in *Moonlight and Valentino*, directed by David Anspaugh and written by Ellen Simon, based on her play; co-starring were Whoopi Goldberg, Gwyneth Paltrow, Kathleen Turner, and Peter Coyote.

On the personal side, he and his wife, Dorothea, became parents of a son, Jesse James Louis. In 1994 they had a daughter, Stephanie Rose.

New Jersey–born Bon Jovi began his career while still in high school, playing in cabaret in Sayreville, his home town. He organized several bands, starting with Atlantic City Expressway, and ultimately organized The Wild Ones, which

changed its name to Bon Jovi and in 1984 released its first album, *Bon Jovi*. The album was a hit, as was *7800 Fahrenheit* (1985). *Slippery When Wet* (1986) and *New Jersey* (1988) were worldwide hits, and generated international tours; his first solo album, *Blaze of Glory* (1990), was also highly successful. The group also issued the album *Keep the Faith* (1992) and the book *Bon Jovi* (1988).

FURTHER READING

"Jonny dangerously. . . ." George Wayne. *Vanity Fair,* Oct. 1995.
"Jon Bon Jovi." David Hochman. *Us,* Aug. 1995.
"You can feel it. . . ." David Hiltbrand. *People,* July 10, 1995.
"From hair to rock eternity." Gwyneth Paltrow. *Interview,* July 1995.
Faithful Followers: Celebrating a Decade of Bon Jovi. Dawn Quinn and Cindy Malachowski. Telstar, 1994.
Bon Jovi: Official Biography. Malcolm Dome. Viking Penguin, 1994.

Botvinnik, Mikhail Moisseyevich (1911–95) St. Petersburg–born Mikhail Botvinnik was from the early 1930s a leading Soviet chess grandmaster. He was also a prominent Soviet electrical engineer, although his attainments as an engineer were far outshone by his status in the world of chess, which after World War II took most of his time and attention. Botvinnik became Soviet chess champion seven times (1931; 1933; 1939; 1941; 1944; 1945; 1952). He became world chess champion in 1948, winning the championship tournament conducted after the death of previous world champion Alexander Alekhine, and was world champion for most of the next 15 years (1948–57; 1958–60; 1961–63) He continued to play competitively after his 1963 loss to Tigran Petrosian, but retired from competition in 1970. In his later years, he focused on the development of electronic chess, taught, and wrote. Among his books were *Selected Games 1926–1968* (1951), *Soviet School of Chess* (1951), *Algorithms of the Game of Chess* (1968), *Computers, Chess and Long-Range Planning* (1971), the autobiography *Reaching the Goal* (1978), *Half a Century of Chess* (1984), and *Mikhail Botvinnik: Master of Strategy* (1992). He was survived by a daughter. (d. Moscow; May 5, 1995)

FURTHER READING

Obituary. *Times* (of London), May 8, 1995.
Obituary. *Independent,* May 8, 1995.
Obituary. *New York Times*, May 7, 1995.

Boutros Ghali, Boutros (1922–)

In the fourth year of his five-year term, on October 20, 1995, United Nations Secretary-General Boutros Boutros Ghali hosted the largest group of world leaders ever assembled, to commemorate the 50th anniversary of the founding of the United Nations.

It was a year in which Boutros Ghali continued to focus on worldwide UN peace-keeping and humanitarian missions, although encountering increasing opposition within the UN over the cost and limited success of many of those missions. The UN did take over the U.S. peace-keeping role in Haiti, played a substantial role in trying to monitor Iraqi compliance with Gulf War peace terms, and continued its worldwide efforts on behalf of refugees and against human rights abuses. But the crucial UN peace-keeping role in Bosnia came very close to failing, and was largely taken over by NATO and the U.S.; and near bankruptcy continued to plague the UN, as many member states refused to meet their financial commitments to it.

Moving into the final year of his term, Boutros Ghali faced several continuing challenges to his leadership, and quite possibly an uphill fight to gain a second term—but seemed ready to take on those challenges and that fight.

Cairo-born Boutros Ghali attended Cairo University and the University of Paris. He was a professor of international law and head of the political science department at Cairo University, and has long been active in international law, political studies, and human rights organizations. He was Egypt's minister of state for foreign affairs (1987–91) and became deputy prime minister (1991). On January 1, 1992, Boutros Ghali began his five-year term as the sixth United Nations secretary-general. He had campaigned long and hard for the job; an experienced mediator who played a significant role in negotiating the 1978 Camp David Accords and the 1979 Egypt-Israel peace treaty, he was thought by many to be a logical choice to continue the expanded worldwide UN mediating role developed so successfully by his predecessor, Javier Pérez de Cuéllar. Boutros Ghali is married to Leia Maria Nadler.

FURTHER READING

"One for. . . ." PATRICIA BEARD. *Town & Country,* Oct. 1995.
"Blue helmets. . . ." BRIAN HALL. *New York Times Magazine,* Jan. 2, 1994.
"Great expectations." ANDREW BILSKI. *Maclean's,* Aug. 30, 1993.
"Alboutros. . . ." MICHAEL LIND. *New Republic,* June 28, 1993.
"A secretary-general. . . ." AHMED MURSI. *World Press Review,* Oct. 1992.
"Challenge for the new boss." BONNIE ANGELO. *Time,* Feb. 3, 1992.
"New U.N. chief. . . ." CAROLE COLLINS. *National Catholic Reporter,* Jan. 10, 1992.
"Hello, Ghali." *Nation,* Dec. 16, 1991.
"A man for all nations." BONNIE ANGELO. *Time,* Dec. 2, 1991.

Bowie, David (David Robert Jones; 1947–)

Always one of the music world's most innovative and thoughtful luminaries, rock star, songwriter, and actor David Bowie in 1995 issued the album *Outside*, a "concept" album that tells in song-and-story about a murder set in the underside of the art world, in which Bowie plays seven different characters. Bowie and his longtime producer, Brian Eno, conceived as the album as Volume One of a multivolume work at the end of the 20th century, that would somehow symbolize the passing of the values of that century. The album itself, the lead-in song "The Heart's Filthy Lesson," and the title song were all respectfully received, appealing especially to Bowie's established core audiences. So, too, was the single "Strangers When We Meet," derived from the album. Album and single were not a great commercial success, however, even though Bowie toured for six weeks, sharing a program with the group Nine Inch Nails, and sometimes working together with them on stage. Bowie also issued *The David Bowie Interactive CD-ROM*, based on Bowie's recent song single and video "Jump They Say."

Whatever the commercial fate of his most recent work, Bowie's status as a great star had long been fixed. In early November, he was selected a member of the Rock and Roll Hall of Fame. On the visual arts side of his career, Bowie had a one-person show of his artworks in London in late April, there also showing two new wallpaper designs done with the Laura Ashley company.

Bowie became a leading rock singer and songwriter in 1969, with publication of his first song, "Space Oddity," followed by such albums as *The Man Who Sold the World* (1970), *Hunky Dory* (1971), *The Rise and Fall of Ziggy Stardust and the Spiders from Mars* (1972), *Pin Ups* (1973), *Young Americans* (1975), *Lodger* (1979), *Let's*

Dance (1983), *Tin Machine* (1989), *Sound + Vision* (1989), and the retrospective *Changesbowie* (1990), which added seven songs and 27 minutes to the original 1976 *Changesonebowie* album. In 1993, he issued the albums *Black Tie White Noise* and *Bowie—The Singles Collection*. As an actor, Bowie also starred as the alien in the film *The Man Who Fell to Earth* (1976), and appeared in such films as *Merry Christmas Mr. Lawrence* (1983), *The Last Temptation of Christ* (1988), and *The Linguini Incident* (1992), and on Broadway in *The Elephant Man* (1980). Among his written works are *David Bowie in His Own Words* (1981), *David Bowie: Tonight* (1984), and the *David Bowie Anthology* (1985). Previously married to Angela Barnett (1970–80), Bowie married the model Iman in 1992; he has one child.

FURTHER READING

"David Bowie." CHRIS MUNDY. *Us*, Nov. 1995.
"Fame, fame." JEREMY HELLIGAR. *People*, Oct. 16, 1995.
"David Bowie." INGRID SISCHY. *Interview*, Sept. 1995.
"Bowie, David." *Current Biography*, Nov. 1994.
"Station to station." DAVID SINCLAIR. *Rolling Stone*, June 10, 1993.
"Bowie light." JERRY STAHL. *Esquire*, May 1993.
"Savage dreams. . . ." KEVIN ZIMMERMAN. *Variety*, Apr. 5, 1993.
Backstage Passes: Life on the Wild Side with David Bowie. ANGELA BOWIE and PATRICK CARR. Putnam, 1993.
"A session with. . . ." JIM JEROME. *Life*, Dec.1, 1992.
"Architectural Digest. . . ." CHRISTOPHER BUCKLEY. *Architectural Digest*, Sept. 1992.

Bowles, Paul Frederick (1910–) The

Paul Bowles boomlet continued in 1995. September saw a Paul Bowles Festival in New York, marked by his first visit to his hometown in nearly three decades. The well-attended festival included two concerts of music by Bowles and some by his favorite composers; a symposium of lectures and panel discussions of his work; a book, *Paul Bowles: Music*; and a screening of the 1993 documentary film *Paul Bowles: The Complete Outsider*, directed by Catherine Warnow and Regina Weinreich. At the first concert he was introduced by Debra Winger, who had starred in the film version of his novel *The Sheltering Sky*. A new CD, *Paul Bowles: Baptism of Solitude*, with readings by Bowles and music by Bill Laswell, was also released.

A recording of Bowles's music, made in September, was scheduled for 1996 release, including his 1946 *Concerto for Two Pianos*; *Suite for Small Orchestra* and his Spanish-style opera (*zarzeula*), *The Wind Remains*, which was premiered by Leonard Bernstein in 1943. A German film, *Halfmoon*, based on three of his short stories, was also scheduled for 1996 release.

New York–born Bowles dropped out of the University of Virginia at age 19, then studied with Aaron Copland in New York City and Berlin (1930–32) and Virgil Thomson in Paris (1933–34). He wrote scores for several films, including *Watch on the Rhine* (1943), *Summer and Smoke* (1961), and *Sweet Bird of Youth* (1962), as well as two operas: *The Wind Remains* and *Yerma*. He also worked as music critic for the *New York Herald Tribune* (1942–46) and made recordings of North African music for the Library of Congress in the late 1950s, but largely ceased composing his own music in the early 1960s.

Bowles is best known for his writings, especially his novels *The Sheltering Sky* (1949; basis for the 1991 Bernardo Bertolucci film), *Let It Come Down* (1952), and *The Spider's House* (1955). Residing in Tangier, Morocco, from the early 1950s, he has also written travel books, notably *Their Heads Are Green and Their Hands Are Blue* (1963), and numerous short stories and translations. His autobiography, *Without Stopping* (1972), was published shortly before the death of his wife and fellow author, Jane Sydney Auer Bowles (1973); they had married in 1938. A revival of interest in Bowles brought the 1993 publication of *In Touch: The Letters of Paul Bowles*, edited by Jeffrey Miller; *Conversations with Paul Bowles*, edited by Gena Dagel Caponi; and *Paul Bowles Photographs: How Could I Send a Picture into the Desert?*. Recent collections of his work include *Too Far from Home: The Selected Writings of Paul Bowles* (1993), *Collected Stories of Paul Bowles* (1993), and *The Portable Paul and Jane Bowles* (1994), edited by Millicent Dillon.

FURTHER READING

"Incidental music." K. ROBERT SCHWARTZ. *Opera News*, Sept. 1995.
Paul Bowles: Romantic Savage. GENA D. CAPONI. Southern Illinois University Press, 1994.
Conversations with Paul Bowles. GENA D. CAPONI, ed. University Press of Mississippi, 1993.
Paul Bowles. ALLEN HIBBARD. Macmillan, 1993.

Paul Bowles by His Friends. GARY PULSIFER, ed. Dufour, 1993.
"Port is playing. . . ." DAVID EHRENSTEIN. *Advocate*, Jan.15, 1991.
The Dream at the End of the World: Paul Bowles and the Literary Renegades in Tangiers. MICHELLE GREEN. HarperCollins, 1991.

Boyer, Ernest Leroy (1928–95) Ohio-born Ernest Boyer, a leading educational administrator, received his 1950 A.B. from Greenwood College and his 1955 M.A. and 1957 Ph.D. from the University of Southern California. He held several teaching and administrative posts at California's Upland College and the University of California, moving east to become executive dean of the State University of New York (SUNY) (1965–68), and then vice chancellor (1968–70) and chancellor (1970–77). He was Federal Commissioner of Education during the Carter administration (1977–79), and then became president of the Princeton-based Carnegie Foundation for the Advancement of Teaching. Among Boyers' books were *High School: A Report on Secondary Education* (1983), *College: the Undergraduate Experience in America* (1987), *Campus Life* (1990), *Ready to Learn* (1991), and *The Basic School* (1995). He was survived by his wife, Kathryn, a daughter, and two sons. (d. Princeton, New Jersey; December 8, 1995)

FURTHER READING

Obituary. *Times* (of London), Dec 29, 1995.
Obituary. *New York Times*, Dec. 9, 1995.

Bradlee, Benjamin Crowninshield

(1921–) Watergate was the story of a lifetime, and it was Ben Bradlee's involvement in that celebrated case, and his part in Robert Woodward and Carl Bernstein's 1974 book, *All the President's Men*, that made him a household name—though often the face people remembered was that of Jason Robards, who played him in the 1976 film. In 1995, that celebrity, and Bradlee's own storytelling ability, translated into best-sellerdom, when he published his memoirs, *A Good Life: Newspapering and Other Adventures*. There was, of course, much more to his life than Watergate, and the book takes Bradlee from Harvard and wartime naval service and through his years at the *Washington Post*, where he became executive editor, talking along the way about his friendships with many of Washington's and America's elite, including President John F. Kennedy and *Post* owner Katherine Graham. Bradlee was widely seen promoting the book, which was serialized in *Newsweek*.

Boston-born Bradlee received his 1943 A.B. from Harvard University, then served in the U.S. Navy (1942–45). After apprenticing at the *New Hampshire Sunday News*, in Manchester (1946–48), he came to the *Washington Post*, where he was a reporter (1948–51) and a press attache in France (1951–53). He switched to *Newsweek* as Paris-based European correspondent (1953–57) and then worked in Washington for the magazine as a reporter (1957–61) and senior editor (1961–65). Returning to the *Washington Post*, he became managing editor (1965–68) and then vice president and executive editor (1968–91), helping to build it into one of the nation's premier newspapers. Two previous books were *That Special Grace* (1964) and *Conversations with Kennedy* (1975). Bradlee married Sally Quinn in 1978; they have one son. From two previous marriages, he also has a daughter and two sons, one his namesake, who is also a newspaperman and author.

FURTHER READING

"Still news." *Psychology Today,* Nov.–Dec. 1995.
"Last of the red hots." DAVID REMNICK. *New Yorker,* Sept. 18, 1995.
"The Bradlee mystique." PETER J. BOYER. *Vanity Fair,* Sept. 1991.
"So long, sweetheart." KEN ADELMAN. *Washingtonian,* Sept. 1991.
"Ben and Sally. . . ." DIANA WEST. *M Inc.,* June 1991.

Bradley, Bill (1943–) On August 16, 1995, New Jersey Senator and former basketball star Bill Bradley announced that he would not seek a fourth senatorial term in 1996. He had signaled the decision earlier in the year, repeatedly criticizing the current programs of both major parties and specifically attacking President Bill Clinton's proposed budget as damaging to mothers and children. The next day, August 17, Bradley declared that he was seriously considering a presidential run as a third-party candidate, and for the balance of the year focused

publicly on such matters as campaign reform, the need for improved racial relations, and the use of governmental power to ensure social justice and economic stability for those displaced by technological unemployment and other economic factors. During 1995, Bradley voted largely with his Democratic colleagues in the Senate, though parting company with them when he felt that the Clinton administration had leaned over too far and compromised the Democratic social welfare program.

Forthcoming in January 1996 was Bradley's autobiography *Time Present, Time Past.*

Missouri-born Bradley received his 1965 B.A. from Princeton University, where he was an All-American basketball player, and his 1968 M.A. from Oxford University, which he attended as a Rhodes scholar. He served with the U.S. Air Force Reserves (1967–78). Bradley was a highly successful professional basketball player with the New York Knicks (1967–77), a mobile forward with an outstanding long shot, who helped his team to two National Basketball Association (NBA) championships (1970 and 1973), and was elected to the NBA Hall of Fame in 1983.

On his retirement from sports, Bradley moved into politics, as a Democratic senator from New Jersey (1979–), and quickly emerged as a leading Senate liberal, active on the finance and energy committees, as well as on the Select Committee on Aging. Although often mentioned as a potential presidential or vice presidential candidate, he decided not to make a run for either post in 1992, instead making one of the three Democratic convention nominating speeches for Bill Clinton and campaigning actively for the Clinton-Gore ticket. He is also a member of the National Advisory Council on Rights of the Child and the National Commission to Prevent Infant Mortality. Among his written works are the autobiographical *Life on the Run* (1976), *The Fair Tax* (1984), and (with several coauthors) *Implications of Soviet New Thinking* (1988). Bradley married Ernestine Schlant in 1974; they have one daughter.

FURTHER READING

"Deep thoughts." MATTHEW COOPER. *New Republic,* Sept. 11, 1995.
" 'This was not. . . .' " STEPHEN B. SHEPARD et al. *Business Week*, Aug. 16, 1993.
"Senator Lazarus. . . ." MORTON KONDRACKE. *New Republic*, Sept. 2, 1991.
"Bill folds. . . ." JOHN B. JUDIS. *New Republic*, Jan. 28, 1991.

Kenneth Branagh (right) and Laurence Fishburne.

Branagh, Kenneth (1960–)

After the critical and commercial disaster that was the 1994 film *Mary Shelley's Frankenstein*, Kenneth Branagh at least temporarily left the world of big-budget Hollywood films behind. In 1995, he played Iago in a well-received film version of Shakespeare's *Othello*, starring Laurence Fishburne in the title role and costarring Irene Jacob as Desdemona, Nathaniel Parker as Cassio, and Michael Maloney as Rodrigo. The work was directed and adapted for film by Oliver Parker. Branagh also wrote and directed the very low-budget British film *In the Bleak Midwinter*, about a provincial theater company preparing to do *Hamlet* in a local church; the cast included Michael Maloney in the lead, Richard Briers, Mark Hadfield, and Nick Farrell.

Forthcoming was another major classical work, Branagh's own film adaptation of Shakespeare's *Hamlet*. Branagh will direct and star; costarring will be Robin Williams as Osric, Derek Jacobi as Claudius, Julie Christie as Gertrude, Billy Crystal as the first Gravedigger, Charlton Heston as the Player King, Rosemary Harris as the Player Queen, Jack Lemmon as Marcellus, Kate Winsley as Ophelia, John Gielgud, and John Mills. In 1995, Branagh and the Renaissance Theatre Company had received a best spoken-word or nonmusical album nomination Grammy for their recording of *Hamlet*.

On the personal side, Branagh and actress Emma Thompson announced their separation in October. They had married in 1989.

Belfast-born Branagh was one of the most promising theater people to come out of the 1980s. After attending the Royal Academy of Dramatic Art (RADA), he debuted in London in *Another Country*, then quickly became a notable Shakespearean actor, starring on stage as *Hamlet* and *Henry V* (at age 23) and directing and producing *Romeo and Juliet*, all in Britain. In 1987, he starred in the highly regarded television series "The Fortunes of War," costarring Emma Thompson, and in the film *A Month in the Country*. After a notable split with the Royal Shakespeare Company, he founded the Renaissance Theatre Company (1987), and two years later brought to the United States stage productions of Shakespeare's *Midsummer Night's Dream* and *King Lear*, and Ibsen's *Ghosts*, starring in the latter two; *Ghosts* also appeared on television. In 1989, he also made his directorial debut and starred in an Oscar-nominated new film version of Shakespeare's *Henry V*.

Branagh's first American film was *Dead Again* (1991). His other films include *Peter's Friends* (1992), *Much Ado About Nothing* (1993), and *Mary Shelley's Frankenstein* (1994).

Branagh published an autobiography, *Beginning*, in 1990, at age 28; he had earlier written and produced a play, *Public Enemy*.

FURTHER READING

"It's a monster!" GRAHAM FULLER. *Interview*, Nov. 1994.
"Kenneth Branagh." DAVID HOCHMAN. *Us*, Nov. 1994.

"Young Frankenstein." JEANIE PYUN. *Mademoiselle*,
  Nov. 1994.
"Much ado about Shakespeare." *Economist*, Oct. 2,
  1993.
"Much ado about Branagh." DINITIA SMITH. *New
  York*, May 24, 1993.
"Branagh. . . ." *Cosmopolitan*, Oct. 1991.
"Vaulting ambition. . . ." F. X. FEENEY. *American
  Film*, Sept.–Oct. 1991.
"Stratford on. . . ." JOHANNA SCHNELLER. *GQ*, Sept.
  1991.
"Renaissance man." GEORGINA HOWELL. *Vogue*, Sept.
  1991.
"L.A. bard." *Esquire*, Sept. 1991.

Brando, Marlon (Marlon Brando, Jr.;
1924–) Now approaching his sixth decade on
stage and screen, Marlon Brando starred as psychiatrist Jack Mickler in the 1995 film *Don Juan
DeMarco*. The story is driven by his relationship
to a would-be suicide, whom he dissuades from
jumping to his death; Johnny Depp plays the
troubled young man, who fancies himself to be
Don Juan DeMarco, the world's greatest lover,
and has gone some distance to prove that it is so.
As the film unrolls, and the two men engage in a
series of theraputic encounters, the young man
convinces his psychiatrist that there may be
something to his point of view. Brando and his
wife, played by Faye Dunaway, revitalize their
stalled marriage, Don Juan recovers his eccentric balance, and all ends well in this gentle,
successful fairy tale. Jeremy Leven wrote and
directed.

Forthcoming was a starring role opposite Val
Kilmer in a film version of H. G. Wells's *The
Island of Dr. Moreau*, directed by Richard Stanley. The projected film *Rapture* was canceled because of financing problems..

On the personal side, Brando's life was
touched again by tragedy in 1995, when his
daughter, Cheyenne Brando, committed suicide,
reportedly after losing custody of her four-year-old son. Dag Drollet, the father of her child, had
been killed in 1990 by her half-brother, Christian Brando, who is serving a ten-year prison
sentence for voluntary manslaughter in the case.

Omaha-born Brando is one of the leading
stage and screen actors of his time. In 1947, he
created the role of Stanley Kowalski in Tennessee Williams's *A Streetcar Named Desire* (recreated in the 1951 film). This major role also
signaled the breakthrough of "method" acting,

the enormously influential American version of
the Stanislavski school, as taught at New York's
Actors Studio. Brando's first best actor Oscar
was for his film role in *On the Waterfront* (1951),
his second for creation of another landmark role,
that of Vito Corleone, in *The Godfather* (1972).
He also starred in such films as *Julius Caesar*
(1953), *One-Eyed Jacks* (1961), *Last Tango in
Paris* (1972), and after some years of seclusion,
The Dry White Season (1989), and *The Freshman* (1990), with a sendup of his own Godfather
role. In 1992, he appeared in *Christopher Columbus: The Discovery*. His autobiography was
Brando: Songs My Mother Taught Me (1994),
written with Robert Lindsey. Brando has been
married to Anna Kashfi and Movita. He has nine
children, one now deceased.

FURTHER READING

Marlon Brando: A Friend of Mine. GEORGE ENGLUND.
  Warner, 1995.
"Translating Brando." HAROLD BRODKEY. *New Yorker*,
  Oct. 24, 1994.
"Bringing up baby." PETER MANSO. *Premiere*, Oct.
  1994.
"Brando's way." PETER MANSO. *Vanity Fair*, Sept.
  1994.
"Marlon Brando and. . . ." NANCY CALDWELL SOREL.
  Atlantic, July 1994.
Marlon Brando: A Portrait. PAUL RYAN. Carroll &
  Graf, 1994.
Brando: The Biography. PAUL MANSO. Hyperion,
  1994.
Marlon Brando: Larger Than Life. NELLIE BLY.
  Windsor, 1994.
Brando. ROBERT TANITCH. Sterling, 1994.
Marlon Brando. DAVID DOWNING. Madison Books,
  1993.
The Films of Marlon Brando, rev. ed. TONY THOMAS.
  Carol, 1992.
"Runnin' into. . . ." WILLIAM A. WELLMAN, JR. *Film
  Comment*, July–Aug. 1991.
Brando: A Life in Our Times. RICHARD SCHICKEL.
  Macmillan, 1991.
Conversations with Brando. LAWRENCE GROBEL.
  Hyperion, 1991.

Brett, Jeremy (Peter Jeremy Huggins;
1935–95) Although British actor Jeremy Brett
was best known by far on both sides of the Atlantic for his portrayal of Sherlock Holmes, he
played in a very wide range of stage and screen
roles during his almost four-decades-long career.

Born in Berkswell, England, Brett studied at the Central School of Speech and Drama, and began to play leads on the London and New York stage in 1956, beginning with Troilus in the Old Vic production of *Troilus and Cressida*. He starred in a very well received *Hamlet* in London in 1961. Among his films were *War and Peace* (1956) and *My Fair Lady* (1964), in which he played Freddie, as well as several starring roles in television films. By far his greatest role was Sherlock Holmes; he appeared in the first of the more than 40 television films in the series in 1984, and was viewed by many as second to none in the classic role, though most often compared to Basil Rathbone. He also played Holmes on the London stage in 1988, in *The Secret of Sherlock Holmes*. His marriage to actress Anna Massey ended in divorce; they had one son, who survives him. He was then married to television producer Joan Wilson, who predeceased him. (d. London; September 12, 1995)

FURTHER READING

"So long, Sherlock " *New Orleans Magazine,* Dec. 1995.
Obituary. *Times* (of London), Sept. 14, 1995.
Obituary. *New York Times*, Sept. 14, 1995.

Breyer, Stephen Gerald (1938–   )

In his first full year on the Supreme Court, Justice Stephen Breyer emerged as an independent-minded legal scholar who, at least at the beginning of his Court career, leaned toward the liberal side on most, though not all issues.

He wrote a strong dissent in *U.S.* v. *Lopez*, a landmark case; in it he sharply disagreed with the majority decision that declared unconstitutional the federal Gun-Free School Zones Act of 1990, which made possession of a gun within 1,000 feet of a school illegal. The ruling, a major conservative reinterpretation of congressional ability to regulate interstate commerce and therefore to legislate on a very broad range of issues, reopened federal-state powers questions that had long been considered settled. Breyer wrote the majority opinion in *O'Neal* v. *McAninch*, ruling that prisoners could obtain *habeas corpus* federal reviews of their state convictions when federal judges had grave doubts as to possible state court errors.

Breyer joined the majority in *U.S. Term Lim-*

its Inc. v. *Thornton*, a landmark decision ruling that to limit congressional terms required a constitutional amendment; 23 state laws imposing terms limits were invalidated and Congress was barred from passing a term limits law. He joined those dissenting in several other key cases, including *Miller* v. *Johnson*, a landmark decision ruling the establishment of Georgia's Eleventh Congressional District unconstitutional because it was organized primarily to provide racial representation, rather than to respond to specific discrimination; the landmark case of *Rosenberg* v. *Rector and Visitors of the University of Virginia*, which ruled that the publicly funded University of Virginia was required to finance a Christian magazine run by students; and another landmark case, *Adarand Constructors* v. *Pena*, which ruled that the federal government was required to use the same strict standards as the states in carrying out affirmative action programs, reversing the Court's long-held position on federal affirmative action programs. The latter decision was widely viewed as a major conservative victory. Breyer also dissented in *Missouri* v. *Jenkins*, which effectively limited the level of state spending to carry out a federally managed school desegregation plan in Kansas City.

Breyer joined the majority in *Babbitt* v. *Sweet Home Chapter of Communities for a Greater Oregon*, ruling that the federal government had the right under the Endangered Species Act to sharply restrict logging and other activities harmful to the northern spotted owl; in *Capital Square Review and Advisory Board* v. *Pinette*, ruling that it was unconstitutional to bar display of a large Ku Klux Klan cross in an Ohio public park; and in *Veronia School District* v. *Acton*, ruling that an Oregon school district's random drug testing program was constitutional.

San Francisco–born Breyer is a graduate of Stanford University, Oxford University, and Harvard Law School. He began his career as a law clerk to Supreme Court Justice Arthur J. Goldberg (1964–65), then became a special assistant to the U.S. attorney general (1967–70). He returned to Harvard Law School as an assistant professor (1967–70) and professor (1970–80), also becoming a Watergate prosecutor (1974–75) and special counsel to the Senate Judiciary Committee (1979–80). He was appointed to U.S. Court of Appeals of the First Circuit by President Jimmy Carter in 1980, and was appointed to the Supreme Court by President Bill Clinton in 1994, replacing retiring Justice Harry A. Blackmun. Among his publications are *Energy Regulation by the Federal Power Commission* (1974; with Paul W. MacAvoy), *Regulation and Its Reform* (1982), *Administrative Law and Regulatory Policy* (2nd ed., 1985; with Richard B. Stewart), and *Breaking the Vicious Circle: Toward Effective Risk Regulation* (1993). Breyer is married to Joanna Hare; they have two daughters and a son.

FURTHER READING

"Breyer restraint. . . ." JEFFREY ROSEN. *New Republic*, July 11, 1994.
"Clinton's zero-risk. . . ." KENNETH T. WALSH and TED GEST. *U.S. News & World Report*, May 23, 1994.

Bridges, Beau (Lloyd Vernet Bridges, III; 1941–) Veteran film and television star Beau Bridges in 1995 presented a far-from-flattering portrait of President Richard M. Nixon, opposite Ron Silver as Henry Kissinger, in the television biography film *Kissinger and Nixon*, directed by Daniel Petrie and based on Walter Isaacson's book *Kissinger: A Biography*.

Bridges also played scientist Dr. Simon Kress in the *Sandkings* episode of the Showtime science fiction series "The Outer Limits," directed by Stuart Gilliard. Costarring were his father Lloyd Bridges, here playing his fictional father; his son, Dylan Bridges, playing his fictional son; and Helen Shaver as his wife. For the Bridges family, it was very much a replay of their earlier lives; Beau had begun his career as a child actor in the late 1940s, sometimes working with his father. For the *Sandkings* role, Beau was nominated for an Emmy as best guest actor in a drama series and a CableAce award as best actor in a dramatic special or series.

Bridges also narrated the five-part television film *5 American Handguns—5 American Kids*, part of the "America Undercover" series, which started with five handguns on a rack and told the stories of the disasters caused by their various uses.

As a child, Beau Bridges appeared in such films as *Force of Evil* (1948) and *The Red Pony* (1949). From his late teens, he emerged as a Hollywood star in such films as *Gaily* (1969), *The Landlord* (1970), *Lovin' Molly* (1974), *The Other Side of the Mountain* (1975), *Norma Rae* (1979), *Heart Like a Wheel* (1983), *The Iron Triangle* (1989), *The Fabulous Baker Boys* (1989), and *Married to It* (1993), and in such telefilms as *The Child Stealer* (1979), *The Runner Stumbles* (1979), *Witness for the Prosecution* (1984), *Space* (1985), *Women and Men: Stories of Seduction* (1989), *Without Warning: The James Brady Story* (1991), *Wildflower* (1991), *The Positively True Adventures of the Alleged Texas Cheerleader-Murdering Mom* (1993), *Secret Sins of the Father* (1994; he also directed), and *Million Dollar Babies* (1994).

Los Angeles–born Bridges is the son of actor Lloyd Bridges and the brother of actor Jeff Bridges, his costar in *The Fabulous Baker Boys*. He attended the University of California at Los Angeles. Previously divorced, he is married to Wendy Bridges; he has five children.

FURTHER READING

"The Bridges of L.A. County." CHRISTA D'SOUZA. *Esquire*, July 1994.

Bridges, Jeff (1949–) Film star Jeff Bridges starred as Wild Bill Hickok in the 1995 film *Wild Bill*, written and directed by Walter Hill and based on Thomas Babe's play *Fathers and Sons* and the Pete Dexter novel *Deadwood*. Ellen Barkin as Calamity Jane, John Hurt, Diane Lane, David Arquette, Christina Applegate, Bruce Dern, and Keith Carradine costarred in

Hill's bitter, sometimes surreal version of the story of the famous Western gunfighter and lawman.

Forthcoming were starring roles opposite Barbra Streisand and Lauren Bacall in the film *The Mirror Has Two Faces*, directed and produced by Streisand; and in the film *White Squall*, directed by Ridley Scott and costarring Caroline Goodall and John Savage. Bridges was also slated to direct the forthcoming science fiction film *The Giver*, adapted from Lynn Lowry's Newberry Award-winning young adult novel.

Los Angeles–born Bridges is one of the leading American film actors of the last two decades, in such films as *The Last Picture Show* (1971; and its 1990 sequel *Texasville*), *Hearts of the West* (1975), *Starman* (1984), *Tucker* (1989), *The Fabulous Baker Boys* (1989; opposite his brother, Beau Bridges), *The Fisher King* (1990), *American Heart* (1992), *Fearless* (1993), *The Vanishing* (1993), and *Blown Away* (1994). Jeff and Beau Bridges are the sons of actor Lloyd Bridges; Jeff played his first screen role at the age of eight, in his father's television series, "Sea Hunt." He is married to photographer Susan Geston; they have three children.

FURTHER READING

"Blast action hero. . . ." BENJAMIN SVETKEY.
　　Entertainment, July 15, 1994.
"The fabulous Bridges boy." LEO JANOS.
　　Cosmopolitan, July 1994.
"The Bridges of L.A. County." CHRISTA D'SOUZA.
　　Esquire, July 1994.
"The reluctant star." JANET MASLIN. *New York Times Magazine*, Oct. 17, 1993.
"Jeff Bridges." JOHN CLARK. *Premiere*, May 1991.
"Bridges, Jeff." *Current Biography*, Mar. 1991.

Brinkley, David (1920–   ) The title of David Brinkley's book of memoirs tells it all: *David Brinkley: 11 Presidents, 4 Wars, 22 Political Conventions, 1 Moon Landing, 3 Assassinations, 2,000 Weeks of News and Other Stuff on Television and 18 Years of Growing Up in North Carolina.* One of the best-known news commentators in America, Brinkley has been reporting the news since the days of President Franklin Roosevelt, and was long paired with Chet Huntley in the *Huntley-Brinkley Report*, the premier NBC evening news show. But beyond his expe-

rience reporting from Washington, many reviewers of the new book lauded Brinkley's stories of his youth in Wilmington, North Carolina, with some readers openly calling for more writings on the life of the pre-famous Brinkley. Meanwhile, he continued to host his Sunday morning news analysis and discussion program, *This Week with David Brinkley.* In 1995, the Museum of Television and Radio honored Brinkley for lifetime achievement.

Brinkley began his newspaper career as a high school intern with the *Wilmington Morning Star* (later the *Star-News*) (1938–41) and attended Vanderbilt University. After World War II army service, he worked as reporter and bureau manager for United Press in various Southern cities (1941–43) before joining NBC as a Washington-based newswriter and radio and television broadcaster. He was White House correspondent from 1951, and then cohost of the nightly *Huntley-Brinkley Report* (1956–70). He remained with NBC News, continuing to appear on the nightly news as rotating anchor (1970–71) and coanchor with John Chancellor (1976–79) until his retirement in 1981. He then moved to ABC, where he became anchor of *This Week with David Brinkley* (1981–   ).

Brinkley has covered every presidential nominating convention and election since 1956, and has received numerous honors and awards, including ten Emmys, three Peabody awards, including a 1990 award for lifetime achievement, and the Presidental Medal of Freedom (1992).

He was inducted into the Academy of Television Arts and Sciences' Television Hall of Fame in 1989. In 1988, he published *Washington Goes to War*. He also wrote and coanchored the Peabody award-winning television special *Pearl Harbor: Two Hours That Changed the World* (1991). Brinkley married Susan Adolph in 1972; they have a daughter. He also has three sons from an earlier marriage.

FURTHER READING

"David Brinkley." POPE BROCK. *People,* July 27, 1992.

Bristow, Lonnie Robert (1930–) On June 21, 1995, Dr. Lonnie Bristow took office as the first African-American president of the American Medical Association (AMA), signaling an extraordinary reversal of position in the 46 years since the organization had admitted the first African-American into its House of Delegates. One of the AMA's first major moves during Bristow's tenure was its July 1995 all-out attack on smoking as addictive and greatly detrimental to health, coupled with an equally sharp attack on the tobacco industry for allegedly concealing information on tobacco's health hazards. A second major move—and a highly controversial one—was the AMA's October condemnation and then about-face endorsement of the Republican Medicare plan.

New York City–born, Bristow received his 1953 B.S. from the City College of New York, and his 1957 M.D. from New York University. He interned in San Francisco, and was a resident physician there and in New York City, beginning his private practice as a specialist in internal medicine at San Pablo, California (1964). From the early 1970s, he became active in a wide range of professional and community organizations. He was a trustee of the American Society of Internal Medicine (1976–83) and president of the society (1981–82). He became a member of the AMA medical service council (1976). He became a delegate to the AMA (1979), the first African-American member of its Board of Trustees (1985), and first African-American chair of that Board (1993). He married Marilyn Hingslage in 1961; they have a daughter and a son; he also has a daughter from his first marriage.

FURTHER READING

"New American Medical Association. . . ." LISA C. JONES. *Ebony,* Aug. 1995.
"Choosing the right medicine. . . ." DENNIS L. BREO. *JAMA, Journal of the American Medical Association,* Feb. 16, 1994.

Matthew Broderick (right) and Jennifer Jason Leigh.

Broderick, Matthew (1962–) Stage and screen star Matthew Broderick scored a triumph in 1995 as the acclaimed star of a Broadway revival of the Frank Loesser-Abe Burrows musical *How to Succeed in Business without*

Really Trying, leading a cast that included Jonathan Freeman, Ronn Carroll, and Megan Mullally. For the role he won a Tony Award, a Drama Desk award, and Outer Circle Award as best actor in a musical. On screen, Broderick directed and starred as real-life scientist Richard Feynman, opposite Patricia Arquette as his wife, in *Infinity*. He also starred as the voice of Tack in the long-delayed animated film *Arabian Knight*, directed by Richard Williams, in a cast that included Vincent Price and Jennifer Beals. Forthcoming was a starring role opposite Jim Carrey in the film *Cable Guy*, directed by Ben Stiller.

New York City–born Broderick, son of actor James Broderick, emerged as a leading young stage and screen actor in the early 1980s. On stage, he won a Tony for *Brighton Beach Memoirs* (1983), and also appeared in such plays as *Torch Song Trilogy* (1981), *Biloxi Blues* (1985), and *The Widow Clare* (1986). On screen, he appeared in several popular films, including *Wargames* (1983), *Ladyhawke* (1985), *Ferris Bueller's Day Off* (1986), *Project X* (1986), *Torch Song Trilogy* (1988), *Biloxi Blues* (1988), *The Freshman* (1989), *Family Business* (1989), *Glory* (1989), *Out on a Limb* (1992), *The Night We Never Met* (1993), *A Life in the Theatre* (1993), *The Road to Wellville* (1994), *Mrs. Parker and the Vicious Circle* (1994), and starred as one of the voices in *The Lion King* (1994).

FURTHER READING

"Matthew Broderick's. . . ." JOSHUA MOONEY. *Mademoiselle*, Oct. 1994.

Brokaw, Tom (Thomas John Brokaw; 1940–) NBC evening news anchor Tom Brokaw was a bridesmaid, not a bride, in 1995. He hosted the Alfred I. DuPont–Columbia University Awards for broadcast journalism in January, but the top award went to his competition: Peter Jennings and ABC News. Brokaw and his "NBC Nightly News" lagged far behind Jennings and ABC's "World News Tonight," but continued in second place, slightly ahead of Dan Rather and the "CBS Evening News"—though all the major network news programs suffered losses in audience share because other channels carried live coverage of the O. J. Simpson trial. In mid-October, after the trial ended, Brokaw and Katie

Couric arranged an exclusive televised interview with Simpson, but the would-be coup fell through when Simpson withdrew at the last minute. In April, Brokaw reported live from the site of the Oklahoma City bombing. He also continued to host occasional prime-time news specials, such as *Tycoon*, a documentary on Microsoft chairman Bill Gates.

Brokaw's contract with NBC runs only into 1997, and he has strongly suggested that he might then give up the pressure of daily news anchoring. Some politicians in South Dakota (where he owns a radio station) and Montana (where he has a ranch) have sought to convince Brokaw to run for the U.S. Senate from their respective states.

South Dakota–born Brokaw began his long career in broadcasting in 1962, and anchored news shows in Atlanta and Los Angeles during the mid-1960s before becoming NBC White House correspondent in 1973. He became a nationally known figure as the host of NBC's "Today" show (1976–82), and has anchored the "NBC Nightly News" since 1982, as one of the three chief American reporters and interpreters of the news. He is also cohost of the prime-time weekly news program, "Now with Tom Brokaw and Katie Couric" (1993–). Brokaw's B.A. was from the University of South Dakota. He married Meredith Lynn Auld in 1962; they have three children.

FURTHER READING

Anchors: Brokaw, Jennings, Rather and the Evening News. ROBERT GOLDBERG and GERALD J. GOLDBERG. Carol, 1990.

Brooks, Garth (1962–) The Garth Brooks phenomenon continues: In 1995 Brooks became the best-selling country music performer of all time, with a total of more than 55 million albums sold; and he was poised to overtake Billy Joel in second place, behind the Beatles, as best-selling recording artist of all time. His parade of awards continued as well, with major American Music, Academy of Country Music, Country Music, Irish Recorded Music, British Country Music, People's Choice, and World Music awards.

Brooks introduced yet another blockbuster work in 1995, the album *Fresh Horses*, released worldwide in late November. It was preceded by two singles, the ballad "She's Every Woman," written by Brooks and Victoria Shaw, and "The Fever," a reworking of an Aerosmith standard. Both became hit singles. *Fresh Horses* included eight more tracks—seven of them coauthored by Brooks—"The Old Stuff," "Cowboys and Angels," "That 'Ol Wind," "Rollin'," "The Change," "The Beaches of Cheyenne," "It's Midnight Cinderella," and "Ireland." A great deal of promotion in support of the album was scheduled, and Brooks was slated for American and world tours through 1998. *Fresh Horses* made its debut in the same week as *The Beatles Anthology I*, coming in second on the Billboard 200 chart.

Oklahoma-born Brooks began his career singing country music in cabaret. He and his wife made an unsuccessful bid to enter the Nashville country music world in 1985. A second try, in 1987, worked spectacularly well, resulting in his first country album, *Garth Brooks* (1989), with the hit singles "Much Too Young," "If Tomorrow Never Comes," and "The Dance," the latter two becoming signature songs. His second album, *No Fences* (1990), contained such hit singles as "The Thunder Rolls" and "Friends in Low Places." That year saw his induction into Grand Ole Opry, and a long string of country music awards, including the Academy of Country Music and Country Music Association entertainer of the year awards, as well as best record awards for *No Fences* and "Friends in Low Places." Brooks went on to issue the hit albums *Ropin' the Wind* (1991), *The Chase* (1992), his Christmas album *Beyond the Season* (1992), *In Pieces* (1993), and *The Hits* (1994). Brooks's B.A. was from Oklahoma State University. He is married to Sandy Mahr, and has two children.

FURTHER READING

"Don't be fooled. . . ." PETER GALVIN. *Interview*, Mar. 1994.
Garth Brooks: No Fences. CAROL CUELLAR and AARON STANG. CPP Belwin, 1994.
"Playboy interview. . . ." STEVE POND. *Playboy*, June 1994.
"The country craze." MARY NEMETH and DIANE TURBIDE. *Maclean's*, Nov. 8, 1993.
"Ropin' the wind. . . ." ANTHONY DeCURTIS. *Rolling Stone*, Apr. 1, 1993.
Garth Brooks: One of a Kind, Workin' on a Full House. RICK MITCHELL. Simon & Schuster, 1993.
Garth Brooks. ROSEMARY WALLNER. Abdo & Daughters, 1993.
Garth Brooks: Straight from the Heart. EDWARD TALLMAN. Dillon/Macmillan, 1993.

"He's Garth Brooks. . . ." CHARLES HIRSHBERG and NUBAR ALEXANIAN. *Life*, July 1992.
"Garth Brooks. . . ." MARJIE McGRAW. *Saturday Evening Post*, July–Aug. 1992.
"Brooks, Garth." *Current Biography*, Mar. 1992.
The Garth Brooks Scrapbook. LEE RANDALL. Carol, 1992.

Brophy, Brigid Antonia (1929–95) British writer and critic Brigid Brophy emerged as a major figure with her first and best-known novel, *Hackenfeller's Ape* (1953); among her later novels were *The King of the Rainy Country* (1956), *Flesh* (1962), *The Snow Ball* (1964), and *In Transit* (1969). She also wrote the short story collection *The Crown Princess* (1953), a play, and studies of Aubrey Beardsley and Ronald Firbank. Brophy also was a highly visible campaigner on a wide range of professional and social issues. She was a leader of the successful British campaign to pay authors royalties for the use of their books in libraries, called Public Lending Right. She was also president of the British National Anti-Vivisection Society and campaigned actively for a considerable range of other causes, not allowing herself to be stopped by the onset of multiple sclerosis in 1981. Brophy briefly attended Oxford University. She was survived by her husband, art historian Michael Levey, and a daughter. (d. Lincolnshire, England; August 7, 1995)

FURTHER READING

Obituary. *New York Times*, Aug. 9, 1995.
Obituary. *Times* (of London), Aug. 8, 1995.
Obituary. *Independent*, Aug. 8, 1995.

Brown, Ron (Ronald Harmon Brown; 1941–) Secretary of Commerce Ron Brown continued to travel widely to promote U.S. foreign trade during 1995, and to attack the discriminatory trading practices of many other countries, especially Japan. These matters, however, were overshadowed by new accusations of financial irregularities while in office. In 1993 and 1994, he had been accused of taking a $700,000 bribe from the Vietnamese government; the accusations were found groundless by a grand jury and the FBI, and President Bill Clinton had defended him. The 1995 allegations

involved possible wrongdoing involving payments from a former business partner, required financial disclosures, and several other matters, which in aggregate caused Attorney General Janet Reno to appoint an independent counsel, Miami attorney Daniel S. Pearson, to examine the possibility of criminal charges. Brown strongly denied any wrongdoing; the investigation was proceeding at year's end.

Born in Washington, D.C., Brown received his 1962 B.A. from Middlebury College, and his 1970 J.D. from St. John's University School of Law. He began his career as a Washington "insider" soon after his graduation, working in a series of increasingly responsible posts at the National Urban League (1971–79); was counsel for the Senate Judiciary Committee (1980); worked in the presidential campaign of Senator Edward Kennedy (1979–80), remaining with him in 1981; and was a partner in the law firm Patton, Boggs and Blow (1981–89).

Brown worked with the Democratic National Committee from 1981. He was Jesse Jackson's 1988 Democratic Convention manager, a Dukakis political adviser during the 1988 presidential campaign, and in February 1989 became the trailblazing first African-American Democratic National Committee chairperson. In that position he played a major role in 1992 presidential politics, developing an unusually unified Democratic National Convention and presidential election campaign. On December 12, 1992, Clinton named Ron Brown to be his secretary of commerce.

Brown married Alma Arrington in 1962; they have two children.

FURTHER READING

"Do you want. . . ." WELD ROYAL. *Sales & Marketing Management,* July 1995.
"Sleazy genius. . . ." JOHN B. JUDIS. *New Republic,* May 15, 1995.
"A talk with. . . ." FRANK MCCOY. *Black Enterprise,* June 1993.
"Unholy trinity. . . ." JOHN B. JUDIS. *Mother Jones,* Mar.–Apr. 1993.
"A pro tries. . . ." BILL HEWITT. *People,* Jan. 18, 1993.
"Talking to. . . ." MARY ANN FRENCH. *Essence,* July 1992.

Browner, Carol (1955–) Environmental Protection Agency (EPA) Administrator Carol Browner spent much of 1995 in a defensive stance, as congressional Republicans mounted

their promised sharp attack on the EPA, as part of their general attack on several decades of environmental protection laws and regulations. In President Bill Clinton's proposed federal budget, detailed in February 1995, the EPA budget was to be increased by more than 5 percent, to $6.6 billion. But the Clinton budget was quite clearly not acceptable to the Republican Congress. On July 27, the president signed a "rescissions" bill, in which $1 billion was cut from the EPA's 1995 clean-water budget and $100 million cut from the EPA's 1995 toxic waste cleanup budget. Four days later, the House voted massive cuts in the 1996 EPA budget, which became part of the wider budget battle fought for the rest of the year. Throughout the budgeting process, Browner sharply and publicly differed with the Republican majority, speaking out especially strongly against the revisions the House made to the 1972 Clean Water Act in May. Congressional Republicans responded to Browner's yearlong barrage of criticism by charging her with illegal lobbying to influence pending legislation, a charge she entirely rejected, as did other federal officials who met the same kinds of charges.

The EPA introduced no major new environmental protection initiatives in 1995. In late September, the EPA prepared a statement of long-term environmental protection goals, but little action was expected, with the agency facing probable massive new funding cuts and possible major revisions of existing environmental protection laws.

Browner began her career as a strongly environmentalist Florida House of Representatives lawyer in 1980, soon after receiving her 1979 J.D. from the University of Florida, where she had also done her undergraduate work. Moving to Washington, she worked for Common Cause on environmental matters, and in the late 1980s as legislative director for then-Senator Al Gore, a congressional leader on environmental issues.

In January 1991, she moved back to her home state, as head of the Florida Department of Environmental Protection; in that post, she negotiated a federal-state settlement aimed at restoring the ecologically damaged Everglades National Park. She also developed a reputation for working with industry and ecologists to simultaneously foster development and preservation, and for speeding the pace of agency decisions, approaches criticized by some ecologists and welcomed by others. Her stated early intentions as head of the Environmental Protection Agency (1993–   ) ran along similar lines; she also very strongly stressed the need to restore public faith in the EPA, which she felt had sagged greatly during the Reagan and Bush years. Browner is married to Michael Podhorzer; they have one son.

FURTHER READING

"Browner, Carol M." *Current Biography*, May 1994.
"Twenty minutes with. . . ." WILL NIXON. *E*, Dec. 1993.
"The sinkable. . . ." FRANCIS WILKINSON. *Rolling Stone*, Oct. 28, 1993.
"Is Carol Browner. . . ." JON BOWERMASTER. *Audubon*, Sept.–Oct. 1993.

Buchanan, Pat (Patrick Joseph Buchanan; 1938–   ) Talk-show host, writer, and politician Pat Buchanan once again became a Republican presidential nomination candidate in 1995, still appealing to the extreme right wing of his party. His platform was much the same as it had been during the 1992 campaign: last-ditch opposition to abortion so fervent that he called the Christian Coalition too weak on the issue; scathing political and personal denunciations of a very wide range of Democrats, moderate Republicans, women in politics, homosexuals, and racial and ethnic group leaders; and threats to form a third party if he were not satisfied with the Republicans. Buchanan drew considerable interest in New Hampshire and other early primary states during 1995, although he was again viewed by many Republican politicians as a potential "spoiler," who might do well in early primaries, but stood no chance of being nominated or elected, while again conveying an upsetting, hard-right Republican image to the great majority of voters during the 1996 presidential campaign. One notable early attack on Buchanan came in July 1995, when conservative Republican William J. Bennett accused Buchanan of "flirting" with fascism, and urged Republicans to reject him and his views. Buchanan placed a distant fourth, with 9 percent of the vote, in the November Florida Republican straw poll.

Washington, D.C.–born Buchanan began his career in journalism as an editorial writer for the *St. Louis Globe Democrat* (1962–66). He moved into politics as an executive assistant to Richard M. Nixon in 1966, and moved into the White House as a special assistant to Nixon in 1969, during the years that followed becoming a leading speechwriter for Nixon and Vice President Spiro Agnew. Although Buchanan left the White House in 1973, he remained loyal to Nixon throughout the Watergate scandals that cost Nixon his presidency. Buchanan became a widely followed syndicated columnist and broadcasting personality from the mid-1970s, most notably as the ultraconservative half of the Cable News Network's "Buchanan-Braden Show" (1978–83) and "Crossfire" (1982–85; 1987–92). He went back into the White House as President Ronald Reagan's communications director (1985–87), then resuming his media career. He participated in the 1992 Republican presidential primary campaign as an ultraconservative, receiving 2.8 million votes and more than 22 percent of the entire Republican primary vote. He later supported the Bush candidacy, though his intemperate Republican national convention speech was thought by many to have harmfully identified the Republican Party with the far right, and to have contributed greatly to the Bush-Quayle defeat in the November election.

Buchanan's books include *The New Majority* (1973), *Conservative Votes, Liberal Victories* (1975), and his autobiography *Right from the Beginning* (1988). Buchanan's 1961 A.B. was from Georgetown University, and his 1962 M.S. in journalism from Columbia University. He is married to the former Shelley Scarney.

FURTHER READING

"The Pat solution." JEFFREY H. BIRNBAUM. *Time*, Nov. 6, 1995.
"Bay watch." RICH LOWRY. "Pat Buchanan. . . ." ROBERT D. NOVAK. *National Review*, Aug. 14, 1995.
"A potent trinity. . . ." DAVID CORN. *Nation*, June 26, 1995.
"A fighter. . . ." JAMIE DETTMER. *Insight on the News*, Apr. 3, 1995.
"Crowded on the right. . . ." NINA BURLEIGH. *Time*, Mar. 13, 1995.
"An old soldier. . . ." MICHAEL RUST. *Insight on the News*, July 19, 1993.
"By heaven inspired. . . ." NORMAN MAILER. *New Republic*, Oct.12, 1992.
"Rot on the right." LAURENCE I. BARRETT. *Time*, Aug. 24, 1992.
" 'Outsiders get. . . .' " PIERRE BRIANCON. *World Press Review*, May 1992.
"Heir apparent. . . ." FRED BARNES. *New Republic*, Mar. 30, 1992.

"Springtime for Buchanan." SIDNEY BLUMENTHAL. *New Republic*, Mar. 9, 1992.
"The case for Buchanan." TOM BETHELL. *National Review*, Mar. 2, 1992.

Burger, Warren Earl (1907–95) Born in St. Paul, Minnesota, Chief Justice Warren Burger worked his way through the St. Paul College of Law, receiving his LL.B. in 1931. He practiced law in St. Paul and also went into Republican state politics. An Eisenhower supporter, he was appointed to the Justice Department during the first Eisenhower administration, and in 1956 was appointed by President Eisenhower to the U.S. Court of Appeals for the District of Columbia. He was President Richard Nixon's first appointee to the U.S. Supreme Court, replacing liberal Earl Warren as Chief Justice (1969–86).

During his long tenure on the Court, Chief Justice Burger, a leading conservative, led an attempt to limit and to some extent reverse the thrust of the far more liberal and activist Warren Court, meeting with mixed success in such areas as the death penalty, which he favored, and in several other criminal law areas. He was, however, far from being a doctrinaire conservative, taking positions on such issues as the validity of busing to help cure segregated schools and on abortion rights that might have been viewed as ultraliberal by the conservatives of a later day. His main focus, especially in his later years, was on administrative reform, aimed at speeding the work of the Court, coupled with criticism of the behavior of the media and many members of the legal profession. Burger published the 1995 book *It is So Ordered: A Constitution Unfolds*. He was survived by a daughter and a son. (d. Washington, D.C.; June 25, 1995)

FURTHER READING

Obituary. *Current Biography*, Aug. 1995.
"Warren Burger. . . ." HUGH SIDEY. *Time,* July 10, 1995.
Obituary. *Economist,* July 8, 1995.
Obituary. *Times* (of London), June 27, 1995.
Obituary. *Independent,* June 27, 1995.
Obituary. *New York Times,* June 26, 1995.
The Burger Court: Political and Judicial Profiles. CHARLES M. LAMB and STEPHEN C. HALPERN, ed. University of Illinois Press, 1991.

Burroughs, William Seward (1914–)

The revival of interest in Beat Generation icons brought William Burroughs back into the public eye in 1995. The year saw publication of two new books by the long-controversial writer. The first was *My Education: A Book of Dreams*, a partly autobiographical work that includes sketches for stories and other fragments of prose. The book is set in a dreamlike framework, though it includes some very real events, such as his 1951 accidental killing of his wife, Joan, during a "William Tell" game, when he was trying to shoot an apple off her head. His second new book was *Ghost of a Chance*, an historical-environmental tale set in Madagascar, ultimately involving a battle between international bureaucrats and people seeking to protect the island's unique flora and fauna. Burroughs also was reader on an audiobook version of his *Naked Lunch*. The Quality Paperback Book Club published a special one-volume edition of his *Junky, Queer,* and *Naked Lunch.*

St. Louis–born Burroughs received his 1936 A.B. from Harvard University. He stayed on at Harvard to do postgraduate work, and then held a series of jobs before serving in the military during World War II. As he later detailed in his work, he became a drug addict in 1944. Burroughs was long an expatriate in Latin America, Europe, and North Africa. His first novel, originally published under the name Robert Lee, was *Junky: Confessions of an Unredeemed Drug Ad-*

dict (1953). In 1959, under his own name, he published by far his best known work, the novel *Naked Lunch*. Its explicit treatment of drugs and sex was very much in tune with the emerging times, and Burroughs became a major figure in the Beat movement and the subsequent countercultural movement of the 1960s. Among his later works were *The Exterminator* (1960), *The Soft Machine* (1961), *The Ticket That Exploded* (1962), *Dead Fingers Talk* (1963), *The Yage Letters* (1963; correspondence with his friend, poet Allen Ginsberg), *Nova Express* (1964), *The Job* (1969), *Wild Boys* (1971), *Exterminator!* (1973), *The Last Words of Dutch Schultz* (1975), *Cities of the Red Night* (1981), *Queer* (1985), *The Western Lands* (1987), and *The Letters of William Burroughs, 1945–59* (1993). He also released *Spare Ass Annie and Other Tales* (1993), a recording of Burroughs reading from his own work, backed by music. He married Joan Vollmer in 1945; they had one son.

FURTHER READING

The Algebra of Need: William Burroughs and the Gods of Death, 2nd ed. ERIC MOTTRAM. M. Boyars, 1994.

"Let's do naked lunch." DAVID GATES. *Newsweek,* Sept. 6, 1993.

William S. Burroughs. KYOICHI TSUZUKI. Books Nippan, 1993.

William Burroughs: El Hombre Invisible. BARRY MILES. Hyperion, 1993.

"David Cronenberg on. . . ." KAREN JAEHNE. *Film Quarterly,* Spring 1992.

"Which is the fly. . . ." LYNN SNOWDEN. *Esquire,* Feb. 1992.

"Cronenberg does. . . ." JOHN H. RICHARDSON. *Premiere,* Feb. 1992.

"Burroughs on. . . ." DAVID EHRENSTEIN. *Advocate,* July 16, 1991.

"Wm. Burroughs. . . ." VICTOR BOCKRIS. *Interview,* Apr. 1991.

Bush, George (George Herbert Walker Bush; 1924–) Former president George Bush continued to be active in retirement during 1995. On May 3, in a very notable action that drew great national attention, he publicly resigned as a Life Member of the National Rifle Association, writing "I was outraged when, even in the wake of the Oklahoma City tragedy, Mr. Wayne La-Pierre, executive vice president of the N.R.A, defended his attack on federal agents as 'jack-booted thugs.' To attack Secret Service agents or A.T.F. people or any government law enforcement people as 'wearing Nazi bucket helmets and black storm trooper uniforms' and wanting to 'attack law abiding citizens' is a vicious slander on good people."

With his wife, Barbara Bush, George Bush visited China in 1995, as he had in 1994. His visit was part of a wider Asian visit (September 4–19), which began with a visit to Vietnam (September 4–7), a month after U.S.-Vietnam diplomatic relations had been resumed; he became the first American president or former president to visit Vietnam since the end of the Vietnam War. He then went to China (September 8–13), and then on to Japan (September 13–19), where his tour, for an unrevealed fee, was sponsored by the highly controversial Women's Federation for World Peace, headed by Hak Ja Han Moon, wife of Rev. Sung Myung Moon.

Bush also accepted President Bill Clinton's invitation to attend the November 6 state funeral of assassinated Israeli Prime Minister Yitzhak Rabin, as did former President Jimmy Carter.

George Bush defeated Michael Dukakis in the bitterly contested 1988 presidential race, becoming the 41st president of the United States in 1989, the climax of a political career that had begun in Texas in the early 1960s. He had grown up in a Republican party family, the son of Connecticut Senator Prescott Bush, and then left New England to enter the oil business in Texas in the early 1950s, cofounding the Zapata Petroleum Company in 1953 and becoming president and then board chairman of the Zapata Off Shore Company in 1956. He was an unsuccessful Republican senatorial candidate from Texas in 1964, but won a House seat in 1966, moving to Washington as a Houston congressman for two terms (1967–71). In 1970, he made another unsuccessful run for the Senate on the Republican ticket.

Bush was United States ambassador to the United Nations during the Vietnam War (1971–72), and then Republican National Committee chairperson (1973–74). He was the chief American liaison officer in Peking (1974–76), then returned to Washington as head of the CIA (1976–77). He made an unsuccessful Republican presidential nomination run in 1980, but withdrew in favor of Ronald Reagan, and subsequently became Reagan's two-term vice president, operating in those eight years in a largely ceremonial and standby fashion, as have most vice presidents. He then succeeded Reagan as president (1989–93).

The early Bush years saw a series of major international triumphs as the Cold War ended and the Soviet empire collapsed. First came the quick and easy late 1989 invasion of Panama that toppled the Noriega dictatorship. Then came a series of major Soviet-American peace moves, with planned troop pullbacks and real progress on arms control and on the ending of a whole series of regional conflicts that had for decades been spurred by Soviet and American sponsorship of the combatants. With both countries acting in concert as peacemakers, and with the direct intervention of George Bush and Mikhail Gorbachev, the continuing conflicts in Nicaragua, Cambodia, Angola, Mozambique, Namibia, Ethiopia, and several other countries moved swiftly toward resolution. Bush's last triumph was the successful prosecution of the 1991 Persian Gulf War. On November 3, 1992, he won only 38 percent of the popular vote in the presidential election, losing his bid for reelection to Arkansas governor Bill Clinton, in a three-way race that included independent candidate H. Ross Perot.

George Bush's 1948 B.A. was from Yale University. A navy pilot in World War II, he married Barbara Pierce in 1945. Their five surviving children are George (elected governor of Texas in 1994), John, Neil, Marvin, and Dorothy; their second child, Robyn, died of leukemia at age three. During the 1988 presidential campaign, Bush published two books, *Man of Integrity* (with Doug Wead) and *Looking Forward: The George Bush Story* (with Victor Gold).

FURTHER READING

"On the 19th hole. . . ." GEORGE PLIMPTON. *New York Times Magazine*, Apr. 24, 1994.
"George Bush speaks out. . . ." VICTOR GOLD. *Washingtonian*, Feb. 1994.
"Revelations of Bush's diary. . . ." FRANCES FITZGERALD. *Nation*, Mar. 8, 1993.
George Bush. WILLIAM E. PEMBERTON. Rourke, 1993.
"Life in Bush hell." JAMES PINKERTON. *New Republic*, Dec. 14, 1992.
"Bush's desperate game." JOE KLEIN. "Face to face." ANN McDANIEL. *Newsweek*, Oct. 19, 1992.
"The case for Bush. . . ." RICHARD VIGILANTE. "The wilderness year." *New Republic*, Aug. 31, 1992.
"Warrior for the status quo." MICHAEL DUFFY and DAN GOODGAME. "Bush on the record." MICHAEL KRAMER and HENRY MULLER. "The fight of his life." DAN GOODGAME. *Time*, Aug. 24, 1992.

"A conversation with. . . ." ANN McDANIEL and TOM DeFRANK. *Newsweek*, Aug. 24, 1992.
"Finding a road. . . ." HILARY MACKENZIE. *Maclean's*, Aug. 24, 1992.
"A visit with. . . ." RICHARD BROOKHISER. *Atlantic*, Aug. 1992.
Chameleon: The Unauthorized Biography of George Bush. JONATHAN SLEVIN and STEVEN WILMSEN. Krantz, 1992.
George Bush: His World War II Years. ROBERT B. STINNETT. Macmillan, 1992.

Butenandt, Adolf Johann Friedrich

(1903–95) German biochemist Adolf Butenandt received his doctorate at the University of Göttingen in 1927, there beginning the sex hormone work that was to win him a Nobel Prize. In 1929, he isolated the hormone estrone, which helps control sexual development in women, and in 1931 isolated androsterone, a male sex hormone. In 1934, he isolated progesterone. He and Leopold Ruzicka were then able to synthesize testosterone, which affects masculine characteristics; this and later work with sex hormones led directly to the development of steroids and birth control pills. In 1939, he and Ruzicka shared the Nobel Prize in chemistry. Butenandt was able to take possession of his Nobel only in 1949, after the Nazi period, as the Nazis had ordered Germans to reject the prizes after the Nobel Peace Prize had been awarded to anti-Nazi German Carl von Ossietzsky in 1935. Butenandt, who remained in Germany and in favor with the government throughout the Nazi period, was director of Berlin's Kaiser Wilhelm Institute of Biochemistry (1936–45), a post he retained after the war (1945–60), when it became the Max Planck Institute, of which he became president (1960–72). No information was available as to survivors. (d. Munich, Germany; January 18, 1995)

FURTHER READING

Obituary. *Times* (of London), Feb. 13, 1995.
Obituary. *Independent,* Feb. 1, 1995.
Obituary. *New York Times*, Jan. 19, 1995.

Buthelezi, Mangosuthu Gatsha

(1928–) During 1995, Zulu leader Gatsha Buthelezi continued to play a major opposition role in the new multiracial South African government led by Nelson Mandela, though he was still home affairs minister in that government. Buthelezi asserted that the Zulu Inkatha Freedom Party, the African National Congress, and the National Party had in April 1994 agreed to international mediation of Zulu demands for the creation of a largely autonomous Zulu homeland in KwaZulu (Natal), and that Mandela had reneged on the agreement. In February 1995, Buthelezi led a withdrawal of Inkatha from Parliament; Inkatha later returned, still demanding mediation. In early April, Inkatha pursued its claim by withdrawing from the Constituent Assembly, demanding autonomy from a government set on creating a much more centralized nation than Inkatha was willing to accept, and creating the very real possibility of civil war if the matter was not solved peacefully. Major government-Inkatha disputes continued throughout the year, as did fighting between Inkatha and government supporters in Natal, the center of Zulu strength. To take up the worsening violence in Natal, President Mandela in June set up a special committee that included himself, Buthelezi, F. W. De Klerk, and Thabo Mbecki; little progress was reported, as the killing in Natal continued.

Buthelezi became chief of the Buthelezi tribe in 1963, succeeding his father, Mathole Buthelezi. He was a Zulu administrator for two decades, becoming chief minister of the Kwa-Zulu in 1976. As the long fight for South African democracy developed during the 1970s and 1980s, he emerged as the main spokesperson and leader of the Zulus, and a third force in South African politics, for he negotiated with the White South African government on behalf of the Zulus, and often opposed the African National Congress (ANC). His followers, organized into the Inkatha movement, carried those disagreements into anti-ANC street fighting throughout the 1980s and early 1990s. Buthelezi emerged as a powerful independent force in South African politics in the early 1990s, as negotiations over the future of the country proceeded between the De Klerk government and the ANC, led by Nelson Mandela. Thought by many to be seeking a Zulu homeland separate from the new South Africa, Buthelezi in the early 1990s allied himself with diehard White racists attempting to prevent the emergence of multiracial democracy; his Inkatha forces sharply escalated their attacks on the ANC and its supporters. He was publicly reconciled with newly inaugurated Mandela in May 1994, and

was named home minister in the new government; he retained that position although he was dismissed from his position as Zulu prime minister in September 1994, after his Inkatha supporters had stoned President Mandela's helicopter and then the Zulu royal palace.

Buthelezi attended Adams College and Fort Hare University. He married Irene Audrey Thandekile Mzila in 1952; they have four daughters and three sons. In 1990, he published *South Africa: My Vision of the Future.*

FURTHER READING

"A moment in time. . . ." VIVIENNE WALT. *Interview,* June 1994.
"Buthelezi. . . ." SCOTT MACLEOD. *Time,* July 6, 1992.
"The chief. . . ." CHRISTOPHER S. WREN. *New York Times Magazine,* Feb. 17, 1991.

Byrne, Gabriel (1950–) In another very busy year, Irish stage and screen actor Gabriel Byrne starred opposite Anjelica Huston and Melanie Griffith in the television miniseries *Buffalo Girls,* directed by Rod Hardy and based on the Larry McMurtry novel. He also appeared in the Western film *Dead Man,* written and directed by Jim Jarmusch. A third starring role came in the crime thriller *The Usual Suspects,* produced and directed by Bryan Singer. Byrne also starred in the film *Frankie Starlight,* directed by Michael Lindsay-Hogg, and was one of the voices in the television film *Out of Ireland,* narrated by Kelly

McGillis, the story of eight emigrants. Bryne also published the autobiographical book *Pictures In My Head*.

Forthcoming were starring roles in the film *The Brylcream Boys*, directed by Terence Ryan, in a cast that includes Bill Campbell, William McNamara, and Joan Butler; and opposite Catherine O'Hara and Stephen Rea in the film *The Last of the High Kings*, directed by David Keating. He was also slated to star opposite Nastassia Kinski in the film *Somebody's Waiting*, written and directed by Martin Donavan.

Dublin-born Byrne attended University College, Dublin, and began acting in his late 20s, becoming a leading player in the Irish theater before emerging as a film star in the mid-1980s. He made his film debut in *The Outsider* (1979). Some of his most notable films were *Hanna K* (1983), *Defence of the Realm* (1986), *Lionheart* (1987), *Siesta* (1987), *A Soldier's Tale* (1988), *Miller's Crossing* (1990), *Point of No Return* (1993), *Prince of Jutland* (1994), *Trial by Jury* (1994), *Little Women* (1994), and *A Simple Twist of Fate* (1994). He married actress Ellen Barkin in 1988. They had a son and a daughter before separating in 1993.

FURTHER READING

"Gabriel Byrne. . . ." CHRIS CHASE. *Cosmopolitan*, Sept. 1993.

C

Cage, Nicolas (Nicholas Coppola; 1965–)
Film star Nicolas Cage starred as an alcoholic
and compulsive Las Vegas gambler who is going
downhill fast in the acclaimed 1995 film *Leaving
Las Vegas*, directed by Mike Figgis, in a cast
that included Elisabeth Shue, Julian Sands,
Richard Lewis, and Valeria Golino. For this role,
Cage was named best actor of the year by the
New York Film Critics Circle and the Los An-
geles Film Critics Association, and received a
Golden Globe nomination as best actor in a
drama.

Cage also starred as the leading criminal
"heavy" in the Barbet Schroeder crime thriller

Nicholas Cage (right) and Samuel L. Jackson.

Kiss of Death, a remake of the 1947 Henry Hath-
away film, with a cast that included David
Caruso, Samuel L. Jackson, Helen Hunt, and
Jay O. Sanders.

Forthcoming were starring roles opposite Annabella Sciorra and Isabelle Rossellini in the
film *The Funeral*, directed by Abel Ferrara; and
opposite Sean Connery and Ed Harris in *The
Rock*.

On the personal side, Cage and actress Patricia Arquette married in April; each has a child
by a previous marriage..

California-born Cage, Francis Ford Coppola's
nephew, began his career with strong supporting roles in such 1980s films as *Valley Girl*
(1983), *Rumble Fish* (1983), *Racing with the
Moon* (1984), *Birdy* (1984), and *The Cotton Club*
(1984), and moved into leads with his role opposite Kathleen Turner in *Peggy Sue Got Married*
(1986). He went on to star in *Raising Arizona*
(1987), in *Moonstruck* (1988) as the one-armed
baker who becomes Cher's lover, *Vampire's Kiss*
(1989), *Firebirds* (1990), in the David Lynch film
Wild at Heart (1990) as Sailor Ripley opposite
Laura Dern as Lula Pace Fortune, *Zandalee*
(1991), *Honeymoon in Vegas* (1992), *Amos & Andrew* (1993), *Red Rock West* (1993), *Guarding
Tess* (1994), *It Could Happen to You* (1994), and
Trapped in Paradise (1994).

FURTHER READING

"Dangerous, dedicated. . . ." FRED SCHRUERS. *Rolling
     Stone*, Nov. 16, 1995.
"Nicolas Cage." MARK MARVEL. *Interview*, Aug. 1994.
"Cage, Nicolas." *Current Biography*, Apr. 1994.

"Nicolas Cage. . . ." RICHARD NATALE. *Cosmopolitan*, Dec. 1992.
"Nicolas Cage." STEVE POND. *Us*, Sept. 1992.

Cahill, Margaret Gorman

(1905–95) In September 1921, at Atlantic City, New Jersey, 16-year-old Margaret Gorman became the first Miss America, inaugurating a contest that was to quickly grow into an American institution. In the post–World War II period, and especially after the heightened feminist consciousness of the 1970s, winners came to be evaluated on several bases, including artistic accomplishment. At the start, though, the contest was purely and openly a "bathing beauty" contest, and it was as a very young bathing beauty, attired in what by 1990s' standards was a very, very modest bathing costume, complete with stockings, that she won the contest. At 5'1", she was the shortest Miss America ever; very slim, her appearance was enhanced by her adoption of the emerging styles of the 1920s liberated women, in rebellion against the constricted, floor-length costumes of a time just ending. In the widest social sense, the first Miss America was a symbol of the new, freer day dawning for the American women of her time. She later married and spent her entire life in the Washington, D.C. area. Her husband predeceased her; she was survived by a brother. (d. Bowie, Maryland; October 1, 1995)

FURTHER READING

Obituary. *New York Times*, Oct. 5, 1995.

Cardoso, Fernando Henrique

(1931–   ) During his first year in office, Brazilian President Fernando Henrique Cardoso focused largely on domestic matters. Elected largely because of his successful anti-inflation programs while finance minister, he immediately upon taking office found himself dealing with trade deficits, inflation, and the prospect of a recession. On top of all this, substantial elements of the military were, as always, mistrustful of a civilian president and were quite ready to try to seize power if Cardoso's presidency destablized the country.

Cardoso proved quite able to deal with the imposition of austerity programs, devaluation of

the *real*, and the threat of recession. In June he broke the month-old oil workers strike, ordering out troops to seize struck refineries and forcing the strikers back to work on threat of dismissal. Early in the year, with then-mounting trade deficits, and caught in the backwash of the Mexican financial collapse, he used government currency-purchasing intervention to turn back a speculative attack mounted by international currency traders, and devalued the *real*, devaluing it again in June. He also raised many import duties sharply; later in the year, he joined other coffee producers in limiting production, to keep prices high. But austerity programs have their political hazards, and by year's end resistance was gathering to his economic policies.

Born in Rio de Janeiro, Cardoso's training was as a sociologist. While a young left-oriented university sociology professor, he was arrested by the Brazilian military in 1969; blacklisted, he founded the São Paulo-based Brazilian Analysis and Planning Center (Cebrap), and also taught abroad as a visiting lecturer during much of the 1970s, most notably at the University of California at Berkeley, Oxford University, Yale University, and Stanford University. He has also been an active author, publishing more than a score of books, among them the seminal *Dependency and Development in Latin America* (1979), coauthored with Enzo Faletto, which very effectively argued the necessity of independent development throughout Latin America, rather than dependence upon foreign aid and financing.

Cardoso entered electoral politics as a senator from São Paulo (1986–92). A Social Democrat, he was a cofounder of Brazil's Social Democratic party in 1988. He became foreign minister in 1992 and finance minister in 1993. He was elected to the presidency October 3, 1994, succeeding President Itamar Franco, and took office on January 1, 1995. He is married to anthropologist Ruth Correa Leite Cardoso; they have three children.

FURTHER READING

" 'What happened. . . .' " IAN KATZ. *Business Week,* Oct. 30, 1995.
"Fulfilling Brazil's promise. . . ." JAMES F. HOGE, JR. *Foreign Affairs,* July 17, 1995.
"Cardoso wins. . . ." *Facts on File*, Oct. 6, 1994.

Carey, Mariah (1970–   ) At the 1995 22nd annual American Music Awards, singer and songwriter Mariah Carey was again named top female pop/rock artist. She also was named best pop artist at the World Music Awards and best female pop artist at the Blockbuster Entertainment Awards. She received two best pop vocal Grammy nominations, for "Hero" and "All I Wanna Do"; and with Luther Vandross received a best pop vocal collaboration Grammy nomination for "Endless Love."

Carey scored an enormous hit in 1995 with the album *Daydream*, which topped the charts. Its songs included the light pop love song "Fantasy"; "One Sweet Day," sung with Boyz II Men; "Melt Away," a duet with Babyface; "I Am Free"; "Looking In"; "Underneath the Stars"; and the popular title song. "Fantasy" was the first single released; it made its debut at the top of the charts, becoming an instant classic. "One Sweet Day," the second single, did the same.

Among Carey's 1995 contributions was a $1 million pledge to the Fresh Air Fund, dedicated to the development of Camp Mariah, a career awareness camp for inner-city children. She is a director of the Fund.

Long Island–born Carey left high school to live and work in New York City in 1987. She worked as a waitress and backup singer before signing her first recording contract, with Columbia Records. She became a star overnight with her first album *Mariah Carey* (1990), which sold well over 9 million copies; its ten songs included "Vision of Love," a number one single, as were the 1991 singles "Someday," and "I Don't Wanna Cry." In 1992 she released the album *Emotions*, which yielded five consecutive number one singles, including the title track. 1993 saw issuance of the chart-topping album *Music Box*, and 1994 of the album *Merry Christmas*. Carey married music company executive Tommy Mottola in 1993.

FURTHER READING

"Pop's princess grows up." CHRISTOPHER JOHN FARLEY. *Time,* Sept. 25, 1995.
Mariah Carey: Her Story. CHRIS NICKSON. St. Martin's, 1995.
"Mariah Carey. . . ." LYNN NORMENT. *Ebony*, Apr. 1994.
"How sweet it is. . . ." STEVE DOUGHERTY. *People*, Nov. 22, 1993.
"Carey, Mariah." *Current Biography*, July 1992.
"Pop meteor. . . ." CHRIS SMITH. *New York*, Sept. 23, 1991.

Carpenter, Mary-Chapin (1959–   )
Singer and songwriter Mary-Chapin Carpenter, a major figure in country music, was greatly honored by her colleagues in 1995. Her 1994 hit album *Stones In The Road* won a Grammy Award as best country album of the year, and for the album she won a Grammy for best female country performance of the year. She also won a country music "Clip of the Year" Billboard Music

Video award for "Shut Up and Kiss Me," a hit single drawn from the album.

Carpenter was named international female vocalist of the year at the first British Country Music Awards. She was also nominated as best female vocalist of the year at Nashville's 29th annual Country Music Awards, and won a Nammie award for outstanding achievement, awarded by the Nashville music industry. She was a best female vocalist nominee at the Academy of Country Music awards.

Much of Carpenter's year was spent on tour, in support of *Stones In the Road*, but she also released several singles. One was the hit ballad "Why Walk When You Can Fly," drawn from *Stones In The Road*. Another was John Lennon's song "Grow Old With Me," on the album *Working Class Hero—A Tribute to John Lennon*. She was also one of the many artists who appeared on the soundtrack album of Tim Robbins' film *Dead Man Walking*, among them Bruce Springsteen, Johnny Cash, Eddie Vedder, Lyle Lovett, and Nusrat Fateh Ali Khan.

Born in Princeton, New Jersey, Carpenter received her 1981 B.A. from Brown University. She played in clubs in the Washington, D.C., area from the early 1980s, before signing with CBS Records in 1987. Her earlier albums include *Hometown Girl* (1988), *State of the Heart* (1989), and *Shooting Straight in the Dark* (1990). She was named best new female vocalist by the Academy of Country Music in 1990, and best female vocalist of the year by the Country Music Association in 1992.

FURTHER READING

"Mary Chapin Carpenter." JAMES BRADY. *Parade*, June 18, 1995.
"Mary Chapin Carpenter. . . ." BOB ALLEN. *Country Music*, May–June 1995.
"Carpenter, Mary-Chapin." *Current Biography*, Feb. 1994.
"City folk." DAVID WILD. *Vogue*, Apr. 1993.

Carrey, Jim (1962–)

Antic comedian Jim Carrey, who became a major commercial film star after his title role in the 1994 hit comedy *Ace Ventura, Pet Detective* was back again with a 1995 sequel, *Ace Ventura: When Nature Calls*, this one just as slapstick as the original. In this one, Carrey goes to Africa—and to the bank; it was a worldwide commercial hit. The film, apparently aimed at young children thrilled by jokes about sex, bodily functions, and excretions, seems also to have appealed to their older siblings and to a startlingly large number of adults, as well. Ian McNeice costarred; Steve Oedekerk wrote and directed.

Carrey also starred in another antic role, as The Riddler in *Batman Forever*, another commercially successful sequel, starring Val Kilmer in the title role, with Tommy Lee Jones as the villain Harvey Two-Face, Nicole Kidman as the love interest, and Chris O'Donnell as Robin; Joel Schumacher directed.

Forthcoming were starring roles in another sequel, *The Mask II*, directed by Charles Russell; opposite Matthew Broderick in the film *Cable Guy*, directed by Ben Stiller; and in the film *The Truman Show*, directed by Peter Weir.

Toronto-born Carrey began his film and television career in the mid-1980s. He appeared in the television series "The Duck Factory" (1984), and scored a major hit in the television series "In Living Color" (1990–94). His films include *Once Bitten* (1985), *Peggy Sue Got Married* (1986), *The Dead Pool* (1988), *Earth Girls Are Easy* (1989), *Ace Ventura, Pet Detective* (1994), *The Mask* (1994), and *Dumb and Dumber* (1994). He was formerly married, to Melissa Womer, and has a daughter.

FURTHER READING

"Renaissance man." MARTHA SHERRILL. *Esquire*, Dec. 1995.
"King of the jungle." DANA KENNEDY and KATE MEYERS. *Entertainment*, Nov. 10, 1995.
"Jim Carrey. . . ." FRED SCHRUERS. *Rolling Stone*, July 13, 1995.
"Let's get physical. . . ." JACK KROLL. "Funny face." JEFF GILES. *Newsweek*, June 26, 1995.
" 'What failure taught me.' " GAIL BUCHALTER. *Parade*, Jan. 15, 1995.
"Jim Carrey's wild ride." BERNARD WEINRAUB. *Playboy*, Dec. 1994.
"Love with the proper. . . ." DAN SANTOW. *People*, Sept. 5, 1994.
"Lord Jim." KEN TUCKER. *Entertainment*, Aug. 5, 1994.
"Lucky Jim." MICHAEL KAPLAN. *Us*, Aug. 1994.

Carter, Jimmy (James Earl Carter, Jr.; 1924–)

Former President Jimmy Carter continued to pursue his worldwide personal peacemaking mission during 1995. The Bosnian War truce he had helped to arrange in late December 1994 expired on May 1, and Bosnian Serb forces refused to renew it. His role in Bosnia, however, continued into late August and early September, when Bosnian Serb leader Radovan Karadzic wrote to Carter accepting the U.S. plan as a basis for peace talks.

Carter scored a more definitive—though perhaps again short-term—success in Sudan, where in March he was able to secure a two-month cease-fire in the Sudanese Civil War. He met with less success in Nigeria, though receiving some promises of clemency for several political prisoners, also in March. While revisiting Haiti with Colin Powell and Sam Nunn on a fact-finding mission in late February, Carter offered to monitor the upcoming June 30 elections, but his offer was refused.

Georgia-born Carter became the 39th president of the United States (1977–81), the climax of a political career that began with his four years in the Georgia Senate (1963–67). He had gone on to become governor of Georgia (1971–75), emerged as the surprise "outsider" winner of the Democratic presidential nomination after a long series of primary campaigns, and defeated incumbent Gerald Ford in the 1976 presidential race. His earlier career included seven years as a naval officer (1946–53), and ten years as a successful Georgia farmer and businessman at Plains, Georgia.

Carter's very difficult presidential term was dominated by largely adverse foreign affairs matters, including the Arab oil embargo of the mid-1970s, the Iran hostage crisis that began in late 1979 and colored the rest of his presidency, and the worsening Soviet-American relations that began with the Soviet invasion of Afghanistan and resulted in the American boycott of the 1980 Moscow Olympics. His major accomplishment was the 1978 Camp David Accords, which paved the way for the 1979 Egyptian-Israeli peace treaty.

After leaving the presidency, Carter initiated several pilot projects aimed at bringing sound low-income housing to decaying American inner cities. He has also been active in international mediation and human rights efforts, as in Nicaragua in 1989; in Ethiopia, the Sudan, and Haiti in 1990; in Zambia and Nicaragua in 1991; and in Paraguay, Sudan, and Somalia in 1992. He has also been a distinguished professor at Emory University.

Carter was a key foreign policy adviser to presidential candidate and then President-elect Bill Clinton. On July 14, 1992, he addressed the Democratic National Convention in support of Clinton, his presence as the only living Democratic former president and his enthusiastic endorsement greatly helping the convention's unity theme. During 1992 and 1993, Carter also developed the massive Atlanta Project, a program to help solve the problems faced by poor people in his home state's capital city.

Carter's 1947 B.S. was from the U.S. Naval Academy. He married Rosalynn Smith in 1946; they have four children. After he left office, they collaborated in writing *Everything to Gain: Making the Most of the Rest of Your Life* (1988). He has also written several other works, including *Keeping the Faith: Memoirs of a President* (1982), *An Outdoor Journal* (1988), *America on My Mind* (1991), *One Man, One Vote: A Candidate and a State Come of Age* (1992), *Turning Point: A Candidate, A State, and a Nation Come of Age* (1993), *Blood of Abraham: Insights into the Middle East* (1993), the young adult book *Talking Peace: A Vision for the Next Generation* (1993), and the poetry collection *Always a Reckoning: And Other Poems* (1994).

FURTHER READING

"What makes Jimmy run?" GARY SMITH and HARRY BENSON. *Life,* Nov. 1995.

"Eyes on the prize." GREGORY JAYNES. *Esquire,* Oct. 1995.

"When the medium. . . ." *Inc.,* Sept. 12, 1995.

"Catching up. . . ." PAUL SCHNEIDER. *Audubon,* Jan–Feb. 1995.

Jimmy Carter: Beyond the Presidency. MELLONEE CARRIGAN. Childrens, 1995.

"Jimmy Carter. . . ." MARK MARVEL. *Interview,* Dec. 1994.

"Trust and respect. . . ." CARL MOLLINS. *Maclean's,* Oct. 3, 1994.

"A man with a mission." ELEANOR CLIFT et al. *Newsweek,* Oct. 3, 1994.

"One very busy ex-prez." GEORGE J. CHURCH. *Time,* Oct. 3, 1994.

"Ex hits the spot." BILL HEWITT. *People,* Oct. 3, 1994.

The Carter Presidency: A Re-Evaluation. JOHN DUMBRELL. St. Martin's, 1993.

The Presidency of James Earl Carter, Jr. BURTON I. KAUFMAN. University Press of Kansas, 1993.

The Carters: First Families Series. CASS A. SANDAK. Macmillan, 1993.

The Presidency and Domestic Policies of Jimmy Carter. HERBERT D. ROSENBAUM and ALEXEJ UGRINSKY, eds. Greenwood, 1993.

Jimmy Carter: Foreign Policy and Post-Presidential

Years. HERBERT D. ROSENBAUM and ALEXEJ UGRINSKY, eds. Greenwood, 1993.
Jimmy Carter and the Politics of Frustration. GARLAND A. HAAS. McFarland, 1992.

"An officer and a gentleman." DAVID HOCHMAN. *Us,* Dec. 1993.
"Three stars are born." HARRY F. WATERS et al. *Newsweek,* Oct. 25, 1993.

Caruso, David (1956–)

Actor David Caruso, a television star who made headlines when he left the hit series "N.Y.P.D. Blue" early in the fall 1994 season, completed his transition to feature films in 1995. His first starring role, in the crime thriller *Kiss of Death*, was as ex-convict Jimmy Kilmartin, who tries and fails to go straight, is sent back to prison, and after serving his additional term ultimately confronts top criminal Little Junior, played by Nicolas Cage. The work, a remake of the 1947 Henry Hathaway film, was directed by Barbet Schroeder. Caruso was moderately well reviewed, but it was Cage who gained the most critical praise—and the film did not do very well at the box office.

Caruso's second starring film role was as San Francisco prosecutor David Corelli in the crime thriller *Jade*, directed by William Friedkin and costarring Linda Fiorentino, Chazz Palminteri, Richard Crenna, and Michael Biehn. The film, a story of corruption, unorthodox sex, and corruption in high places, was not well received, either critically or at the box office, and did not help Caruso's emerging film career.

Forthcoming was a starring role in the suspense thriller *Insider*, directed by Rene Aram.

New York City–born Caruso made his feature film debut in *An Officer and a Gentleman* (1982), and went on to supporting roles in *First Blood* (1982), *Thief of Hearts* (1984), *Blue City* (1986), *China Girl* (1987), *Twins* (1988), *King of New York* (1990), *Hudson Hawk* (1991), and *Mad Dog and Glory* (1993). He has also appeared often in television, emerging as a star in "N.Y.P.D. Blue" (1993–94), for which he won the 1994 Golden Globe Award as best actor in a drama, and an Emmy nomination as best actor in a drama. Twice divorced, he has one daughter.

FURTHER READING

"Kiss and tell." BRUCE FRETTS. *Entertainment,* Apr. 28, 1995.
"David Caruso." DAVID RENSIN. *Playboy,* Sept. 1994.
"In the spotlight. . . ." ALAN W. PETRUCELLI. *First for Women,* June 20, 1994.
"Family ties." JOYCE CARUSO. *Mademoiselle,* Jan. 1994.

Cash, Johnny (John R. Cash; 1932–)

Celebrated country singer and songwriter Johnny Cash continued to be honored by his peers in 1995, on March 23 winning the all-time favorite artist award at the first British Country Music Awards show, held in Birmingham. He, Marty Stuart, and Travis Tritt also received a best country vocal collaboration Grammy nomination for "The Devil Comes Back To Georgia." Cash's 1994 *American Recordings* won a Nammie award as outstanding album at the first annual Nammie Award ceremony, in Nashville.

Cash, Kris Kristofferson, Willie Nelson, and Waylon Jennings, four country singing legends singing as The Highwaymen, issued the country collection album *The Road Goes On Forever*, containing a new song by each of the four stars, along with a selection of standards written by others. They also issued a hit single from the album, the blues song "It Is What It Is." They also released an audiobook dramatization of Louis L'Amour's western novel *Riding For the Brand*. Cash was also one of the many artists who wrote and sang a song for the soundtrack album of Tim Robbins' film *Dead Man Walking*, among them Bruce Springsteen, Eddie Vedder, Mary-Chapin Carpenter, Lyle Lovett, and Nusrat Fateh Ali Khan.

Born in Kingsland, Arkansas, Cash began writing songs and performing on local radio while in high school. After air force service, he settled in Memphis and began recording, with "Cry, Cry, Cry" (1955), "Folsom Prison Blues" (1956), and his first major hit and signature song "I Walk the Line" (1956). Early albums included *With His Hot and Blue Guitar* (1957), *Songs That Made Him Famous* (1958), *Fabulous Johnny Cash* (1959), *Ride This Train* (1960), *Sound of Johnny Cash* (1962), *Ring of Fire* (1963; the title cut another signature song), and *Keep on the Sunny Side* and *I Walk the Line* (both 1964), *Orange Blossom Special* (1965), and *Greatest Hits* (1967). Recovering from drug and alcohol abuse, he had two major hits with June Carter, who became his wife: "Jackson" (1967) and "If I Were a Carpenter" (1970). Cash also produced a million-selling live album, *At Folsom*

Prison (1968), as well as *The Holy Land* (1968), *Jackson* (1969), and another live album, *At San Quentin* (1969), with the hit song "A Boy Named Sue." He starred in television's "The Johnny Cash Show" (1969–71).

Numerous other albums followed. In all, Cash has written more than 400 songs, sold more than 53 million albums, and won six Grammys, as well as the Grammy Living Legend award (1993). He is the only person ever to be named to the "Triple Crown" of the Country Music Hall of Fame (1980), the Songwriter's Hall of Fame (1984), and the Rock and Roll Hall of Fame (1992). Cash has also worked occasionally as an actor, as in *North and South* (1985) and *Stagecoach* (1986). He has published the autobiographical *Man in Black* (1975) and the novel *Man in White* (1986).

Cash's 1954 marriage to Vivian Liberto ended in divorce; they had four daughters, including the singer Rosanne Cash. In 1968, he married June Carter; they have one son.

FURTHER READING

" 'I can sing of death . . . .' " DOTSON RADER. *Parade,* June 11, 1995.
"New adventures of. . . ." MARK JACOBSON. *Esquire,* Aug. 1994.
"Johnny Cash. . . ." CHRIS GILL. *Guitar Player,* July 1994; Sept. 1994.
"Cash unplugged." JOHN MORTHLAND. *Country Music,* July–Aug. 1994.
"Johnny Cash." JANCEE DUNN. *Rolling Stone,* June 30, 1994.
"Dream album." CHRISTOPHER JOHN FARLEY. *Time,* May 9, 1994.
"Next big. . . ." NISID HAJARI. *Entertainment,* Feb. 18, 1994.
Johnny Cash. SEAN DOLAN. Chelsea House, 1994.
Johnny Cash—A Man and His Music. MILTON OKUN, ed. Cherry Lane, 1994.
"Johnny Cash. . . ." PETER GALVIN and KAREN SCHOEMER. *Interview,* Sept. 1993.

Cash, Rosalind (1938–95) New Jersey–born actress and singer Rosalind Cash began her career as a singer in cabaret, making her breakthrough into substantial stage roles in the late 1960s as a member of New York's Negro Ensemble Theater. One very notable role was that of Douglas Turner Ward's daughter in the Lonnie Elder play *Ceremonies in Dark Old Men* (1969),

another that of Goneril opposite James Earl Jones in the title role of *King Lear* (1973). She made her film debut in *Klute* (1971); among her other films were *The Omega Man* (1971), *The New Centurions* (1972), *Hickey and Boggs* (1972), *Uptown Saturday Night* (1974), *Amazing Grace* (1974), *Cornbread Earl and Me* (1975), *The Monkey Hustle* (1976), and *Wrong Is Right* (1982). She also appeared in many television films and series episodes, including a recurring role in "General Hospital." Cash attended New York's City College. She was survived by a sister and two brothers. (d. Los Angeles; October 31, 1995)

FURTHER READING

Obituary. *Jet,* Nov 20, 1995.
Obituary. *Independent,* Nov 17, 1995.
Obituary. *New York Times,* Nov. 3, 1995.

Castro Ruz, Fidel (1926–   ) In the 37th year of his reign, Cuban dictator Fidel Castro faced an ever more difficult and destabilizing economic situation at home, and made no visible progress in his campaign to convince the U.S. to lift the embargo that has increasingly strangled the Cuban economy since the loss of his Russian and Eastern European economic support. In mid-October, with inflation soaring and even necessities very difficult to buy in Cuba without hard foreign currency, he reversed a long-standing policy, and legalized the out-of-control black market in currency, licensing foreign exchange banks in Cuba in an attempt to secure U.S. dollars for the faltering economy. At the same time, he sharply stepped up—though without much success—his attempt to secure foreign investment in Cuba, visiting France in March and throughout the year meeting with the trade representatives of many countries.

On October 22, Castro attended the United Nations 50th anniversary celebration, and—dressed in conservative suit and tie—briefly addressed the General Assembly, while anti-Castro demonstrators crowded the streets outside the UN building. He then changed back to his trademark fatigues to address a pro-Castro rally at Harlem's Hotel Theresa, where he had stayed in 1960.

Castro and the Clinton administration did

reach a new agreement on the question of refugees from Cuba, which provided for the admission of at least 20,000 refugees a year.

Further, most of the refugees detained at the Guantanamo Bay American base in Cuba were to be allowed to settle in the United States. Longstanding American policy on refugees was also reversed; fleeing Cubans were now to be intercepted by American ships and returned to Cuba. But the American embargo remained in place, with congressional Republicans trying to make sanctions even more restrictive and the Clinton administration trying to maintain the embargo while at the same time opening new dialogue aimed at encouraging democratic forces in Cuba.

After leading the successful 1959 revolution against the government of Fulgencio Batista, Castro was a leading figure in world politics until the late 1980s. He survived the U.S.-backed Bay of Pigs invasion of 1961 and also the Soviet missile withdrawal after the1962 Cuban Missile Crisis came very close to igniting World War III, remaining in power as a Soviet ally and economic dependent through the late 1980s. Castro played a major role in supplying and training leftist revolutionaries throughout Latin America, and sent tens of thousands of troops to Angola and Ethiopia in the late 1970s; withdrawal of those forces was agreed upon only in the late 1980s, under pressure from the Soviet Union.

In the early 1990s, with the United States embargo still in place, Soviet subsidies gone, and Eastern European trading partners almost gone, Castro's government was hard pressed to continue vital social services, or even to guarantee adequate food supplies for Cuba. Castro made some attempts to draw foreign investment, gain hard currency from Cubans returning home to visit, and stimulate a partially free economy, but with little success, as the Cuban economy continued to fall apart and his hold on the country weakened.

Castro attended the University of Havana and practiced law in Havana before beginning his political career. He is married to Mirta Diaz-Bilart; they have one son. He also has several other children not publicly acknowledged.

FURTHER READING

" 'Solutions can be found. . . .' " MORTIMER B. ZUCKERMAN and LINDA ROBINSON. *U.S. News & World Report,* May 15, 1995.
"Castro's compromises. . . ." "Will a tighter embargo. . . ." J. F. O. McALLISTER. "Open for business." KEVIN FEDARKO. *Time,* Feb. 20, 1995.
Castro, 2nd ed. SEBASTIAN BALFOUR. Longman, 1995.
"The long, long good-bye. . . ." CHARLES LANE. *New Republic,* Oct. 3, 1994.
"Fidelity. . . ." ARTURO J. CRUZ, JR. and CONSUELO CRUZ SEQUEIRA. *New Republic,* Sept. 12, 1994.
"Castro's legacy." ERNESTO F. BETANCOURT. *Society,* July–Aug. 1994.
"Conversations with Castro." ANN LOUISE BARDACH. *Vanity Fair,* Mar. 1994.
Covering Castro: Rise and Decline of Cuba's Communist Dictator. JAY S. MALLIN, SR. U.S.-Cuba Institute/Transaction, 1994.
Face to Face with Fidel Castro: A Conversation with Tomas Borge. Talman/Ocean Press, 1994.
Fidel: Castro's Political and Social Thought. SHELDON B. LISS. Westview, 1994.
Fidel Castro: Cuban Revolutionary. WARREN BROWN. Millbrook, 1994.
Fidel Castro and the Quest for a Revolutionary Culture in Cuba. JULIE M. BUNCK. Pennsylvania State University Press, 1994.
Fidel Castro. ROBERT E. QUIRK. Norton, 1993.
Castro! DON E. BEYER. Watts, 1993.
Fidel Castro. PAUL MADDEN. Rourke, 1993.
Fidel by Fidel: A New Interview. . . . FIDEL CASTRO et al. Borgo Press, 1993.
Castro's Final Hour. ANDRES OPPENHEIMER. Simon & Schuster, 1993.

Cater, Douglass (Silas Douglass Cater, Jr.; 1923–95) Born in Montgomery, Alabama, writer, politician, and educator Douglass Cater received his 1947 B.A. and 1948 M.A. from Harvard University. He was the Washington editor of *Reporter* magazine (1950–63) and then the magazine's national affairs editor (1963–64), during his tenure with the magazine also engaging in a wide range of other writing and consulting activities, in and out of the federal government. He was a special assistant to President Lyndon B. Johnson (1964–68), left the White House to join Hubert Humphrey's unsuccessful 1968 presidential campaign, and then taught at the University of California (1971–72) and Stanford University (1972–77). He was a senior figure at the Aspen Institute (1978–82), then becoming president of Maryland's Washington College. Cater was a moderate who strongly advocated civility in government. Among his books were *The Fourth Branch of Government* (1959), *Power in Washington*

(1964), *TV Violence and the Child* (1975), and the political novel *Dana: The Irrelevant Man* (1970). He was survived by his wife, Libby, two daughters, two sons, and a brother. (d. Chestertown, Maryland; September 14, 1995)

FURTHER READING

Obituary. *New York Times*, Sept. 14, 1995.

Chandrasekhar, Subrahmanyan

(1910–95) Born in Lahore, India, Subrahmanyan Chandrasekhar was one of the leading astrophysicists of the century. Early recognized as a talented mathematician and physicist, he studied at Presidency College in Madras before winning a scholarship to Cambridge University in 1930. While traveling to Britain by ship in 1930, and following on from the work of Arthur Eddington and Ralph H. Fowler, Chandrasekhar developed the basic theory of stellar evolution that would lead to the "black hole" theory, calculating the "Chandrasekhar limit." This postulates that a star 1.4 times as massive as Earth's sun will, late in its evolution, continue to collapse through what in less massive suns would be the white dwarf stage, into a stage he did not predict; others later would call this later stage a "black hole." His paper was published in 1931 and was ridiculed (among others by Eddington) when he presented it to the Royal Astronomical

Society in 1935, but later became one of the basic documents of modern astrophysics. He won a 1983 Nobel Prize in physics and many other honors. Chandrasekhar taught at the University of Chicago from 1936, and was associated with the university and its Yerkes Observatory until his death. His writings included specialist monographs such as *An Introduction to the Study of Stellar Structure* (1939) and his central work, *The Mathematical Theory of Black Holes* (1983), as well as general works including *Eddington: The Most Distinguished Astrophysicist of His Time* (1984), *Truth and Beauty: Aesthetics and Motivations in Science* (1987), and *Newton's Principia for the Common Reader* (1995). He was survived by his wife, astrophysicist Lalitha Chandrasekhar, and by three sisters and two brothers. (d. Chicago; August 21, 1995)

FURTHER READING

Obituary. *Physics Today,* Nov. 1995.
Obituary. *Current Biography,* Oct. 1995.
Obituary. *Economist,* Sept. 2, 1995.
Obituary. *Times* (of London), Aug. 24, 1995.
Obituary. *Independent,* Aug. 24, 1995.
Obituary. *New York Times*, Aug. 22, 1995.
"Confronting the final limit." JOHN HORGAN. *Scientific American,* Mar. 1994.
Chandra: A Biography of S. Chandrasekhar. KAMESHWAR C. WALI. University of Chicago Press, 1990.

Charles, Prince of Wales
(Charles Philip Arthur George; 1948–) For the Prince of Wales, 1995 was for most of the year a time of somewhat diminished worldwide media coverage—although the impact of the family matters he had aired through the 1994 "authorized" Jonathan Dimbleby documentary film and later biography continued to generate considerable heat. In early January, Camilla Parker Bowles and her husband, Brigadier Andrew Parker Bowles, announced their coming divorce; Charles had in 1994 announced that he and Ms. Bowles had maintained a long adulterous relationship, providing the material for a media circus. Otherwise, Charles provided the media with no new "scandals," though that did not stop enterprising reporters and columnists from publishing the usual mountain of material.

On the other hand, his estranged wife, Princess Diana, provided enough material for a whole new media circus. On November 20, in a long televised interview with BBC reporter Martin Bashir, she talked about Charles's long-term adultery; her isolation and neglect at the hands of her husband, the British royal family, and their set; the damage caused by the media; her own extramarital affair; and her years of bulimia, allegedly brought on by all the rest. An estimated 27 million people saw the interview in Britain, and many millions more abroad—and Prince Charles and the British Royals had another very, very bad year. In late December, Queen Elizabeth wrote to Charles and Diana, urging them to divorce quickly, a course reportedly favored by Charles; they had been separated since 1992.

Charles did make one very notable visit in 1995; underscoring the new, much more cordial relationship between Eire and Britain, he visited Ireland in early June, the first such royal visit to Ireland since that country won independence from Britain in 1922.

Prince Charles is the oldest son of Elizabeth II and Prince Philip, and heir to the British throne. He attended Trinity College, Cambridge, and the University College of Wales. He married Lady Diana Spencer in 1981; they have two children: William Arthur Philip, born June 21, 1982; and Henry Charles Albert David, born September 15, 1984. His books include *The Old Man of Lochnagar* (1980), *A Vision of Britain* (1989), *The Prince of Wales' Watercolours* (1991), and *Highgrove: An Experiment in Organic Gardening and Farming* (1993), written with Charles Glover.

FURTHER READING

"Together at last?" MICHELLE GREEN. *People,* Jan. 23, 1995.
"A greater love. . . ." CHRISTOPHER WILSON. *Cosmopolitan,* Jan. 1995.
"Crown of thorns." BRUCE WALLACE. Dec. 5, 1994. "Can Charles. . . ." BRUCE WALLACE and PATRICIA CHISHOLM. Oct. 31, 1994. *Maclean's.*
"Prince of pique." MICHELLE GREEN et al. Oct. 31, 1994. "Tattle royal." JONATHAN DIMBLEBY. Nov. 7, 1994. *People.*
"Royally screwed." DENIS JUDD. *New Statesman & Society,* Oct. 28, 1994.
Charles: The Untold Story. ROSS BENSON. St. Martin's, 1994.
Prince Charles: An Intimate Portrait of the Man Born to Be King. JONATHAN DIMBLEBY. Morrow, 1994.

Chavis, Benjamin Franklin, Jr.

(1948–) Former National Association for the Advancement of Colored People (NAACP) leader Benjamin Chavis continued to play an active role in African-American affairs during 1995. After serving for 15 months as executive director of the NAACP, he had been fired by the NAACP's Board of Directors in August 1994 for alleged financial irregularities.

Chavis had also encountered sharp opposition for his continuing attempts to include in the mainstream of African-American leadership Nation of Islam leader Louis Farrakhan, highly controversial because of his allegedly racist and anti-Semitic views; Chavis was also criticized for holding closed meetings with militant African-American leaders without informing other NAACP leaders. Cast adrift by the NAACP, Chavis moved even closer to Farrakhan, organizing and leading the National African-American Leadership Summit, which at its second annual meeting, in Houston, Texas (June 9–11, 1995) sponsored Farrakhan's October 16 "Million Man March" of Black men in Washington, D.C. Chavis became national director of the demonstration, attended by several hundred thousand Black men and a few uninvited women. Having become strongly identified with Farrakhan, Chavis's future as an African-American leader seemed linked with that of Farrakhan.

On the personal side, Chavis's mother, Elisabeth Ridley Chavis, died during 1995.

Born in Oxford, North Carolina, Chavis is a veteran of the southern civil rights struggles of the 1960s and 1970s. While a young minister working with the United Church of Christ in 1970, he became one of the "Wilmington 10," charged with complicity in the burning of a White-owned grocery store in Wilmington, North Carolina. He was convicted in 1976 on the basis of false evidence; his conviction was reversed in 1979, after three witnesses admitted lying at his trial. Chavis completed his divinity degree studies at Duke University in 1979, while in the fourth year of his unjustified imprisonment; he later related that he had been taken to his studies on campus in leg irons and handcuffs. He later became director of the United Church of Christ's Commission for Racial Justice. In 1993, he was appointed executive director of the NAACP. He is the author of *Psalms From Prison* (1983). He is married to Martha Chavis.

FURTHER READING

"Unity in the community. . . ." GEORGE E. CURRY. *Emerge*, Sept. 1994.

"Chavis, Benjamin F." *Current Biography*, Jan. 1994.

"He's no gentle Ben. . . ." JACK E. WHITE. *Time*, July 19, 1993.

"Ben Chavis. . . ." LYNN NORMENT. *Ebony*, July 1993.

"Getting real. . . ." *Newsweek*, June 14, 1993.

"Ben again. . . ." W. HAMPTON SIDES. *New Republic*, May 10, 1993.

Chen Yun (Liao Chenyun; 1905–95)

Chen Yun, a printing industry worker born in Shanghai, joined the Communist Party of China in 1925 and quickly became an activist, moving into armed conflict at the outbreak of the Chinese Civil War (1927). He was elected to his party's Central Committee in 1931, and was an increasingly important member of that committee until 1987, then becoming chairman of the Communist Party Central Advisory Committee (1987–92). Chen fought during the Long March to Yenan (1934–35), was a deputy director and then director of his party's Organizing Committee from 1937 through the end of the anti-Japanese and civil wars, and emerged as a major party and government figure in the People's Republic of China. Among his other major positions were the key economic planning position of Vice Premier of the State Council (1949–75; 1978–80), and Vice Chairman of the Communist Party (1956–69). Although he supported Mao Zedong's disastrous Great Leap Forward economic campaign (1958–59), he was one of those who pointed to its failure and convinced Mao to end it. After Mao's death (1976), Chen emerged as a central, somewhat conservative leader of Chinese communism, who supported Deng Xiaoping and helped develop Deng's reforms, but also urged caution, warning of inflation and other consequences of an overheated economy and of damage to Chinese communism's social fabric. He was survived by his wife, Yu Ruomu, three daughters, and two sons. (d. April 10, 1995)

FURTHER READING

Obituary. *Times* (of London), Apr. 12, 1995.
Obituary. *New York Times*, Apr. 12, 1995.

Chernomyrdin, Viktor Stepanovich

(1938–) Russian prime minister and Our Home Is Russia party leader Viktor Chernomyrdin faced an uncertain political future as 1995 drew to a close. On December 17, his party came in third in the Russian parliamentary elections, with less than 10 percent of the vote, behind the Communist Party with 22 percent and Vladimir Zhirinovsky's right-wing Liberal Democratic Party with almost 11 percent—for despite all his attempts to steer an independent reformist course, Chernomyrdin and his party were identified with the extraordinarily unpopular President Boris Yeltsin.

Yeltsin's 1995 was a year of multiple defeats, and the same was therefore so for Chernomyrdin, even though he had, in fact, opposed the highly unpopular Russian invasion of Chechnya and sought to soften the impact of Yeltsin's hard-line market economy policies, with their tremendous negative impact on the savings, pensions, health care, and sense of security of tens of millions of Russians.

In 1995, Chernomyrdin formally took himself out of the 1996 presidential race; whether he would stay out of the race or offer himself as a moderate reformist candidate was a very live question going into 1996.

An ethnic Russian born in Cherny-Otrog, in the Cherny region of what was then the Soviet Union, Chernomyrdin trained as an engineer at the Industrial Institute at Kuybyshev (now Samara), graduating in 1966. After military service (1957–60), he worked in an oil refinery (1960–67), at the same time beginning his long political career. He joined the Communist Party in 1961. He was a political functionary with the Orsk City Committee (1967–73), chief engineer and later director of the Orenburg gas plant (1973–78), and then moved into a series of national Communist Party and Soviet government posts, among them that of Soviet gas minister (1985–89), head of the gas industry (1989–92), and fuel and energy minister (1992). He was a member of his party's central committee (1986–90), and for that part of that period (1987–89) also a Supreme Soviet deputy. In 1992, he became head of the Russian Council of Ministers. He is married and has two sons.

FURTHER READING

"The challenge facing. . . ." MARK HOPKINS. *The New Leader*, Feb. 14, 1994.

Cherry, Don

Cherry, Don (1937–95) Oklahoma-born Don Cherry, who grew up and studied music in Los Angeles, was a leading jazz trumpeter and cornetist. He began his career in the early 1950s, playing with Los Angeles-area bands, and in 1956 began his highly innovative association with Ornette Coleman. He played in the Coleman band in the late 1950s, making a highly regarded series of recordings with Coleman (1958–61). He began his own recording career in 1960, with the album *The Avant Garde*, the first of what would become many albums with other leading jazz musicians, among them Sonny Rollins, John Coltrane, and Gato Barbieri. His best known and by many most highly regarded album was *Complete Communion* (1964). From the mid-1960s and for the rest of his life, Cherry became a world-traveling artist, playing a wide range of instruments in many different musical cultures, his stated aim being to experience and integrate many aspects of world music. He was survived by his wife, four sons, and his stepdaughter, singer Neneh Cherry. (d. Málaga, Spain; October 19, 1995)

FURTHER READING

"Cherry on top." STANLEY CROUCH. *New Republic,* Nov. 20, 1995.
Obituary. *Billboard*, Nov. 4, 1995.
Obituary. STEVE VOCE. *Independent,* Oct. 21, 1995.
Obituary. *New York Times*, Oct. 21, 1995.

Chirac, Jacques René

Chirac, Jacques René (1932–) On May 7, 1995, Paris mayor Jacques Chirac, founder and president of the conservative Rally for the Republic party, defeated Socialist Party candidate Lionel Jospin, winning election to a 7-year term as president of France, with 52 percent of the vote. He was inaugurated on May 17, succeeding Socialist president François Mitterrand, and appointed Alain Juppe as his premier. Chirac quickly moved to formally reassert French commitment to the European Union (EU), as did Juppe. But it soon became clear that Chirac, unlike Mitterrand, was not prepared to swiftly move into a federal European economic and monetary union, instead focusing on reducing France's high rates of unemployment and declining standard of living. In early June, Chirac joined British prime minister John Major in calling for a go-slow European federation policy, calling for a less centralized approach that recognized massive French and British opposition to federation with Germany.

Chirac called for much stronger NATO intervention in the Bosnian War, threatening withdrawal of French forces if NATO did not step up its involvement, and contributing French ground and air forces to the NATO effort when it came. He also triggered an enormous adverse international reaction when he announced in June that France would resume underground nuclear testing at Mururoa Atoll in the South Pacific; he proceeded with the testing, despite very sharp protests from many Pacific nations, including Australia, New Zealand, and Japan. There were large antinuclear demonstrations in many countries, including France, riots in Tahiti, and Greenpeace led an international protest flotilla to Mururoa, where it was broken up by French naval vessels. In France, Chirac's popularity plummeted as the nuclear test outcry grew. By year's end, his popularity had gone down even further, during a long public workers' strike in response to announced social security and other social service net reductions.

Chirac attended the National School of Political Science in the early 1950s and was a summer student at Harvard University (1953). He began his long career in public life after military service during the French-Algerian War. In 1958, he attended the National School of Administration, and worked in government until 1967, when he won election to the National Assembly as a conservative Gaullist. He became Minister of Agriculture in 1972 and was prime minister in the government of Gaullist president Valéry Giscard d'Estaing in 1974. Chirac left the government and founded Rally for the Republic in 1976, then winning election as mayor of Paris (1977–95). He made an unsuccessful run for the presidency against Giscard d'Estaing and Socialist François Mitterrand in 1981; Mitterrand won. Chirac was prime minister again (1986–88) and was defeated again for the presidency by Mitterrand in 1988. He is married to Bernadette Chodron de Courcel; they have two daughters.

FURTHER READING

" 'We are not. . . .' " CHRISTOPHER REDMAN and THOMAS SANCTON. *Time,* Dec. 11, 1995.
"Vive la difference . . ." *Economist,* Nov. 25, 1995.
"Lucky Jacques." CATHY NOLAN. *People,* June 5, 1995.
"Third-time lucky. . . ." ANDREW BILSKI. *Maclean's,* May 22, 1995.

"Can Chirac change France?" *Economist*, May 13, 1995.
"Chirac, Jacques." *Current Biography*, Apr. 1993.

Chopra, Deepak (ca. 1947–   ) In the summer of 1993, Oprah Winfrey devoted a whole hour of her popular television show to a conversation with Indian physician Deepak Chopra, who had just published the book *Ageless Mind, Timeless Body*. As a direct result of his discussion of the role of the mind and spirit in health, his book debuted at the top spot on the *Publishers Weekly* best-seller list and stayed there for nine weeks, selling more than a million copies in hardcover. In 1995, several passages of the book were found to be close in form and content to passages in Dan Georgakas's *The Methuselah Factors* (1981); Chopra's publisher said that attribution had been inadvertently omitted, and that appropriate clarifications and revisions were being made in Chopra's book.

In 1995, Chopra published a new hardcover best-seller *The Seven Spiritual Laws of Success: A Practical Guide to the Fulfillment of Your Dreams*, which by late November had sold more than one million copies. He also inaugurated the "Perfect Health Library" with two new health guides, *Boundless Energy* and *Perfect Digestion*, and a revised version of his 1987 *Creating Health*. All four were also released in audiobook form, with Chopra as reader. He also served as reader in a 1995 audiobook version of Gitanjali Rabindranath Tagore's *Offerings from the Heart*.

But Chopra also turned in quite a new direction with his first novel *The Return of Merlin*. Drawing on a love for English literature, he wrote about the medieval wizard Merlin returning to bring magic to 20th-century Britain. A two-hour lecture given as part of his publicity tour for the book was later run nationally on the Public Broadcasting System.

Another nonfiction work, tentatively titled *The Way of the Wizard: Twenty Spiritual Lessons for Creating the Life You Want*, was scheduled for January 1996 publication. Chopra and fellow physician David Simon were also working on a textbook for physicians on mind-body medicine.

Born and educated in New Delhi, India, Chopra followed his father into medicine, specializing in internal medicine and endocrinology. Coming to America in 1970 with his wife Rita, Chopra did his internship in New Jersey and taught at Harvard and other university medical schools, establishing his own practice in Boston in the mid-1970s. He later turned to Eastern philosophy and medicine, especially the traditional mind-body science called *ayurveda*, originally as a disciple of Mareshi Mahesh Yogi. He established an anti-stress clinic in 1986. He has published numerous books, including *Creating Health: How to Wake Up the Body's Intelligence* (1987; originally self-published), *Return of the Rishi: A Doctor's Story of Spiritual Transformation and Ayurvedic Healing* (1989), *Quantum Healing* (1990), *Perfect Health* (1990), *Unconditional Life* (1991), *Creating Affluence* (1993), *Ageless Body, Timeless Mind* (1993), *Restful Sleep* (1994), *Perfect Weight* (1994), and *Journey Into Healing: A Step-by-Step Personal Guide Compiled from the Timeless Wisdom of Deepak Chopra, M.D.* (1994). In 1993, Chopra became executive director of San Diego's Sharp Institute for Human Potential and Mind-Body Medicine.

FURTHER READING

"Chopra, Deepak." *Current Biography*, Oct. 1995.
"Deepak Chopra. . . ." CHIP BROWN. *Esquire*, Oct. 1995.
"The mind-body problems." ELISE PETTUS. *New York*, Aug. 14, 1995.
"From here. . . ." JAMES MAURO. *Psychology Today*, Nov–Dec. 1993.
"Guru on the go." CATHERINE WINTERS. *American Health*, Jan–Feb. 1992.

Chrétien, Jean (Joseph Jacques Jean Chrétien; 1934–) Canadian Prime Minister Jean Chrétien overcame a massive challenge to the very concept of Canada in 1995. On October 30, with more than 92 percent of Quebec's eligible 5 million voters going to the polls, and by a very narrow 50.5 percent–49.5 percent margin, Quebec voted to stay in Canada, rejecting a massive separatist campaign that might have succeeded in splitting Canada into two nations. The next day, Quebec premier and separatist Parti Québécois leader Jacques Parizeau resigned, while Chrétien and other Canadian leaders began to craft new concessions to Quebecers seeking more autonomy. The immediate secession crisis was over, but separatist sentiment remained very strong in Quebec, with separatist leaders vowing to carry on the fight for independence until it was achieved. Nor had Canada's long economic crisis turned around; unemployment rates continued to be very high, despite a large Canada-U.S. trade surplus, and the Canadian dollar, although buoyed by the Quebec referendum result, was still low and under continuing attack by international currency speculators.

On the personal side, Jean and Aline Chrétien narrowly escaped death on November 5, when a man armed with a knife forced entry into their official residence in Ottawa. It took a reported 10 minutes for the police to arrive after they were called. Chrétien's security arrangements were immediately placed under emergency review.

Born in Shawinigan, Quebec, Chrétien graduated from Laval University and practiced law before going into politics, becoming a Liberal member of the House of Commons (1963–86). He was parliamentary secretary to the prime minister (1965), and then held several cabinet-level positions, his ministries including Finance (1966; 1976–77; 1977–79); Industry, Trade, and Commerce (1976–77); Social Development (1980–82); and Energy, Mines, and Resources (1982–84). He also served as Attorney-General (1979–80), and was Secretary of State for External Affairs and Deputy Prime Minister (both 1984). He resigned in 1986, practiced law, and was then re-elected to Parliament from a New Brunswick constituency (1990–), also becoming national leader of the Liberal party (1990–). His party won a landslide victory in the 1993 Canadian general elections.

Chrétien's books include *Straight from the Heart* (1985) and *Finding a Common Ground* (1992). He is married to Aline Chaîné and has three children.

FURTHER READING

"The making of a leader." LAWRENCE MARTIN. *Maclean's,* Oct. 23, 1995.
"The private prime minister." ANTHONY WILSON-SMITH. "The battles ahead. . . ." E. KAYE FULTON. *Maclean's,* Jan. 24, 1994.
" 'You have to know. . . .' " ROBERT LEWIS and ANTHONY WILSON-SMITH. *Maclean's,* Jan. 3, 1994.
"Jean Chrétien. . . ." ROY MACSKIMMING. *Chatelaine,* Apr. 1991.

Christopher, Warren (1925–) In his third year in office, Secretary of State Warren Christopher continued to travel the world on behalf of his country, covering the entire range of American international concerns. Of necessity, much of his attention was directed to the world's "hot spots" and continuing problems, which in 1995 meant emphasis on Bosnia, the Middle East, Russia, and China.

A major focus throughout the year was the Bosnian War. Christopher played a substantial role in the entire sequence of developments that resulted in deepening American involvement in Bosnia, the Dayton (Ohio) agreements and Paris Peace Accords, and the escalating American involvement in Bosnian peacekeeping activities that, in December, resulted in the dispatch of 20,000 Americans into highly controversial deep-winter peacekeeping duty in Bosnia. Future assessments of his role in the history of his time may well turn on the success or failure of the Bosnian mission.

Christopher also played a considerable role in reviving the Israeli-Syrian peace talks, stalled for most the year, which resumed near Washington in late December. He had been deeply involved with the developing, highly successful Middle East peace process since his appointment, and also with the continuing sanctions against Iraq and Iran.

Despite a continuing dialogue between Christopher and his Chinese counterparts, and to no one's surprise, the secretary of state had no apparent success in convincing the Chinese government to improve its abysmal human rights performance. He did, however, go forward with the normalization of U.S.-Vietnamese relations, himself visiting Vietnam on August 5 to formally reopen diplomatic relations between the two former enemies.

Pennsylvania-born Christopher received his 1945 B.S. from the University of Southern California and his 1949 LL.B. from Stanford University. He began his career as a law clerk to U.S. Supreme Court Justice William O. Douglas (1949–50). Returning to California, he began working for the Los Angeles law firm O'Melveny and Myers, becoming a partner in 1958, and going back to the firm after periods of government service. He was a deputy U.S. attorney general during the Johnson administration (1967–69), and a deputy secretary of state during the Carter years (1977–81), in 1980 becoming heavily involved in negotiations for the release of the Iran hostages, about which he wrote (with others) in *American Hostages in Iran: The Conduct of a Crisis* (1985). In 1991, he chaired the Independent Commission on the Los Angeles Police Department, formed after the Rodney King beating; its report found a pervasive pattern of racism in the department and called for the resignation of police chief Daryl F. Gates.

Christopher played a substantial role in the 1992 presidential elections, as a key Clinton adviser, and was manager of the Clinton presidential transition team before being named secretary of state (1993–). He married Marie Josephine Wyllis in 1956; they have four children.

FURTHER READING

"Christopher, Warren M." *Current Biography,* Nov. 1995.
"Secretary of State. . . ." INA GINSBURG. *Interview,* Nov. 1994.
"Defending his boss." DAN GOODGAME and J. F. O. MCALLISTER. *Time,* Oct. 18, 1993.
" 'A preventer of crises.' " LOUISE LIEF and TIM ZIMMERMAN. *U.S. News & World Report,* July 5, 1993.
"Clothed ambition. . . ." JACOB HEILBRUNN. *New Republic,* Feb. 1, 1993.

Chung, Connie

(Constance Yu-hwa Chung; 1946–) The ax fell for Connie Chung in 1995. In May, she was dropped from the "CBS Evening News" show on which she had been coanchor with Dan Rather since June 1993, and which had dropped into third place among the major network evening news shows. Her low-rated prime-time news magazine program "Eye to Eye" was also cancelled. CBS reportedly offered a demotion to anchoring weekend newscasts, substituting for Rather, and occasional evening news specials. In response, Chung asked to be let out of her contract.

Chung had been widely criticized for her handling of an interview with Newt Gingrich's mother, choosing to broadcast a comment critical of First Lady Hillary Rodham Clinton, which Mrs. Gingrich believed would be off the record—as Chung had put it, "just between you and me." Some of Chung's critics suggested that she had long been known more for her celebrity interviews and "Q" rating (viewer assessment of recognizability and likability) than for her abilities as a reporter of hard news. Chung anchored CBS's coverage of the April 1995 Oklahoma City bombing; some also suggested that poor performance there contributed to her downfall; Rather was also reportedly unhappy that she was sent alone, although he was on vacation. Some of Chung's defenders charged that sexism was involved, and a group of senior television newswomen expressed their support for her, including Jane Pauley, Barbara Walters, Judy Woodruff, Katie Couric, Lesley Stahl, Sylvia Chase, and Cokie Roberts.

On the personal side, Chung and her husband, talk-show host Maury Povich, adopted a son, Matthew Jay Povich, in July, ending a long quest for parenthood; it was her first child and his third.

Born in Washington, D.C., Chung began her broadcasting career in 1969, as a Washington-area television reporter, and moved through a series of increasingly responsible and highly visible jobs in the next two decades, including seven years (1976–83) anchoring KNXT in Los Angeles and a series of anchor assignments with NBC (1983–89), before moving to CBS. There she developed a successful weekly news magazine program, but in 1990 scaled back her activities to a series of specials, under the title "Face to Face with Connie Chung," while attempting to become pregnant. In 1991, she reduced her schedule even further, though continuing to serve as weekend anchor of the "CBS Evening News" and filling in occasionally on CBS morning news programs. She returned to full activity in 1993, joining Rather as the first Asian-American and second woman network nightly news anchor, and beginning her news magazine program "Eye to Eye with Connie Chung." Chung received her B.S. from the University of Maryland in 1969.

FURTHER READING

"Career lessons learned. . . ." ANDREA PEYSER. *Glamour,* Aug. 1995.
"This is her life." MARY C. HICKEY. *Ladies Home Journal*, Oct. 1993.
"Anchor aweigh." SHELLEY LEVITT. *People,* June 21, 1993.
"Connie Chung. . . ." ALAN EBERT. *Good Housekeeping*, June 1993.
Connie Chung: Broadcast Journalist. MARY MALONE. Enslow, 1992.

Çiller, Tansu (1946–) Turkish prime minister and True Path Party leader Tansu Çiller had a very difficult year in 1995, as Turkey's unresolved economic and political problems worsened. She and her coalition government had no real success in curbing Turkey's runaway inflation, estimated to be in 70–80 percent per year range. At the same time, partly because of worsening economic conditions, Muslim fundamentalists gained strength, winning many local elections, making armed attacks on more moderate Muslim groups, and engaging in guerrilla actions against government forces.

The Turkish government's war against Kurdish independence forces in Turkey and northern Iraq also went badly. In early March, government forces totaling 35,000–40,000 invaded Iraq, attacking Kurdish guerrilla forces in northern Iraq, while 15,000–20,000 more attacked Kurdish forces within Turkey. Although they claimed to have inflicted major casualties, the Kurds continued cross-border attacks into Turkey, so much so that the Turks made further unsuccessful attacks into Iraq during the summer. Facing mounting world criticism, the Turks ultimately withdrew.

On October 15, Çiller's ruling coalition collapsed, as government workers, demanding that their wages be indexed to inflation struck, rioted, and partially shut down the government. The opposition, however, was itself very badly divided, and could not form a government, and on October 18, Çiller was back to form a new ruling coalition. But in the December 24 general elections, her party came in second to the Welfare Party, an Islamic group, and she resigned, though remaining in office until a new government could be formed, probably a coalition of non-religious parties. Turkey's major outstanding problems remained, the fundamentalist challenge was growing, and some observers wondered if the Turkish army might once again take power, as it had several times in the nation's modern history.

Istanbul-born Çiller is the child of a prominent and wealthy Turkish family. She graduated from Istanbul's American-run Robert College and from Bogazici University, then in the mid-1970s received her Ph.D. in economics from the University of Connecticut, also studying at Yale University. She returned home to teach at Bosporus University, becoming a full professor by 1983 and publishing various works on economics. She became a True Path Member of Parliament in 1991, and was that year appointed economics minister by Turkish President Suleyman Demirel, whom she succeeded as prime minister in 1993, becoming her country's first woman prime minister. Çiller is married to Ozer Ocuran and has two children.

FURTHER READING

"Turkey's embattled. . . ." JOHN DOXEY. *New Leader*, Mar. 13, 1995.
"Çiller, Tansu." *Current Biography*, Sept. 1994.
"The other new . . . ." ANDREW PHILLIPS. *Maclean's*, July 12, 1993.

Cioran, E. M. (Emil M. Cioran; 1911–95)

Romanian philosopher and writer E. M. Cioran, long resident in France, was generally seen as a philosopher of despair to that generation of French writers and intellectuals that developed existentialism and the theory of the "absurd," and explored the further reaches of noncommunication—although Cioran himself expressed his views in a clear, slashing, entirely communicative style. Born in Rasinari, Romania, Cioran studied at the University of Bucharest. His first five works were in Romanian, beginning with his highly regarded *The Peaks of Despair* (1934). He settled in Paris in 1937, lived modestly on the Left Bank for the rest of his life, and refused several prestigious and lucrative literary honors, opting against any trace of affluence. His first book in French was *A Short History of Decay* (1949); among his further books were *Syllogisms of Bitterness* (1952), *The Temptation to Exist* (1956), *History and Utopia* (1964), *The Fall Into Time* (1964), and *The Trouble With Being Born* (1973). There were no survivors. (d. Paris; June 20, 1995)

FURTHER READING

Obituary. *Independent,* June 24, 1995.
Obituary. *Times* (of London), June 23, 1995.
Obituary. *New York Times*, June 22, 1995.

Clancy, Tom (Thomas L. Clancy; 1947–)

Tom Clancy, whose works have been huge commercial successes in publishing and films, turned to television in 1995, with the two-part miniseries *Tom Clancy's "Op Center"*, which focused on a secret government operations center for dealing with international trouble spots. Directed by Lewis Teague from a script by Steve Sohmer, based on a story and concept by Clancy and Steve Pieczenik, it starred Harry Hamlin, Kim Cattrall, Wilford Brimley, and Lindsay Frost. Though the miniseries received mixed reviews, a sequel was planned. Also appearing were the first two of a projected series of paperback books (and audiobooks), using the characters from the "Op-Center" miniseries, but with new plots: *Reality Check* and *Mirror Image*. Clancy and Pieczenik were also developing original CD-ROM space adventure games, the first to be *Tom Clancy's First Contact: Derelict*. Clancy himself has signed to develop a line of paperback books for children and teens, starting with *Tom Clancy's Net Force* in 1996, with film, television, toy, and video game spin-offs planned. In all of these projects, the works are shaped and supervised by Clancy, but some or all of the writing will be done by others.

Clancy's *Debt of Honor* appeared in paperback in 1995, reaching the top of the best-seller list in its second week. *Publishers Weekly* reported that the novel was the second- best-selling hardcover fiction book of 1994, with over 2.3 million sold.

On the personal side, Clancy's father died, and his wife, Wanda, filed for divorce after 26 years of marriage, charging desertion and adultery.

Baltimore-born Clancy graduated from Loyola College in 1969, then working as an insurance agent until 1980. He emerged as a best-selling novelist with *The Hunt for Red October* (1984), which was followed by *Red Storm Rising* (1986), *Patriot Games* (1987), *The Cardinal of the Kremlin* (1988), *Clear and Present Danger* (1989), *The Sum of All Fears* (1991), *Without Remorse* (1993), and *Debt of Honor*, all number-one best-sellers. He has also published several works in his "Guided Tour" series, focusing on the history and use of various types of military hardware, including *Submarine* (1993) and *Armored Cav: A Guided Tour of an Armored Cavalry* (1994). He is also a part-owner of baseball's Baltimore Orioles. Clancy married Wanda Thomas in 1969; they have three daughters and a son.

FURTHER READING

The Tom Clancy Companion. MARTIN H. GREENBERG, ed. Berkley, 1992.
"The write stuff." *American Legion*, Dec. 1991.

Clark, Grahame (John Grahame Clark; 1907–95)

A leading British archaeologist, Grahame Clark focused primarily on European prehistory, although his later work spanned the early world. He studied at Cambridge University's Peterhouse College, and was at Peterhouse from 1930 until 1980, having held the Disney Chair of Archaeology (1952–74) and been the Master of Peterhouse (1973–80). Clark was a prolific writer from the start of his career, publishing scores of professional papers, and emerged as a major figure in British archaeology with publication of the books *The Mesolithic Age in Britain* (1932) and *The Mesolithic Settlement of Northern Europe* (1936). Among his further works were *Archaeology and Society* (1939), *Prehistoric England* (1940), *From Savagery to Civilization* (1946), *Prehistoric Europe: The Economic Basis* (1952), *World Prehistory: An Outline* (1961), *Aspects of Prehistory* (1970), *The Earlier Stone Age Settlement of Scandinavia* (1975), *Mesolithic Prelude* (1980), *The Identity of Man* (1983), and *Space, Time and Man: A Prehistorian's View* (1992). He was survived by his wife, Mollie, and one son; a son and a daughter predeceased him. (d. Cambridge, England; September 12, 1995)

FURTHER READING

Obituary. *New York Times*, Sept. 18, 1995.
Obituary. *Times* (of London), Sept. 14, 1995.

Clark, Marcia (1953–)

Los Angeles lawyer Marcia Clark became a very familiar face on world television screens in 1995—fully as familiar as any movie or television star. For the entire year, she "starred" as chief prosecutor in the very highly publicized trial of O. J. Simpson for the alleged murders of Nicole Brown Simpson and Ronald Goldman. Until Simpson's acquittal on October 3, 1995, she shared the world's hottest single spotlight, along with Simpson, the other lawyers in the case, Judge Lance Ito, and a parade of witnesses in what became the world's leading media circus—as well as a very serious trial upon which Simpson's life depended. Like so many of the others involved, the media explored every aspect of her life, giving major coverage to a very personal custody fight with her estranged husband, Gordon Clark, who sued for custody of their two sons, arguing that her duties on the Simpson case precluded her from taking adequate care of the children. Even her dress and courtroom demeanor were studied at length; critics complained that she did not dress showily enough, smile enough—in short, that she did not act and dress like the film star they thought she should be. Clark went on to prosecute and ultimately lose the celebrated case, at considerable personal cost.

On the other hand, the conclusion of the case brought an opportunity for considerable personal financial gain. In November, Viking announced that it had purchased for $4.2 million the world rights to publish her as-yet-untitled book about the case, to be written with a ghost-writer.

Deputy Los Angeles District Attorney Clark has spent her entire legal career in criminal law. She is a graduate of the University of California at Los Angeles and Southwestern University Law School (1979). After admission to practice law in California, she worked for two years as a defense attorney before becoming a prosecutor in 1981. While not at all as well known as several of California's celebrity defense lawyers, including her Simpson case opponent Robert Shapiro, Clark had previously prosecuted 21 murder trials, winning 19 of them, including several highly publicized cases, such as the conviction of movie fan Robert John Bardo for the murder of actress Rebecca Schaeffer; and the convictions of Albert Lewis and Anthony Oliver for the shooting murders of two people attending a Bible class at Los Angeles's Mt. Olive Church of God.

California-born Clark moved often as a child, completing high school in Staten Island, New York. She filed for a divorce from her second husband in 1994, and has two sons.

FURTHER READING

"Rites of passage. . . ." THOMAS FIELDS-MEYER. *People*, Nov. 6, 1995.
"Marcia Clark." JIMMY BRESLIN. *Esquire*, Aug. 1995.
"What's next . . . ?" ANNE TAYLOR FLEMING. *Ladies Home Journal*, June 1995.

" 'You have to care for the kids.' " *Newsweek,* Apr. 17, 1995.
"The voice of the victims." MELINDA BECK. *Newsweek,* Jan. 23, 1995.
"The reckoning for Simpson. . . ." BETSY STREISAND and MIKE THARP. *U.S. News & World Report,* Jan. 23, 1995.
"Her day in court. . . ." ELIZABETH GLEICK. *People,* July 18, 1994.

Clayton, Jack (1921–95)

Born in Brighton, England, film director and producer Jack Clayton began his long film career in the mid-1930s, in a series of apprenticeship jobs. He worked in the Royal Air Force film unit during World War II, and after the war moved into film production. He became a director in 1956, with the short film *The Bespoke Overcoat,* which won an Oscar. He emerged as a major director in 1959, with the classic *Room at the Top,* starring Laurence Harvey and Simone Signoret, acclaimed as introducing a new social realism into the British films of the day. His further films included *The Innocents* (1961), *The Pumpkin Eater* (1964), *Our Mother's House* (1967), *The Great Gatsby* (1974), *Something Wicked This Way Comes* (1983), *The Lonely Passion of Judith Hearne* (1987), and *Momento Mori* (1992). He was survived by his third wife, actress Haya Harareet. (d. Slough, England; February 25, 1995).

FURTHER READING

Obituary. *New York Times,* Mar. 1, 1995.
Obituary. *Variety,* Feb. 28, 1995.
Obituary. *Independent,* Feb. 28, 1995.
Obituary. *Times* (of London), Feb. 27, 1995.

Cleary, Beverly Atlee Bunn (1916–)

Writer Beverly Cleary has been best known for creating *human* children, who were pesky, adventurous, and sometimes unlucky, but certainly not goody-two-shoes kids. She has done the same thing in writing her own life, telling it clearly, honestly, and vividly, not painting over the difficult parts, but instead sharing the humor of her own mistakes. The second volume of her autobiography, *My Own Two Feet,* published in 1995, goes from her college years during the Depression through her marriage and early work as a librarian, ending with the 1949 acceptance of her first novel, *Henry Huggins.* That began a career that has encompassed 37 books, which together have sold 75 million copies in 20 countries and in 14 languages. During 1995, her hometown of Portland, Oregon, dedicated the Beverly Cleary Sculpture Garden for Children, including sculptures of favorite characters Ramona Quimby, Henry Huggins, and his dog Rigsby. It is not far from 37th street—model for Henry and Ramona's Klickitat Street—now the site of bus tours for Cleary fans.

After junior college, Oregon-born Cleary received a 1938 B.A. from the University of California and a 1939 B.A. in librarianship from the University of Washington. She was children's librarian in the Yakima, Washington, public library (1939–40), then post librarian at the U.S. Army Regional Hospital, Oakland, California (1942–45). She won wide attention with her first book, *Henry Huggins* (1950); Henry and his dog, Ribsy, appeared in numerous other books. Cleary's Ramona Quimby was introduced in *Beezus and Ramona* (1955), but became a full-fledged star with *Ramona the Pest* (1968), again appearing in numerous sequels. Other notable works included *Ellen Tebbits* (1951), *Otis Spofford* (1953), *The Real Mole* (1960), *Emily's Runaway Imagination* (1961), *The Mouse and the Motorcycle* (1965), *Ralph S. Mouse* (1982), *Dear Mr. Henshaw* (1983; it won the 1984 Newberry Medal), *Janet's Thingamajigs* (1987), *The Growing Up Feet* (1987), *Muggie Maggie* (1990), *Strider* (1991), and *Petey's Bedtime Story* (1993), as well as a play *Socks* (1973). The first volume of her autobiography was *A Girl from Yamhill: A Memoir* (1988). She married Clarence T. Cleary in 1940; they have a son and a daughter.

FURTHER READING

"Perfectly Cleary." CHERYL BOWLAN. *Parenting,* Oct. 1995.
Beverly Cleary. SUSAN ONION. Teacher Created Materials, 1994.
Beverly Cleary. JULIE BERG. Abdo & Daughters, 1993.
Beverly Cleary. Pat Pflieger. Twayne/Macmillan, 1991.

Clinton, Bill (William Jefferson Blythe, IV; 1946–)

For President Bill Clinton, 1995 was a politically and personally difficult year, following as it did his disastrous 1994 defeat on health care reform and the massive Republican victory in the 1994 congressional elections—and because the potentially disastrous Whitewater investigation dragged on.

As it turned out, though, 1995 was a year of surprisingly strong political comeback. He began the year with low popularity ratings, facing the much-heralded "Contract with America" put forward very aggressively by seemingly invincible House Speaker Newt Gingrich—and ended it with popularity ratings far higher than those of any of the possible Republican candidates, facing a largely unsuccessful and unpopular Republican majority led by a Newt Gingrich openly distrusted by the vast majority of American voters, who was himself facing very serious ethics charges. At year's end, runaway congressional Republicans, who had refused to accept a budget "deal" agreed to by their own leaders, Bob Dole and Newt Gingrich, had closed down the federal government, and were locked in a battle with the president that damaged the Republican Party and helped the Democratic president every day it continued, for Clinton was for the first time being seen by most Americans as someone who had the backbone to stand up for what he believed in.

President Clinton was also seen as having firmed up his foreign policy. After the apparently successful 1994 peace-keeping intervention in Haiti, his personal stock went up; it stayed up as he played a highly visible and successful role in bringing forward the Middle East and Bosnian peace processes, while continuing and strengthening the embargos against Iraq and Iran. Even the very risky and largely unpopular Bosnian intervention, with its dispatch of 20,000 Americans to deep-winter peace-keeping duty in Bosnia, did not seem to hurt Clinton's popularity, for here, too, he was seen by many as a leader, who was finally standing up for his beliefs.

It was still a long time until the next presidential elections, in November 1996, and Clinton was still viewed as a presidential campaign underdog by most political analysts. By year's end, the American economy showed signs of weakness, as evidenced by the low Christmas sales figures. The Bosnian intervention remained extraordinarily risky; anyone studying a map of the area saw that dissident Serbs could easily fight a long guerrilla war from the high, rugged mountains covering two thirds of the country. And Whitewater still loomed. Even so, while at the beginning of 1995 it seemed clear to many that Clinton had no political future, at the end it seemed that he might just possibly win re-election.

On November 3, 1992, Bill Clinton was elected 42nd president of the United States, defeating incumbent George Bush and independent candidate H. Ross Perot. Clinton won in an electoral-vote landslide, 370 electoral votes to Bush's 168; Perot won none. However, Clinton won these with only 43 percent of the popular vote (43.7 million votes), to Bush's 38 percent (38.2 million votes) and Perot's 19 percent (19.2 million votes). Clinton's election was widely described as an extraordinary repudiation of George Bush, who had been enormously popular after the Persian Gulf War, in some job-approval polls scoring in the 90+ percent range.

Bill Clinton and Vice President Al Gore were inaugurated on January 20, 1993. During Clinton's first year in office, he encountered some early appointment problems, and was forced to compromise on his promised lifting of the ban on gays in the military, after running into massive opposition, led in the military by General Colin Powell. He also suffered a major congressional defeat when his economic stimulus plan was defeated by a Republican filibuster. He was able to push through his 1993 budget bill, and scored notable victories with passage of the North American Free Trade Agreement (NAFTA) and the Brady gun-control bill. His second year in office was dominated by the health care and congressional campaign defeats.

Arkansas-born Clinton received his 1968 B.S. from Georgetown University, and his 1973 J.D. from Yale University; in between, he was a Rhodes Scholar at Oxford University (1968–70). He taught law at the University of Arkansas Law School and was in private practice (1973–76) before entering politics as state attorney general (1977–79), then becoming governor of his home state (1979–81; and again 1983–92). Born three months after his father's death, he later took his stepfather's surname, Clinton. He and Hillary Rodham met when both were at Yale Law School; they married in 1975 and have one daughter, Chelsea.

FURTHER READING

"Bill Clinton. . . ." LANDON Y. JONES, JR. and GARRY CLIFFORD. *People*, Dec. 25, 1995.
"He's no Bill Clinton." DANIEL FRANKLIN. *Washington Monthly*, May 1995.

"Now for the last campaign." JAMES CARNEY. *Time,* Mar. 13, 1995.

" 'I think we've learned a lot.' " PETER MAAS. *Parade,* Feb. 19, 1995.

"Taking the high road with Congress. . . ." KENNETH T. WALSH and MATTHEW COOPER. "Clinton's many faces. . . ." KENNETH T. WALSH and MATTHEW COOPER. *U.S. News & World Report,* Jan. 30, 1995.

First in His Class: The Biography of Bill Clinton. DAVID MARANISS. Simon & Schuster, 1995.

Everything America Loves about Bill Clinton. MARGO FRASER. Press-Tige, 1995.

The Dysfunctional President: Inside the Mind of Bill Clinton. PAUL FICK. Birch Lane/Carol, 1995.

Bill Clinton: Forty-Second President of the United States. CAROL GREENE. Childrens, 1995.

Clinton Confidential: The Climb to Power—The Unauthorized Biography of Bill and Hillary Clinton. GEORGE CARPOZI. E. Dalton, 1995.

William Jefferson Clinton: 42nd President of the United States. DAVID R. COLLINS. Garrett, 1995.

"What Bill wrought. . . ." MICHAEL LIND. "They blew it. . . ." MICKEY KAUS. *New Republic,* Dec. 5, 1994.

"Clio and the Clintons." CARL SFERRAZZA ANTHONY. *American Heritage,* Dec. 1994.

"How could he recover?" JONATHAN ALTER and BOB COHN. *Newsweek,* Nov. 21, 1994.

"A polarizing president. . . ." KENNETH T. WALSH et al. *U.S. News & World Report,* Nov. 7, 1994.

"Clinton at midterm. . . ." WILLIAM GREIDER. *Rolling Stone,* Nov. 3, 1994.

"Clinton, Bill." *Current Biography,* Nov. 1994.

"Blending force. . . ." DAN GOODGAME and MICHAEL DUFFY. *Time,* Oct. 31, 1994.

"The president's past." MICHAEL KELLY. *New York Times Magazine,* July 31, 1994.

Bill Clinton on Stump, State, and Stage: The Rhetorical Road to the White House. STEPHEN A. SMITH, ed. University of Arkansas Press, 1994.

Bill Clinton's Pre-Presidential Career: An Annotated Bibliography. ALLAN METZ. Greenwood, 1994.

The Bill Clinton Story: Winning the Presidency. JOHN HOHENBERG. Syracuse University Press, 1994.

Bill Clinton: Eyes on the Future. LESLIE KITCHEN. Maryland Historical Press, 1994.

Bill Clinton: United States President. MICHAEL D. COLE. Enslow, 1994.

Bill Clinton: As They Know Him. DAVID GALLEN. Gallen, 1994.

Highwire: From the Back Roads to the Beltway—The Education of Bill Clinton. JOHN BRUMMETT. Hyperion, 1994.

On the Make: The Rise of Bill Clinton. MEREDITH L. OAKLEY. Regnery, 1994.

Slick Willie, Vol. 2: Why America Still Cannot Trust Bill Clinton. CHRISTOPHER MANION. Annapolis, 1994.

Clinton, Hillary Rodham (1947–) As head of the federal Task Force on National Health Care Reform, First Lady Hillary Rodham Clinton had taken the highly visible lead in the failed campaign for the Clinton health care program, and its 1994 defeat was for her also a major personal defeat, made even worse by the huge Republican victory in the 1994 congressional elections. Still popular, although also still threatened by the continuing Whitewater investigation, she largely withdrew from domestic politics during the balance of 1994 and throughout 1995, limiting herself to rather bland speechmaking on the desirability of social and economic justice for children and other such fairly safe issues.

It was somewhat different abroad; apparently, it was thought safe for her to travel widely, expressing her views on a considerable range of issues. On March 7, in Copenhagen, Denmark, she addressed the first United Nations World Summit on Social Development, calling for enhanced international aid for women's education and health. A week later, at the UN's New York headquarters, she addressed a meeting on "Women and the United Nations," calling for more attention to the needs of the world's women, and specifically for employment of a greater number of women by the UN. In late March and early April, she and her daughter Chelsea toured South Asia, visiting five countries, advocating aid to women and children, but clearly trying to avoid controversy. In late August, however, she courted controversy; after touring in Southeast Asia, she publicly considered the advisability of going through with a scheduled trip to China to speak to the Fourth United Nations Conference on Women. She ultimately decided to go, apparently after receiving informal assurances that the Chinese would allow arrested dissenter Harry Wu to leave China. On September 7, in Beijing, she addressed the conference, sharply criticizing world violations of human rights. She never directly criticized China for its abysmally poor human rights record, but her speech clearly implied it.

At year's end, Hillary Rodham Clinton was still being kept very much out of American day-to-day politics. What role, if any, she would play during 1996 was a matter of conjecture.

In November, she published the book *It Takes a Village: And Other Lessons Children Teach Us,* which during her January 1996 book tour reached the top of the best-seller list.

Hillary Rodham Clinton is a distinguished lawyer and law professor, children's advocate, educational reformer, and women's rights leader. Indeed, she kept her own name, Hillary Rodham, until 1982, only adopting her husband Bill Clinton's name for political purposes, because of mounting local objections to her views on the question of keeping her own name.

She received her 1969 B.A. from Wellesley College, where she was president of college government, and her 1973 J.D. from Yale Law School, where she served on the *Yale Review of Law and Social Action*. During and after law school, she worked at Cambridge and then in Washington with Marian Wright Edelman at the Children's Defense Fund; in later years, she was the chairperson of the Fund's board of directors. In 1974, she was a staff member of the Impeachment Inquiry Staff of the House of Representatives Judiciary Committee, investigating the Watergate affair and the possible impeachment of President Richard M. Nixon.

She and Bill Clinton met when both were at Yale Law School. They married in 1975; she then joined him in Arkansas, where she taught law and joined the Rose Law Firm in Little Rock, becoming a successful litigator. She also became a nationally known figure for her work in several areas. Active in her profession, she was chair of the American Bar Association (ABA) Commission on Women in the Professions (1987–91). She also continued her nationwide work with the Children's Defense Fund and several other organizations. In Arkansas, she founded Arkansas Advocates for Children and Families (1977), and chaired the Arkansas Education Standards Committee (1983–84). She grew up in Park Ridge, Illinois. She and Bill Clinton have one daughter, Chelsea.

FURTHER READING

"What's next . . . ?" Liz Tilberis. *Harper's Bazaar*, Sept. 1995.
"The next First Lady." Susan Estrich. *Glamour*, Aug. 1995.
"Being there for Bill." Kenneth T.Walsh. *U.S. News & World Report*, Feb. 27, 1995.
" 'I think we've learned a lot.' " Peter Maas. *Parade*, Feb. 19, 1995.
Clinton Confidential: The Climb to Power—The Unauthorized Biography of Bill and Hillary Clinton. George Carpozi. E. Dalton, 1995.
"Clio and the Clintons." Carl Sferrazza Anthony. *American Heritage*, Dec. 1994.

"Ladies' Home Journal visits. . . ." *Ladies Home Journal*, Nov. 1994.
Hillary Rodham Clinton. Nancy Loewen. Creative Ed., 1994.
Hillary Rodham Clinton: Activist First Lady. Thomas Stacey. Enslow, 1994.
Hillary Rodham Clinton: A First Lady for Our Time. Donnie Radcliffe. Warner, 1994.
Story of Hillary Rodham Clinton: First Lady of the United States. Joyce Milton. Dell, 1994.
Meet Hillary Rodham Clinton. Valeria Spain. Random House, 1994.
First Lady: The Story of Hillary Rodham Clinton. Aaron Boyd. M. Reynolds, 1994.
Hillary Rodham Clinton: First Lady. Suzanne LeVert. Millbrook, 1994.
"Clinton, Hillary Rodham." *Current Biography*, Nov. 1993.
Hillary Clinton: Inside Story. Judith Warner. NAL-Dutton, 1993.
Hillary Clinton. Julie Bach. Abdo & Daughters, 1993.
Hillary Rodham Clinton, a New Kind of First Lady. JoAnn B. Guernsey. Lerner, 1993.
Hillary Rodham Clinton. Victoria Sherrow. Dillon/Macmillan, 1993.

Close, Glenn (1947–) Actress Glenn Close won the 1995 Tony Award for best actress in a musical for her role as aging silent screen star Norma Desmond in Andrew Lloyd Webber's stage musical version of Billy Wilder's 1950 film classic *Sunset Boulevard*. She also won Drama Desk and Outer Critics Circle best actress awards.

Close and Barbra Streisand coproduced and Close starred in the title role of the television film *Serving in Silence: The Margarethe Cammermeyer Story*, directed by Jeff Bleckner and costarring Judy Davis. The fact-based film was the story of Colonel Margarethe Cammermeyer, holder of the Bronze Star, who was discharged from the army after openly declaring herself to be a lesbian during a 1989 army security interview. Close won an Emmy as leading actress in a miniseries or special for the role.

Forthcoming were starring roles in the film *101 Dalmatians*, directed by Stephen Herek; and in Stephen Frears's film *Mary Reilly*, costarring Julia Roberts and John Malkovich.

On the personal side, Close and stage carpenter Steve Beers announced that they were to be married.

Connecticut-born Close, on stage from the

early 1970s, emerged as a stage and screen star in the 1980s, winning a Tony for her Broadway role in *The Real Thing* (1984) and playing leads in such films as *The World According to Garp* (1982), *The Big Chill* (1983), *The Natural* (1984), *Fatal Attraction* (1987), *Dangerous Liaisons* (1988), *Reversal of Fortune* (1990), *Hamlet* (1990), *Meeting Venus* (1991), *The House of the Spirits* (1994), and *The Paper* (1994). She won a Tony award for her 1992 Broadway role in *Death and the Maiden*. Close's 1974 B.A. was from the College of William and Mary. She was twice previously married and has one child.

FURTHER READING

"Glenn Close." JULIANN GAREY. *Us,* Feb. 1995.
"Close to the bone. . . ." JAMES KAPLAN. *New York,* Sept. 12, 1994.
"Kindred spirits. . . ." LISA LIEBMAN. *New Woman,* Apr. 1994.
"Women who run. . . ." DANA KENNEDY. *Entertainment,* Feb. 11, 1994.
"Glenn Close. . . ." RICHARD MERYMAN. *Cosmopolitan,* Feb. 1994.
"Close to her heart." MELANIE BERGER. *Ladies Home Journal,* Jan. 1993.
"Glenn Close." FRANK SPOTNITZ. *American Film,* Nov.–Dec. 1991.
"Getting Close. . . ." STEPHEN FARBER. *Connoisseur,* Aug. 1991.

Connery, Sean (Thomas Connery; 1930–) Still best known by far for his role as the mythical James Bond, film star Sean Connery played a quite different kind of mythical hero in 1995, as King Arthur in the film *First Knight*, directed by Jerry Zucker and costarring Julia Ormond as Guinevere, Richard Gere as Lancelot, Ben Cross as Malagant, and John Gielgud as Oswald, Guinevere's advisor.

Connery also starred in the film *Just Cause,* as Harvard Law School professor Paul Armstrong, who takes the case of Bobby Earl, an African-American convicted of child rape and murder in backcountry Florida, and who now faces execution after eight years on Death Row. Laurence Fishburne, Kate Capshaw, Blair Underwood, Ed Harris, and Ruby Dee costarred; the film was directed by Arne Glimcher.

Forthcoming was a starring role opposite Nicolas Cage and Ed Harris in *The Rock.*

Edinburgh-born Connery was on stage and screen in small roles during the 1950s and early 1960s; he became an instant star as sex-symbol James Bond in *Dr. No* (1962), and went on to become a worldwide celebrity in six more James Bond films: *From Russia with Love* (1963), *Goldfinger* (1964), *Thunderball* (1965), *You Only Live Twice* (1967), *Diamonds Are Forever* (1971), and *Never Say Never Again* (1982). But he soon became far more than a sex symbol, showing himself to be a strong and flexible actor in such films as *A Fine Madness* (1966), *The Molly Maguires* (1970), *The Wind and the Lion* (1975), *The Man Who Would Be King* (1975), *Robin and Marian* (1976), *Cuba* (1979), *The Untouchables* (1986; he won an Academy Award as best supporting actor), *The Name of the Rose* (1987), *Indiana Jones and the Last Crusade* (1989), *Family Business* (1989), *The Hunt for Red October* (1990), *The Russia House* (1990), *Medicine Man* (1992), *Rising Sun* (1993), and *A Good Man in Africa* (1994). Connery has been married twice and has one child, the actor Jason Connery.

FURTHER READING

"You only live twice." *Entertainment,* Feb. 17, 1995.
Sean Connery: A Biography. MICHAEL FREEDLAND. Trafalgar, 1995.
Great Scot: The Life of Sean Connery. JOHN HUNTER. Trafalgar, 1994.
"Great Scot." ZOE HELLER. *Vanity Fair,* June 1993.
Sean Connery. JOHN PARKER. Contemporary, 1993.
The Films of Sean Connery. LEE PFEIFFER and PHILIP LISA. Carol, 1993.
"Finely aged Scot." STEVEN GOLDMAN. *Us,* Mar. 1992.
"Straight talk." JOHN H. RICHARDSON. *Premiere,* Feb. 1992.
Sean Connery: From 007 to Hollywood Icon. ANDREW YULE. Fine, 1992.
The Films of Sean Connery. ROBERT SELLERS. St. Martin's, 1991.

Conroy, Pat (Donald Patrick Conroy; 1945–) In 1995, Pat Conroy debuted at the top of the national and regional best-seller lists across the country with his new novel, *Beach Music*. Like many of his earlier works, this one focuses on the pains and trials of 20th-century life, in particular the narrator's attempts to come to terms with his life after his wife's suicide. Six years past its contractual deadline, the book was originally scheduled for 1994 publication, but

FURTHER READING

"The Conroy saga." JOHN BERENDT. *Vanity Fair,* July 1995.
Parting the Curtains: Interviews with Southern Writers. DANNYE R. POWELL. Blair, 1994.
Who's Writing This?: Notations on the Authorial I, with Self-Portraits. DANIEL HALPERN, ed. Ecco, 1994.
"Waves of success. . . ." DANIEL MAX. *Variety,* Jan. 13, 1992.
"Pat Conroy. . . ." HOLLY MILLEA. *Us,* Jan. 1992.

was delayed after the real-life suicide of Conroy's youngest brother. When the book finally did appear, Conroy went on a 32-city promotional tour, which included appearances on *Charlie Rose, Good Morning America,* and *CBS Sunday Morning*; a 30-minute CNN documentary; and a cover interview in *Vanity Fair.* Paramount bought the film rights to the novel, for which Conroy is to write the screenplay, and also to a screenplay, *Ex,* written by Conroy and Doug Marlette, and Conroy's screen adaptation of Thomas Wolfe's *Look Homeward, Angel. Beach Music* was the first of a two-novel contract, for a reported $4.5 million advance.

Atlanta-born Conroy taught school (1967–70) after receiving his 1967 B.S. from The Citadel. His early work includes *The Boo* (1970) and *The Water Is Wide* (1972; basis of the 1974 film *Conrack,* starring Jon Voight). In 1976, he published *The Great Santini* (modeled on his father), adapted by writer-director Lewis John Carlino into the 1979 film, with Robert Duvall in the title role. Conroy's military school story *The Lords of Discipline* was adapted into the 1983 Franc Roddam film. In 1986, Conroy published *The Prince of Tides*; he and Becky Johnson received an Academy Award nomination for their adaptation of the novel into the 1991 film, directed by Barbra Streisand and starring Streisand and Nick Nolte. Conroy and his first wife had three daughters. He married his second wife, Lenore Guerewitz, in 1981; they have two daughters and a son.

Cook, Elisha Jr. (1902–95) San Francisco-born Elisha Cook, Jr. played supporting roles on stage before fully beginning his long film career. His breakthrough stage role came in the 1933 Theatre Guild production of Eugene O'Neill's *Ah! Wilderness,* as the teenage son, Richard. Cook went to Hollywood in 1936, and played a series of supporting roles through the late 1980s. His breakthrough film role—which made him a memorable figure in film history—came in 1941, as Wilmer, the "gunsel" in John Huston's classic *The Maltese Falcon,* in a cast that included Humphrey Bogart, Mary Astor, Sidney Greenstreet, and Peter Lorre. Of that extraordinary company, Cook was the last to die. He went on to play more than 100 film roles and many television roles; his films included such classics as *Phantom Lady* (1944), *The Big Sleep* (1946), *Shane* (1953), and *Rosemary's Baby* (1968). There were no survivors. (d. Big Pine, California; May 18, 1995)

FURTHER READING

Obituary. *Independent,* May 26, 1995.
Obituary. *Times* (of London), May 22, 1995.
Obituary. *New York Times,* May 21, 1995.

Cook, Peter Edward (1937–95) Born in Torquay, Peter Cook became one of Britain's leading comic writers and actors in the irreverent satirical revue *Beyond the Fringe,* in which he, Dudley Moore, Alan Bennett, and Jonathan Miller opened at the 1960 Edinburgh Festival. The show was a tremendous hit in London in 1961 and on Broadway in 1962, and began major careers for all four of its stars. It also launched a new style of comedy in Britain, where until then

the royal family and many other establishment figures had been out-of-bounds for satirical treatment. Cook and Moore went on to develop a long-lasting comedic partnership, becoming television stars in the "Not Only . . . But Also" series of satirical sketches (1965–71), during the 1970s in the two-character show *Behind the Fridge*, and in several videos and records. Cook also appeared in several films, among them *The Wrong Box* (1966), *Bedazzled* (1967), *The Hound of the Baskervilles* (1970), *The Secret Policeman's Other Ball* (1982), and *Yellowbeard* (1983), and in the television series "The Two of Us" (1981). He was also the proprietor of the Soho cabaret The Establishment, and owner of the satirical magazine *Private Eye*. He was survived by his third wife, Lin Chong Cook, and two daughters. (d. London; January 9, 1995)

FURTHER READING

"Bedazzled." JOHN LAHR. *New Yorker,* Jan. 23, 1995.
"One Cook too few." *People,* Jan. 23, 1995.
Obituary. *Independent,* Jan. 10, 1995.
Obituary. *Times* (of London), Jan. 10, 1995.
Obituary. *New York Times,* Jan. 10, 1995.

Cornfeld, Bernard (1927–95) Istanbul-born Bernard Cornfeld emigrated to the United States with his family in the early 1930s. A graduate of Brooklyn College, his first career was as a social worker. He began a new career selling mutual funds in the early 1950s. After moving to Paris in 1956, he organized a massive mutual funds sales operation, which sold a wide range of mutual finds to American military personnel and other Americans living abroad, and built his company, Investors Diversified Services, into a financial empire, with many highly speculative offshore mutual funds of its own and other insurance, real estate, and investment operations. One of his most prominent funds was the Fund of Funds. Under attack by the Securities and Exchange Commission (SEC) for his illegal activities, Cornfeld agreed to leave the U.S. securities markets in 1967, but continued to build his paper empire abroad, and to live very expensively. Cornfeld's empire collapsed in 1970; he lost control of his company to Robert L. Vesco, who took more than $200 million from what remained of the company and became a fugitive from prosecution. Cornfeld, who in 1973 was jailed for almost a year and then acquitted in Switzerland, spent most of the rest of his life defending himself against lawsuits and tax prosecutions, while unsuccessfully trying to make a comeback. He was survived by a daughter. (d. London; February, 27, 1995)

FURTHER READING

Obituary. *Times* (of London), Mar. 2, 1995.
Obituary. *New York Times,* Mar. 2, 1995.
Obituary. *Independent,* Mar. 1, 1995.

Corrigan, Douglas G. "Wrong Way" (1907–95) On July 10, 1938, pilot Douglas Corrigan flew his patched-up 1929 Curtiss-Robin wreck of a plane solo nonstop from California to New York, setting a new record time for the solo flight. He had done a great deal of work on the plane since buying it for next to nothing in 1935; still, when he applied for permission to fly his plane on to Dublin, he was turned down sharply by the aviation authorities, who called the plane entirely unsafe for the flight. Undaunted, Corrigan filed flight plans for a return trip to California, and on July 17 took off to "California" from Brooklyn's Floyd Bennett Field. California turned out to be Dublin's Baldonnel Airport, 28 hours and 13 minutes later; Corrigan landed in what he claimed to think was California, though few believed him; hence the name "Wrong Way Corrigan." Very lightly penalized by the American aviation authorities, Corrigan became a national hero, complete with massive New York ticker tape parade, autobiography, and the biofilm *Wrong Way Corrigan* (1939). He later worked as a pilot and air freight company operator. He was survived by two sons and a sister; his wife and a son predeceased him. (d. Orange, California; December 9, 1995)

FURTHER READING

Obituary. *Independent,* Dec. 15, 1995.
Obituary. *New York Times,* Dec. 14, 1995.

Costner, Kevin (1955–) Worldwide film figure Kevin Costner in 1995 coproduced and starred as the Mariner in the science fiction special effects film *Waterworld*, directed by Kevin

Reynolds; costarring were Dennis Hopper as his arch-enemy the Deacon, Jeanne Tripplehorn, and Tina Majorino. The story is set in a future world in which there is only ocean, with all land covered by the sea; the Mariner, a land creature, travels that world continually in his ship, like a future-world Ancient Mariner. The film was one of the most expensive ever made, its cost reportedly well over $140 million. Its U.S. revenue was smaller than that necessary to make it profitable, but it had become a worldwide hit by year's end, and was reportedly profitable, as well, with many revenue sources still to be fully explored.

Costner also coproduced and hosted the television miniseries *500 Nations*, narrated by Gregory Harrison, on the invasion and conquest of Native American lands and cultures by invading European-Americans, accenting the misdeeds of the invaders.

Forthcoming was a starring role in the film *Tin Cup*, directed by Ron Shelton

California-born Costner emerged as a film star from the mid-1980s, in *Silverado* (1985), *The Untouchables* (1987), *No Way Out* (1987), *Bull Durham* (1988), *Field of Dreams* (1989), *Dances with Wolves* (1990), *Robin Hood: Prince of Thieves* (1991), *JFK* (1991), *The Bodyguard* (1992), *A Perfect World* (1993), *Wyatt Earp* (1994), and *The War* (1994). Costner made his directorial debut with the enormously successful *Dances with Wolves*, which won seven Oscars out of twelve nominations, including best picture, best director, and best adaptation; he also won the Directors Guild of America's best director award and Golden Globe awards for best picture and director, and published *Dances with Wolves: The Illustrated Story of the Epic Film* (1990). Costner attended California State University. Costner and his wife, Cindy Silva, ended their marriage in 1994; they have three children.

FURTHER READING

"That sinking feeling." CHARLES FLEMING. *Vanity Fair*, Aug. 1995.
" 'You can't always be perfect.' " EDWARD KLEIN. *Parade*, July 23, 1995.
"Dangerous when wet." JESS CAGLE. *Entertainment*, July 14, 1995.
"Trouble in paradise." PAM LAMBERT. *People*, Nov. 7, 1994.
"The private. . . ." DEAN LAMANNA. *Ladies Home Journal*, July 1994.
Kevin Costner: the Unauthorized Biography. TODD KEITH. Oliver Books, 1994.
"You asked for him!" *Teen*, Jan. 1992.
"Into the woods. . . ." STEPHANIE MANSFIELD. *GQ*, July 1991.
"Safe sex symbol. . . ." BARBARA LIPPERT. *M Inc.*, June 1991.

Crichton, Michael (John Michael Crichton; 1942–) In 1995, Michael Crichton left behind gender politics and returned quite literally to the themes of his hugely successful novel and film *Jurassic Park*. The sequel, *The Lost World*, takes place five years later; though all of the bioengineered dinosaurs were supposedly destroyed after *Jurassic Park*, the beaching of recently dead carcasses calls for returning hero Ian Malcolm to investigate possible dinosaur survivors in a "lost world." Launched with a party at New York City's Museum of Natural History and a *Time* magazine cover story, the book had a 2 million-copy first printing and hit the top of the national best-seller charts after less than a week on sale. Audiobook and CD versions, read by Anthony Heald, were released simultaneously with the hardcover.

The year also saw release of the film version of Crichton's 1980 novel *Congo*, based on a screenplay by John Patrick Shanley, directed by Frank Marshall, and starring Dylan Walsh, Laura Linney, Ernie Hudson, and Tim Curry. At the time of the film's opening, the novel was in the top spot on the paperback best-seller charts, with more than 5.4 million copies in print. The film was less warmly greeted, receiving mixed reviews and more modest commercial success. Meanwhile, Crichton was writing the script for a forthcoming film, tentatively titled *Genes*.

Chicago-born, Long Island–raised Crichton received his A.B., summa cum laude in anthropology, and his M.D. from Harvard University, in 1964 and 1969, respectively, then working as a postdoctoral fellow at La Jolla, California's Salk Institute (1969–70), training he was later to use in his medical, scientific, often futuristic thrillers. After a first novel, *A Case of Need*, under the pseudonym Jeffery Hudson, which won an Edgar from the Mystery Writers of America for the best mystery novel and was filmed as *The Carey Treatment* (1972), Crichton quickly established himself as a popular novelist under his own name with books such as *The Andromeda Strain* (1969), *The Terminal Man* (1972), *Five Patients* (1970), *The Great Train Robbery* (1975), *Eaters of the Dead* (1976), *Congo* (1980), *Electronic Life* (1983), *Sphere* (1987), *Travels* (1988), *Jurassic Park* (1990), *Rising Sun* (1992), and *Disclosure* (1994). The latter three were all highly successful films; Crichton cowrote the screenplays for *Jurassic Park* and *Rising Sun*. Crichton also created the characters and wrote the pilot show (1994) for the television medical drama series, "E.R." He has also published the art book *Jasper Johns* (1977; rev. ed. 1994).

Crichton has also developed a second career as a film director. He wrote and directed *Westworld* (1973), *Coma* (1977), *The Great Train Robbery* (1978; based on his own novel), *Looker* (1981), *Runaway* (1984), and directed *Physical Evidence* (1989). Crichton's fourth wife is actress Anne-Marie Martin; he has a daughter.

FURTHER READING

"How good . . . ?" MICHAEL D. LEMONICK. "Meet Mister Wizard." GREGORY JAYNES. *Time,* Sept. 25, 1995.
"Michael Crichton." ALBERT KIM. *Entertainment*, Dec. 30, 1994.
"Pop fiction's. . . ." GREGORY JAYNES. *Time*, Jan.10, 1994.
"Crichton, Michael." *Current Biography*, Nov. 1993.

Crow, Sheryl (1964–) Singer and songwriter Sheryl Crow became a popular performer with her rendition of "All I Wanna Do," the hit single from her 1993 debut album *Tuesday Night Music Club*. She became a major star in 1995, when her "All I Wanna Do" won a Grammy Award as best record of the year. Crow herself was awarded Grammys for best pop vocal performance of the year and as best new artist of the year. She also received a Blockbuster Entertainment Award as best new artist of the year. Among her other awards was an Irish Recorded Music Award as most popular international artist. With that kind of recognition and airplay, and supported by her worldwide touring activities, *Tuesday Night Music Club* went on to sell more than five million copies.

Crow followed up her new success with release of the ballad "Strong Enough," another single drawn from *Tuesday Night Music Club*. The record became a major hit, as was another single from the album, the funk rock "Can't Cry Anymore." Crow also appeared on the soundtrack album of the film *Boys on the Side*, singing "Keep On Growing."

Born in Kennett, Missouri, Crow received her 1984 B.F.A. from the University of Missouri. She moved to Los Angeles in 1986, and in the same year began her touring career, as a backup singer in Michael Jackson's world tour, in support of his "Bad" album. She was also a backup singer with several other groups, including Don Henley and The Eagles.

FURTHER READING

"All she wants. . . ." ELYSA GARDNER. *Rolling Stone*, Dec. 15, 1994.
"As the Crow flies." ROBERT SEIDENBERG. *Entertainment*, Oct. 14, 1994.
"Sheryl Crow." JAMES HUNTER. *Rolling Stone*, Oct. 28, 1993.

Cuomo, Mario Matthew (1932–) After his 1994 loss to George Pataki in the New York gubernatorial race, three-time former governor Mario Cuomo remained very much in the public eye, as one of the nation's leading liberals in a time of conservative ascendancy. But although he disavowed any specific political plans, he was still only in his early 60's and had a large New York State and national following.

During 1995, Cuomo did three of the things that have become familiar for high visibility American politicians out of office. He became a partner in a major law firm, New York City's Wilkie, Farr & Gallagher, where his reputation and probable influence could be counted on to bring major new clients to the firm. He became the host of his own well-received radio talk show. And he wrote the book *Reason To Believe*, published in October, as the political wars heated up once again, domestic political crises multiplied, and the 1996 presidential race seriously began. It was a book that restated his own liberal beliefs, sharply attacked the new conservatism as epitomized by Newt Gingrich's "Contract with America," and called for preserving the social service network that had been built since the days of Franklin D. Roosevelt's 1930s New Deal.

New York–born Cuomo moved into politics after two decades as a practicing lawyer and law teacher. He was New York secretary of state (1975–79) and lieutenant governor (1979–82), before becoming governor in 1983, after defeating then-New York City mayor Ed Koch in a hotly contested primary campaign. He wrote of the gubernatorial contest in his *Diaries of Mario M. Cuomo: The Campaign for Governor* (1984).

As governor, he became a powerful Democratic Party leader. After his keynote address to the 1984 Democratic National Convention, he was thought to be a leading contender for the American presidency, even though he is a much-attacked Catholic liberal who has refused to modify his pro-choice views—in spite of one Catholic cleric's statement that he was "in serious risk of going to hell" because of his pro-choice stand, and in spite of Cardinal John O'Connor's later-denied threat of excommunication. Cuomo has also declined to reverse his long-standing opposition to the death penalty. After a long public debate with himself, Cuomo decided not to seek the 1992 Democratic presidential nomination, but did not endorse Bill Clinton until the nomination fight was over; on July 15, 1992, he delivered a powerful nominating speech at the Democratic National Convention, and then backed Clinton without reservation during the campaign that followed. He has also written *More Than Words: The Speeches of Mario Cuomo* (1993).

Cuomo received his B.A. from St. John's College, in 1953, and his LL.B. from St. John's University. He is married to Matilda Raffa Cuomo; they have five children.

FURTHER READING

"Super Mario." RICHARD BROOKHISER. *National Review*, Oct. 10, 1994.
"Why we've fallen. . . ." JACOB WEISBERG. *New York*, Aug. 8, 1994.
"Governor Cuomo. . . ." *Forbes*, Jan. 31, 1994.
"Cuomo vadis. . . ." JEFFREY ROSEN. *New Republic*, Apr. 26, 1993.
"No justice. . . ." DAVID A. KAPLAN. *Newsweek*, Apr. 19, 1993.
"Message from a kibitzer." GLORIA BORGER and DAVID GERGEN. *U.S. News & World Report*, July 20, 1992.
"The man who. . . ." BARBARA GRIZZUTI HARRISON. *Playboy*, July 1992.
"Why Cuomo said no." GARRY WILLS. *New York Review of Books*, Jan. 30, 1992.
"The state of. . . ." ELIZABETH KOLBERT. *New York Times Magazine*, Feb. 10, 1991.

Curtis, Jamie Lee (1958–) For her role in the 1994 film *True Lies*, Jamie Lee Curtis received a 1995 Golden Globe Award as best actress in a motion picture, musical or comedy.

In 1995, Curtis starred as Heidi Holland in the title role in the television film *The Heidi Chronicles*, adapted by Wendy Wasserstein from her Pulitzer Prize-winning and Tony-winning play. Paul Bogart directed; Tom Hulce, Peter Friedman, and Kim Cattrall costarred. The work follows the life of its protagonist from her days as college student in the early 1970s through the late 1980s, as she develops her life as an art historian and a feminist, finally suffering a near-breakdown, apparently—and not terribly convincingly—because she has not found a husband and also because she has held fast to her feminist ideals while everyone around her has caved in to the "system" they started out rejecting. At the end of the play, she adopts a child, as an affirmation of life and a means of self-regeneration. Curtis received a Golden Globe nomination as best actress in a miniseries or telefilm for the role.

Forthcoming were starring roles in the film *Fierce Creatures*, directed by Robert Young and costarring John Cleese, Kevin Kline, Michael Palin, and Robert Lindsay; and in the film *House Arrest*, directed by Harry Winer and costarring Kevin Pollak and Jennifer Tilly. Also scheduled for 1996 is a new children's book *Tell Me Again*.

Curtis is from a film family, the daughter of actors Janet Leigh and Tony Curtis. She began her career in television guest spots, was in the series "Operation Petticoat" (1977–78), and began appearing in film roles in 1978, starting with *Halloween*. Among her later films are *The Fog* (1980), *Halloween II* (1981), *Trading Places* (1983), *Perfect* (1985), *A Fish Called Wanda* (1988), *Blue Steel* (1990), *Queen's Logic* (1991), *My Girl* (1992), *Forever Young* (1992), *Mother's Boys* (1994), *My Girl 2* (1994), and *True Lies* (1994). She also starred in the television series "Anything But Love" (1990–93) and in several television movies, most notably *Dorothy Stratten: Death of a Centerfold* (1981). She has written an autobiographical book for children, *When I Was Little: A Four-Year-Old's Memoir of Her Youth* (1993). Curtis attended the University of the Pacific. She is married to Christopher Guest and has a daughter.

FURTHER READING

"My low-fat dinner with. . . ." WENDY WASSERSTEIN. *New Woman,* Nov. 1995.
"Playing 'Heidi' go seek. . . ." DANA KENNEDY. *Entertainment,* Oct. 13, 1995.
"Making a splash." PAULA CHIN. *People,* Aug. 22, 1994.
"Tuff enough." ROD LURIE. *Los Angeles,* July 1994.
"Jamie Lee Curtis. . . ." RYAN MURPHY, *Us,* July 1994.

Dalai Lama (Tenzin Gyatso; 1935–) Thirty-five years after leaving his homeland, the Dalai Lama, exiled religious and political ruler of Tibet, and the spiritual leader of an estimated 6 million Buddhists throughout the world, continued to contest Chinese control of Tibet. As Deng Xiaoping's health declined, and the struggle for the succession began in China, the Dalai Lama's campaign and role took on new significance; a less-than-united new Chinese leadership might make concessions denied during the Deng era.

There was a substantial dispute between the Dalai Lama and the Chinese government in 1995, over who would name the Panchen Lama, believed to be a reincarnation of the tenth Panchen Lama, who died in 1989 and is the second most important figure in Tibetan Buddhism, after the Dalai Lama. Two six-year-old boys were named, one by the priesthood, led by the Dalai Lama, the other by the Chinese Communist government, beginning a major dispute that would not soon be settled.

The Dalai Lama visited the United States in 1995, meeting with Democratic and Republican leaders who expressed support for his aims, appearing on several talk shows, including Ted Koppel's "Nightline," and visiting several cities. Mindful of Chinese sensitivities on the issue of Tibet, President Bill Clinton did not meet formally with him, but instead "dropped in" on a meeting between the Dalai Lama and Vice President Al Gore.

In 1995, the Dalai Lama published the lecture collection *The World of Tibetan Buddhism* with the financial help of actor Richard Gere, who also wrote the book's foreword. Late in the year he also published *Awakening the Mind, Lightening the Heart: Core Teachings of Tibetan Buddhism.*

Tenzin Gyatso was born to a Tibetan rural family. He formally became the Dalai Lama in 1940, although Tibet was ruled by a regency until 1950, when he took power. He fled Tibet's capital, Lhasa, in 1950, after attempted Tibetan resistance to the Chinese, but returned to maintain an uneasy nine-year relationship with the Chinese (1950–59). He fled Tibet after the failed 1959 Tibetan insurrection against Chinese rule, then leading the Tibetan exile community in northern India while continuing to be a world religious figure. He was awarded the 1989 Nobel Peace Prize. His works include *My Land and People* (1962), *The Opening of the Wisdom Eye* (1963), *The Buddhism of Tibet and the Opening of the Middle Way* (1975), *Kindness, Charity, and Insight* (1984), *A Human Approach to World Peace* (1984), *The Bodhgaya Interviews* (1988; edited by Jose Ignacio), *Five Point Peace Plan for Tibet* (1988), *Oceans of Wisdom: Guidelines for Living* (1989), *The Dalai Lama at Harvard: Lectures on the Buddhist Path to Peace* (1989; with Jeffrey Hopkins), *Tibet, the Sacred Realm* (1990), *The Nobel Peace Prize and the Dalai Lama* (1990; with Sidney Piburn), *MindScience: An East-West Dialogue* (1993; with others), *The Path to Enlightenment* (rev. ed., 1994), and *The Way to Freedom: Core Teachings of Tibetan Buddhism* (1994). His memoirs were published as *Freedom in Exile: The Autobiography of the Dalai Lama* (1990).

FURTHER READING

Towards a Western Buddhism: Western Buddhist Teachers in Dialogue with the Dalai Lama. THUBTEN CHODRON, ed. Parallax, 1995.
"Extraordinary people." HERBERT BUCHSBAUM. *Scholastic Update,* Dec. 3, 1993.
Dalai Lama: A Policy of Kindness. SIDNEY PIBURN. Snow Lion, 1993.
The Dalai Lama. LOUIS G. PEREZ. Rourke, 1993.
Gentle Bridges: Conversations with the Dalai Lama on the Sciences of Mind. JEREMY W. HAYWARD and FRANCISCO J. VARELA, eds. Shambhala, 1992.
"Hello Dalai . . ." Jim Holt. *New Republic,* Nov. 11, 1991.

Daly, John (1966–)

In 1995, John Daly—for several years the bad boy of the PGA Tour—seemed to be pulling himself together. For the first time since he exploded onto the golf scene by winning the 1991 PGA Championship, his misdemeanors, and especially his drinking, were not dominating his life. Instead it was golf, played well enough to win him one of the sport's most prestigious tournaments, the British Open. It wasn't easy. Daly started the final day four strokes off the lead, fought to a three-stroke lead by the 13th hole, then bogeyed two holes, and finally finished with a one-stroke lead, thinking he had won. But Italy's Costantino Rocca hit an amazing 65-foot putt to pull into a tie, so Daly had to win it again, which he did in convincing fashion, with a four-stroke lead in the four-hole playoff. With this win, he became the only golfer under 30 to have won one two major championships.

On the personal side, in January 1995 Daly married Paulette Dean; it was his third marriage and her first. They later had a daughter. With his life more stable, Daly won reinstatement of two commercial contracts that had been suspended in late 1994 because of his troubled behavior, a 10-year, $30 million contract with Wilson and a $10 million contract from Reebok; he also gained new endorsements.

Arkansas-born Daly is a self-taught golfer, who modeled himself after golf great Jack Nicklaus. He began his professional career playing on the Ben Hogan circuit, a "minor league" developmental tour, where his biggest victory was the Utah Open. He made a notable entry onto the PGA Tour by winning the PGA Championship in 1991, and was named rookie of the year.

In 1992, he won the B.C. Open, and in 1994, the BellSouth Classic. Dubbed "Long John" for his powerful drives, Daly in 1993 took just two shots to hit the 630-yard uphill green on the 17th hole at Baltusrol, the longest hole in U.S. Open history, a feat previously believed impossible. In between, troubles abounded: Daly was suspended briefly late in 1992 for various infractions of PGA rules, and again in late 1993 and early 1994, for quitting in mid-tournament; that suspension was shortened after he underwent treatment for alcoholism. In late 1994, the PGA Tour put him on notice again, after he fought with a spectator; Daly then withdrew from competition for a time. He has published *Grip It and Rip It! John Daly's Guide to Hitting the Ball Farther Than You Ever Have Before* (1992), written with John Andrisani. Daly attended the University of Arkansas. He has a daughter, Shynah, from his second marriage, to Bettye Fulford, which ended in divorce in 1994.

FURTHER READING

"An epic finish." RICK REILLY. *Sports Illustrated,* July 31, 1995.
"Full blast." DAVE KINDRED. *Golf,* Nov. 1991.
"A real long shot." MIKE PURKEY. *Golf,* Oct. 1991.

D'Amato, Alfonse M. (1937–)

New York Senator Alfonse D'Amato moved more onto the national stage in 1995, having become chairperson of the powerful Senate Banking, Housing and Urban Affairs Committee after the Republican victory in the 1994 congressional elections. To a considerable extent because of his new position, he also became chairman of the politically powerful National Republican Senatorial Committee, source of vitally needed money for Republican senatorial candidates, whether incumbents or challengers. Throwing his support to Bob Dole early, and bringing with him the endorsements of New York's top Republicans, he also occupied a powerful position in the Dole presidential campaign.

There was more, as well. As Banking Committee head, he also headed the Senate special committee on the Whitewater matter, with its alleged links to President Bill Clinton and Hillary Rodham Clinton. He opened hearings in late July, once again going over such matters as the 1993 suicide of White House deputy counsel Vin-

cent W. Foster, the subsequent conduct of former White House counsel Bernard Nussbaum, and a complex web of financial charges and dealings. He turned up the heat in late autumn, charging the White House with lack of cooperation and ultimately forcing White House disclosure of the minutes of a key 1993 meeting, while Democrats angrily charged him with conducting a highly political investigation.

D'Amato also figured in a highly publicized media incident. On April 5, while appearing on a talk show, he sharply criticized Judge Lance Ito's handling of the O. J. Simpson trial, indulging publicly in a highly offensive caricature of a supposedly Japanese-American accent. The slur was immediately picked up, drawing national and international attention. D'Amato apologized, brusquely and then at length on the Senate floor, as criticism mounted.

D'Amato in 1995 also published the autobiography *Power, Pasta, and Politics: The World According to Senator Al D'Amato.*

On the personal side, D'Amato and television reporter Claudia Cohen announced their coming marriage; D'Amato and Penelope Ann Collenburg, long legally separated, announced their divorce.

Brooklyn-born D'Amato pursued a career in local politics before entering the national arena. He was receiver of taxes of the Town of Hempstead, on Long Island (1971–77), and a town supervisor (1977–80). He made successful Senate runs (1980; 1986; 1992), weathering charges of

financial irregularity that began with a 1989 *New York Times* exposé, and also a series of unrelated charges that resulted in a 1991 Senate Ethics Committee rebuke.

D'Amato's 1959 B.S. and 1961 J.D. were from Syracuse University. He has four children.

FURTHER READING

Senator Pothole: The Unauthorized Biography of Al D'Amato. LEONARD LURIE. Carol, 1994.
"Senator Pothole. . . ." RICHARD BROOKHISER. *National Review*, Nov. 2, 1992.
"Senator Pothole." ELIZABETH KOLBERT. *New York Times Magazine*, Oct. 27, 1991.

Daschle, Tom (Thomas Andrew Daschle; 1947–) As Senate minority leader and chairperson of the Senate's Democratic Conference in a period of Republican ascendancy, South Dakota Senator Tom Daschle played a largely defensive role during 1995. He and other Senate Democratic leaders did score one major victory early in the budget fight that was to dominate the 104th Congress: on March 2, they turned back the proposed Republican balanced budget constitutional amendment one vote short of the two-thirds majority needed for passage. Beyond that, most of the major issues before Congress went unresolved pending settlement of the budget crisis, or were passed and signed by President Bill Clinton in watered down form. Indeed, Senate Democrats, led by Daschle, had a hard time holding their own, with many Democrats defecting to the Republican position in key issues, and some Democrats announcing that they would not even seek reelection in 1996.

On November 30, Daschle was cleared by the Senate Ethics Committee of any improper conduct relating to federal inspections of an aircraft company owned by a friend.

South Dakota–born Daschle went into politics soon after leaving the air force (1969–72). He became a Washington aide to South Dakota Senator James Abourezk (1973–77), and then won election to Congress (1977–87). He made a successful senatorial run in 1986, and was elected to a second term in 1992. After the Republican victory in the 1994 congressional elections, he narrowly won election as Senate minority leader.

Daschle's 1969 B.A. is from South Dakota State University. He is married to Linda Hall, deputy administrator at the Federal Aviation Administration; they have three children.

FURTHER READING

"Daschle, Tom." *Current Biography,* Oct. 1995.
"Daschle's dash." WESTON KOSOVA. *New Republic,* May 23, 1994.

Davies, Robertson (William Robertson Davies; 1913–95) Canadian novelist, dramatist, essayist and critic Robertson Davies, who also worked in journalism and as an educator, was best known by far as one of Canada's few novelists to become a major international literary figure. Beginning with *Tempest Tost* (1951) he published many Jungian-oriented, sometimes surreal novels, the best-known being *A Mixture of Frailties* (1958). Others include *Fifth Business* (1970), *The Rebel Angels* (1981), *What's Bred in the Bone* (1985), and *The Lyre of Orpheus* (1988). His final novel was *The Cunning Man* (1995). He also wrote several works of nonfiction and more than a dozen plays, some of these highly regarded in Canada. Davies was editor and publisher of the *Peterborough Examiner* (1942–62), and taught English (1960–81) and was master (1962–81) of Ontario's Massey College, a graduate unit of the University of Toronto. He was survived by his wife, Brenda Mathews, and three daughters. (d. Orangeville, Ontario; December 2, 1995)

FURTHER READING

"The magic touch. . . ." JOHN IRVING. "A fond farewell. . . ." PETER C. NEWMAN. *Maclean's,* Dec. 18, 1995.
Obituary. *Economist,* Dec. 9, 1995.
Obituary. *Times* (of London), Dec. 5, 1995.
Obituary. *New York Times,* Dec. 4, 1995.
" 'A moralist. . . .' " MEL GUSSOW. *New York Times Book Review,* Feb. 5, 1995.
Robertson Davies: Man of Myth: A Biography. JUDITH S. GRANT. Viking Penguin, 1995.
"The indiscreet charm. . . ." MICHAEL COREN. *Saturday Night,* Oct. 1994.

Davis, Geena (Virginia Elizabeth Davis; 1957–) Actress Geena Davis was a familiar face on television screens in 1995, as her 1994 film *Speechless* became a hit in home video. Davis also starred as the pirate captain Morgan in the new blood-and-gore Christmas-season special effects spectacular *Cutthroat Island,* opposite Matthew Modine as Shaw, her unsavory lieutenant, and Frank Langella as her uncle Dawg, who tries to seize a treasure trove before she can get to it; Patrick Malahide, Maury Chaykin, Harris Yulin, and Stan Shaw costarred. The big-budget film was directed by her husband, Renny Harlin, who had made his reputation with such thrillers as *Die Hard II* (1990) and *Cliffhanger* (1993), and was presented as a straight adventure film, though with unusually large numbers of explosions, fires, and killings

for what was inevitably seen as a children's holiday-season film.

Forthcoming was a starring role in the action film *The Long Kiss Goodnight*, written by Shane Black and again directed by Harlin.

Massachusetts-born Davis made her film debut in *Tootsie* (1982), and went on to appear in such films as *Fletch* (1985), *Transylvania 6-5000* (1985), *The Fly* (1986), *Beetlejuice* (1988), *The Accidental Tourist* (1988; she won an Academy Award as best supporting actress), *Earth Girls Are Easy* (1989), *Quick Change* (1990), *Thelma and Louise* (1991), *A League of Their Own* (1992), *Hero* (1992), *Speechless* (1994), and *Angie* (1994). Her television appearances include the series "Buffalo Bill" (1983–84) and "Sara" (1985), and the television film *Secret Weapons* (1985). Davis attended Boston University. Twice divorced before her marriage to Harlin, her second husband was actor Jeff Goldblum.

FURTHER READING

"I dream of Geena." MEREDITH BERKMAN. *Mademoiselle*, Dec. 1994.
"The brainy bombshell." GEORGE KALOGERIS. *Vogue*, May 1994.
"Geena soars." RACHEL ABRAMOWITZ. *Premiere*, Feb. 1994.
"Geena tees off." PETER RICHMOND. *GQ*, Feb. 1994.
"Geena Davis. . . ." RUSSELL MILLER. *Ladies Home Journal*, Apr. 1993.
"Geena Davis." FRANK SANELLO. *First for Women*, Nov. 30, 1992.

"Geena's sheen." KEVIN SESSUMS. *Vanity Fair*, Sept. 1992.
"Geena Davis." DAVID RENSIN. *Harper's Bazaar*, June 1992.
"An interview. . . ." TOM HANKS. *Interview*, Mar. 1992.
"Davis, Geena." *Current Biography*, Oct. 1991.

de Klerk, Frederik Willem (1936–)

Though no longer daily in the public eye, former South African president F. W. de Klerk, still at the head of the National Party and now the nation's second deputy vice president, played a major role in the new multiracial South Africa that continued to emerge during 1995. He and his party remained an integral part of the new government, even though there were multiple disputes and abrasions that might have torn apart the African National Congress (ANC)-National Party alliance. One of the most serious occurred very early in the year, when on January 18 President Nelson Mandela voided a secret amnesty that had been granted to thousands of police, military, and government people by the apartheid National Party government. But the alliance endured; to affirm that, Mandela and de Klerk appeared together publicly two days later, while continuing to disagree on the amnesty issue, which had yet to be resolved. De Klerk also had the satisfaction of seeing his 1990 moratorium on the death penalty made permanent by South Africa's new Supreme Court, which ruled the death penalty a violation of the rights provided by the country's new constitution.

De Klerk practiced law in the 1960s and early 1970s, and was elected to the national assembly in 1972. He became Transvaal leader of South Africa's ruling National Party in 1982. He held several Cabinet posts from the mid-1970s, was education minister in the government of Pieter Willem Botha, and succeeded Botha as head of the National Party in February 1989. Botha resigned as president in August 1989; de Klerk became acting president, and was named to a full five-year presidential term in September, bringing with him a new spirit of reconciliation between the races. In October 1989, de Klerk released eight long-term political prisoners, including Walter Sisulu and six other ANC leaders, and Jafta Masemola of the Pan Africanist Congress. On February 2, 1990, he legalized the ANC and several other outlawed organizations, and on February 11 freed ANC leader Nelson

Mandela, opening a new chapter in South African history. On August 7, 1990, the ANC agreed to a full cease-fire, bringing to an end 30 years of guerrilla war. The government, in turn, agreed to free many more political prisoners, allow many exiles to freely return home, and relax several repressive laws—and lived up to its promises.

On November 18, 1993, de Klerk's National Party, the ANC, and 19 other political parties agreed on a historic new constitution that would establish multiparty democracy and—through the adoption of a Bill of Rights—guarantee "fundamental rights" for all South Africans, with a resulting transition to majority, or Black, rule in South Africa. De Klerk then presided over the process that in 1994 resulted in South Africa's first fully free elections and the election of Nelson Mandela to the presidency. Mandela and de Klerk shared the 1993 Nobel Peace Prize.

De Klerk attended Potchefstroom University. He married Marike Willemse in 1959; they have two sons and a daughter.

FURTHER READING

"A prisoner. . . ." HERBERT BUCHSBAUM. *Scholastic Update*, Feb. 25, 1994.
"Nelson Mandela. . . ." PAUL GRAY. "To conquer the past." LANCE MORROW. *Time*, Jan. 3, 1994. (Men of the Year: The Peacemakers)
"de Klerk's. . . ." BILL KELLER. *New York Times Magazine*, Jan. 31, 1993.

Delany, Bessie (Annie Elizabeth Delany; 1891–1995)

In 1993, sisters Bessie and Sadie (Sarah) Delany, then respectively 102 and 104 years old published the best-selling oral history *Having Our Say: The Delany Sisters' First Hundred Years* (coauthored with Amy Hill Hearth), which introduced the two extraordinary women to the world. In 1995, the book was adapted into the Broadway play *Having Our Say*. They also published the best-selling *The Delany Sisters' Book of Everyday Wisdom* (1994).

Bessie Delany was born in Raleigh, North Carolina, graduating from St. Augustine College in 1911. She taught in the South after her graduation. In 1917, she and her sister went north to New York City; they were to live together in the New York area for the rest of their lives; neither married or had children. She graduated from the dental school of Columbia University in 1923, and began her long practice in Harlem (1923–

50); she was the second Black woman dentist in New York City, while Sadie Delany became New York's first Black public high school home economics teacher. Prominent in the Black community, the sisters were an integral part of all the main movements that characterized the American Black community of their day, from the Harlem Renaissance of the 1920s to the civil rights movements of the 1950s. Bessie Delany retired from practice in 1950; in 1957, the sisters retired to a house in Mt. Vernon. She was survived by her 106-year-old sister. (d. Mt. Vernon, New York; September 25, 1995)

FURTHER READING

"Delany, Bessie. . . ." *Current Biography*, Nov. 1995.
"Dr. Annie. . . ." *Jet*, Oct. 16, 1995.
Obituary. *New York Times*, Sept. 26, 1995.
"Bessie and Sadie. . . ." AMY HILL HEARTH. *Smithsonian*, Oct. 1993.

Deng Xiaoping (T'eng Hsiao-ping; 1904–   )

As Deng Xiaoping's health continued to decline during 1995, his potential successors, among them conservative Premier Li Peng and relatively more moderate president and Communist Party head Jiang Zemin, began more and more openly to maneuver for position. But there was no open factional split while Deng lived, for although his daughter, Deng Rong, confirmed that he had very serious medical problems, he still commanded enormous prestige and stood astride China, his presence demanding at least the appearance of unity. In this, he was one with the vast majority of senior government, party, and military leaders, who prized a united China far more than the benefits to be gained by even his own economic reforms. The bitter memory of a century of foreign domination and civil war was still very much alive in China—and that contending group most thought to bring lasting stability was very likely to win the succession struggle already in progress, which would immediatly follow Deng's death.

The essence of Deng's continuing massive influence on the course of events in China was that he continued to be a symbol of unity and simultaneously living proof that the succession, however sharply contested, could proceed in an orderly, peaceful way, when it came. His potential successors, still faced with the tremendous economic and social problems stemming from very rapid economic growth and redirection of economic focus, sought continued growth—but also cracked down on dissidents, stonewalled on worldwide criticism of China's abysmal human rights record, and sharply resisted opening China's internal markets to foreign sellers. With the era of Deng Xiaoping coming to a close, his fast-paced economic reform approach was coming more openly into question, as China's elites prepared for the succession, and for a continuing attempt to couple destablilizing—but necessary—economic change with continuing political repression.

Deng joined the Communist Party of China in the 1920s, while a student in France. He fought through the whole length of the Chinese Civil War (1927–49) and is a survivor of the 1934 Long March. During the Communist ascendancy, he became a major moderate leader, was purged twice (1973 and 1976), and survived to become the primary leader of Chinese communism in the late 1970s. Deng attended the French School in Chongqing, studied in France during the 1920s, and attended Moscow's Far Eastern University. He married Cho Lin; the couple had three daughters and two sons.

FURTHER READING

Deng Xiaoping and the Chinese Revolution: A Political Biography. DAVID S. GOODMAN. Routledge, 1995.

Deng Xiaoping: My Father. DENG MAOMAO. Basic, 1995.

" 'To be rich is glorious'. . . ." ELIZABETH WRIGHT. "Will China's boom go bust?. . . ." JOHN KOHUT and JAN WONG. *World Press Review*, July 1994.

"Deng Xiaoping." *Current Biography*, June 1994.

"The Chinese dream. . . ." CHEN XUNWU. *America*, Feb. 19, 1994.

Buying Mao: Chinese Politics in the Age of Deng Xiaoping. RICHARD BAUM. Princeton University Press, 1994.

Deng Xiaoping: Chronicle of an Empire. MING RUNG. Westview, 1994.

Deng Xiaoping in the Scales of History. DAVID SHAMBAUGH. Oxford University Press, 1994.

Sowing the Seeds of Democracy in China: Political Reform in the Deng Xiaoping Era. MERLE R. GOLDMAN. Harvard University Press, 1994.

Deng Xiaoping: And the Making of Modern China. RICHARD EVANS. Viking Penguin, 1994.

"Can Deng . . . ?" BRIAN CROZIER. *National Review*, July 6, 1992.

The New Emperors: China in the Era of Mao and Deng. HARRISON E. SALISBURY. Little, Brown, 1992.

De Niro, Robert (1945–) Veteran film star Robert De Niro in 1995 played leads in two underworld films, both immediately hailed by many as classics that went far beyond the normal bounds of the genre. In the Las Vegas-set film *Casino*, based on the Nicholas Pileggi book and cowritten and directed by Martin Scorsese, De Niro starred as 1970s mob syndicate-connected gambler and casino operator Sam "Ace" Rothstein, opposite Sharon Stone as his wife, Las Vegas gambler Ginger McKenna. Their violent life together and ultimate breakup supplies much of the drama of the film, although Las Vegas and the illegal world are the sea in which they swim. Joe Pesci costarred as Nicky Santoro, Rothstein's mad-dog killer friend, and James Woods as Ginger's small-time con man lover before and during her marriage, in a cast that also included Don Rickles, Alan King, Kevin Pollak, L. Q. Jones, and Dick Smothers, with several other show business celebrities appearing as themselves.

In the very well received crime film *Heat*, written and directed by Michael Mann, De Niro starred as soon-to-retire super-criminal Neil McCaulay, opposite Al Pacino as top-notch, personally troubled Los Angeles Police Department detective Vincent Hanna, who ultimately defeats De Niro. The film, a highly violent cops-and-robbers genre work, also focuses on the personal lives of many in its large cast of characters, and deepens into Mann's deeply pessimistic view of modern American life. Val Kilmer, Jon Voight, Diane Venora, Tom Sizemore, Amy Brenneman, and Ashley Judd costarred.

Forthcoming was a starring role in the film *Marvin's Room*, directed by Jerry Zaks and costarring Meryl Streep, Leonardo Dicaprio, Hume Cronyn, Gwen Verdon, and Hal Scardino. De Niro is executive producer of the film. Also forthcoming was a starring role in the film *The Fan*, directed by Tony Scott and costarring Wesley Snipes, Ellen Barkin, John Leguizamo, and Renicio Del Toro. De Niro is also slated to star in the film *Sleepers*, written, directed, and produced by Barry Levinson and costarring Kevin Bacon, Brad Pitt, Billy Crudup, Minnie Driver, and Jason Patric.

On the personal side, De Niro and his former companion Toukie Smith were the parents of twins born to a surrogate mother.

New York–born De Niro became one of the leading actors of the American cinema in the mid-1970s, beginning with his strong supporting roles in *Bang the Drum Slowly* (1973), *Mean Streets* (1973), and as the young Vito Corleone in *The Godfather, Part II* (1974), for which he won a best supporting actor Oscar. He went on to star in many films, including *Taxi Driver* (1976), *The Deer Hunter* (1978), *Raging Bull* (1980; he won a best actor Oscar), *Once Upon a Time in America* (1984), *Brazil* (1985), *Midnight Run* (1988), *We're No Angels* (1989), *Stanley and Iris* (1989), *Goodfellas* (1990), *Awakenings* (1990), *Cape Fear* (1991), *Guilty by Suspicion* (1991), *Backdraft* (1991), *Night and the City* (1992), *Mad Dog and Glory* (1993), *This Boy's Life* (1993), and *Mary Shelley's Frankenstein* (1994). He made his directorial debut and starred in *A Bronx Tale* (1993). He was previously married and has two other children. His father was painter Robert De Niro, Sr., who died in 1993.

FURTHER READING

"Mr. Untensity." Kim Cunningham. *People*, Jan. 8, 1996.
"De Niro on De Niro." Robert De Niro, Jr. *Vogue*, Jan. 1995.
"A walk and . . . ." Peter Brant and Ingrid Sischym. *Interview*, Nov. 1993.
"De Niro direct." Julia Reed. *Vogue*, Sept. 1993.
"De Niro, Robert." *Current Biography*, May 1993.
The Films of Robert De Niro. Douglas Brode. Carol, 1993.

Dennehy, Brian (1939–)

Stage, film, and television star Brian Dennehy appeared in all three media in 1995. In the theatrical film *The Stars Fall on Henrietta*, he starred as rich Big Dave, opposite Robert Duvall as the small-time 1930s Texas oil wildcatter who needs a stake to explore a last-chance "sure thing" oil reservoir; James Keach directed. In the theatrical film *Tommy Boy*, directed by Peter Segal, Dennehy starred as the father, opposite Chris Farley as his incompetent son, and David Spader, Bo Derek, Dan Aykroyd, and Julie Warner.

On television, Dennehy directed, produced, cowrote, and starred as lawyer and recovering alcoholic Charlie Sloan in the murder mystery *Shadow of a Doubt*, based on the William J. Coughlin novel and costarring Bonnie Bedelia and Fairuza Balk.

On stage, Dennehy starred as the schoolmaster, Hugh, in a very well received revival of Brian Friel's play *Translations*, set in the 1830s Irish countryside. Howard Davies directed a cast that included Donal Donnelly and Dana Delany.

Connecticut-born Dennehy saw service with the Marine Corps in Vietnam. In the mid-1970s, he emerged as a strong supporting player in a wide range of character roles on stage and screen, with a notable role off-Broadway in *Streamers* (1976) and his film debut in *Semi-Tough* (1977). He became best known for such films as *F.I.S.T.* (1978), *First Blood* (1982), *Gorky Park* (1983), *Never Cry Wolf* (1983), *Finders Keepers* (1984), *Cocoon* (1985), *Silverado* (1985), *F/X* (1986), *Legal Eagles* (1986), *Return to Snowy River* (1988), *Miles from Home* (1988), *Cocoon: The Return* (1988), *The Last of the Finest* (1989), and *Presumed Innocent* (1990). He has also appeared in the television series "Big Shamus, Little Shamus" (1979) and "Star of the Family" (1982–83), as well as in many television films, including *Foreign Affairs* (1993), *Leave of Absence* (1994), and *Jack Reed: A Search for Justice* (1994). Notable stage appearances were in *The Cherry Orchard* (1988) and *The Iceman Cometh* (1990). Dennehy graduated from Columbia University and did postgraduate work at Yale University. He is married to Jennifer Dennehy; he has three children from a previous marriage.

FURTHER READING

"Brian Dennehy." *Playboy*, Nov. 1993.

Denner, Charles (1926–95) Born in Poland, French film star Charles Denner moved to France with his family in 1930. He began his stage career in 1946, and made his film debut in *La Meulleure Part* (1956), directed by Yves Allégret. Denner emerged as a leading player in the title role of the film *Bluebeard* (1963), directed by Claude Chabrol. Another early starring role was in *Upside Down/Inside Out* (1964). He starred again as director Claude Berri's father in the autobiographical film *The Two of Us* (1967). In 1969, he starred in Constantin Costa-Gavras' political thriller *Z*. Among his other films were *The Sleeping Car Murders* (1965), *The Thief of Paris* (1967), *The Bride Wore Black* (1968), *The Crook* (1970), *Such a Gorgeous Kid Like Me* (1972), *The Down-In-the-Hole Gang* (1973), *And Now My Love* (1974), *The Night Caller* (1975), and *The Man Who Loved Women* (1977). He was survived by his wife and two children. (d. Dreux, France; September 10, 1995)

FURTHER READING

"A departure. . . ." STANLEY KAUFFMANN. *New Republic,* Oct. 16, 1995.
Obituary. *Times* (of London), Sept. 13, 1995.
Obituary. *New York Times*, Sept. 12, 1995.
Obituary. *Independent*, Sept. 12, 1995.

Depardieu, Gérard (1948–) Actor Gérard Depardieu starred in 1995 opposite Roman Polanski in the film *A Pure Formality*, directed by Giuseppe Tornatore and written by Tornatore and Pacale Quignard. The story is spare: Depardieu is a captured fugitive, who may be a murderer; Polanski is his antagonist, the police inspector who interrogates him throughout the night in an isolated police station. Their confrontation is meant to be out of time and place, raising existential and other philosophic questions, far more than those encountered in the normal murder mystery.

Forthcoming were starring roles in the film *Unhook the Stars*, directed by Nick Cassavetes and costarring Gena Rowlands and Marisa Tomei; and opposite Bob Hoskins and Patrica Arquette in the film *The Secret Agent*. Depardieu was also slated to star opposite Whoopi Goldberg in an as-yet-untitled film directed by Norman Jewison.

Gérard Depardieu (left) and Roman Polanski.

The seeming antithesis of a romantic star, with his chunky physique, skewed nose, and lantern jaw, French-born Depardieu burst on the French film scene as an amoral *Easy Rider*-style juvenile delinquent in *Going Places* (1974) and then emerged as a leading French actor of the 1970s and 1980s, making more than 60 films, including *Stavisky* (1974), *1900* (1976), *Get Out Your Handkerchiefs* (1978), *The Last Metro* (1980; he won the French César award as best French actor), *My American Uncle* (1980), *Danton* (1982), *The Return of Martin Guerre* (1982), *Tartuffe* (1984), *Jean de Florette* (1986), *Green Card* (1990), *Cyrano de Bergerac* (1990), *Too Beautiful for You* (1990), *Camille Claudel* (1990), *Uranus* (1991), *1492: Conquest of Paradise* (1992), *Germinal* (1993), *My Father, the Hero* (1994), and *Colonel Chabert* (1994). He also became a substantial theater actor in France, and has appeared on television. He is married to the actress, singer, and songwriter Elisabeth Guignot; they have one daughter and one son.

FURTHER READING

Gérard Depardieu: A Biography. PAUL CHUTKOW. Knopf, 1994.
"All gaul." PENELOPE MESIC. *Chicago*, Jan. 1993.
"His passion for wine. . . ." PER-HENRIK MANSSON. *The Wine Spectator*, May 15, 1991.
"Gérard Depardieu. . . ." TOM CONROY. *Rolling Stone*, Mar. 7, 1991.

"Life in a big glass. . . ." RICHARD CORLISS. *Time*, Feb. 4, 1991.
"Gérard Depardieu. . . ." JEANNIE PARK. *People*, Feb. 4, 1991.

Desai, Anita Mazumdar (1937–) In 1995, Indian novelist Anita Desai published *Journey to Ithaca,* her tenth novel, and her first since 1989. The tale of European newlyweds journeying to and around India in search of spiritual enlightenment draws more than a little from Desai's own background. Her mother was a German engineer who met and married a Bengali engineering student in Berlin and returned with him to live in India; the novel's Sophie is a German woman married to an Italian man obsessed with India. Desai skillfully uses her mother's (and her own) experience as an outsider to illuminate this tale of a clash of cultures across two continents.

An earlier Desai novel, *In Custody* (1985), was made into a film in 1994, and marked the directing debut of Ismail Merchant, the film producer famed for his collaboration with director James Ivory. Desai had cowritten the screenplay with Shahrukh Husain.

Born in Mussoorie India, Anita Mazumdar received her B.A. from Delhi University in 1957. She married Ashvin Desai in 1958; they have four children. From the early 1960s, she began building up a notable literary ouevre, including *Cry, the Peacock* (1963), *Voices in the City* (1965), *Bye-Bye Blackbird* (1968), *The Peacock Garden* (1974), *Where Shall We Go This Summer?* (1975), *Cat on a Houseboat* (1976), *Fire on the Mountain* (1977), *Games at Twilight and Other Stories* (1978), *Clear Light of Day* (1980), *The Village by the Sea* (1982), *In Custody* (1985), and *Baumgartner's Bombay* (1989). She has won numerous awards, including the prestigious Winifred Holtby prize of the Royal Society for Literature (1978).

FURTHER READING

"How Odysseus. . . ." MARIANNE BRACE. *Independent* June 1, 1995.
Cultural Imperialism and the Indo-English Novel: Genre and Ideology in the Novels of R. K. Narayan, Anita Desai, Kamala Markandaya, and Salman Rushdie. FAWZIA AFZAL-KHAN. Pennsylvania State University Press, 1993.

Desai, Morarji (1896–1995) Gujarat-born Morarji Desai, Indian prime minister (1977–79), began his long government career in 1918, in the Bombay civil service. He resigned to join the Indian freedom movement in 1930, and during the 1930s became a Congress Party leader and provincial minister in Bombay. He resigned with the other Congress Party ministers in 1939, at the outbreak of World War II, and was with the other leaders of his party imprisoned by the British (1942–45), after endorsing Mahatma Gandhi's demand that the British leave India. After independence, Desai rose within the Indian government; he was Jawaharlal Nehru's minister for commerce and industry (1956–58) and finance minister (1958–63), and was Indira Gandhi's finance minister (1966–69), then splitting with Gandhi and going into opposition. He and other opposition leaders were jailed by Gandhi in 1975, but Desai emerged as the first non–Congress Party Prime Minister of India in the 1977 elections. He was in power for 27 months, a period of considerable civil unrest in India, and was brought down by a faction led by Home Affairs minister Charan Singh in 1979, shortly before Indira Gandhi returned to power. Desai then retired. His autobiography was *The Story of My Life* (1974). No information on survivors was available. (d. Bombay; April 10, 1995)

FURTHER READING

Obituary. *Times* (of London), Apr. 11, 1995.
Obituary. *Independent,* Apr. 11, 1995.

Obituary. *New York Times*, Apr. 11, 1995.
Morarji Desai: The Man and His Ideas. S. R. BAKSHI. South Asia, 1992.

Deutch, John Mark (1938–)

On May 9, 1995, Deputy Secretary of Defense John Deutch was confirmed by the Senate as director of the Central Intelligence Agency. He succeeded R. James Woolsey, who had resigned in January after drawing heavy criticism when Aldrich Ames was exposed as a longtime Russian mole in the CIA. Deutch took the CIA job, which he had earlier declined, after retired Michael Carns had withdrawn his name from nomination by President Clinton.

Deutch inherited a CIA widely seen as riddled with "old-boy" networks and pervasive sexism, careless of legalities, and with its worldwide spy operations thoroughly compromised. He promised large-scale reforms, and pledged to end sexism and racism at the CIA, while at the same time denying any intention to institute a "bloodbath" at the agency. One of his earliest actions was to hire Nora Slatkin as CIA executive director, the first woman to hold that post. The CIA also quickly settled a class action lawsuit alleging sexual discrimination, which had been brought by 450 women on the clandestine, or secret, side of the agency. Some other top-level executive changes were also made. On the other hand, Deutch also quickly moved to propose revitalization of the CIA's covert action capability, source of many past scandals, a move criticized by some critics of the CIA, despite promised safeguards. Whether or not the CIA's old-boy networks would once again survive a new director and generate a new set of scandals remained a matter of conjecture.

Born in Brussels, Belgium, Deutch emigrated to the U.S. with his family in 1940, becoming a naturalized citizen in 1946. He received his 1961 B.A. from Amherst College and his 1961 Bachelors in Chemical Engineering from the Massachusetts Institute of Technology (MIT), and then worked as a systems analyst in the office of the Secretary of Defense (1961–65). He received his 1965 Ph.D. in physical chemistry from MIT, and went on to become a fellow at the National Academy of Sciences (1966–67). He then returned to the academic world, becoming an assistant professor at Princeton University (1967–70). Deutch became a member of the MIT faculty in 1970, becoming a full professor (1971) and department chair (1976). He became dean of science at MIT in 1982, and was also provost (1982–90). From the mid-1970s, he also served in a number of key national posts, dealing with matters of nuclear energy safety and new energy technology, and advising the U.S. Army and the White House on a wide range of military matters. He became of member of the President's Foreign Intelligence Advisory Board in 1990. He has three sons.

FURTHER READING

"The CIA's most. . . ." TIM WEINER. *New York Times Magazine*, Dec. 10, 1995.
"Reforming the Pentagon. . . ." *Technology Review*, Apr. 1994.

DeVito, Danny (Daniel Michael DeVito; 1944–)

Actor, director, and producer Danny DeVito in 1995 appeared as film star Martin Weir and coproduced the well-received, Hollywood-set film comedy *Get Shorty*, starring John Travolta as gangster-turned-movie producer Chili Palmer opposite Gene Hackman as bottom-of-the-barrel movie producer Harry Zimm, and costarring Rene Russo. Barry Sonnenfield directed and coproduced and Scott Franklin adapted the Elmore Leonard novel. The cast also included Dennis Farina and Delroy Lindo, with Bette Midler, Harvey Keitel, and Penny Marshall in cameo roles.

Forthcoming was the film *Matilda*; which De-Vito was scheduled to produce, direct, and star in, along with Rhea Perlman, Mara Wilson, Pam Ferris, and Embeth Davidtz.

New Jersey–born DeVito was a New York stage actor before making his main career in Hollywood. He appeared in such Off-Broadway productions as *The Man with a Flower in His Mouth* (1969) and *One Flew over the Cuckoo's Nest* (1971), re-creating his role in the 1975 film version, and went on to such films as *Car Wash* (1976), and *Goin' South* (1978). Then came his role as Louie DePalma in the long-running television series "Taxi" (1978–83), for which he won a 1981 Emmy, and roles in such films as *Terms of Endearment* (1983), *Romancing the Stone* (1984), *Jewel of the Nile* (1985), *Ruthless People* (1986), *Tin Men* (1987), *Throw Momma from the Train* (1987; he also directed), *Twins* (1988), *The War of the Roses* (1989; he also directed), *Other People's Money* (1991), *Batman Returns* (1992), *Hoffa* (1992; he also directed), *Jack the Bear* (1993), *Look Who's Talking Now* (1993; as the voice of the dog, Rocks), *Renaissance Man* (1994), and *Junior* (1994). DeVito is married to actress Rhea Perlman, and has three children. (For additional photo, see **Travolta, John**.)

FURTHER READING

"Danny DeVito." *Playboy*, Feb. 1993.

Diana, Princess of Wales (Diana Frances Spencer; 1961–   ) In late November, Princess Diana, who during 1995 had been rather quiet, though still the object of enormous media attention, provided the material for a whole new British Royal Family media circus. In a long televised interview with BBC reporter Martin Bashir, televised by the BBC on November 20 (aired in the United States four days later), she talked about her estranged husband's long-term adultery; her own extramarital affair; her isolation and neglect at the hands of her husband, the British royal family, and their set; the damage caused by the constant attention of the media; and her years of bulimia, allegedly brought on by all the rest. The interview, which immediately caused an enormous public outcry, was seen by an estimated 27 million people in Britain, and later by many millions more abroad— and Prince Charles and the British Royals had another very, very bad year. In late December, Queen Elizabeth wrote to Diana and Charles, urging them to quickly divorce, a course reportedly favored by Charles; they had been separated since 1992.

Diana Spencer worked as a kindergarten teacher in London before her marriage. She married Charles, Prince of Wales, heir to the British throne, in July 1981, in a ceremony watched worldwide by hundreds of millions of viewers. During the years that followed, the two remained great celebrities, every step and misstep chronicled and photographed in great detail by the media. In the later years of their marriage, media attention focused on reported marital strains, and in 1992 those strains became public. On December 9, 1992, the Prince and Princess of Wales announced their separation, which was in 1993 followed by her formal withdrawal from public appearances. They have two children: William Arthur Philip, born June 21, 1982; and Henry Charles Albert David, born September 15, 1984.

FURTHER READING

"Diana. . . ." ANDREW MORTON and CAROL HALL. " 'I won't go quietly.' " MICHAEL ELLIOTT and DANIEL PEDERSEN. *Newsweek*, Dec. 4, 1995.
"True confessions. . . ." MICHELLE GREENE. *People*, Dec. 4, 1995.
" 'Well, there were. . . .' " *Guardian*, Nov. 21, 1995.
"Di struts. . . ." *People*, Nov. 6, 1995.
"Diana. . . ." *McCall's*, Apr. 1995.
With Love from Diana: The Princess of Wales'

Personal Astrologer Shares Her First-Hand Account of Diana's Turbulent Years. PENNY THORTON. Pocket Books, 1995.
"Crown of thorns." BRUCE WALLACE. *Maclean's*, Dec. 5, 1994.
"Tattle royal." JONATHAN DIMBLEBY. *People*. Nov. 7, 1994.
"Romantic interlude. . . ." ANNA PASTERNAK. "Diss and tell." MICHELLE GREEN and TERRY SMITH. *People*, Oct. 17, 1994.
"A princess in peril." Sept. 5, 1994. "Let's do lunch. . . ." "Taking the heat." June 13, 1994. MICHELLE GREEN et al. *People*.
"Is Princess Di. . . ." CINDI LEIVE. *Glamour*, June 1994.
Diana: Her New Life. ANDREW MORTON. Simon & Schuster, 1994.
The Tarnished Crown: Princess Diana and the House of Windsor. ANTHONY HOLDEN. Random House, 1993.
Diana, Princess of Wales. JULIA DELANO. Smithmark, 1993.
Princess Diana: Glitter, Glamour, and a Lot of Hard Work. NANCY E. KRULIK. Scholastic, 1993.
Princess Diana: Royal Ambassador. RENORA LICATA. Blackbirch, 1993.

Dickson, Dorothy Schofield (1893–1995)

Kansas City–born Dorothy Dickson, a star in the British musical theater during the 1920s and 1930s, began her career as a dancer, in 1914 forming a ballroom dancing act with Carl Hyson, whom she married in 1920 and divorced in 1936. She made her Broadway debut in Jerome Kern's stage musical *Oh, Boy!* (1917), and danced in several other Broadway shows, including two editions of the Ziegfeld Follies. She emerged as a star overnight in 1921, in the title role of the London version of Jerome Kern's musical *Sally*, singing "Look For the Silver Lining," which had become Marilyn Miller's signature song a year earlier in New York. Staying in Britain, she starred in Kern's musicals *The Cabaret Girl* and *The Beauty Prize*, and then moved into drama in the title role of the play *Peter Pan*. From the mid-1920s through the late 1930's, she was a leading figure in the British musical theater, in such hit musicals as *Tip Toes* (1926), *Peggy Ann* (1927), *Wonder Bar* (1930), *Stop Press* (1935), and *Spread It Abroad* (1936). Dickson continued to appear in musicals and drama through the early 1950s. She was also a recording artist, and appeared in several films. She was survived by a daughter. (d. London; September 25, 1995)

FURTHER READING

Obituary. *New York Times*, Sept. 29, 1995.
Obituary. *Independent,* Sept. 27, 1995.
Obituary. *Times* (of London), Sept. 27, 1995.

Dietz, Robert Sinclair (1914–95)

New Jersey–born Robert Dietz, a leading marine geologist, received his 1937 B.S, 1939 M.S., and 1941 Ph.D. from the University of Illinois. He was a much-decorated Army Air Force pilot during World War II. After the war, he joined the U.S. Navy expedition to Antarctica (1946–47), and then worked at the navy's San Diego Electronic Laboratory (1946–54), the London Office of Naval Research (1954–59), and again at the San Diego laboratory (1959–63). He later worked with the U.S. Coast and Geodetic Survey (1963–70) and the National Oceanic and Atmospheric Administration (1970–77), and then was a professor of geology at Arizona State University (1977–1985), then moving to emeritus status. Dietz made a major contribution to ocean floor studies and validation of the continental drift theory in the 1960s and 1970s, originating the term "sea-floor spreading" to describe the process of sea floor breakup as new matter is thrust up from below to form new sea-floor mountain chains, or mid-ocean ridges. He helped build the bathyscaphe that he, Jacques Piccard, and Don Walsh took to the bottom of the Pacific's seven-mile-deep Challenger Trench in 1960; one result was the Dietz-Piccard book *Seven Miles Down*. Dietz also wrote hundreds of scientific papers and several other books in his field. He was survived by two sons and a brother (d. Tempe, Arizona; May 19, 1995)

FURTHER READING

Obituary. *New York Times*, May 24, 1995.

Dillon, Matt (1964–)

In 1995, actor Matt Dillon starred as the soon-to-be-murdered husband in the dark film comedy *To Die For*, directed by Gus Van Sant, playing opposite Nicole Kidman as the wife who ultimately has him killed by several teenagers. The film was loosely based on the far-from-comedic 1990–91 New Hampshire Pamela Smart case, in which she and three teenage accomplices were convicted of

Matt Dillon (left) and Annabella Sciorra.

conspiring to murder her husband, Gregg Smart, at least partly for the $140,000 insurance policy on his life.

Dillon also starred opposite Anne Parillaud, Gabriel Byrne, Corban Walker (in the title role as an adult), and Alan Pentony (in the title role as a child) in the film *Frankie Starlight*, directed by Michael Lindsay-Hogg. Parillaud plays an Irish single mother in the U.S. after World War II, who gives birth to Frankie, a dwarf. Dillon is a soldier, not the boy's father, who loves her; and Byrne is a U.S. immigration officer who befriends her.

Forthcoming were starring film roles *Albino Alligator*, directed by Kevin Spacey and costarring Faye Dunaway, Viggo Mortenson, and Gary Sinise, and *Beautiful Girls*, directed by Ted Demme and costarring Uma Thurman, Timothy Hutton, and Lauren Holly.

Born in New Rochelle, New York, Dillon began his movie career as a teenager, in *Over the Edge* (1979), quickly followed by *Little Darlings* (1980), which established him as a leading teenage Hollywood star. During the 1980s, he starred in such films as *My Bodyguard* (1980), *Liar's Moon* (1982), *Tex* (1982), *The Outsiders* (1983), *Rumblefish* (1983), *The Flamingo Kid* (1984), *Native Son* (1986), *Kansas* (1988), *Drugstore Cowboy* (1989), *Bloodhounds of Broadway* (1989), *A Kiss Before Dying* (1991), *Singles* (1992), *The Saint of Fort Washington* (1993), *Mr.*

Wonderful (1993), and *Golden Gate* (1994). His younger brother is the actor Kevin Dillon.

FURTHER READING

"From here to maturity. . . ." *Seventeen*, July 1991.
"Matt Dillon." BRENDON LEMON. *Interview*, Apr. 1991.
"The Dillon papers." BRET EASTON ELLIS. *American Film*, Feb. 1991.

Djilas, Milovan (1911–95) Born in Podbisce, Montenegro, Yugoslav writer and politician Milovan Djilas attended Belgrade University in the early 1930s, becoming a lawyer. He joined the Communist Party in 1932 and was imprisoned by the Yugoslav government (1932–35). While in jail, he met several Communist Party leaders and became a leader of that party after meeting and working with Josip Broz (Tito), who would eventually become the leader of Yugoslavia. In 1937, Djilas recruited fighters for the International Brigades in the Spanish Civil War. Djilas became a member of his party's Central Committee and Politburo in 1938, and was a key Communist partisan leader during World War II; he lost his father, two sisters, and two brothers during the war. After the war, he rose swiftly in Communist Yugoslavia, becoming a major Tito associate, and by 1954 was a Yugoslav vice president and head of the federal parliament. It was Djilas whom Tito selected to tell Stalin about the Yugoslav-Soviet split in 1948.

But by 1954 Djilas had become disillusioned with Yugoslav communism. Emerging as a powerful and open critic of Tito's government, he was expelled from his party and all positions in 1954, and was in the decades that followed Yugoslavia's leading dissenter. He became a world figure after his indictment of communism, *The New Class*, was smuggled abroad and published in 1957. It became a classic, and by far his best known work, though he continued to publish a wide range of works for the rest of his life. He was imprisoned (1956–61; 1962–66), then briefly going abroad. From late in 1968, he was for 18 years refused a passport and held prisoner in his own country. Among his other works were his two autobiographies, *Land Without Justice* (1952) and *Memoirs of a Revolutionary* (1973), along with *Conversations With Stalin* (1962), *Montenegro* (1964), and *Beyond the New Class* (1969), as well as a considerable number of other fiction and nonfiction works. He was survived by a daughter and a son. (d. Belgrade; April 20, 1995)

FURTHER READING

Obituary. *National Review,* May 15, 1995.
Obituary. *Independent,* Apr. 21, 1995.
Obituary. *Times* (of London), Apr. 21, 1995.
Obituary. *New York Times*, Apr. 21, 1995.
"A crazy war." PAUL HOCKENOS. *New Statesman & Society,* Sept. 13, 1991.

Dole, Bob (Robert Joseph Dole; 1923–)

Kansas Republican Senator Bob Dole, the Senate majority leader, was the front-running candidate for the Republican presidential nomination throughout 1995. All of his public comments and political actions could be seen clearly only if that fact and his political situation were taken into account. Throughout the year, Dole, a right-leaning Republican moderate, was to be seen trying to occupy the right and the middle at once—to the right to negate a possibly disabling challenge from such ultraconservative candidates as Phil Gramm during the presidential primary process, and to the middle to capture the main mass of middle-ground voters in American politics, whose votes would elect the next president. And so Dole sometimes very uncomfortably tried to lean both ways at once—apparently with considerable success. Actually in the presidential race since early 1994, he formally announced his candidacy on April 10, 1995, and quickly built up major campaign funds and won the support of most of the mainstream of his party, including the overwhelming majority of Republican governors. After a close race with Phil Gramm in Iowa in August, Dole picked up strength, winning the November Florida straw poll as Gramm visibly faded and began to run short of money.

At year's end, Dole was behind Clinton in the presidential candidate popularity polls, but far ahead of all the other Republican candidates. He could be expected to pick up support in 1996, as massive campaign expenditures and heavy media focus kicked in, and was a strong favorite to win the Republican nomination, despite his age and lack of vibrant personal appeal. A great unknown, however, faced any Republican candidate—the specter of a third or fourth party conservative candidacy that would take far larger numbers of Republican than Democratic voters, as Ross Perot had done in 1992.

Kansas-born Dole has spent three decades in Washington, starting with his four congressional terms (1961–69). A leading Republican, he has served in the Senate since 1969, and as Senate Republican leader since 1985. He was chairperson of the Republican National Committee (1971–73), and his party's unsuccessful vice presidential candidate in 1976. He made unsuccessful runs for the Republican presidential nomination in 1980 and 1988. A staunch Republican party supporter, he campaigned hard for the Bush-Quayle ticket in 1992, as he had in 1988, even after his primary defeat by Bush. He was elected to a fifth Senate term in 1992, by a huge majority, with 64 percent of the vote.

On the personal side, Dole "went public" in 1992 when he found that he had prostate cancer, in an attempt to help others understand and openly deal with the problem. His treatment was reportedly entirely successful.

Dole's B.A. and LL.B. were from Topeka's Washburn Municipal University. In 1975, he married Elizabeth Hanford Dole, the American Red Cross president, formerly U.S. secretary of labor. Together they published *Doles: Unlimited Partners* (1988).

FURTHER READING

"The Dole world." HOWARD FINEMAN. *Newsweek*, Jan. 8, 1996
"A taciturn leader. . . ." JERELYN EDDINGS. *U.S. News & World Report,* Dec. 18, 1995.
"The Republicans' choice." *Economist,* Dec. 2, 1995.
"Will the real . . . ?" MICHAEL KRAMER. *Time,* Nov. 20, 1995.
"What they're like at home." Edward Klein. *Parade,* Oct. 15, 1995.
" 'I think I've. . . .' " MICHAEL DUFFY and KAREN TUMULTY. "Medical verdict. . . ." CHRISTINE GORMAN. "Facing the age issue." MICHAEL DUFFY and NANCY GIBBS. *Time,* July 31, 1995.
"The last interventionist. . . ." CHARLES LANE. *New Republic,* July 3, 1995.
"GOP heavyweights. . . ." MICHAEL RUST and LISA LEITER. *Insight on the News,* Apr. 3, 1995.
"The survivor." WALTER SHAPIRO. *Esquire,* Apr. 1995.
"Lots more Mr. Nice Guy." KAREN TUMULTY. *Time,* Mar. 13, 1995.
"Out of the trenches. . . ." JOSETTE SHINER and RALPH Z. HALLOW. *Insight on the News,* Mar. 6, 1995.
Bob Dole. RICHARD BEN CRAMER. Random House, 1995.
Bob Dole: The U. S. Senator Who Was Severely Wounded in WWII. Chelsea House, 1995.

"The hunters." ROBERT PARRY and JEFFREY KLEIN. *Mother Jones*. July–Aug. 1994.

"Let the race begin. . . ." WICK ALLISON and WILLIAM A. RUSHER. *National Review*. Apr. 4, 1994.

"Robert Dole. . . ." J. D. PODOLSKY. *People*, Dec. 13, 1993.

"King Robert. . . ." FRED BARNES. *New Republic*, Apr. 5, 1993.

"Bob Dole speaks. . . ." CORY SERVAAS. *Saturday Evening Post*, July–Aug. 1992.

Dornan, Robert Kenneth (1933–)

California Republican congressman Robert Dornan was censured by his House Republican colleagues in January 1995. Often highly controversial and abrasive, he had in a speech on the House floor accused President Bill Clinton of having given "aid and comfort to the enemy" as a protester during the Vietnam War. Nor was the incident an isolated one; Dornan's conservative political and social views have in many well-documented instances been accompanied by highly personal attacks on those with whose views and lifestyles he disagreed, his targets of choice often being homosexuals, feminists, and opposing politicians, with special emphasis on highly personal attacks on President Clinton.

On April 13, Dornan declared himself a candidate for the Republican presidential nomination; running on a hard-line conservative program that included a school prayer amendment to the Constitution; opposition to any gun control; the outlawing of all but a few abortions; the ending of the Department of Education and many federal social service and arts funding programs; and tougher anticrime and anticriminal alien laws and regulations. He was not expected to be a serious contender for the candidacy, and although some observers thought he might appeal to Republican primary voters to the right of conservative candidate Patrick Buchanan, few thought that he would stay in the race very far into 1996.

New York City–born Dornan attended California's Loyola University (1950–53), served in the military as a fighter pilot (1953–58), and was an Air Force reservist pilot (1958–75). During the Vietnam War, he was a photographer and broadcast journalist, who spent a considerable amount of time in Southeast Asia. He became a talk show host in Los Angeles (1965–73), later producing his own show (1970–73). He served in the House of Representatives (1977–82; 1985–). Dornan published *Judicial Supremacy: The Supreme Court on Trial* (1986), written with Csaba Vedlik. He married Sallie Hansen in 1955; they have three daughters, two sons, and five foster children.

FURTHER READING

"California tirading." JUDITH COLP. *Insight on the News*, Sept. 2, 1991.

"Flying high. . . ." LESLIE KAUFMAN. *California*, May 1991.

Douglas, Michael (Michael Kirk Douglas; 1944–)

Actor and producer Michael Douglas starred as President Michael Shepherd, in the title role of the 1995 film comedy-drama *The American President*. His White House occupant is a liberal, a widower, and an exceedingly decent human being, who is also a very popular president in the fourth year of his term, and ready to run for reelection. However, he manages to supply his opponents with an extraordinarily juicy scandal, by falling in love with environmentalist lobbyist Sydney Wade, played by Annette Bening. Their quite innocent and straightforward love affair, set in the White House, cannot be kept secret, although the White House staff tries very hard, and instead becomes a major scandal, fanned by villainous opposition Senator Bob Rumson, played by Richard Dreyfuss. Martin Sheen costarred as the

president's chief of staff, with Michael J. Fox as an advisor who very much resembles real-life George Stephanopolous, and Anna Deavere Smith as the president's press secretary, in a cast that also included David Paymer and Samantha Mathis. Rob Reiner directed and produced; Aaron Sorkin wrote the screenplay. The film received generally favorable reviews, though some reviewers felt that the gentle comedy should have been something other than it was—perhaps a biting political satire, in their view more in tune with the times. Douglas received a Golden Globe nomination as best actor in a musical or comedy for the role.

Forthcoming was a starring role opposite Kirk Douglas in the film *The Ghost and the Darkness*, directed by Stephen Hopkins, written by William Goldman, and coproduced by Michael Douglas.

Son of actor Kirk Douglas, Michael Douglas first became a star in the television series "The Streets of San Francisco" (1972–75), paired with Karl Malden. Moving into films, he produced the Oscar-winning *One Flew over the Cuckoo's Nest* (1975), produced and starred in the notable nuclear-accident film *The China Syndrome* (1979), and produced and starred in such films as *Romancing the Stone* (1984), *Jewel of the Nile* (1985), and *The War of the Roses* (1989), all three with Kathleen Turner. He also starred in such films as *A Chorus Line* (1985), *Fatal Attraction* (1987), *Wall Street* (1987; he won a best actor Oscar and Golden Globe Award), *Black Rain*

(1989), *Shining Through* (1992), *Basic Instinct* (1992), *Falling Down* (1993), and *Disclosure* (1994). Douglas's 1967 B.A. was from the University of California. He married Diandra Mornell Luker in 1977; they have one son.

FURTHER READING

"Hollywood husbands." MEREDITH BERKMAN and MARK MORRISON. *Ladies Home Journal*, Feb. 1995.
"Michael's full disclosure." NANCY COLLINS. *Vanity Fair*, Jan. 1995.
Michael and Kirk Douglas. SKIP PRESS. Silver Burdett, 1995.
"He said. . . ." REBECCA ASCHER-WALSH and BENJAMIN SVETKEY. *Entertainment*, Dec. 16, 1994.
"Michael and Diandra. . . ." DEBORAH NORVILLE. *McCall's*, Nov. 1992.
"Just your basic. . . ." T. KLEIN. *Cosmopolitan*, May 1992.
"Michael Douglas." JUDITH THURMAN. *Architectural Digest*, Apr. 1992.
"Steaming up the screen." BRIAN D. JOHNSON. *Maclean's*, Mar. 30, 1992.

Douglas-Home, Alexander (Alec) Frederick

(1903–95) London-born Alexander Douglas-Home was the oldest of the five sons of the Earl of Home, one of whom was the playwright William Douglas-Home. He attended Eton and Oxford and began his long political career in 1929, with an unsuccessful run for the House of Commons, and won election in 1931. He was parliamentary private secretary to Prime Minister Neville Chamberlain (1936–40), briefly saw active wartime service before falling ill, and went back into the House of Commons in 1943. He was defeated in the 1945 general elections, and reelected in 1950. In 1951, when his father died, the title passed to him, and he moved into the House of Lords. He was minister of state for Scotland (1951–55) and commonwealth secretary (1955–60), and was Anthony Eden's foreign secretary (1960–63). Douglas-Home was the Conservative Party's startling choice to succeed Eden in 1963, then necessarily renouncing his hereditary peerage. Labour won the 1964 elections, making his tenure in office very brief. He was foreign secretary again (1970–74), then retired from politics. He was then awarded a life peerage as Lord Home of the Hirsel. His autobiography was *The Way the Wind Blows* (1976). He was survived by a son and three daughters; his wife predeceased him. (d. Berwickshire, Scotland; October 9, 1995)

FURTHER READING

Obituary. *Times* (of London), Oct 10, 1995.
Obituary. *Independent*, Oct 10, 1995.
Obituary. *New York Times*, Oct. 10, 1995.

Robert Downey, Jr. (left) and Lili Taylor.

Downey, Robert, Jr. (1965–) Actor

Robert Downey, Jr. starred as 17th-century English doctor Robert Merivel in the 1995 film *Restoration*, set in the freewheeling period that was the Stuart Restoration. Merivel is a much-favored court physician, whom King Charles II (Sam Neill) sets up as the titled, landed, in-name-only husband of one of his mistresses, played by Polly Walker. Charles rejects Merivel when he learns that he has fallen in love with her. Costarring are Meg Ryan, as an insane asylum inmate who has a child by Merivel; Hugh Grant as a treacherous court painter, Ian McKellen, and David Thewlis. Michael Hoffman directed; Rupert Walters wrote the screenplay, based on the Rose Tremain novel.

Downey also appeared as Rivers in a film adaptation of Shakespeare's *Richard III*, starring Ian McKellen in the title role, Annette Bening as Queen Elizabeth, Jim Broadbent as Buckingham, Nigel Hawthorne, Kristin Scott, Maggie Smith, and John Wood. McKellan and director Richard Loncraine wrote the screenplay, which presented the classic work as a murder-laden 1930s gangster film set in English high society. Downey also starred in two other films: *Home for the Holidays*, directed by Jodie Foster and costarring Holly Hunter, Charles Durning, Anne Bancroft, Geraldine Chaplin, and Dylan McDermott; and the animated television film *Mr. Willowby's Christmas Tree*, directed by Jon Stone and costarring Stockard Channing, Leslie Nielsen, and several Muppet characters, including narrator Kermit the Frog.

New York City–born Downey, the son of filmmaker Robert Downey, made his screen debut at the age of five, in his father's film *Pound* (1970), and played in several other children's roles. He emerged as a star in his late teens, in such films as *Baby, It's You* (1983), *Firstborn* (1984), *Tuff Turf* (1985), *Back to School* (1986), *Less Than Zero* (1987), *Johnny Be Good* (1988), *Chances Are* (1989), *True Believer* (1989), *Air America* (1990), and *Too Much Sun* (1991). He then made a major breakthrough in the title role of *Chaplin* (1992), and also starred in *Heart and Soul* (1993), *Only You* (1994), and *Natural Born Killers* (1994). He narrated the documentary *The Last Party*, about the 1992 presidential election campaign. Downey is married to actress Deborah Falconer and has one child.

FURTHER READING

"Irrepressible, irresistible. . . ." NANCY MILLS. *Cosmopolitan*, Mar. 1995.
"Ladies and the tramp." BOB SPITZ. *Us*, Jan. 1993.
"20 questions. . . ." *Playboy*, Aug. 1991.

Drexler, Clyde Austin (1962–) In 1995,

Clyde Drexler came back to Houston to win what had eluded him throughout his notable basketball career: a championship ring. Many sports observers regarded Drexler as "past it" and on the verge of retirement; he had been passed over in the All-Star balloting in both 1994 and 1995. He had expressed his desire to be traded, saying he wanted to play for a contender, and in February 1995 got his wish, going to the Houston Rockets, where he was reunited with his old University of Houston teammate Hakeem Olajuwon. The trade brought the team immediate dividends; in late March and early April, when Olajuwon was out for eight games, Drexler carried the team. Though the team was tipped to be the first defending NBA champions ousted in the first round of the following year's playoffs, the Rockets won three hard-fought Western Conference series, defeating first Utah in five games, then Phoenix in seven games, and finally San Antonio in six games. Many thought the team would be exhausted by these grueling battles, but Houston seemed simply to gain momentum, and swept Orlando in four games for the NBA championship.

In retrospect, Drexler was seen as a major veteran addition to a largely young team, with both his skills and his chemistry with the team being key factors in winning the championship. In the playoffs overall, Drexler averaged 21.5 points a game, second only to Olajuwon, and only slightly less than his season average of 21.8. In May, Drexler and Olajuwon were named to the All-NBA third team. In the new 1995–96 season, the Rockets continued on a strong course that, if Olajuwon and Drexler keep their health, may bring them a shot at a third championship. At year's end, the team was 22-8 and Drexler himself was averaging 20 points a game.

New Orleans–born Drexler attended Sterling High School in Houston, Texas, and then the University of Houston (1980–83). He first came to national attention as a member of the University of Houston basketball team, dubbed "Phi Slamma Jamma," with whom he went to two straight NCAA Final Fours, though without a championship. Leaving Houston after his junior year to turn professional, Drexler had a strong career with the Portland Trail Blazers (1989–95), with whom he went to the NBA Finals twice (1990; 1992); he set team records in ten categories, including points, assists, steals, and rebounds. Drexler has been named to the NBA All-Star Team seven times (1986; 1988–93), and to the all-NBA first team (1992), second team (1988; 1991), and third team (1990; 1995). He was also a member of the celebrated "Dream Team," the U.S. team that won the gold medal in basketball at the 1992 Barcelona Olympics.

FURTHER READING

"Clyde Drexler. . . ." BARRY M. BLOOM. *Sport,* June 1995.
"No more turning away." PAUL ATTNER. *Sporting News,* May 18, 1992.

Dreyfuss, Richard (Richard Stephan Dreyfuss; 1947–) Actor Richard Dreyfuss made the most of a comic villain's role in 1995, as opposition Senator Bob Rumson in Rob Reiner's

gentle film *The American President,* starring Michael Douglas as very popular and very decent President Michael Shepherd. While about to run for reelection, Shepherd has the misfortune to fall in love with environmentalist lobbyist Sydney Wade, played by Annette Bening—thus providing the opposition, led by the mean senator, with a "scandal" to exploit, even though the affair between the widower President and the lobbyist is touchingly innocent and entirely nonpolitical. Reiner directed and produced; Aaron Sorkin wrote the screenplay; the cast included Martin Sheen, Michael J. Fox, and Anna Deavere Smith.

In a quite different vein, Dreyfuss starred in the title role of the film *Mr. Holland's Opus,* portraying the life of an unsuccessful composer who becomes a dedicated high school music teacher. The film is also a commentary on the life of the time, beginning in 1965 and ending with Holland's forced retirement in 1995 due to budget cuts. Stephen Herek directed; the cast included Glenne Headly, Jay Thomas, and Olympia Dukakis. Dreyfuss received a Golden Globe nomination as best actor in a drama for the role. On stage, he also starred opposite Christine Lahti in the play *Three Hotels,* by Jon Robin Baitz, presented at Los Angeles' Mark Taper Forum.

Forthcoming was a starring role in the film *Night Falls On Manhattan,* written and directed by Sidney Lumet and costarring Andy Garcia, Lena Olin, Ian Holm, James Gandolfini, and Ron Leibman.

New York–born Dreyfuss became a leading film star of the 1970s, with his roles in *American Graffiti* (1973), *The Apprenticeship of Duddy Kravitz* (1974), *Jaws* (1975), *Close Encounters of the Third Kind* (1977), and *The Goodbye Girl* (1977), for which he won a best actor Oscar. He went on to star in such films as *Whose Life Is It Anyway?* (1981), *Down and Out in Beverly Hills* (1986), *Tin Men* (1987), *Always* (1989), *Rosencrantz and Guildenstern Are Dead* (1991), *Once Around* (1991), *What About Bob?* (1991), *Lost in Yonkers* (1993), *Another Stakeout* (1993), and *Silent Fall* (1994). On television he coproduced and starred in the HBO telefilm *Prisoner of Honor* (1991), on France's Dreyfus affair, and was the voice of General William T. Sherman in the PBS documentary *Lincoln* (1992). Dreyfuss attended San Fernando Valley State College. Previously married, he has three children.

FURTHER READING

"Richard Dreyfuss." CLAUDIA DREIFUS. *Progressive*, May 1993.

Dudayev, Dzhokhar Mussaevich

(1944–) On December 11, 1994, divisional-strength Russian forces, with air and armor, attacked the breakaway Chechen Republic, led by general Dzhokhar Dudayev. Russian bombers repeatedly attacked the Chechen capital, Grozny, and on December 31, 1994 a 40,000-strong Russian force attacked the city, defended by a small, poorly armed Chechen militia, without air or armor. Surprisingly, that militia held off the attacking Russians for several weeks, long enough for antiwar opposition to grow in Russia and for world condemnation of the Russian action to make itself felt. Reportedly, the Chechens were helped by the virtual refusal of some Russian units, later replaced, to press their attack. Grozny finally fell in early March 1995, to be followed by other towns and villages; but Dudayev's forces were never broken, instead retreating to prepared mountain positions in the Caucasus and waging a guerrilla war against Russian occupation forces. Mindful of their recent Afghanistan experience, Russian forces made no serious attempt to follow, engage, and destroy the Chechens.

After months of negotiations, a Chechen-Russian peace treaty was signed on July 30, 1995. Dudayev did not at first accept the treaty signed by his negotiators, then seemed to accede; but the war never ended. In the months that followed, each side accused the other of breaking the treaty, and fighting again intensified, with Chechen guerrillas also mounting terrorist actions in Moscow and against Russian Chechnya forces. At year's end, the parties were as far apart as ever, with some in the Russian military calling for armed action to end the stalemate and Chechen forces seeming to settle into what might become a long guerrilla war.

Dudayev was a career Soviet military aviator, a graduate of the Tambov Higher Air Force School and the Yuri Gagarin Air Force Academy. Joining the air force in 1966, he swiftly moved up in rank and responsibility to squadron, regimental, and then divisional command. He rose to become the first Chechen Soviet major general, in command of a heavy bomber division headquartered in Estonia (1987–90). After retiring in 1990, he went home to Chechnya and became leader of the pro-independence National Congress of the Chechen People. In the weeks following the failed August 1991 Communist right-wing coup and the breakup of the Soviet Union, Dudayev led a revolt against the government of the Russian Chechen-Ingush Autonomous Republic, and in October 1991 became president of the new Chechen Republic. The new Russian government continued to claim Chechnya as part of Russia, beginning the long dispute that ultimately led to the outbreak of the Chechen War of Independence. Dudayev is married to Alevtina Fedorovna Dudayeva; they have a daughter and two sons.

FURTHER READING

" 'I warned my people. . . .' " ANGUS ROXBURGH. *Guardian*, Dec. 9, 1995.

Duke, Angier Biddle (1915–95) New

York City–born Angier Biddle Duke, an American Tobacco Company heir, dropped out of Yale in 1936, married in 1937, and was one of the leading celebrity playboys of the late 1930s. He emerged from World War II military service a far different man, who from the late 1940s sought public service, which he began as an assistant to Argentina ambassador Stanton Griffis in 1949. He was appointed ambassador to El Salvador (1952–53), was not an appointee during the Eisenhower years, and went to Washington as President John F. Kennedy's chief of protocol (1960–63). President Lyndon B. Johnson appointed him ambassador to Spain (1965–67,) and he was also Johnson's chief of protocol late in 1967. He was ambassador to Denmark (1968–69) and to Morocco (1979–81), then retiring from the foreign service. He was later unpaid chancellor of the Southampton campus of Long Island University. He was survived by his fourth wife, Robin, a daughter, and three sons. (d. Southampton, Long Island; April 30, 1995)

FURTHER READING

Obituary. *Independent,* May 16, 1995.
Obituary. *Times* (of London), May 3, 1995.
Obituary. *New York Times,* May 1, 1995.

Dunaway, Faye (Dorothy Faye Dunaway; 1941–)

Film and television star Faye Dunaway had a busy 1995—far different from 1994, when her year was dominated by her dispute with Andrew Lloyd Webber, who had fired her from the musical *Sunset Boulevard* shortly before the show's scheduled Los Angeles reopening. She and Lloyd Webber settled her $6 million lawsuit out of court for an undisclosed sum in 1995.

Dunaway starred as Marlon Brando's wife in the 1995 film comedy-fantasy *Don Juan DeMarco,* with Johnny Depp as the suicidal world's greatest lover and Brando as the psychiatrist who, while saving Depp's life and sanity, also imbibes some of his philosophy, revitalizing his marriage with Dunaway; Jeremy Leven wrote and directed. She also starred in the television film *A Family Divided,* opposite Stephen Collins as her husband and Cameron Bancroft as their son, involved in a fraternity house gang rape; Donald Wye directed. Her third starring role was again opposite Johnny Depp in the long-delayed New York opening of *Arizona Dream* (1992).

Dunaway also published the autobiography *Looking for Gatsby: My Life,* written with Betsy Sharkey.

Forthcoming were starring roles opposite Jason Alexander in Ken Kwapis's film *Dunston Checks In*; and in Kevin Spacey's film *Albino Alligator,* costarring Matt Dillon, Gary Sinise, and Viggo Mortenson.

Florida-born Dunaway became a film star in 1967 with her portrayal of 1930s midwestern outlaw Bonnie Parker in *Bonnie and Clyde.* She went on to become a leading Hollywood star, in such films as *The Thomas Crown Affair* (1968), *Chinatown* (1974), *Network* (1976; she won a best actress Oscar), as Joan Crawford in *Mommie Dearest* (1981; she decribed the role as "career suicide"), *Barfly* (1987), *The Handmaid's Tale* (1990), *Double Edge* (1992), and *Arizona Dream* (1992). On television, she appeared as revivalist preacher Aimee Semple McPherson in *The Disappearance of Aimee* (1976) and in the title role of *Evita Peron* (1982), going on to roles in *Cold Sassy Tree* (1990), *Silhouette* (1990), and as the disembodied voice of Gaia, the mother goddess of the Earth, in the five-part, ten-hour epic miniseries *Voice of the Planet* (1991). She also starred in the short-lived television series "It Had to Be You" (1993). Dunaway attended Boston University. Formerly married to Peter Wolf, she is married to Terrence O'Neill, and has one child.

FURTHER READING

"Tough act to follow." KAREN S. SCHNEIDER. *People,* May 8, 1995.
"Dorothy Faye Dunaway." GRAHAM FULLER. *Interview,* Feb. 1993.

Dupuy, Trevor Nevitt (1916–95)

New York City–born Trevor N. Dupuy was a leading military historian, the son of military historian and author Ernest Richard Dupuy (1887–1975). Trevor Dupuy was a 1938 West Point graduate, and like his father was a career army officer. He saw Southeast Asia service in World War II, emerging as a lieutenant colonel, and retired in 1968. Also like his father, he was during his years in the military and in retirement a prolific author, beginning with their coauthored book *To the Colors* (1942). Their major collaborative work was *The Encyclopedia of Military History from 3500 B.C. to the Present,* originally published in 1970 and in its fourth edition in 1993. They also published brief histories of the American Revolution and the Civil War. Among Trevor Dupuy's many other works (some written with coauthors) were military histories of World War I, World War II, and the Chinese Civil War, as well as several books on specific aspects of all three wars and on the American Revolution; an encyclopedia of military biography and other works on military biography; a book on the German army; books on the Arab-Israeli Wars; and books and computer models on the forecasting of battle casualties and war material losses. He also published *If War Comes, How to Defeat Saddam Hussein* (1991). He was survived by his wife, Zhang Yun, three daughters, and six sons. (d. Vienna, Virginia; June 5, 1995)

FURTHER READING

Obituary. *New York Times*, June 9, 1995.

Duran, Francisco Martin (1969–) On April 4, 1995, Francisco Duran was convicted of having attempted to assassinate President Bill Clinton by firing at least 27 rounds from a semi-automatic rifle into the White House grounds from Pennsylvania Avenue at approximately 3:00 PM on the afternoon of October 29, 1994. President Clinton was in the White House at the time. Duran, who was standing with the usual crowd of onlookers outside the White House grounds, apparently mistook someone he saw on the grounds for the president, produced the rifle from under his outer clothes and was able to fire many rounds until he was subdued by two bystanders. White House security then arrived. Duran, a Colorado Springs maintenance worker, had been dishonorably discharged from the Army and had served two years in prison for aggravated assault. He had openly told some of his friends that he intended to kill the president and had left his truck, which had anti–gun control bumper stickers, a few blocks from the White House on the day of the attempted assassination, with a note in it telling the world of his plan to shoot the president.

Duran's assassination attempt came only seven weeks after a small plane had slipped through all security to land on the White House lawn. On May 20, a series of new security precautions were put into effect, among them the closing of a section of Pennsylvania Avenue to vehicular traffic, after a study had made it clear that a car bomb detonated on that portion of Pennsylvania Avenue could seriously damage the White House and threaten the life of the president.

FURTHER READING

"Gun-control poster boy of the week." *Time,* Nov. 14, 1994.

Durning, Charles (1923–) Veteran stage and screen star Charles Durning played in several strong character roles in 1995. In the comedy-drama *Home for the Holidays*, directed by Jodie Foster, he played Holly Hunter's father, opposite Anne Bancroft as her mother; Hunter has returned to her childhood home in Baltimore for the Thanksgiving holidays, there finding several members of her rather eccentric family. In a second paternal role, Durning played Sally Field's father in the television miniseries *A Woman of Independent Means*, a fictional biofilm featuring Field as Bess Steed Streeter, produced and directed by Robert Greenwald and based on the Elizabeth Forsythe Halley novel.

In a quite different kind of work, the versatile Durning appeared in the black comedy film *The Last Supper*, a satire on 1990s political matters, directed by Stacy Title; the cast included Cameron Diaz, Ron Eldard, Annabeth Gish, Jonathan Penner, Courtney B. Vance, Jason Alexander, Nora Dunn, and Ron Perlman. Durning also appeared as the town minister in the film *The Grass Harp*, based on Truman Capote's autobiographical novel. The cast included Walter Matthau, Piper Laurie, Sissy Spacek, Jack Lemmon, and Mary Steenburgen, directed by Matthau's son, Charles Matthau.

Durning has been a strong character actor for more than 30 years, creating a wide range of notable roles on stage, screen, and television. In the theater he memorably played the governor in *Best Little Whorehouse in Texas*, and won a Tony as best featured actor in a play for his role as Big Daddy in the 1990 Broadway revival of Tennessee Williams' *Cat on a Hot Tin Roof*. On film, he was especially notable as Jessica Lange's father and Dustin Hoffman's would-be suitor in *Tootsie* (1982). Among his other films are *The Sting* (1973), *Mass Appeal* (1984), *The Rosary Murders* (1987), *Far North* (1988), *Dick Tracy* (1990), *V. I. Warshawski* (1991), *Alien 3* (1992), and *The Hudsucker Proxy* (1994). He has also appeared in many television films, including *Queen of the Stardust Ballroom* (1975) and *The Water Engine* (1992), and had a strong supporting role in the television series "Evening Shade" (1990–94). Durning was born in Highland Falls,

New York, and attended New York University and Columbia University. He married Mary Ann Amelio in 1974.

FURTHER READING

"An actor deals. . . ." DOTSON RADER. *Parade*, Oct. 10, 1993.

Durrell, Gerald Malcolm (1925–95)

Born in Jamshedpur, India, Gerald Durrell moved to Europe with his family in the mid-1930s, and to Britain at the beginning of World War II. He developed the lifelong interest in animals that was to become his vocation while a child living on the island of Corfu, and began his career as an assistant at Whipsnade Zoo during the war. During the postwar period, he emerged as an active collector of animals for zoos and a very popular naturalist and nature writer, who made a major contribution to the preservation of endangered species. The first of his two-score books was the best-selling *The Overloaded Ark* (1953); among his other works were *Three Singles to Adventure* (1954), *My Family and Other Animals* (1956), *A Zoo in My Luggage* (1960), *The Ark's Anniversary* (1991), and *The Aye-Aye and I* (1993). He also wrote several nature-based novels and children's books. Durell's largest audiences stemmed from such film and television works as "Two in the Bush" (1962) and "The Amateur Naturalist" (1983). In 1959, he founded the Jersey Zoo, which focused on the captive breeding of endangered species, which were then released into the wild. He was the younger brother of writer Lawrence Durrell. He was survived by his second wife, Dr. Lee Wilson McGeorge. (d. Jersey, England; January 30, 1995)

FURTHER READING

Obituary. *Independent*, Jan. 31, 1995.
Obituary. *Times* (of London), Jan. 31, 1995.
Obituary. *New York Times*, Feb. 1, 1995.

Duvall, Robert (1931–)

Veteran film star Robert Duvall starred as Roger Prynne opposite Demi Moore as his wife, Hester Prynne, in a 1995 film version of *The Scarlet Letter*, directed by Roland Joffé and very, very loosely adapted by Douglas Day Stewart from the classic Nathaniel Hawthorne novel. The cast included Gary Oldman as Arthur Dimmesdale, Robert Prosky, Edward Hardwicke, and Joan Plowright. The highly erotic film, removed by several lifetimes and cultures from Hawthorne's Puritan New England, was not very well received by critics or at the box office.

Duvall also starred as Mr. Cox, a 1930s Texas oil wildcatter who is trying to find just one more stake to fund another "sure-thing" oil strike, in *The Stars Fall on Henrietta*, directed by James Keach and costarring Brian Dennehy, Aidan Quinn, and Frances Fisher.

Forthcoming were starring film roles in *A Family Thing*, directed by Richard Pearce, playing opposite James Earl Jones; *Phenomenon*, directed by George Bamber and costarring John Travolta, Kyra Sedgwick, and Forest Whitaker; *Something to Talk About*, costarring Julia Roberts, Dennis Quaid, and Gena Rowlands; and *Slingblade*, written and directed by Billy Bob Thornton and costarring John Ritter, Dwight Yoakam, and J. T. Walsh.

San Diego–born Duvall was recognized as a powerful supporting actor in such films as *To Kill a Mockingbird* (1962), *True Grit* (1969), *M*A*S*H* (1970), the first two *Godfather* films (1972; 1974), *Network* (1976), and *Apocalypse Now* (1979). He went on to win a best actor Oscar for his lead in *Tender Mercies* (1983), while continuing to play strong supporting roles and sometimes leads in such films as *Colors* (1988), *Days of Thunder* (1990), *The Handmaid's Tale* (1990), *Rambling Rose* (1991), *Convicts* (1991), *Wrestling Ernest Hemingway* (1993), *Geronimo* (1993), *Falling Down* (1993), and *The Paper* (1994). Among his many television appearances were the title role as a notable Dwight D. Eisenhower in the miniseries *Ike* (1979) and the title role in the 1992 television film *Stalin*. A graduate of Principia College, Duvall is married to Gail Youngs.

FURTHER READING

"Robert Duvall." LAURA DERN. *Interview*, Oct. 1991.

Dylan, Bob (Robert Alan Zimmerman; 1941–)

Legendary singer and songwriter Bob Dylan was once again honored by his peers in 1995, winning a best traditional folk album Grammy Award for his folk and blues album

World Gone Wrong. Dylan also issued the album *MTV Unplugged*, which included new renditions of several of his classic works, including "The Times They Are A-Changin'" and "Like A Rolling Stone," as well as several more recent works. He and his work also appeared in some of the new technological forms; among these were the enhanced CD *Bob Dylan's Greatest Hits, Volume Three,* and the interactive CD-ROM disc *Highway 61,* which included a good deal of unreleased audio and visual material from Dylan's own files and those of his publishers and producers, including several music videos and a group of Dylan's drawings.

Duluth-born Dylan was one of the leading countercultural figures of the early 1960s, an enormously popular folk-rock singer and composer known to millions for many of his own songs, such as "The Times They Are A-Changin'" (1963) and "Blowin' in the Wind" (1963). Later in the 1960s, and through the 1970s and 1980s, he was much more a rock than a folk-rock musician. Although he continued to be a very popular figure in concert and on records, his impact was greatest in the early years, when he burst upon the scene as a 1960s emblem of protest.

Dylan made a substantial comeback on records and in performance, starting in 1989, with his album *Oh Mercy* and its world tour. His 1990 new album *Under the Red Sky* was very well received, as were two *Traveling Wilburys* albums (1988; 1990), made with George Harri-

son, Tom Petty, Jeff Lynne, and (on the first album, made before his late 1988 death) Roy Orbison. Later releases included *The Bootleg Series, Volumes 1–3 (Rare and Unreleased) 1961–91* (1991) and the music video *Bob Dylan: The 30th Anniversary Concert Celebration* (1992). Dylan attended the University of Minnesota, in 1960. His further albums include *Good As I Been to You* (1992) and *World Gone Wrong* (1993). His book *Road Drawings* was published in 1994.

FURTHER READING

"A primitive's portfolio." MALCOLM JONES, JR. *Newsweek,* Mar. 20, 1995.
Bob Dylan. SUSAN RICHARDSON. Chelsea House, 1995.
Bob Dylan: A Descriptive, Critical Discography and Filmography, 1961–1994. JOHN NOGOWSKI. McFarland, 1995.
Bob Dylan's Words: A Critical Dictionary and Commentary. RICHARD D. WISSOLIK and SCOTT McGRATH. Eadmer, 1994.
Bob Dylan: Performance Artist Early Years 60–73. Bob Dylan: Performance Artist Mid Years 74–86. Omnibus, 1994.
Bob Dylan. PAT MATHIAS. Creative Ed, 1994.
"Knockin' on heaven's door. . . ." BOB CANNON. Entertainment, July 30, 1993.
Bob Dylan: A Bio-Bibliography. WILLIAM McKEEN. Greenwood, 1993.
"Bringing folk back home. . . ." JAY COCKS. *Time,* Oct. 26, 1992.
Alias Bob Dylan. STEPHEN SCOBIE. Empire Publication Services, 1992.
Bob Dylan: A Man Called Alias. RICHARD WILLIAMS. Holt, 1992.
Hard Rain: A Dylan Commentary. TIM RILEY. Knopf, 1992.
"Dylan, Bob." *Current Biography,* Oct. 1991.
"Bob Dylan. . . ." TOM PIAZZA. *New York Times Book Review,* May 26, 1991.
Bob Dylan Behind the Shades. CLINTON HEYLIN. Summit, 1991.
Wanted Man: In Search of Bob Dylan. JOHN BAULDIE, ed. Carol, 1991.
Dylan Companion: A Collection of Essential Writing about Bob Dylan. ELIZABETH THOMSON. Delacorte, 1991.
Bob Dylan: Portraits from the Singer's Early Years. DANIEL KRAMER. Carol, 1991.
Bob Dylan, Performing Artist: The Early Years 1960–1973. PAUL WILLIAMS. Underwood-Miller, 1991.
Positively Bob Dylan: A Thirty-Year Discography, Concert and Recording Session Guide, 1960–1989. MICHAEL KROGSGAARD. Popular Culture, 1991.

Eastwood, Clint (1930–) Now a massive figure in world cinema, Clint Eastwood continued to be honored by his peers in 1995. He was awarded the highly prestigious Irving G. Thalberg Award at the March Academy Award ceremonies, was slated to receive the annual American Film Institute's Life Achievement Award in February 1996, and was to be honored at the May 1996 Film Society of Lincoln Center gala.

Eastwood's major film of the year was *The Bridges of Madison County*, adapted for film by Richard LaGravenese from the best-selling Robert James Waller novel. Eastwood directed and

Clint Eastwood (right) and Rene Russo.

starred as photographer Robert Kincaid opposite Meryl Streep as Francesca Johnson, in a cast that included Annie Corley, Victor Slezak, and Jim Haynie. Set in Madison County, Iowa, farm country in 1965, the film straightforwardly tells the story of the brief, passionate love affair between the roving photographer and the farm housewife, whose husband and children are away, an affair that was portrayed as central to their lives, although they never met again. The film was far better critically received than the book had been, and also did well at the box office, although it was not a runaway hit, as the novel had been.

Eastwood also released the soundtrack to *The Bridges of Madison County*; *The Bridges of Madison County Memory Book*, containing his own photographs; and a two-disc biographical multimedia CD-ROM *Eastwood*, which contained a very wide range of video, audio, and written materials on his life and work.

On the personal side, Eastwood won a $150,000 award from a Los Angeles federal jury, which held that *National Enquirer* had fabricated a fictitious interview with him about his personal life. He said he would donate the award to charity.

San Francisco–born Eastwood was a star in television as the lead in the western series "Rawhide" (1958–65). He pursued the same western themes in the Italian-made Sergio Leone "spaghetti westerns" that made him a worldwide star, beginning with *A Fistful of Dollars* (1967). He then went on to become one of the most durable of all international action film stars. Beginning with *Play Misty For Me* (1971), he directed, produced, and starred in many of his films, such as *Honkytonk Man* (1982), *Bird* (1988; about jazz great Charlie Parker), *White Hunter, Black Heart* (1990), and *The Rookie* (1990). He won a best director Oscar for and starred in the Oscar-winning film *The Unforgiven* (1992), directed and starred in *A Perfect World* (1993), and starred in *In the Line of Fire* (1993). Eastwood attended Los Angeles City College. He also served as mayor of Carmel, California (1986–88). Previously divorced, Eastwood has three children; his son, Kyle, appeared in *Honkytonk Man.*

FURTHER READING

"Giving good Clint." DEREK MALCOLM. *Guardian,* Sept. 1, 1995.
"Clint Eastwood." DAVID WILD. *Rolling Stone,* Aug. 24, 1995.
"Clint Eastwood. . . ." JAMES GRANT. *Good Housekeeping,* July 1995.
"Clint Eastwood plays Misty." DOUG STANTON. *Esquire,* June 1995.
Clint Eastwood. ROBERT TANITCH. Sterling, 1995.
Clint Eastwood. Random House, 1995.
Clint Eastwood: A Biography. MINTY CLINCH. Trafalgar, 1995.
Clint Eastwood: The Man and His Films. EDWARD GALLAFENT. Continuum, 1994.
"Eastwood's world." ANNE THOMPSON. *Entertainment,* Dec. 10, 1993.
"Clint Eastwood. . . ." GIL GIBSON. *Ladies Home Journal,* Aug. 1993.
"Architectural Digest. . . ." SUSAN CHEEVER. *Architectural Digest,* July 1993.
"Go ahead. . . ." PAUL A. WITTEMAN. *Time,* Apr. 5, 1993.
"Clint Eastwood. . . ." STUART FISCHOFF. *Psychology Today,* Jan.–Feb. 1993.
Clint Eastwood: Riding High. DOUGLAS THOMPSON. Contemporary, 1993.
Clint Eastwood: Hollywood's Loner. MICHAEL MUNN. Parkwest, 1993.
The Films of Clint Eastwood. BORIS ZMIJEWSKY and LEE PFEIFFER. Carol, 1993.
Clint Eastwood: A Cultural Production. PAUL SMITH. University of Minnesota Press, 1993.

Eazy-E (Eric Wright; 1964–95) Born in Compton, California, Eazy-E was a leading "gangsta rap" pioneer, music company entrepreneur, and record producer. In 1988, he issued his debut hard-core rap album *Eazy-Duz-It,* which propelled him into the top rank of rhythm-and-blues performers, and paved the way for several more solo albums, and for the formation of the hard-core rap group "NWA," which also included Ice Cube, Dr. Dre, M. D. Ren, and Yella. The group became a major element of the new hard-core rap movement, with such albums as *Straight Outta Compton* and *Efil4zaggin.* Its songs, with their antiwoman, anti-authority, pro-violence lyrics drew enormous criticism and also proved enormously attractive to some young audiences. Eazy-E also founded the Ruthless Records label, becoming a successful music industry figure.

Shortly before his death, Eric Wright announced that he had AIDS; he died of complication caused by AIDS. He was survived by his wife, Tomika Woods, and their son; and by his parents, a sister, and a brother. (d. Los Angeles; March 26, 1995)

FURTHER READING

Obituary. *Rolling Stone,* May 4, 1995.
"Gangsta rapper. . . ." *Jet,* Apr. 10, 1995.
"Straight outta time. . . ." *People,* Apr. 10, 1995.
Obituary. *New York Times,* Mar. 28, 1995.

Eckert, John Presper (1919–95) Electrical engineer and computer scientist John Presper Eckert was the coinventor of the ENIAC computer. In 1943, while teaching at the University of Pennsylvania, where he had earned his bachelor's degree in electrical engineering, he joined John W. Mauchly in inventing and—with massive federal funding—developing the pioneering Electronic Numerical Integrator and Computer (ENIAC), to be used in solving artillery ballistics problems. ENIAC, in place by 1945, was also used in the Manhattan Project, to develop nuclear weaponry. For decades, ENIAC was thought to have been the first electronic computer, and Eckert continued to claim that was so, although a federal judge in 1973 voided the ENIAC patent during a lawsuit over disputed royalties. The court found that the first electronic computer had been the Atanasoff-Berry Computer (ABC), developed by John Atanasoff and Clifford Berry (1939–42), which Mauchly had closely studied in that earlier period. In 1946, Eckert and Mauchly founded the Electronic Control Company, forerunner of the modern Unisys company, and developed several other computers, including the UNIVAC. He was survived by his wife, Judith, a daughter, and three sons. (d. Bryn Mawr, Pennsylvania; June 3, 1995)

FURTHER READING

Obituary. *Independent,* June 23, 1995.
Obituary. *New York Times,* June 7, 1995.
"The soul. . . ." BEN YAGODA. *Philadelphia,* Apr. 1992.
"What hath . . . ?" DAVID R. BROUSELL. *Datamation,* Mar. 15, 1991.

Eco, Umberto (1932–) Italian author

and professor Umberto Eco became an international celebrity when his 1981 novel *The Name of the Rose* became a 1983 best-seller, in English translation and then around the world, selling more than 50 million copies. In late 1994, the literary-philosophical murder mystery was published in a new edition, including a postscript in which Eco describes its creation. In 1995, English readers delighted in a new novel by Eco, *The Island of the Day Before,* a mysterious literary tale focusing on 17th-century Italian nobleman Roberto della Griva, shipwrecked in the South Pacific, and his writings aboard an abandoned ship; with the island of the title lying a short distance away, across the international dateline. Though some reviewers criticized the novel for trying to follow too many story lines, others praised its erudite humor, wordplay, and philosophical musings. By December, when the author was on an American promotional tour, the book had reached the best-seller list. During 1995, Eco also saw two other books published in English, *The Search for the Perfect Language,* a wide-ranging and erudite historical study of human ideas about and proposals for a universal language, and *Interpretation and Overinterpretation.*

Italian-born Eco studied at the University degli Studi, at Turin. He worked with Italian Television (1954–59) while beginning his professorial career as a lecturer in aesthetics at the University of Turin (1956–63). He moved on to the faculty of architecture at the University of Milan (1963–65), became professor of visual communication at the University of Florence (1966–69), then professor of semiotics at Milan Polytechnic (1970–71) and then at the University of Bologna (1971–), since that time also serving as editor for *VS* (1971–). He has also been a frequent visiting professor abroad, most notably at New York University (1969–70; 1976), Northwestern University (1972), Yale University (1977; 1980; 1981), Columbia University (1978; 1984), and Harvard University (1993). His first two books, published in 1956 and 1959, were translated into English as *The Aesthetics of Thomas Aquinas* (1988) and *Art and Beauty in the Middle Ages* (1986). Numerous other academic works followed, such as *The Open Work* (1962), *A Theory of Semiotics* (1976), *The Role of the Reader* (1979), and *Semiotics and Philosophy of Language* (1984). But Eco came to wide public attention only with his novels *The Name of the Rose* (1981) and *Foucault's Pendulum* (1988). This gave a wider audience to his later books in English publication, including *The Limits of Interpretation* (1990), *Misreadings* (1993), *Apocalypse Postponed: Essays by Umberto Eco* (1994), and *How to Travel with a Salmon and Other Essays* (1994). His six Norton lectures, given at Harvard University in 1993, were published as *Six Walks in the Fictional Woods* (1994). Eco married Renata Ramge in 1962; they have two children.

FURTHER READING

" 'I went out. . . .' " JOHN HOOPER. *Guardian,* Sept. 30, 1995.
"Tolerance and. . . ." ROGER-POL DROIT. *New Statesman & Society,* Apr. 22, 1994.
"Umberto Eco." FRANCOIS-BERNARD HUYGHE. *UNESCO Courier,* June 1993.

Eddington, Paul (Paul Clark-Eddington;

1927–95) London-born actor Paul Eddington, a Quaker pacifist during World War II, began his theater career with the Birmingham Repertory after the war, also attending the Royal Academy of Dramatic Arts (1951). He toured in repertory and played in supporting roles in the London theater during the 1950s and 1960s, also working in television from the late 1950s. During the 1960s, he worked largely with the Bristol Old Vic company. His breakthrough came with the Jerry Ledbetter role, opposite Penelope Keith as Margo Ledbetter, in television's "The Good Life." (1975–79) He became a major star in the Hacker role in "Yes, Minister," which became "Yes, Prime Minister" in 1986, when Hacker became prime minister in the series. Eddington continued to appear on stage during his years as a television star, most notably in a prize-winning appearance opposite Harold Pinter in a 1993 revival of *No Man's Land.*

Although a television show prime minister during a period of Conservative ascendancy, World War II dissenter Eddington was a lifelong Labour Party member and a supporter of nuclear disarmament. His autobiography was *So Far, So Good* (1995). He was survived by his wife, actress Patricia Scott, a daughter, and three sons. (d. London; November 4, 1995)

FURTHER READING

Obituary. *Independent,* Nov. 7, 1995.
Obituary. *Times* (of London), Nov. 7, 1995.
Obituary. *New York Times*, Nov. 7, 1995.
"Transformation scene." ADAM SWEETING. *Guardian,* Oct. 17, 1995.

Edmonds, Kenneth: See Babyface.

Eisenstaedt, Alfred (1898–1995) One of the leading photojournalists of the century, German-born Alfred Eisenstaedt grew up in Berlin, saw army service in World War I, and began his long career as a photographer in the 1920s. An antifascist, he emigrated to the United States in 1935, after the Nazi takeover. Eisenstaedt became an acclaimed photojournalist and portraitist during his long and celebrated association with *Life* magazine (from 1936 to his death), perhaps most notably for his informal shots, taken largely with a 35-millimeter Leica camera. Although he shot portraits of a wide range of celebrities, from Marlene Dietrich to presidents John F. Kennedy and Bill Clinton, Eisenstaedt's V-J photos in Times Square were by far his best known works. Many of his finest photos are collected in such books as *Witness to Our Time* (1966), *The Eye of Eisenstaedt* (1969), *Eisenstaedt's Album: Fifty Years of Friends and Acquaintances* (1976), *Witness to Our Time* (1980), *Eisenstaedt: Remembrances* (1990). His wife, Kathy Kaye, predeceased him; there were no survivors. (d. Martha's Vineyard, Massachusetts; August 23, 1995).

FURTHER READING

Obituary. *Petersen's Photographic,* Jan. 1996.
"Eisenstaedt, Alfred." *Current Biography,* Oct. 1995.
"The old master." BRAD DARRACH. *Life,* Oct. 1995.
Obituary. *Newsweek,* Sept. 4, 1995.
"A poet and his camera. . . ." *Time,* Sept. 4, 1995.
"A shadow. . . ." ALEXANDER WOLFF and KOSTYA KENNEDY. *Sports Illustrated*, Sept. 4, 1995.
Obituary. *Independent,* Aug. 25, 1995.
Obituary. *Times* (of London), Aug. 25, 1995.
Obituary. *New York Times*, Aug. 25, 1995.

Eisner, Michael Dammann (1942–) On July 31, 1995, Walt Disney Company chairman Michael D. Eisner and Capital Cities/ABC chairman Thomas S. Murphy startled the entertainment and communications worlds by announcing the combination of their two companies into a massive media conglomerate, with Disney acquiring Capital Cities and with it the American Broadcasting Company for $19 billion. The resulting company, controlled by Eisner, owned major broadcast and cable television, film production and distribution, theme park, radio, and publishing properties, immediately becoming the world's largest entertainment company. For Eisner, the acquisition meant becoming one of the world's most influential communications magnates. Two weeks later, Eisner, who had always refused to seriously share power in his companies, made a move that again startled his world, hiring powerful Hollywood agent and corporate dealmaker Michael Ovitz to be his second in command, as president of the Walt Disney Company. At year's end, more surprises were expected, as Eisner and Ovitz developed their new relationship and immense new company.

Eisner has spent his entire working life on the entertainment side of the communications industries. After graduating from Denison University in 1964, his first job was as a clerk at NBC. He soon moved to CBS, where he worked in the children's programming department, and moved to the children's programming department at ABC (1966). There he became a protégé of Barry Diller and rose swiftly, working in program development. At ABC, he was vice president of daytime programming (1971–75), vice president of program planning and development (1975–76), and senior vice president of prime time production and development (1976). He joined Diller at

Paramount Pictures (1976), as president and chief operating officer (1976–84).

In 1984, he moved to the ailing Disney Studios as chairman and chief executive officer; with associates Frank Wells and Jeffrey Katzenberg, he turned Disney around, building its revenues from less than $2 billion to $10 billion a year, and emerged as one of Hollywood's most powerful and best paid company heads. Eisner encountered significant problems in 1994–95. Wells was killed in a plane crash in April 1994; Katzenberg left Disney in August, their bitter breakup stemming from Katzenberg's feeling that Eisner was not willing enough to share corporate power with him. On the personal side, Eisner encountered health problems, needing heart bypass surgery. Eisner was born in Mt. Kisco, New York. He is married to Jane Breckenridge; they have three children.

FURTHER READING

"Call it the great. . . ." RONALD GROVER et al. *Business Week,* Sept. 25, 1995.

"Planetized entertainment." NATHAN GARDELS. *New Perspectives Quarterly,* Fall 1995.

"From heart surgery. . . ." BETSY STREISAND. *U.S. News & World Report,* Aug. 14, 1995.

"Eisner explains everything." JOHN HUEY. *Fortune,* Apr. 17, 1995.

"Of Mickey Mouse and men." JEANNETTE WALLS. *Esquire,* Mar. 1995.

"A mouse divided." KIM MASTERS. *Vanity Fair,* Nov. 1994.

Michael Eisner: Fun for Everyone. SHERILL TIPPINS. Garrett, 1992.

"America's best CEOs." TRACY E. BENSON. *Industry Week,* Dec. 2, 1991.

" 'For every Bruce Willis . . . .' " JOSEPH NOCERA. *GQ,* Oct. 1991.

Prince of the Magic Kingdom: Michael Eisner and the Re-Making of Disney. JOE FLOWER. Wiley, 1991.

The Disney Touch: How a Daring Management Team Revived an Entertainment Empire. RON GROVER. Irwin, 1991.

Elgabrony, Ibraham A.: See Abdel Rahman, Omar.

Elhassan, Tarig: See Abdel Rahman, Omar.

Elizabeth II

Elizabeth II Elizabeth Alexandra Mary; 1926–) For Queen Elizabeth, 1995 seemed to be a year in which she could concentrate on the quiet, methodical rebuilding of her family's very badly battered public image, without new scandals or "revelations" regarding the personal lives of any of her children or their spouses. Until late November, the only matter the media could get its collective teeth into was the tag-end of the media circus generated in 1994 by Prince Charles's highly publicized personal observations about his marriage to Princess Diana, his relationship with his father, and his long adulterous relationship with Camilla Parker Bowles, who with her husband Brigadier Andrew Parker Bowles, announced her coming divorce in early January.

But it was not to be; 1995 was the year of the Diana Interview. In late November, Princess Diana, who had been rather quiet during 1995, though still the object of enormous media attention, provided the material for a whole new British royal family media circus. In a long televised interview with BBC reporter Martin Bashir, she talked about her estranged husband's long-term adultery; her own extramarital affair; her isolation and neglect at the hands of her Prince Charles, the royal family and their set; the damage caused by the constant attention of the media; and her years of bulimia, allegedly brought on by all the rest. The interview, which immediately caused an enormous public outcry, was seen by an estimated 27 million people in Britain, and later by many millions more abroad— and the British royals had another very, very bad year. Widespread calls for a Diana-Charles divorce followed, while Queen Elizabeth faced an even more completely shattered family image. Ultimately, in late December, she wrote to Charles and Diana, urging them to quickly divorce, a course reportedly favored by Charles.

During 1995, Elizabeth made a notable visit to the new South Africa, which—in protest against South Africa's then-racist policies—she had not visited since 1947, five years before she took the throne. She exchanged honors with President Nelson Mandela and toured the country. She also visited Northern Ireland, at least temporarily at peace, in tacit support of the negotiations then in progress. On May 6, she was host to a group of world leaders commemorating the 50th anniversary of V-E Day, the end of World War II in the west.

Elizabeth II is the daughter of George VI and

Elizabeth Angela Marguerite, the queen mother. She succeeded her father to the throne in 1952, becoming Queen of the United Kingdom of Great Britain and Northern Ireland. She married Philip Mountbatten, the Duke of Edinburgh, in 1947, and is the mother of Prince Charles (1948–), Princess Anne (1950–), Prince Andrew (1960–), and Prince Edward (1964–).

FURTHER READING

The Queen: Royality and Reality. KENNETH HARRIS. St. Martin's, 1995.
"Distant relations. . . ." MALCOLM GRAY. *Maclean's,* Oct. 31, 1994.
"Royally screwed." DENIS JUDD. *New Statesman & Society,* Oct. 28, 1994.
Queen Elizabeth II: A Woman Who Is Not Amused. NICHOLAS DAVIES. Carol, 1994.
Queen Elizabeth II. SUSAN AUERBACH. Rourke, 1993.
The Queen: The New Biography. JOHN PARKER. Trafalgar, 1993.
Elizabeth R: The Role of the Monarchy Today. ANTONY JAY. Parkwest, 1993.
Elizabeth and Philip. CHARLES HIGHAM and ROY MOSELEY. Berkley, 1993.
"God save the Queen!" ROBERT K. MASSIE. *Vanity Fair,* Oct. 1992.
The Queen: A Revealing Look at the Private Life of Elizabeth II. DOUGLAS KEAY. St. Martin's, 1992.
Sovereign: Elizabeth II and the Windsor Dynasty. ROLAND FLAMINI. Delacorte, 1991.

Elkin, Stanley (1930–95) New York City–born Stanley Elkin, a novelist, short story writer, and teacher, grew up in Chicago. His 1952 B.A., 1953 M.A., and 1961 Ph.D., all in English literature, were from the University of Illinois. His debut novel was *Boswell* (1964), a absurdist satirical work in which he sets a figure much like that of Scottish biographer James Boswell into the modern world. His second published work was the very well received short story collection *Criers and Kibitzers, Kibitzers and Criers* (1966), which brought him into the first rank of modern American writers. He also published the collections *Searches and Seizures* (1973) and *Van Gogh's Room at Arles* (1992). Elkin's novels also included *A Bad Man* (1967); *The Dick Gibson Show* (1971), set in the world of early radio; *The Franchiser* (1976); *The Living End* (1979); *George Mills* (1982; he won the National Book Critics Circle Award); *The Magic Kingdom* (1985); *The Rabbi of Lud* (1987); *The*

MacGuffin (1993); and *Mrs. Ted Bliss* (1995), published posthumously.

Elkin spent his entire teaching career at St. Louis' Washington University (1960–1995), where he became a full professor in 1969. He was survived by his wife, Joan, a daughter, two sons, and a sister. (d. St. Louis; May 31, 1995)

FURTHER READING

"Remembering. . . ." GEOFFREY WOLFF. *New York Times Book Review,* Sept. 17, 1995.
"Elkin, Stanley Lawrence." *Current Biography,* Aug. 1995.
Obituary. *New York Times,* June 2, 1995.
" 'A hat where. . . .' " PETER J. BAILEY. *The Observer,* May 28, 1995.
Comic Sense: Reading Robert Couver, Stanley Elkin, Philip Roth. THOMAS PUGHE. Birkhauser, 1994.
"The indecorous. . . ." KEN EMERSON. *New York Times Magazine,* Mar. 3, 1991.

Endfield, Cy (Cyril Baker Endfield; 1914–95) Scranton-born Cy Endfield attended Yale University and studied at New York's New Theater School in the late 1930s. After directing several short films in Hollywood in the early 1940s, he saw World War II military service. Returning to Hollywood, he began to direct feature films, beginning with *Gentleman Joe Palooka* (1946). His most notable Hollywood films were *The Un-*

derworld Story (1950) and *The Sound of Fury* (1951). Endfield was blacklisted by the film industry after the House Un-American Activities Committee accused him being a Communist sympathizer; like many other artists and intellectuals of that time, he then fled to England, where he was able to pursue his career—though until 1957 he worked uncredited or under a pseudonym. He emerged as a major British director after the McCarthy period had ended, beginning with *Hell Drivers* (1957), for which he also wrote the screenplay. Among his further films were *Sea Fury* (1958), *Jet Storm* (1959), *Mysterious Island*(1961), *Hide and Seek* (1964), the very notable *Zulu* (1964; which he cowrote and coproduced), *Sands of the Kalahari* (1965), and *Universal Soldier* (1971). He also wrote the screenplay for *Zulu Dawn* (1979). Multitalented Endfield was from his youth also a highly regarded magician. He was survived by his second wife, Maureen, and two daughters. (d. Shipston-on-Stour, England; April 16, 1995)

FURTHER READING

Obituary. *New York Times*, May 2, 1995.
Obituary. *Times* (of London), May 1, 1995.
Obituary. *Independent*, Apr. 21, 1995.
"Pages from. . . ." JONATHAN ROSENBAUM. *Film Comment*, Nov.–Dec. 1993.

Estefan, Gloria Maria (Gloria Maria Fajardo; 1957–)

Pop star Gloria Estefan worked very successfully in both of her musical languages during 1995. In English she continued to build on her 1994 hit album *Hold Me, Thrill Me, Kiss Me*, issuing "Everlasting Love," drawn from the album, which quickly became a hit single, and won a Billboard music video award as "Clip of the Year." From the same source, she issued a second hit single "It's Too Late," a Carole King hit from King's classic *Tapestry*; and a third, "Cherchez La Femme." *Hold Me, Thrill Me, Kiss Me*, well on its way to becoming a classic itself, topped 2 million sales in 1995.

Estefan's new 1995 album was the Spanish-language smash hit *Abriendo Puertas* (*Opening Doors*), which quickly became a top Latino album in the U.S. and was distributed with great success to worldwide Spanish-language audiences, its songs reflecting several Latin-

American and Afro-Caribbean musical traditions. Its title track became a hit single, as did a second single drawn from the album, "Más Allá" ("Beyond").

On the business side, Estefan won a court battle when bandleader Eddie Palmieri's plagiarism suit against her was dismissed; their dispute was over a line in the song "Oye Mi Canto." On the personal side, in late 1995 a college student was killed when he ran his "wet bike" into the rear of a boat piloted by Estefan and her husband, who were judged to be not at fault.

Havana-born Estefan emigrated to the United States with her family at age two, and grew up in the Miami area. She emerged as a very popular composer, singer, and recording star in the late 1980s, with such songs as "Anything for You" (1987), "Rhythm Is Gonna Get You" (1987), "Don't Wanna Lose You" (1989), and "Coming Out of the Dark" (1991), winning several Grammy nominations. Her albums include *Primitive Love* (1985), *Let It Loose* (1987), *Cuts Both Ways* (1989), *Into the Light* (1991), and *Greatest Hits* (1992). In 1987, she sang at the Seoul Olympics and the St. Louis World Series, and in 1992 at the Super Bowl. In March 1990, while touring, she was very seriously injured in a bus accident, but made an extraordinary recovery, returning to her career only a year later. Estefan has been very active in philanthropic activities, as in campaigns against AIDS and leukemia, and for disaster relief, and has received several humanitarian awards. She had her biggest success reaching for her Cuban roots with *Mi Tierra* (1993). Her B.A. was from the University of Miami. She is married to Emilio Estefan, Jr.; they have a son and a daughter.

FURTHER READING

"Clothes encounter." PETER CASTRO. *People,* Nov. 6, 1995.
"Estefan, Gloria." *Current Biography,* Oct. 1995.
"The power and the Gloria." PHILIP SWEENEY. *Guardian,* Oct. 6, 1995.
"Gloria hallelujah!" LAURA MORICE. *McCall's,* July 1995.
Gloria Estefan. JANEL RODRIGUEZ. Raintree Steck-Vaughn, 1995.
Gloria Estefan. DAVID SHIRLEY. Chelsea House, 1994.
"Miami's patron saint." LEONARD PITTS, JR. *Entertainment,* July 30, 1993.
Gloria Estefan: International Pop Star. SHELLY NIELSEN. Abdo & Daughters, 1993.
Gloria Estefan, Cuban-American Singing Star. FERNANDO GONZALEZ. Millbrook, 1993.
"Love and money." ANNA MARIA ARIAS. *Hispanic,* May 1991.
Gloria Estefan. Rebecca Stefoff. Chelsea House, 1991.
Gloria Estefan. GRACE CATALANO. St. Martin's, 1991.

Etheridge, Melissa (1962–) Singer, songwriter, and guitarist Melissa Etheridge added even further to her status as a worldwide rock superstar in 1995. With her 1993 album *Yes I Am* topping 6 million sales and still on the Billboard 200 chart two years after its release, she issued yet another blockbuster album, *Your Little Secret,* which quickly moved into the top ten range, making its debut at number 6 on the Billboard 200 chart. Its title song was also issued as a single; two other songs were clearly also slated to be hits: "I Could Have Been You," and "I Want You To Come Over."

Etheridge won a 1995 Grammy Award for best female rock vocal performance for "Come To My Window." She also received Grammy nominations for best female rock vocal performance for "Supernova," and best rock songwriter for the songs "Come To My Window" and "I'm The Only One." With several other stars ultimately headed for the Hall of Fame, she appeared at the September 3 Cleveland Stadium concert celebrating the opening of the Rock and Roll Hall of Fame and Museum.

Etheridge began composing and performing as a child in her home town, Leavenworth, Kansas. She studied at Boston's Berklee College of Music (1980) and began her professional career singing in cabarets in the Boston area. She moved to Los Angeles in 1982, singing and playing in cabaret. Her debut album was *Melissa Etheridge* (1988), with its hit single "Similar Features"; it was followed by the albums *Brave and Crazy* (1989) and *Never Enough* (1992), with its hit single "Ain't It Heavy," for which she won a 1993 Grammy for best female vocalist. Her third album was *Yes I Am* (1993). She also wrote several songs for the 1987 film *Weeds.*

In January 1993, at the Triangle Ball, one of the Washington, D.C. events honoring the inauguration of President Bill Clinton, Etheridge announced that she was of lesbian sexual preference. Her partner is Julie Cypher.

FURTHER READING

"Melissa Etheridge." FRED SCHRUERS. *Us,* Dec. 1995.
"One of the boys." LUCY O'BRIEN. *Guardian,* Nov. 3, 1995.
"Etheridge, Melissa." *Current Biography,* May 1995.
"Step four. . . ." DANA KENNEDY. *Entertainment,* Mar. 17, 1995.
"Melissa Etheridge. . . ." RICH COHEN. *Rolling Stone,* Dec. 29, 1994.
"Melissa Etheridge." INGRID CASARES. *Interview,* Oct. 1994.
"Melissa. . . ." JUDY WIEDER. *Advocate,* July 26, 1994.
"Melissa Etheridge." STACEU D'ERASMO. *Rolling Stone,* June 2, 1994.

Evers-Williams, Myrlie (Myrlie Louise Beasley; 1933–)

On February 18, 1995, the deeply divided board of directors of the National Association for the Advancement of Colored People (NAACP) voted 30–29 to install Myrlie Evers-Williams as its chairperson, replacing Dr. William F. Gibson. Gibson and several associates had been charged by their detractors with contributing to the huge financial problems faced by the NAACP, and had even been the subject of a highly critical "60 Minutes" television show segment the previous Sunday, which weighed heavily in the vote. The extent of the NAACP debt was unknown; a treasurer's report put it at $2.3 million, while Evers-Williams supporters put it at more than $4 million. In addition, the prestige of the 84-year-old organization had been greatly damaged by the publicity surrounding the 1994 firing of executive director Benjamin Chavis, with its charges of financial irregularities. Evers-Williams faced a set of very difficult tasks in reuniting and revitalizing the NAACP, the leading American civil rights organization of the 20th century.

On the personal side, her husband, retired longshoreman Walter Williams, died of cancer just four days after her election to the office he had urged her to seek.

Born in Vicksburg, Mississippi, Myrlie Beasley attended Alcorn A.& M. College, there meeting and marrying her first husband, Medgar Evers. He ultimately became a lawyer and Mississippi state chairman of the NAACP; she left college after marrying him and became an office worker with the NAACP. On June 12, 1963, he was murdered at their home in Jackson, Mississippi. Almost 31 years and three murder trials later, in 1994, racist Byron De La Beckwith was convicted of the Evers murder and sentenced to life imprisonment.

After her husband's murder Myrlie Evers moved to California with her three children, earned her B.A. degree at Pomona College, and embarked on a long and varied career that included a job as director of planning for Pomona College, executive positions at a New York advertising agency and the Atlantic Richfield oil company, two unsuccessful runs for political office, and a job as Los Angeles commissioner of public works.

FURTHER READING

"Binding the ties. . . ." PAUL RUFFINS. *Nation,* Oct. 30, 1995.

"Evers-Williams, Myrlie." *Current Biography,* Aug. 1995.

"Trials and transformation. . . ." KAREN GRIGSBY BATES. *Emerge,* Feb. 1994.

Ewing, Patrick Aloysius (1962–)

The year 1995 was another heartbreaker for New York Knicks center Patrick Ewing. In the previous year, the basketball team had gone all the way to the NBA Finals, there losing to the Houston Rockets. Throughout the 1994–95 season, Ewing and the Knicks were pointed toward a rematch. But in the end, it was not to be. After defeating Cleveland with relative ease in the first round of the Eastern Conference playoffs, the Knicks fell to Indiana in a grueling seven-game series, losing in the final game by only two points, after a Ewing finger-roll failed to go in. During the regular season, Ewing had been sixth in the league in scoring (averaging 23.9 points a game), eighth in blocked shots (2.01), fourth in rebounding (11.0), and was an All-Star for the ninth time, the oldest player in the All-Star game. He was also one of several NBA stars featured in the new video *NBA Jams: The Music Videos.*

During the summer, Ewing again underwent minor knee surgery, but returned ready to make another try for the elusive championship—this time under new coach Don Nelson. Ewing was one of several key players who were unhappy with the NBA player's union agreement with the league, and led attempts to decertify the union, but eventually accepted the union-wide vote to accept the agreement. His own current contract runs into 1997, but he said in September that he expected to play beyond then. At year's end, the Knicks had a 19-9 record, sixth best in the league, and Ewing himself was sixth in the league in blocked shots, averaging 2.78 a game, and was scoring an average of 21.0 points a game.

Jamaica-born Ewing came to America at age 11. He emerged as one of the leading centers in modern basketball while he was still a college player at Georgetown University, where he took his team to three National Collegiate Athletic Association (NCAA) finals (1982; 1984; 1985), winning the championship in 1984, when he was named Most Valuable Player of the Final Four. In his senior year, he won a host of "player of the year" awards, including the Kodak Award, Rupp Trophy, and Naismith Trophy. After his 1985 graduation, Ewing joined the New York Knicks, beginning a career that would take him to nine All-Star games (1986; 1988–95, as starting center 1990–92). Ewing has also been on two Olympic gold-medal-winning teams, in 1984 and with the "Dream Team" at Barcelona in 1992. He released the video *Patrick Ewing: Standing Tall* in 1993. Ewing married Rita Williams in 1990; they have one daughter; he also has a son from a previous relationship.

FURTHER READING

"Title search. . . ." BARRY M. BLOOM. *Sport,* Feb. 1995.

"Quest for the ring." RICK WEINBERG. *Sport,* May 1994.

Head to Head Basketball: Patrick Ewing and Alonzo Mourning. NEIL COHEN. Bantam, 1994.

Patrick Ewing: Center of Attention. HOWARD REISER. Children's, 1994.

"Michael Jordan vs. . . ." GEORGE CASTLE and GARY BINFORD. *Sport,* May 1993.

Sports Great Patrick Ewing. JACK KAVANAGH. Enslow, 1992.

"Ewing, Patrick." *Current Biography,* May 1991.

Farrakhan, Louis Haleem Abdul

(Louis Eugene Wolcott; 1933–) Nation of Islam head Louis Farrakhan scored a major victory in 1995, when a crowd estimated variously at 400,000 to 2 million Black men and a few uninvited Black women attended his October 16 "Million Man March" rally in Washington, D.C. There they were addressed by a considerable number of Black leaders, including Jesse Jackson and Maya Angelou, and finally by Farrakhan, who spoke for two hours on a wide range of subjects, surrounded on the platform by his Nation of Islam guards, the Fruit of Islam.

Most Black organizations and leaders, including the National Association for Colored People (NAACP) and General Colin Powell, declined to participate in Farrakhan's rally, citing his long record of anti-White, anti-Semitic, antiwoman, anti-Korean, anti-Arab, anti-Vietnamese, and anti-several-other-group utterances. President Bill Clinton left Washington, on that day delivering a widely publicized antibigotry speech in Austin, Texas, in which he did not specifically name Farrakhan. His Republican opponents, led by Bob Dole and Newt Gingrich, were scathing in their denunciations of Farrakhan, as were many others, Black and White, though many also took great care to distinguish between Farrakhan and the vast majority of concerned Black Americans who attended the rally.

Farrakhan was the object of an abortive assassination attempt in 1995. Betty Shabazz, daughter of Black Muslim leader Malcolm X, was arrested in January and charged with hiring an assassin to murder Farrakhan. Her family has long accused Farrakhan of complicity in Malcolm X's 1965 murder. Ultimately, it turned out that Shabazz had been entrapped by a childhood friend and longtime FBI informer; after she agreed to accept responsibility and was placed on probation, the case was ended. Farrakhan stated that he did not believe that Shabazz had tried to hire his murder, and he and Shabazz later appeared together in a gesture of reconciliation. Farrakhan did not admit complicity in Malcolm X's murder, but did state that Nation of Islam members were involved, and apologized to Shabazz.

In late October, Farrakhan's literary agents were reportedly attempting to place his autobiography with a publisher, for an asking price in the $6 million range.

New York City–born Farrakhan grew up in Boston; his birth name was Louis Eugene Wolcott, which he changed to Louis X and then to Louis Haleem Abdul Farrakhan. He attended Winston-Salem Teachers College in North Carolina for two years, then returned to Boston. Before becoming a Black Muslim minister, he was a professional musician. He joined the Nation of Islam in 1955, rose to become leader of the Boston mosque, and in the mid-1960s became a major figure as head of a key Harlem mosque. He became head of the Nation of Islam in 1977.

Farrakhan made a prolonged attempt to move into the mainstream of the African-American community during 1993 and 1994, but his attempt was greatly hampered by the continuing aura of anti-Jewish, anti-White hate that surrounded his organization. In one very notable

1993 incident, one of Farrakhan's chief aides, Khalil Abdul Muhammad, made a hate-filled speech bitterly and personally attacking the Pope, calling Jews "bloodsuckers," praising the murders of the Holocaust, and calling for the expulsion or execution of all Whites from South Africa. Two months later, under intense pressure from a very wide range of Americans, including many African-American leaders, Farrakhan criticized his aide's statements for their manner and removed him from his position, at the same time defending as "truth" many of his statements.

Farrakhan's published works include *Independent Black Leadership in America* (1990), written with Lenora Fulani and Alfred Sharpton, and *A Torchlight for America* (1993). He and his wife, Betsy, have nine children.

FURTHER READING

Prophet of Rage: The Radical World of Louis Farrakhan and Nation of Islam. ARTHUR J. MAGIDA. National Press, 1996.
"Black politics. . . ." ADOLPH REED, JR. *The Progressive,* Dec. 1995.
"After O. J. . . ." MICHAEL LERNER and CORNEL WEST. *Tikkun,* Nov.–Dec. 1995.
"The key to. . . ." ELLIS COSE. " 'My duty is. . . .' " VERN E. SMITH. "An angry 'charmer.' " HOWARD FINEMAN and VERN E. SMITH. "And now what?" MARK WHITAKER. *Newsweek,* Oct. 30, 1995.
"Do not let. . . ." *National Catholic Reporter,* Oct. 27, 1995.
"Why Farrakhan appeals. . . ." DON WYCLIFF. "Why Farrakhan repels." DAVID R. CARLIN, JR. *Commonweal,* Nov. 17, 1995.
"One man's march. . . ." GLENN C. LOURY. "Backward March. . . ." SEAN WILENTZ. *New Republic,* Nov. 6, 1995.
"Demon at the heart. . . ." JONATHAN FREEDLAND. *Guardian,* Oct. 14, 1995.
"Farrakhan, Jesse and Jews." GEORGE E. CURRY. *Emerge,* July–Aug. 1994.
" 'They suck the life. . . .' " SYLVESTER MONROE. "The rift. . . ." LEON WIESELTIER et al. "Pride and prejudice." WILLIAM A. HENRY, III. *Time,* Feb. 28, 1994.
"Louis Farrakhan's. . . ." MICHAEL C. KOTZIN. *The Christian Century,* Mar. 2, 1994.
American Jihad. STEVEN BARBOZA. Doubleday, 1994.
The Life and Times of Louis Farrakhan. C. ALAN MARSHALL. Marshall, 1992.

Farrar, David (1908–95) London-born actor David Farrar began his working life as a journalist, moving into his acting career in the mid-20s, playing largely in supporting stage roles.

He made his film debut in *Death of a Stranger* (1937), then played in supporting roles until scoring a breakthrough in *Meet Sexton Blake* (1944). His emerged as a star opposite Deborah Kerr in the Michael Powell-Emeric Pressburger classic *Black Narcissus* (1947), and went on to star on both sides of the Atlantic in such films as *Frieda* (1947), *The Small Back Room* (1948), *The Wild Heart* (1950), *Cage of Gold* (1950), *Night Without Stars* (1951), *Obsessed* (1951), *The Black Shield of Falworth* (1954), *Escape to Burma* (1955), *The Sea Chase* (1955), *Tears for Simon* (1956), *John Paul Jones* (1959), *Solomon and Sheba* (1959), and *The 300 Spartans* (1962). His autobiography was *No Royal Road* (1947). He was survived by a daughter. (d. South Africa; August 31, 1995)

FURTHER READING

Obituary. *Independent,* Sept. 29, 1995.
Obituary. *New York Times*, Sept. 9, 1995.
Obituary. *Times* (of London), Sept. 8, 1995.

Farrow, Mia Villiers (1945–) Mia Farrow starred in the 1995 film comedy *Miami Rhapsody*, written and directed by David Frankel, with a cast that included Sarah Jessica Parker, Gil Bellows, Antonio Banderas, Paul Mazursky, and Kevin Pollak. Farrow plays the mother in a thoroughly untrustworthy family of adults; she is having an affair with her grandmother's male nurse (Banderas), while several other similarly complex relationships blossom around her.

Farrow also starred in the film *Reckless*, directed by Norman René and written by Craig Lucas, based on his play, in a cast that included Scott Glenn, Mary-Louise Parker, and Tony Goldwyn. The film, a bitterly surreal seemingly-comic look at American life, features Farrow on what ultimately becomes a nightmare journey through what the author sees as the pathological underside of the "American dream."

Forthcoming was a starring role in John Irvin's film *Mattie*.

On the personal side, in the aftermath of the bitter breakup of her relationship with Woody Allen, Allen lost his New York Court of Appeals bid to gain custody of their three children, with Farrow retaining their custody.

Farrow published the book *Mia Farrow: An*

Autobiography. She herself was the subject of the television miniseries *Love and Betrayal: The Mia Farrow Story*, starring Patsy Kensit as Farrow.

Los Angeles–born Farrow became a star in television as Alison Mackenzie in "Peyton Place" (1964–66). In movies, she became a star in *Rosemary's Baby* (1968), going on to such films as *John and Mary* (1969), *The Great Gatsby* (1973), *Death on the Nile* (1978), *Zelig* (1983), *Broadway Danny Rose* (1984), *Hannah and Her Sisters* (1986), *Radio Days* (1987), *Crimes and Misdemeanors* (1989), *Alice* (1990), *Shadows and Fog* (1992), *Husbands and Wives* (1992), and *Widow's Peak* (1994). She also appeared in several leading stage roles in Britain during the mid-1970s, as a member of the Royal Shakespeare Company.

The daughter of actress Maureen O'Sullivan and director John Farrow, she has been married twice, to Frank Sinatra and Andre Previn. She then had a long-term relationship with Allen (1980–92); though they never married, they had three children: their biological son Satchel, an adopted daughter Dylan, and an adopted son Moses. Their breakup and subsequent bitter custody suit was complicated by disclosure of Allen's affair with Farrow's 21-year-old adopted daughter, Soon-Yi Farrow Previn, one of Farrow's six other children, five of whom are adopted Vietnamese; that affair continued in 1995.

FURTHER READING

"Mia Farrow." INGRID SISCHY. *Interview*, Apr. 1994.
Mia and Woody: Love, Betrayal and Heartbreak. KRISTI GROTEKE. Carroll & Graf, 1994.
"Mia's story." MAUREEN ORTH. *Vanity Fair*, Nov. 1992.
"Everything you always. . . ." PHOEBE HOBAN. *New York*, Sept. 21, 1992.
"Woody and Mia. . . ." ERIC LAX. *New York Times Magazine*, Feb. 24, 1991.
Mia: The Life of Mia Farrow. EDWARD Z. EPSTEIN. Delacorte, 1991.

Faulk, Marshall William (1973–)

Running back Marshall Faulk made a notable debut in the National Football League in the 1994 regular season. Playing with the Indianapolis Colts, he gained 1,282 yards rushing and 522 receiving, scoring a total of 12 touchdowns. That was good enough to win him NFL rookie-of-the-year honors. It also won him a trip to the February 1995 Pro Bowl, as the only rookie selected. Even in that illustrious company, Faulk stood out. Pacing the American Football Conference to a decisive 41-13 win over the National Football Conference, Faulk carried the ball 13 times for 180 yards—shattering the 122-yard Pro Bowl record set by O. J. Simpson 22 years earlier. (Surprisingly, that record was broken twice in the same game, the second time by Faulk's AFC colleague Chris Warren, with 127 yards.) A versatile player, Faulk also gained 27 yards on 2 receptions and 37 yards on two kickoff returns, and scored the final touchdown of the game on an electrifying 49-yard run. Not surprisingly, he was named the Pro Bowl's Most Valuable Player.

In the 1995 season, he helped pace Indianapolis to a record of 9-7 and a berth in the playoffs. Faulk himself ended the regular season with 14 touchdowns (11 rushing; 3 receiving) and 1,553 total yards from scrimmage, having gained 1,078 yards rushing on 289 attempts, for an average of 3.7 yards, and 475 yards on 56 receptions, for an average of 8.5 yards. During the October 1 game against St. Louis, Faulk had the AFC's best single-game stats of the season, with 222 total yards (177 rushing) and 3 touchdowns. However, an injury to his left knee kept Faulk out of the final playoff games, where the Colts lost in the AFC championship. Faulk was scheduled for arthroscopic knee surgery in January 1996.

On the personal side, Faulk and Candace Patton had a son in March 1995, named Marshall William Faulk, Jr., but nicknamed Deucie.

Born and raised in one of New Orleans' poorest ghettos, Faulk graduated from George Washington Carver High School there and attended San Diego State, where—as a freshman coming off the bench to replace an injured teammate—he set a 1995 NCAA Division I-A single game rushing record, with 386 yards on 37 carries. He was three times named running back on the *Sporting News* college All-America first team (1991–93). Leaving after his junior year, Faulk was the second pick overall in the 1994 NFL college draft, and signed with the Indianapolis Colts (1994–).

FURTHER READING

"Tales of a Faulk hero." DAN DIEFFENBACH. *Sport*, July 1995.
" 'Who cares . . . ?' " TOM KRASOVIC. *Sporting News*, Dec. 6, 1993.

Faulkner, Shannon (1975–) On August

14, 1995, Shannon Faulkner joined the cadet corps at The Citadel, a previously all-male, state-funded military college in Charleston, South Carolina. Her two-year-long battle against sex discrimination and for admission to the college had been one of the most celebrated women's equality cases of the 1990s. In April 1995, a Fourth Circuit U.S. Court of Appeals panel had upheld a federal district court ruling that she be admitted to the college, and on August 11 Supreme Court Chief Justice William H. Rehnquist and Justice Antonin Scalia had refused The Citadel's final appeal. Faulkner was not to enjoy the fruits of her victory, however. On August 14, she was one of five new cadets who collapsed in 100-degree heat; taken to the infirmary, she was too sick to rejoin the corps, and on August 18, expressing great regret, was forced to resign from The Citadel. Her physical collapse, after two years of great pressure, was hailed as a victory by many in the corps of cadets, who noisily celebrated—but as more than 150 other women had, by then, expressed interest in admission, it was clear that many women were set to follow in her footsteps.

A top high school student and athlete in her hometown of Powdersville, South Carolina, Faulkner had applied and been admitted to The Citadel in 1993, because college admissions officers had not realized that she was a woman. When the sex-discriminating officers discovered their mistake, they tried to keep her out. She went to court to force admission and, despite bitter vilification and attacks on herself and her family, persevered. In November 1993 she won the right to attend classes while her case was being adjudicated. Supreme Court Chief Justice William H. Rehnquist then temporarily barred her entry, but lifted his ban on January 18, 1994. That allowed her to begin classes as a day student on January 20—though confronted with intense harassment by much of the student body throughout the year, and with the complete opposition of the college administration. On July 22, 1994, Federal District Judge C. Weston Houck ruled that the college must grant her full admission; the college responded with a highly publicized order that her head be shaved, contending that head shaving of first-year students was normal practice at the college. But while that was being debated, in and out of court, a federal appeals court stayed the order of admis-

sion, pending the college's appeal, which was settled in her favor in 1995.

FURTHER READING

"Shannon's quest. . . ." ANDREA GROSS. *Ladies Home Journal,* Feb. 1995.
"The Citadel's lone. . . ." CATHERINE S. MANEGOLD. *New York Times Magazine*, Sept. 11, 1994.
"The naked Citadel." SUSAN FALUDI. *New Yorker*, Sept. 5, 1994.

Favre, Brett Lorenzo (1969–) After

three years of maturing with the Green Bay Packers, Brett Favre emerged in the 1995 season as a superb all-around quarterback. So much so that he beat out both Troy Aikman and Steve Young to be named starting quarterback of the National Football Conference squad at the annual Pro Bowl, and at year's end was overwhelmingly named the National Football League's Most Valuable Player. The numbers tell the tale. In the 1995 regular season, despite a late-season severely sprained ankle, Favre scored a league-leading 38 touchdowns and led his team to an 11-5 record. Overall he gained 4,413 yards passing with an average gain of 7.74 yards and a completion percentage of 63.0 (359 completions on 570 attempts). These included a career-best five touchdown passes in a single game and a 99-yard touchdown pass, the longest in NFL history, both in the same game. His 1995 season quarterback rating led the NFC at 99.5, in the league second only to the AFC's Jim Harbaugh. Early in January 1996, Favre led the Packers in a decisive win over the defending Super Bowl champion San Francisco 49ers, but they then lost to the Dallas Cowboys in the NFC championship, just short of their Super Bowl goal.

Born and raised in Pass Christian, Mississippi, where he attended Hancock North Central High School, Favre played college football for Southern Mississippi College. He was selected in the second round of the 1991 NFL college draft by the Atlanta Falcons (1991–92) and then, after a year spent largely on the bench, was traded to the Green Bay Packers (1992–), where he became starting quarterback. He has been named to the Pro Bowl three times (1992; 1993; 1995).

FURTHER READING

"Brett Favre. . . ." DAN DIEFFENBACH. *Sport,* Nov. 1995.

Ferguson, Colin (1958–) On February 17, 1995, Colin Ferguson was convicted of killing six people and wounding 17 on a Long Island Railroad commuter train near Garden City, New York, on December 7, 1993. Ferguson had fired 30 rounds from a nine-millimeter handgun, reloading once; he was captured by surviving passengers when he stopped to reload again. The case had drawn national attention for several reasons. The prosecution alleged that Ferguson, a Black man from Jamaica, had racial motivations for the killings; Ferguson, pleading innocent, claimed that the killings had been done by an unidentified White man, who stole his gun and afterward successfully fled.

Nassau County Judge Donald E. Belfi ruled that Ferguson was fit to stand trial, and then, after Ferguson fired his lawyers, that he was fit to plead his own defense. The lawyers, William M. Kunstler and Ronald Kuby, had sought to have Ferguson declared mentally incompetent, and then had urged that he plead that he had done the murders because of rage over his treatment as a Black. Ferguson, however, chose to deny having done the killings, although many of his victims gave eyewitness accounts testifying as to his guilt. On March 22, Judge Belfi sen-

tenced Ferguson to a series of consecutive terms adding up to the statutory limit of 200 years in prison. After his sentencing, several of his surviving victims and some of the relatives of those murdered held a press conference demanding stronger gun control laws.

FURTHER READING

"The color of rage." ROBERT I.FRIEDMAN. *Vanity Fair,* Jan. 1995.
"Psycho-killer?. . . ." JIM SLEEPER. *New Republic,* Jan. 10, 1994.
"A mass murderer's. . . ." ANASTASIA TOUFEXIS. *Time,* Dec. 20, 1993.
"Rage, resentment and a Ruger." MELINDA BECK. *Newsweek,* Dec. 20, 1993.

Finney, Jack (Walter Braden Finney; 1911–95) Journeyman author Jack Finney was best known by far for his very popular 1970 novel *Time and Again,* a novel using science fiction devices to develop nostalgic themes, in which his protagonist travels back in time to live in New York City in the 1880s; in 1995 he published a sequel, *From Time to Time.*

Milwaukee-born Finney worked in New York advertisng after attending Knox College, and began his writing career as a freelance short story writer. His debut novel was *Five Against the House* (1954), followed in 1955 by the highly successful horror novel *The Body Snatchers,* the basis of Don Siegel's hit 1956 film *Invasion of the Body Snatchers.* His 1963 novel *Good Neighbor Sam* was the basis for David Swift's 1956 film comedy, starring Jack Lemmon in the title role. Other popular novels included *Marion's Wall* (1973) and *The Night People* (1977). He was survived by his wife, Marguerite, a daughter, and a son. (d. Greenbrae, California; November 17, 1995)

FURTHER READING

Obituary. *New York Times,* Nov. 17, 1995.
"A Finney thing. . . ." LUC SANTE. *Vanity Fair,* Feb. 1995.

Fishburne, Laurence (Laurence Fishburne III; 1961–) Versatile and hardworking actor, writer, and director Laurence Fishburne in 1995 starred in the title role in a well-received

film version of Shakespeare's *Othello*, directed and adapted for film by Oliver Parker, and co-starring Kenneth Branagh as Iago, Irene Jacob as Desdemona, and Nathaniel Parker as Cassio.

Fishburne also wrote, directed, and starred on the New York stage in *Riff Raff*, playing a murderer and thief in the one-act play set in a gang-infested, drug-dealing, depressed New York City neighborhood; Titus Welliver and Heavy D co-starred.

Fishburne starred as a Florida back-country police officer in the film *Just Cause*, opposite Sean Connery as a Harvard law professor determined to free a Black prisoner whom he believes was falsely convicted of murder and who has spent eight years on Death Row; Blair Underwood played the prisoner, in a cast that included Kate Capshaw, Ruby Dee, and Ed Harris; Arne Glimcher directed. Fishburne also starred as an ex-CIA operative, opposite Ellen Barkin in the film *Bad Company*, directed by Damian Harris and costarring Frank Langella and Michael Beach. A third theatrical film appearance was in *Higher Learning*, written and directed by John Singleton, a story about college campus racism.

On the home screen, Fishburne starred as a pioneering African-American World War II aviator in the television film *The Tuskegee Airmen*, directed by Robert Markowitz and costarring Allen Payne, Malcolm-Jamal Warner, Courtney Vance, and John Lithgow. Fishburne received a

Golden Globe nomination as best actor in a mini-series or telefilm for the role.

Forthcoming were starring film roles opposite Kiefer Sutherland in *Double Cross*, directed by Sidney Lumet, and in *Fled*, written and coproduced by Preston Whitmore II, directed by Kevin Hooks, and costarring Stephen Baldwin and Salma Hayek.

Born in Augusta, Georgia, Fishburne grew up in New York City. He began his career as a teen-ager, in the television soap opera "One Life to Live," made his stage debut in *Section D* (1975), and his film debut in *Cornbread, Earl and Me* (1975). In 1992, he won a Tony Award as best featured actor in the play *Two Trains Running*. Among the films in which he played supporting roles were *Apocalypse Now* (1979), *Willie and Phil* (1980), *Gardens of Stone* (1987), *Red Heat* (1988), and *King of New York* (1990). His breakthrough role came as the father in *Boyz N the Hood* (1991). He was nominated for an Academy Award nomination as best actor for his role as Ike Turner in *What's Love Got to Do With It* (1993). His later films also included *Searching for Bobby Fischer* (1993), *Double Cross* (1994), and *Just Cause* (1994). Fishburne is married to Majna Mass Fishburne; they have three children. (For additional photo, see **Branagh, Kenneth.**)

FURTHER READING

"Laurence Fishburne." ROGER D. FRIEDMAN. *Us,* Jan. 1996.
"Catching Fishburne." LESLIE BENNETTS. *Vanity Fair,* Dec. 1995.
"Home again." CHRIS SMITH. *New York,* Nov. 6, 1995.
"Laurence Fishburne. . . ." SHEILA BENSON. *Interview,* Jan. 1995.
"A man called Fish." AUDREY EDWARDS. *Essence,* Nov. 1994.
"Laurence Fishburne." *Playboy,* Apr. 1994.
"Searching for Larry Fishburne." JEFF GILES. *Newsweek,* July 26, 1993.

Flanders, Ed (Edward Paul Flanders; 1934–95) Minneapolis-born stage and screen star Ed Flanders began his long association with San Diego's Globe Theatre in 1952. In 1971, he starred as Rev. Daniel Berrigan in the anti–Vietnam War play *The Trial of the Catonsville Nine*, re-creating the role in the 1972 film version of the play. On Broadway, he starred opposite Jason Robards and Colleen Dewhurst in an acclaimed 1974 revival of Eugene O'Neill's *A*

Moon for the Misbegotten, and in 1976 won an Emmy in the television version of the play. He won a second Emmy in 1977, for his portrayal of President Harry S. Truman in the title role of television's *Harry. S. Truman: Plain Speaking.* Flanders is best known to worldwide audiences for his starring role as Dr. Westphall in the long-running television series "St. Elsewhere" (1982–87), for which he won yet another Emmy (1983). He also appeared in many other television films, among them *Eleanor and Franklin* (1976), *Special Bulletin* (1983), and *The Final Days* (1989). He committed suicide. No information as to survivors was available. (d. Denny, California; February 22, 1995)

FURTHER READING

"From Elsewhere. . . ." TOM GLIATTO. *People,* Mar. 20, 1995.
Obituary. *New York Times*, Mar. 2, 1995.
Obituary. *Variety*, Mar. 2, 1995.

Flores, Lola (Dolores Flores; 1923–95)

Spanish flamenco singer and dancer Lola Flores was one of Spain's leading popular artists, and a major figure throughout the Spanish-speaking world. Emphasizing her partly gypsy heritage, she was also a major figure in Spanish gypsy life. Early in her career, she became a Spanish film star, at the same time developing a large and loyal corps of music fans, who later stood by her even though she had, in the Franco years, been much favored by the dictator, and had often performed privately for him. It turned out that she was equally esteemed by many of the democratic leaders that succeeded the dictator, and her continuing popularity in Spain and throughout Latin America was never in question. She was survived by her husband, *El Pescailla* (Antonio González); their daughter Rosario, a leading flamenco and popular singer; their actress daughter Lolita; and their son, leading pop/rock singer Antonio Flores, who died on May 30. (d. Madrid; May 16, 1995)

FURTHER READING

Obituary. *Billboard*, June 3, 1995.
Obituary. *Times* (of London), May 29, 1995.

Ford, Harrison (1942–) Actor Harrison

Ford continued to star on television screens during 1995, as his 1994 film *Clear and Present Danger* became a major hit in home video, join-

ing such previous, still-playing hits as *The Fugitive* (1993) and the now-classic "Star Wars" and "Indiana Jones" series.

In 1995, Ford tried a change of pace, starring in the Humphrey Bogart role opposite Julia Ormond in the title role of the film comedy *Sabrina*, a remake of Billy Wilder's 1954 classic, which had starred Bogart, Audrey Hepburn, and William Holden. Sidney Pollack directed; the cast included Greg Kinnear in the Holden role, John Wood, Nancy Marchand, Richard Crenna, and Angie Dickinson. The film, a major change of pace for action star Ford, received mixed reviews; however, Ford received a Golden Globe nomination as best actor in a musical or comedy for the role.

Forthcoming was a starring role as a New York police officer who inadvertently becomes involved with an Irish Republican Army activist, in the film *Devil's Own*.

Chicago-born Ford played largely in supporting roles, working part-time as a carpenter, for a decade before breaking through to become a leading movie actor as Han Solo in *Star Wars* (1977). He completed the Star Wars trilogy with *The Empire Strikes Back* (1980) and *Return of the Jedi* (1983), meanwhile doing the blockbuster Indiana Jones trilogy: *Raiders of the Lost Ark* (1981), *Indiana Jones and the Temple of Doom* (1984), and *Indiana Jones and the Last Crusade* (1989). Among his other films are *Witness* (1985), *The Mosquito Coast* (1986), *Working Girl* (1988), *Presumed Innocent* (1990),

Regarding Henry (1991), *Patriot Games* (1992), *The Fugitive* (1993), and *Clear and Present Danger* (1994). Ford attended Ripon College. He has been married twice and has two children.

FURTHER READING

"Regarding Harrison." BARBARA LAZEAR ASCHER. *Ladies Home Journal,* Jan. 1996.
"After surviving. . . ." BRUCE FRETTS. *Entertainment,* Aug. 19, 1994.
"Off camera." LAWRENCE GROBEL. *Playboy,* Sept. 1993.
"The fugitive star." DAVID HALBERSTAM. *Vanity Fair,* July 1993.
"Harrison Ford. . . ." MARTHA FRANKEL. *Movies USA,* May 1992.
"Harrison Ford. . . ." NATALIE GITTELSON. *McCall's,* June 1991.

Foreman, George Edward (1950–)

In the eyes of the public, George Foreman was still heavyweight champion, after his stunning November 6, 1994, win over the 19-years-younger Michael Moorer, to take the World Boxing Association (WBA) and International Boxing Federation (IBF) crowns (two of the three heavyweight titles). But in fact, by the end of 1995, Foreman had formally been stripped of his titles. In April, Foreman won a controversial majority decision in a Las Vegas fight against Axel (Sergeant) Schulz of Germany, in which one judge called a draw and the other two gave Foreman the nod, though just barely. Because he had cho-

sen to fight Schulz, instead of making a mandatory defense against the top WBA contender, Tony Tucker, Foreman was stripped of his WBA title. Then after Foreman declined to give Schulz a mandatory rematch by October 3, 1995, he lost his IBF title as well. Late in 1995, a rematch with Moorer was being discussed for early 1996. Foreman said he would fight ex-champ and ex-con Mike Tyson, but not while Tyson was represented by controversial manager Don King.

In April, Foreman was honored as fighter of the year by the Boxing Writers Association of America. In May, Foreman called for headgear to be made mandatory in boxing; this came after the death of superfeatherweight Jimmy Garcia from injuries suffered in the ring; at least three other boxers had died from head injuries in the previous two years.

Foreman spent much of 1995 tending to his other interests, especially traveling widely to promote his new book, *By George: Autobiography of George Foreman*, and his "Lean Mean Fat-Reducing Grilling Machine."

Texas-born Foreman won the heavyweight boxing championship at the 1968 Mexico City Olympics, then turned professional in 1969. He became world heavyweight champion in 1973 by defeating Joe Frazier, but lost the title to Muhammad Ali the following year. After a string of 46 victories was broken with a March 1977 loss to Jimmy Young, he left boxing to become an evangelical minister, but returned to the ring a decade later, in 1987, partly to fund his church, the Church of the Lord Jesus Christ, and community youth center near Houston. Foreman's lifetime professional record through 1994 was 73–4, with 68 knockouts, for an unequaled 93 percent knockout average. With his 1994 win, Foreman became the oldest fighter to win a title in any weight class. Foreman and his wife, (Mary) Joan Foreman, have three children; he also has six children from four previous marriages. His four sons all bear his name, being known as George II through George V.

FURTHER READING

"Playboy interview. . . ." LAWRENCE LINDERMAN. *Playboy,* Dec. 1995.
"Foreman, George." *Current Biography,* Aug. 1995.
"Home on the range. . . ." HANS J. MASSAQUOI. *Ebony,* July 1995.
"Sport lifestyle. . . ." DAN DIEFFENBACH. *Sport,* June 1995.

"Never count him out." DAVID ZINCZENKO. *Men's Health,* Apr. 1995.

"The burger king." MARK KRAM. *Esquire,* Feb. 1995.

"Big. . . ." JAN REID. *Texas Monthly,* Feb. 1995.

"KO'd." RICHARD HOFFER. *Sports Illustrated,* Nov. 14, 1994.

"Foreman's big fall." MIKE DOWNEY. *Sport,* Nov. 1994.

"George Foreman." *Sporting News,* Apr. 22, 1991.

"It's coming back. . . ." JOHN SKOW. *Time,* Apr. 22, 1991.

"Body + soul. . . ." PHIL BERGER. *New York Times Magazine,* Mar. 24, 1991.

Fortier, Michael: See McVeigh, Timothy James.

Foster, Henry W., Jr. (1933–) On February 2, 1995, President Bill Clinton nominated African-American obstetrician and educator Dr. Henry W. Foster to the post of Surgeon General, succeeding Dr. Jocelyn Elders. Dr. Foster, the acting director of Nashville's Meharry Medical College, was thought to bring to the job a particularly strong background in the fight against infant mortality and the prevention of teenage pregnancy. He was also a long-term and leading member of Planned Parenthood.

A political contest over the nomination immediately developed, with Congressional Republicans led by Senator Phil Gramm attacking Foster as pro-abortion. Foster responded by stating that he had performed fewer than a dozen abortions during his three decades of practice. Later, Foster revised his estimate of the number of abortions he had performed to 39. Ultimately, Senate Republicans were able to block the Foster nomination when Democrats and those Republicans supporting Foster, although they formed a majority, could not muster enough votes to cut off debate on the nomination.

Foster received his 1948 B.A. from Morehouse University and his 1958 degree in medicine from the University of Arkansas. After service in the Air Force and a period of internship and residency, he joined the Meharry staff, and became head of Meharry's obstetrics and gynecology department (1973–90). He is married to Clair Anderson; they have a daughter and a son.

FURTHER READING

"The doctor in the lion's den." NINA BURLEIGH. *Time,* May 15, 1995.

"Hanging tough. . . ." DAVID ELLIS. *People,* Mar. 13, 1995.

"Surgical strike. . . ." ELIZABETH GLEICK. *Time,* Feb. 20, 1995.

Jodie Foster (right) and James Garner.

Foster, Jodie (Alicia Christian Foster; 1962–) For her starring role in the 1994 film *Nell,* which she also coproduced, film star, director, and producer Jodie Foster received Screen Actors Guild and Blockbuster Entertainment best actress awards and an Italian David di Donatello award as best actress in a foreign film. She had also been nominated for a best actress Oscar.

In 1995, Foster directed the off-beat comedy-drama film *Home for the Holidays,* starring Holly Hunter as Claudia Larson, visiting her parents in Baltimore for Thanksgiving; Charles Durning and Anne Bancroft played her parents; Robert Downey was Tommy Larson, her hyperactive, gay brother; Geraldine Chaplin was her eccentric aunt, and Dylan McDermott was her brother's lover.

Still forthcoming was the sequel to *The Silence of the Lambs,* with Foster once again slated to star opposite Anthony Hopkins as psychopathic killer Dr. Hannibal "the Cannibal" Lecter. Also forthcoming was *The Dinosaur Man,* based on Dr. Susan Baur's work with schizophrenics; Foster was slated to direct and star in the film, and also to direct and star in the forthcoming *Jean Seberg,* based on the life of the American actress. Yet another forthcoming starring role was as an astronomer who receives the first radio message from space, in the science fiction thriller *Contact*, directed by George Miller and based on Carl Sagan's novel.

Los Angeles–born Foster was a leading child actor in television, beginning with "Mayberry, R.F.D." in 1969. In her early teens, she played major roles in such films as *Alice Doesn't Live Here Anymore* (1975) and *Taxi Driver* (1976). She then made the extremely difficult transition to adult roles, in such films as *The Hotel New Hampshire* (1984), *Five Corners* (1986), *The Accused* (1988; she won a best actress Oscar), *Shadows and Fog* (1992), *Little Man Tate* (1992; which she directed), *Sommersby* (1993), and *Maverick* (1994). Her 1985 B.A. was from Yale University.

FURTHER READING

"Jodie Foster." LAURA MORICE. *Us*, Dec. 1995.
"Calling the shots." SUZANNA ANDREWS. *Working Woman*, Nov. 1995.
"Jodie loses. . . ." MELINA GEROSA. *Ladies Home Journal*, Feb. 1995.
"Pure Jodie." MICHAEL SCHNAYERSON. *Vanity Fair*, May 1994.
"Jodie Foster. . . ." MARK HARRIS et al. *Entertainment*, Apr. 2, 1993.
"Foster, Jodie." *Current Biography*, Aug. 1992.
"What's driving Miss Jodie?" MICHAEL SEGELL. *Redbook*, Nov. 1991.
"Wunderkind." ARION BERGER. *Harper's Bazaar*, Nov. 1991.
"Burden of the gift." JULIE CAMERON. *American Film*, Nov.–Dec. 1991.
"A screen gem turns director." RICHARD CORLISS. *Time*, Oct. 14, 1991.
"Jodie Foster." INGRID SISCHY. *Interview*, Oct. 1991.
"Jodie Foster. . . ." BRIAN D. JOHNSON. *Maclean's*, Sept. 16, 1991.
"Jodie Foster." GEARI HIRSHEY. *Rolling Stone*, Mar. 21, 1991.
"Yet again. . . ." TRACY YOUNG. *Vogue*, Feb. 1991.
"Child of the movies." JONATHAN VAN METER. *New York Times Magazine*, Jan. 6, 1991.

Fowler, William Alfred (1911–95)

Pittsburgh-born William Fowler, a leading astrophysicist, received his 1933 B.S. from Ohio State University and his 1936 Ph.D. from the California Institute of Technology, where he immediately joined the faculty to begin his long association with that institution. He became a full professor at Caltech in 1946 and Institute Professor of Physics in 1970, and retired in 1982, though retaining his affiliation. During World War II, Fowler worked on several projects, among them ordnance and atomic bomb components. After the war, he began his major work, becoming a founder of the new field of nuclear astrophysics, and joining in the development of a body of theoretical work on the evolution of the universe, back to the presumed Big Bang. A major early work was the 1957 paper "Synthesis of the Elements in Stars." Other major works included *Nucleo-synthesis in Massive Stars and Supernovae* (1965), coauthored with astronomer Fred Hoyle, and *Nuclear Astrophysics* (1967). Fowler was awarded a 1983 Nobel Prize in physics. Among his many other honors were a 1974 National Medal of Science. He was survived by his second wife, Mary, and two daughters. (d. Pasadena, California; March 14, 1995)

FURTHER READING

Obituary. *Times* (of London), Mar. 24, 1995.
Obituary. *New York Times*, Mar. 16, 1995.

Fox, Michael J. (1961–)

In Rob Reiner's film comedy-drama *The American President*, Michael J. Fox costarred as a young White House presidential advisor—very much resembling real-life George Stephanopolous—who with the rest of the White House staff is desperately and unsuccessfully trying to keep secret an innocent, nonpolitical, but potentially disastrous affair between his President, played by Michael Douglas, and environmentalist lobbyist Sydney Wade, played by Annette Bening. The gentle comedy, directed and produced by Rob Reiner and written by Aaron Sorkin, received mixed though generally favorable reviews.

Fox also costarred in the Brooklyn-set film *Blue in the Face*, directed by Wayne Wang and Paul Auster, in a cast that included Harvey Keitel, Lou Reed, Roseanne, Jim Jarmusch, Lily Tomlin, and Madonna. He also played a cameo role and coproduced the poorly received film *Coldblooded*, written and directed by Wallace Wolodarsky and costarring Jason Priestley and Peter Riegert. Forthcoming was a starring role in the film *The Frighteners*, directed by Peter Jackson and costarring Trini Alvarado, Peter Dobson, and John Astin.

On the personal side, he and his wife, actress Tracy Pollan, had twin girls; they already had a son.

Vancouver-born Fox became a popular television player as the conservative young son in the series "Family Ties" (1982–89), and a film star in the teenage fantasy-comedies *Back to the Future* (1985), *Back to the Future II* (1989), and *Back to the Future III* (1990). He also starred in the highly regarded *Casualties of War* (1989), *The Hard Way* (1991), *Doc Hollywood* (1991), *For Love or Money* (1993), *Life with Mikey* (1993), *Homeward Bound: The Incredible Journey* (1993), *Greedy* (1994), *Where the Rivers Flow North* (1994), and *Don't Drink the Water* (1994).

FURTHER READING

"Michael J. Fox." JEFF GILES. *Us*, July 1993.
"The return of. . . ." MELANIE BERGER. *Ladies Home Journal*, July 1993.
"Walking tall with. . . ." CHRIS CHASE. *Cosmopolitan*, Apr. 1991.

Franklin, Melvin (David English; 1942–95)

Born in Montgomery, Alabama, popular singer Melvin Franklin was one of the two original members of The Temptations remaining with the group. The deep bass singer began his musical career in Detroit in the mid-1950s, and while still in his mid-teens was singing with the

vocal group The Distants. In 1962, he, Eddie Kendricks, Otis Williams, Paul Williams, and Eldridge Bryant formed The Temptations. Promoted by Berry Gordy's Motown organization, they became a hugely popular group in the mid-1960s, starting with their 1964 hit "The Way You Do the Things You Do," and followed by their 1965 number-one hit "My Girl." Among their further hits were "Beauty's Only Skin Deep" (1966), "I Wish It Could Rain" (1967), the Grammy-winning single "Cloud Nine" (1968), "I Can't Get Next to You" (1969), "Just My Imagination" (1971), and "Papa Was a Rolling Stone" (1972). Though there were fewer top hits after the early 1970s, and many personnel changes, the group continued to tour and record through 1995. Franklin was survived by his wife and five children. (d. Los Angeles; February 23, 1995).

FURTHER READING

"Rites held. . . ." *Jet*, Mar. 13, 1995.
Obituary. *Billboard*, Mar. 11, 1995.

Franz, Dennis (Dennis Schlachta; 1944–)

Television star Dennis Franz was honored by his peers in 1995 for his role in the highly successful television crime series "N.Y.P.D. Blue," which maintained its popularity in the fall 1995 season despite the replacement of his former costar, David Caruso, with Jimmy Smits. For his role as detective Matty Sipowicz, Franz won a Golden Globe award as best television actor in a drama series and a Screen Actors Guild award as best actor in a drama series; he also received an Emmy nomination as best lead actor in a drama series, an award he had won for the role in 1994.

Franz also starred as a defense lawyer in the television film *Texas Justice*, directed by Peter Lowry and costarring Peter Strauss and Heather Locklear as a warring couple, with Strauss charged of attempting to murder Locklear. Forthcoming was a starring role opposite Dustin Hoffman in the film version of David Mamet's play *American Buffalo*, directed by Michael Corrente.

Born in Maywood, Illinois, Franz began his acting career in Chicago regional theater, most notably playing a wide range of roles in the Organic Theatre Company (1973–78). He made his film debut in *The Fury* (1978). His first television series role was in "Chicago Story" (1982). His breakthrough role was as detective Sal Benedetto in the television series "Hill Street Blues" (1982–83). The role, which began as a series of guest appearances, ultimately became a lead (1985–87), and Franz became a star. He went on to play starring roles in the shortlived series "Beverly Hills Buntz" (1987), "Nasty Boys" (1990), and "N.Y.P.D. Mounted" (1991). He then began his long starring run in "N.Y.P.D. Blue" (1993–). Among his film appearances were supporting roles in *Dressed to Kill* (1980), *Body Double* (1984), *Die Hard II* (1990), and *The Player* (1992). Franz attended Wright Junior College and Southern Illinois University. He is married to Joanie Zeck.

FURTHER READING

"Franz, Dennis." *Current Biography,* July 1995.
"Dennis Franz." Bruce Fretts. *Entertainment,* Dec. 30, 1994.

Freeh, Louis Joseph (1950–) Federal Bureau of Investigation (FBI) Director Louis Freeh found himself very much on the defensive in 1995, because of two situations predating his 1994 appointment to the post. The first was the 1992 Ruby Ridge, Idaho siege and gunfight between federal agents and Randall Weaver, in which Weaver's wife and son and a federal marshal were killed. As Justice Department prosecutors and Senate Judiciary Committee staff dug into the facts, it became clear that highranking FBI personnel had attempted a coverup, withholding documents from the Justice Department. Freeh suspended several officials pending resolution of the continuing investigation, among them Larry A. Potts, key FBI supervisor of the siege, whom he had earlier in 1995 promoted to the post of deputy director of the FBI and then demoted as a parallel investigation developed. In August, the Justice Department agreed to a $3.1 settlement of Weaver family claims against the government. The parallel probe of FBI actions that had resulted in Potts' demotion was the Justice Department and Senate Judiciary Committee investigation of the use of deadly force in the 1993 Waco, Texas Branch Dravidian siege, in which four government agents and 86 Branch Dravidians reportedly died.

While on the defensive, however, Freeh and the FBI continued to deal with the entire range of federal law enforcement matters, most visibly with the continuing threat of terrorism, as in the April Oklahoma City bombings, in which 169 people died; the World Trade Center bombing case, which resulted in multiple convictions; and the unsolved Unabomber letter bombings. After the Oklahoma City bombing, Freeh supported President Clinton's call for a wide range of new antiterrorism laws, moderating his stance later, after many in Congress and civil liberties groups sharply criticized some of the proposals as major infringements of civil liberties.

Jersey City–born Freeh was an FBI agent (1975–81), then became a federal prosecutor in the southern district of New York, where his reputation was greatly enhanced by his role in the successful Mafia prosecutions of the mid-1980s. In 1989, he headed the southern district's organized crime strike force. He was appointed a federal district judge in 1991 by President George Bush. President Bill Clinton appointed Freeh director of the FBI in 1994, replacing William S. Sessions. Freeh's J.D. was from Rutgers University. He is married to Marilyn Freeh, and has four children.

FURTHER READING

"A former G-man. . . ." Brian Duffy. *U.S. News & World Report,* May 1, 1995.
"The squeaky-clean G-man." James Carney. *Time,* Aug. 2, 1993.
"The new G-man. . . ." Brian Duffy. *U.S. News & World Report,* Aug. 2, 1993.

Freeman, Morgan (1938–) Stage and screen star Morgan Freeman played a veteran homicide detective opposite Brad Pitt as his young partner in the 1995 serial-murder thriller film *Seven,* directed by David Fincher, in a cast that included Gwyneth Paltrow, Richard Rountree, and Kevin Spacey. He also starred in the film *Outbreak,* directed by Wolfgang Petersen, in a cast that included Dustin Hoffman, Rene Russo, Cuba Godding, Jr., Patrick Dempsey, Donald Sutherland, and Kevin Spacey; the story is about a deadly virus that threatens to generate a massive epidemic. Freeman also narrated the television miniseries *The Promised Land,* which told the story of the long African-American migration from the South to Chicago,

part of the massive internal migration that began in the 1920s.

For his role in *The Shawshank Redemption* (1994), Freeman was nominated for an Academy Award as best actor and a Screen Actors Guild award as best leading actor in a motion picture.

Forthcoming were starring roles in the film *Moll Flanders*, written and directed by Pen Densham, and costarring Robin Wright, Stockard Channing, and Brenda Fricker; and opposite Keanu Reeves in the Andrew Davis film *Dead Drop*.

Freeman has spent most of his long career in the theater, winning a 1978 Tony nomination for his role in *The Mighty Gents*, and appearing in a considerable range of Shakespearean and other classical roles. He emerged as a leading screen and stage player late in his career, beginning with his lead Off-Broadway as Hoke Colburn, the Black chauffeur in *Driving Miss Daisy* (1987), and in strong supporting roles in such films as *Street Smart* (1987) and *Clean and Sober* (1988). His major breakthrough came in 1989, with his film re-creation of his *Driving Miss Daisy* role, for which he won a 1990 best actor Oscar nomination. In the same year, he appeared in *Glory*, and played the Joe Clark role in *Lean On Me*. In 1990, he appeared as Petruchio opposite Tracey Ullman in the New York production of *The Taming of the Shrew*. In 1991, he played Azeem in *Robin Hood: Prince of Thieves*, and in 1992 played in *The Power of One* and *The Unforgiven*. He has also appeared as a regular on two television series: public television's children's show "The Electric Company" (1971–76) and for a time in the early 1980s on "Another World," a daytime soap opera. He made his feature film directorial debut with the South Africa-set *Bopha* (1993).

FURTHER READING

"Spotlight. . . ." *People*, Oct. 16, 1995.
"Alternate roots." MEREDITH BERKMAN. *Entertainment*, Oct. 22, 1993.
"Freeman, Morgan." *Current Biography*, Feb. 1991.

Freleng, Friz (Isadore Freleng; 1906–95)

Kansas City–born Friz Freleng, a self-taught artist who became a leading film animator and director, began his long Hollywood career in 1927 with the Walt Disney studio. He soon left Disney and Hollywood for New York, where he worked on the "Krazy Kat" cartoon series. He returned to Hollywood in 1930 to join Warner Bros., and in the three decades that followed created many cartoon characters, among them the world-famous Porky Pig, Speedy Gonzalez, and Yosemite Sam. In 1963, he and David DePatie founded the animation production company DePatie-Freleng Enterprises, and created several successful television cartoon series, among them "The Pink Panther." Freleng won four Academy Awards and three Emmys. Among the films he directed were *Bugs Bunny and the Three Bears* (1944), *Tweety Pie and Sylvester* (1947), *Bugs Bunny Rides Again* (1948), *Speedy Gonzalez* (1955), *Knightly Knight Bugs* (1968), and *Daffy Duck's Movie* (1983). Freleng published *Animation: The Art of Friz Freleng* (1993), written with David Weber. He was survived by his wife, Lily, and two daughters (d. Los Angeles; May 26, 1995)

FURTHER READING

Obituary. *Times* (of London), May 30, 1995.
Obituary. *Independent,* May 29, 1995.
Obituary. *New York Times*, May 28, 1995.

Friedrich, Otto (Alva Otto Friedrich; 1929–95)

Boston-born journalist, author, and editor Otto Friedrich received his 1948 A.B. from Harvard University. He began his career on the *Stars and Stripes* copydesk in the early 1950s, and later worked for the United Press, *New York Daily News*, and *Newsweek*. He spent seven years with the *Saturday Evening Post* (1962–69), the last four of them as managing editor, and after the magazine expired wrote the well-regarded book *Decline and Fall* (1970). He joined *Time* magazine in 1970 as a senior editor and became a senior writer for the magazine in 1980. A prolific writer, he also wrote many freelance articles, several novels and nonfiction works, and with his wife, Patricia Broughton, many children's books. He was survived by his wife, three daughters, a son, two sisters, and a brother. (d. North Shore, Long Island; April 26, 1995)

FURTHER READING

"Adagio, ma non troppo." LEWIS H. LAPHAM. *Harper's,* Aug. 1995.

"To our readers." JAMES R. GAINES. *Time*, May 8, 1995.
Obituary. *New York Times*, Apr. 28, 1995.

Frondizi, Arturo (1908–95) Argentinian lawyer and politician Arturo Frondizi began his political work as a Radical Party activist while still a law student at the University of Buenos Aires in the late 1920s. After his 1930 graduation, he became a leading liberal and reformist member of his party, who in 1936 was shot and wounded at a party conference after accusing some officeholders of corruption in the awarding of utilities concessions to foreign companies. In the same period, he became a leading political defense lawyer, noted for his representation of arrested Communists and liberals. Frondizi was elected to the Argentine national parliament in 1946, and became a national figure after his unsuccessful 1951 vice presidential campaign. After Juan Perón's 1955 overthrow, Frondizi became the Radical Party presidential candidate. He made a secret agreement with Perón that won him Perón's unstated support, and was elected to the presidency in 1958. Upon taking office, he abandoned his nationalist and populist positions, courted foreign investment, and introduced pro-business economic austerity programs. In 1962, with a resurgence of Perónist political strength, the Argentine military forced Frondizi to resign. Although he remained in politics, he was from then on a minor figure in Argentine public life. There were no survivors. (d. Buenos Aires; April 18, 1995)

FURTHER READING

Obituary. *Independent*, Apr. 20, 1995.
Obituary. *Times* (of London), Apr. 19, 1995.
Obituary. *New York Times*, Apr. 19, 1995.

Fuentes, Carlos (1928–) Though labeled as fiction, Carlos Fuentes' book *Diana: The Goddess Who Hunts Alone*, about a brief 1970 affair, was more than "semi" autobiographical, with some reviewers describing it as a thinly veiled memoir. This characterization is suggested by the main character being a young Mexican novelist named Carlos; by the appearance of named celebrities such as William Styron, Luis Bunuel, Tina Turner, and Clint Eastwood; and by the title character, actress Diana Soren, whose life description and personal relationships leave little doubt that she is based on the late and troubled actress Jean Seberg. Some reviewers greeted the book warmly, while others found it unsuccessful and unsatisfying as either novel or memoir. Translation for the 1995 English publication was done by Alfred MacAdam.

Mexico City–born Fuentes, a much-honored writer and diplomat, is a leading figure in Latin-American literature. He began his career as a Mexican delegate to the International Labor Organization (1950–52), held several government and university posts during the 1950s, and was Mexican ambassador to France (1974–76). He has also edited several literary magazines. He taught comparative literature at several universities during the late 1970s and early 1980s, from 1984 at Harvard University, where he became Robert F. Kennedy Professor of Latin American Studies (1987–). He is best known by far for his novels, his breakthrough coming with *Where the Air Is Clear* (1958), a sharply critical study of the upper-class Mexican life that was his own heritage. Among his other best-known works are the novels *The Death of Artemio Cruz* (1962), *A Change of Skin* (1967), *Terra Nostra* (1975), *Old Gringo* (1985; basis of the 1989 film starring Gregory Peck and Jane Fonda), *Cristobal Nonate* (1987), *The Campaign* (1991), and the 5-novella collection *The Orange Tree* (1993). He has also written short stories, several volumes of essays, and a controversial television series *The Buried Mirror: Reflections on Spain and the New World by Carlos Fuentes* (1991). Fuentes married his second wife, Sylvia Lemus, in 1973; they have a son and a daughter. He also has a daughter from his first marriage.

FURTHER READING

"Chiapas. . . ." NATHAN GARDELS. *New Perspectives Quarterly*, Spring 1994.
Author, Text and Reader in the Novels of Carlos Fuentes. KRISTINE IBSEN. P. Lang, 1994.
"Daring dreamer." GUY GARCIA. *Time,* June 29, 1992.
"Carlos Fuentes." FERNANDO AINSA. *UNESCO Courier,* Jan. 1992.
"Carlos Fuentes. . . ." MARTA MESTROVIC. *Publishers Weekly,* Oct. 25, 1991.
"The new world disordered." ELISABETH HICKEY. *Insight on the News,* Sept. 30, 1991.

Fujimori, Alberto (1938–) Sharply rebutting earlier reports that he had been losing popularity because of his country's continuing massive poverty and unemployment rates, Peru's President Alberto Fujimori was in April returned to office for a second five-year term, in an election considered by foreign observers to be substantially free of fraud. Fujimori won by an absolute majority of the votes cast, defeating his main rival, former United Nations secretary general Javier Pérez de Cuéllar by almost three to one. Fujimori's ruling coalition also won an absolute congressional majority. His estranged wife, Susana Higuchi, was denied a place on the ballot. The victory came after armed border clashes between Peru and Ecuador during January and February, which had mobilized Peruvian opinion behind Fujimori, though the magnitude of his electoral victory made it clear that his authoritarian government had the support of the great majority of those voting.

Fujimori's economic policy successes continued during 1995, as foreign investment grew. At the same time, his policies had little visible impact on the rate of unemployment, or on the increasing problem of mass poverty—and although the Shining Path and Tupac Amaru Communist insurgencies were hit hard by army attacks, they both continued.

Though the Catholic leader of a largely Catholic country, Fujimori made a notable appearance in Beijing in September, at the UN World Conference on Women, strongly attacking the Vatican's opposition to contraception, and seeking the support of other South American leaders in the formation of a continent-wide coalition in support of enhanced family planning and birth control education.

Peruvian-born Fujimori, the son of Japanese-Peruvian immigrants, attended La Molina, the National Agrarian University, graduating in 1961, and then taught at the university. His 1969 master's degree was in mathematics, from the University of Wisconsin. He became dean of the science faculty at La Molina in 1984, was principal of the university (1984–89), and was president of the Peruvian National Council of Principals (1987–89). He scored an upset victory over novelist Mario Vargas Llosa in the 1990 presidential election. On April 5, 1992, with the support of the military, he seized dictatorial power, dissolving the federal Congress, the regional assemblies, and the courts, and ruling by decree. On September 12, 1992, he scored a major victory in his country's civil war, with the capture of Shining Path leader Abimael Guzmán Reynoso; but the civil war continued, although diminishing in intensity during 1993 and 1994.

Fujimori and his estranged wife, civil engineer Susana Higuchi, married in 1974; they have four children.

FURTHER READING

"Saving the state in Peru." NATHAN GARDELS and ABRAHAM LOWENTHAL. *New Perspectives Quarterly,* Fall 1993.
"The unshining path. . . ." GUSTAVO GORRITI. *New Republic,* Feb. 8, 1993.
"Casting stones." MIKE MOORE. "Can Fujimori save Peru?" MICHAEL RADU. *Bulletin of the Atomic Scientists,* July–Aug. 1992.
"The 'Karate Kid'. . . ." TOM VOGEL, JR. *Commonweal,* Jan. 11, 1991.

Fukuda, Takeo (1905–95) Former Japanese prime minister and Liberal Democratic Party leader Takeo Fukuda joined his country's Ministry of Finance in 1929, after receiving his law degree from the University of Tokyo. He held a succession of increasingly responsible government financial positions through the 1930s and 1940s, serving in Europe and occupied China, and in the postwar period rising to head the Finance Ministry's budget bureau. He resigned in

1950, after being indicted for allegedly taking bribes from the Showa Denko company, though he was later acquitted of the charges. Fukuda won election to Japan's House of Representatives in 1952, held several Cabinet posts, and rose to become concurrently president of the Liberal Democratic Party and prime minister (1976–78). His chief achievement as prime minister was the signing of a peace and friendship treaty with China, laying the formal basis for extended commercial ties. He continued to be a leading figure in his party until his death. He was survived by his wife, Mie Arai Fukuda, two daughters, and two sons. (d. Tokyo; July 5, 1995)

FURTHER READING

Obituary. *Current Biography,* Sept. 1995.
Obituary. *Economist,* July 15, 1995.
Obituary. *Independent,* July 8, 1995.
Obituary. *Times* (of London), July 6, 1995.
Obituary. *New York Times,* July 6, 1995.
Statesman and Pragmatic Humanist—In Honor of Takeo Fukuda on the Occasion of His 90th Birthday. HANS D'ORVILLE, ed. InterAction Council, 1995.

Fulbright, J. William (James William Fulbright; 1905–95) Missouri-born J. William Fulbright studied as a Rhodes Scholar at Oxford after graduating from the University of Arkansas in 1925, an experience that was to be central to his later political career. It resulted very directly in his initiation of the Fulbright exchange scholarship program in 1946, during his first term in the U.S. Senate. On returning to the U.S. from Britain, he became a lawyer, and began his career with the Justice Department in 1934. He became president of the University of Arkansas in 1939, and was fired by a new governor in 1941, then turning to politics. He served in the House of Representatives (1941–45), and then began his long Senate career (1945–75).

In the Senate, Fulbright focused on foreign affairs, as the highly independent and internationalist chair of the Foreign Relations Committee becoming one of the most influential Senators of his time. He supported the formation of the United Nations, the Marshall Plan, the Korean War, and strong U.S. action during the Cuban Missile Crisis. He was also a powerful opponent of McCarthyism, playing a key role in McCar-

thy's ultimate disgrace. Fulbright was from the early 1960s very doubtful about the wisdom of American involvement in the Vietnam War, but went along with presidents John F. Kennedy and Lyndon B. Johnson, even sponsoring the Tonkin Gulf resolution that enabled Johnson to escalate the war in 1964. In the mid-1960s, Fulbright turned into a steadfast opponent of the war. On domestic matters, he often voted as a Southern conservative, in several instances voting against civil rights laws. Fulbright strongly influenced the career and views of President Bill Clinton, who was once a member of his staff (1966; 1967). Among Fulbright's published works were *Old Myths and New Realities: And Other Commentaries* (1964), *Arrogance of Power* (1967), *The Future of the United Nations* (1977), *The Crippled Giant* (1981), and *The Price of Empire* (1989), written with Seth P. Tillman. He was survived by his second wife, Harriet Mayor, and two daughters. (d. Washington, D.C.; February 9, 1995)

FURTHER READING

"Crippled giant." JACOB HEILBRUNN. *New Republic,* Mar. 6, 1995.
"Fulbright's legacy." SIDNEY BLUMENTHAL. *New Yorker,* Mar. 6, 1995.
"A contrary voice. . . ." *People,* Feb. 27, 1995.
"A politican of principle." JONATHAN ALTER. *Newsweek,* Feb. 20, 1995.
Obituary. *Independent,* Feb. 10, 1995.
Obituary. *Times* (of London), Feb. 10, 1995.
Obituary. *New York Times,* Feb. 10, 1995.
Fulbright: A Biography. RANDALL B. WOODS. Cambridge University Press, 1995.
J. William Fulbright: A Bibliography. BETTY AUSTIN. Greenwood, 1995.

Furculo, Foster (1911–95) New Haven–born politician and writer Foster Furculo received his 1933 B.A. and 1936 LL.B from Yale University. He began his law practice in Springfield, Massachusetts in 1937, saw Navy service during World War II, and after the war began to build his political career, winning election as a Democrat to the U.S. House of Representatives in 1948 and a second term in 1950. He was appointed Massachusetts state treasurer and receiver by Governor John Dever in 1952, and four years later, running as a liberal Democrat, won the first of his two gubernatorial terms. As governor, he stressed such programs as student aid, expanded the state's social service network, developed pioneering antidiscrimination legislation, and greatly expanded the University of Massachusetts. He later taught courses at several Massachusetts colleges, and wrote a wide range of articles, essays, and fiction, including several plays. He was survived by his wife, Constance Gleason Furculo, and by a daughter, three sons, and a brother. (d. Cambridge, Massachusetts; July 5, 1995)

FURTHER READING

Obituary. *New York Times*, July 6, 1995.

G

Gabor, Eva (1919–95) Hungarian actress Eva Gabor was the youngest of the three celebrity Gabor sisters, and the first of the three to emigrate to the United States, in 1939. She had in Hungary been a cabaret singer and skater; in the U.S., she quickly moved into Hollywood films, among them *Forced Landing* (1941), *A Royal Scandal* (1945), *The Last Time I Saw Paris* (1954), *Don't Go Near the Water* (1957), *Gigi* (1958), and *A New Kind of Love* (1963). She became a star on stage in *The Happy Time* (1950). Gabor became a major television star in the long-running situation comedy "Green Acres" (1965–71), playing a bored sophisticate in a rustic setting, opposite Eddie Albert as her country-loving husband. Gabor was also a successful businesswoman who developed her own wig company. Her autobiography was *Orchids and Salamis* (1951). She was survived by her mother, and her two sisters, Zsa Zsa and Magda. (d. Los Angeles; July 4, 1995)

FURTHER READING

Obituary. *Current Biography,* Sept. 1995.
Obituary. *Variety,* July 10, 1995.
Obituary. *Times* (of London), July 6, 1995.
Obituary. *New York Times,* July 5, 1995.
Obituary. *Variety,* July 5, 1995.

Garcia, Jerry (Jerome John Garcia; 1942–95) San Francisco–born Jerry Garcia, the guitarist and leading figure of The Grateful Dead and a popular rock composer, began his career in

Jerry Garcia (front left) with members of The Grateful Dead.

the late 1950s, playing guitar and banjo in Bay area bluegrass bands. In 1965, he, Bob Weir, Ron McKernan, Phil Lesh, and Bill Kreutzmann formed The Grateful Dead, which was in its early years a strongly drug-oriented alternative culture Haight-Ashbury blues-folk-rock group. Their first album was *The Grateful Dead* (1967), followed by such albums as *Anthem of the Sun* (1968), *Aoxomoxoa* (1970), *Workingman's Dead* (1970), *American Beauty* (1970), *The Grateful Dead* (1971), and many others. The band, with Garcia writing much of their material, became a very popular alternative culture group in the late 1960s, beginning a free-swinging touring career that would last three decades, each concert unplanned and different, with little regard for commercial considerations. They attracted a uniquely loyal following, the "Deadheads," many of whom followed them on tour. The Grateful Dead became one of the most notable survivals of the 1960s alternative culture, for its fans serving as a symbol of artistic and personal freedom—and Garcia was its leading figure. Garcia also formed his own band, touring in between Grateful Dead tours, and recording several albums. He was survived by his third wife, Deborah Koons, and four daughters. (d. Forest Hills, California; August 9, 1995)

FURTHER READING

"Live and let die. . . ." JOHN TAYLOR. *Esquire,* Dec. 1995.
Obituary. *Guitar Player,* Dec. 1995.
Obituary. *Current Biography,* Oct. 1995.
"Jerry Garcia, RIP." WILLIAM F.BUCKLEY, JR. *National Review,* Sept. 25, 1995.
"Dead reckoning. . . ." BILL BARICH. "Playing in the band. . . ." DAVID FRICKE. "Land of the Dead. . . ." BEN FONG-TORRES. "End of the beginning. . . ." ROBERT STONE. " 'We were just. . . .' " "Jerry Garcia. . . ." MIKAL GILMORE. "And we bid you. . . ." " 'He had faced. . . .' " DAVID FRICKE. "Funeral for. . . ." ALEC FOEGE et al. *Rolling Stone,* Sept. 21, 1995.
"Last rites. . . ." CHRIS WILLMAN. *Entertainment,* Aug. 25, 1995.
"What a long, strange. . . ." STEVE DOUGHERTY. *People,* Aug. 21, 1995.
"The trip ends. . . ." RICHARD CORLISS. "No longer. . . ." *Time,* Aug. 21, 1995.
Obituary. *Times* (of London), Aug. 11, 1995.
Obituary. *New York Times*, Aug. 10, 1995.
Obituary. *Independent,* Aug. 10, 1995.
Obituary. *Variety*, Aug. 10, 1995.
Captain Trips: A Biography of Jerry Garcia. SANDY TROY. Thunders Mouth, 1994.
"Still truckin'." BILL BARICH. *New Yorker,* Oct. 11, 1993.
"The Grateful." HOWARD RHEINGOLD. *Interview,* July 1991.
"Love and money." ANNA MARIA ARIAS. *Hispanic,* May 1991.

García Márquez, Gabriel (1928–) Colombian Nobel Laureate Gabriel García Márquez retains his title of master of magical realism with his latest novel, *Of Love and Other Demons.* Set in colonial South America, the work explores the cruelty of ignorance and intolerance through the story of 12-year-old Sierva Maria, who is bitten by a rabid dog and assumed therefore to be possessed by demons; handed over to the church for exorcism, she is blamed for all manner of evil events, especially as she tells of strange dreams and premonitions, but finds temporary salvation in the person of her exorcist, Cayetano Delaura, who comes to love the child. A prelude to the novel describes an incident said to have sparked the book: the 1940s disinterment of bones from an old convent that included the bones of a child whose full and long head of coppery hair was still attached to the skull 200 years after her burial.

A leading Latin American novelist, García Márquez won the Nobel Prize for literature in 1982, in recognition of a body of novels and short stories that by then had made him a world figure, including the novels *One Hundred Years of Solitude* (1967), *Death of a Patriarch* (1975), and *Love in the Time of Cholera* (1984). His most recent major work includes the novel *The General in His Labyrinth* (1989) and *Strange Pilgrims: Twelve Stories* (1993). Politically an independent, critical of both socialism and capitalism, García Márquez was influenced by Marxism in the early 1960s and became a close personal friend of Cuban leader Fidel Castro; as a result he was for 33 years, until 1991, officially barred by immigration laws from entering the United States. He attended the National University at Bogotá. He is married to Mercedes García Márquez; they have two children.

FURTHER READING

"Love and other demons." ROSA MORA. *World Press Review,* July 1994.

Garcia Marquez. ROBIN FIDDIAN, ed. Longman, 1995.

Gabriel Garcia Marquez: Colombian Writer. SEAN DOLAN. Chelsea House, 1994.

Bibliographic Guide to Gabriel Garcia Marquez, 1986–1992. NELLY S. DE GONZALEZ. Greenwood, 1994.

Gabriel Garcia Marquez: Solitude and Solidarity. MICHAEL BELL. St. Martin's, 1993.

The First Garcia Marquez: A Study of His Journalistic Writing from 1948–1955. ROBERT L. SIMS. University Press of America, 1992.

"Gabriel Garcia Marquez." MANUEL OSORIO. *UNESCO Courier,* Oct. 1991.

Garner, James (James Baumgarner; 1928–)

Still one of the world's most familiar faces for his perennial "Maverick" and "Rockford Files" series and many theatrical film reruns, film and televison star James Garner starred in yet another major screen work in 1995. In the very well received five-hour television miniseries "Streets of Laredo," a sequel to Larry McMurtry's acclaimed 1989 miniseries "Lonesome Dove," Garner played former Texas Ranger Captain Woodrow Call, now retired and a bounty hunter, who is on the track of several train robbers, the worst of them young killer Joey Garza, played by Alexis Cruz. Costarring were Sissy Spacek as a former prostitute turned schoolteacher, Sam Shepherd as bounty hunter and former Ranger Pea Eye Parker, Sonia Braga as Joey's mother, Ned Beatty as Judge Roy Bean, Billy Williams, Randy Quaid, and Wes Studi. Joseph Sargent directed; Larry McMurtry and Diana Ossana coproduced and cowrote the script, based on the McMurtry novel.

Garner also received a Screen Actors Guild Award nomination as best actor in a television film or miniseries for *The Rockford Files: I Still Love L.A* (1994).

Oklahoma-born Garner began his long career in the mid-1950s, in a small, nonspeaking role in *The Caine Mutiny Court Martial* (1954), and in bit parts in television. He quickly emerged as a major television series star, in the title role of the western "Maverick" (1957–61), and later as private investigator Jim Rockford in "The Rockford Files" (1974–80). His wide range of films included *Sayonara* (1957), *The Great Escape* (1963), *The Americanization of Emily* (1964), *Marlowe* (1969), *They Only Kill Their Masters* (1972), *Victor/Victoria* (1982), *Murphy's Romance* (1985), *Sunset* (1987), and *Maverick* (1994). He also starred in such telefilms as *Promise* (1986; it won five Emmys, including best drama), *My Name Is Bill W* (1989), *Barbarians at the Gate* (1993), and *Breathing Lessons* (1994). Garner attended the University of Oklahoma. He married Lois Clarke in 1956; they have three children. (For photo, see **Foster, Jodie.**)

FURTHER READING

"James Garner. . . ." MARK MORRISON. *Ladies Home Journal,* July 1994.

"Filmographies." ANDY WEBSTER. *Premiere,* June 1994.

Gates, William Henry, III (1955–)

Computer software magnate William Gates, founder of the Microsoft Corporation, in 1995 once again topped *Forbes* magazine's list of the world's richest people, his net worth estimated at $12.9 billion, $2.2 billion more than the runner-up, Warren E. Buffet.

Gates continued to build Microsoft, already a giant in computer software, as the worldwide communications industries merged and new competition developed from immense communications companies even larger than his. Among his many projects was the introduction of Microsoft's long-awaited Windows 95 software, accompanied by a massive worldwide marketing campaign. Another was the introduction of Microsoft's electronic online service, expected to jump into a commanding position in the online field and to soon provide television and movies through the computer. Gates also accelerated his quest for content, through his Corbis company scouring the world for deals with museums and other image sources, preferably on an exclusive basis—though relatively few were willing to grant exclusives. In October, Corbis announced acquisition of the Bettman Archive, one of the world's great stores of millions of still historical photos.

There were setbacks, though. Microsofts's highly touted 1994 acquisition of the Intuit software company was challenged by the U.S. Justice Department, and Microsoft quickly withdrew from the $2 billion deal, to the surprise of most observers. Microsoft's 1994 settlement of a lawsuit charging that the company unfairly and illegally exploited its position as the world's dominant supplier of computer software was upset by a federal judge, reopening the case, a major threat to Microsoft.

Late in the year, Gates published *The Road Ahead*, written with John Ottavino, which quickly reached the top of the best-seller list; the authors also served as readers of the audio version.

After his 1973 graduation from high school in Seattle, Washington, Gates attended Harvard University, where he started producing computer software. He cofounded the Microsoft Corporation in Redmond, Washington (1976), which survived early lean years to become the dominant software producer for personal computers. He married Microsoft executive Melinda French in 1994.

FURTHER READING

"Online with. . . ." LYNNE POVICH. *Working Woman,* Jan. 1996.
"Whose Internet . . . ?" BRENT SCHLENDER. *Fortune,* Dec. 11, 1995.
" 'Software is my life.' " MARK WHITAKER and STEVEN LEVY. "Bill's new vision." STEPHEN LEVY. *Newsweek,* Nov. 27, 1995.
"Gates wins respect." GEORGE TANINECZ. *Industry Week,* Nov. 20, 1995.
"Bill Gates. . . ." BRENT SCHLENDER. *Fortune,* Oct. 2, 1995.
"The billionaires." *Forbes,* July 17, 1995.
"Hard drive." PHILIP ELMER-DEWITT and DAVID S. JACKSON. "Mine, all mine. . . ." PHILIP ELMER-DEWITT. *Time,* June 5, 1995.
"A democratic media market." NATHAN GARDELS. *New Perspectives Quarterly,* Spring 1995.
"What Bill Gates. . . ." BRENT SCHENDLER. *Fortune,* Jan. 16, 1995.
Smart Money: The Story of Bill Gates. AARON BOYD. M. Reynolds, 1995.
"Billionaires." Oct. 17, 1994. "On the road with. . . ." RICH KARLGAARD. Feb. 28, 1994. *Forbes.*
"Playboy interview. . . ." *Playboy,* July 1994.
"Bill's excellent future." RICHARD M. SMITH. *Newsweek,* Oct. 11, 1993.
"Billionaire brain. . . ." HENRY PORTER. *Observer,* Apr. 19, 1992.
"Genius at work." BRENDA DALGLISH. *Maclean's,* May 11, 1992.
Hard Drive: Bill Gates and the Making of the Microsoft Empire. JAMES WALLACE and JIM ERICKSON. Wiley, 1992.
William H. Gates: From Whiz Kid to Software King. RALPH ZICKGRAF. Garrett, 1992.
"Mr. Software." FRED MOODY. *New York Times Magazine,* Aug. 25, 1991.
"Gates, William Henry, III." *Current Biography,* May 1991.

Gazzo, Michael V. (1924–95) Playwright, screenwriter, and actor Michael V. Gazzo was the author of the Broadway hit drama *A Hatful of Rain* (1955), an early treatment of the drug problem, starring Ben Gazzara as a narcotics addict fighting to win his battle against addiction, and costarring Shelley Winters, Frank Silvera, and Anthony Franciosa. Gazzo adapted his play into the 1957 Fred Zinneman film, starring Don Murray and Eva Marie Saint.

As an actor, Gazzo appeared in several films, most notably in *The Godfather, Part II,* for which he won a best supporting actor Oscar nomination. His screenwriting credits included *King Creole* (1958), starring Elvis Presley, and his playwrighting credits included the Off-Broadway play *Night Circus* (1958). He was survived by his wife, Grace, a daughter, two sons, a sister, and a brother. (d. Los Angeles; February 14, 1995)

FURTHER READING

Obituary. *Variety,* Feb. 28, 1995.
Obituary. *New York Times,* Feb. 24, 1995.

Gellhorn, Walter (1906–95) St. Louis–born legal scholar and civil libertarian Walter Gellhorn received his 1927 B.A. from Amherst College and his 1931 LL.B. from Columbia University. After graduation, he clerked for Supreme Court Justice Harlan Fiske Stone and was attached to the U.S. solicitor general's office. He began his long teaching career at Columbia Law School in 1933 and retired in 1973, though continuing on in a very active emeritus status until just before his death. From the late 1930s until the end of World War II, Gellhorn worked with several federal agencies and departments, among them the Social Security system, the attorney general's office, the Office of Price Administration, and the War Labor Board. After the war, he helped write the new Japanese Constitution.

Gellhorn was best known by far for his book *Administrative Law: Cases and Comments* (1940), which has gone through many editions and is the standard work in its field. He was also a leading figure in introducing the ombudsman concept into American law. Throughout his life, he was also a leading defender of the Bill of Rights and civil rights, through his work with the American Civil Liberties Union (ACLU) and the National Association for the Advancement of Colored People (NAACP)—and as the author of *Security, Loyalty, and Science* (1950), *The States and Subversion* (1952), *Individual Freedoms and Government Restraints* (1956), *The Freedom to Read* (1956), *American Rights* (1960), and *Ombudsmen and Others: Citizen's Protectors in Nine Countries* (1966). He was survived by his wife, Kitty, two daughters, a sister and a brother. (d. New York City; December 9, 1995)

FURTHER READING

Obituary. *New York Times*, Dec. 11, 1995.

Gephardt, Richard Andrew (1941–)

Former Democratic House Majority Leader Richard Gephardt remained a familiar face on the nation's television screens in 1995, though no longer as one of the leaders of the dominant party, but rather as the leader of a badly rattled minority party during a period of aggressively conservative House Republican ascendancy. Gephardt and other House Democratic leaders spent much of the year fighting a series of defensive actions aimed at blunting the Republican legislative drive—and succeeded in doing this far more effectively than most observers had expected. In this, they were greatly helped by the fact that the Republicans, led by House Speaker Newt Gingrich, did not have enough votes to overcome presidential vetoes of most conservative legislation, and that such conservative goals as the abolition of social security and abortion were not even formally proposed. Late in the year, as the focus of the massive budget fight swung to President Clinton, House Democrats took something of a back seat, although their support of a presidential veto was still an essential element of administration planning.

As the year developed, Gephardt continued to distance himself from President Clinton, probably in anticipation of his own future presidential candidacy. However, as Clinton late in the year seemed to make a comeback, Gephardt fought strongly for the administration's domestic policies, although he was still reserved in several matters of foreign policy, including the proposed supply of American troops for peace-keeping purposes in Bosnia.

St. Louis–born Gephardt began his political career as a St. Louis alderman (1971–76), then began his congressional career in 1979. He was a strong contender for the Democratic presidential nomination in 1988. He was elected House Democratic majority leader in 1989. In July 1991, he took himself out of the 1992 presidential race, though he nearly returned in February 1992, as President George Bush began to look far less invulnerable. He endorsed Bill Clinton in April 1992 and addressed the Democratic National Convention in Clinton's favor in July. Gephardt had encountered some bad publicity because of his 28 overdrafts on the House bank, but was in no way seriously damaged, as attested by his landslide reelection victory in November 1992, with 66 percent of the vote to his opponent's 34 percent. After the Republican victory in the 1994 congressional elections, Gephardt won election as House minority leader in the new Republican-dominated House of Representatives, and became top House Democratic leader, replacing former House Speaker Tom Foley, who had lost his reelection bid.

Gephardt received his 1962 B.S. from Northwestern University, and his 1965 J.D. from the University of Michigan. He married Jane Ann Byrnes in 1966; the couple has three children.

FURTHER READING

"Chameleon. . . ." RICHARD BLOW. *Mother Jones*, Sept.–Oct. 1994.

Gere, Richard (1949–)

Film star Richard Gere appeared as Lancelot, opposite Sean Connery as Arthur and Julia Ormond as Guinevere in the 1995 film *First Knight*, a straightforward, romantic retelling of the King Arthur story, directed by Jerry Zucker. Ben Cross costarred as the evil knight Malagant and John Gielgud appeared as an advisor to the queen. Gere's Lancelot is in this story a rather rough, roving outsider, who falls in love with the steadfastly chaste Guinevere, repeatedly defeats Malagant, and ultimately joins Arthur's Round Table. The costume drama was respectfully received by the critics and did modestly well at the box office, although Gere's outsider was thought by some to be somewhat out of synch with the rest of the production.

Still forthcoming were starring roles opposite Michelle Pfeiffer in the film *Higgins Beach*, directed by Jon Amiel; and in the film *Primal Fear*, directed by Gregory Hoblit and costarring Leonardo DiCaprio. Also slated was a starring role in the film *The Hundredth Monkey*, directed by Alfonso Cuaron.

Continuing to pursue his deep interest in Buddhism and the Dalai Lama, Gere wrote the foreword and contributed money to help publish the Dalai Lama lecture collection *The World of Tibetan Buddhism*. Gere also exhibited a collection of his photos, *Tibet: the Pure Realm*.

Philadelphia-born Gere began his theater career in the early 1970s, and became a star in such films as *Report to the Commissioner* (1975), *Looking for Mr. Goodbar* (1977), *Yanks* (1979), *An Officer and a Gentleman* (1982), and *Internal Affairs* (1989). After several years in the doldrums, Gere's career received an enormous boost from the unexpected popularity of *Pretty Woman* (1990), the *Pygmalion*-like romantic comedy in which he costarred with Julia Roberts. Later films included *Rhapsody in August* (1992), *Final Analysis* (1992), *Sommersby* (1993), *Mr. Jones* (1993), *And the Band Played On* (1993), and *Intersection* (1994). Long interested in Buddhism and Eastern philosophy, Gere is the founder and chairman of Tibet House. Gere attended the University of Massachusetts and married model Cindy Crawford in 1991; they separated in 1994.

FURTHER READING

"Even Richard Gere. . . ." MICHAEL GROSS. *Esquire,* July 1995.
"Richard Gere." TOM O'NEILL. *Us,* July 1995.
"True romance." KAREN S. SCHNEIDER. *People,* Oct. 18, 1993.
"The model and. . . ." HERB RITTS and JULIA REED. *Vogue,* Nov. 1992.

Gibson, Mel (1956–) In 1995, Mel Gibson produced, directed, and starred in the huge costume drama *Braveheart*, set in 13th-century Scotland, playing Scottish independence leader

William Wallace, opposite Patrick McGoohan as conquering English king Edward the Longshanks and Sophie Marceau as the French princess he marries for reasons of state. Angus McFayden played Scottish leader Robert the Bruce. Gibson received a Golden Globe nomination as best director for the film.

Gibson also starred as one of the voices in the animated film *Pocahontas*, directed by Mike Gabriel and Eric Goldberg. He narrated the televised documentary *Australia's Outback: The Vanishing Frontier*, filmed and written by Hugh Piper and Helen Barrow, about a cattle station in western Australia. He also again hosted the children's story series "Rabbit Ears Radio" for National Public Television.

Forthcoming was a starring role in the film *Ransom*, directed by Ron Howard.

Born in Peekskill, New York, Gibson emigrated to Australia with his family in 1968. He appeared on stage and screen in Australia from 1977, in South Australian regional theater in the classics, in several television series, and most notably in the film *Tim* (1979). He soon became a popular worldwide film star in such action films as *Mad Max* (1979), and its two sequels: *The Road Warrior* (1982) and *Mad Max Beyond Thunderdome* (1985); the dramas *Gallipoli* (1981) and *The Year of Living Dangerously* (1983); the *Lethal Weapon* films (1987; 1989; 1992); *Bird on a Wire* (1990); and *Air America* (1990). In 1993, he made his directorial debut with the film *The Man Without a Face*, in which he starred with Nick Stahl. In 1994, he starred in the film *Maverick*. Gibson attended the Australian National Institute of Dramatic Arts. He married Robyn Moore in 1979; they have six children.

FURTHER READING

"Playboy interview. . . ." LAWRENCE GROBEL. *Playboy,* July 1995.
"Wild at heart." JANCEE DUNN. *Us,* June 1995.
"Thistle do nicely." GRAHAM FULLER. *Interview,* May 1995.
"Mad Mac." STEPHANIE MANSFIELD. *GQ,* May 1995.
"Mel Gibson. . . ." WENSLEY CLARKSON. *Cosmopolitan,* Apr. 1994.
"Mad Mel." RACHEL ABRAMOWITZ. *Premiere*, Sept. 1993.
"To Mel and back." ALLEN BARRA. *Entertainment,* Aug. 20, 1993.
Lethal Hero: Mel Gibson Biography. ROLAND PERRY. Oliver, 1993.
"Mel Gibson. . . ." JEANNE MARIE LASKAS. *Redbook,* Nov. 1992.
Mel Gibson. NEIL SINYARD. Outlet, 1992.

Gielgud, John (Arthur John Gielgud; 1904–) Universally recognized as one of world's greatest living actors, John Gielgud, now 91 and in the 74th year of his very long career, continued to work in the screen and broadcast forms in 1995—although now no longer appearing in more physically demanding stage roles. In the King Arthur film *First Knight*, directed by Jerry Zucker, he played a counselor to Queen Guinevere (Julia Ormond), in a cast that included Sean Connery as Arthur, Richard Gere, and Ben Cross. Gielgud also appeared in Mel Gibson's National Public Radio series "Rabbit Ears Radio," reading *The Emperor's New Clothes*, with music by Mark Isham.

Forthcoming was a starring role opposite Lynn Redgrave in the film *Shine*, directed by Scott Hicks. He was also slated to costar in Kenneth Branagh's film adaptation of Shakespeare's *Hamlet*; Branagh will direct and star in the title role, played so notably by Gielgud earlier in the century.

London-born Gielgud, grandnephew of the celebrated actress Ellen Terry, made his stage debut in 1921, and by 1929 had become a highly regarded Shakespearean actor at the Old Vic, going on to play major roles in Shakespeare from then on. He directed a legendary 1935 *Romeo and Juliet* in London, alternating with Laurence Olivier in the Mercutio and Romeo roles. Late in his career, he created several modern roles, in plays such as *Nude with Violin* (1956), *Tiny Alice* (1964), *Home* (1970), and *No Man's Land* (1970). Although Gielgud made his film debut in 1921 and played leads in the films *Secret Agent* (1936) and *Julius Caesar* (1970), he has for most of his career been primarily a theater actor. In recent years, however, he has played numerous strong supporting roles, in such films as *Murder on the Orient Express* (1974), *Arthur* (1981; he won a best supporting actor Oscar), *Chariots of Fire* (1981), and *Shining Through* (1992), and in such television productions as *Brideshead Revisited* (1981), *War and Remembrance* (1988), and *Scarlett* (1994). London's West End Globe Theatre was renamed the Gielgud Theatre in 1994.

Among Gielgud's writings are *Early Stages: A Theatrical Reminiscence* (1939), *Stage Directions* (1963), *An Actor in His Time* (1981), *Backward Glances: Times for Reflection and Distinguished Company* (1990), and *Acting Shakespeare* (1992).

FURTHER READING

"Peerless prince. . . ." *Observer*, Apr. 3, 1994.
John Gielgud: A Celebration. GYLES BRANDRETH. Trafalgar, 1994.

Gill, Vince (1957–) It was a year of many, many awards for celebrated country singer and songwriter Vince Gill. He won a best male country vocal performance Grammy for the song "When Love Finds You," the title song from his Grammy-nominated album of that name. He had received a second nomination in the same category for "I Swear." At Nashville's 29th Annual Country Music Awards, Gill won his fifth straight award as best male vocalist of the year, along with nominations as entertainer of the year, best album, and best music video for *When Love Finds You.*

At the 22nd Annual American Music Awards, he won the best country single award for "Whenever You Come Around," an album of the year nomination for *Who I Am*, a best single record nomination for "Tryin' To Get Over You," a song of the year nomination for "When Love Finds You," and a best male vocalist nomination. Among his other awards were a Nammie for outstanding achievement, and the Nashville Song-writers Association annual songwriter/artist of the year award.

In 1995, Gill issued the hit album *Souvenirs*, a retrospective containing fifteen songs, among them "Never Alone," "Liza Jane," "Never Knew Lonely," "When I Call Your Name," "Look At Us," "Pocket Full of Gold," and "I Will Always Love You." He also issued three hit singles: "Which Bridge To Cross," the country rock song "You Better Think Twice," and "Go Rest High On That Mountain."

Oklahoma-born Gill emerged as a country music star in the late 1980s, on tour and with the solo albums *The Way Back Home* (1987), *When I Call Your Name* (1990), *Pocket Full of Gold* (1991), *I Never Knew Lonely* (1992), and *When Love Finds You* (1994). He won his first Grammy in 1990, for best male country performance, and won two Country Music Association awards in 1991. For his 1992 album *I Still Believe in You*, Gill won three Grammys, as top male country vocalist performance for the song and for the album, and for the song itself, cowritten with John Barlow Jarvis; and five Country Music Association awards, including entertainer, male vocalist, song, songwriter, and album of the year. He is married to Janis Gill; they have one child.

FURTHER READING

"Vince Gill. . . . " *Country Music,* Jan.–Feb. 1995.
Vince Gill: When Love Finds You. Warner, 1994.
"Vince Gill. . . ." JON SIEVERT. *Guitar Player,* Mar. 1992.

Gingrich, Newt (Newton Leroy McPherson Gingrich; 1943–) House Minority Leader Newt Gingrich began 1995 still seemingly on top of his world, although the clouds on his horizon included substantial voter mistrust, continuing questions as to possible financial irregularities, and little progress on passage of the conservative "Contract with America." Still, he was widely thought to be a strong possible 1996 presidential candidate, and talked as if he, too, thought a presidential run might be in prospect.

For a considerable variety of reaons, the year turned out to be not very good for Gingrich. Although he had soft-pedaled such radical and distasteful statements as his proposal that some poor children be taken from their mothers and

put into orphanages, and foregone the controversial $4.5 million in book advances from a publishing company owned by Rupert Murdoch, much of the damage to his reputation seemed to have been done—and there were no signs of it being undone. A November 19, 1995 *Washington Post/ABC* poll showed only 27 percent of those polled holding a favorable view of Gingrich, and 65 percent disapproved of his performance as Speaker of the House of Representatives. On November 27, he said that he would not be a 1996 presidential candidate.

During 1995, Gingrich continued to press for passage of the Republican legislative program, as outlined in his "Contract with America." At year's end, the overwhelming bulk of the program had yet to be enacted, much of it part of the budget deadlock that had shut down the federal government. An index of the change in Gingrich's fortunes was that maverick Republicans in the House of Representatives had refused to honor the agreements Gingrich and Bob Dole had made with President Bill Clinton in an attempt to end the budget deadlock. The House Republican refusal to compromise ended up hurting the Republican party. It seemed likely that a good deal of Gingrich's program would indeed ultimately be enacted into law, but at year's end much remained to be done.

Much also remained to be seen as to the charges of financial irregularity that had pursued Gingrich during much of his tenure as Speaker. On November 29, the Federal Elections

Commission formally charged that the Gopac political action committee, then led by Gingrich, had used funds improperly in relation to Gingrich's 1990 congressional election. On December 6, the House Ethics Committee voted unanimously to hire a special counsel to investigate other persistent financial irregularity charges.

Gingrich also published the best-selling book *To Renew America* and *1945*, written with William Forstchen. Forthcoming was a science fiction novel being written with Jerry Pournelle. In addition to his other cable television appearances, notably on conservative networks, Gingrich even appeared on MTV, in the special *Newt Raw*.

Pennsylvania-born Gingrich taught at West Georgia College before his election to the House of Representatives in 1979. He drew national attention (1987–88) as chief accuser charging financial irregularities by Democratic House Speaker Jim Wright, who ultimately resigned from the House. In August 1989, Gingrich urged ethics probes of 17 other congressional Democrats, as well. He himself was accused of earlier ethics violations in April 1989, soon after his March 1989 selection as House Republican whip, and faced further ethics charges in October 1989; but all charges against him were dropped in March 1990.

During 1992, Gingrich was heavily criticized for his 22 overdrawn checks in the House of Representatives banking scandal, and for his expensive government-supplied limousine and driver, which he gave up during the primary campaign. He played a notably abrasive attack role during the 1992 presidential campaign. At a late-August Bush campaign rally in Georgia he even went so far as to compare Governor Bill Clinton to Woody Allen, who at the time was involved in a widely publicized child custody battle, calling Allen "a perfect model of Bill Clinton's Democratic values," implying that the Democratic platform encouraged incest.

Adopted by his stepfather, Gingrich attended Emory and Tulane universities. With David Drake and Marianne Gingrich, he published *Window of Opportunity: A Blueprint for the Future* (1984). With House Majority Leader Dick Armey, he coauthored the best-selling *Contract with America: The Bold Plan* (1994). He has two daughters from his first marriage, to his high school geometry teacher, Jackie Battley, which ended in divorce. He married Marianne Ginther in 1981.

FURTHER READING

"Taking his measure. . . ." DORIS KEARNS GOODWIN et al. "Good Newt, bad Newt. . . ." JOHN F. STACKS. "Newt's universe. . . ." " 'I am not in a teaching job.' " "Master of the House." NANCY GIBBS and KAREN TUMULTY. "Newt's world." LANCE MORROW. *Time,* Dec. 25, 1995. (Man of the Year Issue.)

"Washington is. . . ." GLORIA BORGER et al. *U.S. News & World Report,* Dec. 25, 1995.

"Who's shrinking whom?" RICH LOWRY. *National Review,* Dec. 25, 1995.

"Gingrich's future. . . ." *Economist,* Dec. 23, 1995.

"Tantrums, taxes. . . ." BRUCE B. AUSTER and KENNETH T. WALSH. *U.S. News & World Report,* Nov. 27, 1995.

"Rivals or partners?" *Economist,* Nov. 4, 1995.

"Thinkalong with Newt." JOHN TAYLOR. *Esquire,* Nov. 1995.

"Man and woman. . . ." ARIANNA HUFFINGTON. *Ladies Home Journal,* Nov. 1995.

"The trouble with. . . ." VIVECA NOVAK. *Time,* Oct. 16, 1995.

"The politics of perception." CONNIE BRUCK. *New Yorker,* Oct. 9, 1995.

"The inner quest. . . ." GAIL SHEEHY. *Vanity Fair,* Sept. 1995.

"Newt warns. . . ." JAMIE DETTMER and LISA LEITER. *Insight on the News,* July 17, 1995.

"Plain talk from. . . ." *Business Week,* June 12, 1995.

"The executive. . . ." FRED BARNES. *New Republic,* May 22, 1995.

" 'The parallel is F.D.R.' " *Time,* Apr. 10, 1995.

"Mud path." GEORGE TOBIN. *National Review,* Apr. 3, 1995.

"Hail to thee . . . !" *Esquire,* Apr. 1995.

"Newt Gingrich. . . ." NOEL E. PARMENTEL, JR. *Nation,* Mar. 13, 1995.

"The future. . . ." MARGOT ADLER. *Utne Reader,* Mar.–Apr. 1995.

"National heartthrob." PAULA POUNDSTONE. "Why Newt now?" JEFFREY KLEIN. *Mother Jones,* Mar.–Apr. 1995.

"Newt's futurist. . . ." THOMAS M. DISCH and MICAH L. SIFRY. *Nation,* Feb. 27, 1995.

"The Speaker . . . ?" WILLIAM D. HARTUNG. *Nation,* Jan. 30, 1995.

"Master of the. . . ." JAMES CARNEY and KAREN TUMULTY. *Time,* Jan. 16, 1995.

"The warrior." HOWARD FINEMAN. *Newsweek,* Jan. 9, 1995.

"Man with a mission." KAREN TUMULTY. *Time,* Jan. 9, 1995.

"Gingrich comments. . . ." *Insight on the News,* Jan. 2, 1995.

Newt Gingrich: Speaker to America. JUDITH WARNER and MAX BERLEY. NAL-Dutton, 1995.

Ginsburg, Ruth Bader (1933–) In her
second year on the Supreme Court, Justice Ruth Bader Ginsburg continued to emerge as one of the Court's leading scholars, still very much on the liberal side in a series of sharply contested decisions. Among Ginsburg's major opinions was the dissent in *Miller* v. *Johnson*, a landmark case ruling that Georgia's eleventh congressional district was unconstitutional because it was organized primarily to provide racial representation, rather than to respond to specific discrimination. The decision was widely viewed as threatening the legality of scores of recently redistricted congressional districts. She wrote a second major dissenting opinion in the landmark case of *Adarand Constructors* v. *Pena*, declaring the Court's established position on affirmative action sound. The majority decision, which ruled that the federal government was required to use the same strict standards as the states in carrying out affirmative action programs, reversed the Court's long-held position on federal affirmative action programs, and was widely viewed as a major conservative victory. Another dissenting opinion came in *Missouri* v. *Jenkins*, which effectively limited the level of state spending to carry out a long-disputed, federally-managed school desegregation plan in Kansas City. In *Capital Square Review and Advisory Board* v. *Pinette*, she wrote a dissent in a decision ruling it unconstitutional to bar display of a large Ku Klux Klan cross in an Ohio public park.

Ginsburg wrote the majority opinion in *City of Edmonds* v. *Oxford House*, ruling that residential zoning laws in the city of Edmonds, Washington could not be used to discriminate against the establishment of group homes for people with disabilities. She also wrote the majority opinion in the consumer-protection case *American Airlines* v. *Wolens*, ruling that airlines were not protected by federal law from class action lawsuits, and that American Airlines could therefore be sued for making changes in frequent flyer contracts. Writing for a unanimous Court, she ruled in *Nations Bank of North Carolina* v. *Variable Annuity Life Insurance Co.* that federally chartered banks had the right to sell annuities.

Ginsburg joined the strong dissent in *U.S.* v. *Lopez*, a landmark decision that declared unconstitutional the federal Gun-Free School Zones Act of 1990, which made possession of a gun within 1,000 feet of a school illegal, ruling that this was an invalid extension of congressional ability to regulate interstate commerce. The ruling was widely seen as a major conservative reinterpretation of the power of Congress to legislate on a very broad range of issues, reopening formerly long-settled federal-state powers questions. She also joined the dissent in *Rosenberg* v. *Rector and Visitors of the University of Virginia*, a landmark decision ruling that the publicly funded University of Virginia was required to finance a Christian magazine run by students, apparently a sharp change of Court direction on a basic constitutional issue.

Ginsburg joined the majority in *U.S. Term Limits Inc.* v. *Thornton*, a landmark decision ruling that to limit congressional terms required a constitutional amendment; 23 state laws imposing terms limits were invalidated and Congress was barred from passing a term limits law. She also joined the majority in *Veronia School District* v. *Acton*, which found that an Oregon school district's random drug testing program was constitutional. In *Babbitt* v. *Sweet Home Chapter of Communities for a Greater Oregon*, she joined the majority in ruling that the federal government had the right under the Endangered Species Act to sharply restrict logging and other activities harmful to the northern spotted owl.

New York City–born Ginsburg received her B.A. from Cornell University. She attended Harvard Law School and then Columbia Law School, receiving her LL.B. and J.D. from the latter. She clerked with U.S. District Court Judge Edmund Palmieri (1959–61), and then taught law at Rutgers Law School (1963–72) and Columbia Law School (1972–80), becoming the first woman to become a tenured professor there. During the late 1960s and early 1970s, while director of the American Civil Liberties Union Women's Rights Project, Ginsburg fought and won several of the most important women's rights cases of the modern period, winning five of the six cases she argued before the Supreme Court. She was appointed to the federal Court of Appeals for the District of Columbia by President Jimmy Carter in 1980, and was appointed to the Supreme Court by President Bill Clinton in 1993, replacing retiring Justice Byron R. White. Ginsburg is married to lawyer Martin D. Ginsburg and has two children, a son and a daughter, who is also a lawyer.

FURTHER READING

Ruth Bader Ginsburg: Supreme Court Justice. CARMEN BREDESON. Enslow, 1995.

Women Chosen for Public Office. ISOBEL V. MORIN. Oliver Press, 1995.

"The big time! . . ." *Cosmopolitan*, May 1994.

"Ginsburg, Ruth Bader." *Current Biography*, Feb. 1994.

Ruth Bader Ginsburg. ELEANOR H. AYER. Macmillan, 1994.

Ruth Bader Ginsburg. BOB ITALIA. Abdo & Daughters, 1994.

Ruth Bader Ginsburg: Associate Justice of the United States Supreme Court. CHRISTOPHER E. HENRY. Watts, 1994.

Ruth Bader Ginsburg: Supreme Court Justice. JACK L. ROBERTS. Millbrook, 1994.

"Meet our new. . . ." ANGELA HUNT. *Glamour*, Oct. 1993.

"Justice for women." ELAINE SHANNON. *Vogue*, Oct. 1993.

"The book of Ruth. . . ." JEFFREY ROSEN. *New Republic*, Aug. 2, 1993.

"Two lives. . . ." STEVEN V. ROBERTS. *U.S. News & World Report*, June 28, 1993.

Giuliani, Rudolph W. (1944–) Mayor

Rudolph Giuliani, like so many other New York City mayors before him, had a hard time making ends meet in 1995. Indeed, his was an even harder time than most, for the city was to receive almost $700 million less in New York State aid than expected, and there were mandated increases in some kinds of expenditures. The total projected current deficit came to more than $3 billion. In June, Giuliani and the city council agreed on a budget for the fiscal year starting July 1 that would cut expenditures by more than $1 billion—if such hoped-for savings as those resulting from "increased productivity" were actually realized. Critics called the budget another exercise in smoke and mirrors, with paper-and-number-shuffling replacing needed tax dollars and real economies, while supporters called it an austerity budget, carrying the largest spending cuts since the Great Depression. Standard and Poor's, the bond rating service, leaned toward the "smoke and mirrors" theory, and in July cut the city's credit rating from A minus to BBB plus, a vote of no confidence that would result in raising the interest rates for any future city borrowing. Moody's, the other top bond rater, had long since lowered the city's credit rating.

Meanwhile, the city's ongoing problems continued. Major transit fare increases went into effect late in the year. Drinking water pollution reportedly increased, while the massive $10 billion new filtration plant needed to solve the problem remained unfinanced. Instead, with the help of Governor George Pataki, a new agreement that would cost only a tenth of that was reached within the cities and counties of the New York watershed, and was hailed by some as a major breakthrough.

On the positive side, the murder rate continued to decline, and the quality of life on the city's streets was said by many to have improved a good deal.

One very notable incident involving mayor Giuliani occurred during the United Nations 50th anniversary celebration, when he insisted that Yasir Arafat leave a concert given by the New York Philharmonic, saying that he could not forget Arafat's former role as a terrorist. Giuliani's action was condemned by the White House and many in the UN community, and praised by several right-wing Jewish organizations.

New York City–born Giuliani began his long career as a government prosecutor in the early 1970s, as an assistant U.S. attorney for the Southern District of New York, then moving up to become an associate deputy U.S. attorney in the Justice Department (1975–77). He was in private practice during the Carter years, in the New York City law firm of Patterson, Belknap, Webb and Tyler, moving back into government during Ronald Reagan's administration as U.S. attorney for New York's southern district (1983–89), there achieving prominence as an aggressive and successful prosecutor in a wide range of cases. He left government to make an unsuccessful New York City mayoral run in 1989, then practiced with White & Case (1989–90) and Anderson Kill Olick & Oshinsky (1990–93). In 1993, running as a Republican-Liberal candidate, he defeated incumbent Democratic mayor David Dinkins by a 51 percent to 48 percent majority, in a campaign that played heavily on racial themes in a highly polarized city, although Giuliani strongly denied any play to racist sentiments.

Giuliani received his B.A. from Manhattan College, and his J.D. from New York University. Giuliani's second wife is newscaster Donna Hanover; they have a son and a daughter.

FURTHER READING

"Police mayor in FIRE City." JOE CONASON. *Nation*, Dec. 18, 1995.

"The holy terror. . . ." JOHN TIERNEY. *New York Times Magazine*, Dec. 3, 1995.

"Our loser. . . ." ERIC POOLEY. *New York*, Nov. 21, 1994.

"What made. . . ." DOUGLAS HARBRECHT et al. *Business Week*, Nov. 7, 1994.

"Paring Rudy's apple." MAGGIE MAHAR. *Barron's*, Aug. 22, 1994.

"The tolerant bully." CHRIS BULL. *Advocate*, June 28, 1994.

"Apple juice." JIM SLEEPER. *New Republic*, May 9, 1994.

"Radicals at work." *Economist*, Nov. 6, 1993.

"Rudolph Giuliani. . . ." TODD S. PURDUM. *New York Times Magazine*, July 25, 1993.

"Change partners." ANDY LOGAN. *New Yorker*, June 14, 1993.

Glavine, Tom (Thomas Michael Glavine; 1966–) Pitcher Tom Glavine had a dream year in 1995. He did not win the Cy Young award; that went to his teammate Greg Maddux. But as pitcher for the Atlanta Braves, he won two games in the World Series, including the sixth and final game, in which he had eight strikeouts and gave up only one hit, as Atlanta won its first World Series. Glavine himself was named Most Valuable Player of the series, a rare honor in the careers of even the most illustrious players. During the regular season, he was seventh in the National League with a record of 16-7, for a winning percentage of .696, and an earned-run average of 3.08. Glavine had been somewhat overshadowed by his teammate, Maddux, in the past four years, but Atlanta manager Bobby Cox points out that Glavine—the last person to win the Cy Young award before Maddux—has won more games in the previous five years than any other pitcher in baseball, and is the last to have three consecutive 20-game winning seasons.

Earlier in the year, during the 1994–95 strike, Glavine was a key spokesman for the players' association.

Born in Concord, Massachusetts, Glavine graduated from Billerica High School. He was selected by the Atlanta Braves in the 1984 free-agent draft (also selected in the hockey draft) and played in the minor leagues (1984–87), with the GC Braves, Sumter, Greenville, and Richmond, until called up to the Atlanta Braves (1987–), where he has spent his entire major league career. In 1991, he won the Cy Young award and was named *Sporting News* National League pitcher of the year. He led the National League in pitching victories for three years (1991–93), with 20, 20, and 22 wins respectively, and was twice named to *Sporting News* All-Star team (1991–92). In 1993, he had the best winning percentage in the major leagues, at .786, on a record of 22 and 6. Glavine married Carri Dobbins in 1992.

FURTHER READING

"The two sides of. . . ." STEVE MARANTZ. *Sporting News,* May 1, 1995.

Glennan, Thomas Keith (1906–95) After his 1927 graduation from Yale University as an electrical engineer, North Dakota–born Thomas Glennan entered the film industry, where he played a substantial role in the introduction of sound, the era of the "talkies," and went on to develop a major career as a Hollywood studio manager. During World War II, he put his training and administrative talents to much different uses, becoming director of the Navy's sound laboratory at New London, Connecticut. Glennan became president of Cleveland's Case Institute of Technology in 1947, holding that post for 18 years, with two interruptions for public service. The first came when President Harry S. Truman appointed him one of the five members of the U.S. Atomic Energy Commission (1950–52). In 1958, President Dwight D. Eisenhower appointed him the first head of the U.S. National Aeronautics and Space Administration (NASA);

it was during his period of administrative leadership that astronaut Alan Shepard made the first manned American suborbital space flight, on May 5, 1961. Glennan was also the space program's key early recruiter, responsible for the hiring of NASA's formative staff. After leaving NASA, Glennan went back to Case Reserve, retiring in 1966, and was then U.S. representative to the International Atomic Energy Agency. He was survived by his wife, Ruth, three daughters, and a son. (d. Mitchellville, Maryland; April 11, 1995)

FURTHER READING

Obituary. *Physics Today,* Nov. 1995.
Obituary. *Times* (of London), Apr. 18, 1995.
Obituary. *New York Times,* Apr. 12, 1995.

Glover, Danny (1947–) Film star Danny Glover became an even more familiar face on television screens in 1995, as his baseball fantasy film *Angels in the Outfield* proved a substantial hit in home video. Glover's major 1995 film was *Operation Dumbo Drop,* directed by Simon Wincer and costarring Ray Liotta and Denis Leary. Set during the Vietnam War, the film is a comedy-fantasy about a group of American soldiers who set out to do a good deed by supplying a Vietnamese village with an elephant to replace one that has been killed in the war. Glover also starred as classic detective Philip Marlowe in *Red Wind,* a Showtime television movie in the series "Fallen Angels," directed by Agnieszka Holland and costarring Kelly Lynch.

Forthcoming was a starring role opposite Joe Pesci and Rosanna Arquette in the film *Gone Fishin',* directed by John Avildsen.

San Francisco–born Glover, a civil rights activist during his late-1960s college years, entered the theater through appearances as an amateur in the works of such playwrights as Amiri Baraka and Athol Fugard, and worked as a professional in supporting roles on stage throughout the 1970s. He appeared in a Yale Repertory Theater production of Fugard's *Master Harold and the Boys* (1982). On screen, he played in such films as *Escape from Alcatraz* (1979), *Chu Chu and the Philly Flash* (1981), *Out* (1982), and *Iceman* (1984), before his breakthrough starring role as Moze opposite Sally Field in *Places in the Heart* (1984). In 1985, he starred opposite Whoopi Goldberg in *The Color Purple,* and also in *Witness* and *Silverado.* He then reached huge audiences in the thrillers *Lethal Weapon* (1985), *Lethal Weapon II* (1987), *Predator II* (1990), and *Lethal Weapon III* (1992), also starring in such films as *To Sleep with Anger* (1990), *Flight of the Intruder* (1991), *Grand Canyon* (1991), *A Rage in Harlem* (1991), *Bopha* (1993), and *The Saint of Fort Washington* (1993) Glover's B.S. was from San Francisco State University. He is married to Asake Bomani, and has one child.

FURTHER READING

"What a man!" KEVIN POWELL. *Essence,* July 1994.
"An everyman. . . ." KITTY BOWE HEARTY. *Premiere,* Feb. 1992.
"Danny Glover." *Playboy,* Sept. 1991.

Godunov, Alexander (1949–95) Dancer Alexander Godunov grew up in Riga, Latvia, and there began his ballet training, moving to Moscow in his mid-teens. After dancing with the Young Ballet Company for three years, he joined the Bolshoi Ballet in 1971, becoming the company's youngest principal dancer. In 1972, he became the principal dance partner of Maya Plisetskaya, the greatest Russian ballerina of her time. Godunov became a very popular figure abroad from the early 1970s, when he toured the United States with the Bolshoi. He became yet another prominent defector from the Soviet Union in 1979, leaving the Bolshoi during its run in New York at the Metropolitan Opera House. His wife, ballerina Ludmila Vlasova, did not join him, though she was not allowed to leave the United States until it was clear she was not being forced to go. Vlasova later divorced Godunov.

Godunov continued his career abroad, joining the Ballet Theater in the U.S, and was a principal dancer with that company until 1982, until he and artistic director Mikhail Baryshnikov fell out, and Godunov was fired. Although he continued to dance with several companies, he also turned to a film career, starring opposite Harrison Ford in *Witness* (1982), and also appearing in several other films, including *The Money Pit* (1986) and *Die Hard* (1988). He also starred in his own television show: "Godunov: The World to Dance In" (1983–84). There were no survivors. (d. Los Angeles; May 18, 1995)

FURTHER READING

"Fallen from grace." SHELLEY LEVITT. *People,* June 5, 1995.
Obituary. *Independent,* May 20, 1995.
Obituary. *Times* (of London), May 20, 1995.
Obituary. *New York Times*, May 19, 1995.
Obituary. *Variety*, May 19, 1995.

Goldberg, Whoopi (Caryn Johnson; 1950–   ) It was another busy year for versatile screen star Whoopi Goldberg. She starred as a lesbian cabaret singer opposite Mary-Louise Parker and Drew Barrymore in the film *Boys on the Side*, written, directed, and coproduced by Herbert Ross; it told the story of three women who meet partly by chance, travel across the country, and ultimately find themselves living together as an extended family. Goldberg also starred in the film drama *Moonlight and Valentino*, directed by David Anspaugh and adapted from her own play by Ellen Simon, in a cast that included Elizabeth Perkins, Gwyneth Paltrow, Kathleen Turner, Peter Coyote, and Jon Bon Jovi in his film debut.

Goldberg appeared in the star-studded documentary *The Celluloid Closet*, which reviewed the treatment of homosexuality in Hollywood films, from their beginnings until the present; Rob Epstein and Jeffrey Friedman directed; Lily Tomlin narrated. She also appeared as an interviewer in the ABC After-school Special *Bonnie Raitt Has Something to Talk About*. In November, Goldberg, Billy Crystal, and Robin Williams hosted *Comic Relief VII*, their fundraising marathon to benefit the homeless.

Forthcoming were starring roles in the films *Eddie*, directed by Steve Rash; *T. Rex*, written and directed by Jonathan Betuel; and opposite Gerard Depardieu in an as-yet-untitled film to be directed by Norman Jewison. Goldberg was also slated to once again host the annual Academy Award television show, as she had in 1994.

New York City–born Goldberg, who had previously worked as a popular comedian and cabaret and stage entertainer, emerged as a film star in *The Color Purple* (1985; she received an Oscar nomination), and went on to such films as *Jumpin' Jack Flash* (1986), *Fatal Beauty* (1987), *Burglar* (1988), *The Long Walk Home* (1990), *Sarafina* (1992), *Sister Act* (1992), *Made in America* (1993), *Sister Act II* (1993), *Corrina, Corrina* (1994), *The Lion King* (1994), *Star Trek Generations* (1994), *The Pagemaster* (1994), and *Naked in New York* (1994). In 1990, she scored a major success—including a best supporting actress Oscar—as the Harlem-based psychic in the year's surprise top-grossing film *Ghost*. She also starred opposite Jean Stapleton in the short-lived television series "Bagdad Cafe" (1990), and hosted a short-lived television interview show (1992–93). She had a one-woman show on Broadway (1984) and later toured in a second one-woman show (1988). Goldberg was married to union organizer Lyle Trachtenberg in 1994. It was her second marriage; she has one child.

FURTHER READING

"Whoopi. . . ." MICHELE WILLENS. *McCall's,* Mar. 1995.
"Whoopi Goldberg. . . ." LEA DELARIA. *Advocate,* Feb. 7, 1995.
"This sister's act." JANN WENNER. *Us,* Apr. 1994.
Whoopi Goldberg. JUDY DEBOER. Creative Education, 1994.
Whoopi Goldberg: Entertainer. ROSE BLUE. Chelsea House, 1994.
"Whoopi Goldberg." ROD LURIE. *Los Angeles,* May 1993.
Whoopi Goldberg: From Street to Stardom. MARY A. ADAMS. Dillon/Macmillan, 1993.
"Witty, gritty. . . ." JAMIE DIAMOND. *Cosmopolitan,* Nov. 1992.
"Funny lady." MELANIE BERGER. *Ladies Home Journal,* Oct. 1992.
"The joy of being Whoopi." JOHN SKOW. *Time,* Sept. 21, 1992.
"Whoopi Goldberg." MATTHEW MODINE. *Interview,* June 1992.

Goldblum, Jeff (1952–) In 1995, actor Jeff Goldblum starred in the film *Powder*, opposite Mary Steenburgen as the teacher and Sean Patrick in the title role as a mutant teenage genius and saint; Victor Salva wrote and directed. Goldblum also starred opposite Christine Lahti as his wife in the techno-thriller *Hideaway*, based on the Dean Koontz novel, its story revolving around occult pheomena following his near-death car accident experience. Brett Leonard directed; the cast included Alicia Silverstone, Rae Dawn Chong, Jeremy Sisto, and Alfred Molina. Another starring role was in the film comedy *Nine Months*, written and directed by Chris Columbus and costarring Hugh Grant, Julianne Moore, Tom Arnold, Joan Cusack, and Robin Williams, a story about a pregnant woman and her reluctant child psychiatrist lover.

Forthcoming were starring roles in the film *Independence Day*, written, directed, and produced by Roland Emmerich, and costarring Will Smith, Bill Pullman, Randy Quaid, Judd Hirsch, and Mary McDonnell; and opposite Samuel L. Jackson in the film *The Great White Hype*, directed by Reginald Hudlin.

Pittsburgh-born Goldblum played in the New York theater in the early 1970s, most notably in *Two Gentlemen of Verona* (1971). His wide range of films includes *Invasion of the Body Snatchers* (1978), *The Big Chill* (1983), *The Right Stuff* (1983), *Silverado* (1985), *The Fly* (1986), *Beyond Therapy* (1987), *Earth Girls Are Easy* (1989), *Twisted Obsession* (1990), *The Tall Guy* (1990),

Mr. Frost (1990), *The Favor, the Watch and the Very Big Fish* (1991), *Fathers and Sons* (1992), *Deep Cover* (1992), and *Jurassic Park* (1993). He also appeared in the television series "Tenspeed and Brownshoe" (1980), and in the telefilms *The Race for the Double Helix* (1987) as scientist James Watson, and *Framed* (1990). Goldblum attended the Neighborhood Playhouse. He was previously married to actress Geena Davis (1987–91).

FURTHER READING

"Jeff Goldblum. . . ." SABINE DURRANT. *Independent*, July 22, 1993.

Goldman, Ronald L.: See Simpson, O. J.

John Goodman (right) and Simon Fenton.

Goodman, John (1952–) Screen star John Goodman remained a very popular television figure in 1995, still starring opposite Roseanne in her very popular long-running situation comedy series. For his role in "Roseanne," he received an Emmy nomination as best lead actor in a comedy series and a Screen Actors Guild nomination as best actor in a comedy series, telefilm, or miniseries.

Goodman also starred as corrupt, charismatic Louisiana politician Huey Long in the title role of the well-received television biofilm *Kingfish: A Story of Huey P. Long*, directed by Thomas Schlamme, in a cast that included Matt Craven,

Ann Dowd, Jeff Perry, and Bob Gunton. For this role, he received an Emmy nomination as best lead actor in a miniseries or special and a CableAce nomination as best actor in a movie or miniseries. Goodman also re-created his 1992 stage role as Mitch in a 1995 television production of Tennessee Williams' classic play *A Streetcar Named Desire*.

Before his "Roseanne" role catapulted him to stardom, Missouri-born Goodman had played in strong character roles, on Broadway in such plays as *Loose Ends* (1979) and *Big River* (1985), and in such films as *Eddie Macon's Run* (1983), *True Stories* (1986), and *Raising Arizona* (1987). His other films include *Sea of Love* (1989), *Always* (1989), *Stella* (1990), *King Ralph* (1991), *Barton Fink* (1991), *The Babe* (1992; as baseball star Babe Ruth), *Born Yesterday* (1993), and *The Flintstones* (1994). Goodman attended Southwest Missouri State College. He married Anna Elizabeth (Annabeth) Hartzog in 1989; they have one daughter.

FURTHER READING

"Stoned again." PATRICK GOLDSTEIN. *Premiere*, May 1994.
"John Goodman." JAMES GREENBERG. *Us*, Apr. 1992.
"The Babe." VIC ZIEGEL. *Life*, Apr. 1992.
"John Goodman is. . . ." PETE RICHMOND. *GQ*, Apr. 1992.
"Being the big. . . ." PETER DE JONGE. *New York Times Magazine*, Feb. 10, 1991.
"John Goodman. . . ." ERIC SHERMAN. *Ladies Home Journal*, Feb. 1991.

Gordon, Gale

Gordon, Gale (Charles T. Aldrich; 1906–95) New York City–born Gale Gordon, the child of a theater family, began his acting career in the theater, moving into radio in the 1930s, most notably as Mayor La Trivia in "Fibber McGee and Molly." He became a very familiar face in early television, most notably as Osgood Conklin in "Our Miss Brooks" (1952–56), and in "The Brothers" (1956–57), "Pete and Gladys" (1960–62), and "Dennis the Menace" (1962–63). Gordon became an enduring figure in television in the role of banker Theodore J. Mooney, supporting Lucille Ball in "The Lucy Show" (1963–68), and then as Harrison Otis Carter in Ball's "Here's Lucy" (1968–74). Both shows were among the most successful in television history, still playing in syndication throughout the world.

He also appeared as Curtis McGibbon in Ball's series "Life With Lucy" (1986). Gordon also played in several films. Late in his career, he took on few television roles, instead returning to the stage in regional theater. His wife, Virginia, had died a few weeks earlier. He was survived by a sister. (d. Escondido, California; June 30, 1995)

FURTHER READING

Obituary. *Independent*, Aug. 2, 1995.
Obituary. *Variety*, July 10, 1995.
Obituary. *New York Times*, July 3, 1995.

Gordone, Charles

Gordone, Charles (1927–95) Cleveland-born playwright and actor Charles Gordone began his New York stage career in the early 1950s, appearing in many supporting roles during the years that followed, while—like so many other actors—working at a series of other jobs to make a living while staying in the acting profession. In 1970, Gordone's first play was produced—and on Broadway. It was *No Place to Be Somebody: A Black Comedy*, the story of a small-time Black saloonkeeper and con man who unsuccessfully tries to buck the White mob. Gordone's play won a Pulitzer Prize, and Drama Desk, Critics Circle, and Vernon Rice awards; and he was hailed as an extraordinary new talent. Unfortunately, no more hit plays followed, although Gordone did write, direct, and appear in several more plays, and worked with many regional theaters. Active in Black theater affairs, he cofounded the Committee for Employment of Negro Performers in 1962. He taught at Texas A&M University (1986–95). He was survived by his companon, Susan Kouyomjian, two daughters, and two sons. (d. College Station, Texas; November 17, 1995).

FURTHER READING

Obituary. *Jet*, Dec. 11, 1995.
Obituary. *New York Times*, Nov. 19, 1995.

Gore, Al

Gore, Al (Albert Gore, Jr.; 1948–) During his third year in office, Vice President Al Gore continued to play a significant role in the Clinton administration. Gore traveled a good deal, often performing the vice president's traditional ceremonial role, as at the European celebrations of the 50th anniversary of V-E Day in May. He also often traveled essentially as a special envoy for President Bill Clinton.

Gore also performed some other formal and informal functions at home and abroad, as when he held a formal Washington meeting with the Dalai Lama, with President Clinton only "dropping in" in order to upset the Chinese as little as possible. Gore attended and sometimes chaired international conferences, such as the March UN "social summit" in Copenhagen; acted as a high-level peace negotiator, as in Bosnia and the Middle East; was an informal trade negotiator, as in his visits to Japan and Russia; and spoke for the president on a considerable range of domestic issues, from the baseball strike to the telecommunications bill. In 1995, Gore published the book *Common Sense Government: Works Better and Costs Less.*

He also stood by, ready to take office as president if necessary, as is the primary constitutional role of every vice president, however otherwise active he or she may be. In a lighter vein, he and President Clinton appeared on the 10th-anniversary special of "The Larry King Show."

Gore is the son of longtime Tennessee representative and later senator Albert Gore, Sr., and grew up in Washington, D.C. Like his father, he opposed the Vietnam War, and thought of leaving the country to avoid the draft, but in the end volunteered, seeing army service in Vietnam (1969–71). He returned home to a job as an investigative reporter for Nashville's *The Tennessean* (1971–76). Turning to politics, he served four terms in the House of Representatives (1977–85), and was elected to the Senate in 1984. He made an unsuccessful presidential primary run in 1988, and in 1989 was positioning himself for a 1992 run when his youngest child, Albert Gore III, was seriously injured in an automobile accident. Gore spent much of his discretionary time after that focusing on his son's recovery and related family matters, and in 1991 declared himself out of the presidential race—only to find himself running with Bill Clinton in 1992.

Gore played a moderate's role during his congressional career, voting for arms control, for only some defense cuts, for civil rights, and for education, child support, and welfare reform. While focusing on his son's recovery, Gore developed a very special interest in the environment, which resulted in the book *Earth in the Balance: Ecology and the Human Spirit,* a 1992 best-seller. Also published under the names of Clinton and Gore was the campaign book *Putting People First* (1992).

Gore attended Washington, D.C.'s St. Albans preparatory school. His 1969 B.A. was from Harvard University. He also attended the Vanderbilt University School of Religion (1971–72). He and Mary Elizabeth (Tipper) Aitcheson married in 1970; their four children are Karenna, Kristin, Sarah, and Albert III.

FURTHER READING

"Why White House. . . ." KENNETH T. WALSH. *U.S. News & World Report,* Dec. 25, 1995.
"Al Gore." GENE KOPROWSKI. *Forbes,* Dec. 4, 1995.
"In step with. . . ." JAMES BRADY. *Parade,* Apr. 16, 1995.
"Al Gore. . . ." RICHARD LOUV. *Parents Magazine,* Feb. 1995.
"Getting smaller. . . ." LEE WALCZAK and SUSAN B. GARLAND. *Business Week,* Jan. 23, 1995.
"Gore's dilemma." PETER J. BOYER. *New Yorker,* Nov. 28, 1994.
"The good son. . . ." RICHARD L. BERKE. *New York Times Magazine,* Feb. 20, 1994.
Al Gore: United States Vice President. BETTY M. BURFORD. Enslow, 1994.
Al Gore: Vice President. REBECCA STEFOFF. Millbrook, 1994.
"Where are you Al?" L. J. DAVIS. *Mother Jones,* Nov.–Dec. 1993.
"Has anyone seen. . . ." WALTER SHAPIRO. *Esquire,* Sept. 1993.
"Gore. . . ." ELEANOR CLIFT. *Newsweek,* Jan. 25, 1993.
Al Gore: Vice President of the United States. BOB ITALIA. Abdo & Daughters, 1993.
Story of Bill Clinton and Al Gore. Dell, 1993.
Al Gore, Jr.: His Life and Career. HANK HILLIN. Birch Lane/Carol, 1992.

Gould, Laurence McKinley (1896–1995)

Michigan-born Laurence Gould, a polar explorer and college president, saw World War I action in the Army Ambulance Service. After the war, he attended the University of Michigan, earned his Ph.D. in geology in 1925, and began his work in polar exploration in northern Canada and Greenland. In 1928, he was assistant to Admiral Richard E. Byrd on Byrd's first expedition to Antarctica, and continued to work in polar exploration throughout his career, in later years becoming the much honored longtime chairman of the National Academy of Sciences

Committee on Polar Research, and a board member or trustee of several major philanthropic organizations. Gould was the highly innovative president of Carleton College (1945–62), a small liberal arts college in Northfield, Minnesota, dedicated to bridging the growing gap between the sciences and the arts and humanities. There were no immediate survivors. (d. Tucson, Arizona; June 20, 1995)

FURTHER READING

Obituary. *Current Biography*, Aug. 1995.
Obituary. *Times* (of London), July 10, 1995.
Obituary. *New York Times*, June 22, 1995.

Graf, Steffi (Stephanie Maria Graf; 1969–   ) Professionally, 1995 was a very good year for Steffi Graf; personally, it was a disaster. She began and ended the year ranked number one—in the latter few months coranked with Monica Seles, who finally returned to professional play, after having been knifed in the back in 1993 by a German fan obsessed with Graf. Though troubled by an aching back and foot, Graf won at the November WTA Tour Championships, doing rare publicity—including appearances on "Good Morning, America" and "Late Night with David Letterman"—in support of the WTA Tour's new sponsor, Corel (formerly Virginia Slims). That capped a year in which she won nine tournaments, including three Grand Slam titles—the French Open, over Mary Pierce; Wimbledon, over Arantxa Sánchez Vicario; and the U.S. Open, over Seles—bringing her total Grand Slam titles to 18. (She had withdrawn from the other Grand Slam event, the Australian Open, because of a pulled calf muscle.) Her yearly earnings topped $2 million, and she was named *Tennis* magazine's player of the year.

Privately, Graf's year was dominated by tax evasion charges leveled at her and at her father and manager, Peter Graf. In mid-July, German authorities raided the family compound in Brühl, Germany, taking away cartons of documents for investigation. In the wake of the raid, Graf said she was considering moving away from Germany because of the tax problems. In August, Peter Graf was arrested and a family tax advisor was also taken into custody; the government claims that they failed to re-

port $35.2 million of Steffi Graf's earnings over several years. Despite rumors that Graf herself might be arrested, the prosecutors in October said that she had undergone lengthy questioning, but there was no reason to arrest her at that time. Graf's main corporate sponsor, among others, called for Graf to take control of her own affairs, and urged Peter Graf to step aside as his daughter's manager, and to make clear that she had not been involved in the handling of her own finances.

At year's end, Graf was scheduled to miss the Australian Open, since she required foot surgery.

Steffi Graf emerged as a leading under-14 tennis player in the early 1980s, turning professional at age 13. She won the German Open in 1986 and from 1987 was the world's dominant tennis player, with a string of 66 consecutive victories. She took the French Open in 1987, and became World Champion in 1988, the year she won the U.S. Open, Wimbledon, and the Australian and French opens, along with the Olympic championship. Among her succeeding major victories were the U.S. Open, Wimbledon, and the German Open again in 1989; the Australian Open in 1990; and Wimbledon in 1991 and 1992. During that period, she held the number one world ranking for a record 186 consecutive weeks, before losing it to Monica Seles in 1991, and regaining it only temporarily later that year. After Seles was attacked and sidelined by an obsessed Graf fan in 1993, Graf was again dominant, winning eight out of nine events entered that year, including the French Open, Wimbledon, the German Open, the Canadian Open, and the U.S. Open. She was coached from her earliest years by her father, Peter, and then by Pavel Slozil (1987–91), and later Heinz Gunthardt. In 1994, she won a record 27 matches without losing a set.

FURTHER READING

"The Martina and. . . ." Mark Marvel. *Interview*, July 1995.
Sports Great Steffi Graf. Ron Knapp. Enslow, 1995.
"6 lessons from. . . ." DENNIS VAN DER MEER and ALEXANDER MCNAB. *Tennis*, Aug. 1994.
"Dark star." HARM CLUEVER and PETER RIEBSCHLAEGER. *Tennis*, Nov. 1992.
"The spirit of '88." ANDREA LEAND. *World Tennis*, Feb. 1991.
Steffi Graf. JAMES R. ROTHAUS. Child's World, 1991.

Graham, Billy (William Franklin Graham, Jr.; 1918–) One of the world's leading evangelists settled a key succession question in November 1995, when he announced that his eldest son, **Franklin Graham** (William Franklin Graham III; 1952–), had been elected first vice chairperson of the board of directors of the Billy Graham Evangelistic Association, and would succeed to the leadership if the elder Graham became incapacitated. Franklin Graham has been on the board of the association since 1979. Billy Graham continued as chairman and chief executive of the organization—he had once said that only God could choose his successor—but the announcement recognized his physical frailty. He has Parkinson's disease; in June he was hospitalized after he collapsed during a Toronto appearance, as a result of flu and a bleeding colon; in December he was again hospitalized, where he was treated for four fractured ribs, sustained during a fall. Billy Graham's 1975 best-seller *Angels: God's Secret Agents* was reissued in late 1994, and was once again found on 1995 best-seller lists.

Franklin Graham published his own book in 1995: *Rebel With a Cause: Finally Comfortable Being Graham*, written with Cecil Murphy. It describes his troubled adolescence, including smoking, drinking, and fighting, and his conversion to born-again Christianity at age 22.

In March, Billy Graham's crusade in Puerto Rico was carried by satellite to some 175 countries, with translations into more than 40 languages; called the Global Mission, it was billed as the largest evangelical outreach ever. In April 1995, Graham led a memorial service for victims of the Oklahoma City bombing. Father and son appeared together for the first time in October 1995 in Saskatoon, during a Canadian crusade. Evangelistic crusades were planned for 1996 in Australia, New Zealand, Minneapolis, and Charlotte, North Carolina.

Born in Charlotte, North Carolina, Billy Graham came to evangelical Christianity in 1934, inspired by traveling revivalist Mordecai Ham. In 1940 he graduated from the Florida Bible Institute (now Trinity College) and was ordained by the Southern Baptist Convention, later receiving his 1943 A.B. from Wheaton College. He served as minister of the First Baptist Church at Western Springs, Illinois (1943–45), then embarked on what was to be a worldwide career, becoming a vice president of Youth for Christ International (1945–48). He was also president of Northwestern Schools in Minneapolis (1947–52). He became a widely popular touring evangelist with his 1949 Los Angeles crusade, the first of many. From 1950, the year he founded the Minneapolis-based Billy Graham Evangelistic Association, he was also one of the leading radio preachers of his day, whose weekly "Hour of Decision" radio program won an audience of millions; later in his career, he also drew huge audiences for his television specials.

From 1952 he published the syndicated newspaper column "My Answer." He has also published numerous books, among them *Peace with God* (1953), *The Secret of Happiness* (1955), *World Aflame* (1965), *How to Be Born Again* (1977), *Till Armageddon* (1981), *Approaching Hoofbeats: The Four Horsemen of the Apocalypse* (1983), *Facing Death and the Life After* (1987), *Answers to Life's Problems* (1988), *Hope for the Troubled Heart* (1991), and *Storm Warning* (1992). Graham was married to Ruth McCue Bell in 1943; they have three daughters and two sons.

Franklin Graham, often dubbed the "rebellious Graham," had a wild youth that included high-speed chases and confrontations with the police and resulted in his expulsion from LeTourneau College in Longview, Texas. But at age 22, a religious experience in Jerusalem turned him back in the family direction. He joined the board of the mission organization Samaritan's Purse in 1978, becoming its president; he also founded and leads the World Medical Mission. Ordained by the Grace Community Church, a nondenominational evangelical Christian congregation in Tempe, Arizona, he made his evangelical preaching debut in Juneau, Alaska, in 1989, and has been preaching widely since. He and his wife, Jane Austin Graham, have four children, the oldest being William Franklin Graham IV.

FURTHER READING

"The son also rises." JOHN W. KENNEDY. *Christianity Today,* Dec. 11, 1995.

"Grace under fire." GARTH M. ROSELL. "Fifty years with. . . ." WILLIAM MARTIN. "Billy Graham." *Christianity Today,* Nov. 13, 1995.

"The eternal crusader." CHARLES HIRSHBERG and HARRY BENSON. *Life,* Nov. 1994.

"God's Billy pulpit." NANCY GIBBS and RICHARD N. OSTLING. *Time,* Nov. 15, 1993.

Billy Graham. NATHAN AASENG. Zondervan, 1993.

"The second coming of. . . ." PETER BECKER. *M,* Dec. 1991.

"My own Christmas. . . ." BILLY GRAHAM and MEL LORENTZEN. *Christian Herald,* Nov.–Dec. 1991.

"Billy and Lyndon." WILLIAM MARTIN. *Texas Monthly,* Nov. 1991.

"America's crusader." JOE TREEN. *People,* Oct. 7, 1991.

A Prophet with Honor: The Billy Graham Story. WILLIAM MARTIN. Morrow, 1991.

Graham, Franklin: See Graham, Billy.

Graham, William Franklin: See Graham, Billy.

Gramm, Phil (William Philip Gramm, 1942–) On February 24, 1995, Texas Republican Senator Phil Gramm formally declared himself a candidate for the 1996 Republican presidential nomination. He had clearly by then been in the race for many months and was well on the way to building very substantial campaign funds and a nationwide campaign organization. Gramm, who in the early days of his campaign seemed top contender for the nomination, ran as a right-wing conservative who also

wanted to stress his ties to the middle ground voter, on a program that included a constitutional amendment outlawing abortion; opposition to all gun control; opposition to all National Endowment for the Arts (NEA) funding; massive cuts in social service programs; the flat tax; the balanced budget, promised in five, rather than seven years; school prayer; and opposition to U.S. participation in United Nations peacekeeping forces.

In the Senate during 1995, Gramm engaged in what amounted to a duel with Bob Dole for the Republican conservative primary vote, charging Dole again and again with compromising key conservative positions. To the surprise of many observers, Gramm's very well-financed campaign did not prosper as predicted. Although he did well in several early straw polls, his ratings vis-a-vis Dole had slipped a great deal by the turn of the year, and he was in some states being challenged by Lamar Alexander and Patrick Buchanan, while running far behind Dole overall. Public perception of Gramm as extremely abrasive in personal style did not help his campaign; nor were many conservatives pleased by the revelation that in 1974 he had invested a small sum in the development of a soft-core pornographic film.

Georgia-born Gramm's 1964 B.A. and 1967 Ph.D. in economics were from the University of Georgia. He taught economics at Texas A&M (1967–78) and was a partner in Gramm Associates (1971–78). He was a Texas Democratic congressman (1978–83), resigning in January 1983 when he changed sides to support President Ronald Reagan, and quickly winning reelection to the House as a Republican. A two-term senator, he was first elected to the Senate in 1985. He is married to Wendy Lee, former chair of the Commodity Future Trading Commission; they have two sons.

FURTHER READING

"Gramm gets going." RICH LOWRY. *National Review,* Oct. 23, 1995.

"Phil's alibi. . . ." WILL SALETAN. *Mother Jones,* Sept.–Oct. 1995.

"The maverick." JAMES SRODES. *Financial World,* Aug. 29, 1995.

"On the record." WILLIAM SALETAN. "Phil's felon. " WILLIAM SALETAN. *Mother Jones,* July 17, 1995.

"The porn broker." JOHN B. JUDIS. *New Republic,* June 5, 1995.

"The ironman cometh." MARJORIE WILLIAMS. *Vanity Fair,* May 1995.

"GOP heavyweights. . . ." MICHAEL RUST and LISA LEITER. *Insight on the News,* Apr. 3, 1995.

"How right thou art. . . ." S. C. GWYNNE. *Time,* Mar. 13, 1995.

"Phil Gramm's. . . ." ROBERT SHERRILL. *Nation,* Mar. 6, 1995.

"Righter than Newt." DAVID FRUM. *Atlantic,* Mar. 1995.

"The Gramm reaper." WALTER SHAPIRO. *Esquire,* July 1994.

"The real leader. . . ." DAVID SEGAL. *Washington Monthly,* Mar. 1994.

"Senator spite." ROBERT DRAPER. *Texas Monthly,* Feb. 1993.

Grammer, Kelsey (ca. 1955–)

For ten years, Kelsey Grammer developed the role of Dr. Frasier Crane, the insecure, pedantic, often overwhelmed psychiatrist on the popular television series "Cheers." When that series died in 1993, Grammer moved the now-divorced Crane from Boston to his hometown of Seattle, where he became a radio psychiatrist, and reconnected with his father and pompous brother, also a psychiatrist. The resulting series, "Frasier," became a major commercial and critical success. In both its first and second seasons, Grammer won an Emmy as lead actor in a comedy series; the show itself won a 1995 Peabody Award. Grammer also received 1995 nominations for a People's Choice Award as favorite male television performer (he

had won in 1994), and a Screen Actors Guild Award for best actor in a comedy series, telefilm, or miniseries.

In the 1995–96 season, "Frasier" continued its popularity. At year's end, Grammer was nominated for a Golden Globe award as best actor in a musical or comedy series. Grammer also hosted and cowrote the television special *Kelsey Grammer Salutes Jack Benny,* which aired in late November, and was the voice for mad scientist Dr. Frankenollie in *Runaway Brain,* the first new Mickey Mouse cartoon in 42 years. Forthcoming was a film, *Down Periscope,* directed by David Ward, in which Grammer stars with Bruce Dern and Lauren Holly.

Grammer also published the autobiographical book *So Far,* and was reader on the simultaneously released audio version. He helped promote the book, most notably with a December appearance on "The Oprah Winfrey Show." Less happily, he faced charges of sexual assault, after a teenager said he had had sex with her when she was 15; in February, a New Jersey court declined to indict him. In the late 1980s, Grammer had been convicted on charges of possessing cocaine. In October, he joined Tony Danza and John Larroquette in hosting a benefit for Columbia University's Center on Addiction and Substance Abuse (CASA).

Born on St. Thomas, in the Virgin Islands, and raised in New Jersey and Florida, Grammer studied at the Julliard School and played in regional theater, often in classical roles, most notably three years at San Diego's Old Globe Theatre (1976-79), and in the title role in *Richard II* at Los Angeles's Mark Taper Forum (1992). He also played in numerous productions on and off Broadway, including Cassio to James Earl Jones's *Othello* (1982), and was a guest on many television series, miniseries, and made-for-television movies, such as *The Innocent* (1994). His breakthrough role was as Dr. Frasier Crane on the television series "Cheers" (1984–93). Grammer has been twice divorced and has two daughters.

FURTHER READING

"Beyond therapy." BRET WATSON. *Entertainment,* Nov. 3, 1995.

"Kelsey Grammer." MARGY ROCHLIN. *Playboy,* Dec. 1994.

"Kelsey Grammer. . . ." JOSH MOONEY. *Cosmopolitan,* Sept. 1994.

"The doctor is in." TOM O'NEILL. *Us,* Mar. 1994.

"'Cheers' and. . . ." MICHAEL A. LIPTON. *People,* July 5, 1993.
"Scenes from. . . ." TIM APPELO. *Entertainment,* Nov. 6, 1992.
"Kelsey Grammer. . . ." ROD LURIE. *Los Angeles Magazine,* Feb. 1991.

Grant, Hugh (1960–)

In 1995 British actor Hugh Grant won best actor British Academy of Film & Television Arts (BAFTA) and Golden Globe awards for his 1994 starring role in the film *Four Weddings and a Funeral.*

He also played in several new roles. In the comedy *Nine Months,* he starred as a child psychiatrist who reacts very badly to the news that his woman friend is pregnant; the film was written and directed by Chris Columbus and costarred Julianne Moore, Tom Arnold, Joan Cusack, Jeff Goldblum, and Robin Williams.

Grant also starred in the comedy *The Englishman Who Went up a Hill but Came Down a Mountain,* directed and adapted from his own novel by Christopher Monger, about two cartographers (Grant and Ian McNeice) in early 20th-century Wales who, while mapping the countryside, decide that what the local people call a mountain is really definable as just a hill, causing considerable local upset. A third starring role was as a theater company manager opposite Alan Rickman as a second-rate star in Mike Newell's Liverpool-set, bitterly realistic film *An Awfully Big Adventure,* set on the seedy side of the British theater.

Grant costarred as Edward Ferrars, sometime suitor of Elinor Dashwood (Emma Thompson) in *Sense and Sensibility,* a period comedy adapted from the classic Jane Austen novel. He also costarred, as a treacherous Court painter, in Michael Hoffman's film *Restoration.*

On the personal side, Grant was arrested in Hollywood in June while consorting with a prostitute in his car, receiving a great deal of short-lived media attention.

A graduate of Oxford University, London-born Grant began his career in supporting roles at the Nottingham Playhouse, and cofounded the comedy group The Jockeys of Norfolk (1985). He made his professional film debut in a supporting role in James Ivory's *Maurice* (1987) and went on to supporting roles in *White Mischief* (1988), *The Lair of the White Worm* (1988), *The Dawning* (1988), *Remando al Viento* (1988), *La Nuit Bengali* (1988), *Impromptu* (1991), *Crossing the Line* (1991), *Bitter Moon* (1992), and *The Remains of the Day* (1993). His breakthrough starring role came in *Four Weddings and a Funeral* (1994). He has also appeared in several television films and miniseries, and in the series "Sirens" (1994).

FURTHER READING

"Grant, Hugh." *Current Biography,* Sept. 1995.
"If your boyfriend . . . ?" *Glamour,* Sept. 1995.
"The Americanization of. . . ." TRISH DEITCH ROHRER. *Us,* Aug. 1995.
"It had to be. . . ." ANTHONY LANE. *New Yorker,* July 24, 1995.
"What's a guy. . . .?" BENJAMIN SVETKEY. *Entertainment,* July 21, 1995.
"A night to remember. . . ." KAREN S. SCHNEIDER. *People,* July 10, 1995.
"Hugh Grant. . . ." DAVID GRITTEN. *Cosmopolitan,* Jan. 1995.
"Hugh Grant." DAVID SVETKEY. *Entertainment,* Dec. 30, 1994.
"Grant's Zoom." LUCY KAYLIN. *GQ,* Dec. 1994.

Grant, James Pineo (1922–95)

Beijing-born James Grant was the child of American medical missionaries working in China, and grew up in that country. After his 1943 graduation from the University of California, he returned to China as an American military officer, and stayed on in China after the war as a United Nations Relief and Rehabilitation official (1946–

47) and as a consultant to the U.S. Economic Aid mission (1948–49). Returning to the U.S., he earned his law degree from Harvard in 1951, practiced law in Washington (1951–54), and then held a series of international jobs, including that of deputy assistant secretary of state for Near Eastern and South Asian affairs (1962–64). He was a founder and first president of the Overseas Development Council (1969–80).

He then headed the United Nations Children's Fund (UNICEF; 1980–95), in that period emerging as one of the world's leading humanitarian figures; his contributions were credited with saving the lives of tens of millions of children, through such measures as oral rehydration therapy to treat children afflicted with diarrhea, a major cause of death among the world's children. Grant quite properly called his multiple campaigns for children a "revolution" in child survival, enlisted such celebrities as Audrey Hepburn as worldwide UNICEF health-care ambassadors, and built UNICEF into a highly respected international force, publishing an annual *State of the World's Children* report. Among his accomplishments were the 1990 World Summit for Children and the United Nations Convention on the Rights of the Child. He was survived by his wife, Ellen Young, and three sons. (d. Mt. Kisco, New York; January 28, 1995)

FURTHER READING

Obituary. *Times* (of London), Feb. 1, 1995.
Obituary. *New York Times*, Jan. 29, 1995.

Gray, Georgia Neese Clark (1900–95)

The first woman treasurer of the United States, Georgia Neese Clark, was born in Richland, Kansas, near Topeka, where her family owned the Richland State Bank. She pursued a career in the theater after graduating from Topeka's Washburn University, touring in repertory until the early 1930s. Then returning home, she became active in the family bank and in New Deal Democratic politics, becoming a Democratic national committeewoman in 1936 and president of the bank in 1937. Until her resignation from the national committee in 1964, she was a major figure in the Democratic Party. In 1949, President Harry S. Truman named her the first woman to hold the post of treasurer of the United

States, a position she held for the balance of his adminstration. From 1964, she focused on family banking and business interests. She was survived by a nephew. (d. Topeka, Kansas; October 26, 1995)

FURTHER READING

Obituary. *New York Times*, Oct. 28, 1995.

Gray, John (1952–)

John Gray has become something of a publishing phenomenon, helped in part by several visits to television's "The Oprah Winfrey Show." In 1995, his *Men Are from Mars, Women Are from Venus: A Practical Guide for Improving Communication and Getting What You Want in Your Relationship* (1992) celebrated its second birthday on the hardcover best-seller lists, for some months in the top spot, with more than 3 million copies in print. In late November, *Publishers Weekly* reported that the book was marking its 137th week on its best-seller list, "the best performance by a nonfiction author this decade." The audiobook version also was a number-one best-seller. An interactive CD-ROM version, including video clips, activities, and a paperback, was also published in 1995.

Gray's 1994 book, *What Your Mother Couldn't Tell You and Your Father Didn't Know: Advanced Relationship Skills for Lasting Intimacy,* did not match the original's success, though it also reached the best-seller list and was reprinted in paperback in 1995. However, his new 1995 offering, *Mars and Venus in the Bedroom: A Guide to Lasting Romance and Passion*—focusing on the differences in men's and women's sexual responses and how that understanding can help overcome sexual miscommunication and lead to more satisfying sexual relations—came closer and was also high on the best-seller lists. Gray was widely seen in promotion for the book, as on the "Today Show," and on the CNN, CNBC, and Fox networks. Also a best-seller was the audiobook version, read by Gray.

Houston-born Gray was a follower of Maharishi Mahesh Yogi during the 1970s, living largely abroad until returning to the United States in 1979. He and author Barbara DeAngelis married and ran a relationship advice business in the early 1980s; after they divorced in 1984, he continued to run the business, giving nationwide seminars. Gray's earlier books include *What You Feel You Can Heal: A Guide for Enriching Relationships* (1984) and *Men, Women, and Relationships: Making Peace with the Opposite Sex* (1990). Gray received his bachelor's and master's degrees in Eastern philosophy from the Maharishi European Research University in Switzerland, and a 1982 correspondence-course Ph.D. in psychology from Columbia Pacific University. He married his second wife, Bonnie Josephson, in 1985; they have one child; she also has two daughters from a previous marriage.

FURTHER READING

"Talking with. . . ." J.D. REED. *People,* May 1, 1995.

Greenspan, Alan (1926–) During 1995, Federal Reserve System head Alan Greenspan continued to try to balance the falling international real value of the dollar against the impact of high interest rates on the U.S. economy. His explanation that interest rates must remain high in order to combat inflation had begun to wear thin, though, and was being questioned even by those most sympathetic to his position. The Federal Reserve Board raised interest rates in February, citing the danger of inflation, even though signs of inflation were absent from all

the major economic reports. Greenspan continued to publicly defend his anti-inflation policy through much of the year, finally lowering rates by a quarter of a percent in December.

On June 20, speaking before the Economics Club of New York, Greenspan finally made it clear that a major motivating force in keeping interest rates high was the fear that the sharp decline in the value of the dollar, if coupled with lower U.S. interest rates, might cause a flight of international investment dollars from the U.S. In fact, with the sharp decline of the dollar during much of 1995, interest rates on dollar-denominated international debt obligations had fallen quite sharply, as measured against interest paid in stronger currencies, notably the German mark and the Japanese yen. Throughout the year, as trade deficits continued to pile up, the national debt continued to grow, the stability of the dollar remained uncertain, and Washington lawmakers created a major budget crisis, Greenspan continued to talk about inflation and to try to stabilize the value of the dollar, which is a central concern for America and for the world economy.

Greenspan, a leading free-market economic conservative, was a key economic consultant to presidents Richard Nixon and Gerald Ford, and was chairperson of the National Council of Economic Advisors (1974–76). He moved into the center of national economic activity when he was appointed head of the Federal Reserve System by President Ronald Reagan. He was reappointed to a second term by President George Bush in 1991. During 1992, as the deep recession worsened and unemployment grew, Greenspan began to revise his long-held optimistic view of the economy; by September 1992, the Federal Reserve had lowered its discount rate and federal funds rate to 3 percent—and to little immediate avail, much to the discomfort of President Bush, who lost the White House in November largely on economic issues. In 1993, Greenspan publicly endorsed Clinton's deficit reduction package and financial stimulus plans, held interest rates low, and took many steps to aid economic growth. In 1994, he sharply changed his position; the Federal Reserve Board increased short-term interest rates six times, taking the federal funds rate from 3 percent to 5.5 percent, and the discount rate from 3 percent to 4.75 percent, thereby forcing U.S. business and consumer interest rates up sharply, while the dollar continued to fall.

A New Yorker, Greenspan received his B.S. in 1948, his M.A. in 1950, and his Ph.D. in 1977, all from New York University.

FURTHER READING

"What Greenspan. . . ." GEORGE P. BROCKWAY. *The New Leader,* July 17, 1995.
"Greenspan's ho-hum. . . ." *World Press Review,* May 1995.
"Greenspan's quest. . . ." DAVID M. JONES. *Challenge,* July–Aug. 1994.
"Was Greenspan. . . ." OWEN ULLMANN. *Business Week,* Apr. 18, 1994.
"Look who's talking, too." ALAN GREENBLATT. "Why Alan Greenspan. . . ." WILLIAM GREIDER. *Washington,* Dec. 1993.

Griffith, Melanie (1957–   ) Film star Melanie Griffith continued to be a very familiar face on American television screens in 1995, as her 1994 film *Milk Money* continued to successfully unroll in home video. In 1995, she starred in the television miniseries *Buffalo Girls,* as Dora Dupran, a madam in an Old West house of prostitution and the best friend of Calamity Jane, played by Anjelica Huston. Directed by Rod Hardy and based on the Larry McMurtry novel, the miniseries included Gabriel Byrne as Griffith's lover Teddy Blue, Sam Elliott as Wild Bill Hickok, Peter Coyote as Buffalo Bill Cody, Reba McEntire as Annie Oakley, and Native American activist Russell Means as Sitting Bull. Grif-

fith received a Golden Globe nomination as best supporting actress in a miniseries or telefilm for the role. Griffith also played the adult Tina Tercell in the coming-of-age film *Now and Then,* starring Thora Birch as the young Teeny, one of the four young girls the film is about; Leslie Linka Glatta directed.

Forthcoming were starring roles opposite Jeremy Irons and Dominique Swain in the film *Lolita,* directed by Adrian Lyne, with screenplay by Harold Pinter; opposite Nick Nolte in the film *Mulholland Falls,* directed by Lee Tamahori; in the film *The Gaslight Addition,* costarring Demi Moore, Rosie O'Donnell, and Rita Wilson; and in the film *Two Much,* directed by Fernando Trueba and costarring Antonio Banderas, Daryl Hannah, Danny Aiello, and Eli Wallach.

On the personal side, Griffith affirmed her intention to go through with her second divorce from actor Don Johnson, filed in 1994; they had previously been married and divorced in the mid-1970s.

New York City–born Griffith got off to a quick start, playing strong young supporting roles in three 1975 films—*Night Moves, The Drowning Pool,* and *Smile*—but then encountered personal and professional problems. She reemerged as a leading dramatic actress in the mid-1980s, in such films as *Something Wild* (1986), *The Milagro Beanfield War* (1988), and *Stormy Monday* (1988); scored a major hit opposite Harrison Ford in *Working Girl* (1988; she won an Oscar nomination); and followed up with starring roles in *Pacific Heights* (1990), *The Bonfire of the Vanities* (1990), *Paradise* (1991), *Shining Through* (1992), *A Stranger Among Us* (1992), *Born Yesterday* (1993), *Milk Money* (1994), and *Nobody's Fool* (1994). Griffith has one child.

FURTHER READING

"From pleasingly plump. . . ." BONNIE SIEGLER and ANGELA EBRON. *Family Circle,* Aug. 8, 1995.
"Griffith's true grit." JIM JEROME. *Ladies Home Journal,* Oct. 1994.
"Melanie Griffith." MARK MORRISON. *Us,* Sept. 1994.
"Thoroughly modern Melanie." MIMI AVINS. *New Woman,* Sept. 1994.
"Melanie unplugged." ERIC ALTERMAN. *Vanity Fair,* June 1994.
"Melanie Griffith. . . ." MARTHA SHERRILL. *McCall's,* June 1994.
"Rocky Mountain low." *People,* Mar. 28, 1994.
"The hottest. . . ." STEVE DITLEA and NANCY STEDMAN. *Redbook,* Mar. 1993.

Grinkov, Sergei (1967–95)

On November 20, while training at Lake Placid, New York for a professional tour and the upcoming world skating championships, Russian skater Sergei Glinkov suddenly collapsed and died of a totally unexpected heart attack. There had been no previous hint of a health problem, and no trace of drugs or other contributing factors. Grinkov, early in his career a singles skater, paired with Russian skater Yekatereina Gordeyev; they went on to become acclaimed leading pairs skaters, winning Olympics gold medals in Calgary in 1988 and in Lillehammer in 1994. They married in 1991; their daughter, Daria, was born in 1992. He was survived by his wife and daughter. (d. Lake Placid, New York; November 20, 1995)

FURTHER READING

"Soulmates on ice. . . ." WILLIAM PLUMMER. *People,* Dec. 11, 1995.
"Love story. " LEIGH MONTVILLE. *Sports Illustrated,* Dec. 4, 1995.
"Short but sweet program." STEVE WULF. *Time,* Dec. 4, 1995.
Obituary. *Times* (of London), Nov. 23, 1995.
Obituary. *Independent,* Nov. 22, 1995.
Obituary. *New York Times,* Nov. 22, 1995.
"Gordeeva and Grinkov." E.M. SWIFT. *Sports Illustrated,* Feb. 28, 1994.

Grisham, John (1955–)

John Grisham's 1995 best-seller, *The Rainmaker,* stayed in the legal vein of his previous novels, but was the first to be written in the first-person point of view and the first since his debut to be set largely in a courtroom. The David-and-Goliath tale has young attorney Rudy Baylor handling an insurance case against the law firm that broke its contract with him—for which he was suing them. Some surprised reviewers lauded the book for its gritty realism. A film was scheduled, with Grisham set to coproduce. Grisham also sold his first original screenplay, *The Gingerbread Man,* reportedly for more than $1.5 million.

Meanwhile, the paperback version of *The Chamber* debuted at the top of the best-seller lists; it had been the best-selling work of hardcover fiction in 1994, with more than 3 million sold, a new record even for this extremely popular author. The 1993 novel and 1994 film *The Client* found new life in 1995 as a television series, starring John Heard, Polly Holliday, David Barry Gray, Terry O'Quinn, Ossie Davis, and JoBeth Williams as family-law attorney Reggie Love.

Grisham's longtime agent Jay Garon died in August 1995, and his editor David Gernert left Doubleday to become an agent, with Grisham as his first and most major client, focusing not only on books but also on film scripts and CD-ROMs. Unusually, under special arrangement with Doubleday, Gernert will continue to act as Grisham's editor.

Grisham began his writing career with a courtroom drama involving paternal revenge, *A Time to Kill* (1989). That book became a bestseller only after the enormous success of his next three books, *The Firm* (1991) and *The Pelican Brief* (1992), both film successes in 1993, and *The Client* (1993). Grisham's J.D. was from the University of Mississippi. He practiced law in Mississippi, and was elected to the Mississippi House of Representatives in 1984, resigning during his second term, when his books began to be lucrative. In 1994, he became publisher and key financial supporter of the Mississippi literary magazine *The Oxford American.* He is married to Renee Grisham; they have two children.

FURTHER READING

"Grisham's law." MARTHA DUFFY. *Time,* May 8, 1995.
"Attorney's privileges." MARK HARRIS. *Entertainment,* May 5, 1995.
"Grisham, John." *Current Biography,* Sept. 1993.

"The Grisham brief." ROBIN STREET. *Writer's Digest*, July 1993.

"John Grisham. . . ." MICHELLE BEARDEN. *Publishers Weekly*, Feb. 22, 1993.

Groom, Winston (1943–) Eight years after first emerging in public, Winston Groom's Forrest Gump became a household name, with Tom Hanks' Oscar-winning portrayal of the low-IQ but ubiquitous country icon. As the success of the 1994 film became apparent, Groom weighed in with a spin-off book, *Gumpisms: The Wit and Wisdom of Forrest Gump* (1994). In 1995, he produced a real sequel, *Gump & Co.*, which has Gump—as usual—appearing everywhere, as from the Iran-Contra affair to the breaking down of the Berlin Wall, and featuring his son, Little Forrest. The work was simultaneously released in audiobook form, read by Will Patton. Film rights were sold for a reported $2 million, though other details about a possible film sequel were unsettled.

One thing for sure: Groom will not again sign a "net" contract, to be paid largely out of profits, as he did for the original contract. By Hollywood bookkeeping, the third-highest-grossing film of all time in mid-1995 still had not shown a profit, even after earning more than $650 million worldwide. Groom was retaining a lawyer to see that he received an equitable share of the proceeds.

Groom also published an historical work, *Shrouds of Glory: From Atlanta to Nashville: The Last Great Campaign of the Civil War*, inspired by his great-grandfather's participation in the 1864 campaign. Though he hewed to the historical record, reviewers noted that he brought his story-telling skills to the task. Groom's success has meant new life for his earlier works, as well, such as *As Summers Die*, reprinted in paperback in 1995.

Born in Washington, D.C., Groom received his 1965 B.A. from the University of Alabama, and then saw military service (1965–67) that included duty as an Army officer in Vietnam. He was a reporter with the *Washington Star* (1967–76). Groom's Vietnam experience was the center of his first novel, *Better Times Than These* (1976), and also of his first nonfiction work, *Conversations with the Enemy; the Story of PC Robert Garwood* (1983; with Duncan Spencer). His novels include *As Summers Die* (1980), *Only* (1984), *Forrest Gump* (1986), and *Gone the Sun* (1988). His second wife is Anne Clinton. He has two children.

FURTHER READING

"Winston Groom. . . ." MICHELE BEARDEN. *Publishers Weekly,* Apr. 17, 1995.

"Surprise package. . . ." JOSEPH OLSHAN. *People,* Sept. 5, 1994.

Guardino, Harry (1925–95) New York City–born Harry Guardino was a versatile film, television, and stage player. He began his long career after seeing Naval service in World War II, studying at the New York Dramatic Workshop while playing in television and stage supporting roles. He made his film debut in *Flesh and Fury* (1952); among his further films were *Hold Back Tomorrow* (1955), *Houseboat* (1958), *Pork Chop Hill* (1959), *King of Kings* (1961), *The Pigeon That Took Rome* (1962; he received a Golden Globe best supporting actor nomination), *The Treasure of San Gennaro* (1966), *Madigan* (1968), *Lovers and Other Strangers* (1970), *Dirty Harry* (1971), *They Only Kill Their Masters* (1972), *Capone* (1975), *St. Ives* (1976), *Any Which Way You Can* (1980), and *The Neon Empire* (1989). His hundreds of television appearances included starring roles in the series "The Reporter" (1964), "Monty Nash" (1971), and the

Hamilton Burger role in "Perry Mason" (1973–74). He was survived by his wife, Elyssa, a daughter, three sons, two sisters, and two brothers. (d. Palm Springs, California; July 17, 1995)

FURTHER READING

Obituary. *Variety*, July 24, 1995.
Obituary. *Independent*, July 19, 1995.
Obituary. *New York Times*, July 18, 1995.

Gur, Mordechai (1930–95) Jerusalem-born Mordechai Gur was a leading Israeli military officer and politician. He began his military career while still in his mid-teens, joining the Haganah, which was an underground force during the British occupation. He fought with the Haganah through the Israeli War of Independence (First Arab-Israeli War), left the army to study at Hebrew University, and returned as the Arab-Israeli guerrilla war intensified in the early 1950s. Gur's army career included service as a parachutist commando, and as an army general staff officer and military college administrator. In 1967, during the Six-Day War (Third Arab-Israeli War), he commanded the forces that took the Old City of Jerusalem. He became Israeli chief of staff in 1974, and was credited with having planned the Israeli commando attack that freed hijacked airline passengers at Entebbe, Uganda in 1976. He retired from the military in 1978. Gur then entered politics, serving as a Labor Party Member of Parliament, and was minister of health in the Likud-Labor coalition government (1984–86). He also published books on military history and several children's books. Long ill with cancer, Gur committed suicide. He was survived by his wife, Rita, two daughters, and two sons. (d. Tel Aviv; July 16, 1995)

FURTHER READING

Obituary. *Times* (of London), July 17, 1995.
Obituary. *Independent*, July 17, 1995.
Obituary. *New York Times*, July 17, 1995.

Guthrie, Robert (1917–95) Missouri-born doctor, medical researcher, and professor of medicine Robert Guthrie in the early 1960s made a major breakthrough that was to save tens of thousands of children all over the world from mental retardation. He introduced a very simple, inexpensive test that, for a few cents and with a few minutes spent in analyzing test results, would screen newly born children for the inherited disease of phenylketonuria (PKU). If undetected, PKU causes brain damage and therefore mental retardation; if detected in the newly born, a special, carefully observed diet can prevent the damage and retardation. At the time of his discovery, Guthrie was at the State University of New York at Buffalo, where he taught (1958–86); he had previously held posts at the National Institutes of Health, the University of Kansas, and two research centers. Guthrie's several degrees were from the University of Minnesota and the University of Maine. He was survived by his wife, Margaret, three daughters, two sons, and a brother. (d. Seattle; June 24, 1995)

FURTHER READING

Obituary. *New York Times* June 25, 1995.

Gwynn, Tony (Anthony Keith Gwynn; 1960–) The strike that ended the 1994 baseball season also ended Tony Gwynn's chance to reach a .400 batting average, which no one has done since Ted Williams batted .406 in 1941. Gwynn had pushed his average up to .394 when the season was prematurely cut off. He had strongly supported the union, however. In 1995, Gwynn was not nearly so close, ending the season with a .368 batting average. However, that was enough to make him the National League's leading batsman for the second consecutive year, and the sixth time in his career. He continues to have the highest batting average of any active player over the last ten years. Gwynn also tied with Dante Bichette as the year's hitting leader, both having gained 197 hits; Gwynn had led the league outright in 1994 with 165 hits. Gwynn also played in his eleventh All-Star game, as starting right-fielder on the National League team. In 1994, Gwynn had extended his contract with the Padres through 1997, with an option year.

Los Angeles–born Gwynn graduated from Long Beach Polytechnic High School and attended San Diego State University. Selected by San Diego in the 1981 free-agent draft, he played in the minor leagues (198–82) in Walla Walla, Amarillo, and Hawaii, before coming up to the Padres (1982). Recovering from a fractured wrist, he played briefly in the minors in Las Vegas (1983), then returned to the Padres, where he had twelve straight years of hitting .300 or over (1984–95). Gwynn has been a member of the All-Star team eleven times (1984–87; 1989–95) and has won the National League batting title six times (1984; 1987–89; 1994–95). With Jim Rosenthal, he wrote *Tony Gwynn's Total Baseball Player* (1992). He is married to Alicia Cureton; they have a son and a daughter. His brother, Chris Gwynn, also plays major league baseball, as an outfielder with the Kansas City Royals.

FURTHER READING

"The unnatural." MIKE LUPICA. *Esquire,* Aug. 1995.

"Tony Gwynn. . . ." BARRY M. BLOOM. *Sport*, Sept. 1994.

"Tony Gwynn. . . ." ROBERT E. HOOD. *Boys' Life*, Sept. 1992.

"Mr. contact." JEFF SILVERMAN. *California*, Sept. 1991.

Hackett, Albert (1900–95) New York City–born Albert Hackett began his long acting career as a child, making his stage debut at age six. He ultimately moved into adult theater and silent film roles. In 1924, he and Frances Goodrich began their long writing partnership; their first play was *Up Pops the Devil* (1930), followed by *Bridal Wise* (1932). Married in 1931, Goodrich and Hackett went to Hollywood in the early 1930s, beginning their long screen-writing careers with *The Secret of Madame Blanche* (1933). Among their further films were *The Thin Man* (1934), *Naughty Marietta* (1935), *Ah! Wilderness* (1935), *Rose Marie* (1936), *After the Thin Man* (1936), *Another Thin Man* (1939), *Lady in the Dark* (1944), *It's A Wonderful Life* (1946), *The Virginian* (1946), *Easter Parade* (1948), *In the Good Old Summertime* (1949), *Father of the Bride* (1950), *Father's Little Dividend* (1951), *Seven Brides for Seven Brothers* (1954), and *Five Finger Exercise* (1962). Their most celebrated work by far was the play *The Diary of Anne Frank* (1956), which won a Tony Award and a Pulitzer Prize. They adapted the play into the 1959 film version. Goodrich (1891–1984) predeceased Hackett. He was survived by his second wife, Gisele Svetlik Hackett. (d. New York City; March 16, 1995)

FURTHER READING

Obituary. *Variety,* Mar. 28, 1995.
Obituary. *Independent,* Mar. 21, 1995.
Obituary. *New York Times,* Mar. 18, 1995.

Hackman, Gene (1930–) Veteran actor Gene Hackman starred in 1995 as bottom-of-the-barrel producer Harry Zimm opposite John Travolta as gangster-turned-movie producer Chili Palmer in the well-received, Hollywood-set film comedy *Get Shorty*, costarring Rene Russo and Danny DeVito, who also coproduced. Barry Sonnenfield directed and coproduced and Scott Franklin adapted the Elmore Leonard novel. The cast also included Dennis Farina and Delroy Lindo, with Bette Midler, Harvey Keitel, and Penny Marshall in cameo roles.

Hackman also starred in the post-Cold War thriller *Crimson Tide*, as captain of the American nuclear submarine *Alabama*, opposite Denzel Washington as his new executive officer. With civil war underway in Russia, dissident nationalists have seized a Russian nuclear installation, and are threatening to begin World War III by attacking the U.S. Hackman moves toward a pre-emptive strike against the Russians; Washington organizes a mutiny to prevent a humanity-destroying war.

Hackman also starred as killer sheriff Herod opposite Sharon Stone as an avenging gunwoman in the film *The Quick and the Dead*, directed by Sam Raimi; it was the story of a murderous annual duellist tournament in an Old West town, which Herod always wins by killing the surviving contestants—until Stone appears.

Forthcoming was a starring role in the film *The Birdcage*, directed by Mike Nichols and costarring Robin Williams, Nathan Lane, and Dianne Wiest.

California-born Hackman became a star in his best actor Oscar-winning role as Popeye Doyle in *The French Connection* (1971), a role he repeated in *The French Connection II* (1975). Among his other films are *The Poseidon Adventure* (1972), *The Conversation* (1974), *Night Moves* (1975), the notable *Mississippi Burning* (1988), *The Package* (1989), *Postcards from the Edge* (1990), *Narrow Margin* (1990), *Loose Cannons* (1990), *Class Action* (1991), *Company Business* (1991), *The Unforgiven* (1992), *The Firm* (1993), *Geronimo* (1993), and *Wyatt Earp* (1994). In 1992, he starred on Broadway opposite Glenn Close and Richard Dreyfuss in Ariel Dorfman's play *Death and the Maiden*. Hackman was previously married to Faye Maltese, and has three children. (For additional photo, see **Travolta, John**.)

FURTHER READING

"Gene Hackman's. . . ." JOHN CULHANE. *Reader's Digest*, Sept. 1993.

Hallowes, Odette Brailly (1912–95)

Born in Picardy, Odette Brailly grew up in France, married Englishman Roy Sansom in 1931, and raised their three daughters in London during the 1930s. After the fall of France, in May 1940, she volunteered for the British Special Operations Executive (SOE), was trained for intelligence work, and returned to France as an SOE courier in October 1942. She and an SOE colleague, Peter Churchill, were captured by the Germans in April 1943. She revealed nothing to the Germans, despite prolonged torture by the Gestapo. She and Churchill were then sent to the infamous Ravensbrück concentration camp, where, under a continuing death sentence, her torture and defiance continued until the camp was taken by the Allies. She became a much-honored heroine after the war, receiving the British George Cross and the French Legion of Honor, while always insisting that she was only a symbol of all those like her who had fought and defied the Nazis. She was played by Anna Neagle in the 1950 biofilm *Odette*. She married Peter Churchill in 1947, after the death of her first husband. Divorced in 1956, she later married former SOE operative Geoffrey Hallowes. She was survived by her husband and her three daughters. (d. Walton-on-Thames, England; March 13, 1995)

FURTHER READING

Obituary. *New York Times*, Mar. 21, 1995.
Obituary. *Times* (of London), Mar. 17, 1995.

Hampton-El, Clement: See Abdel Rahman, Omar.

Hanks, Tom (1956–) It was another extraordinary year for actor Tom Hanks. For his title role in the film *Forrest Gump*, he won his second consecutive best actor Academy Award; he had won his first best actor Oscar a year before, for *Philadelphia*. For the Forrest Gump role, he also won the Screen Actors Guild, Golden Globe, People's Choice, and Blockbuster Entertainment best actor awards.

In 1995, Hanks starred as astronaut Jim Lovell in yet another acclaimed film and Academy Award contender, *Apollo 13*, directed by Ron Howard and costarring Kevin Bacon and Bill Paxton as his fellow astronauts, with Gary Sinise, Ed Harris, Kathleen Quinlan, and Jean Speegle Howard. Based on the autobiographical book *Lost Moon*, by Lovell and Jeffrey Kluger, the film tells the story of the Apollo 13 moon flight, in which the American spaceship *Odyssey* came very close to landing on the moon, but was forced to abort by explosions causing loss of power and oxygen in the spacecraft; the astronauts then took refuge in their lunar module, the *Aquarius*, and ultimately piloting the craft back to Earth. Hanks, Ron Howard and Brian Grazer announced late in 1995 that they would produce a 13-part HBO docudrama on the Apollo space program.

Hanks also starred as the voice of the toy cowboy Woody in the very successful Christmas season Disney computer-animated film *Toy Story*. He also appeared in the documentary *The Celluloid Closet*, which reviewed the treatment of homosexuality in Hollywood films.

Forthcoming was the film *That Thing You Do*, written, directed by, and starring Hanks.

California-born Hanks appeared in the television series "Bosom Buddies" (1980-82), then emerged as a film star in the mid-1980s, with *Splash* (1984), and went on to star in such films as *Bachelor Party* (1984), *Volunteers* (1985), *The Man with One Red Shoe* (1985), *The Money Pit* (1986), *Every Time We Say Goodbye* (1986), *Big* (1988), *Punchline* (1988), *Turner and Hooch* (1989), *Joe Versus the Volcano* (1990), *The Bonfire of the Vanities* (1990), *Radio Flyer* (1991), *A League of Their Own* (1992), *Sleepless in Seattle* (1993), and *Philadelphia* (1993). Hanks attended California State University at Sacramento. He married Rita Wilson in 1988; they have one son and expect another child early in 1996; he also has two children from a previous marriage.

FURTHER READING

"Shooting the moon. . . ." SKIP HOLLANDSWORTH. *Texas Monthly,* July 1995.
"What appeals to. . . ." JEFF GORDINIER. *Entertainment,* June 23, 1995.
"Tom Hanks. . . ." GERRI HIRSHEY. *GQ,* June 1995.
"Hollywood husbands." MEREDITH BERKMAN and MARK MORRISON. *Ladies Home Journal,* Feb. 1995.
Tom Hanks: Journey to Stardom. TRAKIN. St. Martin's, 1995.
"Tom Hanks." JEFF GORDINIER. *Entertainment,* Dec. 30, 1994.
"The evolution of. . . ." MARK MORRISON. *Us,* Aug. 1994.
"Peaking Tom." BRIAN D. JOHNSON. *Maclean's,* July 11, 1994.
"Tom terrific." KEVIN SESSUMS. *Vanity Fair,* June 1994.
"Tom Hanks." INGRID SISCHY. *Interview,* Mar. 1994.
"Playing the part. . . ." *Newsweek,* Feb. 14, 1994.
Tom Hanks. ROSEMARY WALLNER. Abdo & Daughters, 1994.
"Tom Hanks. . . ." JENNET CONANT. *Esquire,* Dec. 1993.
"The players." ANDREW CORSELLO and AMY DONOHUE.
"Tom, Denzel and me." DAVID BERTUGLI. *Philadelphia,* Dec. 1993.

Hardy, Bert (Albert Hardy; 1913–95)

London-born Bert Hardy was one of the leading British photojournalists of his time. Child of a very poor family, he left school at the age of 13, a year later went to work as a messenger for Central Photo Service, and soon began his career as a photographer, making his professional debut with a photo in *Bicycle* magazine. A pioneer whose tool was a Leica, rather than the customary plate glass camera of the day, Hardy brought a sense of spontaneity to his street scenes and photo stories. After working for photo agencies through the 1930s, he went on his own in 1939. In 1941, he joined *Picture Post*, and soon became the magazine's chief photographer. Hardy became an acclaimed photojournalist as an army photographer during World War II. After the war, he went back to *Picture Post*, traveling Britain and the world, most notably as a war correspondent, whose Korean War pictures were particularly prized. After the magazine ceased publication in 1957, he worked as an advertisng photographer, retiring in 1964. He published *Bert Hardy: My Life* (1986). Hardy was survived by his wife, Sheila, and two sons. (d. Oxted, England; July 3, 1995)

FURTHER READING

Obituary. *New York Times,* July 7, 1995.
Obituary. *Independent,* July 5, 1995.
Obituary. *Times* (of London), July 5, 1995.

Harris, Neil Patrick (1973–) Though

still a familiar face on the world's television screens in reruns of his television series "Doogie Howser, M.D," actor Neil Patrick Harris, now in his early 20s, is no longer playing teenagers. In the very well received television film version of Willa Cather's novel *My Antonia*, directed by Joseph Sargent, he played Jim Burden, a young man growing up in the American West early in the century, opposite Jason Robards, Eva Marie

Saint, and Elina Lowensohn as the young Bohemian-American girl with whom he falls in love. Harris also starred in the title role opposite Anne Archer and Len Cariou in the television film *The Man in the Attic*, directed by Greame Campbell; he played the lover of a married woman, who hides him in her attic for 20 years, while she has many other lovers, as well.

Forthcoming was a starring role in the film *The Animal Room*, directed by Craig Singer and costarring Matthew Lillard, Gabriel Olds, Catherine Hicks, and Stephen Pearlman.

In late 1989 Harris became a major television figure, starring in the imaginative role of "Doogie Howser," a teenage doctor who graduated from medical school at the age of 14. In the early 1990s, as Harris and the show grew up, he and the show were acclaimed for their emphasis on frank talk about AIDS, safe sex, and other serious matters, which proved appealing to wide audiences. Harris grew up in Ruidoso, New Mexico, acted in school productions, and was discovered by playwright Mark Medoff at a summer drama camp, then going into his first film, *Clara's Heart* (1988). He later played in such telefilms as *Cold Sassy Tree* (1989), *Leave Her to Heaven* (1989), *A Family Torn Apart* (1993), and *Snowbound: The Jim and Jennifer Stolpa Story* (1994), and has also appeared in guest roles in several television series.

FURTHER READING

"Three hot actors. . . ." KEVIN KOFFLER and CLAIRE CONNORS. *Seventeen*, Jan. 1992.

Harris, Phil (1906–95) Indiana-born bandleader, singer, and actor Phil Harris, child of a show business family, began his career as a child in Nashville, working as a drummer in his family's vaudeville act. He became a successful touring big band leader and radio personality in the early 1930s, and in 1936 joined Jack Benny's enormously popular radio show. With his breezy personal style and talent for comedy, Harris soon became a household name. He stayed with Benny until 1952, also developing his own radio show and costarring with his wife, movie star Alice Faye, in their shared radio show (1946–54). He also appeared in several films, among them *Man About Town* (1939), *Buck Benny Rides Again* (1940), *Wabash Avenue* (1950), *The*

High and the Mighty (1954), and *The Jungle Book* (1967), the last a highly successful late-career role as the voice of Baloo the Bear in the Disney classic. He was survived by Alice Faye, and their two daughters. (d. Rancho Mirage, California; August 11, 1995)

FURTHER READING

Obituary. *Independent,* Aug. 23, 1995.
Obituary. *Times* (of London), Aug. 14, 1995.
Obituary. *Variety*, Aug. 14, 1995
Obituary. *New York Times*, Aug. 13, 1995.

Harrison, George (1943–) Former Beatle George Harrison, an historic figure in world popular music, joined two other living legends, former Beatles Paul McCartney and Ringo Starr, in a three-segment, six-hour television biography of the group, *The Beatles Anthology*, broadcast on ABC November 19, 20, and 22, 1995. The show, which included the world premiere of the 1977 John Lennon song "Free As a Bird," drew enormous audiences. It was followed by release of their two-disc set *The Beatles Anthology, Volume. 1*; volumes 2 and 3 were to be released in 1996. Volume 1 contained more than 40 selections drawn from the years 1958–64, including some from the period when they were still called the Quarrymen, and others before Ringo Starr replaced Pete Best as drummer. Included were the unreleased Lennon–McCartney songs "Hello Little Girl" and "Like Dreamers Do," as well as "Free As a Bird." Two other Lennon songs, "Real Love" and "Grow Old With Me," were scheduled to be released in the 1996 volumes. A *Beatles Anthology* book was also to be released in 1996, as was a ten-hour home video version of the anthology. The anthology albums and a "Free As a Bird" single were released in early December; both immediately became record-breaking chart toppers.

Liverpool-born Harrison joined The Quarrymen as a guitarist in 1958, and in 1960, with Paul McCartney, John Lennon, and Pete Best (replaced by Ringo Starr in 1962) formed the Beatles; Harrison was lead guitarist and sometimes a singer. As a member of the group, he helped trigger a revolution in popular music and in the early 1960s emerged as a worldwide celebrity. He also played a special role, studying with Indian musician Ravi Shankar, learning the sitar and several other Indian instruments, introducing Indian strains into the work of the Beatles, and thereby helping to bring Indian music into Western popular music of his time. Harrison organized the 1971 *Concert for Bangladesh*, the landmark first international rock music benefit for humanitarian goals.

Harrison's main work as a songwriter developed after the Beatles years. He also formed his own film production and rock management companies. He scored a substantial comeback with the album *Cloud Nine* (1987), and in 1988 was prime mover in the organization of the extraordinary "new" group, The Traveling Wilburys, consisting of Harrison, Bob Dylan, Roy Orbison (until his death), Tom Petty, and Jeff Lynne, all longtime stars, who produced two well-received albums (1988; 1990). In 1992, he was the first recipient of Billboard's Century Award, for lifetime creative achievement. In the same year, he issued the two-CD set *George Harrison Live in Japan*. Harrison has been married twice, and has one child.

FURTHER READING

"Get back. . . ." RICHARD CORLISS. *Time,* Nov. 20, 1995.
The Lost Beatles Interviews. GEOFFREY GIULIANO.
    NAL-Dutton, 1994.
Illustrated George Harrison. GEOFFREY GIULIANO.
    Book Sales, 1993.

Hatch, Orrin Grant (1934–) Utah Senator Orrin Hatch, a leading Republican conservative, served as chair of the Senate Judiciary Committee during 1995. He had become a very familiar face on American television screens in 1991, as one of that committee's chief supporters of Clarence Thomas against the sexual harassment accusations of Anita Faye Hill, and was ranking minority member of the committee in 1993 and 1994. As chair, he was able to set much of the committee's agenda, which included heavy emphasis on hearing testimony about several militia organizations after the Oklahoma City bombings, and on the 1993 siege at Ruby Ridge, Tennessee, at which a federal officer and two family members of besieged Randall Weaver were killed. On the floor of the Senate, Hatch was one of the leaders of the fight for the failed balanced budget amendment, as well as a leader in the battle for the whole range of Republican budget proposals.

Hatch's 1959 B.S. was from Brigham Young University, and his 1962 J.D. from the University of Pittsburgh. After practicing law in Pittsburgh and Salt Lake City, he won the first of his four senatorial terms in 1976. Hatch was long the ranking Republican minority member of the Senate's Labor and Human Resources Committee. He married Elaine Hansen in 1967; they have six children.

FURTHER READING

Orrin Hatch and Twenty Years of America. LEE RODERICK. Gold Leaf Press, 1994.

Heaney, Seamus Justin (1939–) Seamus Heaney and his wife, Marie, were on vacation in rural Greece and for a full day did not know what the world already knew: that he had been awarded the 1995 Nobel Prize for Literature. Born, educated, and long resident in Northern Ireland, Heaney has since 1972 lived primarily in Dublin, with a country residence in County Wicklow, but considers himself simply Irish. He said that he was gratified to be honored in a new time for Ireland, since the 1994 ceasefire was announced by the Irish Republican Army (IRA). In addition to the honor, the Nobel Prize itself is today worth more than $1 million.

Coincidentally, Heaney published two new books in 1995. *The Redress of Poetry* is a collection of his lectures as Professor of Poetry at Oxford University, while *Laments* is a collection of poems by the 16th-century Polish writer Jan Kochanowski, translated by Heaney and Stanislaw Baranczak. A new book of Heaney's own poems, *The Spirit Level*, was scheduled for summer 1996 publication.

Born near Castledaw, in Northern Ireland's County Derry, Heaney received his 1961 B.A. in English language and literature from Queen's University in Belfast and a teaching certificate at nearby St. Joseph's College (1961-62). He began publishing poems while at university, under the pseudonym Incertus. His first book, *Eleven Poems*, was published in 1965, but his second, *Death of a Naturalist* (1966), brought him wide attention, winning the 1967 Somerset Maugham and 1968 Cholmondeley awards. His other works of poetry include *Door into the Dark* (1969), *Wintering Out* (1972), *North* (1975; it won the W.H. Smith award and Duff Cooper prize), *Stations* (1975), *Bog Poems* (1975), *Field Work* (1979), *Poems: 1965-1975* (1980), *Station Island* (1984), *The Haw Lantern* (1987; it won the Whitbread award), *Selected Poems: 1966-1987* (1990), and *Seeing Things: Poems* (1991). His other works include *Preoccupations: Selected Prose 1968-1978* (1980); *The Government of the Tongue* (1988); *The Place of Writing* (1990); *The Cure at Troy* (1990), a version of Sophocles' play *Philoctetes*; and *Sweeney Astray* (1984), his version of the medieval Irish narrative poem *Buile*

Suibhne, published in a revised version as *Sweeney's Flight* (1992), with Rachel Geise's photographs of Northern Ireland

Throughout most of his career, Heaney has also continued teaching, at St. Thomas's Secondary School (1962-63), St. Joseph's College of Education (1963-66), and Queen's University (1966-72), all in Belfast, and at Carysfort College (1975-81). Since 1985, he has been Boylston professor of rhetoric and oratory at Harvard University, where he teaches one semester a year; he was also professor of poetry at Oxford University (1989-94). Heaney married Marie Devlin in 1965; they have two sons and a daughter.

FURTHER READING

"Seamus Heaney. . . ." JONATHAN BING. *Publishers Weekly,* Dec. 4, 1995.
"A poet. . . ." PAUL GRAY. "The arts and media." *Time,* Oct. 16, 1995.
"The guttural muse." BLAKE MORRISON. "Son of the soil. . . ." DAVID SHARROCK. *Guardian,* Oct. 6, 1995.
Critical Essays on Seamus Heaney. ROBERT F. GARRATT. G. K. Hall, 1995.
The Art of Seamus Heaney, 3rd ed. TONY CURTIS, ed. Dufour, 1994.
More on the Word-Hoard: The Work of Seamus Heaney. STEPHEN WADE. Borgo, 1994.
Seamus Heaney: Poet and Critic. ARTHUR E. McGUINNESS. P. Lang, 1994.
Seamus Heaney and the Language of Poetry. BERNARD O'DONOGHUE. Prentice Hall, 1994.
Questioning Tradition, Language, and Myth: The Poetry of Seamus Heaney. MICHAEL R. MOLINO. Catholic University Press, 1994.
Seamus Heaney: The Making of the Poet. MICHAEL PARKER. University of Iowa Press, 1993.
Seamus Heaney: A Collection of Critical Essays. ELMER ANDREWS, ed. St. Martin's, 1993.
"A soul on the washing line." *Economist,* June 22, 1991.
Seamus Heaney, Poet of Contrary Progressions. HENRY HART. Syracuse University Press, 1991.

Hechinger, Fred M. (1920–95) Born in Nuremberg, Germany, *New York Times* education editor Fred Hechinger emigrated to the United States in 1936. A graduate of New York's City College, he served in military intelligence during World II, and took graduate courses at the University of London after the war. He began his newspaper career as a reporter for the Overseas News Agency, and then worked for several magazines and newspapers in the U.S. and

abroad before joining the *New York Times* in 1959. As the prolific and highly respected education editor of the *Times* from then until his retirement in 1980, Hechinger became a significant reforming force in American education; his column "About Education" was closely followed by many in education, and by many parents, as well. In 1977, he also became president of the New York Times Company Foundation and The New York Times Neediest Cases Fund. After retiring and until his death, he became a senior advisor to the Carnegie Corporation of New York, a major philanthropic organization. Among his many publications was *Fateful Choices: Preparing American Adolescents for the 21st Century* (1993). He was survived by his wife, Grace Bernstein Hechinger, and two sons. (d. New York City; November 7, 1995)

FURTHER READING

Obituary. *New York Times*, Nov. 7, 1995.

Helms, Jesse Alexander (1921–   ) Republican North Carolina Senator Jesse Helms warred with the Clinton administration—and often with his Republican colleagues—on a wide range of matters during 1995, although his direct attacks on the President were somewhat less flamboyant than in 1994. Now chairman of the powerful Senate Foreign Affairs Committee, he demanded major structural changes in the State Department and related federal foreign policy organizations; when rebuffed, he openly blocked Senate consideration and possible confirmation of several key international agreements, held up hundreds of State Department and related promotions and appointments, and blocked confirmation proceedings for more than 30 nominated ambassadors, leaving posts vacant around the world. He also opposed the administration on a very wide range of foreign policy matters, among them aid to Haiti, Cuba sanctions, the Mexican loan package, and immigration policy. Helms and the Democrats reportedly reached a compromise set of agreements in early December, and long-stalled appointments and appropriations began to go forward.

Helms also unsuccessfully attempted to block reauthorization of the Ryan White Care Act, a major federal AIDS-assistance law, in a widely quoted *New York Times* interview calling AIDS victims responsible for having the disease because of their "deliberate, disgusting, revolting conduct." His all-out attack on homosexuals was largely rejected by his Republican and Democratic colleagues, who voted to reauthorize the act for five years, by a vote of 97-3. Helms was able to secure an amendment barring the use of the federal funds appropriated to promote intravenous drug use or homosexuality.

After a career in business, four years as a Raleigh city councilman, and twelve years in broadcasting (1961-73), North Carolina–born Helms began his senatorial career in 1973. After the Republican victory in the 1994 congressional elections, Helms became the chairman of the Senate Foreign Relations Committee. He also became an acute embarrassment to many in his own party, for his extraordinarily abrasive public attacks on President Bill Clinton, even going so far as to say, on November 22, 1994, that the president was unpopular on North Carolina military bases, and that "Mr. Clinton better watch out if he comes down here. He'd better have a bodyguard." His remarks were published on the anniversary of the assassination of President John F. Kennedy.

Helms attended Wingate College and Wake Forest College. He married Dorothy Jane Coble in 1942; they have three children.

FURTHER READING

"What you need. . . ." ERIC BATES. *Mother Jones,* May 15, 1995.
One-Hundred-One Proof Pure Old Jess: Jesse Helms Quoted. News & Observer, 1993.
"The senator. . . ." CHARLES HORNER. *Commentary,* Jan. 1992.

Hemphill, Julius (1940–95) Fort Worth–born Julius Hemphill, a leading jazz saxophonist and composer, studied music and began his professional career in Fort Worth, and lived in St. Louis from 1966. In 1968, he was a founder of the Black Artist Group. In 1972, he recorded his seminal album *Dogon A.D.,* and in 1975 released *Coon Bid'ness.* Taken together, these works were a major musical contribution, greatly influencing many other musicians. He also began to create mixed media works, among them *The Orientation of Sweet Willie Rollbar* (1972). In 1973, he moved to New York City, then focusing on mixed media works for several years. In 1976,

Hemphill was a founder of the World Saxophone Quartet; he left the quartet in 1989, and founded the Julian Hemphill Sextet in 1989. Among his later works was *Long Tongues: A Saxophone Opera*, which premiered in New York in 1990. He was survived by his companion, Ursula Oppens, and two sons. (d. New York City; April 2, 1995).

FURTHER READING

"Julius Hemphill. . . ." JOHN CORBETT. *Down Beat*, Aug. 1995.
"Julius Hemphill. . . ." HOWARD MANDEL. *Down Beat*, July 1995.
Obituary. *Down Beat*, June 1995.
"Julius Hemphill. . . ." GENE SANTORO. *Nation*, Mar. 7, 1994.
Obituary. *Billboard*, Apr. 15, 1995.
Obituary. *New York Times*, Apr. 4, 1995.

Herriot, James (James Alfred Wight; 1916–95) Glasgow-born Alf Wight became—as the writer James Herriot—far and away the best-known veterinarian in history. After graduating from Glasgow Veterinary College, he began his practice in Thirsk (Darrowby in his books), Yorkshire in 1940. He was to practice there for more than four decades, with a break for World War II military service. From his earliest years in practice, he kept a daily diary, which provided the basis for his wealth of anecdotes and stories, at first delivered verbally, then—from about age 50, at his wife's urging—written down in a string of enormously popular books that found worldwide audiences. His first publications, in Britain, were *If Only They Could Talk* (1970) and *It Shouldn't Happen to a Vet* (1972), both collections of loosely connected stories drawn from his Yorkshire experiences. But his first great success came with the 1972 American publication of these works in a single volume: *All Things Great and Small*. Ultimately, he would write almost a score of books, many of his later ones for children; a dog story collection was in the publishing process at the time of his death. He became at least as well known for the several "All Things Great and Small" television series based on his work, which are still running on the world's television screens. He was survived by his wife, Joan, whom he married in 1941, and by their daughter Rose, a doctor in Thirsk, and son, James, who carries on the veterinary practice. (d. Thirsk, Yorkshire; February 23, 1995)

Donald Vaughan Sinclair (ca. 1912–95), Herriot's longtime veterinary partner, known in the books and series as Siegfried Farnon, died after a drug overdose only four months later, and only three weeks after the death of Audrey Weston Sinclair, his wife of 53 years. Sinclair had founded the Thirsk veterinary practice in 1939 and hired Wight in 1940; the two shared the practice for decades, sometimes with others, including Sinclair's brother Brian (in the books, Tristan Farnon), who died in 1988. (d. Thirsk, Yorkshire; June 28, 1995)

FURTHER READING

"Small wonders. . . ." *People*, Mar. 13, 1995.
"Barnside manner." JESSICA SHAW. *Entertainment*, Mar. 10, 1995.
Obituary. *Times* (of London), Feb. 24, 1995.
Obituary. *New York Times*, Feb. 24, 1995.
Obituary. *Independent*, Feb. 24, 1995.
All Things Herriot: James Herriot and His Peaceable Kingdom. SANFORD STERNLICHT. Syracuse University Press, 1995.

Heston, Charlton (Charles Carter; 1923–) Now late in his long career, screen and stage star Charlton Heston continued to appear in a wide range of roles, including some starring roles. In 1995, he starred as Brigham Young opposite Tom Berenger as an armed Mormon Danite (Avenging Angel) in the television film *The Avenging Angel*, directed by Craig R. Baxley and costarring James Coburn and Fay Masterson, about early Mormon settlement times and conflicts in Utah.

Heston also narrated the television miniseries *James A. Michener's Texas*, based on the Michener novel and directed by Richard Lang, and costarred in the worldwide disaster fantasy film *In the Mouth of Madness*, directed by John Carpenter and costarring Julie Carmen and Jurgen Prochnow. He also talked about his life and career in a new book *In the Arena: An Autobiography*.

Forthcoming were starring film roles in *Alaska*, directed by his son, Fraser Heston; and opposite Carrie Snodgress in *Lord Protector*, directed and produced by Ryan J. Carroll. He is also slated to play the role of the Player King in Kenneth Branagh's adaptation of Shakespeare's *Hamlet*.

Illinois-born Heston began his long stage and screen career in the late 1940s. On stage, his work has included three appearances as *Macbeth* (1954, 1959, 1976), and leads in *A Man for All Seasons* (1965 and 1987) and *The Caine Mutiny Court Martial* (1985). On screen, he has been a star since the early 1950s, in such films as *Julius Caesar* (1950 and 1970), *The Greatest Show on Earth* (1952), *The Far Horizons* (1955), *The Wreck of the Mary Deare* (1959), *Ben-Hur* (1959), *El Cid* (1961), *Diamond Head* (1962), *55 Days at Peking* (1962), *The Greatest Story Ever Told* (1965), *Khartoum* (1966), *Planet of the Apes* (1967; and the 1969 sequel), *Soylent Green* (1973), and *Midway* (1975). Late in his career, he appeared in supporting roles in such films as *Wayne's World 2* (1993), *Tombstone* (1993), *True Lies* (1994). He has also worked extensively in television, as in *Treasure Island* (1990), produced and directed by his son, Fraser Heston, and as Sherlock Holmes in *Crucifer of Blood* (1991). Heston attended Northwestern University. He married Lydia Clark in 1944; the couple have one child, producer-director Fraser Heston.

FURTHER READING

"Heston and Vidal. . . ." CHRIS PETRIKIN. *Variety,* Oct. 16, 1995.
"Revenge of a nerd." TED ALLEN. *Chicago,* Sept. 1995.
"The Heston commandments. . . ." GEORGE WAYNE. *Vanity Fair,* Sept. 1994.

Highsmith, Patricia (1921–95) Texas-born Patricia Highsmith grew up in New York City, and entered on a writing career immediately after her graduation from Barnard in 1942. Her first published novel was *Strangers on a Train* (1950), adapted by Raymond Chandler into Alfred Hitchcock's 1951 classic suspense film, starring Robert Walker and Farley Granger as the two men who meet and hatch a plot to create dual alibis for two unrelated murders. Much of her further work was in the mystery genre, most notably the five "Ripley" novels, beginning with *The Talented Mr. Ripley* (1957) and ending with *Ripley Under Water* (1991). Her work, often perceived by some of her critics as bitter and amoral, included such novels as *The Glass Cell* (1965) and *Found in the Street* (1986), and several short story collections. Highsmith moved to England in the early 1960s, then to

France, and from 1982 lived near Locarno, Switzerland. There were no survivors. (d. Locarno, Switzerland; February 4, 1995)

FURTHER READING

Obituary. *Variety*, Feb. 16, 1995.
Obituary. *Times* (of London), Feb. 6, 1995.
Obituary. *New York Times*, Feb. 5, 1995.

Hijuelos, Oscar (1951–) Pulitzer Prize-winning novelist Oscar Hijuelos weighed in with a new work in 1995. *Mr. Ives' Christmas: A Novel* focuses on the life and faith of New York City foundling Edward Ives, with his adoptive parents, his wife, Annie MacGuire, and his son Robert, whose death, alluded to briefly in the beginning of the book, haunts the story. Some reviewers have noted a similarity between Hijuelos and Charles Dickens (reinforced in this work by Ives' love for Dickens), and suggest that if Hijuelos's earlier novels were more like Dickens' "big books," such as *Great Expectations*, this new one was more in the vein of shorter morality tales, such as *A Christmas Carol*. An audiobook version was released simultaneously with the hardcover. Hijuelos himself went on a 10-city promotional tour in November.

Born in Manhattan of Cuban immigrant parents, Hijuelos received his B.A. and M.A. from City College of New York. While working on inventory control in an advertising agency, he wrote his first novel, *Our House in the Last*

World (1984), a semi-autobiographical work set among Cuban emigrés in Spanish Harlem; it won him a National Endowment of the Arts (NEA) grant and the American Academy of Arts and Letters Rome Prize, including a year in Italy. He did not gain wide public attention until his second novel, *The Mambo Kings Play Songs of Love* (1989), about two Cuban musicians, brothers, seeking to make it big in 1950s New York, who find love along the way. It won the 1990 Pulitzer Prize (he was the first Hispanic writer to do so), was nominated for the National Book Award and the National Book Critics Circle Award, was translated into ten languages, and was the basis of Arnold Glimcher's 1992 film *The Mambo Kings,* scripted by Cynthia Cidre and starring Armand Assante and Antonio Banderas as the brothers, Cesar and Nestor. His third novel was the well-received *The Fourteen Sisters of Emilio Montez O'Brien* (1994). Hijuelos is divorced.

FURTHER READING

" 'A house filled with women.' " SUSANNAH HUNNEWELL. *New York Times Book Review*, Mar. 7, 1993.
" 'Sisters' act." DINITIA SMITH. *New York*, Mar. 1, 1993.
Growing up Latino: Memoirs and Stories. HAROLD AUGENBRAUM and ILAN STAVANS, eds. Houghton Mifflin, 1993.

Hill, Grant Henry (1972–) Because he had been part of the Duke University basketball team that won two consecutive NCAA championships (1991–1992), Grant Hill was one of the best-known rookies in the 1994–95 NBA season. But it was his own solid performance as a forward for the Detroit Pistons—averaging 19.9 points, 6.4 rebounds, and 5.0 assists a game—that won him co-Rookie of the Year honors (shared with Dallas's Jason Kidd). More than that, Hill became the first rookie ever to be the leading vote-getter for the All-Star game, where he scored a respectable 10 points, and was the only unanimous selection for the NBA's All-Rookie team.

Hill's public recognition and his attractive personal style also brought him substantial commercial endorsements, more than any other NBA player except Michael Jordan and Shaquille O'Neal. For Fila USA, a footwear company, he appeared throughout the season in a series of spots called "Rookie's Journal." In March, Hill also joined Jay Leno on "The Tonight Show." A book, tentatively titled *Change the Game*, was scheduled for 1996 publication.

Inspired by his mother, lawyer and consultant Janet Hill, he has plans to go to law school after his NBA career is over. He is also active in the NBA's Stay in School program.

Born in Dallas, where his father, Calvin Hill, was a running back with the Dallas Cowboys, Grant Hill attended South Lakes High School in Reston, Virginia, before going on to Duke University (1990–94), where he averaged 14.9 points, 6.0 rebounds, and 3.6 assists a game. Duke reached the NCAA Finals again in 1994, but lost to Arkansas. Hill was named to the *Sporting News* All-America first team (1994), and was the third pick overall in the 1994 NBA draft, joining the Detroit Pistons (1994–).

FURTHER READING

"Sugar Hill. . . ." CHRISTOPHER JOHN FARLEY. *Essence,* Nov. 1995.
"Grant Hill. . . ." JOHN SINGLETON. *Interview,* Apr. 1995.
"The savior." TOM JUNOD. *GQ,* Apr. 1995.
"Amazing Grace." MIKE LUPICA. *Esquire,* Feb. 1995.
"Shooting star. . . ." WILLIAM PLUMMER. *People,* Jan. 23, 1995.
"The name of. . . ." MICHAEL P. GEFFNER. *Sporting News,* Jan. 16, 1995.
"A leader is born. . . ." MICHAEL BRADLEY. *Sporting News,* Apr. 4, 1994.

Hobby, Oveta Culp (1905–95) Born in Killeen, Texas, Oveta Culp began her public career as the protégée of her father, Texas legislator Isaac Culp. She worked in several state jobs from the mid-1920s, in the Democratic Party as a campaign worker in the late 1920s, and in family businesses during the 1930s. In 1931, she married William P. Hobby, former governor of Texas (1917–21). In 1942, weathering powerful male opposition, she founded and became head of the trailblazing Women's Army (Auxiliary) Corps (WAAC). In 1943, she founded and headed the successor organization, the Women Army Corps (WAC), which provided a way for more than 100,000 women to enter the war effort in a wide range of non-combat army jobs at pay and rank equal to that of male reservists. In 1945, she was the first woman to be awarded the Ar-

my's Distinguished Service Medal. She went back to Texas after the war, working at her family's *Houston Post* and radio stations. A Democrat, she campaigned for Republican Dwight D. Eisenhower in 1952; he then appointed her head of the Federal Security Agency (1953), which during her tenure became the Department of Health, Education, and Welfare, with Hobby as its first head and only the second woman to become a Cabinet member. After leaving Washington in 1955, she returned to the *Houston Post* and other family businesses. She was survived by a daughter and a son. Her husband died in 1964; he had been publisher of the *Houston Post-Dispatch*. (d. Houston; August 16, 1995)

FURTHER READING

Obituary. *Current Biography,* Oct. 1995.
Obituary. *Times* (of London), Aug. 18, 1995.
Obituary. *New York Times*, Aug. 17, 1995.

Hockenberry, John (ca. 1956–) As a Middle East correspondent, John Hockenberry has traveled in some dangerous foreign places, including Jerusalem, Kurdistan, Iran, and Somalia, but in some ways the most dangerous and foreign place for him is what he calls the "crip world"—for Hockenberry is a paraplegic, who became paralyzed from the mid-chest down after an automobile accident when he was just 19. In 1995, the man best-known as a National Public Radio (NPR) correspondent and more recently

as an ABC television journalist described how he has managed his life since that accident, in the book *Moving Violations: War Zones, Wheelchairs, and Declarations of Independence.* More than just a story about overcoming disabilities, it is also a remarkable portrait of an individual's struggle for freedom and self-determination in the face of blatant discrimination and such practical obstacles as escalators, who develops the wisdom to understand how his own pride and drive could—if untempered—warp his life. Hockenberry toured widely promoting the book.

During 1995, Hockenberry also became engaged to Alison Craiglow, an "ABC News" producer. The news program "Day One" was canceled late in the year; Hockenberry was to be reassigned.

Born in Dayton, Ohio, Hockenberry studied mathematics and anthropology at the University of Chicago (1975–78), and music composition and harpsichord performance at the University of Oregon (1979–81). He joined NPR in 1980, working in Seattle (1980–81) and Chicago (1985–87), but primarily in Washington, D.C. (1981–84; 1987–88; 1991–92), as a reporter for "All Things Considered." He then hosted various programs, originating NPR's arts and public affairs program "Heat" (1990) and the on-air call-in show "Talk of the Nation" (1991). He was NPR's Middle East correspondent (1988–90), winning a duPont-Columbia award for his reporting. He has also won several other awards, including the prestigious Benton Fellowship in Broadcast Journalism (1985), two Peabody Awards (1987; 1990), and an Emmy (1994). He joined ABC as correspondent for "Day One" (1992–95). His first marriage ended in divorce.

FURTHER READING

"Man in the driver's seat. . . ." MICHAEL A. LIPTON. *People,* June 6, 1994.
"On a roll." *New Yorker,* Nov. 23, 1992.

Hoffman, Dustin Lee (1937–) Entirely in tune with uncertain times, veteran actor Dustin Hoffman in 1995 starred as Dr. Sam Daniels in the very well received and popular film *Outbreak,* directed by Wolfgang Petersen, about the threat of a massive epidemic posed by release of a deadly virus. Costarring were Rene Russo as Dr. Roberta Keough, Morgan Freeman as Gen-

HOLMES, HAMILTON E.

Dustin Hoffman (right) and Susie Cusack.

eral Billy Ford, Cuba Gooding, Jr., Patrick
Dempsey, Donald Sutherland, and Kevin
Spacey. Lawrence Dworet and Robert Roy Pool
wrote the screenplay, based on Laurie Garrett's
book *The Coming Plague* and Richard Preston's
book *The Hot Zone*. Hoffman was also honored
by induction into the French Order of Arts and
Letters.

Forthcoming was a starring role opposite Dennis Franz in the film version of David Mamet's
play *American Buffalo*, directed by Michael Corrente.

Los Angeles–born Hoffman has been a major
film star since his breakthrough role as *The
Graduate* (1967), which he followed with such
films as *Midnight Cowboy* (1969), *Little Big Man*
(1971), *Lenny* (1974), *All the President's Men*
(1976), *Marathon Man* (1976), *Kramer vs.
Kramer* (1979; he won a Best Actor Oscar),
Tootsie (1982), *Rain Man* (1988; and a second
Best Actor Oscar), *Family Business* (1989), *Dick
Tracy* (1990), *Billy Bathgate* (1991), *Hook*
(1992), and *Hero* (1992). On stage, he was a notable Willy Loman in the 1984 revival of *Death
of a Salesman* (televised in 1985), and in 1990
brought his Shylock from London to Broadway
in Peter Hall's production of *The Merchant of
Venice*. Hoffman attended Santa Monica City
College. He was formerly married to Anne
Byrne, married Lisa Gottsegen in 1980, and has
five children.

FURTHER READING

"Midnight Cowboy. . . ." STEVE DALY. *Entertainment,*
  Mar. 1995.
"Tales of Hoffman." GREG KILDAY. *Entertainment,*
  Mar. 4, 1994.

Holmes, Hamilton E. (1941–95) Atlanta-
born Hamilton E. Holmes was a leading citizen
of Atlanta, a distinguished orthopedic surgeon
and educator, who headed the orthopedic section
of Atlanta's Grady Memorial Hospital and
taught at and was associate dean of Atlanta's
Emory University Medical School. He was also
the first African-American trustee of the University of Georgia. Therein lies an extraordinary
American story—and, some would say, an extraordinary irony—for only 33 years earlier,
when he was 19, he and 18-year-old Charlayne
Hunter-Gault were the two African-Americans
who desegregated the University of Georgia and
then fought through to honors and careers second to none, he in medicine, she in broadcast
journalism.

Holmes and Hunter-Gault were high school
classmates at an all-Black high school; he was
valedictorian of his class and a leading school
athlete. On January 9, 1961, after the U.S. Supreme Court had ended more than two years of
attempts to bar them from admission, they arrived on the school's Athens campus, and were
soon the objects of a violent demonstration by
thousands of racist students and others, which
riot police finally ended, with many arrests.
Holmes and Hunter-Gault were suspended, re-
admitted the next day, and went on to graduate,
despite years of racist ostracism, taunts, and
threats. Holmes then fulfilled his childhood
dreams, becoming the first African-American
student at the Emory University Medical School
and later a much-honored surgeon. He was survived by his wife, Marilyn Vincent Holmes, a
daughter, three sons, his mother, a sister, and
three brothers. (d. Atlanta; October 26, 1995)

FURTHER READING

Obituary. *Jet,* Nov. 13, 1995.
Obituary. *New York Times,* Oct. 28, 1995.
*An Education in Georgia: Charlayne Hunter,
  Hamilton Holmes and the Integration of the
  University of Georgia.* CALVIN TRILLIN. University
  of Georgia Press, 1991.

hooks, bell (Gloria Jean Watkins; 1952–)
Cultural critic bell hooks seemed to be omnipresent in 1995. First came her new book *Killing Rage: Ending Racism*, a series of mostly never-before-published essays on race and racism from a Black and feminist perspective. The title was drawn from the lead essay, "Killing Rage." She also published *Art on My Mind: Visual Politics*, addressing such concerns as the lack of Black artists and Black critics in America, and the minimal role of art in the lives of most African-Americans. She was also one of three main contributors to *Andres Serrano Body and Soul*, edited by Brian Wallis, interpreting the work of the controversial Serrano as an attack on a patriarchal church and state antagonistic to the human body. Late in 1994 she had also published *Outlaw Culture: Resisting Representations* and *Teaching to Transgress: Education as the Practice of Freedom*.

Hooks was born in Hopkinsville, Kentucky. She received her 1973 B.A. from Stanford University, 1976 M.A. from the University of Wisconsin, and 1983 Ph.D. from the University of California at Santa Cruz. Her first published book was the poetry collection *And There We Wept* (1978). It was followed by her best-known work, *Ain't I a Woman? Black Women and Feminism* (1981). Among her further works are *Feminist Theory: From Margin to Center* (1984), *Talking Back: Thinking Feminist, Thinking Black* (1989), *Yearning: Race, Gender, and Cultural Politics* (1990), *Breaking Bread: Insurgent Black Intellectual Life* (1991), *Black Looks: Race and Representation* (1992), *A Woman's Mourning Song*, (1992), *Sisters of the Yam: Black Women and Self-Recovery* (1993), and *Changing the Subject: Paintings and Prints 1992–94* (1994). She was also coauthor (with Julie Dash and Toni C. Bambara) of *Daughters of the Dust: The Making of an African American Woman's Film*. Hooks has taught at several colleges and universities, and became a professor of English at the City College of New York in 1994.

FURTHER READING

"Bell Hooks." INGRID SISCHY. *Interview,* Oct. 1995.
"Sister Knowledge." CARL POSEY. *Essence,* May 1995.
"Books—and more. . . ." CALVIN REID. *Publishers Weekly,* Mar. 27, 1995.
Bearing Witness: Selections from 150 Years of African-American Autobiography. HENRY L. GATES, ed. Pantheon, 1991.

Hoon, Shannon (Richard Shannon Hoon; 1967–95) Musician Shannon Hoon, lead singer of the recently successful rock band Blind Melon, died in the band's tour bus in a New Orleans parking lot on October 21, 1995, reportedly because of an accidental drug overdose. Born in Lafayette, Indiana, Hoon had started his singing career while still in high school. He, guitarist Roger Stevens, and bassist Brad Smith had founded their band in Los Angeles in 1990, and scored a major success in 1992 with their first album, *Blind Melon*, and its hit single and video "No Rain." The band was touring to promote its second album, *Soup*. He was survived by his companion, Lisa Crouse, and their daughter, and by his mother, father, sister, and brother. (d. New Orleans; Oct. 21, 1995)

FURTHER READING

Obituary. *Rolling Stone,* Nov. 30, 1995.
Obituary. *Independent,* Oct. 27, 1995.
Obituary. *New York Times,* Oct. 23, 1995.
"New Hoon rising." ANDREW ABRAHAMS. *People,* Aug. 21, 1995.

Hopkins, Anthony (1937–) Celebrated actor Anthony Hopkins in 1995 starred in the title role of the film *Nixon*, the highly controversial film biography of the former president, directed, cowritten, and coproduced by Oliver

Stone. Costarring were Joan Allen as Pat Nixon, James Woods as H. R. Haldeman, Bob Hoskins as J. Edgar Hoover, Powers Boothe as Alexander Haig, Ed Harris as E. Howard Hunt, E. G. Marshall as John Mitchell, Paul Sorvino as Henry Kissinger, and Mary Steenburgen as Hannah Nixon, in a large cast that also included David Paymer, David Hyde Pierce, J. T. Walsh, Brian Bedford, Kevin Dunn, Larry Hagman, Tony Goldwyn, Ed Herrman, and Madeleine Kahn as Martha Mitchell. The work, liberally using flashbacks, ultimately presented Stone's view of Nixon's life history, motivations, and development from early days in California through to Watergate and his forced resignation in disgrace, to avoid impeachment and dismissal. Hopkins received a Golden Globe nomination as best actor in a drama for the role.

Hopkins also starred as an American officer in Berlin in the espionage thriller *The Innocent*, directed by John Schlesinger and costarring Campbell Scott and Isabella Rossellini; Ian McEwan's screenplay was based on his own novel.

Forthcoming was a starring role in the Merchant-Ivory film *Surviving Picassso*, directed by James Ivory, with screenplay by Ruth Prawer Jhabvala. Costarring are Natasha McElhone, Julianne Moore, Diane Venora, Joan Plowright, and David Margulies.

Hopkins played in repertory during the early 1960s; he joined the National Theatre in 1967, the same year he made his film debut in *The Lion in Winter*. A few of his most notable theater roles were in the title role of *Macbeth* (1972; National Theatre), *Equus* (1974–75; on Broadway); *Pravda* (1985; National Theatre), *King Lear* (1986; National Theatre), and *Antony and Cleopatra* (1987; title role, National Theatre). He has appeared in such films as *The Looking Glass War* (1967), *A Bridge Too Far* (1976), *Magic* (1978), *The Elephant Man* (1978), *The Bounty* (1984; as Captain Bligh), *84 Charing Cross Road* (1987), *Desperate Hours* (1989), *The Silence of the Lambs* (1991; he won a best actor Oscar), *Spotswood* (1991), *Howard's End* (1992), *Bram Stoker's Dracula* (1992), *The Remains of the Day* (1993), *The Trial* (1993), *Shadowlands* (1993), *The Innocent* (1993), and *Legends of the Fall*; and in a wide range of television roles, winning Emmys in *The Lindbergh Kidnapping Case* (1975) and *The Bunker* (1980), and playing such title roles as *Kean* (1980) and *Othello* (1981). He made his directorial debut with the play *August* (1994), in which he also starred.

Hopkins attended the Welsh College of Music and Drama and the Royal Academy of Dramatic Art. His second wife is Jennifer Lynton; he has one daughter. (For additional photo, see **Stone, Oliver.**)

FURTHER READING

"Playboy interview. . . ." LAWRENCE GROBEL. *Playboy*, Mar. 1994.
"The flowering of. . . ." DAVID ANSEN. *Newsweek*, Jan. 17, 1994.
Anthony Hopkins: The Authorized Biography. QUENTIN FALK. Interlink, 1994.
Anthony Hopkins: A Biography. MICHAEL F. CALLAN. Macmillan, 1994.
"Nicholson? Brando? . . ." LISA LIEBMANN. *Interview*. Apr. 1992.
" 'Call me Tony.' " RITA GAM. *World Monitor*, Apr. 1992.
"Anthony Hopkins'. . . ." MARTHA FRANKEL. *Movies USA*, Mar.–Apr. 1992.

Hordern, Michael (1911–95) Celebrated British actor Michael Hordern began his long career in the mid-1930s. After playing as an amateur for several years, he made his London debut as Lodovico in *Othello*. After World War II naval service, he returned to the theater, emerging as a major figure in the title role of Chekhov's *Ivanov* (1950). In the decades that followed, he played in more than 80 stage roles, at least an equal number of film roles, and late in his career starred in television. On stage, he played in a wide range of classic and modern roles, ranging from his Malvolio in *Twelfth Night* (1954) to his notable title role in *King Lear* (1969), which was followed by two television productions of *Lear*. He also played in such modern classics as John Mortimer's *The Dock Brief* (1958), Harold Pinter's *The Collection* (1962), Alan Ayckbourn's *Relatively Speaking* (1967), and Tom Stoppard's *Enter a Free Man* (1968) and *Jumpers* (1972). Among his films were *Passport to Pimlico* (1949), *A Christmas Carol* (1951), *The Heart of the Matter* (1953), *Cleopatra* (1963), *The Spy Who Came In From the Cold* (1956), *A Funny Thing Happened on the Way to the Forum* (1966), and *Gandhi* (1982). Very late in his career, he starred in television as Joseph Featherstone in the television series "Middlemarch" (1994). He was survived by a daughter. (d. Oxford; May 2, 1995)

FURTHER READING

Obituary. *Times* (of London), May 4, 1995.
Obituary. *New York Times*, May 4, 1995.
Obituary. *Independent,* May 4, 1995.
Obituary. *Variety*, May 3, 1995.

Horgan, Paul (Paul George Vincent O'Shaughnessy Horgan; 1903–95) Buffalo-born Paul Horgan, a prolific and wide-ranging writer and historian, moved to the Southwest with his family at the age of 12; the region was to be the setting of many of his later novels and short stories. He initially set out to pursue a career in music; the first two of his 17 novels, *The Fault of Angels* (1935) and *No Quarter Given* (1937), were set in the world of music. Among his other novels were *Main Line West* (1936), *Lamp on the Plains* (1937), *The Habit of Empire* (1939), *A Distant Trumpet* (1960), the trilogy *Things as They Are* (1964), *Everything to Live For* (1969), and *The Thin Mountain Air* (1977). His history of the Rio Grande, *Great River* (1954), won a Pulitzer Prize, as did his biography *Lamy of Santa Fe* (1975). He also published several volumes of short stories, plays, essays, poetry, and several children's books. Horgan also taught at several colleges and universities, including Yale

and Wesleyan University. There were no survivors. (d. Middletown, Connecticut; March 8, 1995)

FURTHER READING

Obituary. *Times* (of London), Apr. 6, 1995.
Obituary. *Independent,* Mar. 25, 1995.
Obituary. *New York Times*, Mar. 9, 1995.
Nueva Granada: Paul Horgan and the Southwest.
    ROBERT F. GISH. Texas A&M University Press, 1995.

Hoskins, Bob (Robert William Hoskins, 1942–) British film star Bob Hoskins appeared in 1995 as FBI director J. Edgar Hoover in the highly controversial biographical film *Nixon*, directed, cowritten, and coproduced by Oliver Stone and starring Anthony Hopkins as disgraced, very nearly impeached President Richard M. Nixon.

In a rather different kind of role, Hoskins also starred as the voice of the snow goose Boris in the animated Alaskan action film *Balto*, costarring Kevin Bacon as the voice of the half-dog, half-wolf title character, Bridget Fonda as the voice of the husky Jenna, Jim Cummings as the voice of the dog Steele, and Phil Collins as the voices of the polar bears Muk and Luk; Simon Wells directed. Hoskins also appeared on Mel Gibson's American public radio children's show *Rabbit Ears Radio*, telling the story of *The Bremen Town Musicians*.

Forthcoming was a starring role in the film *The Secret Agent*, costarring Patricia Arquette and Gérard Depardieu.

A cockney, Hoskins left school at age 15, and then worked at jobs from manual labor to plumbing, with a stint in the merchant navy; while working on a kibbutz, he became involved in amateur theatre, where he was discovered by an agent. From the mid-1980s, he emerged as a leading British film actor, making his debut in *National Health* (1974) and going on to such movies as *Royal Flash* (1975), *Zulu Dawn* (1980), *The Long Good Friday* (1980), *The Honorary Consul* (1984), *Lassiter* (1984), *The Cotton Club* (1985), *Sweet Liberty* (1986), *Mona Lisa* (1986), *A Prayer for the Dying* (1987), *The Lonely Passion of Judith Hearne* (1988), *Who Framed Roger Rabbit?* (1988), *Heart Condition* (1990), *Mermaids* (1990), *Shattered* (1991), *Hook* (1991), *Passed Away* (1992), *The Favor, the Watch and the Very Big Fish* (1992), *Super Mario Bros.* (1993), and *The Changeling* (1994). He wrote, directed, and appeared in *The Raggedy Rawney* (1988). Hoskins has also appeared often on television, most notably in his powerful lead in the miniseries *Pennies from Heaven* (1979). His second wife is Linda Banwell; he has two daughters and two sons.

FURTHER READING

"The life and times. . . . " DALYA ALBERGE. *Times* (of London), July 24, 1995.
"Hoskins, Bob." *Current Biography*, Sept. 1990.

Houston, Whitney

(1963–) Singer and actress Whitney Houston had another major hit in 1995—the hit single "Exhale (Shoop Shoop)," from the original soundtrack album of her film *Waiting to Exhale*, which opened for the Christmas season. The song made its debut at the top of the charts, and the album was not far behind. The album contained 15 songs by Babyface (Kenny Edmonds); other artists include Toni Braxton, Aretha Franklin, Brandy, TLC, Mary J. Blige, Chaka Khan, SWV, Chanté Moore, Patti LaBelle, For Real, CeCe Winans, Sonja Marie, Faith Evans, and Shanna.

In the film *Waiting to Exhale*, Houston starred as Savannah, one of four Phoenix-based African-American women, who share their life stories and experiences during the course of a year, with emphasis upon their relationships with men. Angela Bassett, Loretta Devine, Lela Rochon, and Gregory Hines costarred; the film was directed by Forest Whitaker and based on the bestselling Terry McMillan novel.

Forthcoming was a starring role opposite Denzel Washington in the film *The Preacher's Wife*, directed by Penny Marshall, a remake of *The Bishop's Wife* (1947), which starred Cary Grant, Loretta Young, and David Niven. Also forthcoming was a film based on the book *Dorothy Dandridge: A Biography*, by Donald Bogle; Houston purchased an option on the work, and announced plans to coproduce and star in a film version, to be written by Bogle.

Houston received a CableAce nomination for best performance in a music special or series for her 1994 HBO television special *Whitney—The Concert for a New South Africa*.

New Jersey–born Houston suddenly emerged as a leading popular singer in the mid-1980s with her first album, the Grammy-winning *Whitney Houston* (1985), followed by *Whitney* (1986), and with such songs as "Didn't We Almost Have It All," "The Greatest Love of All," and "How Will I Know." In 1990, her single "I'm Your Baby Tonight," from the album of the same name, also hit number one, as did her 1991 "All the Man That I Need." In 1992, she and Kevin Costner costarred in the hit film *The Bodyguard*, which generated the Grammy-winning soundtrack, *The Bodyguard, Original Soundtrack Album*. Her soundtrack rendition of Dolly Parton's "I Will Always Love You" became enormously popular, spending 14 weeks at the top of the *Billboard* 100 chart, and Houston won 1994 Grammys for record of the year and best pop vocal performance, while the soundtrack won a best album Grammy. Houston is the daughter of singer Cissy Houston, and the cousin of singer Dionne Warwick. Houston is married to singer Bobby Brown; they have one daughter.

FURTHER READING

"Fame. . . . " JESS CAGLE. *Entertainment*, Dec. 22, 1995.
"Not who. . . . " PAM LAMBERT. *People*, Dec. 18, 1995.
"Whitney Houston. . . . " *Jet*, Oct. 9, 1995.
"Whitney's toughest. . . . " ANN ELLIOT. *Redbook*, May 1995.
"Whitney and Cissy. . . . " LYNN NORMENT. *Ebony*, May 1995.

"The real Whitney. . . ." M. C. PATTERSON. *McCall's,* June 1994.

"It must be love!" JOY DUCKETT CAIN. *Essence,* Feb. 1994.

Whitney Houston. ROSEMARY WALLNER. Abdo & Daughters, 1994.

"WH. . . ." ANTHONY DECURTIS. *Rolling Stone,* June 10, 1993.

"Thoroughly modern. . . ." LYNN HIRSCHBERG. *Vanity Fair,* Nov. 1992.

"20 questions. . . ." *Playboy,* May 1991.

Howard, Ron (1954–)

Director, actor, writer, and producer Ron Howard scored a triumph in 1995, directing the film *Apollo 13.* The film starred Tom Hanks as astronaut Jim Lovell, Kevin Bacon as astronaut Jack Swigert, and Bill Paxton as astronaut Fred Haise, in a cast that included Gary Sinise, Ed Harris, Kathleen Quinlan, and Jean Speegle Howard. Based on the autobiographical book *Lost Moon,* by Lovell and Jeffrey Kluger, the film tells the story of the Apollo 13 moon flight, in which the American spaceship *Odyssey,* captained by Lovell, came very close to landing on the moon, but was forced by an oxygen tank explosion and electrical failures to turn away. The astronauts then took refuge in their lunar module, the *Aquarius,* which was not programmed for a return to Earth; ultimately, on very short rations of all kinds, they piloted the craft back to Earth. The film was extraordinarily well received by the critics and the public, immediately becoming a major Academy Award contender, as did Howard and its players. Howard received a best director Golden Globe nomination for the film.

Howard was slated to direct the forthcoming film *Ransom,* starring Mel Gibson. Also still forthcoming was an as-yet-undeveloped film based on a John Grisham novel.

Oklahoma-born Howard was a child star in television, as Opie in "The Andy Griffith Show" (1960–68), and later in "The Smith Family" (1971–72) and "Happy Days" (1974–80). He also appeared in such films as *The Music Man* (1962), *American Graffiti* (1973), and *The Shootist* (1976). As an adult, he directed, and in several instances cowrote and coproduced, such films as *Splash* (1984), *Cocoon* (1985), *No Man's Land* (1987), *Clean and Sober* (1988), *Willow* (1988), *Parenthood* (1989), *Backdraft* (1991), and *The Paper* (1994). Howard was also, with longtime associate Brian Glazer, executive producer and writer of the television series spun off from *Parenthood* (1990). Howard attended the University of Southern California. He married Cheryl Alley in 1975; they have five children.

FURTHER READING

"Howard, Ron." *Current Biography,* Aug. 1995.

"Shooting the moon. . . ." SKIP HOLLANDSWORTH. *Texas Monthly,* July 1995.

"Ron Howard." *Playboy,* May 1994.

"Paper boy." MEREDITH BERKMAN. *Entertainment,* Apr. 1, 1994.

"Ron Howard." JOHN CLARK. *Premiere,* Apr. 1991.

Hunter, Holly (1958–)

Film star Holly Hunter starred as homicide detective M. J. Monahan in the well-received crime thriller *Copycat,* directed by Jon Amiel. The film also starred Sigourney Weaver as psychologist Helen Hudson, and costarred Dermot Mulroney as Hunter's partner; Harry Connick, Jr. as a serial killer; and William McNamara. The film's storyline followed a familiar course; Weaver helps Hunter and Mulroney to find the serial killer, who in turn is stalking Weaver.

Hunter also starred in the film *Home for the Holidays,* directed by Jodie Foster. Hunter, as Claudia Larson, is home for Thanksgiving, visiting her parents in Baltimore; Charles Durning and Anne Bancroft are her parents, Robert Downey is her gay brother, Dylan McDermott is her brother's lover, and Geraldine Chaplin is her eccentric aunt. Hunter also appeared in the television miniseries *The American Experience: "The Way West."*

Forthcoming was a starring role in the film *Crash*, directed by David Cronenberg and costarring James Spader, Rosanna Arquette, and Elias Koteas.

Georgia-born Hunter appeared in several regional theater productions and in New York in the Beth Henley plays *Crimes of the Heart* (1981) and *The Wake of Jamey Foster* (1982) before beginning her film career. She made her film debut in *Raising Arizona* (1987), and scored an early breakthrough in a starring role in *Broadcast News* (1987). She went on to several less-well-received films, including *Always* (1990), *Miss Firecracker* (1989), and *Once Around* (1991), and emerged as a leading actress with her Oscar-winning starring role as Ada McGrath opposite Harvey Keitel and Sam Neill in Jane Campion's acclaimed 1993 film *The Piano.*

Hunter has also starred in several television films, winning an Emmy as best actress in a miniseries or special in 1990 for her starring role in *Roe v. Wade*, and another best actress Emmy in 1993 for the title role in *The Positively True Adventures of the Alleged Texas Cheerleader-Murdering Mom.* Her 1980 B.F.A. was from Carnegie-Mellon University.

FURTHER READING

"Holly Hunter." MANOHLA DARGIS. *Us,* Nov. 1995.
"Hunter, Holly." *Current Biography,* July 1994.
" 'Tis the season. . . ." BERNARD WEINTRAUB.
    Cosmopolitan, Jan. 1994.
"The return of Holly's comet." JACK KROLL.
    Newsweek, Nov. 15, 1993.
"Hunter season." JEANNINE STEIN. *Advocate*, July 27, 1993.

Hussein I (Hussein ibn Talal; 1935–   ) In a far more secure position than he had been at any other time in the 1990s, Jordan's King Hussein spent much of 1995 consolidating his country's new peace with Israel, developing a new set of relationships with the emerging Palestinian state led by Yasir Arafat, and redeveloping his relations with the moderates in the Arab world. That included King Fahd of Saudi Arabia; Saudi-Jordanian relations had been strained since Jordan's support of Iraq during the Persian Gulf War.

Hussein took great care to distance himself from Saddam Hussein during 1995; on one occasion, in late August, state-controlled Iraqi radio even broadcast one of his anti-Saddam speeches. Very notably, he granted asylum to two major Iraqi military defectors, Lt. General Hussein Kamel and Lt. Colonel Saddam Kamel—and their wives, Saddam Hussein's two oldest daughters. Jordan's grant of refuge and refusal to extradite the defectors put King Hussein squarely back into the moderate Arab camp. King Hussein also called for Saddam Hussein's ouster, while Jordanian and U.S. troops carried on joint maneuvers in Jordan.

King Hussein also continued to participate in the Middle East peace process, meeting with President Hosni Mubarak of Egypt, participating in a February Cairo peace summit with Mubarak, Israeli Prime Minister Yitzhak Rabin, and Arafat, and making a detailed agreement with Arafat that covered the status and future of previously disputed Muslim religious sites in East Jerusalem and Jordanian-Palestinian administrative and financial matters.

Hussein became king of Jordan in 1953, succeeding his father, Abdullah Ibn Hussein, who was the son of Hussein Ibn Ali, head of the 1916 Arab revolt against the Turks during World War I, which had been assisted by British officer T. E. Lawrence ("Lawrence of Arabia"). For almost four decades, Hussein survived as a moderate in the turbulent politics of the Middle East, although he was drawn into the 1967 Six-Day War (Third Arab-Israeli War), and lost control over the West Bank and Jerusalem, which Israel has occupied ever since. He gave up all territorial claims to these areas in 1988, during the Palestinian Intifada, to pave the way for a Palestinian declaration of independence. In 1970, he fought and won a war against the Palestine Liberation Organization (PLO), then headquartered in his country, although by 1990 the relatively large Palestinian population of Jordan strongly influenced his position on the Iraqi invasion of Kuwait, which was supported by most Palestinians. Hussein emerged from the Persian Gulf War greatly damaged, with subsidies withdrawn by the rich Arab nations, led by Saudi Arabia, and with the U.S. relationship all but severed. But in 1992 and 1993, he re-emerged as a leading Arab moderate.

On July 25, 1994, he and Israeli Prime Minister Yitzhak Rabin signed the Washington Declaration, a statement of intent to end the 46-

year-long state of war that had existed between the two countries. On July 26, the two addressed a joint session of the U.S. Congress, and in a joint news conference condemned terrorism. Later in the year, Jordan outlawed the fundamentalist, violently anti-peace organization Hamas. On October 26, he and Rabin signed a full peace treaty, formally ending the state of war, at an Israeli-Jordanian border crossing ceremony attended by President Bill Clinton.

Hussein attended Britain's Victoria College and Sandhurst. He has been married four times, since 1978 to Lisa Halaby, now Queen Noor, and has eleven children.

FURTHER READING

" 'We cannot turn back.' " TAD SZULC. *Parade*, Apr. 2, 1995.

"Smoke signals. . . ." MARTIN PERETZ. *New Republic*, Nov. 28, 1994.

"Stalked by. . . ." FOUAD AJAMI. *U.S. News & World Report*, Aug. 1, 1994.

" 'Trying to catch. . . .' " CHRISTOPHER DICKEY. *Newsweek*, Aug. 19, 1991.

"The great survivor. . . ." JOHN STACKS and DEAN FISCHER. *Time*, July 22, 1991.

Hussein, Saddam (1937–) Despite continuing United Nations sanctions, coup attempts and threats of coups, major defections, and damaging admissions, Saddam Hussein continued to rule in Iraq in 1995. But his rule was shaken, despite a contrived "election" in October, in which he received almost all of the "votes" cast. In late August, when Egyptian president Hosni Mubarak offered Hussein asylum, should he decide to flee Iraq, the offer was taken by many observers quite seriously.

Underlying all of the specific threats to Hussein's regime was the fact of Iraq's isolation, and with it the continuing damage being caused by United Nations economic sanctions. Hussein's regime grew more repressive in order to survive repeated coup attempts from within the ranks of his own military, who seemed increasingly convinced that Hussein's overthrow was the only event that could bring Iraq back into the world community. Perhaps the most damaging single event was the defection of Lt. General Hussein Kamel, chief of Iraq's biological, chemical, and nuclear weapons establishment, and his brother, Lt. Colonel Saddam Kamel, head of Saddam

Hussein's own personal guard—and their wives, Saddam Hussein's two oldest daughters, along with many other high-ranking officers. These high-level defectors were granted asylum by Saddam Hussein's former ally, King Hussein of Jordan, who also openly attacked Saddam Hussein, calling on him to step down. After their defections, the Kamel brothers set about the task of organizing the overthrow of Saddam Hussein; Hussein Kamel also told the world about Iraq's stockpiles of deadly biological weapons, forcing Iraq to disclose some facts about the weapons, which it long ago claimed to have destroyed.

Born in Takrit, Iraq, Hussein joined the Ba'ath socialist party in 1957, and went into Egyptian exile in 1958, after taking part in the failed attempt to assassinate General Karim Kassem, premier of the Iraqi republic. He returned to Iraq in 1963, after the army coup in which Kassem was killed. Hussein was a leader of the Ba'ath coup of 1968, and took full power in 1971, then surrounding himself with followers from his home village, instituting a reign of terror in his country, and becoming the dictator of Iraq. He also began to develop a massive cult of personality around himself.

In 1980, Hussein's forces attacked Iran, instigating the Iran-Iraq War (1980–88); his forces used large amounts of poison gas against the Iranians, although chemical warfare had been outlawed throughout the world. In the late 1980s, after the 1988 cease-fire with Iran, his forces continued to use poison gas, this time against Iraq's own rebellious Kurdish population, killing thousands of civilians, and forcing hundreds of thousands to flee into exile. With the end of the Iran-Iraq War, Hussein emerged as a strongman in the Middle East.

On August 2, 1990, Hussein's armies invaded and took over oil-rich Kuwait. He then turned toward far richer Saudi Arabia, either to invade or simply to intimidate, and was met by the American-led multinational response, coupled with United Nations action, which resulted in sanctions, a blockade, and ultimately the Persian Gulf War. He lost that war in 1991, but his opponents left him in control of his country, where he defeated Shiite and Kurdish insurrections and attacked civilian populations. He also resisted international surveillance of his nuclear weapons program, and unsuccessfully called for an end to UN sanctions.

Hussein attended Cairo University and

Baghdad's al-Mujstanseriya University. He married Sajidal Khairalla in 1963, and has four children.

FURTHER READING

Saddam Hussein: Absolute Ruler of Iraq. REBECCA STEFOFF. Millbrook, 1995.
Saddam and Uncle Sam. DAVID W. FELDER. Felder, 1995.
With Friends Like These: Reagan, Bush, and Saddam, 1982–1990. BRUCE W. JENTLESON. Norton, 1995.
"Gun barrel. . . ." TIM ZIMMERMAN et al. *U.S. News & World Report*, Oct. 24, 1994.
"Saddam Hussein's gamble." *Economist*, Oct. 15, 1994.
Iraq Speaks: Documents of the Gulf Crises. SADDAM HUSSEIN. Diane, 1994.
"High time." ALBERT WOHLSTETTER. *National Review*, Feb. 15, 1993.
Saddam Hussein. JANE CLAYPOOL. Rourke, 1993.
Saddam Hussein. NITA RENFREW. Chelsea House, 1993.
"Saddam's best ally." LESLIE COCKBURN and ANDREW COCKBURN. *Vanity Fair*, Aug. 1992.
" 'Back from the living dead'. . . ." RAY WILKINSON. "The stalking of Saddam." CHARLES LANE. *Newsweek*, Jan. 20, 1992.
Saddam Speaks on the Gulf Crisis: A Collection of Documents. OFRA BENGIO, ed. Syracuse University Press, 1992.
Saddam Hussein: A Political Biography. EFRAIM KARSH and INARI RAUTSI. Pergamon, 1991.

Huston, Anjelica (1952–) Film star Anjelica Huston played a major role in television in 1995, starring as Calamity Jane at the center of the miniseries *Buffalo Girls*, directed by Ron Hardy, and adapted by Cynthia Whitcomb from the Larry McMurtry novel. Costarring were Melanie Griffith; Sam Elliott as Wild Bill Hickok, the probable father of her child; Gabriel Byrne; Peter Coyote as Buffalo Bill Cody; country singer Reba McEntire as Annie Oakley; and Native American activist Russell Means as Sitting Bull. For the role, Huston received an Emmy nomination as best lead actress in a miniseries or special.

Huston also starred as Jack Nicholson's former wife in the film *The Crossing Guard*, written and directed by Sean Penn, a story about a man planning to murder a drunken driver who had killed his son. She received a best supporting actress in a musical or comedy Golden Globe

Anjelica Huston (right), Marisa Tomei (left), and Alfred Molina.

nomination for the role. A third costarring role came the film *The Perez Family*, directed by Mira Nair, and costarring Alfred Molina as her husband, just released from 20 years in a Cuban prison by the Mariel boatlift, and Marisa Tomei, a prostitute who pretends to be his wife after they have arrived in Miami.

Forthcoming was Huston's directorial debut, the television film *Bastard Out of Carolina*, adapted by Anne Meredith from the Dorothy Allison novel, the story of a young girl suffering parental abuse. Jennifer Jason Leigh will star.

Born in Los Angeles but raised in Ireland, Huston took a critical pounding when her father, actor-director John Huston, cast the 15–year-old in his film *A Walk With Love and Death* (1967). She retreated from film to the stage, emerging as a leading dramatic film actress in the mid-1980s by winning a best supporting actress Oscar as Maerose Prizzi in John Huston's *Prizzi's Honor* (1985). She later starred in *Gardens of Stone* (1987), *The Dead* (1987; screenplay by brother Tony Huston); *A Handful of Dust* (1988), John Huston's last film; *Enemies, A Love Story* (1989); *Crimes and Misdeameanors* (1989); *The Grifters* (1990); *The Witches* (1990); *The Addams Family* (1991); *Addams Family Values* (1993); *Manhattan Murder Mystery* (1993); and *And The Band Played On* (1993).

Huston is the granddaughter of actor Walter Huston. She studied with acting coach Peggy

Feury. In 1990, she ended a 17-year relationship with Jack Nicholson. She married sculptor Robert Graham in 1993.

FURTHER READING

"Class actress." PILAR VILADES. *Town & Country,* Oct. 1994.
"Anjelica." SOFIA COPPOLA. *Interview,* Oct. 1994.
"Anjelica Huston. . . ." JEFF SILVERMAN. *Cosmopolitan,* Mar. 1993.
"Anjelica Huston." NANCY GRIFFIN. *Harper's Bazaar,* June 1992.
"Anjelica Huston. . . ." *People,* Dec. 30, 1991.
"Anjelica Huston." SUSAN MORGAN. *Interview,* Dec. 1991.
"Huston Addams." SUSAN MORGAN. *Interview,* July 1991.

I

Ice Cube (O'Shea Jackson; 1970–) Rap singer, composer, and actor Ice Cube appeared in several films during 1995. In *Friday*, a neighborhood story set in South Central Los Angeles, he wrote, coproduced, and starred opposite Chris Tucker and Nia Long. The film generated the hit album *Friday: Original Motion Picture Soundtrack*, which featured several popular rap stars and groups, including Ice Cube's with "Friday" and 2 Live Crew with "Hoochie Mama."

Ice Cube also starred in the film *The Darker Side of Black*, written and directed by Isaac Julien and costarring Chuck D., Buju Banton, Shabba Ranks, and Cornel West, an exploration of the bitterly anti-woman, anti-homosexual rap and dance-hall music worlds.

A third film role was in John Singleton's *Higher Learning*, about bitter race relations on a college campus, which also generated a hit soundtrack album. Ice Cube also played an innocent Arican-American charged with the murder of a White woman in the film *The Glass Shield*.

Forthcoming were the film *Player's Club*, which he wrote and was slated to direct, and a starring role in the film *Anaconda*.

Los Angeles–born Ice Cube began his career as a rap songwriter with the pioneer hard-core rap group NWA, founded by Eazy-E, which also included Dr. Dre, M. D. Ren, and Yella. He wrote many of the songs on their early hit album *Straight Outta Compton* (1989). He left the group to go solo in 1990, then releasing the rap albums *Amerikka's Most Wanted* (1990), *Kill At Will* (1991), *Death Certificate* (1991), *The Pred-*

ator (1992), and *Lethal Injection* (1994). His works proved very appealing to many young African-Americans and many Whites, as well; they were also highly controversial, repeatedly expressing violently anti-White, anti-Jewish, anti-Asian, anti-woman, and homophobic sentiments. Ice Cube has appeared as an actor in the films *Boyz N the Hood* (1991), *Trespass* (1992), and *The Glass Shield* (1994).

FURTHER READING

"Ice Cube." *Current Biography,* Aug. 1995.
"Generation rap." SHEILA RULE. *New York Times Magazine,* Apr. 3, 1994.

"Ice capades." MEREDITH BERKMAN. *Entertainment,* Dec. 18, 1992.
"Ice Cube. . . ." FRANK OWEN. *Us,* Jan. 1992.
"Ice." EHRLICH DIMITRI. *Interview,* Dec. 1991.

Irons, Jeremy (1948–)

British actor Jeremy Irons ventured into what was for him new territory in 1995, starring in a violent action film: *Die Hard With a Vengeance.* The third of the "Die Hard" films, this sequel, directed and coproduced by John McTiernan, again starred Bruce Willis, leading a cast that included Samuel L. Jackson, Graham Greene, Colleen Camp, Larry Bryggman, and Anthony Peck. Irons plays the film's leading "heavy," a terrorist bomber, the brother of the leading terrorist of the first of the "Die Hard" films. The work was not very well received by the critics, but went on to be a box office hit.

Forthcoming were starring roles opposite Melanie Griffith and Dominique Swain in the film *Lolita,* directed by Adrian Lyne, with a screenplay by Harold Pinter; in Bernardo Bertolucci's film *Stealing Beauty*; and in the film *Acts of Love,* directed by Bruno Barreto and costarring Amy Irving, Dennis Hopper, Julie Harris, and Gary Busey.

Irons emerged as a screen and stage star in the early 1980s. In 1981, he created the Charles Ryder role in the television miniseries "Brideshead Revisited," the celebrated adaptation of the Evelyn Waugh novel. In the same year, he played opposite Meryl Streep in *The French Lieutenant's Woman.* He went on to star in such films as *Moonlighting* (1982), *Betrayal* (1983), *The Wild Duck* (1983), *Swann in Love* (1984), *The Mission* (1986), *Dead Ringers* (1989), *Frankenstein Unbound* (1989), *A Chorus of Disapproval* (1989), *Reversal of Fortune* (1990; he won a best actor Oscar for his portrayal of Claus von Bülow), *Kafka* (1991), *Damage* (1992), *Waterland* (1992), *M. Butterfly* (1993), *The House of the Spirits* (1994), and *The Lion King* (1994). Irons won a Tony as best leading actor in a drama for *The Real Thing* (1984). He married actress Sinead Cusack in 1978; they have two children.

FURTHER READING

"A question of character." GEORGINA HOWELL. *Vogue,* Jan. 1993.
"Metamorphosis." HARLAN KENNEDY. *American Film,* Nov.–Dec. 1991.

Ives, Burl Icle Ivanhoe (1909–95)

Illinois-born Burl Ives, a leading folk musician and actor, began his singing career as a child. He moved to New York City to pursue a career in music in the early 1930s and began his acting career in the late 1930s, making his Broadway debut in *The Boys From Syracuse* (1938). Ives emerged as a leading folksinger in the late 1930s; his first major hit was the song "Wayfarin' Stranger," which became his signature song and also the title of his 1940 radio show and his 1948 autobiography. Some of his later great hits were the songs "Blue Tail Fly," "Big Rock Candy Mountain," and "Foggy Foggy Dew." His parallel stage career included appearances in *This Is the Army* (1942), *Sing Out Sweet Land* (1944), *Show Boat* (1954), and by far his most notable role, that of Big Daddy in Tennessee Williams' play *Cat on a Hot Tin Roof,* which he re-created in the 1958 film version. Among his other films were *East of Eden* (1948), *Desire Under the Elms* (1958), *The Big Country* (1958; he won a best supporting actor Oscar), and *Our Man in Havana* (1959). He also appeared in television, most notably as the star of the series "O. K. Crackerby" (1965–68) and "The Lawyers" (1969–72). He was survived by his second wife, Dorothy Koster, a daughter, and three sons. (d. Anacortes, Washington; April 14, 1995)

FURTHER READING

"So long, Big Daddy. . . ." MARK GOODMAN. *People,*
    May 1, 1995.
Obituary. *Billboard,* Apr. 29, 1995.
Obituary. *Variety,* Apr. 17, 1995.
Obituary. *Times* (of London), Apr. 15, 1995.
Obituary. *New York Times,* Apr. 15, 1995.

Ivory, James Francis (1928–   ) Director
James Ivory added another major film to his long
list of highly regarded works in 1995—although
many reviewers judged this one to be not quite
as successful as previous works. The film was
Jefferson in Paris, produced by Ismail Merchant,
with a screenplay by Ruth Prawer Jhabvala.
Nick Nolte played the title role, leading an accomplished cast that included Greta Scacchi,
Thandie Newton, James Earl Jones, Jean-Pierre
Aumont, Simon Callow, Michael Lonsdale,
Nancy Marchand, and Gwyneth Paltrow. Although the film was set in the five years that
Thomas Jefferson was U.S. ambassador to
France (1784–89), the work was far more concerned with Jefferson's personal life during that
period than about the great affairs of state in
which he was involved. Many critics thought it
was somewhat caught between the political and
the personal, and not quite fully realized in either sphere, although most treated the film and
its celebrated director with very real respect.

Ivory and Ismail Merchant directed a segment
of the film *Lumière and Company,* directed by
Sarah Moon; a century-of-film celebration in
which a worldwide selection of almost 40 modern directors each created a 52-second film, using an original Lumière camera, re-created
original film emulsion, natural light, and worked
in a continuous shot.

Forthcoming was the film *Surviving Picassso,*
directed by Ivory, with a screenplay by Ruth
Prawer Jhabvala. Anthony Hopkins was set to
star in the title role, in a cast that includes
Natasha McElhone, Julianne Moore, Diane Venora, Joan Plowright, and David Margulies.

California-born Ivory began his long, fruitful
collaboration with Merchant and Jhabvala in the
early 1960s, with such films as *Shakespeare
Wallah* (1965), *Bombay Talkie* (1970), and *Autobiography of a Princess* (1975), all of them
largely set in India. His later films included *The
Europeans* (1979), *Heat and Dust* (1983), *A
Room with a View* (1986), *Maurice* (1987),
Slaves of New York (1989), *Mr. and Mrs. Bridge*
(1990), *Howards End* (1992), and *The Remains
of the Day* (1993). Ivory's 1951 B.F.A. was from
the University of Oregon, his M.A. from the University of Southern California.

FURTHER READING

"Doing it right the hard way. . . ." RICHARD CORLISS.
    Time, Mar. 16, 1992.
Films of Merchant Ivory. ROBERT E. LONG. Abrams,
    1991.

Jackson, Alan (1958–) Country singer Alan Jackson was again highly honored by his colleagues in 1995. At Nashville's 29th annual Country Music Awards, he was named best entertainer of the year. He received five other nominations as well: best male vocalist, best singer of a single for "Keeper of the Stars," best album for *Who I Am*, best music video for "I Don't Even Know Your Name," and best vocal event for "A Good Year For the Roses" (with George Jones). Jackson also received a Nashville Music Award nomination as best artist/songwriter and shared a best international song British Country Music Award with Jim McBride for their song "Chattahoochee."

Jackson's recordings continued to sell very well throughout the year, with his 1991 album *Don't Rock the Jukebox* topping 4 million sales, his 1992 album *A Lot About Livin' (and a Little 'bout Love)* topping 6 million, and his 1994 album *Who I Am* topping 3 million. His single "Summertime Blues" was the most performed song of the year, according to BMI (the Broadcast Music Institute), and his singles "If I Could Make a Living" and "Livin' On Love" were also among the most performed songs of the year. In 1995, Jackson issued the hit single "Song For The Life," and in late autumn, a "Greatest Hits" collection, which was still going strong in the top ten of *Billboard*'s Top 200 albums chart at year's end.

Born in Newnan, Georgia, Jackson was a student at West Georgia College and worked various jobs while playing in local clubs. In 1988 he became the first artist signed in Arista's new

Nashville division. Writing or cowriting many of his own songs, he won a substantial audience with his debut album *Here in the Real World* (1990), and built a larger audience with *Don't Rock the Jukebox* (1991), which was named 1992 album of the year; the title track was also named 1992 song of the year by the Academy of Country Music. They were followed by *A Lot About Livin' (and a Little 'bout Love)* (1992), *Honky Tonk Christmas* (1993), and *Who I Am* (1994). Jackson joined the Grand Ole Opry in 1991. He is married to Denise Jackson, a teacher; they have two daughters.

FURTHER READING

"Southern comfort." KAREN SCHOEMER. *Us*, Aug. 1994.
"Alan Jackson. . . ." MICHAEL MCCALL. *Country Music*,
May–June 1994.

Jackson, Janet (1966–)

Singer Janet Jackson participated fully in the enormous burst of attention generated by the June 1995 release of *HIStory: Past, Present, and Future, Book I*, the latest album of her brother, Michael Jackson. Their media-attacking single "Scream," written, produced, and sung as a duet, was released two weeks before the album and became an instant hit. Their video for the song was one of the major music video events of the year, winning several MTV video award nominations and *Billboard*'s award as top pop/rock "clip of the year."

Janet Jackson also issued her own very well received 1995 album, *Design of a Decade: 1986/96*; largely a "great hits" collection, it introduced two new songs "Twenty Foreplay" and "Runaway," both issued as hit singles.

On the film side of her career, Jackson's song "Again," from the film *Poetic Justice*, won an ASCAP award as one of the most performed songs from motion pictures. Jackson herself won a Billboard Music Artist Achievement Award. She also received Soul Award nominations for her song "Any Time, Any Place" and her music video "You Want This."

As a child, Jackson appeared with her brothers in the popular group the Jackson Five. She made three albums in the early 1980s: *Janet Jackson* (1982), *Dream Street* (1984), and *Control* (1986); the latter introduced several hit singles, and hinted at the major career that would blossom a few years later. She scored a major success in 1989, with the hit album *Rhythm Nation: 1814*. Her "Love Will Never Do (Without You)" became a number-one pop single in 1991. Her hit 1993 album was *Janet*. Jackson made her film debut in *Poetic Justice* (1993), and sang the Oscar-nominated "Again" in the film's soundtrack album. She was formerly married.

FURTHER READING

"Janet on. . . ." PAMALA JOHNSON. *Essence*, Jan. 1996.
"Janet Jackson's. . . ." *Jet*, Nov. 6, 1995.
"Janet." STEVE POND. *Us*, Nov. 1995.
"Janet. . . ." LYNN NORMENT. *Ebony*, Jan. 1995.

"Sexual healing. . . ." DAVID RITZ. *Rolling Stone*, Sept. 16, 1993.
"Jackson, Janet." *Current Biography*, June 1991.

Jackson, Jesse Louis (1941–)

Hard-pressed to find a constituency, African-American politician Jesse Jackson tried to build an independent stance and body of support during 1995. Touring widely, he fashioned an appeal to African-American audiences that focused more on self-help and the development of family values than on the social service network, which was shrinking rapidly under the attack by the new Republican Congressional majority and many state legislatures. At the same time, he called for defense of what had been previously won, criticized President Bill Clinton for being half-hearted in his defense of social justice, and repeatedly threatened to mount an independent presidential campaign, which some Democrats thought might draw away enough votes to deny Clinton wins in several key states.

Jackson did not, however, seem to draw a great deal of support for his political ambitions. This was especially so before Colin Powell's announcement that he would not run in the 1996 presidential election; Powell had been clearly favored over Jackson by the overwhelming majority of African-American voters. On October 16, Jackson publicly allied himself with highly controversial Nation of Islam leader Louis Farrakhan, at Farrakhan's Washington, D.C. "Million Man March," speaking in full support of Farrakhan's role in creating the demonstration, and otherwise in the most general terms about several kinds of equality. Whether or not Jackson emerged with an enhanced constituency was a matter of debate among observers.

Jackson published the 1995 book *Legal Lynching: Racism, Injustice and the Death Penalty*. In 1995, his son, Jesse Jackson, Jr. was elected to the House of Representatives from Illinois.

South Carolina–born Jackson received his 1964 B.A. from North Carolina Agricultural and Technical University. After postgraduate work at the Chicago Theological Seminary, he became a Baptist minister in 1968. Long active in the civil rights movement, Jackson directed the Southern Christian Leadership Operation Breadbasket (1967–71), and in 1971 founded Operation PUSH (People United to Save Humanity), and later the Rainbow Coalition. He made an unsuccessful bid for the Democratic presidential nomination in 1984, but emerged as a major figure; he campaigned again in 1988, making an electrifying speech at the 1988 Democratic National Convention. In 1991, he became one of two new "shadow" senators representing Washington, D.C., active in lobbying for statehood. In 1988, he published *A Time to Speak: The Autobiography of the Reverend Jesse Jackson*. Jackson married Jacqueline Brown in 1964; they have five children.

FURTHER READING

"What not to be. . . ." DAVID CORN. *Nation,* July 31, 1995.
"The contender. . . ." JONATHAN FREEDLAND. *Guardian,* June 3, 1995.
"Jesse Jackson. . . ." JOHN NICHOLS. *The Progressive,* Jan. 1995.
"Farrakhan, Jesse and Jews." GEORGE E. CURRY. *Emerge,* July–Aug. 1994.
"Stand and deliver." ELIZABETH GLEICK. *People,* Apr. 11, 1994.
"Action Jackson. . . ." HANNA ROSIN. *New Republic,* Mar. 21, 1994.
"A new civil rights. . . ." PAUL GLASTRIS and JEANNYE THORNTON. *U.S. News & World Report,* Jan. 17, 1994.
"An older, grimmer Jesse." HOWARD FINEMAN. *Newsweek,* Jan. 10, 1994.
Jesse Jackson and Black People. AMIRI BARAKA. Third World, 1994.
I Am Somebody!: A Biography of Jesse Jackson. JAMES HASKINS. Enslow, 1992.
Jesse Jackson and Political Power. TERESA CELSI. Millbrook, 1991.
Jesse Jackson. ROBERT JAKOUBEK. Chelsea House, 1991.
Jesse Jackson: A Biography. PATRICIA C. MCKISSACK. Scholastic, 1991.

Jackson, Michael Joseph (1958–) Superstar Michael Jackson had encountered major personal problems in 1993, with charges of child sexual abuse brought by the family of a 13-year-old boy. He denied all charges but, facing enormous adverse publicity, canceled the balance of an international tour, and in January 1994 settled the civil charges out of court for an undisclosed sum, reportedly well over $10 million, while no criminal charges were filed. He and Lisa Marie Presley, only child of the late Elvis Presley, were married in May 1994, and during

1994 and early 1995 Jackson worked to rebuild his shattered career and reputation, a campaign that included a joint television interview with Diane Sawyer.

In June 1995, Jackson began a massive career comeback, with release of the two-disk album *HIStory: Past, Present, and Future, Book I*; it became a worldwide best-seller, and several of the singles drawn from it went on to become even greater hits. The album was preceded by one of its hit singles, "Scream," an attack on the media that was a duet written, produced, and sung by him and his sister, Janet Jackson. The later video version was one of the major video hits of the year, winning several MTV video award nominations and *Billboard*'s award as top pop/rock "clip of the year."

HIStory carried 15 new Jackson songs and 15 "greatest hits." Among the other new songs were "You Are Not Alone," a major hit single; "Stranger in Moscow," "This Time Around," "Earth Song," "D. S.," "Money," "Childhood," "Tabloid Junkie," "1 Bad," "Little Susie," and "They Don't Care About Us," which immediately created a storm because it included anti-Semitic lyrics. Jackson quickly apologized for the lyrics, and said that he would substitute inoffensive language on future copies of the albums.

On the personal side, Jackson was hospitalized, reportedly with heart problems, while rehearsing for an HBO special in early December, and canceled all public appearances, at least until year's end.

Indiana-born Jackson began his extraordinary career in 1969, as the 11-year-old lead singer of his family's singing group, the Jackson Five. He became a leading popular soloist in the late 1970s, with such albums as *Off the Wall* (1979); *Thriller* (1982), the best-selling album in history, with more than 24 million sales through 1994; *Bad* (1987); and such singles as "I Can't Stop Loving You," along with many popular videos. His 1991 album *Dangerous* generated the hit singles "Black or White," "Remember the Time," "In the Closet," "Jam," and "Heal the World." Jackson starred in the film version of *The Wiz* (1978), opposite Diana Ross, and in *Moonwalker* (1988). In 1993, he was awarded the Grammy Legend Award.

FURTHER READING

"The Jackson jive. . . ." MAUREEN ORTH. *Vanity Fair,* Sept. 1995.
"Hooked. . . ." STANLEY CROUCH. *New Republic,* Aug. 21, 1995.
"Michael Jackson. . . ." *Jet,* July 3, 1995.
"Can he beat it?" DANA KENNEDY. *Entertainment,* June 16, 1995.
"Did Michael do it?" MARY A. FISCHER. *GQ,* Oct. 1994.
"Michael tells. . . ." ROBERT E. JOHNSON. *Ebony,* Oct. 1994.
"Neverland meets Graceland." TOM GLIATTO. *People.* Aug. 15, 1994.
"Dodging the bullet. . . ." BILL HEWITT. *People.* Feb. 7, 1994.
Michael Jackson: Entertainer. Chelsea House, 1994.
Michael Jackson—The King of Pop: His Darkest Hour. LISA CAMPBELL. Branden, 1994.
Michael Jackson Unauthorized. CHRISTOPHER ANDERSEN. Simon & Schuster, 1994.
Michael Jackson: Entertainer. LOIS NICHOLSON. Chelsea House, 1994.
Michael Jackson. Andrews & McMeel, 1993.
Michael Jackson: King of Pop. LISA CAMPBELL. Branden, 1993.
Michael Jackson: The Magic and the Madness. J. RANDY TARABORRELLI. Carol, 1991.

Jackson, Samuel L. (1949–)

For his role in the 1994 film *Pulp Fiction,* rising film star Samuel L. Jackson received Academy Award and Screen Actors Guild best supporting actor nominations, and won a best supporting actor award from the British Academy of Films and Television Arts (BAFTA).

In 1995, he appeared in several films. In *Die Hard with a Vengeance,* directed by and coproduced by John McTiernan, he costarred opposite Bruce Willis and Jeremy Irons. In *Kiss of Death,* directed and produced by Barbet Schroeder, he costarred with David Caruso, Nicolas Cage, and Helen Hunt. Jackson also appeared in Stephen Gyllenhaal's film *Losing Isaiah,* starring Jessica Lange and Halle Berry as adoptive and natural mothers locked in a custody battle. A fourth film appearance was in the fantasy *Fluke,* starring Matthew Modine as a man who dies in a car accident and is reincarnated as a golden retriever.

Forthcoming were starring roles opposite Jeff Goldblum in Reginald Hudlin's film *The Great White Hype* and in the film *A Time To Kill,* directed by Joel Schumacher and costarring Sandra Bullock, Matthew McConaughey, Kevin Spacey, Charles S. Dutton, and Donald Sutherland. He was also slated to star opposite Geena Davis in the film *The Long Kiss Goodnight,* directed by Renny Harlin.

Jackson made his film debut in *Ragtime* (1981), and went on to play strong supporting roles in several films, among them *Eddie Murphy Raw* (1987), *Mo' Better Blues* (1990), and *Goodfellas* (1990). A breakthrough role was that of the brother in *Jungle Fever* (1991), for which he won several awards, including best supporting actor at the Cannes Film Festival. Among his other early 1990s films were *Strictly Business* (1991), *White Sands* (1992), *Patriot Games* (1992), *Fathers and Sons* (1992), *Amos & An-*

drew (1993), *Jurassic Park* (1993), and *True Romance* (1993). He has also appeared in several television films. Jackson is a graduate of Morehouse College and a cofounder of Atlanta's Just Us Theatre Company. He is married to LaTanya Richardson; they have one child. (For additional photo, see **Cage, Nicolas**.)

FURTHER READING

"Samuel L. Jackson. . . ." *Jet,* June 12, 1995.
"Sam I am." CLAUDIA DREIFUS. June 1995.
"Samuel L. Jackson." DAVID RENSIN. *Playboy,* Apr. 1995.
"Samuel L. Jackson." JED SPINGARN. *Entertainment,* Mar. 1995.
"Samuel L. Jackson." NANCY MILLS. *Cosmopolitan,* Oct. 1994.
"Harlem on his mind. . . ." DIANE GOLDNER. *People,* July 1, 1991.

Mick Jagger (second from left) and the Rolling Stones.

Jagger, Mick (Michael Philip Jagger; 1941–) After 33 years of recording and touring, Mick Jagger and the Rolling Stones were still going strong. They toured worldwide throughout the year in support of their 1994 hit album *Voodoo Lounge,* and planned to continue touring right on through 1996, including an Australian tour for the first time in 22 years. They also issued a very well received CD-ROM version of *Voodoo Lounge.* They were also honored by their peers in 1995, winning Grammys for best rock album for *Voodoo Lounge* and best short-form video for "Love Is Strong."

During their world tour, the Stones recorded the album *Stripped,* a collection of classics pre-sented in studio settings, during rehearsals, and live from their their appearances at Paris's Olympia Theatre and Amsterdam's Paradiso Club. Included were such standards as "Street Fighting Man," "I'm Free," "Let It Bleed," "Slipping Away," "Angie," "Love In Vain," and the Bob Dylan classic "Like a Rolling Stone," recorded for the first time by the Stones and later in the year issued as a single.

Jagger was the chief organizer of the Rolling Stones, in 1962; he and Keith Richards were the group's main songwriters, and Jagger its leading performer, portraying an angry, deeply alienated, uncontrollably violent, mythic sexual figure, a model for the scores of other such rock figures who would follow. Such albums as *The Rolling Stones* (1964; and two 1965 sequels), *Aftermath* (1966), and *Their Satanic Majesties Request* (1967), coupled with their worldwide tours, established them as one of the century's leading popular musical groups. In 1969, after a murder by their Hell's Angels security guards at an Altamont, California, Stones concert, the group toned down their image somewhat. Although they continued to tour and record throughout the 1980s, their popularity lessened after the mid-1970s. Yet their very successful 1989–90 world tour showed that the rock group still had enormous vitality and drawing power.

Jagger appeared in the film *Ned Kelly* (1969), and in the film of the group's Altamont concert, *Gimme Shelter* (1972). He has also done several solo recordings, most recently *Wandering Spirit* (1993). Jagger attended the London School of Economics. He was formerly married to Bianca Jagger (1971–79), and married his longtime companion, model Jerry Hall, in 1990. Jagger has five children, the three youngest with Hall.

FURTHER READING

"Jagger remembers." JANN S. WENNER. *Rolling Stone,* Dec. 14, 1995.
"Now, Mick!" DIMITRI EHRLICH. *Interview,* Oct. 1994.
"Some boys!" BRIAN D. JOHNSON. *Maclean's,* Aug. 8, 1994.
Mick Jagger: Primitive Cool. CHRISTOPHER SANDFORD. St. Martin's, 1994.
"Mick Jagger." KURT LODER. *Esquire,* Apr. 1993.
Mick Jagger: The Story Behind the Rolling Stone. DAVIN SEAY. Birch Lane/Carol, 1993.
Jagger Unauthorized. CHRISTOPHER ANDERSEN. Delacorte, 1993.
Time Is on My Side: The Rolling Stones Day-by-Day, 1962–1984. ALAN STEWART and CATHY SANFORD. Popular Culture, 1992.

Jenkins, Dorothy (1914–95) San Diego–
born Dorothy Jenkins, an award-winning screen and stage costume designer, attended art school in Los Angeles, and held several design jobs during the 1930s and early 1940s. She won her first costume design Academy Award for *Joan of Arc* (1948) starring Ingrid Bergman in the title role; her second for *Samson and Delilah* (1948), starring Victor Mature and Hedy Lamarr; and her third for *Night of the Iguana* (1964), starring Ava Gardner and Richard Burton. Among her other films were *The Misfits*, starring Clark Gable and Marilyn Monroe; *The Sound of Music*, starring Julie Andrews; *Elmer Gantry*, starring Burt Lancaster and Jean Simmons; *The Greatest Show on Earth*, starring Betty Hutton and Charlton Heston; and *The Music Man*, starring Robert Preston and Shirley Jones. She also costumed many plays, including *South Pacific* and *The World of Suzie Wong*, and worked in television. She was survived by two sons and a brother. (d. Santa Barbara, California; November 21, 1995)

FURTHER READING

Obituary. *New York Times*, Nov. 30, 1995.

Jennings, Peter Charles (1938–) ABC
News and evening news anchor Peter Jennings were honored by their peers in 1995, winning the top award, the Gold Baton, at the Alfred I. duPont-Columbia University Awards for broadcast journalism, for "depth and range of its news coverage" and "outstanding television journalism." One of the five ABC reporting segments especially cited were his own 1994 special "Peter Jennings Reporting: While America Watched—The Bosnian Tragedy." His occasional series of news specials continued in 1995, most notably with "In the Name of God," on evangelical churches, and "Hiroshima: Why the Bomb Was Dropped," in late July, shortly before the 50th anniversary of the atomic bombing. Jennings and his evening news program also maintained their comfortable ratings lead over their main competitors at CBS and NBC, who were far behind, battling for second place—though all the major network news programs suffered losses in audience shares because cable channels carried live coverage of the O. J. Simpson trial.

Outside of ABC, Jennings served as chairman of the Coalition for the Homeless, a day-long benefit in New York City, involving tours of artists' studios and auctions of donated works.

Toronto-born Jennings worked in Canadian broadcasting before joining ABC News in 1964. During the next two decades, much of that time spent abroad, he rose to become chief London correspondent for ABC, and in 1983 became the anchor of "World News Tonight," one of the three chief American reporters and interpreters of the news. Jennings attended Carleton University, and his LL.D. is from Rider College. His third marriage, to writer Kati Marton, ended in 1993; he has two children.

FURTHER READING

"How 'Stanley Stunning'. . . ." ALAN EBERT. *Good Housekeeping*, Apr. 1991.

Jhabvala, Ruth Prawer (1927–) Novelist, short story writer, and screenwriter Ruth Prawer Jhabvala, a longtime collaborator of director James Ivory and producer Ismail Merchant, wrote the screenplay of *Jefferson in Paris*, which opened in 1995. It was directed by Ivory, produced by Merchant, and starred Nick Nolte in the title role. The film, set in the five years that Thomas Jefferson was U.S. ambassador to France (1784–89), focused more on the personal than the political, with emphasis on his relationships with two women: Maria Cosway, played by Greta Scacchi, and 15-year-old African-

American slave Sally Hemings, played by Thandie Newton. The cast also included James Earl Jones, Jean-Pierre Aumont, Simon Callow, Michael Lonsdale, Nancy Marchand, and Gwyneth Paltrow.

Jhabvala also wrote the screenplay for Ivory's forthcoming film *Surviving Picassso*, starring Anthony Hopkins in the title role, in a cast that includes Natasha McElhone, Julianne Moore, Diane Venora, Joan Plowright, and David Margulies.

In 1995, she also published the very well-received multigenerational novel *Shards of Memory*.

German-born Jhabvala lived in India (1951–75), where much of her work is set, and in the United States thereafter. A distinguished novelist and short story writer, she has also written several classic screenplays, many of them directed by James Ivory. Some of her best known novels are *The Nature of Passion* (1956), *The Householder* (1960), *Heat and Dust* (1975), *In Search of Love and Beauty* (1983), *Three Continents* (1987), and *Poet and Dancer* (1993). Her filmscripts include *The Householder* (1963), *Shakespeare Wallah* (1965), *The Guru* (1969), *Bombay Talkie* (1971), *Autobiography of a Princess* (1975), *Roseland* (1977), *Hullabaloo over Georgie and Bonnie's Pictures* (1978), *Jane Austen in Manhattan* (1980), *Quartet* (1981), *Heat and Dust* (1983), *The Bostonians* (1984), *Room With A View* (1986; she won a best screenplay Oscar), *Mr. and Mrs. Bridge* (1990), *Howards End* (1992), and *The Remains of the Day* (1993; she won a best adapted screenplay Oscar). Her M.A. is from the University of London. She is married to Indian architect Cyrus S. H. Jhabvala, and has three children.

FURTHER READING

"A cinematic sensibility." JAMES ATLAS. *Vogue*, Mar. 1993.
"The book of Ruth." JOSEPHINE HART. *Vanity Fair*, Mar. 1993.
Silence, Exile and Cunning: The Fiction of Ruth Prawer Jhabvala, 2nd ed. YASMINE GOONERATNE. Apt, 1993.
"Doing it right the hard way. . . ." RICHARD CORLISS. *Time*, Mar. 16, 1992.
Ruth Prawer Jhabvala: Fiction and Film. JAYANTI BAILUR. Arnold/South Asia, 1992.
Ruth Prawer Jhabvala. RALPH J. CRANE. Twayne, 1992.

Jiang Zemin (1926–) Chinese president and Communist Party head Jiang Zemin, long the protégé of Deng Xiaoping, seemed in 1995 to be a front-runner in the succession struggle already under way; with Deng's death nearing, the onset of a bitter succession battle seemed imminent. However, being Deng's protégé and a leading economic reformer was no longer necessarily a prime asset in the struggle over who was to lead China, for the country was experiencing many of the problems resulting from very quick growth, as its overheated economy brought with it a huge, 20 percent-plus annual inflation rate, savings and pension losses for hundreds of millions of Chinese, a massive internal migration from country to city, the regrowth of crime and prostitution, and even lessened ability to enforce China's very harsh population control laws, as a more mobile people became harder to trace and fully control.

Jiang responded by urging some measures to help cool the economy, while at the same time projecting a somewhat toughened image, imprisoning dissidents, sharply resisting worldwide criticism of China's terrible human rights record, and taking a hard line on trade matters. On October 24, he and President Bill Clinton met in New York, during the United Nations 50th-anniversary celebration, and after a two-hour discussion that included human rights matters and the status of Taiwan, apparently agreed on nothing of any substance. Whether Jiang would, indeed, succeed Deng remained a matter of conjecture.

Born in Yangzhou City, Jiangsu Province, Jiang received his 1947 electrical engineering degree from Shanghai's Jiaotong University. He was a Communist during the final stages of the Chinese Civil War and began his public career as a commercial attaché at the Chinese embassy in Moscow (1950–56). Jiang returned to China in 1956, and worked in the Ministry of Machine Building until 1959, the year that Mao Zedong's extraordinarily damaging Great Leap Forward industrialization campaign became fully operative. He continued to work in industrial management in the two decades that followed, though not in any highly visible government position. In the late 1970s, he emerged as a protégé of Deng Xiaoping, then in power, and held a series of key national industrial posts (1980–85), also becoming a member of the Communist Party Central Committee in 1982. In 1985, Deng appointed him mayor of Shanghai. In 1989, after the

Tienanmen Square Massacre, Jiang was elevated by Deng to the positions of general secretary of the Communist Party and commander-in-chief of the armed forces. In 1993, still supported and directed by Deng, Jiang became president of the People's Republic of China. He is married to Wang Yeping; they have two sons.

FURTHER READING

" 'The problem is. . . .' " MORTIMER B. ZUCKERMAN et al. "The new look. . . ." SUSAN V. LAWRENCE and EMILY MACFARQUHAR. *U.S. News & World Report,* Oct. 23, 1995.
"Jiang Zemin." *Current Biography,* May 1995.
" 'China's arms sales. . . .' " MORTIMER B. ZUCKERMAN et al. *U.S. News & World Report,* Mar. 15, 1993.
" 'The United States. . . .' " MORTIMER B. ZUCKERMAN et al. *U.S. News & World Report,* May 27, 1991.

John, Elton Hercules (Reginald Kenneth Dwight; 1947–) Singer and songwriter Elton John was greatly honored by his peers in 1995. He and lyricist Tim Rice won an Academy Award for best original song for "Can You Feel the Love Tonight" from the film *The Lion King.* John himself won a Grammy for best pop vocal performance for the song, and the two collaborators received several other Grammy nominations for that song and for the song "Circle of Life." On quite another kind of prize front, he and celebrated Russian cellist and conductor Mstislav Rostropovich received Polar Music Prizes from the king of Sweden, sharing the $265,000 award.

John, who continues to be one of the most prolific and best-selling artists in world music, issued yet another hit album in 1995, *Made In England,* with such new hits as the title song, "Cold," "Blessed," "House," and "Believe," which became a hit single. He toured in concert throughout the year in support of that album and his many other best-selling albums; one of them, his *Greatest Hits* collection, topped 13 million sales. He also appeared in the television concert film *A Special Evening With Elton John,* winning a CableAce award for the show.

Born in Pinner, Middlesex, England, John won a scholarship at age 11 to study classical music at London's Royal Academy of Music (1959–64), but turned toward popular music, working as songwriter and member of various groups, beginning with Bluesology (1965), beginning his collaboration with his frequent songwriting partner, Bernie Taupin. After an unsuccessful debut album, *Empty Sky* (1969), John scored a major success with *Elton John* (1970); the hit "Your Song" became his signature song. In the years of his greatest success, he toured widely and his major albums included *Tumbleweed Connection, 11.17.70, Friends,* and *Madman Across the Water* (all 1971); *Honky Chateau* (1972); *Don't Shoot Me I'm Only the Piano Player* and *Goodbye Yellow Brick Road* (both 1973); *Caribou* (1974); *Empty Sky, Captain Fantastic and the Brown Dirt Cowboy,* and *Rock of the Westies* (all 1975); and *Here and There* and *Blue Moves* (1976). He also appeared in the movie version of The Who's rock-opera, *Tommy* (1975).

After taking a break, he slowed his production to more or less one album a year, including *A Single Man* (1978), *Victim of Love* (1979), *21 at 33* (1980), *Jump Up* (1982), *Too Low for Zero* and *The Fox* (both 1983), *Breaking Hearts* (1984), *Ice on Fire* (1985), *Leather Jackets* (1986), *Reg Strikes Back* (1988), and *Sleeping with the Past* and *The Thom Bell Sessions* (1989). In the early 1990s, John publicly talked about drug and alcohol problems which, by then, he had largely overcome. His most recent albums include *The One* (1992) and *Duets* (1993). He won the 1981 Grammy award for best instrumental composition for "Basque," from *The Wind Beneath My Wings,* and was given the Brits award as best British male artist in 1991. In 1994, he was inducted into the Rock and Roll Hall of Fame.

FURTHER READING

"Elton John. . . ." INGRID SISCHY. *Interview,* Apr. 1995.
"Roaring back." RICHARD CORLISS. *Time,* Mar. 13, 1995.
Rocket Man: The Encyclopedia of Elton John. CLAUDE BERNARDIN and TOM STANTON. Greenwood, 1995.
Elton John. MICK ST. MICHAEL. Smithmark, 1994.
"Architectural Digest. . . ." SUSAN CHEEVER. *Architectural Digest,* Jan. 1993.
Elton John: The Definitive Biography. PHILIP NORMAN. Simon & Schuster, 1993.
The Many Lives of Elton John. SUSAN CRIMP and PATRICIA BURSTEIN. Carol, 1992.
Elton John. PHILIP NORMAN. Crown, 1992.

John Paul II, Pope (Karol Wojtyla; 1920–) Though clearly in fragile health, Pope John Paul II resumed his worldwide travels in 1995; he had broken his shoulder during a fall at the Vatican in November 1993, broke his right thigh in another fall at the Vatican in April 1994, and had curtailed his travel schedule in 1994. He made a major trip to Australia and Asia in January 1995, visiting the Philippines, Australia, Papua New Guinea, and Sri Lanka; in Manila, an estimated 3–4 million attended his mass. In September, he visited Africa, speaking in Cameroon, Kenya, and making his first trip to South Africa; he had refused to visit South Africa until the apartheid system was ended. In October, he visited the United States, where he spoke in New Jersey, New York, and Maryland, at New York addressing the general assembly of the United Nations.

On March 30, Pope John Paul II issued the encyclical letter *Evangelium Vitae* (*Gospel of Life*), in which he very sharply attacked abortion and euthanasia, calling upon Catholics to practice conscientous objection to laws permitting either. He also expressed grave doubts about the death penalty, and commented on a wide range of other matters. His 1994 book *Crossing the Threshhold of Hope* continued to be a worldwide best-seller.

John Paul II is the first pope of Polish origin, and the first non-Italian pope of the past four centuries. He was ordained as a Catholic priest in 1946, and then moved steadily upward in the Polish Catholic Church, becoming a professor of the-ology in the 1950s, and ultimately archbishop of Krakow (1963–78). He became a cardinal in 1967, and then pope in 1978. He has been largely a very conservative pope, strongly opposing abortion and strongly discouraging liberal social action on the part of the priesthood. He attended Krakow's Jagellonian University and Rome's Angelicum.

FURTHER READING

"John Paul II. . . ." AVERY DULLES. *America,* Dec. 9, 1995.
"Keeping faith. . . ." JEFFREY L. SHELER et al. *U.S. News & World Report,* Oct. 9, 1995.
"Pope risks furor. . . ." *National Catholic Reporter,* May 5, 1995.
"Papal secrets." TAD SZULC. "Life, death and the Pope." Kenneth L. Woodward. *Newsweek,* Apr. 10, 1995.
"John Paul II. . . ." LEO D. LEFEBURE. *The Christian Century,* Feb. 15, 1995.
The Young Life of Pope John Paul II. CLAIRE J. MOHAN. Young Sparrow, 1995.
Pope John Paul II: The Biography. TAD SZULC. Simon & Schuster, 1995.
Pope John Paul II and the Church. PETER HEBBLETHWAITE. Sheed and Ward, 1995.
Letter to a Jewish Friend: The Simple and Extraordinary Story of Pope John Paul II and His Jewish School Friend. GIAN F. SVIDERCOSCHI. Crossroad, 1995.
"Empire of the spirit." PAUL GRAY. "Kitchen pope. . . ." PAUL JOHNSON. "Lives of the pope." JOHN ELSON. *Time,* Dec. 26, 1994. (Man of the Year issue.)
"The pope in crisis." DAVID REMNICK. *New Yorker,* Oct. 17, 1994.
Pope John Paul II's Theological Journey to the Prayer Meeting of Religions in Assisi: From the Second Vatican Council to the Papal Election. JOHANNES DORMANN. Angelus Press, 1994.
At the Center of the Human Drama: The Philosophical Anthropology of Karol Wojtyla—Pope John Paul II. KENNETH L. SCHMITZ. Catholic University Press, 1994.
God's Politician: Pope John Paul II, the Catholic Church, and the New World Order. DAVID WILLEY. Thomas Dunne/St. Martin's, 1993.
Pope John Paul the Second: Religious Leader. JAY WILSON. Chelsea House, 1993.

Johnson, Helene (1909–95) Boston-born Helene Johnson, one of the younger African-American poets of the Harlem Renaissance, grew up in Massachusetts, attended Boston University, and moved to New York City in 1927, taking some extension courses at Columbia Univerisity. In the late 1920s, her poems appeared in several magazines, among them *Vanity Fair* and *Opportunity*. Although much of her work was written in "University English," some, including her highly regarded "Poem," was written in then-pioneering colloquial (or "street language") style. For her modest, moving body of published work, she was later acclaimed as a substantial figure in the Harlem Renaissance, a major Black cultural movement of the 1920s that directly included such literary and artistic figures as Langston Hughes, Countee Cullen, Claude McKay, and Jean Toomer, and in a somewhat wider sense such notables as Paul Robeson and James Weldon Johnson. She was survived by a daughter. (d. New York City; June 30, 1995)

FURTHER READING

Obituary. *New York Times*, June 11, 1995.

Johnson, Randy (Randall David Johnson; 1963–) Seattle Mariners pitcher Randy Johnson finally stepped up to the top of his profession in 1995, when he won the American League's Cy Young award. Known for his intimidating fastballs, and earlier in his career for frequent wild pitches, Johnson credits pitching great Nolan Ryan with advice during the 1993 season that helped him to diversify his mound repertoire, adding a slider and a changeup. At 6′10″ the tallest pitcher in the game, Johnson had 18 wins (tied for second in the league) in the 1995 regular season, against two losses, for a league-leading winning percentage of .900, and an earned-run average of 2.48. The formidable left-hander also led the league in strikeouts, with 294, almost 90 more than the second-place pitcher, becoming the first pitcher in 54 years (and only the fourth ever) to lead the major leagues in strikeouts for four straight years. Johnson also set a major league record for most strikeouts per nine innings, with 12.35; and was the first pitcher ever to average ten or more strikeouts per nine innings (1991–95). In addition, he pitched three shut-outs, which was second in the league; and overall pitched 214 1/3 innings, fourth in the league. Not surprisingly, he was named starting American League pitcher at the 1995 All-Star game.

Johnson was one of the main reasons that the Mariners were considered strong contenders to get to and win the World Series. And, indeed, Johnson won some key games down the stretch, but it was not to be. The Mariners behind Johnson defeated the California Angels for the American League West title, then overcame the New York Yankees 3–2 in the divisional play-offs, again with Johnson winning key games, sometimes pitching after just a one-day rest. But the Mariners finally fell to Cleveland in six games for the league championship, with Johnson pitching two games for a total of 15 1/2 innings and an earned run average of 2.35.

Born in Walnut Creek, California, Johnson was educated at the University of Southern California. He began his career with the Montreal Expos (1988–89), before joining the Seattle Mariners (1989–). He led the American League in strikeouts for four consecutive years (1992–95) and has been named to the All-Stars four times (1990; 1993; 1994; 1995).

FURTHER READING

"Fastball." BRUCE ALLAR. *Sporting News,* July 11, 1994.
"Picture perfect pitcher." RICHARD HOFFER. *Sports Illustrated,* May 4, 1992.

Jones, James Earl (1931–) Celebrated actor James Earl Jones in 1995 starred as Father Stephen Kumalo in a powerful film adaptation of Alan Paton's 1948 classic South African

anti-apartheid novel *Cry, the Beloved Country.* Richard Harris costarred as James Jarvis, a White landowner whose civil rights activist son has been murdered; together, Jones and Harris symbolize the racial unity that, almost half a century later, would produce a new South African nation. Darrell James Roodt directed; Ronald Harwood adapted the Paton novel for the screen; the cast included Charles S. Dutton, Leleti Khumalo, Vusi Kunene, and Eric Miyeni. A 1951 film version of the book had been directed by Vincent Korda, and starred Canada Lee, Charles Carson, and Sidney Poitier. In another work on South African themes, Jones and Alfre Woodard narrated the television documentary *Countdown to Freedom: 10 Days That Changed South Africa*, on the events that led to the ending of apartheid and the emergence of a new South Africa.

Jones also costarred as narrator Madison Hemings, a descendant of President Thomas Jefferson, in the film *Jefferson in Paris*, directed by James Ivory and starring Nick Nolte as Jefferson during his five years as American ambassador to France (1784–89); costarring were Greta Scacchi, Thandie Newton, Jean-Pierre Aumont, and Simon Callow. Jones also inaugurated a short-lived new Seattle-set African-American network television series "Under One Roof," costarring Joe Morton, Vanessa Bell Calloway, Essence Atkins, and Merlin Santana.

Forthcoming were starring roles opposite Robert Duvall in *A Family Thing*, directed by Richard Pearce; and in *Lone Star*, written and directed by John Sayles and costarring Matthew McConaughey, Joe Morton, and Frances McDormand.

Mississippi-born Jones has been a leading figure in the American theater since his starring role as African-American heavyweight champion Jack Jefferson (inspired by the real-life Jack Johnson) in *The Great White Hope* (1968; on film 1970). A classical actor of enormous range, Jones is highly regarded for such roles as *Macbeth* (1962), *King Lear* (1973), Hickey in *The Iceman Cometh* (1973), *Othello* (1982), and his starring role in *Fences* (1988), for which he won a Tony. He was the voice of Darth Vader in *Star Wars* (1977), played Alex Haley in television's miniseries *Roots II* (1979), and played major roles in such films as *Gardens of Stone* (1987), *Field of Dreams* (1989), *The Hunt for Red October* (1990), *Convicts* (1991), *Excessive Force* (1993), *The Sandlot* (1993), *The Lion King* (1994), *Clear and Present Danger* (1994), and *Clean Slate* (1994). He published the autobiography *James Earl Jones: Voices and Silences* (1993). Jones's 1957 B.A. was from the University of Michigan. Son of actor Robert Earl Jones, he married actress Cecilia Hart in 1982; they have one son. (For additional photo, see **Mandela, Nelson**.)

FURTHER READING

"James Earl Jones . . . ." *Jet,* Mar. 27, 1995.
"When his sound. . . ." WALLACE TERRY. *Parade,* Dec. 25, 1994.
"Jones, James Earl." *Current Biography,* Nov. 1994.
"How James Earl Jones. . . ." JOHN CULHANE. *Reader's Digest* (Canadian), Nov. 1994.
"James Earl Jones." JOHN CLARK. *Premiere,* June 1992.

Jones, Jerry (Jerral Wayne Jones; 1942–   )

During 1995, Dallas Cowboys' owner Jerry Jones was still living with the consequences of having split with ex-Cowboys' coach Jimmy Johnson, after two consecutive Super Bowl championships, and then hiring in his stead Barry Switzer. Though Switzer's first regular season was successful, the Cowboys fell apart in the National Football Conference championship game against the San Francisco 49ers in mid-January 1995. Though the Cowboys looked strong early in the 1995 regular season, they suffered another devastating loss to the 49ers in mid-November and from then on looked vulnerable, though they rallied to end with a 12–4 record and home-field advantage throughout the playoffs. The question was: Would Dallas be able to win another Super Bowl, and would Jones fire Switzer if they did not? To help the team during 1995, Jones brought aboard the talented Deion Sanders; the two were widely seen in a commercial joking about Sanders' $35 million contract.

Jones also moved into direct confrontation with the National Football League in 1995. He signed lucrative sponsorship deals with Nike, Pepsi, and Dr. Pepper. The NFL charged that this was in direct competition with NFL Properties, owned by the team owners themselves, which makes cooperative marketing and licensing deals using team names, logos, and trademarks, and has current deals with now-unhappy sponsors such as Reebok and Coca-Cola. Jones denied this, saying these were deals with Texas Stadium, not the Cowboys as a team; he is one of only three league owners who own their own stadium. In September, the NFL filed a suit for $300 million in damages against Jones; in November, Jones filed a $750 million counter-suit.

Los Angeles–born Jones was raised in Arkansas and won a football scholarship to the University of Arkansas; he was guard and co-captain on the 1964 undefeated championship team, on which ex-Cowboys' coach Johnson was a teammate and Switzer an assistant coach. After Jones' 1965 graduation and his 1970 M.B.A. from Arkansas, he built a fortune in insurance, real estate, and oil and gas exploration. He bought the Dallas Cowboys in 1989, a year when they had a 1–15 record; after that the team turned around, winning the Super Bowl in the 1992 and 1993 seasons. Jones was named *Inc.*'s Entrepreneur of the Year in 1993. Jones and his wife, Gene Jones, have two sons and a daughter.

FURTHER READING

"Lone Cowboy." PETER CASTRO. *People,* Oct. 23, 1995.
"The ringmaster." PAUL ATTNER. *Sporting News,* Mar. 13, 1995.
"Playboy interview. . . ." LAWRENCE LINDERMAN. *Playboy,* Oct. 1994.
"Vain glory. . . ." GARY CARTWRIGHT. *Texas,* June 1994.
"Men will be boys. . . ." PAUL A. WITTEMAN. *Time,* Apr. 11, 1994.
"The man. . . ." CURRY KIRKPATRICK. *Newsweek,* Dec. 6, 1993.
"America's owner." DAVID WHITFORD. *Inc.,* Dec. 1993.

"King Cowboy." FRANK DEFORD. *Vanity Fair,* Nov. 1993.

Jones, Quincy (Quincy Delight Jones, Jr.; 1933–   ) In 1995 multifaceted popular entertainment figure Quincy Jones received one of the greatest of film industry honors, the Jean Hersholt Humanitarian Award, presented during the Academy Awards show.

Jones continued to pursue a wide range of entertainment business interests, including QwestBroadcasting, Qwest Records, rap music's *Vibe* magazine, QDE Entertainment, the Montreux Jazz Festival, syndicated television shows, and several films in development. At the same time, he focused on producing new records, a lifelong occupation. His 1995 album was the very well received *Q's Juke Joint,* in which he gathered a wide range of recording artists, from such classic figures as Ray Charles and Stevie Wonder to such popular figures as Gloria Estefan, Brandy, and a new voice, that of star-to-be Lamia, whose "Put a Move On My Heart" became a hit single that promised to begin a major career. Forthcoming were a series of works generated from the album, including a CD-ROM, a television movie version, and Lamia's debut album, slated for release in 1996. Jones was also working on an autobiography.

Chicago-born Jones has had a varied career, which over four decades has included arranging and working as a trumpeter with Lionel Hampton and Dizzy Gillespie, and arranging music for many of the leading singers of the 1950s and 1960s. In the 1960s, he was music director and producer for Mercury Records. He has composed and conducted many film scores. From 1969, he was a prolific recording artist, with such albums as *Walking in Space* (1969), *Smackwater Jack* (1971), and *Mellow Madness* (1975). He was also a producer, most notably of the Michael Jackson records *Off the Wall* (1980) *Thriller* (1982), and *Bad* (1987). Jones' 1989 album *Back on the Block* sold over a million copies and brought him six Grammy awards in 1991, making him the most honored pop artist in the history of the awards, with a total of 25 Grammys during his long career. His documentary *Listen Up: The Lives of Quincy Jones* was widely distributed in 1990. He produced incoming President Bill Clinton's inaugural show *An American Reunion: The People's Inaugural Celebration* (1993).

Jones attended the Berkeley College of Music and the Boston Conservatory. He and his wife, actress Nastassja Kinski, have a daughter.

FURTHER READING

"The piano next door. . . ." *Economist*, July 20, 1991.

Jones, Tommy Lee (1946–) Stage and screen actor Tommy Lee Jones made his writing and directing debuts in 1995 with the television film *The Good Old Boys*, in which he also starred. The cast included Sissy Spacek, Terry Kinney, Frances McDormand, Wilford Brimley, and Sam Shepard. Jones played modern cowboy Hewey Calloway, home visiting his brother in West Texas, who stays to help the family beat foreclosure and eviction.

Jones also starred in the commercial blockbuster *Batman Forever*, sequel to *Batman*, this time starring Val Kilmer in the title role, with Jones as villain Harvey Two-Face, Nicole Kidman as the love interest, Jim Carrey as the Riddler, and Chris O'Donnell as the teenage Boy Wonder, Robin.

Forthcoming was a starring role in Barry Sonnenfeld's film *Men in Black*, costarring Will Smith and Vincent D'Onofrio.

Texas-born Jones made his Broadway debut in *A Patriot for Me* (1969) and his film debut in *Love Story* (1970). He also appeared in several other New York stage productions, including *Ulysses in Nighttown* and *True West*. Among his films are *Jackson County Jail* (1976), *Rolling Thunder* (1977), *Coal Miner's Daughter* (1980), *Back Roads* (1981), *Nate and Hayes* (1983), *The River Rat* (1984), *Black Moon Rising* (1986), *The Big Town* (1987), *Stormy Monday* (1988), *The Package* (1989), *Fire Birds* (1990), *Blue Sky* (1991), *JFK* (1991; he received an Oscar nomination), *Heaven and Earth* (1993), *The Fugitive* (1993), *House of Cards* (1993), *Cobb* (1994), *Blue Sky* (1994), *The Client* (1994), *Blown Away* (1994), and *Natural Born Killers* (1994). He won an Emmy in the television film *The Executioner's Song* (1982); his many television appearances also include *Lonesome Dove* (1989). Jones's B.A. was from Harvard University. He is married to Kimberlea Cloughley, and has two children.

FURTHER READING

"Jones, Tommy Lee." *Current Biography,* Oct. 1995.
"Tommy Lee Jones." ELMER KELTON. *Interview,* June 1995.
"Texas ranger. . . ." ALLEN BARRA and MARION HART. *Entertainment,* Dec. 23, 1994.
"The good old boy." LUCY KAYLIN. *GQ,* Mar. 1994.
" 'Somebody's gonna. . . .' " GAVIN SMITH. *Film Comment,* Jan.–Feb. 1994.
"The fugitive. . . ." MIMI SWARTZ. *Texas,* Oct. 1993.
"Hot damn, he's good." RICHARD CORLISS. *Time,* Sept. 6, 1993.

Jordan, Michael Jeffrey (1963–) Rumor became reality in 1995, when Michael Jordan returned to the game at which he has so excelled: basketball. In early 1995, he was preparing for spring training as a minor leaguer in his second sport, baseball; it is unclear whether he would have remained had there not been a baseball strike. However, Jordan declared himself unwilling to get in between baseball's union and management, and by March he had decided to return to basketball and the Chicago Bulls, making his comeback, after 18 months, against the Indianapolis Pacers on March 19, 1995. His legs were a bit wobbly and his shot was a bit off, but even so Jordan posted an average of 26.9 points per game during the remainder of the regular season. What he was not able to do was fulfill his own dream and that of Bulls' fans: to

win another championship. Jordan and the Bulls got past Charlotte in the first round of the Eastern Conference playoffs, but in a hard-fought semifinals contest lost to Orlando in six games, despite Jordan's average of 31.5 points per game in the playoffs.

At the start of the 1995–96 season, the Bulls again looked strong and Jordan was in better basketball shape. At year's end, the team had a league-leading record of 25-3 and Jordan was tops in scoring, with an average of 30.0 points per game, and third in steals, with 2.39 a game. In the eyes of many, the Bulls were the team to beat in the Eastern Conference, and were tipped to meet the two-time defending champion Houston Rockets in the NBA Finals at season's end. Jordan's current contract expires at the end of the season.

Personally, Jordan continued his highly lucrative commercial endorsements, which bring him an estimated $30 million annually, and which make him the highest-paid athlete in the world, according to *Forbes* magazine. In August, during the off-season, Jordan played himself in a movie tentatively titled *Space Jam*, costarring cartoon characters such as Bugs Bunny, Daffy Duck, and Yosemite Sam, scheduled for late 1996 release.

He also published *I'm Back: More Rare Air*, an updated version of his best-selling memoir *Rare Air: Michael on Michael* (1993), both edited by Mark Vancil.

In April 1995, teenager Larry Martin Demery pleaded guilty to a first-degree murder charge in the 1993 killing of Jordan's father, James Jordan. He agreed to testify for the prosecution in the trial of the other person accused of the murder, Daniel Andre Green, (now known as Lord D. As-saddiq Al-amin Sallam U'allah), scheduled to start in January 1996. Both could face the death penalty. Jordan has said he would not attend out of concern that his appearance would turn the trial into a media circus.

Born in Brooklyn, Jordan graduated from Emsley A. Laney High School in Wilmington, North Carolina, then starred at the University of North Carolina (1981–84), on the team that won the NCAA national championship in 1982. Jordan himself was twice named *Sporting News* college player of the year (1983; 1984) and won the Naismith Award (1984). Leaving school after his junior year, he was—astonishingly—selected third in the NBA college draft, by the Chicago Bulls. He was NBA rookie of the year (1985); was named the league's Most Valuable Player three times (1988; 1991; 1992); was elected to the All-Star starting team for seven straight years (1987–93); and was also Most Valuable Player in the All-Star Game (1988), defensive player of the year (1988), and a member of the NBA All-Defense first team six straight times (1988–93). He led the Bulls to three straight championships (1991–93), being named MVP in all three playoffs, and won seven straight scoring titles (1987–93), only the second player ever to do so.

On October 6, 1993, Jordan voluntarily retired from basketball, and then decided to pursue a career in baseball, joining the "farm" system of the Chicago White Sox. In 1994, his No. 23 was retired and a 12-foot statue of him unveiled outside the Bulls' new United Center. At his 1993 retirement, Jordan was professional basketball's 15th leading scorer of all time, with 21,541 points, and held records for career scoring averages for the regular season (32.3 points per game), the playoffs (34.6), and the All-Star Game (21.0). He had scored 50 or more points 33 times, with a playoff record of 63 points in a 1986 game, and a record 23 consecutive points in a 1987 game. He was also on gold-medal-winning teams at the Olympics in 1984 and, with the "Dream Team," in 1992. Jordan's baseball performance, however, was generally mediocre, though he at least quadrupled attendance at every game he played. In 1994, he published *I Can't Accept Not Trying: Michael Jordan on the Pursuit of Excellence*, based on interviews with

Mark Vancil. Jordan and his wife, Juanita, have two sons and a daughter.

FURTHER READING

"Bull Market." DARRYL HOWERTON. *Sport,* Jan. 1996.

"The road home. . . ." BOB GREENE. *People,* Oct. 9, 1995.

"The greatest. . . ." WALTER LEAVY. *Ebony,* June 1995.

"Fresh air. . . ." LACY J. BANKS. *Sport,* June 1995.

"Two champs are back." STEVE WULF. *Time,* Apr. 3, 1995.

"Resurrection." PHIL TAYLOR. *Sports Illustrated,* Mar. 27, 1995.

"Hoop dreams." JOHN LELAND. *Newsweek,* Mar. 20, 1995.

"Chicago hope." MARK VANCIL. *Sporting News,* Mar. 20, 1995.

Michael Jordan. JAMES BECKETT. Ballantine, 1995.

Michael Jordan: A Biography. BILL GUTMAN. Pocket Books, 1995.

Michael Jordan: Basketball to Baseball and Back, rev. ed. BILL GUTMAN. Millbrook, 1995.

Rookie: When Michael Jordan Came to the Minor Leagues. JIM PATTON. Addison-Wesley, 1995.

Michael Jordan: Beyond Air. PHILIP BROOKS. Childrens, 1995.

Michael Jordan: A Shooting Star. GEORGE BEAHM. Andrews & McMeel, 1994.

Michael Jordan: A Life Above the Rim. ROBERT LIPSYTE. HarperCollins, 1994.

Sport Shots: Michael Jordan. CHIP LOVITT. Scholastic, 1994.

Michael Jordan: Star Guard. RON KNAPP. Enslow, 1994.

Michael Jordan, Basketball Great. SEAN DOLAN. Chelsea House, 1994.

"The untouchable." GEORGE CASTLE. "The golf course." STEVE GORDON. "Giving back." TERRY MULGANNON. "The price of fame." LACY J. BANKS. "Courting greatness." BOB RYAN. "The Jordan years." WILLIAM LADSON. *Sport,* Dec. 1993.

"A truly death-defying. . . ." RICHARD LAPCHICK. "Europe loses. . . ." IAN THOMSEN and TED RODGERS. "Retired or just tired?" PAUL ATTNER. "One loss. . . ." WILLIAM C. RHODEN. " 'The desire isn't there.' " JACK MCCALLUM. *Sports Illustrated,* Oct. 18, 1993.

Michael Jordan. CHIP LOVITT. Scholastic, 1993.

Hang Time: Days and Dreams with Michael Jordan. BOB GREENE. St. Martin's, 1992.

The Jordan Rules: The Inside Story of a Turbulent Season with Michael Jordan and the Chicago Bulls. SAM SMITH. Simon & Schuster, 1992.

Taking to the Air: The Rise of Michael Jordan. JIM NAUGHTON. Warner, 1992.

K

Kantor, Mickey (1939–) After 1994 Senate confirmation of the General Agreement on Tariffs and Trade (GATT), several massive and immediate trade deficit problems remained. Although U.S. trade representative Mickey Kantor hailed American export figures, it seemed clear that the 1995 trade deficit would once again exceed $100 billion, with Japanese and Chinese trade imbalances leading the way. Even the North American Free Trade Agreement (NAFTA) seemed headed for a combined $25 billion-plus trade deficit.

Kantor spent 1995 working on the specific imbalances, with his main focus on Japan and China, and a secondary focus on Canada; with Mexico in financial crisis, Mexican exports to the U.S. far exceeded imports. In late June, after U.S.-Japanese automotive trade talks had broken down, and just before punitive U.S. tariffs on imported Japanese cars were to go into effect, Kantor and Japanese trade minister Ryutaro Hashimoto announced an agreement that averted the threatened trade war. However, Kantor's version of the substance of the modest, nonbinding agreement was immediately disputed by the Japanese. Kantor and Chinese trade minister Wu Yi also signed a wide-ranging agreement on U.S.-Chinese trade issues, which did not perceptibly alter the pace or amount of the growing trade imbalance between the two countries. Several long-running Canadian-U.S. agricultural product trade disputes continued.

Nashville-born Kantor received his 1961 B.A. from Vanderbilt University, and his 1967 LL.B. from Georgetown University. In 1967, he and Valerie Kantor, then his wife, founded the federally funded South Florida Migrant Labor Services organization, and during the Carter years he served on the board of directors of the Legal Services Corporation, there meeting and becoming a friend of Hillary Rodham Clinton. In 1975, Kantor became a partner in the Los Angeles law firm of Manatt, Phelps, Phillips, and Kantor, also becoming active in California Democratic politics. In 1992, he was a leader of the Clinton presidential campaign. After the election, he was appointed U.S. trade representative by President Bill Clinton.

FURTHER READING

"Kantor, Mickey." *Current Biography*, Mar. 1994.
"Trade warrior." Dan Goodgame. *Time*, Mar. 15, 1993.

Kasparov, Gary (Garry [Garri] Kimovich Kasparov; 1963–) Gary Kasparov has been acknowledged as the world's greatest living chess player for ten years, since he became the youngest chess champion ever in 1985, at 22. In 1993, he and British chess-player Nigel Short left the International Chess Federation (FIDE) to found the Professional Chess Association, attempting to establish a regular competitive circuit, like those in tennis and golf, with commercial sponsorship, large prizes, and television fees. As part of this move, the PCA sponsored a highly publicized 20-game tournament, starting in September 1995, between Kasparov and Indian chess-player Vishy (Viswanathan) Anand, who ranked second in the world and who had defeated Kasparov earlier in 1995 as part a World Chess Grand Prix speed tournament.

Played in a soundproof booth at the World Trade Center in New York City, the Kasparov-Anand match was televised around the world with move-by-move analysis by grandmasters, with moves also carried live on the Internet. After 30 days and 18 games, Kasparov eventually won the tournament, 10 1/2-7 1/2, taking the $900,000 purse (Anand got $450,000). Whether Kasparov succeeded in his wider objective remained to be seen. Unfortunately, an unprecedented series of eight draws at the start of the tournament caused considerable loss of the public interest initially generated by the charismatic Kasparov.

Though hard feelings existed between FIDE adherents and PCA, Kasparov seemed to have arranged a rapprochement with the better-established group, with the possibility of a future championship between titleholders from the two organizations. At year's end, the FIDE title remained in limbo, Kasparov and Short having been stripped of their FIDE credentials, and a new FIDE champion not having been recognized.

Early in 1995, Kasparov the latest in his series of chess books: *Garry Kasparov's Chess Puzzle Book.*

Born in Baku, Azerbaijan, Kasparov has been a leading chess player since the mid-1970s. He won the Azerbaijan championship and the Soviet junior championship in 1975, was World junior champion in 1980, and Soviet champion in 1981. Between 1984 and 1990, Kasparov and Anatoly Karpov played five world championship matches. The 1984 match was discontinued because both players were ill, so Karpov retained his world title. But in 1985, Kasparov defeated Karpov, successfully fighting off Karpov's attempts to retake the title in 1986, 1987, and 1990, as well as Nigel Short's 1993 challenge. In 1989, he won the World Chess Cup; in that year, his world life chess rating reached a record-breaking 2,795, passing Bobby Fischer's rating of 2,780. Kasparov has published several books on chess, including *Kasparov vs. Karpov, 1990* (1991; with several co-authors), *Learn Chess with Gary Kasparov* (1994), and works on great chess openings. He is separated from Maria Kasparova, whom he married in 1989; they have a daughter.

FURTHER READING

Mortal Games: The Turbulent Genius of Garry Kasparov. FRED WAITZKIN. Putnam, 1993.
Gary Kasparov's Best Games. RAYMOND KEENE. Holt, 1993.
"The new opposition." WILLIAM D. EGGERS. *Reason,* July 1991.
Kasparov's Chess Openings: A World Champion's Repertoire. Otto Borik. Trafalgar, 1991.

Kay, Ulysses (1917–95) Tucson-born composer and educator Ulysses Kay received his 1938 B.A. in music at the University of Arizona and his 1940 M.A. at the Eastman School, doing postgraduate work at Yale and Columbia. He was an editorial advisor to Broadcast Music, Inc. (BMI) in the 1950s and 1960s, and was a professor of music for more than two decades at the Herbert H. Lehman College of the City University of New York, starting in 1968. A prolific composer, largely in the modernist, dissonant styles of his time, African-American Kay was often reviewed as a Black composer, although only some of his work reflected African-American historical concerns, notably two operas: *Jubilee* (1976) and *Frederick Douglass* (1991), both featuring anti-slavery and Civil War themes. Among his other works were the operas *The Boor, The Juggler of Our Lady,* and *The Capitoline Venus;* "Overture to New Horizons," generated by a 1958 Soviet-American cultural exchange; the ballet *Danse Calinda; Concerto for Orchestra,* and other symphonic, chamber, and choral works. He was survived by his wife and three daughters. (d. Englewood, New Jersey; May 20, 1995)

FURTHER READING

Obituary. *Down Beat,* Sept. 1995.
Obituary. *New York Times,* May 23, 1995.
Ulysses Kay: A Bio-Bibliography. CONSTANCE T. HOBSON and DEBORRA A. RICHARDSON. Greenwood, 1994.

Keaton, Diane (1946–) Actress and director Diane Keaton in 1995 again starred as Nina Banks in the film comedy *Father of the Bride Part II,* directed by Charles Shyer and cowritten by Nancy Meyers and Shyer. A sequel to *Father of the Bride* (1991), it costarred Steve

Martin in the title role as her husband and Kimberley Williams as their daughter. The film's comic possibilities spring from the fact that both mother and daughter are pregnant. Keaton also directed the very well received comedy-drama film *Unstrung Heroes*, starring John Turturro and Andie MacDowell, in a cast that included Nathan Watt, Michael Richards, Maury Chaykin, and Kendra Krull.

Keaton was nominated for an Emmy as best lead actress for her title role in the television film *Amelia Earhart: The Final Flight* (1994), a role that also brought her a Screen Actors Guild nomination as best actress in a television film or miniseries

Forthcoming were starring roles in the film *Marvin's Room*, directed by Jerry Zaks and co-starring Robert De Niro, Meryl Streep, Leonardo Dicaprio, Hume Cronyn, Gwen Verdon, and Hal Scardino; and opposite Bette Midler in the film *The First Wives Club*, directed by P. J. Hogan.

California-born Keaton made the transition from the New York theater to Hollywood in Woody Allen's *Play It Again Sam*, starring opposite Allen on Broadway in 1971 and again in the 1972 film version. She was Michael Corleone's wife in the classic *Godfather* films (1972; 1974), won a best actress Oscar for Allen's *Annie Hall* (1977), and also starred in his *Interiors* (1978) and *Manhattan* (1979). She went on to star in such films as *Reds* (1981), *The Little Drummer Girl* (1984), *Crimes of the Heart* (1986), *Radio Days* (1987), *The Godfather Part III* (1990, reprising her Kay Corleone role), *The Lemon Sisters* (1990), *Father of the Bride* (1991), *Manhattan Murder Mystery* (1993), and *Look Who's Talking Now* (1993). In 1991, she directed *Wildflower*, her first full-length television film. Her starring roles in television also include *Running Mates* (1992) and *Amelia Earhart: The Final Flight* (1994). She was a student at New York's Neighborhood Playhouse in 1968.

FURTHER READING

"Annie Hall. . . ." Nancy Collins. *Vanity Fair,* Nov. 1995.
"Undone heroes." Nancy Jo Sales. *New York,* Sept. 18, 1995.
"Plane speaking." Benjamin Svetkey. *Entertainment,* June 10, 1994.
"Keaton's comeback." Sean Elder. *Vogue,* Sept. 1993.
"Diane in La-La Land." Patrick Pacheco. *Connoisseur,* Jan. 1992.

Keitel, Harvey (1941–) Actor Harvey Keitel starred in one of the few 1995 movies likely to become a film classic. The work was *Ulysses' Gaze*, produced and directed by Theo Angelopoulos, a story set in the Bosnian War, with Keitel as a documenary filmmaker in search of the work of two turn-of-the-century Greek filmmakers. His search takes him to besieged Sarajevo and to the Bosnian film archivist, played by Erland Josephson, who ultimately becomes the center of the film. Angelopoulos' work was thought by many to be the best artistic portrayal so far of the Bosnian tragedy and of the greater tragedy that is the nearly perpetual series of wars that has plagued the Balkans for many centuries, with no end in sight.

In a wholly different kind of role, the versatile star played a homicide detective in the film *Clockers*, Spike Lee's study of the violence within African-American communities that often accompanies the drug trade and is inspired by the macho, moneyed images conveyed to young people by drug dealers. Costarring were John Turturro as his partner, Delroy Lindo as a drug dealer, Mikti Phifer in the killer's role, and Isaiah Washington as Phifer's brother, who tries to make a false confession to save him.

A third starring role came as Brooklyn cigar store owner Augie in Wayne Wang's film *Smoke*, costarring William Hurt, Stockard Channing, Harold Perrineau, Forest Whitaker, and Ashley Judd. Keitel starred again as Augie in Wang's quickly-made sequel, *Blue in the Face*, in a cast that included Roseanne, Lily Tomlin, Madonna, Lou Reed, Michael J. Fox, and Jim Jarmusch. He also played a cameo role in Barry Sonnenfeld's Hollywood-set film comedy *Get Shorty*, starring John Travolta and Gene Hackman.

Forthcoming was a starring role in the film comedy *Head Above Water*, directed by Jim Wilson and costarring Cameron Diaz and Craig Sheffer.

Brooklyn-born Keitel spent the early part of his career in supporting roles in the theater. He made his film debut in *Who's That Knocking at My Door?* (1968), and broke through into strong supporting film roles in Martin Scorsese's *Mean Streets* (1973), followed by such films as *Alice Doesn't Live Here Anymore* (1975), *Taxi Driver* (1976), *Mother Jugs and Speed* (1976), *Buffalo Bill and the Indians* (1976), *The Border* (1981), *Nemo* (1983), *Wise Guys* (1986), *The Last Temptation of Christ* (1988), *The Two Jakes* (1990), *Bugsy* (1991; he received an Oscar nomination),

Thelma and Louise (1991), *Sister Act* (1992), *Reservoir Dogs* (1992), *The Piano* (1993), *Rising Sun* (1993), *Snake Eyes* (1993), *Pulp Fiction* (1994), *Somebody to Love* (1994), *Monkey Trouble* (1994), and *Imaginary Crimes* (1994). He has also appeared in many television films. Keitel studied acting with several leading teachers and at the Actors Studio. He was formerly married.

FURTHER READING

"Harvey Keitel." LAWRENCE GROBEL. *Playboy,* Nov. 1995.
"Keitel, Harvey." *Current Biography,* Mar. 1994.
"Heaven, hell. . . ." NICK TOSCHES. *Esquire*, Sept. 1993.
"Harvey Keitel. . . ." JULIAN SCHNABEL. *Interview*, Dec. 1992.

Kelly, Nancy (1921–95) Massachusetts-born Nancy Kelly grew up in New York City, where she became a child actress and model; one of her earliest major roles was in Rachel Crothers' Broadway play *Susan and God* (1937). She also played children's roles in several films of the late 1920s and early 1930s. From the late 1930s through the mid-1940s, she played leading and strong supporting adult roles in several films, among them *Jesse James* (1939), *Stanley and Livingstone* (1939), and *To the Shores of Tripoli* (1942). She emerged as a leading actress on Broadway in the 1950s, in her Tony-winning role as the mother of a psychotic child in Maxwell Anderson's play *The Bad Seed* (1954). She re-created the role in the 1956 film version of the play, winning an Oscar nomination. Much of her later career was in the theater. She was survived by a daughter. (d. Bel Air, California; January 2, 1995)

FURTHER READING

Obituary. *Independent,* Jan. 20, 1995.
Obituary. *Variety,* Jan. 18, 1995.
Obituary. *New York Times*, Jan. 14, 1995.

Keneally, Thomas Michael (1935–) Best-known as the man who wrote *Schindler's List*, Thomas Keneally published his 21st work of fiction in 1995: *The River Town*, a novel based on his grandparents' life as Irish immigrants in a small town in New South Wales, Australia. He envisions the work as the first part of a trilogy, which will follow Tim and Kitty Shea and their son Johnny through the beginnings of World War I. Keneally is also working on a nonfiction book that focuses on political prisoners transported by the British from Ireland to Australia who later escaped and came to America; it was partly inspired by research into the career of a great-uncle who made a new life in Los Angeles, after being transported to Australia in 1865.

The continuing popularity of the film *Schindler's List* boosted sales of Keneally's novel, and *Publishers Weekly* reported in 1995 that it was the best-selling trade paperback of 1994, with more than 1.1 million copies sold. Late 1994 also saw publication of the second edition of his children's book *Ned Kelly and the City of Bees*. In July 1995, Keneally ended his four-year tenure as Distinguished Professor of English at the University of California at Irvine, returning to his home in Australia.

Sydney-born Keneally is one of Australia's leading authors. After initially studying for the priesthood, he became a writer. His first major work was the novel *Bring Larks and Heroes* (1967), followed by *The Survivor* (1969), *The Chant of Jimmie Blacksmith* (1972), *Blood Red, Sister Rose* (1974), *Season in Purgatory* (1976), *Passenger* (1978), and *Confederates* (1979). He became a world figure with publication of *Schindler's Ark* (1982; in America *Schindler's List*), written at the urging of a Los Angeles shopkeeper who had been one of those saved; the work won Britain's prestigious Booker Prize (1983) and became the basis of Steven Spielberg's classic, Academy Award-winning film *Schindler's List* (1993). Among Keneally's other fictional works are *Outback* (1983), *The Playmaker* (1987), *To Asmara* (1990), *Flying Hero Class* (1991), *A Family Madness* (1993), and *Woman of the Inner Sea* (1993). He has also published *The Place Where Souls Are Born: A Journey into the Southwest* (1992) and *Now and in Time to Be: Ireland and the Irish* (1992). Keneally is also founder and past chairperson of the Australian Republic Movement, seeking to end constitutional ties with Britain. He is married to Judith Mary Martin; they have two daughters.

FURTHER READING

"Thomas Keneally. . . ." SYBIL STEINBERG. *Publishers Weekly*, Apr. 3, 1995.
Australian Melodramas: Thomas Keneally's Fiction. PETER PIERCE. International Specialized Book Services, 1995.

Kennedy, Anthony McLeod (1936–)

Although often described as a "swing" vote on the Court in previous years, Justice Anthony Kennedy moved decisively toward conservative positions on several key issues during 1995, and therefore had a great deal to do with the Court's pronounced conservative cast.

Kennedy wrote two landmark majority opinions: In *Rosenberg Rector and Visitors of the University of Virginia*, writing for a 5–4 majority, he found that the publicly funded University of Virginia was required to finance a Christian magazine run by students, signaling a sharp change of Court directon on a basic constitutional issue. And in *Miller* v. *Johnson*, again writing for a 5–4 majority, he found that Georgia's eleventh congressional district was unconstitutional because it was organized primarily to provide racial representation, rather than to respond to specific discrimination. The decision was widely viewed as threatening the legality of scores of recently redrawn congressional districts.

Kennedy also joined the 5–4 majority in the landmark *U.S.* v. *Lopez* case, declaring unconstitutional the federal Gun-Free School Zones Act of 1990, which made possession of a gun within 1,000 feet of a school illegal, as an invalid extension of the congressional ability to regulate interstate commerce; in the landmark *Adarand Constructors* v. *Pena* ruling, which required that the federal government use the same strict standards as the states in carrying out affirmative action programs, reversing the Court's long-held position on federal affirmative action programs; and in the *Missouri* v. *Jenkins* decision, effectively limiting the level of state spending to carry out a federally managed school desegregation plan in Kansas City. Kennedy swung toward the liberal side in the landmark *U.S. Term Limits Inc.* v. *Thornton* case, writing a concurring opinion as part of a 5–4 majority, ruling that to limit Congressional terms required a constitutional amendment; 23 state laws imposing term limits were invalidated and Congress was barred from passing a term limits law.

Kennedy joined the majority in *Capital Square Review and Advisory Board* v. *Pinette*, ruling that it was unconstitutional to bar display of a large Ku Klux Klan cross in an Ohio public park; in *Veronia School District* v. *Acton*, ruling that an Oregon school district's random drug testing program was constitutional; and in *Babbitt* v. *Sweet Home Chapter of Communities for a Greater Oregon*, ruling that the federal government had the right under the Endangered Species Act to sharply restrict logging and other activities harmful to the northern spotted owl. He wrote a sharp dissent in *Florida Bar* v. *Went For It Inc.*, a decision that found valid a Florida state law barring lawyers from direct mail solicitation of people injured in accidents and their relatives for 30 days after the accident, calling the law a violation of First Amendment free speech guarantees.

California-born Kennedy was appointed to the Sacramento-based Ninth Circuit U.S. Court of Appeals in 1975; he had been recommended for the post by then-California governor Ronald Reagan. Thirteen years later, in 1988, President Reagan appointed him to the Supreme Court, after the earlier nomination of Robert Bork was rejected by the Senate. Kennedy's 1958 B.A. was from Stanford, his 1961 LL.B. from Harvard. He is married to Mary Davis; they have three children.

FURTHER READING

Anthony Kennedy. BOB ITALIA. Abdo and Daughters, 1992.
"A new day in court." LAUREN TARSHIS and JAMES EARL HARDY. *Scholastic Update*, Nov. 1, 1991.

Kennedy, Edward: See Kennedy, Ted.

Kennedy, Rose Fitzgerald (1890–1995)

Boston-born Rose Fitzgerald was the daughter of Boston mayor John "Honey Fitz" Fitzgerald; she was to lead a politics-filled life, starting with her experience of the Boston Irish political world of her youth. After graduating from Manhattanville College, Rose Fitzgerald returned to Boston, there in 1914 marrying Joseph Patrick Kennedy, who was to become a major financier; a leading Democrat, in 1934 he became the first head of the Securities and Exchange Commission, and was ambassador to Great Britain (1937–40). Among their nine children were John, Robert, and Edward Kennedy. She published an autobiography, *Times to Remember* (1974).

Rose Kennedy became part of an American legend on the death of her son, John Fitzgerald Kennedy, the 35th president of the United States, who was assassinated in Dallas, Texas on November 22, 1963. Five years later, another one of her sons, presidential candidate Robert (Bobby) Francis Kennedy was assassinated. She was survived by her son Senator Edward Kennedy and four daughters. Several of her grandchildren are following political careers, in what has become the family tradition. (d. Hyannis Port, Massachusetts, January 22, 1995).

FURTHER READING

"The sorrow and the strength." BRAD DARRACH. *Life,* Mar. 1995.
"Death of a matriarch. . . ." ELIZABETH GLEICK. *Time,* Feb. 6, 1995.
"The last matriarch." MARK GOODMAN. *People,* Feb. 6, 1995.
"Rose Kennedy. . . ." COLMAN MCCARTHY. *National Catholic Reporter,* Feb. 3, 1995.
Obituary. *Times* (of London), Jan. 24, 1995.
Obituary. *Independent,* Jan. 24, 1995.
Obituary. *New York Times,* Jan. 23, 1995.
Rose: The Life and Times of Rose Fitzgerald Kennedy. CHARLES HIGHAM. Pocket Books, 1995.
Rose Kennedy. SUSAN B. SIMONELLI. Chelsea House, 1992.

Kennedy, Ted (Edward Moore Kennedy; 1932–)

After coming from behind to win reelection in 1994, Massachusetts Democrat Senator Ted Kennedy resumed his position as a major liberal figure in the Senate. Throughout 1995, he maintained a set of classic liberal positions, while in speech after speech, on and off the Senate floor, he extolled the virtues of conscience, the New Deal social service network, civil rights, a national healthcare program—in short, he functioned as a liberal Democratic and Kennedy family elder statesman for American liberals in a time of conservative Republican ascendancy. During 1995, Kennedy was often one of a small group of senators who sharply opposed some of President Bill Clinton's concessions to the Republican majority, as on many aspects of the Republican welfare bill, which they felt warred on children and poor women; and on the administration's proposed antiterrorism bill, which Kennedy felt might go much too far in damaging civil liberties, a position also taken by many Senate conservatives.

On the personal side, Kennedy's mother, Rose Fitzgerald Kennedy, died at the age of 105.

Boston-born Kennedy is the fourth son of Joseph and Rose Fitzgerald Kennedy, and the brother of President John Fitzgerald Kennedy, assassinated in 1963, and Senator Robert Francis Kennedy, assassinated while a presidential candidate in 1968. He has represented Massachusetts in the Senate since 1963. He probably would have been his party's presidential candidate in 1972 or later elections, but for the 1969 Chappaquiddick incident, in which he left the scene of a fatal accident.

After U.S. Army service (1952–53), Kennedy received his 1956 B.A. from Harvard University, studied at the International Law School in The Hague, and received his 1959 LL.B. from the University of Virginia. Kennedy was formerly married to Virginia Joan Bennett, and has a daughter and two sons. In 1992 he married Washington lawyer Victoria Reggie, who has a daughter and a son.

FURTHER READING

"Last hurrah. . . ." DOUG IRELAND. *Nation,* Nov. 14, 1994.
"Steady Teddy. . . ." DAVE BRUDNOY. *National Review,* Nov. 7, 1994.
"Kennedy diplomacy." LESLIE COCKBURN and ANDREW COCKBURN. *Vanity Fair,* Nov. 1994.
"November song." BURTON HERSH. *Esquire,* Sept. 1994.
"Is Ted Kennedy's. . . ." GEORGE HOWE COLT and KEN REGAN. *Life,* Aug. 1994.
"Chappaquiddick's. . . ." MICHAEL R. BESCHLOSS. *New Yorker,* July 25, 1994.

"Biography or soap opera?" PAUL GRAY. *Time*, July 12, 1993.

The Last Brother. JOE MCGINNISS. Simon & Schuster, 1993.

Senator: My Ten Years with Ted Kennedy. RICHARD E. BURKE. St. Martin's, 1993.

Good Ted, Bad Ted: The Two Faces of Edward M. Kennedy. LESTER DAVID. Birch Lane/Carol, 1993.

Kessler, David Aaron (1952–) Continuing to make an extraordinary contribution to the health and safety of Americans and to the quality of American life, Food and Drug Administration (FDA) director David Kessler in 1995 once again pursued a very wide range of health and safety issues, focusing even more on tobacco addiction and going forward on such matters as the safety and effectiveness of new drugs and vaccines, some of them genetically engineeered; truth in labeling; clear and complete consumer drug information; and the multifold inspection and compliance tasks that comprise most of the FDA's day-to-day work.

By far the most controversial and far-reaching of Kessler's projects in 1995 was his—and the FDA's—attack on cigarettes as the cause of nicotine addiction. Reflecting that view, President Bill Clinton in early August accepted the FDA's view that nicotine was a naturally addictive drug, and therefore could lawfully be regulated by the FDA, and approved the issuance of new FDA rules aimed at cutting teenage smoking, which had been on the rise. Antismoking advocates welcomed the proposed rules; the major tobacco companies immediately sued to prevent their adoption.

A magna cum laude graduate of Amherst College, Kessler received his 1978 LL.B. from the University of Chicago and his 1979 medical degree from Harvard University Medical School. He also took courses at the New York University Graduate School of Business Administration. His residency was in pediatrics at Johns Hopkins, while in the same period he was a consultant to the Senate Labor and Human Resources Committee (1981–84). He was attached to New York's Montefiore Medical Center (1984–91), the last six years as director of the Jack D. Weiler Hospital, part of the Montefiore-Albert Einstein Hospital complex. He also taught food and drug law at Columbia Law School (1986–90) and served on a Health and Human Services commission set up to review the operation of the

FDA before taking over as its director in 1991. Kessler reorganized and revitalized the FDA, quickly and effectively moving against false and misleading food labeling, speeding up evaluation and approval procedures, greatly limiting the use of silicon gel breast implants, and turning the agency into a strongly activist health protector. Incoming President Bill Clinton asked him to stay on. Kessler is married to lawyer Paulette Steinberg; they have two children.

FURTHER READING

"Under a microscope. . . ." MAGGIE MAHAR. *Barron's*, Mar. 2, 1992.

"An apple a day." MARLENE CIMONS. *Runner's World*, Feb. 1992.

"Kessler, David Aaron." *Current Biography*, Sept. 1991.

"A shot in the arm. . . ." HERBERT BURKHOLZ. *New York Times Magazine*, June 30, 1991.

"The enforcer. . . ." *Newsweek*, May 27, 1991.

Kevorkian, Jack (1928–) During 1995, Dr. Jack Kevorkian continued to press his campaign for physician-assisted suicide, which he calls *medicide*, and for which he has invented various types of suicide devices. In 1995, the U.S. Supreme Court refused to hear Kevorkian's appeal of a Michigan Supreme Court ruling that a state law barring assisted suicide was unconstitutional. That made it possible for the state to try Kevorkian on several pending charges, including murder; trial was set for early 1996. Despite that, Kevorkian assisted in several more suicides during the year. In one case, Kevorkian left the body near a county sheriff's office; in another in a hospital parking lot; in a third in a county medical examiner's parking lot. In the latter case, he used the homemade "suicide machine" he had used in his first two assisted suicides; in others, he used carbon monixide, his choice in most of the assisted suicides. Also in the last case, the county medical examiner disputed Kevorkian's diagnosis, saying that the woman who committed suicide was not ill with terminal cancer. The national dispute over the legality and humanity of assisted suicide continued, with Kevorkian at its center.

Born and educated in Michigan, Kevorkian was licensed as a physician in 1953; he worked as a pathologist at the Pacific Hospital in Long Beach, California, until 1982, and is now retired.

He first came to public attention in April 1990, when he described his suicide machine on the "Donahue" show. Janet Adkins, a 54-year-old English professor suffering from the early stages of Alzheimer's disease, saw the show and two months later used his machine to kill herself. First-degree murder charges were brought against Kevorkian, but then dropped. He has in all assisted at 26 suicides. An advocate of euthanasia throughout his medical career, he has published various books and articles on the subject, most notably *Prescription: Medicine: The Goodness of Planned Death* (1991).

FURTHER READING

"Getting to know . ." MARK JANNOT. *Playboy*, Aug. 1994.
"Death becomes him." JACK LESSENBERRY, *Vanity Fair*, July 1994.
"The real. . . ." MARK HOSENBALL. *Newsweek*, Dec. 6, 1993.
"Kevorkian speaks. . . ." "Rx for death." NANCY GIBBS. *Time*, May 31, 1993.
"A conversation with. . . ." FRANK WASHINGTON and TODD BARRETT. *Newsweek*, Mar. 8, 1993.
Dr. Death: Murder or Mercy? Jack Kevorkian's Rx: Death: The Trials of Jack Kevorkian. THOMAS OEHMKE. Lifetime, 1993.

Khallafalla, Fares: See Abdel Rahman, Omar.

Khomeini, Hojatoleslam Ahmad

(1945–95) The son of Iran's late fundamentalist leader Ayatollah Ruhollah Khomeini, Ahmad Khomeini was born and grew up in Qom, in northern Iran. When his father was exiled during the reign of Shah Mohammed Reza Pahlevi in the mid-1960s, Ahmad remained in Iran, until the death of his elder brother, Mustafa, in 1977. He then joined Ayatollah Khomeini in exile, becoming his father's key aide, and continuing in that capacity through the 1979 return to Iran, the Iranian Revolution, Khomeini's seizure of power, the Iran hostage crisis, and the Iran-Iraq war. He spoke always as a fundamentalist radical militant, and was particularly prominent during the 1979-1980 Iran hostage crisis. Like his father, Ahmad Khomeini was a Muslim cleric. After his father's death in 1989, he waged a political struggle to take power, but was quickly defeated by Hashemi Rafsanjani, who was elected to the presidency in 1989. Ahmad Khomeini retained his great prestige, and was a member of Iran's National Security Council and administrator of his father's memorial, near Tehran. He was survived by his wife and three sons. (d. Tehran; March 17, 1995)

FURTHER READING

Obituary. *Times* (of London), Mar. 20, 1995.
Obituary. *New York Times*, Mar. 18, 1995.

Kilmer, Val

(1959–) Film star Val Kilmer in 1995 played the title role in the second "Batman" sequel, *Batman Forever*, which became a worldwide commercial hit. Costarring were Tommy Lee Jones as the villainous Harvey Two-Face; Nicole Kidman as the love interest; Jim Carrey as The Riddler; Chris O'Donnell as the teenage Boy Wonder, Robin; Michael Gough; Pat Hingle; and Drew Barrymore.

Kilmer also starred in the very well received underworld film *Heat*, written and directed by Michael Mann. He played Chris Shiherlis, second in command to master criminal Neil McCauley (Robert De Niro), both of them playing opposite Al Pacino as top-notch Los Angeles detective Vincent Hanna, who ultmately defeats them. While a highly violent cops-and-robbers genre work, the film also focuses on the personal lives of many of its large cast of characters, and conveys Mann's deeply pessimistic view of modern American urban life.

Kilmer also appeared in a small role as a pioneer aviator in the docudrama adventure film *Wings of Courage*, produced, directed, and co-written by Jean-Jacques Annaud. Forthcoming were starring roles opposite Michael Douglas in the film *The Ghost and the Darkness*, directed by Stephen Hopkins; and as Simon Templar in the film *The Saint*, based on the Leslie Charteris mystery novel series.

On the personal side, he and his wife, Joanne Whalley-Kilmer, announced in mid-1995 that they were divorcing after seven years of marriage; they have a son and a daughter.

Los Angeles-born Kilmer began his acting career on stage, in 1981 appearing in *Electra and Orestes* and *Henry IV, Part One*. He made his

Broadway debut in *Slab Boys* (1983). His film debut came in *Top Secret* (1984), and he played supporting roles in the films *Real Genius* (1985), *Top Gun* (1986), *Willow* (1988), and *Kill Me Again* (1989). His breakthrough starring role came as rock star Jim Morrison in *The Doors* (1991). He also appeared in *Thunderheart* (1991), *True Romance* (1993), *The Real McCoy* (1993), and *Tombstone* (1993), and in several television films. Kilmer attended the Hollywood Professional School and the Juilliard School.

FURTHER READING

"Forget forever. . . ." JENNIFER KORNREICH. *People,* Aug. 7, 1995.
" 'The more we love . . . .' " ELINOR KLEIN. *Parade,* July 9, 1995.
"Val Kilmer." REBECCA ASCHER-WALSH. *Entertainment,* June 30, 1995.

King, Stephen (1947–) Stephen King's works have always been notable for their strong characterizations of women. His 1995 novel, *Rose Madder*, continued that tradition, the title character being a battered wife who finally flees, only to be stalked by her chillingly portrayed, deadly husband. Not surprisingly, given King's track record, the book became a best-seller, even though King declined to do a promotional tour.

Taking a lead from 19th-century writers, King has signed to do a book to be serialized in monthly installments, starting in 1996. The novel, tentatively titled *The Green Mile*, features death row inmates in a 1930s Southern penitentiary.

A number of King's novels have been tapped for Spanish-language American publication, both as print and audio books. The first of them, *Los Langoliers*, was published in May to coincide with the television miniseries *The Langoliers*, starring Patricia Wettig, Bronson Pinchot, Dean Stockwell, David Morse, and 12-year-old Kate Maberly, and scripted and directed by Tom Holland. The novella was originally published in a four-story collection *Four Past Midnight* (1990).

The feature film version of King's *Dolores Claiborne* was released in 1995, starring Kathy Bates in another notable King role, along with Jennifer Jason Leigh, Judy Parfitt, Christopher Plummer, David Strathairn, and Eric Bogosian; it was scripted by Tony Gilroy and directed by Taylor Hackford. In the works was *Stephen King's Thinner*, written and directed by Tom Holland; with a cast including Robert John Burke, Michael Constantine, and Lucinda Jenney. King himself appeared on television as a contestant on *Celebrity Jeopardy* in November 1995.

Maine-born King received his 1970 B.S. from the University of Maine, then taught English at the Hampden Academy (1971–73) before embarking on his writing career. Among his many novels are *Carrie* (1974), *Salem's Lot* (1975), *The Shining* (1976), *The Stand* (1978; republished uncut, 1990), *Firestarter* (1980), *Danse Macabre* (1981), *Cujo* (1981), *Pet Sematary* (1983), *The Talisman, Cycle of the Werewolf* (1985), *Skeleton Crew* (1986), *The Eyes of the Dragon* (1987), *Misery* (1987), *The Tommyknockers* (1987), *The Dark Half* (1989), *Four Past Midnight* (1990), *Needful Things* (1991), *Gerald's Game* (1992), *Dolores Claiborne* (1992), *Insomnia* (1994), and the *Dark Tower* series: *The Gunslinger* (1982), *The Drawing of the Three* (1987), and *The Waste Lands* (1991). He has also published many short stories and short screenplays, as well as novels under the name of Richard Bachman, including *Rage* (1977), *The Long Walk* (1979), *Roadwork* (1981), *The Running Man* (1982), and *Thinner* (1984).

Many of King's works have been adapted for film or television, among them *Carrie* (1976), *The Shining* (1980), *Christine* (1983), *The Dead Zone* (1983), *Stand By Me* (1986; based on *The Body*), *The Running Man* (1987), *Pet Sematary* (1989), *Misery* (1990), *The Dark Half* (1993),

Needful Things (1993), *The Tommyknockers* (1993), *The Stand* (1994), and *The Shawshank Redemption* (1994), based on King's novella, *Rita Hayworth and Shawshank Redemption*; King himself directed from his own scripts *Children of the Corn* (1984) and *Maximum Overdrive* (1986). He also wrote an original screenplay for *Stephen King's Sleepwalkers* (1992). King married Tabitha Jane Spruce in 1971; they have three children.

FURTHER READING

The Stephen King Companion, rev. ed. GEORGE BEAHM. Andrews and McMeel, 1995.
Stephen King. AMY KEYISHIAN and MARJORIE KEYISHIAN. Chelsea House, 1995.
Scaring Us to Death: The Impact of Stephen King on Popular Culture, 2nd ed. MICHAEL R. COLLINS. Borgo, 1995.
Stephen King A to Z: A Dictionary of People, Places and Things in the Works of the King of Horror. STEPHEN J. SPIGNESI. Popular Culture, 1995.
Observations from the Terminator: Thoughts on Stephen King and Other Modern Masters of Horror Fiction. TYSON BLUE. Borgo, 1995.
The Work of Stephen King: An Annotated Bibliography and Guide. MICHAEL R. COLLINGS. Borgo Press, 1994.
The Films of Stephen King. ANN LLOYD. St. Martin's, 1994.
Writers Dreaming—Dreamers Writing: 25 Writers Discuss Dreams and the Creative Process. NAOMI EPEL. Crown, 1993.
Stephen King: Master of Horror. ANNE SAIDMAN. Lerner, 1992.
"Stephen King." MARK MARVEL. *Interview*, Oct. 1991.
Stephen King: Man and Artist, rev. ed. CARROL F. TERRELL. North Lights, 1991.
The Stephen King Story. GEORGE BEAHM. Andrews & McMeel, 1991.

Kingsley, Sidney (1906–95) New York City–born Sidney Kingsley began writing plays while still a student at Cornell University. After his 1928 graduation, he was briefly an actor, and then worked as a film and theater play reader for several years while continuing to develop his craft. His first Broadway play was his Pulitzer Prize-winning hit *Men in White* (1933), produced by the Group Theater, and starring Alexander Kirkland as the incorruptible young doctor at the center of the piece. Clark Gable and Myrna Loy starred in the 1934 film version. His second

play—and second Broadway hit—was *Dead End* (1935), his classic Depression-era study of New York slum life. Lillian Hellman adapted it into William Wyler's equally classic 1937 film, starring Sylvia Sydney, Humphrey Bogart, and Joel McCrea, with the Dead End Kids. Another very popular Kingsley play was *Detective Story* (1949), starring Ralph Bellamy; Kirk Douglas starred in the 1951 film version. A fourth hit was his adaptation of Arthur Koestler's 1940 novel *Darkness at Noon*. Kingley's other plays included the antiwar *Ten Million Ghosts* (1936), *The World We Make* (1939), *The Patriots* (1943), *Lunatics and Lovers* (1954), and *Night Life* (1962). Kingsley also served as president of the Dramatists Guild. His wife, the actress Madge Evans, predeceased him. There were no survivors. (d. Oakland, New Jersey; March 20, 1995)

FURTHER READING

Obituary. *Variety*, Mar. 29, 1995.
Obituary. *New York Times*, Mar. 21, 1995.

Kingsolver, Barbara Ellen Barbara Kingsolver's fans are still waiting for her next novel, but in the meantime they were rewarded with the 1995 publication of *High Tide in Tucson: Essays from Now or Never*, which one reviewer described as to be "savored like quiet afternoons with a friend." Its subjects range from the hermit crab that stowed away in her luggage to "How Mr. Dewey Decimal Saved My

Life" (based on a 1993 talk at the American Library Association) to her tours with the Rock Bottom Remainders. The latter is an ad hoc rock group originally formed at the 1992 American Booksellers Association by a group of writers, including Dave Barry, Amy Tan, Stephen King, Matt Groening, Robert Fulghum, and others, celebrated in a 1994 book, *Mid-Life Confidential: The Rock Bottom Remainders Tour America with Three Chords and an Attitude*, edited by band member Dave Marsh. Kingsolver herself read the audiobook version of *High Tide* and did numerous radio interviews promoting the book. *Publishers Weekly* reported that her *Pigs in Heaven* was among the best-selling trade paperbacks of 1994, with more than 400,000 copies sold.

Born in Annapolis, Maryland, Kingsolver received a 1977 B.A. magna cum laude from De-Pauw University and a 1981 M.S. from the University of Arizona, where she studied population biology, and worked as a technical writer in the office of arid lands studies (1981–85). She became a free-lance journalist in 1985, then a full-time writer in 1987, gaining wide attention with her first novel, *The Bean Trees* (1988) and its popular sequel *Pigs in Heaven* (1993). Her other works include *Holding the Line: Women in the Great Arizona Mine Strike of 1983* (1989); *Homeland and Other Stories* (1989); the novel *Animal Dreams* (1990); and the poetry collection *Another America* (1992). Kingsolver married chemist Joseph Hoffman in 1985; they have a daughter.

FURTHER READING

"Kingsolver, Barbara." *Current Biography,* July 1994.
"La pasionaria. . . ." MICHAEL NEILL. *People*, Oct. 11, 1993.
"In life. . . ." MICHAEL J. FARRELL. *National Catholic Reporter*, May 22, 1992.

Knox, Alexander (1907–95) Actor and writer Alexander Knox was born in Strathroy, Ontario. After graduating from the University of Western Ontario, he pursued an acting career, making his 1929 stage debut in Boston and then spending the 1930s in England, where he made his film debut in *The Ringer* (1931) and appeared in the films *The Gaunt Stranger* (1938) and *The Four Feathers* (1939), as well as many theater roles. He began the Hollywood portion of his career in *The Sea Wolf* (1941), appeared in several other wartime films, and made his major breakthrough as President Woodrow Wilson in the biofilm *Wilson* (1944). He cowrote and co-starred in *Sister Kenny* (1946) before returning to Europe to star opposite Ingrid Bergman in Roberto Rossellini's *Europa 51* (1952). From the mid-1950s, he played in many strong supporting roles; among his films were *The Divided Heart* (1954), *The Wreck of the Mary Deare* (1959), *Khartoum* (1966), *You Only Live Twice* (1967), *Nicholas and Alexandra* (1971), and *Gorky Park* (1983). Knox also wrote/cowrote several other screenplays, plays, and novels. He was survived by his wife, actress Doris Nolan. (d. London; April 26, 1995)

FURTHER READING

Obituary. *Times* (of London), May 9, 1995.
Obituary. *Independent,* May 6, 1995.
Obituary. *New York Times*, Apr. 29, 1995.

Koch, Howard (1901–95) New York City–born playwright, radio scriptwriter, and screenwriter Howard Koch was best known by far as one of the three Academy Award-winning screenwriters (the others were Julian and Philip Epstein) of the classic film *Casablanca* (1942). Koch's early plays included *Great Scott!* (1929) and *Give Us This Day* (1933). The most notable of his many radio scripts was Orson Welles's *The War of the Worlds* (1938), adapted from the H. G. Wells Martian-invasion novel, which caused an enormous public sensation. In 1941, Koch and John Huston cowrote the Broadway play *In Time to Come*. Among Koch's other screenplays, some of them cowritten, were *The Sea Hawk* (1940), *In This Our Life* (1942), *Mission to Moscow* (1943), *In Our Time* (1944), *Rhapsody In Blue* (1945), *Three Strangers* (1946), *The Best Years of Our Lives* (uncredited; 1946), *Letter From an Unknown Woman* (1948), *No Sad Songs For Me* (1950), and *The Thirteenth Letter* (1951).

Koch's career was almost destroyed when he was blacklisted in 1950, after being an unfriendly witness before the House Un-American Activities Committee. He and his wife, Anne, moved to France in 1952 and then to Britain, where he wrote the screenplay for the film *The Intimate Stranger* (1956), under the pseudonym Peter Howard. Although he returned to Hollywood in 1956, he was never able to fully resume his career, though his later films included *The Greengage Summer* (1961), *The War Lover* (1962), *633 Squadron* (1964), and *The Fox* (1967). His autobiography was *As Time Goes by: Memoirs of a Writer in Hollywood, New York and Europe* (1979). To raise funds, he sold his *Casablanca* Oscar at auction in 1994.

Koch was a graduate of St. Stephens (now Bard) College and Columbia Law School, who practiced law before turning to his writing career. He was survived by his wife, a daughter, and a son. (d. Kingston, New York; August 17, 1995)

FURTHER READING

Obituary. *Economist,* Aug. 26, 1995.
Obituary. *Times* (of London), Aug. 19, 1995.
Obituary. *Independent,* Aug. 19, 1995.
Obituary. *New York Times,* Aug. 18, 1995.
Obituary. *Variety,* Aug. 18, 1995

Kohl, Helmut (1930–) German Chancellor Helmut Kohl gained strength at home during 1995, as the 1994 German recession faded, the mark continued to be stable, and the strong German economy began to successfully absorb the huge costs that had resulted from unification, which had brought massive government-encouraged investment into eastern Germany. The narrow victory of his coalition in the October 1994 elections no longer seemed a prelude to a quick change of government; Kohl was still the acknowledged leader of a united Germany.

At the same time, Kohl's overarching view of a united Europe, with Germany at its center, was in very serious trouble. With the replacement of pro-European Union president François Mitterrand by far less Europe-oriented president Jacques Chirac, the essential unity of France and Germany on the European Union was at least temporarily shattered. In Britain, too, prime minister John Major, facing a largely hostile electorate, moderated his pro-Europe stance—and both France and Britain refused to go ahead on Kohl's cherished European Monetary Union (EMU), forcing indefinite postponement of that plan. Even in Germany, many voices, including some in his own coalition, urged a go-slow attitude on the EMU. At year's end, Kohl's leadership of Germany was stable, and his place in history as the architect of German unification was assured—but his long campaign for European Union was far from fruition.

Kohl began his political career in the Rhineland, becoming Christian Democratic party chairperson there (1966–73), then deputy national chairperson of his party in 1969 and national chairman since 1973. He was opposition leader in the West German parliament (1976–82), and then succeeded Chancellor Helmut Schmidt. Throughout his career he has been a rather careful centrist, much concerned with the development of the European Community, and pursuing a Western-oriented, but also independent course. He played a major role in modern German history, seizing the opportunity presented by the end of the Cold War to unify Germany (1989–90), and then spent the early 1990s dealing with the economic, social, and political consequences of unification, and the related rise of neo-Nazism.

Kohl attended the University of Frankfurt and the University of Heidelberg. He married Hannelore Renner in 1960; the couple has two children.

FURTHER READING

"The fat man. . . ." CHARLES LANE. *New Republic*, Oct. 24, 1994.
"Kohl. . . ." ROBERT J. DOWLING et al. *Business Week*, May 18, 1992.
"King Kohl." T. S. ALLMAN. *Reader's Digest* (Canadian), May 1991.
"Helmut Kohl. . . ." BRUCE W. NELAN. *Time*, Jan. 7, 1991.

Köhler, Georges

Köhler, Georges (1946–95) Munich-born research biologist Georges Köhler graduated from Freiberg University in 1971, received his doctorate at the Basel Institute of Immunology, and did post-doctoral work with Dr. Cesar Milstein at Cambridge's Laboratory of Molecular Biology. In 1974, while at Cambridge, he invented a trailblazing technique with which biologists could produce pure antibodies. His monoclonal antibody technique, also called the hybridoma technique, was a major step forward in the diagnosis and treatment of many diseases. For many years, Dr. Milstein, his mentor, was given full credit for Köhler's invention, including cash awards and professional honors, although Köhler insisted that it was he who conceived and developed the technique. Ultimately, he was vindicated, sharing the 1984 Nobel Prize for medicine for his discovery. Köhler's later career included a return to the Basel Institute of Immunology (1976–83); he directed Freiberg's Max Planck Institute for Immune Biology from 1984 until his death. He was survived by his wife and three children. (d. Freiberg, Germany; March 1, 1995)

FURTHER READING

Obituary. *Independent,* Apr. 4, 1995.
Obituary. *New York Times,* Mar. 4, 1995.

Koppel, Ted

Koppel, Ted (1940–) Ted Koppel's ABC news show "Nightline" continued to be a strong contender for late-night audiences in 1995. Even though much focus was on the battle between Jay Leno and David Letterman in that time slot, Koppel led one or both of his competitors for much of the year; indeed, for the 1994–95 season overall, Koppel finished second to Letterman. ABC gave local stations incentives to carry Koppel live, rather than delaying him; as a result 78 percent of all ABC stations playing the program live, up from 61 in 1992, when Koppel suggested he might quit if he did not receive more network support.

"Nightline" ratings were helped by strong coverage of the Oklahoma City bombing and O. J. Simpson trial, providing a late-night wrap-up and analysis of the latter at least once a week. At one point, Koppel reports, he received a joking cable from Leno saying, "Stop the O. J. stuff; you're killing us!" But the show covered far more than that. Topics ranged from interviews with Norma McCorvey, better known as Jane Roe of

Roe v. *Wade*, on her about-face on abortion, to analysis of 1993 Waco raid on the Branch Davidian compound, to an in-depth analysis of Mexico's economic and political problems on the show's 15th anniversary, in lieu of a retrospective of clips. Koppel also continued to host occasional "Nightline" town meetings, most notably in Jerusalem after the November assassination of Israeli Prime Minister Yitzhak Rabin and earlier after the Simpson verdict. Koppel also gave his own view on the show's history in a new book *Nightline: History in the Making and the Making of Television,* written by Kyle Gibson.

British-born Koppel emigrated to the United States with his German refugee family in 1953. He began his broadcasting career at New York's WMCA Radio in 1963, in that year moving to ABC News, where he has spent his entire career. He went to Vietnam as an ABC correspondent, worked in Hong Kong and Miami as an ABC bureau chief, was ABC's chief diplomatic correspondent (1971–80), and anchored the "ABC Saturday Night News" (1975–77). In March 1980, he emerged as a leading figure in American broadcast journalism, as ABC turned its nightly reports on the Iran hostage crisis into the Koppel-anchored Monday-to-Friday "Nightline" (1980–). In 1992, he was inducted into the Academy of Television Arts and Sciences' Hall of Fame. With Marvin Kalb, he wrote *In National Interest* (1977). Koppel's B.A. in journalism was from Syracuse University, his M.A. in journalism from Stanford. He is married to Grace Anne Dorney; they have four children.

FURTHER READING

"Long day's journey. . . ." HARRY JAFFE. *Playboy,* Sept. 1995.
"Anchor monster. . . ." JOHN KATZ. *Rolling Stone,* Jan. 10, 1991.

Kozol, Jonathan

Kozol, Jonathan (1936–) For only the second time in its history, *Publishers Weekly* recommended a specific book to its readers: Jonathan Kozol's *Amazing Grace: The Lives of Children and the Conscience of a Nation.* The action was more notable because the first time was for Kozol's 1991 book *Savage Inequalities: Children in America's Schools.* The new book is the result of a more than a year spent in the poorest part of the poorest congressional district in America, in New York's devastated South Bronx. There he visited churches, schools, hospitals, homes, and the homeless, and talked with parents, children, and people who work with them, seeking to understand how they can cope with the violence, destitution, and despair—and how others can tolerate such social conditions among their fellow Americans. Kozol himself was a featured guest at the American Booksellers Association, where he ended up protesting against another guest, House Speaker Newt Gingrich, whose political and social policies are of the type Kozol most strongly criticizes. The work also appeared in audiobook form simultaneously with the hardcover publication in October.

Boston-born Kozol taught in the Boston public school system (1964–65), and in the Newton system (1966–68). His experience was the basis for his highly acclaimed book *Death At An Early Age: The Destruction of the Hearts and Minds of Negro Children in the Boston Public Schools*, which won a 1968 National Book Award. He went on to become a leading educator and education writer, lecturing widely, writing many essays, and publishing such books as *Free Schools* (1972), *The Night Is Dark and I Am Far from Home: A Political Indictment of the U. S. Public Schools* (1975), *Children of the Revolution: A Yankee Teacher in the Cuban Schools* (1978), *Prisoners of Silence: Breaking the Bonds of Adult Illiteracy in the United States* (1980), *On Being A Teacher* (1981), *Alternative Schools: A Survivor's Guide* (1982), *Illiterate America* (1985), *Rachel and Her Children: Homeless Families in America* (1988), and *Blueprint for a Democratic Education* (1992). His B.A. was from Harvard, in 1958; he was a Rhodes Scholar at Oxford from 1958 to 1959. He was formerly married.

FURTHER READING

"Rebuilding the schoolhouse. . . ." VICKI KEMPER. *Common Cause Magazine*, Spring 1993.
"A simple matter. . . ." LARRY HAYES. *Phi Delta Kappan*, Dec. 1992.
"Meet. . . ." ANITA MERINA. *NEA Today*, Sept. 15, 1992.
"Jonathan Kozol." *Playboy*, Apr. 1992.
"Jonathan Kozol. . . ." JOE AGRON. *American School & University*, Feb. 1992.
"Savage inequalities . . ." Peter Schrag. *New Republic*, Dec. 16, 1991.
"Jonathan Kozol." Gordon W.E. Nore. *Progressive*, Dec. 1991.
"Save the children." William Plummer and Maria Speidel. *People*, Oct. 7, 1991.

Kray, Ron (1934–95) British crime figure Ron Kray and his twin brother, Reg Kray, both former professional boxers, became top London gangsters in the late 1950s, building a criminal organization called "The Firm," which by 1959 had reached a dominant position in the East End's protection rackets, and was also involved in a wide range of other criminal activities. Ron Kray played the more openly violent role in their partnership, as the gang's chief "enforcer." Both apparently enjoyed publicity, seeking the company of celebrities and media publicity. For ten years (1959–69), they were by far Britain's most highly publicized gangsters. In 1969, both were convicted of murder—Ron of gangster George Cornell and Reggie of gangster Jack McVitie—and both were sentenced to terms of not less than 30 years in prison. They were sent to separate prisons to serve their terms. Ron Kray was survived by his brother, who was allowed out of Maidstone Prison for what was likened to a state funeral. Ron Kray had been married and divorced twice while in prison. (d. Broadmoor Prison, England; March 17, 1995)

FURTHER READING

"East End honours. . . ." ALAN HAMILTON and STEWART TENDLER. *Times* (of London), Mar. 30, 1995.
Obituary. *New York Times*, Mar. 19, 1995.
Obituary. *Times* (of London), Mar. 18, 1995.
Obituary. *Independent*, Mar. 18, 1995.
Obituary. *Guardian*, Mar. 18, 1995.
Born Fighter. REG KRAY. Trafalgar, 1991.

Kristofferson, Kris (1936–) Singer, songwriter, and actor Kris Kristofferson had a fine year on the music side of his career during 1995. In August, he issued the album *A Moment of Forever*, for the first time in five years containing all his own new songs, most of them love songs, rather than the heavily political material with which he had previously been identified. The record, produced by Don Was for the independent label Justice Records, was a very well received artistic success, praised for both songs and performance, although it was not very strong commercially.

Kristofferson, Johnny Cash, Willie Nelson, and Waylon Jennings, four country singing legends singing as The Highwaymen, issued the country collection album *The Road Goes On Forever*, containing a new song by each of the four stars, along with a selection of standards by others. They also issued a hit single from the album, the blues song "It Is What It Is." The four also read an audiobook dramatization of Louis L'Amour's western novel *Riding For the Brand*.

On the acting side of his career, Kristofferson starred as Abraham Lincoln opposite Jane Curtin as Mary Todd Lincoln and Bug Hall in the title role as their son, in the television film *Tad*, set in the White House during the Civil War. Kristofferson also appeared in the television film *Big Dreams and Broken Hearts: The Dottie West Story*, starring Michele Lee as the country singer and costarring several leading country singers, among them Willie Nelson, Dolly Parton, Chet Atkins, Loretta Lynn, and Kenny Rogers.

Forthcoming was a starring role in the film *He Ain't Heavy*, produced and directed by Dean Hamilton and costarring Danny Aiello, Mickey Rooney, and Robert Prosky.

Texas-born Kristofferson has appeared in such films as *Cisco Pike* (1972), *Blume in Love* (1973), *Alice Doesn't Live Here Anymore* (1974), *The Sailor Who Fell From Grace With The Sea* (1976), *Heaven's Gate*, (1981), *Rollover* (1981), *Welcome Home* (1990), and *Christmas in Connecticut* (1992). He has also appeared in such telefilms as *Stagecoach* (1986), *Amerika* (1987), *Pair of Aces* (1990; and the 1991 sequel), *Miracle in the Wilderness* (1991), *Paper Hearts* (1993), and *Sodbusters* (1994). He is also a well-known country singer and songwriter, with numerous songs and albums, starting with *Kristofferson* (1970); in 1992, he issued a two-CD set, each containing 17 of his songs, on one sung by him, on the other sung by others. Kristofferson attended Pomona College and was a Rhodes Scholar at Oxford University. He has been married three times, and has three children.

FURTHER READING

"Kristofferson." ROSA JORDAN. *Progressive*, Sept. 1991.

Kuchma, Leonid Maximovich

(1938–) Ukraine president Leonid Kuchma pursued three related goals during 1995. His major effort at home was to carry through his drive toward a market economy and away from centralized command economic control, although he continued to encounter stiff opposition to his program, especially from parliament, controlled largely by centralist ex-communists. In April, parliament voted to fire Kuchma's cabinet; but in spite of that, Kuchma was able to push through a new austerity budget and called for an acceleration of his programs. In a set of related developments abroad, Kuchma won commitments of more than $2 billion in loans from the International Monetary Fund and the United States, and renegotiated $2.5 billion of Ukraine's debt to Russia.

Ukraine's cordial new relationship with the United States, strengthened by the 1994 Ukrainian ratification of the Nuclear Non-Proliferation Treaty, served to underscore Kuchma's resolve to pursue an independent international course. Although wary of an expansion of NATO, he was also sharply critical of the Commonwealth of Independent States (CIS), and Ukraine refused to join the projected CIS mutual security agreement, instead seeking U.S. political guarantees. President Bill Clinton visited Ukraine in May and promised economic aid.

Born in the Chernigov region, Kuchma was an industrial manager and Communist party leader during the Soviet period. After attending Dniepropetrovsk State University, he went to work at Yuzhmash, the large missile plant in Dniepropetrovsk, rising over a period of three decades into top positions at the plant and in the Communist Party. In 1981, he became a member of the Central Committee of the Communist Party of the Ukraine (1981–92), then deputy director of the plant (1982–86), and later director general of the plant (1986–92). After the dissolution of the Soviet Union, he expanded his role, becoming a Member of Parliament in October 1991 and premier in October 1992. He went into opposition in September 1993, was elected to parliament from Chernigov, and on July 10, 1994 defeated president Leonid Kravchuk in a runoff election for the presidency. In office, he privatized many state-owned enterprises, allowing huge increases in the prices of several basic commodities and attempting to cut deficits, stabilize the currency, cut enormous inflation rates, and move toward private land ownership. In a major international move, he convinced his parliament to ratify the Nuclear Non-Proliferation Treaty in 1994.

FURTHER READING

"Like Albania. . . ." *Economist*, May 29, 1993.

Kuhn, Maggie (Margaret E. Kuhn; 1905–95) Buffalo-born Gray Panthers founder Maggie Kuhn began her long career as an association executive and activist in social causes while still a student at Case Western Reserve University. A lifelong feminist, she organized a college chapter of the League of Women Voters, successor to the National American Woman Suffrage Association. After her 1926 graduation, she devoted her life to social service, working with the YWCA and the General Alliance of Unitarian Women, and then for 25 years with the United Presbyterian Church, where she was an editor and writer for the church magazine *Social Progress* and a church observer at the United Nations.

She retired when she reached the mandatory retirement age of 65, in 1970—and began her major work, the founding and development of the Gray Panthers, formally organized in 1971. In the decades that followed, she emerged as a leading and exceedingly vital spokesperson for older Americans, especially older women, on a wide range of issues, going far beyond "retirement" issues to urge a set of major changes in American society, among them the ending of sexism, racism, and other discriminatory practices and attitudes, as well as the passage of a set of social welfare laws that included fully paid national health insurance. Kuhn was also a prominent opponent of the Vietnam War. A major Gray Panthers victory was the abolition of mandatory retirement. Kuhn's books included *Get Out There and Do Something About Injustice* (1972), *Maggie Kuhn On Aging* (1977), and her autobiography *No Stone Unturned: The Life and Times of Maggie Kuhn* (1991), written with Christina Long and Laura Quinn. There were no survivors. (d. Philadelphia; April 22, 1995)

FURTHER READING

"Corliss and. . . ." BRUCE SHAPIRO. *Nation,* May 29, 1995.
Obituary. *New York Times*, Feb. 2, 1995.

Kukrit Pramoj (1911–95) Thai politician and former premier Kukrit Pramoj spent his teenage years in Britain and graduated from Oxford University. On his return to Thailand in 1933, he went into banking, and stayed in that profession until 1946, when he began his political career with election as a Member of Parliament. However, that career was put largely on hold by a succession of Thai military governments throughout the early 1970s. With defeat of the military by the democratic rising of 1973, Kukrit became a leader of Thai democratic forces, founding the Social Action party, and becoming a leader of the Thai legislature. He became prime minister of Thailand in March 1975, and in his fourteen months in office swiftly moved to preserve Thai independence, making a full opening toward China by establishing diplomatic relations, while at the same time securing quick withdrawal of American forces from his country in the wake of Communist victories in Vietnam, Laos, and Cambodia. As Social Action party leader, he continued to participate in a series of governments through the early 1980s. He was survived by his wife, Pakpring Thongyai, a daughter, a son, and a brother. (d. Bangkok; October 9, 1995)

FURTHER READING

Obituary. *Economist*, Oct. 21, 1995.
Obituary. *Times* (of London), Oct. 16, 1995.
Obituary. *Independent*, Oct. 11, 1995.
Obituary. *New York Times*, Oct. 10, 1995.

Kumaratunga, Chandrika Bandaranaike

(ca. 1946–) Sri Lankan president Chandrika Bandaranaike Kumaratunga saw her campaign to bring the 12-year-old Sri Lankan Civil War to a peaceful end fail in 1995, the result being intensified war between government forces and the rebel Tamil Tigers. Kumaratunga intensely pursued peace initiatives after her November 1994 presidential election, and had seemed very successful; a ceasefire was signed on January 3, 1995 that went into effect on January 8, and held, while the sides began full-scale peace negotiations. But the Tigers broke off negotiations and ended the truce on April 19, sinking government gunboats and downing government planes. Government forces responded by going back to war, mounting air, sea, and land attacks against rebel forces. Kumaratunga denounced Tamil Tiger leader Velupillai Prabhakaran, and went on to accuse him of ordering the 1991 murder of Indian leader Rajiv Gandhi, as had been charged by the Indian government, which sought his extradition. The war escalated; in August, the rebels rejected a new government peace proposal, and stepped up their attacks. In September, heavily armed government forces began a major attack on Tamil strongholds on the Jaffna peninsula, as a reported 300,000–400,000 refugees fled the area. Government forces claimed that their capture of the city of Jaffna in November was a decisive event in the long war, but that remained to be seen, as the Tigers continued to fight an intense guerrilla war in many parts of the country.

Kumaratunga's father, Solomon Bandaranaike (1899–1959) was prime minister of Sri Lanka (then Ceylon) when he was assassinated. He had been succeeded by her mother, Siramavo Bandaranaike, who was the world's first woman prime minister; out of power since 1977, she was stlll president of her daughter's party. Chandrika Kumaratunga and her husband, actor Vijaya Kumaratunga, established the People's Party in 1984; he was assassinated in 1988. Afterward she fled repeated assassination threats, living abroad until 1991, and then returned home, re-entering Sri Lankan political life, which was dominated by the long civil war. She became Sri Lankan prime minister in August 1994, and won election to the presidency in November 1994.

FURTHER READING

"Kumaratunga's turn." GABRIELE VENZKY. *World Press Review*, Dec. 1994.

Kunitz, Stanley Jasspon

(1905–) The 1995 National Book Award for poetry went to Stanley Kunitz, for his recently published *Passing Through: Later Poems, New & Selected*. The author expressed his gratitude at receiving the award "even though I've waited 90 years to get it," and delight that his editor had offered him a three-book contract, showing faith in his life expectancy. The well-received collection covers a wide range of themes, from ancient to modern, international to individual, real to mythical, with topics as diverse as fights by Roman gladiators, the flight of Apollo 13, and his own father, who committed suicide shortly after Kunitz was born.

In 1995, Kunitz was also awarded the Poetry Society of America's Shelley Memorial Award. In November, Kunitz was honored by his peers at a celebration for his 90th birthday.

Massachusetts-born Kunitz received both his 1926 A.B. (summa cum laude) and his 1927 M.A. from Harvard University, where he also received the Garrison medal for poetry. He was editor of the *Wilson Library Bulletin* (1928–43), while beginning his career as a writer. After World War II military service (1943–45), he turned to university teaching at schools such as Bennington College, Potsdam State Teachers College, and The New School for Social Research, before settling in at Columbia University (lecturer, 1963–66; adjunct professor of writing 1967–85). Throughout these years he was producing poetry, including *Intellectual Things* (1930), *Passport to the War* (1944), *Selected Poems, 1928–1958*

(1958; it won the Pulitzer Prize for poetry), *The Testing-Tree* (1971), *The Terrible Threshold* (1974), *The Coat Without a Seam* (1974), *The Poems of Stanley Kunitz 1928–1978* (1979), *The Wellfleet Whale and Companion Poems* (1983), and *Next-To-Last Things: New Poems and Essays* (1985). Other works included *Poems of John Keats* (1964), *A Kind of Order, A Kind of Folly: Essays and Conversations* (1975), *The Essential Blake* (1987), *Interviews and Encounters* (1993), and numerous literary reference works. Kunitz has also worked with others to translate the works of poets such as Andrei Voznesensky and Yevgeny Yevtushenko, edited the Yale Younger Poets series (1969–77), and was poetry consultant to the Library of Congress (1974–76). He was awarded the prestigious Bollingen prize in 1987. After two previous divorces, he married Elise Asher in 1958. He has one daughter, by his second marriage.

FURTHER READING

Interviews and Encounters with Stanley Kunitz.
Stanley Moss, ed. Sheep Meadow, 1993.

Kunstler, William Moses (1919–95)

New York City–born William Kunstler, a leading and highly visible defense attorney, graduated from Yale University in 1941, won a Bronze Star during his World War II military service, and graduated from Columbia Law School in 1948. He emerged as a prominent political and civil rights defense attorney in the late 1950s, defending a very wide range of clients. Though early identifed with the defense of civil rights activists and dissident political figures, Kunstler in practice defended a much wider range of those accused. Among his very many clients were Martin Luther King, Jr., subway vigilante Bernard Goetz, civil rights leader Stokeley Carmichael, alleged Mafia figure Joseph Bonnano, some of the prisoners tried in the aftermath of the Attica Prison riots, antiwar activist Philip Berrigan, and alleged Atlanta child murderer Wayne Williams. His biggest early victory was the trial of the Chicago Seven, following the 1968 Democratic National Convention; his clients were all acquitted on appeal, and his own contempt sentence was canceled. Kunstler was also a prolific writer; among his books were *Beyond a Reasonable Doubt?: The Original Trial of Caryl Chessman* (1961), *And Justice For All* (1963), *Deep In My Heart* (1966), *Trials and Tribulatons* (1985), *Hints and Allegations: Sonnets from the Amsterdam News* (1994), and *My Life As a Radical Lawyer* (1994), written with Sheila Isenberg. He was survived by his second wife Margaret Ratner, four daughters, and a sister. (d. New York City; September 4, 1995)

FURTHER READING

Obituary. *Current Biography,* Nov. 1995.
Obituary. *Rolling Stone,* Oct. 19, 1995.
"The pariah's farewell." ALEXANDER COCKBURN. *Nation,* Oct. 2, 1995.
Obituary. *Nation,* Sep. 25, 1995.
Obituary. *Jet,* Sep. 25, 1995.
"The rhetorical. . . ." ALEX WILLIAMS. *New York,* Sep. 18, 1995.
"The death of. . . ." JAMES TRAUB. *New Yorker,* Sep. 18, 1995.
"Defending the despised." *People,* Sep. 18, 1995.
Obituary. *Economist,* Sep. 16, 1995.
Obituary. *Times* (of London), Sep. 6, 1995.
Obituary. *Independent,* Sep. 6, 1995.
Obituary. *New York Times,* Sept. 5, 1995.
"Gunning for. . . ." PETER LENNON. *Guardian,* Apr. 29, 1993.
"The most hated. . . ." RON ROSENBAUM. *Vanity Fair,* Mar. 1992.

Kuralt, Charles Bishop (1934–)

Charles Kuralt is retired only in the sense of having left his longtime job as host of "CBS News Sunday Morning." But he views that "retirement" as freeing him to do some of the other things he loves. In particular, he completed a long-planned project: a trip to his favorite places in America and publication of a new book, *Charles Kuralt's America*, describing his experiences and the people he met there, from Key West to Alaska, from New York at Christmas to New Orleans and jazz people such as Ellis Marsalis, head of the Marsalis clan. Kuralt was widely seen promoting the book, and it quickly became a best-seller. Kuralt was reader of the

audio version and also served as narrator for a six-part television documentary, *The Revolutionary War*, which aired on the Learning Channel. Meanwhile, the "On the Road" features that first made him famous in the 1960s were being rerun on various television channels. In January 1995, Kuralt was honored with a Silver Baton at the Alfred I. duPont-Columbia University Awards for broadcast journalism.

On the personal side, Kuralt underwent coronary bypass surgery late in 1995.

Born in Wilmington, North Carolina, Kuralt received his B.A. from the University of North Carolina in 1955. After working as a reporter and columnist at the *Charlotte News* (1955–57), he joined CBS News, where he would remain throughout his career, as writer (1957–59), then longtime correspondent (1959–94), producing his famous "On the Road" features in the 1960s and 1970s, and host of "CBS News Sunday Morning" (1979–94). His many awards include the Ernie Pyle Memorial award (1956), the George Foster Peabody Broadcasting Award (1969; 1976; 1980), the International Radio-Television Society's Broadcaster of the Year award (1985), and ten Emmys. On his 1994 retirement, Kuralt was celebrated in a television special *One for the Road with Charles Kuralt and Morley Safer*. Among his written works are *To the Top of the World* (1968), *Dateline America* (1979), *On the Road with Charles Kuralt* (1985), *Southerners* (1986), *North Carolina Is My Home* (1986), and *A Life on the Road* (1990). Kuralt married Suzanna Folsom Baird in 1962; he has two daughters from a previous marriage.

FURTHER READING

"Charles Kuralt. . . ." ILEANE RUDOLPH. *TV Guide*, Nov. 11, 1995.

Kurtz, Efrem (1900–95) St. Petersburg–born Efrem Kurtz, a conductor, studied at the St. Petersburg Conservatory, fled St. Petersburg for Riga, Latvia as the Russian Revolution approached, and ultimately settled with the rest of his family in Berlin. He graduated from Berlin's Stern Conservatory. He made his conducting debut in Berlin in 1921 as a substitute conductor for visiting American dancer Isadora Duncan, and in 1924 became music director of the Stuttgart Philharmonic. He toured widely with dancer Anna Pavlova (1928–31). In 1933, he fled Nazi Germany, becoming music director of the Ballets Russes de Monte Carlo (1933–41). When war came, he fled to the United States and was music director of the Kansas City Symphony (1943–47), becoming an American citizen in 1944. He was music director of the Houston Symphony (1948–54) and conducted with the Liverpool Philharmonic (1955–57). After that, he was for more than 30 years one of the world's leading touring conductors, and at the same time a highly regarded recording artist. He was survived by his wife, Mary Lynch. (d. London; June 27, 1995)

FURTHER READING

Obituary. *Current Biography,* Sept. 1995.
Obituary. *Variety,* July 24, 1995.
Obituary. *Independent,* July 15, 1995.
Obituary. *New York Times,* June 29, 1995.
Obituary. *Times* (of London), June 28, 1995.

L

Lamont, Corliss (1902–95) New Jersey–born Corliss Lamont, the child of wealth as the son of J. P. Morgan and Co. chairman Thomas Lamont, was a leading American civil libertarian and Left dissenter. He graduated from Harvard in 1924, and taught philosophy at Columbia while earning his 1932 Ph.D. During the 1930s, he joined the board of the American Civil Liberties Union (ACLU), leaving that organization in 1954 when he felt its reponse to McCarthyism inadequate. He was president of the Bill of Rights Fund (1954–69) and chairman of the National Emergency Civil Liberties Committee (1965–95).

He visited the Soviet Union in the 1930s, coming back greatly impressed with communism, and was chairman of the National Council for American-Soviet Friendship (1943–46), but Lamont declared himself a Socialist and not a Communist. He was long attacked as a Communist, especially during the McCarthy period. Appearing before McCarthy's Senate committee in 1953, Lamont denied ever having been a Communist and pleaded the then-uncertain protection of the First Amendment, rather than the certain protection of the Fifth Amendment; he was cited for contempt of Congress and won his court case. In 1965, he won lawsuits against the postmaster-general and the CIA for opening his mail. Lamont unsuccessfully ran for the U.S. Senate in 1952 on the American Labor Party ticket and in 1958 on the Independent Socialist ticket.

A prolific writer, Lamont's books included *Issues of Immortality* (1932), *You Might Like Socialism: A Way of Life for Modern Man* (1939), *The Peoples of the Soviet Union* (1946), *A Humanist Funeral Service* (1947), *The Philosophy of Humanism* (1949), *Civil Liberties in America* (1956), and his autobiography *Yes to Life: Memoirs of Corliss Lamont* (1981). He was survived by his third wife, Beth Keehner, and by three daughters and a son. (d. Ossining, New York; April 26, 1995)

FURTHER READING

"Corliss and. . . ." BRUCE SHAPIRO. *Nation,* May 29, 1995.
Obituary. *Independent,* May 12, 1995.
Obituary. *Times* (of London), May 10, 1995.
Obituary. *New York Times*, Apr. 28, 1995.

Landau, Martin (1934–) For his role as Bela Lugosi in the 1994 film *Ed Wood*, veteran actor Martin Landau won a best supporting actor Academy Award. He also won best supporting actor honors at the Golden Globe awards and from the Screen Actors Guild and the National Society of Film Critics.

In 1995, Landau starred as Jacob in the television series *Joseph,* starring Paul Mercurio as Joseph, Ben Kingsley, Lesley Ann Warren, and Alice Krige; Roger Young directed. Forthcoming was a role in the film *City Hall,* directed by Harry Becker and starring Al Pacino, in a cast that includes John Cusack, Bridget Fonda, Danny Aiello, and David Paymer; and a starring role in Steve Barron's film *Pinocchio*.

Brooklyn-born Landau was a staff artist and cartoonist at the New York *Daily News* before turning to an acting career. He studied at the Actors Studio while in the early 1950s beginning his career in supporting roles on the New York stage and in television. Landau emerged as a star opposite Barbara Bain, then his wife, as Rollin Hand in the television series "Mission Impossible" (1966–69), winning a 1967 Emmy in the role. He also starred in the series "Space 1999" (1975–77). He has played supporting roles in many theatrical films, among them *Pork Chop Hill* (1959), *North by Northwest* (1959), *Cleopatra* (1962), *The Greatest Story Ever Told* (1965), *They Call Me Mr. Tibbs* (1970), *Strange Shadows in an Empty Room* (1977), *Beauty and the Beast* (1981), *Tucker: The Man and His Dreams* (1988; he received a best supporting actor Academy Award nomination), *Crimes and Misdemeanors* (1989; he received a Golden Globe Award and a best supporting actor Academy Award nomination), *Eye of the Widow* (1991), *Sliver* (1993), and *Intersection* (1994).

FURTHER READING

"Martin Landau." LAWRENCE O'TOOLE. *Entertainment,* Mar. 1995.
"Interview with. . . ." ROBERT SEIDENBERG. *Entertainment,* Oct. 21, 1994.

Lane, Priscilla (Priscilla Mulligan; 1917–95) Born in Indianola, Indiana, actress and singer Priscilla Lane was the youngest of the three Lane sisters (the other were Rosemary and Lola). She began her career in the mid-1930s as a big-band singer, joining Fred Waring's Pennsylvanians, along with Rosemary. Both made their film debuts as singers with the Pennsylvanians in *Varsity Show* (1937), then joined their sister Lola as long-term Warner Brothers players. The sisters starred together in several popular films, including *Four Daughters* (1938), *Daughters Courageous* (1939), *Four Wives* (1939), *Ladies Must Live* (1941), and *Four Mothers* (1941). Priscilla Lane also starred in several very popular films of Hollywood's golden age, including *Brother Rat* (1938), *The Roaring Twenties* (1939), and *Arsenic and Old Lace* (1944). She retired in 1948 and married air force colonel Joseph Howard. In 1958, she hosted television's "The Priscilla Lane Show" in Boston. She was

survived by two daughters and two sons. (d. Andover, Massachusetts; April 4, 1995)

FURTHER READING

Obituary. *Times* (of London), Apr. 14, 1995.
Obituary. *New York Times*, Apr. 6, 1995.

lang, k. d. (Kathy Dawn Lang; 1962–) Singer and songwriter k. d. lang issued the 1995 album *All You Can Eat,* coproduced with her longtime collaborator, Ben Mink. A change of pace from the highly imaginative, sometimes surreal approach of her 1992 hit album *Ingenue, All You Can Eat* was a simply presented, back-to-basics group of love songs, which included "If I Were You," "Maybe," "Acquiesce," "Sexuality," "World of Love," and "Infinite and Unforeseen." "If I Were You" was also issued as hit single and as a video.

Lang received a Grammy nomination for best pop vocal collaboration for "All for Love," sung as a duet with Tony Bennett. She was also nominated at the British Awards as best international female solo artist.

Born in Consort, Alberta, Canada, lang began her career singing country music while still at Alberta's Red Deer College. She made her professional singing debut in cabaret in Edmonton, Alberta, and in 1984 formed her first group, the Reclines. Moving to Toronto and gaining in popularity as she toured, she also cut her first country music album, *A Truly Western Experience* (1984). She made her U.S. debut in New York City in 1985, and from that appearance came her association with Sire Records, which issued her albums *Angel with a Lariat* (1986) and *Shadowland* (1988), neither a great commercial hit, but both critically acclaimed. Lang won a 1990 best female country vocalist Grammy award for her fourth album, *Absolute Torch and Twang* (1990). She then took a two-year break from recording, returning as a popular, rather than country, artist with the hit album *Ingenue,* with such singles as "Constant Craving," "The Mind of Love," and "Miss Chatelaine." In 1994, she issued the album *Music from the Motion Picture Soundtrack: Even Cowgirls Get the Blues.*

During her two-year break, lang starred in Percy Adlon's film *Salmonberries,* in large part a lesbian love story. In June 1992, she publicly declared herself to be a lesbian—although she had previously made her sexual orientation clear and had attracted a devoted lesbian audience, in addition to her much larger country and crossover popular music audiences. An activist in many social causes, including animal rights, lang has sparked considerable controversy, most notably with her antimeat ads.

FURTHER READING

"K. D. Lang." LORRAINE ALI. *Rolling Stone,* Nov. 30, 1995.
"Talking with. . . ." JEREMY HELLIGAR. *People,* Nov. 13, 1995.
"A lighter side of lang." BRIAN D. JOHNSON. *Maclean's,* Nov. 6, 1995.
In Her Own Words: K. D. Lang. DAVID BENNAHUM. Omnibus, 1995.
K. D. Lang. PAULA MARTINAC. Chelsea House, 1995.
K. D. Lang: All You Get Is Me. VICTORIA STARR. St. Martin's, 1994.
"k.d. lang cuts it close." LESLIE BENNETTS. *Vanity Fair*, Aug. 1993.
K.D. Lang: Carrying the Torch. WILLIAM ROBERTSON. InBook, 1993.
"K.D. gets real." PETER GODDARD. *Chatelaine*, Sept. 1992.
"Lang, K.D." *Current Biography*, Sept. 1992.
"Virgin territory. . . ." BRENDAN LEMON. *Advocate,* June 16, 1992.
"Midnight cowgirl." KRISTINE MCKENNA. *Us,* May 1992.

Lange, Jessica (1949–) For her role in *Blue Sky,* Jessica Lange won an Academy Award and a Golden Globe award for best actress, and was also nominated as best actress by the Screen Actors Guild. The long-delayed film had originally been made in 1991, but was not released until 1994.

In 1995, she starred in Stephen Gyllenhaal's film *Losing Isaiah,* as a social worker who, with her husband, adopts a little boy left in a garbage dump by his crack-addicted mother, played by Halle Berry. The later contest of the two mothers for custody of the child drives the film's story line; their emotional responses are the heart of the work. The cast included David Strathairn, Cuba Gooding, Jr., Daisy Eagan, Marc John Jefferies, and Samuel L. Jackson. She also starred as the hero's wife in the costume drama *Rob Roy,* set in Scottish history, opposite Liam Neeson in the title role, in a cast that included John Hurt, Tim Roth, and Eric Stoltz; Michael Caton-Jones directed.

Lange recreated her 1992 stage role as Blanche DuBois in a 1995 television production of Tennessee Williams's classic play *A Streetcar Named Desire,* opposite Alec Baldwin as Stanley Kowalski, with John Goodman as Mitch and Diane Lane as Stella Kowalski. Glenn Jordan produced and directed the very well received work. Lange received a Golden Globe nomination as best actress in a miniseries or telefilm for the role.

Minnesota-born Lange became one of the leading movie stars of the late 1970s and of the 1980s, with such films as *All That Jazz* (1979), *The Postman Always Rings Twice* (1981), *Frances* (1982), *Tootsie* (1982), *Crimes of the Heart* (1986), *Music Box* (1989), *Men Don't Leave* (1990), *Cape Fear* (1991), *Night and the City* (1992), and *Blue Sky* (1994). She starred on Broadway as Blanche DuBois in a notable revival of *A Streetcar Named Desire* (1992), and in television in *O Pioneers!* (1992).

Lange attended the University of Minnesota. She was formerly married to Paco Grande, and has three children, one from a former relationship with ballet star Mikhail Baryshnikov, two from her relationship with actor-playwright Sam Shepard.

FURTHER READING

"Jessica Lange." TRISH DEITCH ROHRER. *Us,* Apr. 1995.
"Lange on life." KEVIN SESSUMS. *Vanity Fair,* Mar. 1995.
"Jessica." VALERIE MONROE. *Harper's Bazaar,* Jan. 1991.

Larkin, Barry Louis (1964–)

Barry Larkin was named the National League's Most Valuable Player in 1995, although his numbers did not top the league's lists. He was second in stolen bases, with 51 in 56 attempts; sixth in batting average, with .319; fifth in runs scored, with 98; and tenth in total hits, with 158. Overall his batting average was .319, with 15 home runs and 66 runs batted in. But altogether the voters judged that Larkin's contribution to his Cincinnati Reds team was greater than that of any other single player in the league. Noted for his inspirational team meetings, he was the first shortstop to win the award since 1962. In the All-Star game, Larkin was starting shortstop for the National League team.

Larkin helped the Reds to a record of 85-59 to win the National League's Central Division by nine games. The Reds defeated the Los Angeles Dodgers 3–0 in the divisional playoffs, with Larkin hitting .385, and were picked by many to go to and win the World Series, but were surprisingly swept by the Atlanta Braves 4–0 in the league championship. During that series, Larkin had 7 hits on 18 at bats, for a batting average of .389, and scored one run. At the turn of the year, Larkin signed a three-year, $16.5 million contract extension, with possible options extending to the year 2000 and $21.2 million.

Larkin was born in Cincinnati, where he graduated from Moeller High School, before going on to the University of Michigan (1982–85). He left after three years, but continued his education; late in 1995, he was just three courses short of earning his degree in economics. While in college, he was named to the *Sporting News* college All-America team (1985) and was also a member of the silver medal–winning U.S. Olympic team (1984). Selected by the Cincinnati Reds in the 1982 draft, he did not sign, but was again drafted by the Reds in 1985. After early experience in the minor leagues (1985–86), in Vermont and Denver, he came to the majors (1986–), becoming the team's regular shortstop in 1987. He has been selected to the All-Star team seven times (1988–95), but was unable to play due to injury in 1989 and 1994. Larkin is married to Lisa Davis.

FURTHER READING

"Cincinnati Reds. . . ." *Jet,* Dec. 4, 1995.
"There's no argument. . . ." BOB NIGHTENGALE. *Sporting News,* Nov. 27, 1995.

"By the numbers." TIM KURKJIAN. *Sports Illustrated,* July 8, 1991.
"Barry Larkin." JERRY CRASNICK. *Sporting News,* Apr. 1, 1991.

Lawson, Yank (John Rhea Lawson; 1911–95)

Missouri-born trumpeter and bandleader Yank Lawson attended the University of Missouri, and began his long professional career in the early 1930s. From then through the early 1940s, he played and recorded with some of the leading big-band leaders of his day, among them Ben Pollack, Bob Crosby, Tommy Dorsey, and Benny Goodman. From the early 1940s, he was a much sought-after studio musician who recorded with many top singers, including Frank Sinatra, with whom he recorded a notable 1944 "Stormy Weather," and Louis Armstrong; Lawson appeared as King Oliver in Armstrong's 1957 *Satchmo: A Musical Biography.* Lawson and bassist Bob Haggart, a longtime recording partner, in 1968 founded The World's Greatest Jazz Band. Lawson toured and recorded into the early 1990s. He was survived by his wife, Harriet, and by three daughters and a son. (d. Indianapolis; February 18, 1995)

FURTHER READING

Obituary. *Times* (of London), Mar. 1, 1995.
Obituary. *New York Times,* Feb. 24, 1995.

Leakey, Richard Erskine Frere (1944–)

Paleontologist-conservationist Richard Leakey assumed a new role in his native Kenya in May 1995, when he and other dissident Kenyans formed a new political party, Safina, in opposition to President Daniel arap Moi's ruling Kenya African National Union Party (KANU). It was a move full of danger. Moi, whose government Leakey had until 1994 served as director of the Kenya Wildlife Service, denounced Leakey as a White colonialist with foreign ties, and charged that Safina was training armed guerillas in nearby Uganda, charges denied by Leakey and others. Later in May, some 100 armed government loyalists attacked the Leakey family compound, encircling the house and demanding that the "colonialist" (a third-generation Kenyan) leave. In August, Leakey was severely

cessful plans to save endangered elephant and rhinoceros populations from poachers by obtaining international funding for their protection and by making Kenya a major tourist destination for wildlife safaris, but came into conflict with Kenyan politicians, including Moi, which led him to resign in 1994 in protest over government corruption and mismanagement. Among Leakey's many publications are *People of the Lake: Man, His Origins, Nature and Future* (1979; with Roger Lewin), *The Making of Mankind* (1981; basis for a television series), *Human Origins* (1982), *Origins Reconsidered* (1982; also with Lewin), and *The Origins of Humankind* (1994). Diagnosed with terminal kidney disease in 1968, Leakey's life was saved by the 1980 transplant of a kidney donated by his younger brother, Philip. Both of Richard Leakey's legs had to be amputated after a 1993 airplane crash; he now uses artificial legs. He married Maeve Gillian Epps in 1970; they have three daughters.

FURTHER READING

"Leakey, Richard." *Current Biography,* Oct. 1995.
"Into the ark." *Economist,* June 24, 1995.
Ancestral Passions: The Leakey Family and the Quest for Humankind's Beginnings. VIRGINIA MORELL. Simon & Schuster, 1995.
"The elephant man. . . ." MARK HUBAND. *Observer,* Mar. 27, 1994.
"Skulls and numskulls." *Economist,* Nov. 21, 1992.

beaten in public and in view of police officers, who took no action; three men, believed to be members of KANU, were later charged with the beatings, pleaded not guilty, and were freed on bail. Leakey did not propose to take a leadership role in Safina, but was acting as interim secretary general for the party, which was awaiting registration. Other Safina members and some journalists were also beaten, in that and other incidents.

Pursuing his scientific life, Leakey and longtime collaborator Roger Lewin published a new book in 1995, *The Sixth Extinction: Patterns of Life and the Future of Humankind,* which warns of a coming wave of extinctions equal to that in which the dinosaurs perished. Richard's wife, Maeve Leakey, who now leads the family paleontological dig, announced in 1995 the discovery of fossils 4 million years old; these pushed far back the date at which humans are believed to have been walking upright on two legs.

Son of noted paleontologists Louis Leakey and Mary Nicol Leakey, Nairobi-born Richard Leakey was leading his own paleontological expeditions before he was 20, notably in Tanzania, Kenya, and Ethiopia. He became administrative director (1968–74), then director (1974–89) of the National Museums of Kenya. Increasingly turning toward conservation, he chaired the Wildlife Clubs of Kenya (1969–84) and the East African Wildlife Society (1985–), before becoming director of the Kenya Wildlife Service (1989–94). There he orchestrated largely suc-

le Carré, John (David John Moore Cornwell; 1931–) Spy novelist extraordinaire John le Carré is still coming to terms with the post–Cold War world. In his 1995 novel *Our Game,* his main character Timothy Cranmer is forcibly retired by the British Secret Service, which also ends the activities of his double agent and friend, Larry Pettifer. When Cranmer's lover, Emma, and Pettifer both disappear, Cranmer goes on a journey of exploration and confrontation (with himself, among others) that lands him in the middle of Chechnya, then in the process of rebelling against Russia. Though not the overwhelming success of some of le Carré's earlier works, this new novel quickly landed on the bestseller lists. Meanwhile, le Carré's son, Stephen Cornwell, a film director, took his first turn in the family trade, writing the script for, as well as directing, *Block Party,* a film set in postearthquake Los Angeles, scheduled to air on Showtime early in 1996. Cornwell is also scheduled to be producer for the planned film of *Our Game,* for Francis Coppola's Zoetrope Studios and England's Majestic Films.

Born in Poole, Dorset, England, le Carré studied at Switzerland's Bern University (1948–49), then took a B.A. in modern languages at Oxford University's Lincoln College (1956). After teaching at Eton College (1956–58), he joined the British Foreign Service (1959–64), stationed in Germany from 1961. His first novel, *Call for the Dead* (1960), basis for the film *The Deadly Affair* (1967), starring James Mason and Simone Signoret, introduced the spymaster who would be his most famous character: George Smiley. This was followed by *A Murder of Quality* (1962); *The Spy Who Came in from the Cold* (1963), basis for the 1965 film, which won both the Mystery Writers of America and British Crime Writers novel-of-the-year awards; *The Looking-Glass War* (1965); *A Small Town in Germany* (1968); and *The Naive and Sentimental Lover* (1971).

Le Carré is best known for his Karla trilogy, the first and third parts of which were made into television miniseries (1977 and 1982), starring Alec Guinness as George Smiley: *Tinker Tailor Soldier Spy* (1973); *The Honorable Schoolboy* (1977), which won the James Tait Black Memorial prize and the Crime Writers Association gold dagger; and *Smiley's People* (1980). His other novels include *The Little Drummer Girl* (1983);

A Perfect Spy (1986); *The Russia House* (1989), basis for the 1990 film; *The Secret Pilgrim* (1991), the final tales of George Smiley; and *The Night Manager* (1994). Le Carré's 1954 marriage to Alison Ann Sharp ended in divorce in 1972; they had three sons. He married Valerie Jane Eustace in 1972; they have one son.

FURTHER READING

" 'We distorted. . . .' " WALTER ISAACSON and JAMES KELLY. *Time,* July 5, 1993.
John le Carré. LYNNDIANNE BEENE. Twayne, 1992.
" 'I was heartily. . . .' " CRAIG R. WHITNEY. *New York Times Book Review,* Jan. 6, 1991.

Lee, Spike (Shelton Jackson Lee; 1957–) African-American filmmaker Spike Lee directed, coproduced, and cowrote the 1995 film *Clockers,* his study of violence within African-American communities, often accompanying the drug trade and often inspired by the macho, moneyed images conveyed to young people by drug dealers. His cast included Harvey Keitel and John Turturro as homicide detectives, Delroy Lindo as a drug dealer, Mikti Phifer in the killer's role, and Isaiah Washington as his brother, who tries to make a false confession to save Phifer.

Lee also directed a segment of the film *Lumière and Company,* directed by Sarah Moon. The work was a century-of-film celebration, in which a worldwide selection of almost two-score modern directors each created a 52-second film, using an

Spike Lee (right) and Annabella Sciorra.

original Lumière camera, re-created original film emulsion, natural light, and in a continuous shot.

Forthcoming was the film biography *Jackie Robinson,* directed by Lee and starring Denzel Washington in the title role. Also forthcoming was the film *Girl 6,* directed by, produced, and starring Lee, in a cast that includes Halle Berry, John Turturro, Madonna, Quentin Tarantino, Naomi Campbell, and Ron Silver.

Atlanta-born Lee has made several films, including *She's Gotta Have It* (1986) and *School Daze* (1988); with Lisa Jones, he wrote books about the making of both films. He became a notable and very controversial filmmaker in 1989, with release of his film *Do the Right Thing,* a fictional story that sharply explored racial tensions in his home area of Bedford-Stuyvesant, in Brooklyn. Denzel Washington starred in Lee's equally controversial 1990 film *Mo' Better Blues,* attacked by many as anti-Semitic for its story of the exploitation of African-American artists by two Jewish club owners. His further films included *Jungle Fever* (1991), *Malcolm X* (1992), *Crooklyn* (1994), and *Drop Squad* (1994). Lee's 1979 B.A. was from Morehouse College, and his 1983 M.A. in filmmaking was from New York University.

FURTHER READING

"Why do the white thing?" *Guardian,* Nov. 18, 1995.
"Spike speaks." ALAN FRUTKIN. *Advocate,* Oct. 31, 1995.
"Spike Lee talks about his best films." *Jet,* Oct. 9, 1995.
"Spike." ANNA DEAVERE SMITH. *Premiere,* Oct. 1995.
"Spike on sports. . . ." DARRYL HOWERTON. *Sport,* Feb. 1995.
Spike Lee: Entertainer. NATHAN I. HUGGINS, ed. Chelsea House, 1995.
"Spike Lee. . . ." HENRY LOUIS GATES. *Interview,* Oct. 1994.
Spike Lee: Filmmaker. Chelsea House, 1994.
Spike Lee. KATHLEEN F. CHAPMAN. Creative Education, 1994.
Spike Lee: Filmmaker. BOB BERNOTAS. Enslow, 1993.
Spike Lee. G. DINERO. Dell, 1993.
"Words with Spike." JANICE C. SIMPSON. *Time,* Nov. 23, 1992.
"Great Xpectations." RALPH WILEY. *Premiere,* Nov. 1992.
"Spike Lee. . . ." BARBARA GRIZZUTI HARRISON. *Esquire,* Oct. 1992.
Spike Lee. ALEX PATTERSON. Avon, 1992.
Five for Five: The Films of Spike Lee. TERRY McMILLAN. Stewart Tabori & Chang, 1991.

Lehrer, Jim (James Charles Lehrer; 1934–)

PBS evening news anchor Jim Lehrer carried on alone in 1995, after his longtime partner, Robert MacNeil, retired as coanchor of the "MacNeil/Lehrer Newshour" on October 20, 1995. The show was renamed "The Newshour with Jim Lehrer," with Lehrer supported by various subanchors, and now was based entirely in Washington, D.C. The two remained partners in MacNeil/Lehrer Productions, which (along with *The Wall Street Journal*) announced plans to produce a half-hour late-evening news show in 1996, in time for the presidential campaign.

Meanwhile, Lehrer continued his literary career with a new novel, *The Last Debate,* set during a presidential campaign, in which candidates have veto power over potential moderators; the plot thickens when the moderator selected decides to reveal some explosive information about one of the candidates during the debate. Reviewers pointed out that Lehrer was better prepared than most to give verisimilitude to the setting, since he had hosted not one but two presidential debates in the 1992 campaign.

Kansas-born Lehrer was a reporter for the *Dallas Morning News* (1959–61), then moving to the *Dallas Times Herald* as reporter and later city editor (1961–70). He moved into broadcast journalism as a correspondent and producer for KERA-TV, Dallas (1970–72). He joined the Public Broadcasting System in 1972, and in 1973 began his long association with Robert MacNeil; they won an Emmy for their live coverage of the Senate Watergate hearings. The "Robert MacNeil Report," featuring Lehrer as Washington correspondent, began in 1975, and became their award-winning "MacNeil/Lehrer Report" in 1976 and "The MacNeil/Lehrer NewsHour" in 1983. Lehrer's many awards include several Emmys, a George Polk Award, and a Peabody Award.

His other novels include *Viva Max* (1966), *We Were Dreamers* (1975), *Kick the Can* (1988), *Crown Oklahoma* (1989), *The Sooner Spy* (1990), *Short List* (1992), *Blue Heart* (1993), and *Fine Lines* (1994), the latest in his series of offbeat political novels featuring One-Eyed Mack, lieutenant governor of Oklahoma. He has also written the plays *Chili Queen* (1986) and *Church Key Charlie Blue* (1987) and the memoir *A Bus of My Own* (1992). His 1956 journalism degree was from the University of Missouri. He is married to author Kate Staples Lehrer, and has three children.

FURTHER READING

"Flying solo." Barbara Matusow. *Washingtonian*, Oct. 1995.
"The news about. . . ." Paul Burka. *Texas Monthly*, Oct. 1995.
"MacNeil/Lehrer. . . ." Morgan Strong. *Playboy*, June 1991.

Leigh, Janet (Jeannette Helen Morrison; 1927–) That shower scene in which she was savagely killed was filmed more than 35 years ago but it still reverberates in the American psyche—not least in that of Janet Leigh, who (she confirms) has never since taken a shower. In 1995 Leigh published *Psycho: Behind the Scenes of the Classic Thriller,* written with C. Dickens, giving her own version of the making of the movie and seeking to correct "some of the myths, misconceptions and outright lies" that have surrounded Alfred Hitchcock's 1960 horror film. Leigh also made her debut as a novelist in 1995 with *House of Destiny,* a tale of Hollywood and Sun Valley from the mid-1930s to today, focusing on two longtime friends.

Born in Merced, California, Leigh attended the College of the Pacific, but left to begin her film career with MGM, making her film debut in *The Romance of Rosy Ridge* (1947). She quickly moved into starring roles, and appeared in scores of feature and television films, into the mid-1990s. Although many of her roles were undemanding, she demonstrated range and power

in such classics as Orson Welles's *Touch of Evil* (1958) and Alfred Hitchcock's *Psycho* (1960). Among her other films were *That Forsythe Woman* (1949), *Scaramouche* (1952), *The Naked Spur* (1953), *Houdini* (1953), *My Sister Eileen* (1955), *Pete Kelly's Blues* (1955), *The Vikings* (1958), *The Manchurian Candidate* (1962), *Bye Bye Birdie* (1963), and *Harper* (1966). She has also played in many television movies and series episodes. Among her other books are *Murder Among Friends* (1976), *There Really Was a Hollywood* (1984), and *Love Letters* (1991). Leigh's first husband was actor Tony Curtis (1952–62); they had two children, one of them the actress Jamie Lee Curtis. She married Robert Brandt in 1962.

FURTHER READING

"Coming clean. . . ." Cynthia Sanz and E. X. Feeney. *People*, Aug. 7, 1995.

Leigh, Jennifer Jason (Jennifer Morrow; 1962–) Emerging film star Jennifer Jason Leigh scored a triumph in 1995, starring in the highly regarded film *Georgia*, directed by Ulu Grosbard, and written by Barbara Turner, Leigh's mother, with whom she also coproduced the film. Leigh played young, untalented rock and roll singer Sadie, who returns home to Seattle and to her lifelong, wholly unsuccessful, corrosive, frustrating competition with her benign, very talented folk-rock-singing sister, played by Mare Winningham. Leigh's portrayal of Sadie won her critical acclaim, including a best actress award at the Montreal Film Festival, the best actress award of the New York Film Critics Circle, and considerable mention as a possible Academy Award contender.

Leigh also costarred in the film *Dolores Claiborne,* based on the Stephen King novel and directed by Taylor Hackford, in a cast that included Kathy Bates in the title role as her mother, who has been accused of murder, Christopher Plummer, and Judy Parfitt.

Forthcoming were starring roles opposite Harry Belafonte in Robert Altman's film *Kansas City* and in the television film *Bastard Out of Carolina,* directed by Anjelica Huston.

Los Angeles–born Leigh, the daughter of the late actor Vic Morrow and screenwriter Barbara Turner, began her career with guest appearances in television while in her mid-teens. Leaving high school shortly before graduation, she made her film debut in the horror film *Eyes of a Stranger* (1981), in the first of a long series of roles portraying physically and psychologically battered women. Her breakthrough role came a year later, in *Fast Times at Ridgemont High* (1982). She went on to star in such films as *Easy Money* (1983), *Grandview U.S.A.* (1984), *Flesh + Blood* (1985), *The Hitcher* (1986), *The Men's Club* (1986), *Sister, Sister* (1987), *Under Cover* (1987), *Heart of Midnight* (1988), *Last Exit to Brooklyn* (1989), *Miami Blues* (1990), *Crooked Hearts* (1991), *Single White Female* (1992), *The Prom* (1992), *Map of the Human Heart* (1992), *Short Cuts* (1993), *Mrs. Parker and the Vicious Circle* (1994), and *The Hudsucker Proxy* (1994). In television, she starred as an anorexic teenager in *The Best Little Girl in the World* (1981), and on stage Off-Broadway in *Sunshine* (1989). (For additional photo, see **Broderick, Matthew.**)

FURTHER READING

"Jennifer Jason Leigh." JANCEE DUNN. *Rolling Stone,* Nov. 30, 1995.
"Jennifer Jason Leigh. . . ." LYNN DARLING. *Esquire,* Dec. 1994.
"Single white phenomenon." KEVIN SESSUMS. *Vanity Fair,* July 1993.
"Not the girl next door." JEFFREY RESSNER. *Us,* Sept. 1992.
"Leigh, Jennifer Jason." *Current Biography,* Aug. 1992.
"Jennifer Jason Leigh." *Playboy,* Feb. 1992.
"Jennifer Jason Leigh. . . ." TOM GREEN. *Cosmopolitan,* May 1991.
"Jennifer Jason Leigh." JEFF YARBROUGH. *Interview,* Apr. 1991.

Lemieux, Mario (1965–) Of the many sports comebacks in 1995, perhaps none was so remarkable as that of hockey star Mario Lemieux. He had been forced out of action for 18 months, during which time he underwent two operations on his perennially problematic back, continued treatment for Hodgkins' disease (a type of cancer affecting the lymphatic system, first diagnosed in January 1993), and was also treated for a rare bone infection and anemia. It was not his first comeback. He had lost large chunks of the 1990–91 and 1993–94 seasons because of disk problems in his back and, in the latter, cancer surgery and radiation treatment. Indeed, when he announced his leave of absence in mid-1995, he himself thought his career was over. Even after his return, he was not trying to play every game, especially two in a row on long road trips.

The question for hockey fans and for Lemieux himself was: Did the 30-year-old still have his old skills? The answer showed in the numbers: in mid-January 1996, nearly halfway through the 1995–96 season, Lemieux overwhelmingly led the league in scoring, with 39 goals and 60 assists in 37 games, and a total of 99 points. His Pittsburgh Penguins had the second-best record in the league and were prime candidates for the Stanley Cup at season's end. Lemieux himself was named starting center for the Eastern Conference team in the National Hockey League All-Star game, to be played in late January 1996. He is playing under a seven-year, $42 million contract with the Penguins, signed in late 1992.

Outside of hockey, Lemieux also plays in occasional events on the Celebrity Golf Association tour.

Montreal-born Lemieux has spent his whole professional career with the Pittsburgh Penguins (1984–), winning two Stanley Cups (1991; 1992). Four-time league scoring leader (1988; 1989; 1992; 1993), he also won the Hart Memorial trophy for Most Valuable Player (1988; 1989), and the Conn Smythe trophy for Most Valuable Player in the playoffs (1991; 1992). Lemieux married Nathalie Asselin in 1993; they have a daughter.

FURTHER READING

" 'I'm not coming back . . . .' " LARRY WIGGE. *Sporting News,* Oct. 2, 1995.*Mario Lemieux, Ice Hockey Star.* JEFF Z. KLEIN. Chelsea House, 1995. *Sports Great Mario Lemieux.* RON KNAPP. Enslow, 1995.
"More than magnificent." D'ARCY JENISH. *Maclean's,* Apr. 26, 1993.
"The legend grows." JON SCHER. *Sports Illustrated,* Apr. 19, 1993
Mario Lemieux (Super Mario). TED COX. Childrens, 1993.
Mario Lemieux: Wizard with a Puck. BILL GUTMAN. Houghton Mifflin, 1992.
Mario Lemieux. BOB ITALIA. Abdo & Daughters, 1992.
Mario Lemieux: Wizard with a Puck. BILL GUTMAN. Millbrook, 1992.

Jack Lemmon (left) and Walter Matthau.

Lemmon, Jack (John Lemmon III; 1925–) Actors Jack Lemmon and Walter Matthau teamed up again in 1995; Lemmon once more starred as John opposite Walter Matthau as Max and Ann-Margret as Ariel in the offbeat film comedy *Grumpier Old Men,* directed by Howard Deutsch and costarring Sophia Loren, Burgess Meredith, Daryl Hannah, Kevin Pollack, and Ann Guilbert. The film is set six months after the earlier *Grumpy Old Men* (1993); Loren is introduced as a new love interest for Max, Lemmon and Ann-Margret are married, and the two great friends fall out acrimoniously over their children.

Lemmon also appeared in the film *The Grass Harp,* based on Truman Capote's autobiographical novel. The cast included Walter Matthau, Piper Laurie, Sissy Spacek, Mary Steenburgen, and Charles Durning, and was directed by Matthau's son, Charles Matthau.

Forthcoming was a role as Marcellus in Kenneth Branagh's film adaptation of Shakespeare's *Hamlet,* with Branagh directing and in the title role; Robin Williams, Derek Jacobi, Julie Christie, Billy Crystal, Charlton Heston, Rosemary Harris, Kate Winslet, John Gielgud, and John Mills were set to costar. Also forthcoming was a starring role in the film *Temecula,* directed by Martin Bergman and costarring Richard Lewis, Christine Lahti, and Rita Rudner.

Boston-born Lemmon played in early television, and began his long film career by winning a best supporting actor Oscar for his portrayal of Ensign Pulver in *Mister Roberts* (1954). Nineteen years later, he won a best actor Oscar for *Save the Tiger* (1973). Among his other films, some of the most notable were *Bell Book and Candle* (1958), *Some Like It Hot* (1959), *The Apartment* (1960), *Days of Wine and Roses* (1962), *Irma La Douce* (1963), *The Odd Couple* (1968), *The Prisoner of Second Avenue* (1975), *The China Syndrome* (1978), *Missing* (1981), *Mass Appeal* (1984), *Dad* (1989), *Glengarry Glen Ross* (1992), and *Short Cuts* (1993). Lemmon's B.A. and B.S. were from Harvard. Formerly married to Cynthia Boyd Stone, he married Felicia Farr in 1962, and has two children.

FURTHER READING

"Saint Jack." MICHAEL WILMINGTON. *Film Comment,* Mar.–Apr. 1993.
"Jack Lemmon." JOHN CLARK. *Premiere,* Nov. 1992.
"An everyman. . . ." PHILIP FRENCH. *Observer,* Oct. 25, 1992.
"Laughing on the outside." TOM JUNOD and MICHAEL O'NEILL. *Life,* Oct. 1992.

Leno, Jay (James Douglas Muir Leno; 1950–) It was a very good year for Jay Leno. For more than 90 weeks, he had been beaten in the late-night television wars by CBS rival David Letterman and sometimes also by Ted Koppel and "Nightline" on ABC. But in late July 1995, Leno and NBC's "The Tonight Show" won the ratings race for the first time, the occasion being the first public appearance of actor Hugh

Grant after his arrest with a prostitute. By late November, though "Nightline" sometimes took the lead, Leno was routinely besting Letterman in the ratings. At the 47th annual Emmy Awards, where Leno was a presenter, "The Tonight Show" (produced by Leno's Big Dog Productions) was honored as the outstanding variety, music, or comedy series, an award won by Letterman's show in 1994. The turnaround was largely credited to the new, more spontaneous, high-energy style and club-type setting (including celebrity walk-ons) Leno developed in 1994, and his on-screen relationship with new musical sidekick Kevin Eubanks (who permanently replaced Branford Marsalis in 1995). Leno's 1994 contract, which had run into early 1997, was extended to the year 2000. In February, Leno appeared live online in the NBC Forum of America Online, which also served to publicize the start of the "Tonight Show with Jay Leno" page on the Internet's World Wide Web, featuring guest listings, jokes, quotes, "headlines," and behind-the-scenes footage. In production at HBO was a film on the late-night battles between Leno and Letterman, *The Late Shift*.

Born in New York's suburbs and raised in Massachusetts, Leno began his career as a stand-up comic at Boston nightclubs while studying for a speech degree at Emerson College. He later worked New York clubs and wrote for television's "Good Times." He has toured widely, hosted two of his own NBC specials, made numerous guest appearances, and published five books of odd or absurd newspaper cuttings, many sent by fans. He was a frequent guest on both Johnny Carson's "Tonight Show" and Letterman's "Late Night" from 1977, and was a guest host on the "Tonight Show" from 1986, exclusively from 1987, before succeeding Carson in 1992. Leno married scriptwriter Mavis Nicholson in 1980.

FURTHER READING

"Leno lives!" BIL ZEHME. *Esquire*, Oct. 1995.
"Jay Leno. . . ." STEVE BUCKLEY. *Boston*, May 1992.
"Midnight's mayor. . . ." RICHARD STENGEL. *Time*, Mar. 16, 1992.
The World of Jay Leno: His Humor and His Life. BILL ADLER and BRUCE CASSIDAY. Birch Lane/Carol, 1992.
"Wipe that smirk. . . ." PETER W. KAPLAN and PETER STEVENSON. *Esquire*, Sept. 1991.

Lester, Jerry (1911–95) Chicago-born comedian and early television host Jerry Lester began his career in variety as a child, and turned fully professional after his graduation from Northwestern University. He worked in vaudeville, cabaret, and radio in the 1930s and 1940s, winning small supporting roles in several Broadway musicals and Hollywood films. His breakthrough came in early television, where a talk show guest appearance led to an NBC offer of a show of his own. That show was "Broadway Open House" (1950–51), a pioneering late-night talk show hosted by Lester; its cabaret routines, combined with celebrity guests and musical segments, proved enormously popular. Although the show lasted for only a year, its pattern was to be adopted by such diverse and long-running hosts as Jack Paar, Steve Allen, Johnny Carson, and David Letterman. Lester went on to star in several other television shows until the mid-50s, and later worked largely in cabaret. His career ended in 1975, when he contracted Alzheimer's disease. He was survived by his wife, Alice, two daughters, and a son. (d. Miami; March 23, 1995)

FURTHER READING

Obituary. *Variety*, Mar. 30, 1995.
Obituary. *New York Times*, Mar. 25, 1995.

Letterman, David (1947–) The bloom went slightly off the David Letterman rose in 1995. The first sign of trouble was at the Academy Awards in March; though the televised show had high ratings, many critics and viewers panned Letterman's performance as host, especially his habit of ridiculing people's names; he was not asked back for 1996. Then after the "Late Show with David Letterman" had led late-night rival Jay Leno and "The Tonight Show" in the ratings for more than 90 weeks, Letterman was beaten by Leno for the first time in late July; by late 1995, Letterman was routinely being beaten by Leno. During the year one or both often ran behind Ted Koppel's "Nightline," especially during the Oklahoma City bombing and the O.J. Simpson trial. Part of the problem was CBS's overall programming weakness, meaning poor lead-ins to Letterman's show, as well as weaker affiliates and fewer affiliates overall.

Letterman himself retained a high "Q rating,"

measuring recognizability and likability among audiences, and often continued to best Leno among younger viewers, prized by advertisers. Letterman had won the 1994 Emmy for the outstanding variety, music, or comedy show, but saw the 1995 award go to Leno. Plans for 1996 included a new set, new opening graphics, a new featured guest, Chris Elliott (a regular on Letterman's old NBC show), and the return of writer Rob Burnett. In production at HBO was a film on the late-night battles between Leno and Letterman, *The Late Shift*.

Letterman's own production company, Worldwide Pants, Inc., produced various shows, including a talk show hosted by Tom Snyder, which follows Letterman's own show in the lineup, which debuted in January, and "The Bonnie Hunt Show," which debuted on CBS in October. A buddy comedy called "Emmett and Earl" was also scheduled. Letterman's mother, Dorothy, received a reported $1 million for a book called *Home Cookin' with Dave's Mom*.

Letterman began his career as an announcer in his hometown of Indianapolis. Moving to Los Angeles in the mid-1970s, he worked as a comedy writer for many television performers, performed as a comedian with The Comedy Store, appeared in many guest roles, and was a frequent guest on the "Tonight Show." In 1980, he emerged as a substantial television personality in his own NBC morning show, the "David Letterman Show." Moving to late night, following NBC's "Tonight Show," he wrote and starred in his long-running "Late Night with David Letterman" (1982–93). He debuted on CBS with the "Late Show with David Letterman" in August 1993. He has published several collections of "Top Ten" lists from his show. A highly respected figure in television, Letterman has won seven Emmys. His B.A. was from Ball State University.

FURTHER READING

"Waiting to exhale." KEN TUCKER. *Entertainment*, Dec. 1, 1995.
"Oscar '95. . . ." KEN TUCKER. *Entertainment*, Apr. 7, 1995.
David Letterman. Chelsea House, 1995.
Dave's World: The Unauthorized Guide to the Late Show with David Letterman. MICHAEL CADER. Warner, 1995.
"Letterman lets. . . ." BILL ZEHME. *Esquire*, Dec. 1994.
"Playboy interview. . . ." TOM SHALES. *Playboy*, Jan. 1994.

Lunatic Guide to the David Letterman Show: Watching Television as a Pathway to Radical Self. BRADFORD KEENEY. Station Hill Press, 1994.
David Letterman. ROSEMARIE LENNON. Windsor, 1994.
"New Dave. . . ." RICHARD ZOGLIN and RICHARD CORLISS. *Time*, Aug. 30, 1993.
"David Letterman. . . ." *Cosmopolitan*, Apr. 1993.
"David Letterman. . . ." BILL ZEHME. *Rolling Stone*, Feb. 18, 1993.

Lindfors, Viveca (Elsa Viveca Torstendsdotter Lindfors; 1920–95) Swedish stage and screen actress Viveca Lindfors began her career in Stockholm, at the Royal Dramatic Theater (1937–40), and made her Swedish film debut in *The Spinning Family* (1940). She made seven more Swedish films and appeared in many plays before going to Hollywood in 1946, making her English-language film debut in *To the Victor* (1948). From then until the early 1990s, she appeared in scores of films, largely in costarring roles, among them *The Adventures of Don Juan* (1948), *Four in a Jeep* (1951; she was named best actress at the Berlin Film Festival), *The Damned* (1961), *No Exit* (1962; best actress, Berlin Film Festival), *The Way We Were* (1973), *Unfinished Business* (1987; she also wrote and directed), and *Last Summer in the Hamptons* (1996). In the English-speaking theater, she became a star, making her very notable 1955 Broadway debut in the title role of *Anastasia*. Among her other theater works were *Miss Julie* (1955), *Brecht on Brecht* (1961), and her acclaimed one-woman show *I Am a Woman* (1973). She published the autobiography *Viveca: An Actress, a Woman, a Life* (1981). She was survived by a daughter and two sons. (d. Uppsala, Sweden; October 25, 1995)

FURTHER READING

Obituary. *Variety*, Oct. 30, 1995
Obituary. *New York Times*, Oct. 26, 1995.

Li Peng (1928–) Chinese Premier Li Peng during 1995 expressed increasingly deep concerns about the pace and direction of China's "economic miracle," accompanied as it was by a

large, destabilizing rate of inflation, in the annual 20 percent plus range. In his opening speech to the March meeting of the People's Congress, he called for a sharp change of policy on economic reform, accompanied by measures aimed at cooling down China's overheated economy. Communist China was encountering huge and growing social and economic problems, as runaway inflation destroyed the savings and pensions of hundreds of millions of people, the flight from country to city reached enormous proportions, and even China's draconian birth control laws proved harder and harder to enforce as the population became more mobile and hard to track and fully control.

Clearly, Li Peng and his conservative colleagues were throughout the year also positioning themselves for the inevitable succession struggle that would occur on the death of Deng Xiaoping, stressing that it was they who would bring renewed stability to China—a powerful argument for government, party, and military elites still very mindful of the hundred years of foreign domination and civil war that had preceded the victory of Chinese communism.

Li Peng began his long, steady rise in the Chinese Communist bureaucracy as a young protégé of Premier Zhou En-lai. He emerged as a major figure in the 1980s, serving as minister of power in 1981 and as a Politburo member in 1985. In the late 1980s, as great tension developed between the liberal and conservative wings of the Chinese leadership, he became a conservative faction leader. Throughout the world, he is viewed as the chief architect of the 1989 Tiananmen Square massacre. He was reelected to a second five-year term at the March 1993 meeting of the National People's Congress. Li attended the Moscow Power Institute. He married Zhu Lin in 1958; they have three children.

"Premier Li. . . ." *Beijing Review*, Oct. 30, 1995.
"Circling the Wagons. . . ." PATRICK E. TYLER. *New York Times*, Dec. 15, 1995.

Lithgow, John Arthur (1945–) For stage, screen, and television star John Lithgow, 1995 was largely a television year. In the television film *My Brother's Keeper,* he played dual roles, as the true-life gay twin brothers Bob and

Tom Bradley. After Tom Bradley tests positive for the HIV virus, his insurance company refuses to pay for a bone marrow transplant from his twin that might help prevent the development of AIDS; the brothers then sue the insurance company, "going public" to seek help. Glenn Jordan produced and directed; Ellen Burstyn, Annette O'Toole, and Veronica Cartwright costarred. Lithgow received an Emmy nomination as best lead actor in a miniseries or special.

Lithgow also starred in the "Hallmark Hall of Fame" television film *Redwood Curtain,* as the American adoptive father of an Asian woman, played by Lea Salonga, who searches for her biological father, an American soldier. A third leading role came in the *You, Murderer* episode of television's "Tales from the Crypt," a remake of the 1947 Humphrey Bogart–Lauren Bacall film *Dark Passage,* directed by Robert Zemeckis and costarring Robert Sacchi, Isabella Rossellini, and Sherilyn Fenn. Lithgow also hosted "American Cinema," a ten-part public television film history series. Forthcoming was a new television series on Fox, "Third Rock from the Sun."

Rochester-born Lithgow began playing substantial roles on the New York stage in the early 1970s, in such plays as *The Changing Room* (1972), *Beyond Therapy* (1982), *Requiem for a Heavyweight* (1985), and *M. Butterfly* (1988). His most notable films include *The World According to Garp* (1982; he received an Oscar nomination), *Terms of Endearment* (1983; and a second Oscar nomination), *The Manhattan Project* (1986), *Memphis Belle* (1990), *At Play in the Fields of the Lord* (1991), *Raising Cain* (1992), *Cliffhanger* (1993), *The Pelican Brief* (1993), *The Wrong Man* (1993), *Silent Fall* (1994), *A Good Man in Africa* (1994), and *Princess Caraboo* (1994). He has also appeared in several television films, including *The Day After* (1983), *Amazing Stories* (1987; he won an Emmy), *The Boys* (1991), and *World War II: When Lions Roared* (1994).

Lithgow is a 1967 Harvard University graduate, and also attended the London Academy of Music and Dramatic Art (LAMDA). He has been married twice, last to Mary Yeager in 1981, and has two children.

"Ready to go. . . ." DEVON JACKSON. *People*, July 5, 1993.

Lobo, Rebecca (1973–) For a woman basketball star to become a household name is extremely rare, but that is what happened to Rebecca Lobo in 1995. In her fourth and final year at the University of Connecticut, the 6'4" center and her teammates—notably Jen Rizzotti, Jamelle Elliott, and Kara Wolters, coached by Geno Auriemma—took their basketball team to an unbeaten season (35-0) and the school's first national championship. It was not easy, and in the final game against powerful Tennessee, the Connecticut Huskies trailed with only about two minutes left, but came back to win 70–64. Lobo herself was named the most outstanding player of the NCAA Final Four. She ended the season averaging 17.1 points, 9.8 rebounds, and 3.5 blocks; was consensus national player of the year; won the U.S. Basketball Writers Association Naismith Award as 1995 national player of the year; was a unanimous pick and the top vote-getter for the Associated Press All-America first team; and won numerous other awards, including Big East Player of the Year and Scholar-Athlete of the Year, for the second consecutive year. She was inducted into Phi Beta Kappa, the national honor society, in April 1995, and also won the Wade Trophy, honoring the senior player who best demonstrates academic achievement and leadership *off* the court. She was even a guest on the "Late Show with David Letterman."

Late in 1995, Lobo played *against* some of her old teammates, as a member of the USA Basketball Women's National Team that was touring the country playing exhibition games against college teams, in preparation for the 1996 Atlanta Olympics. At that event, in November, Lobo joined her old teammates on the sidelines of Connecticut's Gampel Pavilion as the championship banner was unfurled, and then joined her new teammates to hand her old school's team its first defeat since its European tour in summer 1994. In the 1995 U.S. Basketball League draft, she was selected in the tenth round by the New Jersey Turnpikes.

Lobo was raised in Southwick, Massachusetts. She was a member of the 1993 USA Junior World Championship Team. Over her four-year career at Connecticut, her team had a 106-25 record. With all her athletic activities, Lobo—a political science major—has maintained a high academic average in her four years at Connecticut (1991–95), in the fall of 1994 achieving a perfect 4.0, and has won various academic honors as well.

FURTHER READING

"The enforcer." ANDREW ABRAHAMS. *People,* Mar. 20, 1995.
"The post with. . . ." RICK TELANDER. *Sports Illustrated,* Mar. 20, 1995

Logan, Onnie Lee (ca. 1910–95) Born in Sweet Water, Alabama, Onnie Lee Logan was the child of a large, poor Black farming family. She had little opportunity for formal education and from early in life did domestic work. From her early 20s, she was also a highly successful midwife, who pursued her career in the largely Black town of Prichard, Alabama, near Mobile, practicing there from 1931 for more than six decades, beginning before formal state licensing came in 1949, and continuing on long after the state formally banned midwifery. In the late 1980s, with author Katherine Clark, she taped her recollections, which became the basis for their highly regarded book *Motherwit: An Alabama Midwife's Story* (1989). She was survived by her husband, Roosevelt Logan, a son, and a sister. (d. Mobile, Alabama; July 11, 1995)

FURTHER READING

Obituary. *New York Times,* July 13, 1995.
"Driving Miss Onnie." MICHAEL LEWIS. *New Republic,* Aug. 16, 1993.

Louganis, Greg E. (1960–) When, in February 1995, diver Greg Louganis announced that he had AIDS, many people immediately flashed back to television images of the 1988 Seoul Olympics and the bloody head injury Louganis sustained when hitting his head on the diving board—and of the U.S. team doctor who treated him barehanded, stitching the cut so he could compete on his next dive. Louganis made the announcement first in an interview with Barbara Walters on "20/20," at publication of his autobiography, *Breaking the Surface: A Life,* written with Eric Marcus. Telling his story "while I still have the chance," Louganis described the agony of being an unacknowledged homosexual, seeing his companion dying of AIDS, and learning (early in 1988) that he himself was HIV-positive—and feeling that he could not tell these things honestly and openly, for fear of being barred from competitive diving and losing commercial endorsements. Louganis had not informed those who treated him at the 1988 Olympics that they were at risk, for which he made late apology in 1995. Dr. James Puffer, who stitched Louganis at Seoul, has remained HIV-negative. Other divers are thought to have been in little or no danger, since the virus was highly diluted in water and also deactivated by chlorine.

That Louganis's story touched many people was evident in the book's appearance on bestseller lists, at times in the top spot. Louganis himself went on a 20-city promotional tour and was widely interviewed on programs such as "The Oprah Winfrey Show," "Good Morning America," "The Larry King Show," "Today," and "CBS This Morning."

San Diego–born Louganis began his extraordinary diving career in his early teens, and won his first Olympic honor, a silver medal for platform diving, at the 1976 Montreal Olympics. He would win 48 American national diving titles, become the 1986 platform and springboard World Diving Champion, and win many other platform and springboard world titles. He won platform and springboard gold medals at both the 1984 and 1988 Olympics, the first diver in 60 years to win both medals in consecutive Olympics. Louganis attended the University of Miami (1978–80) and received his 1983 B.A. in theater from the University of California. He retired from competitive diving after 1988, turning to a career in the theater. In 1994, at the New York City Gay Games, he revealed his homosexual preference.

FURTHER READING

"Below the surface." PETER GALVIN. *Advocate,* Apr. 4, 1995.
"Disclosure." CHRIS BULL. *Advocate,* Mar. 21, 1995.
"Heart of the diver." STEVE WULF. *Time,* Mar. 6, 1995.
"To the man who. . . ." JEFFREY SLONIM. *Interview,* Jan. 1994.

Lovell, Jim (James Arthur Lovell, Jr.; 1928–) For millions of people, American astronaut Jim Lovell will always wear the face of Tom Hanks, the actor who portrayed Lovell in the 1995 hit movie *Apollo 13*. Directed by Ron How-

ard, the film dramatized the experiences of Lovell and his two fellow astronauts, Tom Haise and Jack L. Swigert, Jr., on the 1970 flight, when they lost oxygen and power in the main spacecraft, after an explosion in space. The crew were forced to use the lunar module, with its limited power and oxygen, for 3 days and 15 hours, while maneuvering the craft for a return to Earth, and faced the possibility of being lost in space or incinerated on reentering the Earth's atmosphere. The movie's script, by William Broyles, Jr., and Al Reinert, was based on the 1994 book *Lost Moon: The Perilous Voyage of Apollo 13,* by Lovell and Jeffrey Kluger, which was reissued in paperback in December 1994 under the title *Apollo 13*. Both film and book reached the top spot on their respective lists. An audio version of the book was also released, with Lovell's own voice joining that of the main reader, Edward Herrmann, as well as original recordings between Mission Control and the Apollo spacecraft. In June 1995, Lovell received the Congressional Space Medal of Honor from President Bill Clinton. In July 1995, Universal Studios Hollywood opened a new exhibit, "Making of *Apollo 13*," which Lovell attended, even judging a children's model rocket competition.

Born in Cleveland, but largely raised in Milwaukee, Lovell was fascinated by space travel from his teens. He graduated from the U.S. Naval Academy in 1952, and served as an aircraft-carrier pilot, test pilot, and instructor, before joining the National Aeronautic and Space Administration (NASA) as an astronaut in 1962. Lovell left NASA in 1973 and later worked for a marine company and then in telecommunications, before retiring in 1991. Lovell married Marilyn Gerlach in 1952; they have four children.

FURTHER READING

"Shooting the moon. . . ." SKIP HOLLANDSWORTH. *Texas Monthly,* July 1995.
"When it comes to 'naut." BRUCE FORER. *Entertainment,* June 30, 1995.
"Splashback." CINDY PEARLMAN. *Chicago,* June 1995.
"Remembering Apollo." TIM FOLGER et al. *Discover,* July 1994.

Loy, Nanni (Giovanni Loy; 1925–95) Italian film and television director and actor Nanni Loy began his film career as a documentarian, moving into fiction films in 1957 with *Fiasco in Milan.* His breakthrough film was *Four Days in Naples* (1962), a story about the 1943 World War II Italian Resistance–led rebellion against German forces in Naples. Among his other films were *The Head of the Family* (1967), *Situation Normal All Fouled Up* (1970), *Black Is Beautiful* (1973), *Caffe Express* (1980), and *Picone Sent Me* (1983). Loy was a prolific television director, also often appearing as an actor. At the time of his death, a forthcoming film starring Sidney Poitier was in development. He was survived by his companion, Elvira Carteny, and four children. (d. Rome; August 21, 1995)

FURTHER READING

Obituary. *Independent,* Aug. 22, 1995.
Obituary. *New York Times,* Aug. 23, 1995.

Lugar, Richard Green (1932–) On April 19, 1995, Indiana Republican Senator Richard Lugar announced his candidacy for the 1996 Republican presidential nomination. He ran his campaign very much as a middle-of-the-road conservative, avoiding many of the most inflammatory issues before the country and stressing the stability that his long experience in foreign policy matters and generally conservative positions would contribute. Deeply interested in the international aspects of the president's job, he urged American contributions to the Bosnian conciliation process and nuclear and chemical nonproliferation, while also opposing abortion; called for large social service network and other budgetary cuts; advocated a national sales tax to replace the current tax system; and supported the balanced budget amendment. Lugar's candidacy did not flourish during 1995, and at year's end he was not expected to do well in the presidential primary race.

Indianapolis-born Lugar began his political career in his hometown, as a member of the Indianapolis School Board (1964–67). He was mayor of Indianapolis (1968–75) and president of the National League of Cities (1970–71). He was a keynote speaker at the 1972 Republican National Convention. Lugar won election to the U.S. Senate in 1976, and has served in the Senate since 1977. He was chairman of the National Republican Senatorial Committee (1983–84) and chairman of the Senate Foreign Relations Committee (1985–86). Lugar's 1954 B.A. was from Denison University. He was a Rhodes Scholar at Oxford University, receiving his M.A. from Oxford in 1956. Lugar has published *Letters to the Next President* (1988). He is married to Charlene Smeltzer; they have four sons.

FURTHER READING

"Bland ambition. . . ." MATTHEW COOPER. *New Republic,* Sept. 18, 1995.
"Lugar takes. . . ." RALPH Z. HALLOW. *Insight on the News,* Apr. 3, 1995.
"But seriously. . . ." MARGARET CARLSON. *Time,* Mar. 13, 1995.

Lundberg, Ferdinand Edgar (1905–95) Chicago-born Ferdinand Lundberg attended Chicago City College (1921–23), and then began his career in journalism with the *Chicago Daily Journal* (1924–26). He moved to United Press International (1926–27) and then to the *New York Herald Tribune* (1927–34). During World War II, he worked at the War Shipping Administration (1941–45). After the war, while working as an editor at the Twentieth Century Fund (1946–51), he completed his formal education, with a 1948 B.S. from Columbia University and a 1952 M.A. from Columbia. Lundberg emerged as a highly regarded author and social critic in the mid-1930s, with publication of his sharply critical work on William Randolph

Hearst: *Imperial Hearst: A Social Biography* (1936). He followed it with *America's Sixty Families* (1937), which propounded the very popular Depression-era view that a few wealthy families controlled every significant aspect of life in the United States. Three decades later, he pursued the same theme in *The Rich and the Super-Rich* (1968), which became a best-seller. In a wholly different area, he and Marynia Farnham co-authored *Modern Women: The Lost Sex* (1947), highly regarded in its time, though later attacked by many feminists as sexist. Among Lundberg's other works were *The Rockefeller Syndrome* (1976) and *The Natural Depravity of Mankind: Observations on the Human Condition* (1994). He was survived by his wife, Elizabeth Young Lundberg, and two sons. (Mt. Kisco, New York; March 1, 1995)

FURTHER READING

Obituary. *New York Times*, Mar. 3, 1995.

Lupino, Ida (1918–95) London-born Ida Lupino, an actress, director, writer, and producer, made her film debut in *Her First Affaire* (1933). She played in supporting roles in Hollywood from 1934, making her breakthrough opposite Ronald Colman in *The Light That Failed* (1939), and playing in her classic role opposite Humphrey Bogart in *High Sierra* (1941). Among her other films were *They Drive by Night* (1940), *The Sea Wolf* (1941), *Ladies in Retirement* (1941), *The Hard Way* (1943), *In Our Time* (1944), and *Devotion* (1946). Later in her career, she produced and starred opposite her third husband, Howard Duff, in the television comedy series "Mr. Adams and Eve" (1957–58). In the late 1940s, Lupino emerged as a pioneering woman Hollywood producer, director, and screenwriter, with such films as *Not Wanted* (1949), *Never Fear* (1950), *Outrage* (1950), *Hard, Fast and Beautiful* (1951), *The Hitch-Hiker* (1953), *The Bigamist* (1953), and *The Trouble with Angels* (1956).

Her three marriages, to actor Louis Hayward, producer Collier Young, and Howard Duff, ended in divorce. She was the daughter of actor Stanley Lupino and the niece of actor Lupino Lane; all were members of the historic Lupino British stage family. She attended the Royal Academy of Dramatic Art. She was survived by a daughter and a sister. (d. Burbank, California; August 3, 1995)

FURTHER READING

Ida Lupino: A Biography. WILLIAM J DONNATI. University of Kentucky Press, 1996.
Obituary. *Current Biography*, Oct. 1995.
Obituary. *Independent*, Aug. 7, 1995.
Obituary. *Times* (of London), Aug. 7, 1995.
Obituary. *Variety*, Aug. 7, 1995.
Obituary. *New York Times*, Aug. 5, 1995.
Queen of the "B"s: Ida Lupino Behind the Camera. ANNETTE KUHN. Greenwood, 1995.
"Ida Lupino. . . ." GAVIN LAMBERT. *Architectural Digest*, Apr. 1994.

Lynn, Jeffrey (Ragnar Godfrey Lind; 1909–95) Massachusetts-born actor Jeffrey Lynn attended Bates College. He was a high school teacher before beginning his film, stage, and television career. He became a Warner Brothers contract player in 1937, making his breakthrough to costarring and starring roles in *Four Daughters* (1938). Among his other pre–World War II films were *Yes, My Darling Daughter* (1939), *The Roaring Twenties* (1939), *The Fighting 69th* (1940), *All This and Heaven Too* (1940), and *Million Dollar Baby* (1941). After war service as an intelligence officer, he returned to his screen career, with such films as *Whiplash* (1948), *A Letter to Three Wives* (1949), *Up Front* (1951), *Butterfield 8* (1960), and *Tony Rome* (1967). He also appeared in several Broadway plays, and during the latter part of his career appeared in many television series, including "My Son Jeep," "Star Stage," "Secret Storm," and "Barnaby Jones." He was survived by his wife, Helen, a daughter, seven adopted children, three sisters, and two brothers. (d. Burbank, California; November 24, 1995)

FURTHER READING

Obituary. *New York Times*, Dec. 2, 1995.
Obituary. *Independent*, Nov. 28, 1995.

Lytle, Andrew Nelson (1902–95) Tennessee-born Andrew Lytle, a novelist, literary critic, biographer, editor, and teacher, was associated while a student at Vanderbilt University with the Fugitives, a group of poets. He joined with several of them in the late 1920s in forming the Agrarian movement in southern literature; their 1930 statement "Where I Stand," pioneering in its time, foreshadowed later quality-of-life concerns in an increasingly citified United States. Long the editor of the literary magazine *The Sewanee Review,* Lytle was a teacher at several colleges and universities who influenced at least two generations of American writers. His own works included the novels *The Long Night* (1936), *At the Moon's Inn* (1941), and *The Velvet Horn* (1957), as well as several shorter works of fiction; an essay collection, *The Hero with the Private Parts* (1966); and the autobiographical *A Wake for the Living* (1975). He was survived by two daughters and a sister. (d. Monteagle, Tennessee; December 14, 1995)

FURTHER READING

Obituary. *New York Times*, Dec. 15, 1995.

M

McCartney, Paul (1942–) Former Beatle Paul McCartney, a major and very active figure in world music, joined two other living legends, former Beatles George Harrison and Ringo Starr, in a three-segment, six-hour television biography of the group, *The Beatles Anthology*, broadcast on ABC November 19, 20, and 22, 1995. The show, which included the world premiere of the John Lennon song "Free as a Bird," drew enormous audiences. It was followed by the release of their two-disc set *The Beatles Anthology, Volume. 1;* volumes 2 and 3 were to be released in 1996. Volume I contained more than 40 selections drawn from the years 1958–64, including some from the period when they were still called the Quarrymen and others before Ringo Starr replaced Pete Best as drummer. Included were the unreleased Lennon-McCartney songs "Hello Little Girl" and "Like Dreamers Do," as well as the 1977 John Lennon song "Free as a Bird." Two other Lennon songs, "Real Love" and "Grow Old with Me," were scheduled to be released in the 1996 volumes. A *Beatles Anthology* book was also to be released in 1996, as was a ten-hour home video version of the anthology. The anthology albums and a "Free as a Bird" single were released in early December; both immediately became record-breaking chart toppers.

McCartney also continued his work on behalf of British music, premiering his solo piano work "A Leaf" at a Royal College of Music benefit in March, and continuing his work on behalf of the Liverpool Institute for Performing Arts (LIPA).

Liverpool natives McCartney, John Lennon, George Harrison, and Ringo Starr (from 1962) were the world-famous Beatles (1960–70), with McCartney as rhythm guitarist and then bass guitarist. He and Lennon wrote a great many of the Beatles' songs, such as "Yesterday," "Strawberry Fields Forever," and "Sgt. Pepper's Lonely Hearts Club Band," and he was often the group's lead singer. After the Beatles dissolved in 1970, he went on his own and in 1971 formed Wings, continuing to compose, perform, and record for worldwide audiences during the next two decades. In 1989, he went on the road for the first time in 13 years with a highly successful world tour, which also produced a live album, *Tripping the Live Fantastic* (1990), and in 1993 issued the albums *Off the Ground* and *Paul Is Live. The Liverpool Oratorio*, his first classical work, premiered in 1991. In 1984, McCartney published *Give My Regards to Broad Street*. He married Linda Eastman in 1969; they have four children.

FURTHER READING

"Get back. . . ." RICHARD CORLISS. *Time*, Nov. 20, 1995.
"The music man. . . ." JEFF GILES. *Newsweek*, Oct. 23, 1995.
Lennon and McCartney: Their Magic and Their Music. BRUCE GLASSMAN. Blackbirch, 1995.
The Day John Met Paul: An Hour-by-Hour Account of How the Beatles Began. JIM O'DONNELL. Hall of Fame Books, 1994.
The Lost Beatles Interviews. GEOFFREY GIULIANO. NAL-Dutton, 1994.
The Walrus Was Paul: The Great Beatle Death Clues of 1969. R. GARY PATTERSON. Excursion, 1994.
Turn Me On, Dead Man: The Complete Story of the

Paul McCartney Death Hoax. ANDRU J. REEVE. Popular Culture, 1994.

Paul McCartney: Behind the Myth. ROSS BENSON. Trafalgar, 1993.

Illustrated Paul McCartney. GEOFFREY GIULIANO. Book Sales, 1993.

"Winged Beatle. . . ." *Economist,* June 13, 1992.

"Rock meets classical." DENNIS POLKOW. *Musical America,* Jan.–Feb. 1992.

Blackbird: The Life and Times of Paul McCartney. GEOFFREY GIULIANO. NAL-Dutton, 1991.

Strange Days: The Music of John, Paul, George and Ringo Twenty Years On. WALTER PODRAZIK. Popular Culture, 1991.

McClure, Doug

(Douglas Osborne McClure; 1935–95) California-born actor Doug McClure made his film debut in *The Enemy Below* (1957) and began to play strong supporting roles and second leads in television in the 1960s, beginning with a costarring role opposite William Bendix in the western series "The Overland Trail" (1960). His next series was the detective thriller "Checkmate" (1960–62). He emerged as a major television star as the cowboy Trampas in the long-running, very popular western series "The Virginian" (1962–71). He played in several other series, including "The Search" (1975–76), "Barbary Coast" (1975), and the miniseries *Roots* (1977). His television success also brought him several substantial film roles, as in *Shenandoah* (1965), *Beau Geste* (1966), *The Land That Time Forgot* (1974), and *At the Earth's Core* (1976). McClure also appeared in several plays. He was survived by his wife, Diane, two children, his mother, and a brother. (d. Los Angeles; February 5, 1995)

FURTHER READING

"Easy rider. . . ." *People,* Feb. 20, 1995.

Obituary. *New York Times,* Feb. 8, 1995.

Obituary. *Independent,* Feb. 7, 1995.

Obituary. *Times* (of London), Feb. 7, 1995.

Obituary. *Variety,* Feb. 7, 1995.

McCurry, Michael Demaree

(1954–) On January 5, 1995, President Bill Clinton named Mike McCurry to be White House press secretary, succeeding Dee Dee Myers. McCurry's was a very familiar face to the public, as he had been State Department spokesperson since 1993. His was also a familiar face and style to the Washington press corps, as he had held a series of political public relations posts in Washington since 1976. During 1995, McCurry handled the whole range of White House concerns, issues, and announcements professionally and without a noticeable hitch or personal misstep, while developing considerably more amicable White House–press corps relations than had characterized the first two years of the Clinton administration.

Born in Charleston, South Carolina, McCurry grew up in California. After receiving his 1976 B.A. from Princeton University, he went to Washington as press secretary to New Jersey Democratic Senator Harrison Williams (1976–81). After Williams's indictment in the Abscam scandal, McCurry became press secretary for Senator Patrick Moynihan (1981–83), Senator John Glenn (1984), and Bruce Babbitt (1986–88), and then Democratic National Committee communications director (1988–90). From 1990–93, he worked as a public relations consultant before becoming spokesperson for the State Department (1993–95). McCurry received his M.A. from Georgetown University in 1985. He is married to Debra Lyn Jones; they have a daughter and a son.

FURTHER READING

"Michael McCurry. . . ." DAVID ELLIS. *People,* Oct. 23, 1995.

MacDowell, Andie

(Rose Anderson MacDowell; 1958–) Film star Andie MacDowell became a very familiar face on American television screens in 1995, as both of her 1994 films, *Bad Girls* and *Four Weddings and a Funeral,* did well in home video.

In 1995, MacDowell starred opposite John Turturro in the Los Angeles–set comedy-drama *Unstrung Heroes,* costarring Nathan Watt, Michael Richards, Maury Chaykin, and Kendra Krull. The film premiered at the Cannes Film Festival, and at its autumn opening in New York received mixed reviews. MacDowell played the mother opposite Turturro's inventor-father; their son, played by Michael Richards, runs away to live with his eccentric uncles after his mother becomes ill, providing the storyline for the gentle film, directed by Diane Keaton.

Forthcoming was a starring role opposite John Travolta in the film *Michael,* directed by Nora Ephron, in which MacDowell is a dog expert who is trying to track an angel, played by Travolta. Also forthcoming was a starring role opposite Michael Keaton in the film *Multiplicity,* directed by Harold Ramis.

South Carolina–born MacDowell was a model before making her film debut in *Greystoke: The Legend of Tarzan, Lord of the Apes* (1984). Her breakthrough role came in *sex, lies, and videotape* (1989); she then went on to star in *Green Card* (1990), *Hudson Hawk* (1991), *The Object of Beauty* (1991), *Deception* (1993), *Short Cuts* (1993), *Groundhog Day* (1993), *Bad Girls* (1994), and *Four Weddings and a Funeral* (1994). MacDowell attended Winthrop College. She is married to actor and model Paul Qualley, and has three children.

FURTHER READING

"Secrets of a natural beauty." Elizabeth Gaynor. *Parade,* Oct. 15, 1995.

"The two lives of. . . ." Ellen Welty. *Redbook,* Oct. 1995.

" 'I love being. . . .' " Martin Jones. *First for Women,* July 11, 1994.

"Southern comfort." Kevin Sessums. *Vanity Fair,* Mar. 1993.

Andie MacDowell. Bob Italia. Abdo & Daughters, 1992.

"Andie gets real." Dawn Cotter and Christina Ferrari. *McCall's,* Aug. 1991.

McEntire, Reba (1955–) Veteran country singer Reba McEntire again gathered a good many honors in 1995. She was named Academy of Country Music entertainer of the year, the first woman to win that honor since 1980, and was also the Academy's female vocalist of the year. She won an American Music Award as best country female artist of the year, a Country Music Association award as top touring artist of the year, a Blockbuster Entertainment award as best female country artist, and a People's Choice award as best female musical performer. She also received Grammy nominations for best country album for her *Read My Mind,* and for best female country vocal performance for "She Thinks His Name Was John."

McEntire issued several singles during 1995. Among them were "And Still," a highly emotional ballad about a woman who meets a long-ago lover, feels a surge of sentiment, and realizes that it is truly over when she meets his wife. A second was "The Heart Is a Lonely Hunter," about a woman searching for love. A third was a four-singer collaboration with Trisha Yearwood, Linda Davis, and Martina McBride on the single "On My Own."

On the acting side of her career, she played Annie Oakley in the television miniseries *Buffalo Girls,* starring Anjelica Huston as Calamity Jane in a cast that included Melanie Griffith, Gabriel Byrne, Russell Means, and Sam Elliott.

Oklahoma-born McEntire began her career as a recording artist in 1978 with the debut album

Reba McEntire, and emerged as one of the leading country music singers of her time with the album *My Kind of Country* (1984), a hit that brought the first of her many major awards as Country Music Association female vocalist of the year, an award repeated in 1985. Her other albums include *Have I Got a Deal for You* (1985); *Whoever's in New England* and *What Am I Gonna Do About You* (both 1986); *The Last One to Know* and *Reba McEntire's Greatest Hits* (both 1987); *Reba* (1988); *Reba Live!* and *Sweet 16* (both 1989); *Rumor Has It* (1990); *For My Broken Heart* (1991), memorializing her tour manager and seven band members, killed in a 1991 airplane accident; *It's Your Call* (1992); *Greatest Hits, Volume 2* (1993), and *Read My Mind* (1994). She has also appeared in the films *Tremors* (1990), *North* (1994), and *Is There Life Out There?* (1994), and the television films *The Man from Left Field* (1993) and *Reba* (1994). Previously married, McEntire is now married to her manager, Narvel Blackstock, with whom she runs Starstruck Enterprises; she has one child.

FURTHER READING

"Reba's gift of love. . . ." JIM JEROME. *Ladies Home Journal,* Dec. 1995.
"Changing Nashville's tune." SUZANNA ANDREWS. *Working Woman,* Aug. 1995.
"What Reba did for love." CANDACE BUSHNELL. *Good Housekeeping,* July 1995.
"McEntire, Reba." *Current Biography,* Oct. 1994.
"Reba. . . ." LINDA SANDERS. *Ladies Home Journal,* Mar. 1994.
"Heaven on Earth. . . ." MARTHA FRANKEL. *McCall's,* Dec. 1993.
"Educating Reba." JESS CAGLE. *Entertainment,* Oct. 29, 1993.
"Reba McEntire. . . ." MARJIE McGRAW. *Country Music,* Jan.–Feb. 1993.
Reba: Country Music's Queen. DON CUSIC. St. Martin's, 1991.

McHaney, James M. (1919–95) Arkansas-born James McHaney was a graduate of Columbia College and Columbia Law School. In 1946, while employed by a New York law firm, he became assistant prosecutor to Telford Taylor in the Allied military court prosecutions at Nuremberg, Germany, in the trials of 23 prominent Nazi death camp doctors, scientists, and managers, all accused of mass murder and complicity in mass murder, and many of them accused of having conducted ghastly "experiments" that were in reality mass torture and murder. Taylor charged the accused before the court; McHaney put in the specifics of the cases, largely from the records so carefully kept by the accused, which detailed the murders of hundreds of thousands of innocent people in the name of science. Among the defendants was Dr. Karl Brandt, Hitler's personal doctor; he and six of the others were hanged, and nine others were convicted. McHaney later prosecuted other death camp trials. After a brief period of government employment following the Nuremberg trials, Haney went home to Arkansas, where he practiced law for the balance of his career. He was survived by his wife, Marilyn, a daughter, a son, two sisters, and a brother. (d. Little Rock, Arkansas; April 20, 1995)

FURTHER READING

Obituary. *New York Times,* Apr. 26, 1995.

McKellen, Ian (1939–) British stage and screen star Ian McKellen brought his acclaimed London stage title role in Shakespeare's *Richard III* to the screen in 1995, cowriting the screenplay with director Richard Loncraine. This version was presented as a murder-laden 1930s gangster film set in English high society. Annette Bening as Queen Elizabeth, Jim Broadbent as Buckingham, Robert Downey, Jr., as Rivers, Nigel Hawthorne, Kristin Scott, Maggie Smith, and John Wood costarred in the very well received production. McKellen received a Golden Globe nomination as a best actor in a drama for the role.

McKellen also appeared in the film *Restoration,* a story of sexual decadence set in the Stuart court late in the 17th century. Michael Hoffman directed a cast that included Robert Downey, Jr., Sam Neill, Polly Walker, Meg Ryan, Hugh Grant, and David Thewlis.

On television, McKellen appeared in John Schlesinger's 1930s-set comedy *Cold Comfort Farm,* based on the 1932 Stella Gibbons novel, in a cast that included Kate Beckinsale, Sheila Burrell, and Eileen Atkins. He also narrated the London-set AIDS-crisis telefilm *Heaven's a Drag,* starring Thomas Arklie and Ian Williams. For his role in the 1993 television film *And The*

Band Played On, McKellen won a 1995 CableAce award as best supporting actor in a movie or miniseries. Forthcoming was a starring role in the telefilm *Rasputin,* opposite Alan Rickman and Isabella Rossellini.

A leading British actor since the early 1960s, McKellen has played on stage in a wide range of leading roles. He made his stage debut in 1961, joined the National Theatre Company in 1965, made his Broadway debut in 1966 in *The Promise,* and was a founder of the Actor's Company in 1972. His debut with the Royal Shakespeare Company came in 1974, with his role in *Dr. Faustus.* He further developed his international reputation with *Bent* (1979) and *Amadeus* (1980), for which he won a Tony on Broadway. He toured in his one-man show *Acting Shakespeare* in 1984, played in a series of major roles with the National Theatre during the 1980s, and was an associate director of the National Theatre (1984–86). His films include *Alfred the Great* (1965), *Plenty* (1985), *Scandal* (1988), *Six Degrees of Separation* (1993), *The Ballad of Little Jo* (1993), and *The Last Action Hero* (1993). He has also appeared often on television, perhaps most notably in the AIDS-crisis film *And The Band Played On* (1993). In 1991, he was Cameron Mackintosh professor of contemporary theatre at Oxford University.

In 1991, McKellen accepted a knighthood, becoming Sir Ian. The honor was especially notable because he had been openly working on behalf of gay rights in Britain since announcing his own homosexuality on a BBC program three years earlier. Some fellow gay activists criticized him for accepting the honor from a Conservative government they felt was antigay. But he was publicly defended by many other gay artists, who felt that the honor was "a significant landmark in the history of the British gay movement."

FURTHER READING

"Out and about. . . ." BEN BRANTLEY. *Vanity Fair,* June 1992.
"Sympathy for the devil." LAWRENCE O'TOOLE. *New York Times Magazine,* Apr. 5, 1992.
"McKellen. . . ." JACK PITMAN. *Variety,* Jan. 7, 1991.

MacLaine, Shirley (Shirley MacLean Beaty; 1934–) Veteran film star, cabaret and concert entertainer, and author Shirley MacLaine in 1995 starred as aging widow Margaret

Mary Elderdice in the television film *The West Side Waltz,* a story about age and multigenerational relationships set on Manhattan's Upper West Side. The film was written and directed for television by Ernest Thompson, based on his play, and costarred Liza Minnelli as her neighbor Cara Varnum, Jennifer Grey as Cara's younger live-in companion, Robert Pastorelli, and Kathy Bates as a homeless neighborhood woman. MacLaine also appeared in the documentary *The Celluloid Closet,* which reviews the treatment of homosexuality in Hollywood films, from their beginnings until the present; Rob Epstein and Jeffrey Friedman directed; Lily Tomlin narrated.

MacLaine also published the autobiographical *My Lucky Stars: A Hollywood Memoir,* which became a best-seller.

Still forthcoming was a reprise of her Oscar-winning role as Aurora Greenway in *Terms of Endearment* in a 15-years-later sequel, *The Evening Star,* written and directed by Robert Harling and based on the Larry McMurtry novel. Also forthcoming was a starring role in the film *Mrs. Winterbourne,* directed by Richard Benjamin and costarring Ricki Lake and Brendan Fraser.

Virginia-born MacLaine, the sister of actor Warren Beatty, became a Hollywood star in the 1960s in such films as *The Apartment* (1960), *Two for the Seesaw* (1962), *Irma La Douce* (1963), and *Sweet Charity* (1969). Later in her career, she became a leading dramatic actress in such films as *The Turning Point* (1977), *Being There* (1979), *Terms of Endearment* (1983; she won a best actress Oscar), *Madame Souszatska* (1988), *Steel Magnolias* (1989), *Waiting for the Light* (1990), *Postcards from the Edge* (1990), *Used People* (1992), *Wrestling Ernest Hemingway* (1993), and *Guarding Tess* (1994). She also produced, codirected, and appeared in the documentary film *The Other Half of the Sky: A China Memoir* (1975), and has written several very popular books, including *Many Happy Returns* (1984), *Dancing in the Light* (1985), *Don't Fall Off the Mountain* (1987), and *Dance While You Can* (1991). She was previously married, and has one child.

FURTHER READING

"Oh, brother." Kɪм Cᴜɴɴɪɴɢʜᴀᴍ. *People*, Jan. 8, 1996.
"Shirley's lucky stars. . . ." Mᴇʟɪɴᴀ Gᴇʀᴏsᴀ. *Ladies Home Journal*, June 1995.
"Shirley MacLaine. . . ." Mᴏʟʟʏ Hᴀsᴋᴇʟʟ. *Film Comment*, May-June 1995.
"Write while you can. . . ." Bɪʟʟ Gᴏʟᴅsᴛᴇɪɴ. *Publishers Weekly*, Aug. 8, 1991.
"The real MacLaine." Nᴀɴᴄʏ Cᴏʟʟɪɴs and Aɴɴɪᴇ Lᴇɪʙᴏᴠɪᴛz. *Vanity Fair*, Mar. 1991.

McMartin, Virginia (1907–95) Virginia McMartin was the founder of the Virginia McMartin Pre-School in Manhattan Beach, California, and one of the defendants in a set of six California cases that stemmed from allegations of the sexual molestation of 11 children at the school (1979–83). Her school was closed in 1984, pending disposition of the cases. The cases lasted six years and cost the state of California well over $17 million; not one conviction was secured, although the cases had from the start drawn huge national attention, starting as they did with sensational charges of devil worship, animal sacrifices, pornographic photo sessions, and widespread sexual abuse involving scores of young children and seven of their teachers. In 1986, all charges against Virginia McMartin and her granddaughter were dropped for lack of evidence. The cases against her daughter, Peggy McMartin Buckey, and her grandson, Raymond Buckey dragged on; her daughter spent two years in jail and her grandson five, neither able to raise millions in bail. Ultimately, both were acquitted on 52 counts and Raymond Buckey

was not convicted on 8 final counts. In cases from around the country involving similar charges, where convictions resulted, many have been voided by the courts in recent years, citing tainted evidence from social workers, police, and prosecution. The McMartin cases were the subject of the 1995 television film *Indictment: The McMartin Trial*.

Virginia McMartin was survived by her daughter, Peggy McMartin Buckey, and two grandchildren, one of them Raymond Buckey. (d. Torrance, California; December 17, 1995)

FURTHER READING

Obituary. *New York Times*, Dec. 19, 1995.
The Abuse of Innocence: The McMartin Preschool Trial. Pᴀᴜʟ Eʙᴇʀʟᴇ and Sʜɪʀʟᴇʏ Eʙᴇʀʟᴇ. Prometheus, 1993.

McMurtry, Larry (1936–) In 1995 Larry McMurtry published *Dead Man's Walk: A Novel*, the long-awaited "prequel" to his 1985 novel *Lonesome Dove*, basis for the 1989 television miniseries. Focusing on the early lives of Woodrow Call and Gus McCrae, the new book became a best-seller in hardcover, and was also released in audiobook form, read by Will Patton. A second new work was *The Late Child: A Novel*, a sequel to his 1983 *The Desert Rose*, about aging Las Vegas showgirl Harmony; this work received more mixed reviews and was not as successful commercially. Unlike *Pretty Boy Floyd* (1994), cowritten by McMurtry and Diana Ossana, both 1995 novels were published solely under McMurtry's name, although Ossana edited both.

McMurtry and Ossana continue to collaborate on screenplays. Most notably, they scripted *Larry McMurtry's Streets of Laredo*, the five-hour miniseries that aired in November, starring James Garner as Call (the role originated by Tommy Lee Jones), Sissy Spacek as Lorena, and Sam Shepard as Pea Eye Parker, and directed by Joseph Sargent. This is McMurtry's own sequel to the 1989 miniseries *Lonesome Dove*, not to be confused with John Wilder's 1993 miniseries *Return to Lonesome Dove*. Another *Lonesome Dove* series is also scheduled for 1997. McMurtry and Ossana were also working on a screen version of *Dead Man's Walk*. Another television miniseries, *Buffalo Girls,* based on McMurtry's 1990 novel, was directed by Rod Hardy and starred Anjelica Huston as Calamity Jane, Sam Elliott as Wild Bill Hickok, Melanie Griffith, Gabriel Byrne, Peter Coyote, Jack Palance, Russell Means, and Reba McEntire; it was also released on video. Meanwhile, the film version of his *The Evening Star* was in production; this sequel to *Terms of Endearment* stars Shirley MacLaine, reprising her 1983 Oscar-winning role, again opposite Jack Nicholson.

Texas-born McMurtry received his B.A. from North Texas State College in 1958 and his M.S. from Rice University in 1960. After teaching at Texas Christian University in Fort Worth (1961–62), he returned to Rice to teach English and creative writing (1963–69) and was later a visiting professor at George Mason College (1970) and American University (1970–71). He is by far best known for his fiction, including *Horseman, Pass By* (1961), *Leaving Cheyenne* (1963), *The Last Picture Show* (1966), *Moving On* (1970), *All My Friends Are Going to Be Strangers* (1972) and its sequel *Some Can Whistle* (1989), *Terms of Endearment* (1975; basis of the Oscar-winning 1983 film) and its sequel *The Evening Star* (1992), *Somebody's Darling* (1978), *Cadillac Jack* (1982), *The Desert Rose* (1983), the Pulitzer Prize–winning *Lonesome Dove* (1985), *Anything for Billy* (1988), *Buffalo Girls* (1990), *Streets of Laredo* (1993), and *Pretty Boy Floyd* (1994; novel and screenplay written with Diana Ossana).

Also a prolific screenwriter, McMurtry wrote the script for *The Last Picture Show* (1971), sharing the Academy Award for best adaptation with director and cowriter Peter Bogdanovich; and its sequel *Texasville* (1987). Among his other screenplays are *Montana* (1989), *Memphis* (with Cybil Shepard; 1991), and *Falling From Grace* (1992). McMurtry has also written numerous articles, essays, and book reviews, some collected in *In a Narrow Grave: Essays on Texas* (1968) and *Film Flam: Essays on Hollywood* (1988).

McMurtry served as president of the literary organization PEN (1989–91), the first non–New Yorker in the post since the 1920s. He is co-owner of the Booked Up Book Store, Washington, Texas (1970–) and two other identically named bookstores. Formerly married to Josephine Ballard (1959–66), he has one son.

FURTHER READING

"Return of the native son." JAN REID. *Texas,* Feb. 1993.

McNally, Terrence (1939–) Playwright

Terence McNally's acclaimed new play *Master Class* opened at Broadway's Golden Theater on November 5, 1995. Directed by Leonard Foglia, it starred Zöe Caldwell as legendary singer Maria Callas, in a cast that included Karen Kay Cody, Audra McDonald, Jay Hunter Morris, David Loud, and Michael Friel. Caldwell was widely praised for her stage creation of a difficult, dedicated, powerful artist, and McNally for many aspects of his play, most of all for providing Caldwell with the role of Callas. The play, Caldwell, and McNally were immediately centers of Tony Awards speculation. *Master Class* further established McNally as one of the major American playwrights of the late 20th century.

His 1994 comedy-drama *Love! Valour! Compassion!* won the 1995 Tony and Drama Desk best play awards, and McNally was awarded a best playwright Obie for the work. The work, set among a group of AIDS-threatened gay men in a country house, was directed by Joe Mantello and starred Nathan Lane, John Glover, Stephen Bogardus, and Anthony Heald.

Born in St. Petersburg, Florida, McNally graduated from Columbia University in 1960, then worked as a tutor at the Actor's Studio and as an editor and film critic while he pursued his career as a playwright. His theater awards include a best play Obie for *The Ritz,* and a best book of a musical Tony for *Kiss of the Spider Woman.* Among his many plays are *The Lady of the Camellias* (1963), *And Things That Go Bump in the Night* (1964), *Witness* (1968), *Next* (1969), *Bringing It All Back Home* (1971), *Whiskey* (1973), *The Tubs* (1974), *The Ritz* (1975), *The Lisbon Traviata* (1979), *The Rink* (1984), *Frankie and Johnny in The Clair de Lune* (1988; he also wrote the screenplay for the 1991 film *Frankie and Johnny*), *Kiss of the Spider Woman* (1990), *Lips Together, Teeth Apart* (1991), and *A Perfect Ganesh* (1993). He won an Emmy for *Andre's Mother* (1990).

FURTHER READING

"Success is his best revenge." RICHARD CORLISS. *Time,* Aug. 23, 1993.
"Playwright's progress." KIM HUBBARD. *People,* Oct. 14, 1991.

McNamara, Robert Strange (1916–)

One of the most notable books of 1995 was *In Retrospect: The Tragedy and Lessons of Vietnam,* by Robert McNamara, secretary of defense in the cabinets of presidents John F. Kennedy and Lyndon B. Johnson (1961–68). McNamara had been a leading warhawk in both administrations, strongly urging increased American support for South Vietnam and then massive American intervention in the war, which came in 1964–65. He had developed doubts about the war after that, by 1967 was privately urging President Johnson to withdraw from the war, and left the cabinet in 1968. But he had been publicly silent about the war since then, for 27 years. In his book, written with Brian Vandemark, he for the first time stated that the Vietnam War had been a mistake, for which he and other leaders shared responsibility, and that the U.S. should have left Vietnam in the early 1960s, before the main American buildup there even began. McNamara also stated that he and his colleagues had been consistently badly informed as to the true state of affairs in Vietnam; as 1995 wore on, he continued to make that claim in the months that followed—although many came forward to dispute it, among them several senior military officers and administration military analysts of that period. For most of McNamara's legion of detractors, the book was too little and far too late; the general consensus was that McNamara could far more fruitfully have "gone public" more than a generation earlier, when tens of thousands of lives might have been saved.

San Francisco–born McNamara received his 1937 A.B. from the University of California, and his 1939 M.B.A. from Harvard University, then taught business administration at Harvard (1940–43). McNamara became a major figure in American industry during his fifteen years with the Ford Motor Company. After World War II Army Air Force service, he joined Ford in 1946, rising swiftly to controller (1949–53), and then through a series of general management positions, becoming a group vice president in 1957 and company president in 1960. He left Ford in 1961 to begin his public life, as President John F. Kennedy's secretary of defense, and stayed through 1968. He continued to be a world figure as president of the World Bank (1968–81). His previous books include *The Essence of Security* (1968), *One Hundred Countries—Two Billion People* (1973), *The McNamara Years at the World Bank* (1986), *Blundering into Disaster:*

Surviving the First Century of the Nuclear Age (1986), and *Out of the Cold* (1989). McNamara has two daughters and a son.

FURTHER READING

"The vindicator. . . ." EUGENE McCARTHY. *New Republic,* May 15, 1995.
" 'I sweated blood. . . .' " "Confessing the sins of Vietnam." JONATHAN ALTER. *Newsweek,* Apr. 17, 1995.
Promise and Power: The Life and Times of Robert McNamara. DEBORAH SHAPLEY. Little, Brown, 1993.
Uncertain Warriors: Lyndon Johnson and His Vietnam Advisers. DAVID M. BARRETT. University Press of Kansas, 1993.
"On the mistakes. . . ." CARL BERNSTEIN. *Time,* Feb. 11, 1991.

MacNeil, Robert Breckenridge

(1931–) On October 20, 1995, the 20th anniversary of the "MacNeil/Lehrer Newshour," Robert MacNeil retired from the PBS evening news program he had founded, leaving his longtime partner to carry on in Washington, under the title "The Newshour with Jim Lehrer." MacNeil chose instead to continue the writing career that he has pursued in tandem with broadcasting for some years. On his retirement MacNeil went on a promotion tour for his latest novel, *The Voyage,* which focuses on Canadian diplomat David Lyon, his "ideal" wife and daughters, and his explosive former lover, whose mysterious disappearance leads Lyon on the voyage of the title and threatens his personal life and career. Mac-Neil and Lehrer continue as partners in Mac-Neil/Lehrer Productions, which (along with *The Wall Street Journal*) announced plans to produce a half-hour late-evening news show in 1996, in time for the presidential campaign.

Montreal-born MacNeil graduated from Ottawa's Carleton University and began his broadcasting career as an actor in radio, and a radio and television announcer in Halifax, Nova Scotia (1951–55). He moved into journalism as a Reuters editor in London (1955–60) and was an NBC news correspondent (1960–67), successively based in London, Washington, and New York. He was a London-based BBC correspondent with the "Panorama" series (1967–71), also in that period working in U.S. public television, which became a full-time affiliation in 1971. Originally sole anchor on the evening news report, largely shaping the format, MacNeil began his long association with Jim Lehrer in 1973 with their Emmy-winning daily live coverage of the Senate Watergate hearings on PBS. The "Robert MacNeil Report" began in 1975, with MacNeil originally as sole anchor, largely shaping the format, and MacNeil as Washington correspondent; this became the award-winning "MacNeil/Lehrer Report" in 1976 and "The MacNeil/Lehrer Newshour" in 1983.

MacNeil was coauthor and host of the Emmy- and Peabody-winning nine-part series "The Story of English" (1986), and coauthor of the accompanying book, written with Robert McCrum and William Cran (revised 1993). He has also hosted several PBS specials. His other published works include *The People Machine, The Influence of Television on American Politics* (1968), *The Right Place at the Right Time* (1982), *The Way We Were: 1963, the Year Kennedy Was Shot* (1988), *Wordstruck* (1989), and the novel *The Burden of Desire* (1992). Twice divorced, MacNeil is married and has four children, including the stage designer Ian MacNeil.

FURTHER READING

"Good night, Robin." LARRY REIBSTEIN. *Newsweek,* Oct. 30, 1995.
"The news and. . . ." DANIEL WACKERMA. *America,* Oct. 21, 1995.
"Robert MacNeil. . . ." JOHN F. BAKER. *Publishers Weekly,* Oct. 16, 1995.
"A father and son. . . ." GEORGIA DULLEA. *New York Times,* May 5, 1994.

"Stranger to fiction." BRUCE HEADLAM. *Saturday Night,* Mar. 1992.
"MacNeil/Lehrer. . . ." MORGAN STRONG. *Playboy,* June 1991.

McQueen, Butterfly (Thelma McQueen; 1911–95) Born in Tampa, Florida, Thelma McQueen grew up in the New York City area, studied nursing, and then opted for a career in the theater. Her breakthrough role came in George Abbott's Broadway play *Brown Sugar;* it was followed by a role in Abbott's play *What a Life.* In 1939, she made her film debut in the film role for which she became by far best known, that of Prissy, a young African-American slave, who was Scarlett O'Hara's shaken, crying personal maid in *Gone With the Wind.* While the role brought her fame, it also brought her lifelong criticism from those who called the film racist history from a Confederate point of view. Unfortunately, it also brought McQueen the worst kind of typecasting, in a Hollywood far from hospitable to Black artists. She did play small roles in several more films, among them *The Women* (1939), *Cabin in the Sky* (1943), *Since You Went Away* (1944), *Mildred Pierce* (1945), and *Duel in the Sun* (1947), but after that her film career died. In television, she appeared in the series "Beulah" (1950–53) and much later won a 1980 Emmy as best performer in a children's program for the AfterSchool Special "The Seven Wishes of a Rich Kid." Unable to make a living as a performer, McQueen later held a series of jobs, went back to school and earned her B.A. in 1966 (at the age of 64), and became active in Harlem community affairs. No information about survivors was available. (d. Augusta, Georgia; December 22, 1995)

FURTHER READING

"Escaping Prissy." *People,* Jan. 8, 1996.
Obituary. *Variety,* Dec. 26, 1995.
Obituary. *New York Times,* Dec. 23, 1995.

McVeigh, Timothy James (1968–) On April 19, 1995, at 9:02 A.M., a massive car bomb carried in a rented truck was detonated outside the Alfred P. Murrah Federal Building in Oklahoma City, Oklahoma. The bomb, composed of ammonium nitrate fertilizer, diesel fuel, and other explosives, killed at least 169 people in and

around the largely destroyed building, 19 of them children, making it the worst such event in American history. No one claimed "credit" for the atrocity.

On the same morning, at approximately 10:00 A.M., in Perry, Kansas, about an hour's drive north of Oklahoma City, Timothy McVeigh was arrested for motor vehicle violations and jailed pending bail. On April 21, two days later, federal agents, who had put together small pieces of the exploded truck and found part of a vehicle identification number, located and arrested McVeigh. As the country continued to mourn its dead, investigators and prosecutors began to build a case against McVeigh, who denied all charges.

On August 10, an Oklahoma grand jury handed down an 11-count indictment, charging McVeigh and Terry Lynn Nichols with multiple murders and conspiracy, leaving open the question of whether others were also involved. McVeigh and Nichols were charged with buying, stealing, storing, and mixing the explosives, and renting a Ryder rental truck; McVeigh was charged with driving the truck to the federal building and actually detonating the bomb. Both men continued to be held, awaiting trial. Indicted on lesser charges was a third army friend, Michael Fortier. As the result of a plea bargain with federal authorities, Fortier pleaded guilty on four Oklahoma City-related charges, including knowledge of the plot. He had reportedly agreed to turn state's evidence and testify as a prosecution witness in the trials of McVeigh and Nichols.

Timothy McVeigh was born and raised in Pendleton, New York, near Buffalo. After graduating from high school, he worked as an armed guard for an armored car company. He, Nichols, and Fortier enlisted in the U.S. Army on the same day (March 24, 1988), and became close friends during basic training at Fort Benning, Georgia. McVeigh became a gunner in a Bradley, a tanklike troop carrier. Nichols was discharged from the army in the spring of 1989. McVeigh remained in the army, serving in the Gulf War. In the spring of 1990, he began a course of training for the Green Berets, but was within two days rejected for psychological reasons. After leaving the army, he went back to work as an armed guard. He lived in Kingman, Arizona, for several months in 1993, then joined Nichols in Michigan for a time before returning to Arizona. He was reportedly active in right-wing militias in Michigan and Arizona.

Terry Lynn Nichols (1950–   ), born in Lapeer, Michigan, graduated from Lapeer High School and briefly attended Central Michigan University, then became a farmer in Decker, Michigan, sometimes working with his older brother, James Nichols. A survivalist, he reportedly became a right-wing activist in the early 1990s, and prior to the Oklahoma City bombing had worked on a ranch in Kansas. He reportedly became closely associated with McVeigh in mid-1994. Nichols has a son, Joshua, from his marriage to real estate broker Lana Padilla, which ended in divorce in 1988. In 1991, he married Marife Torres, a 17-year-old "mail-order bride" from the Philippines. She became pregnant abroad while waiting clearance to enter the U.S., and bore a son, who died in a possible accident in 1993; the couple had a daughter in 1993.

Michael Fortier (1969–   ) and McVeigh were close friends, serving together at Fort Riley, Kansas, and remained friendly after both left the military. McVeigh often visited Fortier's home in Kingman, Arizona. Fortier's wife, Lori, and their two-year-old daughter were, during 1995, reportedly exploring the possibility of entering the federal witness protection program, after she and her parents had received numerous threats.

FURTHER READING

By Blood Betrayed: My Life with Terry Nichols and Timothy McVeigh. LANA PADILLA with RON DELPIT. HarperCollins, 1996.
"Good soldier, bad soldier." *People,* Dec. 25, 1995.
"Awaiting his day in court." PATRICK COLE. *Time,* Aug. 14, 1995.
"The suspect speaks out." DAVID H. HACKWORTH and PETER ANNIN. *Newsweek,* July 3, 1995.
"Inside the plot." EVAN THOMAS. *Newsweek,* June 5, 1995.
"The plot." EVAN THOMAS. *Newsweek,* May 8, 1995.
" 'Something big . . .' " ELIZABETH GLEICK. *Time,* May 8, 1995.
"Shadow warriors. . . ." Michael Green. *People Weekly,* May 8, 1995.
"Cleverness—and luck." Evan Thomas and Russell Watson. *Newsweek,* May 1, 1995.
"Who are they?" Elizabeth Gleick. *Time,* May 1, 1995.
"An ex–army man . . ." IAN KATZ. *Guardian,* Apr. 24, 1995.

Maddux, Greg (Gregory Alan Maddux; 1966–   )

His fastball may not be the fastest, but he makes up for it with an extraordinary mound repertoire. Greg Maddux was once again the National League's leading pitcher, with a league-leading record of 19-2, for a remarkable winning percentage of .905, becoming the first major league pitcher ever to top .900 over 20 or more games. To no one's surprise, the man *Sports Illustrated* has called the "best right-hander in the past 75 years" was named winner of the Cy Young award, the first pitcher ever to win four straight Cy Young awards (1992–95); no other pitcher had ever won three straight, though Steve Carlton won four nonconsecutively. He was also a unanimous selection for the second year in a row (as only Sandy Koufax had been before him). Maddux was also named the Associated Press baseball player of the year, the first pitcher ever so honored. He also was named *Sporting News* National League pitcher of the year for the fourth consecutive time (1992–95).

Maddux's 1995 earned run average was 1.63, the league's lowest for the third year in a row, compared to the league average of 4.21; he also became the first major league pitcher since Walter Johnson (1918–19) to have an ERA of under 1.80 two seasons in a row. Maddux led the league in shutouts as well, tying Hideo Nomo with 3, and was third in the league in strikeouts, with 181. He was also remarkably durable (apart from a preseason bout with chicken pox), leading the league in complete games with 10, and number of innings pitched, tied with Denny Neagle for 209 2/3; walking only 23 people, for a league-leading average of 0.99 walks per nine innings; and setting a new major league record for consecutive road victories with 17, building that to 18 at season's end.

Beyond that, Maddux had the thrill of winning the first game of the World Series, without walking a single player, helping his Atlanta Braves to win their first series. Maddux also pitched in the fifth game, but lost. Earlier in the season Maddux had been named to the All-Star team for the fourth time, but was unable to play because of a pulled groin muscle.

After graduating from Las Vegas's Valley High School in 1984, Texas-born Maddux made his professional debut in the minor leagues (1984–86), playing for Pikeville, Peoria, Pittsfield, and Iowa, before joining the Chicago Cubs (1986–92). Later he moved to the Atlanta Braves as a free agent (1993–   ). In addition to his Cy Young awards, Maddux has been named to the All-Star team four times (1988, 1992, 1994, 1995). Maddux and his wife, Kathy, have one daughter. Greg's brother, Mike Maddux, is a pitcher for the New York Mets.

FURTHER READING

"A swing. . . ." DAVE KINDRED. *Sporting News,* Oct. 30, 1995.
" 'I just pitch.' " MICHAEL P. GEFFNER. *Sporting News,* Oct. 9, 1995.
"The right stuff." "Once in a lifetime." TOM VERDUCCI. *Sports Illustrated,* Aug. 14, 1995.
"Drive for show. . . ." TOM VERDUCCI. *Sports Illustrated,* May 1, 1995.
Greg Maddux: Ace Pitcher. TED COX. Childrens, 1995.
"Greg Maddux." George Castle. *Sport,* May 1993.

Madonna (Madonna Louise Ciccone; 1958–)

Though far from the overpowering pop music figure she was in the 1980s and early 1990s, Madonna remained a major figure in 1995. Her 1994 album *Bedtime Stories* remained on the Billboard 200 list for much of the year, still generating hit singles, including the smash hits "Take a Bow," "Bedtime Story," and "Human Nature." She received a Grammy nomination for longform video best music for *The Girlie Show—Live Down Under,* and an MTV dance video award nomination for *Human Nature.* Her records continued to sell well worldwide, with *Like a Virgin* topping 9 million and *Bedtime Stories* topping 2 million during the year.

Her 1995 album was *Something to Remember,* a retrospective that also introduced her renditions of Marvin Gaye's "I Want You," and the new songs "You'll See" and "One More Chance," cowritten with David Foster. "You'll See" became a hit single.

Madonna also pursued the film side of her career. In the anthology *Four Rooms,* she played one of a coven of witches in the *Strange Brew* segment, written and directed by Allison Anders. In *Blue in the Face,* she acted in a cameo role as a singing cigarette girl. Forthcoming was the title role as Evita Perón in the film *Evita,* adapted from the Andrew Lloyd Webber/Andrew Rice hit stage musical, and costarring Jonathan Pryce as Argentine dictator Juan Perón and Antonio Banderas as Che Guevara; Alan Parker will direct. Also forthcoming was a role in Spike Lee's film *Girl 6.*

Michigan-born Madonna has been one of the best-known celebrities of her time, both for concert performances and for such albums as *Madonna* (1983), *Like a Virgin* (1983), *True Blue* (1986), *You Can Dance* (1987), *Like a Prayer* (1989), *The Immaculate Collection* (1990), and *Erotica* (1992), released simultaneously with publication of her picture book *Sex*. Madonna is also a competent actress, as demonstrated in such films as *Desperately Seeking Susan* (1985) and *Who's That Girl?* (1987), and in her Broadway stage debut in *Speed-the-Plow* (1988). Her role as Breathless Mahoney in Warren Beatty's *Dick Tracy* (1990) sparked her "Blond Ambition" world concert tour, the album *I'm Breathless* (1990), and the documentary film *Truth or Dare: In Bed with Madonna* (1991). She also appeared in the films *A League of Their Own* (1992), *The Player* (1992), *Body of Evidence* (1993), and *Dangerous Game* (1993), produced by her own company, Maverick. Madonna attended the University of Michigan (1976–78). She was formerly married to actor Sean Penn (1985–89).

FURTHER READING

"Madonna. . . .?" DAVE KARGER. *Entertainment,* Nov. 10, 1995.
"Bedtime story." LINDA O'KEEFFE. *Metropolitan Home,* Mar. 13, 1995.
"Like a lady." NORMAN MAILER. *Esquire,* Aug. 1994.
Madonna. NICOLE CLARO. Chelsea House, 1994.
Deconstructing Madonna. FRAN LLOYD, ed. Trafalgar, 1994.
"Chameleon in motion." MIKE MYERS and HERB RITTS. *Interview,* June 1993.
Madonna: Portrait of a Material Girl. REBECCA GULICK. Courage, 1993.
Desperately Seeking Madonna: In Search of the Meaning of the World's Most Famous Woman. ADAM SEXTON. Delacorte, 1993.
Madonna: The Early Days. MICHAEL MCKENZIE. Worldwide Televid, 1993.
Madonna. Andrews & McMeel, 1993.
Madonna Speaks. BRUCE NASH et al. Tribune, 1993.
Material Girl: Madonna in the 90s. TIM RILEY. Disney, 1992
Madonna: The Book. NORMAN KING. Morrow, 1992.
Madonna Revealed: The Unauthorized Biography. DOUGLAS THOMPSON. Dorchester, 1992.
Madonna: Blonde Ambition. MARK BEGO. Harmony/Crown, 1992.

Mailer, Norman (1923–   ) Always controversial, Norman Mailer provided his own take on an American conundrum in 1995, with *Oswald's Tale: An American Mystery*. This massive work is really, as some reviewers pointed out, two books in one. The first focuses on Lee Harvey Oswald's life in Russia and his tangled relations with the KGB and FBI, the second on Oswald in America, leading to his death in Dallas, while attempting to make sense of his role in the 1963 assassination of President John F. Kennedy. Though initially drawn by conspiracy theories, Mailer finally inclined toward the notion that Oswald was a lone gunman—or *thought* he was. *Oswald's Tale* was also published in audiobook form, read by Mailer and Norris Church Mailer, his wife. In a very different vein, though still biographical, Mailer also published a long-delayed book on the early life of artist Pablo Picasso, *Portrait of Picasso as a Young Man*.

New Jersey-born Mailer attended Harvard University. His World War II military service was the basis for his first published novel, *The Naked and the Dead,* (1948), which launched him as a major writer. The book was later adapted into the 1958 Raoul Walsh film. Some of his best-known later novels included *Barbary Shore* (1951), *The Deer Park* (1955), *An American Dream* (1965), *The Executioner's Song* (1979; he was awarded a 1980 Pulitzer Prize), *Ancient Evenings* (1983), *Tough Guys Don't Dance* (1983), which he adapted into the 1983 film and directed, and *Harlot's Ghost* (1991). Mailer has written numerous nonfiction works, most notably *Advertisements for Myself* (1959) and *Armies of the Night* (1968), which won a Pulitzer Prize for nonfiction. He also won a 1969

National Book Award. Mailer was a cofounder of *The Village Voice* (1954), an editorial board member of the magazine *Dissent* (1953–69), and president of the American branch of PEN (1984–86). His sixth wife is Norris Church; he has six daughters and three sons.

FURTHER READING

"Norman conquest. . . ." REBECCA ASCHER-WALSH. *Entertainment,* Nov. 10, 1995.
"Kindred spirits. . . ." PETE HAMILL. *ARTnews,* Nov. 1995.
"Black and white justice." *New York,* Oct. 16, 1995.
"Callow young genius." *New York,* Sept. 11, 1995.
"No ordinary secret agent." RAY SAWHILL. *Newsweek,* Apr. 24, 1995.
Norman Mailer. MICHAEL K. GLENDAY. St. Martin's, 1995.
Norman Mailer, rev. ed. ROBERT MERRILL. Twayne/Macmillan, 1992.
"Patriarchs don't pummel." HELLE BERING-JENSEN. *Insight,* Oct. 28, 1991.
"Mailer's alpha and omega." TOBY THOMPSON. *Vanity Fair,* Oct. 1991.
"Stormin' Norman." CHRISTOPHER HITCHENS. *Vogue,* Oct. 1991.
"The old man. . . ." SCOTT SPENCER. *New York Times Magazine,* Sept. 22, 1991.
"His punch is. . . ." BONNIE ANGELO and PAUL GRAY. *Time,* Sept. 30, 1991.
"Mailer and Vidal . . ." CAROLE MALLORY. *Esquire,* May 1991.
The Lives of Norman Mailer: A Biography. CARL ROLLYSON. Paragon, 1991.

Major, John (John Major Ball; 1943–) Al-
though British Prime Minister John Major scored a substantial personal success within his own Conservative Party in 1995 and his electoral popularity ratings rose somewhat late in the year, his high ratings were still under 30 percent, while his chief opponent, Labour Party leader Tony Blair, scored more than 55 percent and seemed to be gaining strength. Indeed, Blair and Labour seemed very close to capturing the center of British politics, moving the Labour Party away from its longtime socialist platform toward a far more popular liberal democratic stance.

Beset by scandals within his own party, and sharply opposed by leading right-wing figures, even in his own Cabinet, Major took a great political risk in June, resigning his Conservative Party leadership to force a new leadership election that he hoped would serve as a vote of confidence in his leadership. It worked; he was reelected to leadership, defeating challenger John Redwood 219–89. He then reshuffled his Cabinet to include more of his supporters and at the same time convince the country that he and his party were moving toward more centrist positions. In foreign affairs, he still expressed support for the projected European Monetary Union, while in fact recognizing powerful domestic opposition by agreeing to an indefinite further delay in putting it into effect. He joined in the American-led Bosnian peace initiative and tried, with some apparent success, to move forward the stalled Northern Ireland peace process.

London-born Major's first career was with the Standard Chartered Bank (1965–79). He joined the Conservative Party in 1960, was a Lambeth borough councillor (1968–71), and became a Member of Parliament in 1979, after two unsuccessful tries. His rise in the Thatcher government was very rapid; by 1985, he was a junior minister at the Department of Health, and by 1986 social security minister. He became treasury chief secretary in 1987, foreign secretary in July 1989, chancellor of the exchequer in October 1989, and then at 47 the youngest British prime minister of the 20th century, succeeding Margaret Thatcher on November 27, 1990. In office, he quickly canceled the enormously unpopular poll tax and developed a more moderate Conservative government than that of Thatcher. He supported the Persian Gulf War without reservation, sending British heavy armor into the ground offensive when it came to join the air and sea forces already in place. He led the Conservative Party to electoral victory in the April 1992 general elections, but with his party soon lost much of his popularity, as his approval ratings dropped into the 16–21 percent range and did not rise much above that in the years that followed, as he and his party continued to be plagued by Britain's worsening economic circumstances, recurrent political scandals, and public resentment of deep cuts in social services. Major married Norma Johnson in 1970; they have two children.

FURTHER READING

"Tories for Washington." GARY L. McDOWELL. *National Review,* Dec. 11, 1995.
"Rover declared it over. . . ." JULIA LANGDON. *Guardian,* Feb. 8, 1995.

"Leave it to beaver. . . ." MATTHEW PARRIS. *New Republic*, Jan. 3, 1994.

"The curious case. . . ." STEVE PLATT and NYTA MANN. *New Statesman & Society*, Jan. 29, 1993.

"John Major at bat." CRAIG WHITNEY. *New York Times Magazine*, Mar. 29, 1992.

"Major. . . ." DANIEL PEDERSEN. *Newsweek*, Mar. 23, 1992.

John Major: The Making of the Prime Minister. BRUCE ANDERSON. Trafalgar Square, 1992.

John Major: Prime Minister. PRESS ASSOCIATION STAFF and JOHN JENKINS. Trafalgar Square, 1991.

Malkovich, John (1953–)

In 1995 actor John Malkovich starred opposite Catherine Deneuve in the critically praised film *The Convent,* directed and written by Portuguese filmmaker Manoel de Oliveira. In the film, in part the director's modern retelling of the Faust story, Malkovich is an American professor, who with his wife, played by Deneuve, explores the library of a Portuguese convent, while both also explore other relationships.

Malkovich also starred as a filmmaker and the narrator of the four episodes comprising the film *Beyond the Clouds,* codirected by Michelangelo Antonioni and Wim Wenders, with a cast that includes Kim Rossi Stuart, Ines Sastre, Fanny Ardant, and Peter Weller, with Marcello Mastroianni and Jeanne Moreau in cameo roles.

Forthcoming were starring roles in the German film *The Ogre,* directed by Volker Schlondorff and and costarring Armin Mueller-Stahl, Marianne Sagebrecht, and Heino Ferch; and in the film *Mulholland Falls,* directed by Lee Tamahori and costarring Nick Nolte, Melanie Griffith, and Daniel Baldwin. He is also slated to star in the film *Portrait of a Lady,* directed by Jane Campion and costarring Nicole Kidman, Mary-Louise Parker, Shelley Winters, and Shelley Duvall. Still forthcoming was a starring role as Dr. Jekyll and Mr. Hyde in the film *Mary Reilly,* directed by Stephen Frears and costarring Julia Roberts, Glenn Close, George Cole, and Kathy Staff.

Before becoming a New York stage player, Illinois-born Malkovich was from 1976 a leading member of Chicago's Steppenwolf Theater Company. He won an Obie Off-Broadway for his role in *True West* (1982), appeared as Biff to Dustin Hoffman's Willy Loman in the 1984 Broadway revival of *Death of a Salesman,* and took his highly praised stage performance in Lanford Wilson's *Burn This* from New York to London late in 1990, making his British stage debut. He began his film career in 1984 with *Places in the Heart,* and went on to strong dramatic roles in such films as *The Killing Fields* (1984), *Eleni* (1985), *The Glass Menagerie* (1987), *Empire of the Sun* (1987), *Dangerous Liaisons* (1988), *The Sheltering Sky* (1990), *The Object of Beauty* (1991), *Of Mice and Men* (1992), *Shadows and Fog* (1992), *Jennifer Eight* (1992), *In the Line of Fire* (1993), and *Heart of Darkness* (1994). Malkovich has also acted and directed in regional theater and appeared on television. Malkovich attended Illinois State University. He was formerly married to actress Glenne Headly.

FURTHER READING

"Character/actor." *Psychology Today*, July-Aug. 1994.

"Odd man. . . ." LUKE CLANCY. *Guardian*, June 29, 1994.

"The touch of evil. " JESS CAGLE. *Entertainment*, Aug. 6, 1993.

"What is. . . ." DAVID GRITTEN. *Cosmopolitan*, Nov. 1992.

Malle, Louis (1932–95)

French director Louis Malle left his political science studies at the Sorbonne to study at the Cinematography Institute. He entered the film world as assistant to Jacques Cousteau; they codirected and Malle shot part of *The Silent World* (1956), the classic documentary of life in the sea. His first fiction film was *Frantic* (1958), followed by his breakthrough film *The Lovers* (1958), starring Jeanne Moreau and highly controversial because of its then-daring sexual content. Among his further films were *Zazie in the Underground* (1960), *The Fire Within* (1963), *The Thief of Paris* (1967), *Lacombe, Lucien* (1973), *Pretty Baby* (1978), *Atlantic City* (1980), *My Dinner with Andre* (1981), and the classic *Au Revoir les Enfants* (1987), based on an incident in his own life as a child, in which a Jewish boy hidden in his boarding school was captured and later murdered by the Nazis. His later films included *May Fools* (1989) and *Damage* (1992). He was survived by his wife, actress Candice Bergen, two daughters, and a son. (d. Beverly Hills, California; November 23, 1995)

FURTHER READING

"As winter comes. . . ." PAM LAMBERT. *People,* Dec. 11, 1995.

Obituary. *Economist,* Dec. 2, 1995.
Obituary. *Times* (of London), Nov. 27, 1995.
Obituary. *Independent,* Nov. 27, 1995.
Obituary. *New York Times,* Nov. 25, 1995.
Obituary. *Variety,* Nov. 27, 1995.
"A hard act. . . . " VANESSA FRIEDMAN. *Vogue,* Nov. 1994.
Malle on Malle. Philip French, ed. Faber & Faber, 1992.

Mamet, David Alan (1947–) Though a

versatile playwright, screenwriter, and director, David Mamet's major work is in the theater, and 1995 was for him mostly a theater year. He wrote and directed the play *The Cryptogram,* a dark, bitter family drama presented on a single, minimal set. Its three characters were a woman he perceives largely in her role as a damaged mother, whose husband has betrayed and left her, played by Felicity Huffman; her damaged young son, played by Shelton Dane; and a male family friend, played by Ed Begley, Jr. The work won an Obie Award as best American play of the year.

Mamet also wrote two one-act plays produced in 1995. *An Interview,* directed by Michael Blakemore, starred Paul Giulfoyel and Gerry Becker in a single dialogue on an almost bare stage; it was presented as part of a group of three one-acters (the others were by Elaine May and Woody Allen) titled *Death Defying Acts.* His second one-act play was *No One Will Be Immune,* another two-character work, starring David Rasche and Robert Joy, also as a single dialogue in a minimal setting. Mamet also rewrote and directed J. B. Priestley's play *Dangerous Corner.*

He also wrote the brief book *Passover,* illustrated by Michael McCurdy, about a grandmother telling the story of a pogrom to her granddaughter, while they are preparing food for a seder, the Jewish Passover holiday meal.

Among Chicago-born Mamet's plays are *Sexual Perversity in Chicago* (1973), *American Buffalo* (1976), *A Life in the Theater* (1976), *The Woods* (1977), *Edmond* (1983), *Glengarry Glen Ross* (1984; he won the Pulitzer Prize for drama), *Speed-The-Plow* (1987), and *Oleanna* (1992; and the 1994 screenplay). His screenplays include *The Postman Always Rings Twice* (1981), *The Verdict* (1982), *The Untouchables* (1987), *We're No Angels* (1989), *Homicide* (1991), and *Vanya on 42nd Street* (1994). He cowrote and directed the film *House of Games* (1987), and wrote and

directed *Things Change* (1988). His first novel was *The Village* (1994). Among his nonfiction works are *Writing in Restaurants: Essays and Prose* (1986), *On Directing Film* (1990), and the autobiographical *The Cabin: Reminiscence and Diversions* (1992). Mamet's B.A. was from Goddard College. Previously married to actress Lindsay Crouse, Mamet is married to actress-singer-songwriter Rebecca Pidgeon.

FURTHER READING

"Playboy interview. . . ." GEOFFREY NORMAN and JOHN REZEK. *Playboy,* Apr. 1995.
David Mamet and Film: Illusion-Disillusion in a Wounded Land. GAY BREWER. McFarland, 1993.

Nelson Mandela (center) with James Earl Jones (right) and Richard Harris.

Mandela, Nelson Rolihiahia (1918–)

In his first full year in office, South African President Nelson Mandela, in alliance with the formerly ruling National Party, continued to build a new multiracial South Africa. Although he paid a good deal of attention to righting some of the wrongs of the apartheid period, his main attention by far was on the present and future, for the vast majority of Black South Africans were desperately poor and only newly free, and much needed to be financed and accomplished. Among his priorities were the securing of meaningful foreign investment, a vastly expanded national education system, and a great increase in the national social service and accompanying adult education network.

On the political side, early autumn local elections brought an African National Congress (ANC) sweep and, for the first time, large numbers of Black local officeholders, completing the move to fully equal multiracial democracy. Democracy and the rule of law also emerged with the appointment of South Africa's new multiracial Supreme Court. Mandela also took steps to prosecute some officials of the former police and government, in January voiding a secret amnesty granted by the apartheid government before the 1994 elections, and in July setting up a national Truth and Reconciliation Commission to formally address the wrongs of the apartheid era. Throughout the year, and despite many disputes, as over the voiding of the amnesty and the pace of school integration, the ANC–National Party alliance held, although the Inkatha Zulu–ANC alliance as always continued to be, at best, tenuous. In sum, Mandela and the new democracy went forward.

On the personal side, Nelson Mandela in April fired his wife, Winnie Mandela, from her post as deputy minister of arts, culture, science, and technology, on grounds of insubordination. In August, he filed for divorce; in October, she contested the divorce. They had been separated since 1992.

Early in his career, Mandela was a leading advocate of nonviolence (1944–60), but both he and the previously nonviolent ANC turned to violence after the 1960 Sharpeville Massacre. He was sentenced to life imprisonment in 1962 and jailed for 28 years, during that time becoming a worldwide symbol of the long fight against South African racism. His release by F. W. de Klerk's new South African government on February 11, 1990, ushered in a new period in South African history, leading to a full cease-fire after 30 years of guerrilla warfare. Mandela was elected president of the ANC in 1991. On November 18, 1993, the ANC, de Klerk's National Party, and 19 other political parties agreed on a historic new constitution that would establish multiparty democracy and, through the adoption of a Bill of Rights, guarantee "fundamental rights" for all South Africans, with a resulting transition to majority, or Black, rule in South Africa. Mandela and National Party leader de Klerk shared the 1993 Nobel Peace Prize.

The ANC swept the 1994 national elections, and on May 10, 1994, Mandela was sworn in as president of the new multiracial South African state in a ceremony that brought together scores of world leaders. He immediately called for conciliation, established a multiparty government of national unity, began the work of rebuilding South Africa's damaged economy and infrastructure, and traveled the world to build international ties and secure financial support. In October 1994, he addressed the United Nations General Assembly and a joint session of the U.S. Congress, and met with President Bill Clinton.

Mandela attended the University College of Fort Hare and the University of the Witwatersrand, and practiced law in Johannesburg in the early 1950s. He married Winnie Mandela, his second wife, in 1958; he has three children from his first marriage. His written works include *No Easy Walk to Freedom* (1986), *Nelson Mandela: The Struggle Is My Life* (rev. ed., 1986), *How Far We Slaves Have Come!* (1991; written with Fidel Castro), *Nelson Mandela Speaks: Forging a Democratic, Nonracial South Africa* (1993), and the autobiography *Long Walk to Freedom* (1994).

FURTHER READING

"Mandela vow. . . ." CAMERON DOUDU. *The Observer,* Nov. 26, 1995.

" 'People have forgotten. . . .' " *Newsweek,* Nov. 6, 1995.

"Mandela, Nelson." *Current Biography,* Nov. 1995.

"Africa's role model." *Economist,* Aug. 12, 1995.

"Rebuilding a nation." MKHONTO MKHONDO. *Emerge,* June 1995.

Opposition in South Africa: The Leadership of Z. K. Matthews, Nelson Mandela and Stephen Biko. Tim J. Juckes. Greenwood, 1995.

"15 days. . . ." LERONE BENNETT, JR. "From prisoner. . . ." HANS J. MASSAQUOI. *Ebony,* Aug. 1994.

"Full Nelson. . . ." JOSEPH CONTRERAS. *New Republic,* May 9, 1994.

"The man of the moment." *E,* May 9, 1994.

"The making of a leader." RICHARD STENGEL. "Birth of a nation." BRUCE W. NELAN and LANCE MORROW. *Time,* May 9, 1994.

" 'My followers heeded my call.' " JOSEPH CONTRERAS. "Black power!" RUSSELL WATSON et al. *Newsweek,* May 9, 1994.

"From prisoner. . . ." BRUCE WALLACE. "A model. . . ." CHRIS ERASMUS. *Maclean's,* Apr. 25, 1994.

"Mandela. . . ." JACQUES GOLDING. *World Press Review,* Mar. 1994.

"The man in cell no. 7." BILL HEWITT. *People,* Feb. 28, 1994.

"Nelson Mandela and F. W. de Klerk." PAUL GRAY.

"To conquer the past." LANCE MORROW. *Time*, Jan. 3, 1994. (Men of the Year: The Peacemakers)

Nelson Mandela: Freedom for South Africa. PAMELA DELL. Childrens, 1994.

Chained Together: Mandela, De Klerk, and the Struggle to Remake South Africa. DAVID B. OTTAWAY. Random House, 1993.

Nelson Mandela: The Fight Against Apartheid. STEVEN OTFINOSKI. Millbrook, 1992.

Nelson Mandela: Voice of Freedom. LIBBY HUGHES. Macmillan, 1992.

Nelson Mandela: The Man, the Struggle, the Triumph. DOROTHY HOOBLER and THOMAS HOOBLER. Watts, 1992.

Mandela, Winnie

Mandela, Winnie (Winnie Nomzano; 1934–) Still a powerful symbol of the South African freedom movement to many Black militants and to large numbers of poor people in South Africa, Winnie Mandela had overcome the scandals of the early 1990s to win election to South Africa's first freely elected parliament in 1994. In a gesture of unity to the militant wing of his movement, Nelson Mandela had named her deputy minister of arts, culture, science, and technology in the new government, although she remained sharply critical of the new government. In December 1994, she was elected to the African National Congress (ANC) national executive committee. She also became president of the ANC's Women's League.

But in 1995 her opposition became a direct confrontation with Nelson Mandela, and she also faced new and very serious charges of financial corruption in office. In protest, 11 members of the Women's League executive resigned in February 1995. In March, Nelson Mandela removed her from her Cabinet post; she won reinstatement by the courts on procedural grounds in April, but was immediately fired again by Nelson Mandela and left the government, although she continued to be a Member of Parliament and a focus of opposition.

In August, Nelson Mandela filed for divorce; in October, she contested his action. They had been separated since 1992.

Winnie Mandela was a social worker before becoming active in the ANC in 1956. She married Nelson Mandela in 1958; the couple then joined their work in the South African freedom movement. Like him, she became a worldwide symbol of resistance to racism, as she pressed for his release during his 28 years in prison and at the same time continued her antiapartheid work. She was forced into silence for long periods by the South African government, and was internally exiled in 1977. From 1985, however, she was able to defy the government, due to growing worldwide condemnation of apartheid and of the imprisonment of Nelson Mandela.

Her situation changed greatly in 1989, when she was publicly censured by the leadership of the ANC and other leaders after her alleged involvement in the beating and murder of a young boy and the beatings of several other young boys in Soweto. Two of her bodyguards were convicted of murder in May 1990. She was charged with kidnapping and assault in September 1990 and convicted in May 1991; but she won reversal of her five-year prison sentence on appeal. Although Nelson Mandela supported her throughout the trial, there were apparently other problems, and in April 1992, Nelson Mandela announced that he and Winnie Mandela would separate, and later that year she resigned her ANC positions. Among her writings is *A Part of My Soul Went with Him* (1985).

FURTHER READING

"Devil or angel?. . . ." DAN RATHER. *Rolling Stone*, Oct. 20, 1994.

"Winnie Mandela. . . ." NOKWANDA SITHOLE. *Essence*, Apr. 1994.

"Winnie . . . ?" JOHN CARLIN. *World Press Review*, Mar. 1994.

"Nelson Mandela. . . ." BARBARA GRIZZUTI HARRISON. *Mademoiselle*, Aug. 1992.

"Blood soccer. . . ." JOHN CARLIN. *New Republic*, Feb. 18, 1991.

Mantle, Mickey Charles

Mantle, Mickey Charles (1931–95) Born in Spavinaw, Oklahoma, legendary baseball star Mickey Mantle was a child of near-poverty who worked in the zinc mines with his father and played semipro baseball while still in high school. He was signed by the New York Yankees in 1949, played on several Yankee farm teams, and made his big-league debut in 1951. Mantle emerged as a star in 1952, playing that year in the first of his 14 All-Star games (1952–65), hitting .311 with 23 home runs. In 1956, he hit .353, with 52 home runs and 130 runs batted in, to win the Triple Crown; he was a three-time American League Most Valuable Player (1956, 1957, 1962) and led the league in home runs four times (1955, 1956,

1958, 1960). He retired in 1968, and was elected to baseball's Hall of Fame in 1974.

There was another side to his life; Mantle was an alcoholic even during his playing career, and for decades afterward. In the early 1990s he became doubly afflicted when his health began to fail. In 1994, he entered the Betty Ford Center, and successfully became a recovering alcoholic. But his health continued to fail. In June 1995, he received a liver transplant; but (unknown to the doctors) by then he had cancer, which had spread and was inoperable, soon causing his death. He had published *The Education of a Baseball Player* (1967); *Whitey and Mickey: A Joint Autobiography of the Yankee Years,* written with Joseph Durso (1977); *The Mick* (1985), written with Herb Gluck; *Mickey Mantle: My Favorite Summer, 1956* (1990), written with Phil Pepe; *All My Octobers: My Memories of 12 World Series When the Yankees Ruled Baseball* (1994); and the autobiography *Mickey Mantle: The American Dream Comes to Life* (1994), written with Lew Rothgreb. He was survived by his wife, Merlyn, and three sons; a fourth son predeceased him. (d. Dallas; August 13, 1995)

FURTHER READING

"Live and let die. . . ." JOHN TAYLOR. *Esquire,* Dec. 1995.

Obituary. *Current Biography,* Oct. 1995.

"Courage at. . . ." RICHARD JEROME. *People,* Aug. 28, 1995.

"The Mantle of. . . ." JACK KROLL. *Newsweek,* Aug. 21, 1995.

Obituary. *Sports Illustrated,* Aug. 21, 1995.

"Superman in pinstripes. . . ." STEVE WULF. *Time,* Aug. 21, 1995.

"A career. . . ." MIKE LUPICA. "He graced. . . ." BOB COSTAS. "Remembering. . . ." ROGER KAHN. " 'Like a damn. . . .' " DAVE KINDRED. *Sporting News,* Aug. 21, 1995.

Obituary. *Independent,* Aug. 14, 1995.

Obituary. *New York Times,* Aug. 14, 1995.

"My time in a bottle." MICKEY MANTLE and JILL LIEBER. *Reader's Digest* (Canadian), Feb. 1995.

Mickey Mantle: Classic Sports Shots. BRUCE WEBER. Scholastic, 1993.

Mickey Mantle Memorabilia. MARK LARSON et al., eds. Krause, 1993.

Mickey Mantle. RICK WOLFF. Chelsea House, 1991.

Marino, Dan

Marino, Dan (Daniel Constantine Marino, Jr.; 1961–   ) National Football League records continued to fall before Miami Dolphins quarterback Dan Marino in 1995. In October, Marino

broke Fran Tarkenton's all-time career record of 3,686 completions. In November, he broke two of Tarkenton's records, of 47,003 career passing yards and of 342 career touchdown passes. (Another Tarkenton record, 6,467 career pass attempts, was within reach for 1996, if he maintains his current health and pace.) In December, Marino had his 52nd game with 300 or more passing yards, breaking a record he shared with Dan Fouts. Marino ended the regular season with a quarterback rating of 90.8, second in the American Football Conference and eighth in the league; he had thrown 24 touchdown passes which gained 3,668 yards and had a completion percentage of 64.1 (309 completions for 482 attempts), with 15 interceptions. He also topped the league in most passing yards in a single game, with 450. Marino was named starting quarterback for the AFC team at the Pro Bowl, to be played in February 1996.

All this came after Marino had had arthroscopic surgery in early October. It was the first surgery on his right knee; his left knee has been operated on five times, most recently in 1991. He had missed virtually all of the 1993 season with an Achilles tendon injury, which left some permanent injury to his right calf muscle.

The problem was, as Marino succinctly put it, "We're not winning games." In January 1995, in the playoffs ending the 1994 season, the Dolphins were expected to advance to the Super Bowl, but lost in the final minute of the AFC championship game to the San Diego Chargers.

Super Bowl expectations were also high for the 1995 regular season, but the team stumbled, losing several close games, some to seemingly weaker teams, and ended with a record of 9-7. Even so, they squeaked into the playoffs, but were again eliminated, this time by the Buffalo Bills. After that defeat, longtime Dolphins coach Don Shula resigned and was replaced by Jimmy Johnson, and Marino began looking toward the 1996 season, seeking to shake the tag "greatest quarterback never to win the Super Bowl." He had been there just once, in Super Bowl XIX, ending the 1984 season, when he and the Dolphins lost to Joe Montana and the San Francisco 49ers.

Born in Pittsburgh, Pennsylvania, Marino graduated from Central Catholic High School there and received his 1983 degree in communications from the University of Pittsburgh, where he was named *Sporting News* All-America team quarterback in 1981. Only the fifth quarterback selected in the celebrated 1983 NFL college draft, Marino joined the Miami Dolphins (1983–) and was named Rookie of the Year. He was named the league's Most Valuable Player (1984–85) and was selected to the Pro Bowl team nine times (1983–87, 1991–92, 1994–95), but played only in 1984 and 1992, in other years being unable to play due to injury. Marino holds numerous career records, including the most games with 400 or more yards passing (12); games (18) and consecutive games (4) with four or more touchdown passes; most seasons with 4,000 or more passing yards (6) and 3,000 or more passing yards (11); and consecutive seasons with 3,000 or more passing yards (9). Among other marks, he also holds several single-season records from his extraordinary 1984 season, including most passing yards (5,084), touchdown passes (48), consecutive games with four or more touchdown passes (4), and games with 400 or more passing yards (4).

Marino and his wife, Claire, have three sons and a daughter.

FURTHER READING

"Dan Marino. . . ." JEFF RYAN. *Sport*, Aug. 1994.
Dan Marino Sports Shots. Scholastic Inc., 1992.
"His time is passing." RICK TELANDER. *Sports Illustrated*, Nov. 4, 1991.

Marsalis, Wynton (1961–) Trumpeter, bandleader, composer, and educator Wynton Marsalis, in the process of becoming a celebrated figure on the American musical scene, had—as

usual—a varied and productive year. Although with the end of the Wynton Marsalis Septet he toured far less, he still pursued a very full concert schedule, which in 1995 included his Duke Ellington–oriented Lincoln Center Jazz Orchestra concert. As Lincoln Center's artistic director, Marsalis also pursued a wide range of other Lincoln Center–related activities. On the educational side, Marsalis developed a highly praised televised four-part public broadcasting series *Marsalis on Music,* which was also to generate a book, a home video, and a music CD.

Marsalis' new string quartet, "At the Octoroon Ball," premiered on May 7, played by the Chamber Music Society of Lincoln Center. He also issued the very well received jazz single "Linus & Lucy."

New Orleans–born Marsalis is the son of pianist and teacher Ellis Marsalis, younger brother of saxophonist Branford Marsalis, and older brother of trombonist Delfeayo Marsalis and drummer Jason Marsalis. After briefly playing with Art Blakey's Jazz Messengers, Wynton Marsalis emerged as one of the leading trumpet soloists of his time, functioning equally well in the classics and in jazz, although he has focused on jazz from the late 1980s. A few of his many notable albums are *Fathers and Sons* (1982), *Wynton Marsalis* (1982), *Trumpet Concertos* (1983), *Black Codes from the Underground* (1985), *Standard Time* (Vol. 1, 1987; Vol. 2, 1990; Vol. 3, 1991, *The Resolution of Romance*), *Majesty of the Blues* (1989), *Soul Gestures in*

Southern Blue (1991), *Baroque Duet* (1992; with Kathleen Battle), and *Blue Interlude* (1992). The 32-minute-long *Citi Movement* is the product of his 1991 collaboration with choreographer Garth Fagan. *In This House, On This Morning* (1992) is an impressionistic suite, portraying an African-American church service. Peter Martins's ballet *Jazz,* to Marsalis's music, premiered in 1993. *Blood on the Fields* (1994) is his three-hour suite for jazz orchestra, on African slaves in America; and Marsalis has published *Sweet Swing Blues on the Road: A Year with Wynton Marsalis and His Septet* (1994). Marsalis studied at the Juilliard School of Music (1979–81).

FURTHER READING

"What is jazz?" TONY SCHERMAN and GEOFFREY C. WARD. *American Heritage,* Oct. 1995.
" 'My home is the road.' " CARL VIGELAN. *Down Beat,* May 1995.
"Wynton and. . . ." A. JAMES LISKA. *Down Beat,* Feb. 1994.
"Wynton Marsalis. . . ." TONY SCHERMAN. *Life,* Aug. 1993.
"The cool world." ERIC POOLEY. *New York,* Dec. 21, 1992.

Martin, Dean

(Dino Paul Crocetti; 1917–95) Ohio-born singer and actor Dean Martin began his career singing in cabaret, with indifferent success. He and comedian Jerry Lewis met in 1946, and developed a hit comedy act, with Lewis as comic and Martin as straight man. They quickly became headliners in cabaret and television, and in 1949 made the first of their 16 very popular films, *My Friend Irma.* Martin also became a major recording artist, with such hit singles as "That's Amore" (1953) and "Memories Are Made of This" (1955). When Martin and Lewis parted in 1956, Martin was widely expected to fade away, but did nothing of the kind, going on to build a successful career in films and television, as a solo headliner in cabaret, and as an even more successful recording artist, beginning with his best-selling "Everybody Loves Somebody" (1964). On television, he starred in "The Dean Martin Show" (1965–73) and later hosted several "celebrity roasts." Among his almost three-score films were *The Young Lions* (1958), *Rio Bravo* (1959), *The Sons of Katie Elder* (1963), *Five Card Stud* (1968), and *Airport* (1970). He was survived by four daughters and two sons. (d. Beverly Hills, California; December 25, 1995)

FURTHER READING

"The song of the soused." TY BURR. *Entertainment,* Jan. 12, 1996.
"Dino. . . ." KAREN SCHOEMER. *Newsweek,* Jan. 8, 1996.
"Burden of sorrow. . . ." J. D. REED. *People,* Jan. 8, 1996.
"Crooning towards. . . ." RICHARD CORLISS. *Time,* Jan. 8, 1996.
Obituary. *New York Times,* Dec, 26, 1995.
Obituary. *Variety,* Dec. 26, 1995
Dino. NICK TOSCHES. Doubleday, 1992.

Martin, Ernest H.

(1919–95) Pittsburgh-born Ernest Martin grew up in Los Angeles and attended the University of California there. He went into radio in the late 1930s. In the late 1940s, he and Cy Feuer began a highly successful joint career as the producers of Broadway musicals, beginning with their 1948 production of Frank Loesser's *Where's Charley?* Among their further smash hits were Loesser's Tony-winning musical *Guys and Dolls* (1950), *Can-Can* (1953), *The Boy Friend* (1954), *Silk Stockings* (1955), *How to Succeed in Business Without Really Trying* (1961), *Little Me* (1962), and *The Goodbye People* (1968). They also produced the film versions of *Cabaret* (1968), *Piaf* (1975), and *A Chorus Line* (1985). Martin was survived by his wife, Twyla, and three daughters. (d. Los Angeles; May 7, 1995)

FURTHER READING

Obituary. *Variety,* May 10, 1995.

Martin, Steve

(1945–) Versatile actor and writer Steve Martin again starred as George Banks in the title role of the film comedy *Father of the Bride Part II,* directed by Charles Shyer, who cowrote with Nancy Meyers. The film, a sequel to the 1991 film, costarred Diane Keaton as his wife, Nina Banks, who in this film becomes pregnant; Kimberley Williams as his daughter, who also becomes pregnant; George Newbern as her husband; Martin Short; B. D. Wong; Eugene Levy; and Jane Adams. The broad and sentimental comedy received mixed reviews. Spencer

Brains (1983), *The Lonely Guy* (1984), *All of Me* (1984), *Three Amigos* (1986), *Little Shop of Horrors* (1986), *Planes, Trains and Automobiles* (1987), *Roxanne* (1987; he also wrote and produced), *Dirty Rotten Scoundrels* (1988), *Parenthood* (1989), *My Blue Heaven* (1990), *Father of the Bride* (1991), *L.A. Story* (1991), *Grand Canyon* (1991), *Leap of Faith* (1992), *Housesitter* (1992), *Mixed Nuts* (1994), and *A Simple Twist of Fate* (1994). On stage, he and Robin Williams starred in an acclaimed 1989 New York revival of *Waiting for Godot.* Martin attended the University of California. He was formerly married to actress Victoria Tennant.

FURTHER READING

"Steve Martin." *Playboy,* Jan. 1993.
"Cool jerk." Peter de Jonge. *New York Times Magazine,* May 31, 1992.

Tracy had originally created the Banks role in *Father of the Bride* (1950) and *Father's Little Dividend* (1952). Martin received a Golden Globe nomination as best actor in a musical or comedy for the role.

On a wholly different front, Martin's 1994 one-act play, *Picasso at the Lapin Agile,* opened in New York. The work, a comedy about a fictional 1904 meeting in Paris between Pablo Picasso and Albert Einstein, was generally well received by the critics. The cast included Harry Groener, Carl Don, Rondi Reed, Mark Nelson, and Tim Hopper. Martin also wrote *Wasp and Other Plays,* a group of four short plays that opened December 17 at New York's Public Theater: *Guillotine, The Zigzag Woman, Patter for a Floating Lady,* and *Wasp.* Barry Edelman directed a cast that included Don McManus, Carol Kane, Peggy Pope, Nesbitt Blaisdell, Amelia Campbell, and Kevin Isola.

Still forthcoming was a starring role in the film *Sgt. Bilko,* directed by Jonathan Lynn.

Texas-born Martin was a television comedy writer and comedian in cabaret before emerging as a leading television, film, and recording comedian in the late 1970s, most notably as a prominent guest and sometimes host on "Saturday Night Live," and with his Grammy-winning albums *Let's Get Small* (1977) and *A Wild and Crazy Guy* (1978). He became a leading comedy film star with *The Jerk* (1979), and went on to such films as *Pennies from Heaven* (1981), *Dead Men Don't Wear Plaid* (1982), *The Man with Two*

Martinez, Edgar (1963–) In 1995, Seattle Mariners third baseman Edgar Martinez was for the second time American League batting champion, posting the highest batting average: .356. He also led the league in on-base percentage, with .479, and was tied with Albert Belle to lead the league in most runs scored, with 121, and doubles, with 52. Martinez was also second in the league with total hits, with 182; second in slugging percentage, at .690; second in total bases on balls, with 116; third in total bases, with 321; and fourth in runs batted in, with 113. Martinez was starting designated hitter for the American League team in the All-Star game. At season's end, he came in third in voting for Most Valuable Player, behind Mo Vaughn and Belle.

Martinez was a key figure in helping the Mariners reach the playoffs, but in the American League Championship series, he went into a slump, getting only 2 hits in 23 at bats, for an average of .087, and no runs batted in. The Mariners lost the series in six games to the Cleveland Indians.

Born in New York City, Martinez was educated at Dorado High School and American College, both in Puerto Rico. He was initially signed as a nondrafted free agent in 1982 and played in the minor leagues (1983–87), in Belling, Wausau, Chattanooga, and Calgary; he first came up to the majors with Seattle in 1987, returned to Calgary for parts of 1988 and 1989, then came to

Seattle to stay (1990–   ), except for rehabilitation in Jacksonville (1993). In 1992, his best year prior to 1995, Martinez led the American League with a batting average of .343, and was named to the All-Star team. With Greg Brown, he wrote *Edgar Martinez: Patience Pays* (1992).

FURTHER READING

"This is. . . ." STEVE MARANTZ. *Sporting News,* Sept. 25, 1995.

Matthau, Walter (Walter Matuschanskavasky; 1920–   ) Veteran screen and stage actor Walter Matthau in 1995 starred as Max opposite Jack Lemmon as John and Ann-Margret as Ariel in the offbeat film comedy *Grumpier Old Men,* directed by Howard Deutsch and costarring Sophia Loren, Burgess Meredith, Daryl Hannah, Kevin Pollack, and Ann Guilbert. The film is set six months after the earlier film *Grumpy Old Men* (1993); Loren is introduced as a new love interest for Max, Lemmon and Ann-Margret are married, and Max and John fall out spectacularly over their children.

Matthau also starred in the film *The Grass Harp,* directed by his son, Charles Matthau, and based on Truman Capote's autobiographical novel. The cast included Piper Laurie, Sissy Spacek, Jack Lemmon, Mary Steenburgen, and Charles Durning.

Forthcoming was a starring role in the film version of the play *I'm Not Rappaport,* written and directed by Herb Gardner and costarring Ossie Davis and Amy Irving.

New York City–born Matthau made his Broadway debut in *Anne of the Thousand Days* (1948), and his film debut in *The Kentuckian* (1955). Among his plays were *Once More with Feeling* (1958), *A Shot in the Dark* (1961), and his Tony-winning lead in *The Odd Couple* (1964), which he re-created on screen in 1968. He won a best actor Oscar for *The Fortune Cookie* (1966); among his many other films are *Charade* (1963), *Fail Safe* (1964), *Kotch* (1971), *Pete n' Tillie* (1972), *Charley Varrick* (1973), *The Sunshine Boys* (1975), *California Suite* (1979), *Hopscotch* (1980), *First Monday in October* (1981), *I Ought to Be in Pictures* (1982), *The Couch Trip* (1988), *Grumpy Old Men* (1993), and *Dennis the Menace* (1993). He is married to Carol Marcus, and has had two children, one of whom died. (For additional photo, see **Lemmon, Jack**.)

FURTHER READING

"The grump who. . . ." TESS CAGLE. *Entertainment,* Jan. 28, 1994.
"Rumpled Royalty." LILLIAN ROSS. *New Yorker*, May 31, 1993.
"Carol in wonderland." BEN BRANTLEY. *Vanity Fair*, May 1992.
Among the Porcupines: A Memoir. CAROL MATTHAU. Random House, 1992.

Mau, Carl Henning (1922–95) Lutheran minister Carl Mau was born in Seattle and attended Washington State University. When he was ordained in 1946, he became the sixth generation of Lutheran ministers in his family. A German-American, he spoke German fluently, which was to help him enormously in his rise in the largely German international Lutheran church hierarchy. After serving as pastor to several congregations in Oregon and Washington, Mau in 1950 became director of the Lutheran World Federation office in Hanover, Germany. He became Federation associate general secretary (1964), American general secretary (1972), and then general secretary of the world federation (1974–85). While general secretary, he was widely credited with building the 60 million strong, 68-country federation into a more cohesive whole, and with moving the African and Eastern European components of the church into more equal partnership within the federation, to

that end holding the 1977 world assembly in Tanzania, and the 1984 assembly in Hungary. At Budapest, he led the successful fight to condemn apartheid, which led to the expulson of the South African church from the federation. He was survived by his wife, Thilda, a daughter, and two sons. (d. Des Moines, Washington; March 31, 1995)

FURTHER READING

Obituary. *Times* (of London), Apr. 19, 1995.
Obituary. *New York Times*, Apr. 5, 1995.

Maxwell, William (1908–) Sometimes dubbed one of the best-kept secrets of American letters, writer and longtime *New Yorker* staffer William Maxwell was honored by his peers in 1995. In April, he was given the Ivan Sandrof Award for Lifetime Achievement from the National Book Critics Circle, and in May he received the Gold Medal for Fiction, awarded every six years by the American Academy of Arts and Letters. Bringing Maxwell's work to fresh audiences was his *All the Days and Nights: The Collected Stories of William Maxwell,* a gathering of 23 stories and 21 "improvisations" written over more than five decades; it includes all the tales in his *The Old Man at the Railroad Crossing and Other Stories* (1966) and *Billie Dyer and Other Stories* (1992), set in the Illinois of his boyhood, along with a number of previously unpublished sketches. In a change of pace, he also published

a children's book, *Bun (Mrs. Donald's Dog Bun and His Home Away from Home),* illustrated by James Stevenson. Maxwell's *They Came Like Swallows* (1937) was also reprinted in a new edition.

Born in Lincoln, Illinois, Maxwell was educated at Harvard University and the University of Illinois, where he taught English (1931–33). His first notable published work was *Bright Center of Heaven* (1934). He then joined *The New Yorker* magazine, where he was a longtime member of the editorial staff (1936–76). His other published works include *The Folded Leaf* (1945), *Heavenly Tenants* (1946), *Time Will Darken It* (1948), *Stories* (1956; with Jean Stafford, John Cheever, and Daniel Fuchs), *The Chateau* (1961), *Ancestors* (1971), *Over by the River* (1977), *So Long, See You Tomorrow* (1979; it won a 1980 American Book Award), and *The Outermost Dreams: Essays and Reviews* (1989). He also edited Charles Pratt's *The Garden and the Wilderness* (1980) and *Letters of Sylvia Townsend Warner* (1982), and has published numerous stories and book reviews. Maxwell married Emily Gilman Noyes in 1945; they have two daughters.

FURTHER READING

"A modest, scrupulous. . . ." HARVEY GINSBERG. *New York Times Book Review*, Jan. 22, 1995.

Mayle, Peter (ca. 1939–) British writer Peter Mayle, whose name has in recent years been synonymous with Provence, no longer lives in that attractive area of southern France— partly because his own works have made it (and him) so popular. But though he now resides on Long Island, his 1995 offering harked back to his Provençal writings. *A Dog's Life* is the purported autobiography of his dog, Boy, who was originally introduced in *Toujours Provence* (1991). Abused and abandoned, Boy is adopted by Mayle's wife and thereafter lives a luxurious life, though he thinks little of her "other half," Mayle himself, and is much given to sly and cynical observations about the people and world around him. Illustrated with drawings by Ed Koren, *A Dog's Life* became a best-seller and Mayle was widely seen on a promotional tour. An audiobook version also appeared.

Born in Surrey, England, but raised in the West Indies, Mayle made his first career in advertising, most notably at New York's Ogilvy, Bensen & Mather, a period he later humorously recalled in his *Up the Agency: The Funny Business of Advertising* (1993). He became a full-time writer in 1975, publishing numerous books and essays. Among his many children's books were *Where Did I Come From?* (1973), *Grownups and Other Problems: Help for Small People in a Big World* (1982), and *Sweet Dreams and Monsters:*

A Beginner's Guide to Dreams and Nightmares and Things That Go Bump in the Night (1987). Adult fare included *How to Be a Pregnant Father* (1977), *Divorce Can Happen to the Nicest People* (1988), and *Wicked Willie's Low-Down on Men* (1987), with cartoonist Gray Jolliffe. He first became widely popular with the surprise bestsellers *A Year in Provence* (1989) and *Toujours Provence* (1991), together the basis for the television miniseries (1993), starring John Thaw and Lindsay Duncan. Mayle's first novel, *Hotel Pastis: A Novel of Provence,* was published in 1993; he followed that with *Provence* (1994), with photographs by Jason Hawkes. Some of Mayle's many short pieces, notably for *GQ—Gentlemen's Quarterly,* were collected in *Expensive Habits* (1991) and *Acquired Tastes* (1992). Twice divorced, Mayle is married to former advertising exective Jennie Hayes and has five children.

FURTHER READING

"Peter Mayle. . . ." MICHELE FIELD. *Publishers Weekly,* Oct. 11, 1993.

"How to eat. . . ." PATRICK DUFFY. *Time,* July 22, 1991.

Meade, James Edward (1907–95)

Somerset-born James Meade was a 1930 graduate of Oriel College, Oxford, and did postgraduate work at Trinity College, Cambridge, there becoming an influential Keynesian. Throughout his life, he was a leading left liberal economist. He taught at Hertford College, Oxford (1931–37). In 1938, he joined the League of Nations economics staff, preparing the League's annual world economic surveys. During World War II, he developed a wide range of economic reports for the British government, and after the war was director of the Economic Section of the Cabinet Office (1946–47), in that position functioning as the postwar Labour government's chief economics officer, whose work was central to the development of the government's nationalization and social services network policies. He then resumed teaching, at the London School of Economics (1947–57), and then held the Cambridge University Chair of Political Economy (1957–68). He was president of the Royal Economic Society (1964–66). A prolific author, many of his works were collected in the two volumes of his *The Theory of International Economic Policy* (1951; 1956). He was awarded the 1977 Nobel Prize in economics. Meade was survived by his wife, Elizabeth, three daughters, and a son. (d. Cambridge, England; December 22, 1995)

FURTHER READING

Obituary. *Economist,* Jan. 6, 1996.
Obituary. *Times* (of London), Dec. 28, 1995.
Obituary. *New York Times,* Dec. 28, 1995.

Merrill, James Ingram (1926–95)

New York City–born James Merrill was a leading poet and novelist whose work also included plays and essays. After his 1947 graduation from Amherst College, Merrill turned to his writing career; his first book was *Poems* (1951); it was followed by a period in which he focused on plays and novels, including his first play *The Immortal Husband* (1955) and his first novel, *The Seraglio* (1957). Returning to poetry, he emerged as a major figure, whose poetic works also in-

cluded *The Country of a Thousand Years of Peace* (1959), *Water Street* (1962), *Nights and Days* (1966; it won a National Book Award), *The Fire Screen* (1969), *Braving the Elements* (1972), *The Yellow Pages* (1974), *Divine Comedies* (1976; it won a Pulitzer Prize); *Mirabell* (1978), *Scripts for the Pageant* (1980), *From the First Nine Poems* (1982), *The Changing Light at Sandover* (1982), *New Selected Poems* (1992), *Selected Poems, 1946–1985* (1993), and the posthumously published *A Scattering of Salts* (1995). He was awarded the 1973 Bollingen Prize. Merrill also published the novel *The Diblos Notebook* (1965). His autobiography was *A Different Person: A Memoir* (1993). Merrill was survived by his mother, two sisters, and a brother. (d. Tucson, Arizona; February 6, 1995)

FURTHER READING

"In memory of. . . ." *Poetry,* Sept. 1995.
"Poets and parents." MARY JO SALTER. *New Republic,* Mar. 6, 1995.
"Poetry. . . ." DAVID GATES. *Newsweek,* Feb. 20, 1995.
"Radiant in. . . ." BRAD LEITHAUSER. *Time,* Feb. 20, 1995.
Obituary. *Times* (of London), Feb. 15, 1995.
Obituary. *Independent,* Feb. 9, 1995.
Obituary. *New York Times,* Feb. 7, 1995.

Mfume, Kweisi (1948–   ) On December 9, 1995, the board of directors of the National Association for the Advancement of Colored People (NAACP) named Maryland Congressman

Kweisi Mfume, chairman of the Congressional Black Caucus, to be its president and chief executive officer. In so doing the NAACP took a major step toward effecting the kind of revitalization and rededication so needed by the severely damaged organization. Since at least 1994, when former executive director Benjamin Chavis was fired for alleged financial irregularities, the NAACP, the leading American civil rights organization of the 20th century, had been afflicted by a mountainous debt, severely damaged prestige, and intense internal conflicts. Board chairperson Dr. William F. Gibson had been replaced by Myrlie Evers-Williams in February 1995, and debts totaled more than $3 million. Mfume—a highly prestigious African-American politician with impeccable credentials, no shadow of any kind of scandal, and demonstrated political savvy—looked to the beleaguered NAACP leadership to be heaven-sent.

Given the recent history of the NAACP, Mfume did impose conditions. One was that his title be president and chief executive officer, rather than the lesser-sounding executive director. Another was that the historic power of the NAACP director to hire and fire staff be restored; it had been removed by the board in earlier years, severely damaging the director's ability to function effectively. A third was that he would report to a small executive committee, rather than to the faction-ridden 64-member board.

That accomplished, Mfume set about the task of putting his new house in order and attempt-

ing to set the NAACP back on its historic track. Now he stood in the shoes of former NAACP leaders William E. Du Bois, James Weldon Johnson, Walter White, and Roy Wilkins, at a time of new racial crises in the United States; much remained to be done.

Baltimore-born Mfume, a graduate of Morgan State University, with an M.A. from Johns Hopkins University, was a popular Baltimore talk show host and disk jockey before settling into his political career. He served on the Baltimore City Council (1979–87), then entered Congress from Maryland's Seventh District and won reelection four times, by huge majorities. He became chairperson of the Congressional Black Caucus in 1992. He has been an adjunct professor of political science at Morgan State. Formerly married, he has five children.

FURTHER READING

"A child of. . . ." JEANNYE THORNTON and JERELYN EDDINGS. *U.S. News & World Report*, Dec. 25, 1995.
"The rise of. . . ." PETER J. BOYER. *New Yorker*, Aug. 1, 1994.
"From table-pounder. . . ." RON STODGHILL, II. *Business Week*, Mar. 1, 1993.

Michener, James Albert (1907–) For his new 1995 novel, slimmer than his earlier "big books," James Michener returned to Spain, the site of an earlier work, *Iberia,* with a tale of bullfighting and religious faith: *Miracle in Seville.* Told by sports journalist Shenstone, the tale flashes back two decades to a bullfighting festival in Seville, scene of a confrontation between Don Cayetano Mota, who has been praying for his bulls to redeem his family's honor, and the disreputable matador Lázaro López. The work was illustrated with two-color drawings by John Fulton, an American-born Seville matador. It was also released in audiobook and large-print editions. The year also saw a television miniseries, *Texas,* based on Michener's 1985 novel; directed by Richard Lang from a script by Sean Meredith, it starred Stacy Keach as Sam Houston, Patrick Duffy as Stephen F. Austin, and David Keith as Jim Bowie, along with Chelsea Field, Benjamin Bratt, Maria Conchita Alonso, Rick Schroder, and voice-over narration by Charlton Heston.

Michener was a teacher and editor during the late 1930s and 1940s. He emerged as a major

American popular author with his Pulitzer Prize–winning first novel *Tales of the South Pacific* (1947); the book was adapted into the musical *South Pacific* (1949). He went on to write numerous best-sellers, many of them historical novels and several of them adapted into hit movies. Some of his best-known novels are *The Bridges at Toko-ri* (1953), *Sayonara* (1954), *The Bridge at Andau* (1957), *Hawaii* (1959), *The Source* (1965), *Iberia* (1968), *Centennial* (1974), *Chesapeake* (1978), *The Covenant* (1980), *Space* (1982), *Texas* (1985), *Alaska* (1988), *Caribbean* (1989), *The Novel* (1991), *Mexico* (1992), and *Recessional* (1994). He has also written several nonfiction works, including *Pilgrimage: A Memoir of Poland and Rome* (1990), *The World Is My Home: A Memoir* (1992), and *Literary Reflections: Michener on Michener, Hemingway, Capote, and Others* (1993). Michener attended Swarthmore College. He has been married three times, since 1955 to Mari Yoriko Sabusawa.

FURTHER READING

James A. Michener: A Bibliography. DAVID A. GROSECLOS. State House Press, 1995.
James A. Michener: A Checklist of His Works, with a Selected, Annotated Bibliography. F. X. ROBERTS and C. D. Rhine, eds. Greenwood, 1995.
James A. Michener: The Beginning Teacher and His Textbooks. G. L. DYBWAD and JOY V. BLISS. Book Stops Here, 1995.
Who's Writing This?: Notations on the Authorial I, with Self-Portraits. Daniel Halpern, ed. Ecco, 1994.
"The man who. . . ." LYNN ROSELLINI. *U.S. News & World Report*, June 17, 1991.

Midler, Bette (1945–) Returning to her musical roots, singer and actress Bette Midler in 1995 made her first nonsoundtrack album since 1990, comprised of new popular ballads. It was *Bette of Roses,* which included the hit title song and several other well-received songs, among them "In This Life," "As Dreams Go By," "Bottomless," and "To Deserve You," Maria McKee's hit pop ballad, the first single generated by the album. In 1995, Midler also returned to her professonal roots, relocating in New York, the Hollywood years now behind her. Midler was also continuing to develop film and television projects with her company All Girls Productions.

Forthcoming was a starring role in Woody Allen's as-yet-untitled next film, written and directed by Allen and costarring Tim Roth, Julia Roberts, Judy Davis, Alan Alda, Ed Norton, Drew Barrymore, and Billy Crudup. Also forthcoming was a starring role opposite Diane Keaton in the film *The First Wives Club,* directed by P. J. Hogan. A major film project being discussed at year's end was a possible leading role in a Martin Scorsese film about cabaret figure Texas Guinan.

Hawaii-born Midler, on stage and screen from 1965, was in the early 1970s the long-running lead singer at New York's Continental Baths, a gay men's health club. She began her recording career with the album *The Divine Miss M* (1973), also recording such albums as *Bette Midler* (1973), *Thighs and Whispers* (1979), *Divine Madness* (1980), and *Some People's Lives* (1990), as well as the soundtrack album for *The Rose* (1980), her first starring film role. Her single "Wind Beneath My Wings" won a 1990 Grammy award for best song. Midler went on to play in such films as *Jinxed* (1982), *Down and Out in Beverly Hills* (1986), *Ruthless People* (1986), *Outrageous Fortune* (1987), *Beaches* (1989), *Stella* (1990), *Scenes from a Mall* (1991), *For the Boys* (1992), and *Hocus Pocus* (1993). She has also appeared in television, most notably in the title role of the television version of the stage musical *Gypsy* (1994; she won a Golden Globe Award). She published *A View from a Broad* (1980). Midler attended the University of Hawaii. She married Martin von Haselberg in 1984; they have one child.

FURTHER READING

Bette: An Intimate Biography of Bette Midler. George Mair. Carol, 1995.
" 'Experience the Divine.' " RICHARD DAVID. *New York,* Sept. 13, 1993.
"A sure Bette." SALLY OGLE DAVIS. *Ladies Home Journal,* July 1993.
"La belle Bette." KEVIN SESSUMS. *Vanity Fair,* Dec. 1991.
"A fashion fairy tale extravaganza." JONATHAN VAN METER. *Vogue,* Dec. 1991.
"Bette Midler and. . . ." EMILY YOFFE. *Newsweek,* Nov. 25, 1991.
"Bette." VERNON SCOTT. *Good Housekeeping,* Mar. 1991.

Miller, Arthur (1915–) American playwright Arthur Miller was much celebrated in 1995, on the occasion of his 80th birthday. On October 17 PEN American Center, the U.S.

branch of the international writers' union, hosted a gala evening of readings and speeches in New York, featuring such fellow luminaries as Nadine Gordimer, Vaclav Havel, Harold Pinter, Edward Albee, and Carlos Fuentes. Another celebratory event was held at the Arthur Miller Center for American Studies in Norwich, England. Viking Penguin issued a special gift edition of his *Homely Girl, A Life: And Other Stories,* which includes the title novella and two other stories, "Fitter's Night" and the brief "Fame." It also published a revised edition of the *Portable Arthur Miller,* a paperback edition of his autobiography *Timebends,* and a new edition of *The Crucible,* which is also available on CD-ROM. During 1995, Miller completed his one-year term as professor of contemporary theater at Oxford University.

Miller has been a leading American playwright since the 1947 production of *All My Sons,* which won a New York Drama Critics' Award. He became a world figure with his Pulitzer Prize–winning *Death of a Salesman* (1949), in which Lee J. Cobb originated the memorable Willy Loman. Miller's most notable further work included the Tony-winning *The Crucible* (1953), the Pulitzer-winning *A View from the Bridge* (1955), *After the Fall* (1963), *Incident at Vichy* (1965), *The Price* (1968), *The American Clock* (1979), *The Last Yankee* (1991), and *Broken Glass* (1994). He wrote the screenplay for *The Misfits* (1961), which starred Marilyn Monroe, his second wife (1956–61), who committed suicide in 1962. His second screenplay was for Karel Reisz's *Everybody Wins* (1990), starring Nick Nolte and Debra Winger. Miller's recent work also includes an Americanized adaptation of Ibsen's *An Enemy of the People* (1990), done in a televised production for PBS's "American Playhouse." In 1987 he published *Timebends: A Life.*

Miller attended the University of Michigan. He has been married three times, since 1962 to photographer Inge Morath, with whom he has collaborated on two travel books; he has two children.

FURTHER READING

"Master of. . . ." JUDITH THURMAN. *Architectural Digest,* Nov. 1995.
"Arthur Miller. . . ." SUSAN CHEEVER. *New Choices for Retirement Living,* Oct. 1994.
Arthur Miller in Conversation. STEVE CENTOLA. Contemporary Research, 1993.
"Miller's crossing." JAMES KAPLAN. *Vanity Fair,* Nov. 1991.

Milosevic, Slobodan (1941–) On December 15, 1995, Serbian President Slobodan Milosevic, Croatian President Franco Tudjman, and Bosnian President Alija Izetbegovic signed a Bosnian peace treaty, which had been pressed upon them by international great power intervention, led by President Bill Clinton. The agreement had been negotiated at Dayton, Ohio, on November 21; it was signed in Paris. A NATO peace-keeping force of 60,000, which included 20,000 Americans, was to be sent to Bosnia; it would be supported by tens of thousands of others in naval, air, and supply forces stationed in neighboring countries and at sea.

No Bosnian Serb leaders signed the agreement, and many expressed dismay and disagreement with some of its terms. Whether President Milosevic would honor the treaty for long and keep the very fragile peace agreed upon was a matter of worldwide conjecture, as it was he who bore by far the greatest responsibility for starting and pursuing the war, which had cost at least 250,000 lives and created at least 2 million refugees. Nor would the task be an easy one: large numbers of Bosnian Serbs now viewed him as a traitor who had sold them out; many of these had not given up their weapons and were entirely capable of waging war for years more from the high, rugged mountains that made up most of Bosnia. However, other world leaders were apparently placing reliance on Milosevic's promises, perhaps relying on the war-weariness of all sides, the ravaged state of the Serbian economy after years of international sanctions and war, and his dictatorial control over his country and the Bosnian Serbs' sources of military supply. At year's end, peace-keeping forces were being deployed in Bosnia; how it would work out remained to be seen.

Born in Pozarevac, near Belgrade, Milosevic followed a very orthodox career path in Tito's Communist Yugoslavia. He became a member of the League of Communists of Yugoslavia in 1959, attended Belgrade University, and moved up as a protégé of Serbian Communist leader Ivan Stambolic. Milosevic worked in the Belgrade city administration during the 1960s, and then became deputy director of the government industrial gas monopoly Technogas (1969–73). He ran a state bank (1978–83) and headed the Belgrade Communist organization (1984–86), then becoming president of the League of Communists of Serbia in 1986. In 1987, resurgent Serbian nationalism created an opportunity for him to take a hard line and gain massive popular and armed forces support. He became known as "The Butcher of the Balkans" in late 1992 and 1993, as Serbian forces turned Bosnia-Herzegovina into a slaughterhouse, with hundreds of thousands of people dead, millions in flight, and the world once again faced with the reality of genocide, this time called "ethnic cleansing." He was reelected to his presidency in 1993. Milosevic is married to League of Communists leader Marjana Markovic.

FURTHER READING

" 'I am just. . . .' " *Time,* July 17, 1995.
"The last ambassador. . . ." WARREN ZIMMERMAN. *Foreign Affairs,* Mar.–Apr. 1995.
"A profile of. . . ." ALESKA DJILAS. *Foreign Affairs,* Summer 1993.
"The butcher of. . . ." "The world's other. . . ." JAMES WALSH. *Time,* Jan. 4, 1993. (Man of the Year issue)
"The butcher of. . . ." JAMES GRAFF. *Time,* June 8, 1992.
"Carving out. . . ." STEPHEN ENGELBERG. *New York Times Magazine,* Sep. 1, 1991.

Mirabella, Grace (1930–) Not many people have a magazine named after them, but that is precisely what Grace Mirabella did, founding the fashion magazine *Mirabella* (with backing from publishing magnate Rupert Murdoch) when she was ousted from *Vogue* after 17 highly successful years as its chief editor. In 1995, Mirabella published her version of that piece of fashion magazine history in her new book *In and Out of Vogue: A Memoir,* written with Judith Warner. Beyond that, she describes how the daughter of poor Italian immigrants came to the center of the fashion world at a time when a fashion revolution was under way. In March 1995, the money-losing *Mirabella* suspended publication; in October it resumed publication, as a bimonthly, with a new owner and a new editor. Though Mirabella's name still appeared on the masthead as founder, she had essentially retired from it.

Born and raised in Newark, New Jersey, Mirabella received her 1950 B.A. from Skidmore College, then joined the executive training program at Macy's (1950–51) before moving on to Saks Fifth Avenue (1951–52). She came to *Vogue* in 1952 and, except for two years in Rome on the public relations staff of Simonetta & Fabiani (1954–56), stayed there until 1988, as associate editor (1965–71), then editor in chief (1971–88). She then started her own magazine, *Mirabella* (1989–   ). Mirabella married William G. Cahan in 1974.

FURTHER READING

"Mirabella, Grace." *Current Biography,* Oct. 1991.
"True Grace. . . ." JEFF SHEAR. *Insight on the News,* June 10, 1991.

Helen Mirren (left) and Ron Rifkin.

Mirren, Helen (1940–   ) Stage and screen

star Helen Mirren was honored by her peers in 1995. She won the Cannes Film Festival best actress award for her role in *The Madness of King George;* she had also received an Oscar nomination as best supporting actress for the role.

On stage, Mirren received a Tony Award nomination as best leading actress for her role as Natalya Petrovna in Ivan Turgenev's play *A Month in the Country,* which won her an Outer Critics Circle award for best debut of an actress. Scott Ellis directed and Richard Freeborn translated the play, which costarred Ron Rifkin, F. Murray Abraham, and Kathryn Erbe.

Mirren again played British detective Jane Tennison in another segment of the "Prime Suspect" series, this one a set of three discrete two-hour television films. In the first of the three, "The Lost Child," Tennison is pregnant while

working on a child abuse case; John Madden directed.

London-born Mirren's long theater career began in the mid-1960s with the National Youth Theatre. She joined the Royal Shakespeare Company (RSC) in 1967, quickly moving into major roles with the RSC and in other productions. She also worked in films and television, as in the films *O Lucky Man!* (1973), *Cal* (1984), *The Comfort of Strangers* (1989), *Prince of Jutland* (1994), and *The Madness of King George* (1994). She became a popular star as London detective Jane Tennison in "Prime Suspect" (1991), "Prime Suspect II" (1992), and "Prime Suspect III" (1994).

FURTHER READING

"Mirren, Helen." *Current Biography,* July 1995.
Helen Mirren: Prime Suspect. AMY RENNERT. KQED, 1995.
"The prime of. . . ." DAVID ANSEN. *Newsweek,* May 16, 1994.
"Mirren and 'Middlemarch.' " CHRISTOPHER HITCHENS. *Vanity Fair,* May 1994.
"In step with. . . ." JAMES BRADY. *Parade,* Apr. 10, 1994.
"An interview with. . . ." AMY RENNERT. *New Orleans,* Apr. 1994.
"Prime time." LISA SCHWARZBAUM. *Entertainment,* Jan. 22, 1993.
"Helen Mirren." JAMES SAYNOR. *Interview,* Jan. 1993.

Mitchell, Joni (Roberta Joan Anderson;

1943–   ) For celebrated Canadian folksinger, composer, and guitarist Joni Mitchell, 1995 was a year of long-overdue recognition and continuing artistic revival. At the December 6 Billboard Music Awards, she received *Billboard*'s Century Award for her whole body of still-unfolding creative work, in recognition of her massive contribution to folk music and the blues, beginning in the late 1960s and continuing today with her currently released album *Turbulent Indigo,* made in 1991, which contains such new songs as "Love Puts On a Face."

In 1995, Mitchell also began what may be a new stage of her performing career. Afflicted in childhood with polio, and suffering from difficult physical problems caused by post-polio syndrome, she had for many years found it physically very difficult to handle the scores of tunings required for her repertoire in each concert, and

so had performed little. But by moving from an acoustic guitar to a specially modified electric guitar hooked up to a portable computerized information bank, containing all the tunings needed for her massive repertoire, she became able to perform easily once again—indeed, perhaps more easily than ever before. One early result was her surprise, extraordinarily successful November 6 appearance at New York's Fez cabaret, accompanied by drummer Bryan Blade, which on very little notice drew many music-world luminaries.

Mitchell was in the late 1960s and early 1970s one of the leading figures of the folk and blues revival. She and several of her songs, such as "Both Sides Now" (1968) and "Woodstock" (1970), also became emblematic of the counter-cultural movements of the day. Some of her best-known early albums were *Clouds* (1969), *Ladies of the Canyon* (1970), *Blue* (1971), *For the Roses* (1972), *Court and Spark* (1974), and *Hejira* (1976). A very notable later work was her collaboration with jazz great Charles Mingus in the award-winning album *Mingus* (1979). Her later albums included *Shadows and Light* (1980), *Wild Things Run Fast* (1982), *Dog Eat Dog* (1985), *Chalk Mark in a Rainstorm* (1988), and *Night Ride Home* (1991). Some of her songs were the basis of children's books, including *Both Sides Now* (1992) and *The Circle Game* (1992). Born in Ft. Macleod, Alberta, Mitchell studied at Alberta College. Previously divorced, she married Larry Klein in 1982.

FURTHER READING

"Mood indigo. . . ." MARTIN SIMPSON. *Guitar Player,* Feb. 1995.
Joni Mitchell: Turbulent Indigo. CAROL CUELLAR, ed. Warner, 1995.
"Joni Mitchell." JANCEE DUNN. *Rolling Stone,* Dec. 15, 1994.
"Lady of the canyon. . . ." NICHOLAS JENNINGS. *Maclean's,* Oct. 31, 1994.
"Joni Mitchell. . . ." DIMITRI EHRLICH. *Interview,* Apr. 1991.

Mitnick, Kevin D. (1964–)

A new kind of criminal drew national headlines early in 1995: the computer hacker turned thief and spoiler. After a two-year hunt, and with the help of computer security expert Tsutomu Shimomura, Kevin Mitnick was traced by computer to Raleigh, North Carolina, where on February 15 he was arrested by federal agents for a series of alleged major computer-generated crimes, and for violating the terms of his 1992 California parole. His downfall came when he electronically invaded Shimomura's San Diego home computer, taking thousands of Shimomura's personal files, and so bringing Shimomura into the continuing hunt for Mitnick. Within two weeks, Shimomura, working with federal agents, had traced Mitnick to a Raleigh apartment, where he was arrested. A July plea bargaining agreement provided that Mitnick plead guilty to one count of a 23-count indictment.

Mitnick began his computer criminal career in a small way while still in his teens, and drew national attention in 1982, when he was able to break into a presumably secure North American Air Command computer system. By the late 1980s, he was routinely—and illegally—breaking into telephone company and other communications company files, allegedly stealing millions of dollars worth of software and causing damage costing millions of dollars. In July 1989, he was convicted of computer crimes in California and sentenced to a year in prison. On his release in 1990, his probation terms prohibited him from touching computers or modems. He allegedly soon violated the terms of his parole; a California arrest warrant for him was issued in 1993.

FURTHER READING

"Kevin Mitnick. . . ." KATIE HAFNER. *Esquire,* Aug. 1995.

"The samurai and. . . ." JEFF GOODELL. *Rolling Stone,* May 4, 1995.

"Cyberscoop!" ANDREW L. SHAPIRO. *Nation,* Mar. 20, 1995.

"Interview with the cybersleuth." STEVEN LEVY. *Newsweek,* Mar. 6, 1995.

"Kevin Mitnick's. . . ." JOSHUA QUITTNER. *Time,* Feb. 27, 1995.

Cyberpunk. JOHN MARKOFF and KATIE HAFNER. Simon & Schuster, 1991.

Mitterrand, François Maurice Marie

(1916–) On June 17, French Socialist President François Mitterrand completed his second term in office and was succeeded by conservative Jacques Chirac. During his final months in office, Mitterrand had continued to play an active but wholly unsuccessful role in trying to bring peace to Bosnia, where French, British, and other international forces were being harassed by Bosnian Serb forces, their peacekeeping role all but destroyed. In these final days of his 14-year-long tenure, he also attempted to further develop a federated European Union (EU), although it was becoming increasingly clear that British Prime Minister John Major would, because of internal opposition, be forced to greatly weaken his support of European economic and monetary union, and that Chirac would join Major in calling for a much weaker commitment—which they did, calling for a more "decentralized" approach in early June, not least because France faced substantial economic problems of its own as the Chirac years began.

A soldier during World War II, Mitterrand was captured early, but escaped from the Germans and became an active Resistance fighter. He entered politics after the war and was a Socialist deputy in the national assembly (1946–58; 1962–81), holding many Cabinet positions in the early years, when his party held power. At the same time, he rose within the Socialist Party and was its first secretary (1971–81), while also becoming a vice president of the Socialist International (1972–81). In 1981, he was elected president of France, and was reelected to a second seven-year term in 1988. Although his party was decisively defeated in the March 1993 general elections, Mitterrand remained in office until the end of his term in 1995, with undiminished responsibility for foreign policy defense issues, focusing on such matters as the Bosnian War and French intervention in Rwanda.

Mitterrand attended the University of Paris. He married Danielle Gouze in 1944; they have two children. His brother is General Jacques Mitterrand.

FURTHER READING

"Bye-bye, Mitterrand." DAVID A. BELL. *New Republic,* Mar. 20, 1995.

"The long march. . . ." RICHARD VINEN. *History Today,* Mar. 1995.

"Mitterrand's legacies." RONALD TIERSKY. *Foreign Affairs,* Jan.–Feb. 1995.

François Mitterrand: The Making of a Socialist Prince in Republican France. Sally Baumann-Reynolds. Greenwood, 1995.

"Mitterrand le Petit." DANIEL SINGER. *Nation,* Oct. 10, 1994.

"Playing with. . . ." JANICE VALLS-RUSSELL. *New Leader,* Sept. 12, 1994.

"Setting of. . . ." ANDREW GUMBEL. *New Statesman & Society,* Sept. 23, 1994.

"Remembrance of things past." PAUL GRAY. *Time,* Sept. 12, 1994.

François Mitterrand: A Study in Political Leadership. ALISTAIR COLE. Routledge, 1994.

Mitterrand: A Political Biography. WAYNE NORTHCUTT. Holmes & Meier, 1992.

Modine, Matthew

(1959–) Actor Matthew Modine starred in 1995 in the film comedy *Bye Bye, Love,* as one of three divorced fathers whose problems provide the film's story line. Costarring were Randy Quaid and Paul Reiser as the other two fathers, along with Janeane Garofalo, Amy Brenneman, Eliza Dushku, and Rob Reiner; Sam Weisman directed.

Modine also starred as a pirate lieutenant opposite Geena Davis as pirate Captain Morgan in the Christmas season special effects adventure film *Cutthroat Island,* directed by Renny Harlin and costarring Frank Langella as her unscrupulous uncle Dawg, Patrick Malahide, Maury Chaykin, Harris Yulin, and Stan Shaw. A third starring role was as a man who is killed in an automobile accident and is immediately reincarnated as a dog, in the film *Fluke,* directed and cowritten by Carlo Carlei and costarring Eric Stoltz, Nancy Davis, Max Pomeranc, Samuel L. Jackson, Ron Perlman, and the dog Comet, star of the "Full House" television series.

Modine also appeared in Vic Burns's television documentary miniseries *The Way West,* an unsympathetic "revisionist" view of the winning of the American West; and as narrator of "The Combat Film," a segment of the television series "American Cinema."

California-born Modine emerged as a star in the late 1980s. He made his film debut in *Baby, It's You* (1983), and in the same year won a Venice Film Festival best actor award for his role in *Streamers* (1983). His breakthrough role came in the following year, as a Vietnam War veteran in *Birdy.* Among his further films were *Full Metal Jacket* (1987), *Married to the Mob* (1988), *Gross Anatomy* (1989), *Pacific Heights* (1990), *Memphis Belle* (1990), *Wind* (1992), *And The Band Played On* (1993), *Short Cuts* (1993), *The Browning Version* (1994), and *Jacob* (1994). Modine studied acting with Stella Adler.

FURTHER READING

"Matthew Modine." RICHARD NATALE. *Cosmopolitan,* Nov. 1990.

Monette, Paul (1945–95) Massachusetts-born novelist and screenwriter Paul Monette was an English teacher at private schools in New England after his graduation from Yale. He moved to Los Angeles in 1974 with his companion, Roger Horwitz, for the first time publicly stating his gay sexual preference. Horwitz died because of AIDS in 1985; Monette chronicled the final period of their lives together in his highly regarded book *Borrowed Time: An AIDS Memoir*

(1988). He also wrote the poetry collection *Love Alone: 18 Elegies for Rog* (1987). He followed these works with several novels on gay men afflicted with AIDS, the last of these *Halfway Home* (1991). Monette's autobiography was the acclaimed *Becoming a Man: Half a Life Story,* which won a 1992 National Book Award. After Monette was diagnosed as having an active case of AIDS in 1993, he continued to write, even though dying. His last works were *West of Yesterday, East of Summer: New and Selected Poems, 1973–1993* (1994) and the posthumously published *Last Watch of the Night: Essays* (1995). He was survived by his companion, Winston Wilde, and by his father and brother. (d. West Hollywood, California; February 10, 1995)

FURTHER READING

"Winning the war." BOHDAN ZACHARY. *Advocate,* Mar. 21, 1995.
Obituary. *Variety,* Feb. 16, 1995.
Obituary. *New York Times*, Feb. 12, 1995.
" 'We all have closets.' " JOSEPH A. CINCOTTI. *New York Times Book Review,* July 26, 1992.
"Paul Monette. . . ." LISA SEE. *Publishers Weekly,* June 29, 1992.
"Paul Monette. . . ." MICHAEL LASSELL. *Advocate,* June 2, 1992.

Montana, Joe (Joseph C. Montana, Jr.; 1956–) Perhaps the greatest quarterback ever to play the game of football, Joe Montana called it quits in 1995. What turned out to be his final game was a wild card contest in the AFC playoffs on December 31, 1994, with Montana leading the Kansas City Chiefs against Dan Marino and the Miami Dolphins. The first half of that game was vintage Montana and Marino, and the winner seemed destined to be whichever had the ball last, but the second half resolved into a series of errors by Chiefs veterans, starting with an interception thrown by Montana. After that defeat, Montana said he would later announce whether or not he would return for the 1995 season.

On April 18 came the decision: retirement. The announcement was made at a public noontime news conference in San Francisco, home of his longtime team, the 49ers. Many of his former 49er teammates (though not backup and later competitor Steve Young) were invited to the retirement ceremony, along with family and local officials. He then flew to Kansas City for a similar news conference. Montana still had one year to go on the three-year, $10.15 million contract he signed with the Chiefs in 1993. He said his main reason for retiring was that he did not feel he could play a full season without injury. He underwent surgery on his right knee in January 1995, hoping to avoid knee replacement; he also continued to suffer periodic headaches, believed to be associated with the 8-10 concussions he received as a quarterback. His left foot has been partly numb since 1986 back surgery to remove a ruptured disk.

Montana later signed with NBC as a part-time studio analyst on the "NFL Live" television show, for six regular season and four playoff games. He published a pictorial autobiography *Montana,* written with Dick Schaap, touring widely to promote the book. He was also the subject of a tribute by NFL Films, *Joe Montana: The Fire Inside,* which aired on TNT in September.

After graduating from Ringgold High School in Monongahela, Pennsylvania, Montana had a notable career as quarterback at the University of Notre Dame, where he received his 1978 B.A. in business administration and marketing. Selected by the San Francisco 49ers in the third round of the 1979 NFL draft, 82nd pick overall, "Joe Cool" developed into a fine all-around quarterback, an extraordinary leader in big games, and a specialist in comebacks, engineering 31 fourth-quarter come-from-behind career wins. He led his team to four Super Bowl championships (1982, 1985, 1989, 1990) without a single Super Bowl loss, and became the only person ever named Most Valuable Player of the Super Bowl three times (1982, 1985, 1990). Among other Super Bowl career records he set were most career touchdown passes (11), consecutive completions (13), highest pass rating (127.8), lowest interception rating (0.0), total pass attempts and total without an interception (122), career passing yardage (1,142), and passes completed (83). He also set single-game records for most touchdowns (5), passing yards (357), and most passes attempted without an interception (36), and holds postseason career records for most touchdown passes (45), passing yards (5,772), passes attempted (734), and passes completed (460), and (shared) games with 300 or more yards passing (6).

After 1986 back surgery that threatened to end his career, Montana returned seemingly as strong as ever. He was named the league's Most Valuable Player, Associated Press's male athlete of the year, and *Sporting News* man of the year in 1989, the year he set the record for highest quarterback rating ever, at 112.4 (not surpassed until 1994, by Steve Young), and *Sports Illustrated*'s sportsman of the year in 1990. He then lost virtually all of the 1991 and 1992 seasons to a career-threatening elbow injury, during which time replacement quarterback Steve Young became the league's highest-rated quarterback and the league's Most Valuable Player. Rather than staying on as a backup to Young, Montana chose to leave for a team where he could start: Kansas City (1993–94).

Montana retired with NFL records for most consecutive games with 300 or more passing yards (5; set in 1982), and most consecutive passes completed (22, in 1987). He had a career pass rating of 92.3, on a total of 3,409 completions on 5,391 attempts (a record 63.2 percentage), for 40,551 yards and 273 touchdowns, with 139 interceptions, and a total of 117 regular-season wins. He was also named to the Pro Bowl eight times (he played in 1981, 1983, 1984, and 1987; he did not play in 1985, 1989, 1990, and 1993, due to injury).

He has published *Audibles: My Life in Football* (1986), written with Bob Raissman, and *Cool Under Fire: Reflections on the San Francisco 49ers—How We Came of Age in the 1980's* (1989), with Alan Steinberg. Twice divorced, Montana married Jennifer Wallace in 1984; they have two daughters and two sons.

FURTHER READING

"The bottom line." BILL PLASCHKE. "The best." DAVE KINDRED. *Sporting News,* Apr. 24, 1995.
"All hail the king." MICHAEL SILVER. *Sports Illustrated,* Apr. 24, 1995.
Joe Montana, The Comeback Kid. JIM SPENCE. Rourke, 1995.
Joe Montana. G. S. PRENTZAS. Chelsea House, 1994.
"Joe Montana." RANDY COVITT. *Sport,* Sept. 1993.
Joe Montana. BOB ITALIA. Abdo & Daughters, 1992.
Sports Great Joe Montana. JACK KAVANAGH. Enslow, 1992.
Joe Montana. JAMES R. ROTHAUS. Childs World, 1991.
Joe Montana. MARC APPLEMAN. Little, Brown, 1991.
Joe Montana. Scholastic, 1991.

Montgomery, Elizabeth

Montgomery, Elizabeth (1933–95) Los Angeles–born Elizabeth Montgomery, a star in television, was the daughter of actor Robert Montgomery and actress Elizabeth Allan. She made her television debut in 1951, in her father's television drama series "Robert Montgomery Presents," and continued to appear in a wide range of television roles during the 1950s and early 1960s. She made her theatrical film debut in *The Court Martial of Billy Mitchell* (1955), and also appeared in *Johnny Cool* (1963) and *Who's Been Sleeping in My Bed?* (1963); but she was primarily a television figure. Her major breakthrough came as the star of the long-running comedy series "Bewitched" (1964–1972), as the witch Samantha Stevens, the role with which she was always identified. The series producer, William Asher, was her second husband. After "Bewitched," she went on to star in many television films and miniseries, among them *A Case of Rape* (1974), *The Legend of Lizzie Borden* (1965), *Dark Victory* (1976), *A Killing Affair* (1977), *The Awakening Land* (1978), *Act of Violence* (1978), *The Rules of Marriage* (1983), *Second Sight* (1986), *Face to Face* (1990), and *Black Widow Murders* (1993). Montgomery was active in a considerable range of social causes, among them AIDS research and humanitarian treatment of those afflicted by the disease; gay and lesbian rights; ecological preservation; and animal rights. She was survived by her fourth husband, actor Robert Foxworth, and three children. (d. Los Angeles; May 18, 1995)

FURTHER READING

"That Magic feeling." Tom Gliatto et al. *People,* June 5, 1995.
"Master of. . . ." Jess Cagle. *Entertainment,* June 2, 1995.
Obituary. *Independent,* May 20, 1995.
Obituary. *Times* (of London), May 20, 1995.
Obituary. *New York Times,* May 19, 1995.
Obituary. *Variety,* May 19, 1995.
"The legend of. . . ." Robert L. Pela. *Advocate,* July 30, 1992.

Moore, Demi (Demi Guynes; 1962–)

Actress Demi Moore in 1995 starred as Hester Prynne in a film version of *The Scarlet Letter,* directed by Roland Joffrey and very, very loosely adapted by Douglas Day Stewart from the Nathaniel Hawthorne novel. Gary Oldman costarred as Arthur Dimmesdale; the cast included Robert Duvall as her husband, Robert Prosky, Edward Hardwicke, and Joan Plowright. The

highly erotic film, removed by several lifetimes and cultures from Hawthorne's Puritan New England setting, was not very well received by the critics or at the box office.

Moore also played the adult Samantha Albertson in the coming-of-age film *Now and Then,* starring Ashleigh Anton Moore as young Samantha, one of the four young girls the film is about. Melanie Griffith appeared as the adult Tina Tercell; Leslie Linka Glatta directed.

For her role in *Disclosure* (1994), Moore received the Blockbuster Entertainment award as best actress in a theatrical film drama. She was also People's Choice Award nominee as favorite woman actress in a drama.

Forthcoming were starring roles opposite Burt Reynolds in the film *Striptease,* written and directed by Andrew Bergman, and in the film *The Gaslight Addition,* costarring Melanie Griffith, Rosie O'Donnell, and Rita Wilson. She was also slated to star opposite Alec Baldwin in the film *The Juror,* directed by Brian Gibson and written by Ted Tally.

New Mexico–born Moore played reporter Jackie Templeton in television's "General Hospital," and appeared in such 1980s films as *Choices* (1981), *Parasite* (1982), *St. Elmo's Fire* (1985), *Wisdom* (1986), *The Seventh Sign* (1988), and *We're No Angels* (1989). Her breakthrough came in 1990 with a starring role opposite Patrick Swayze and Whoopi Goldberg in the fantasy *Ghost,* which became the surprise top-grossing film of the year, making her a bankable star. She also starred in *A Few Good Men* (1992), *Indecent Proposal* (1993), and *Disclosure* (1994).

Having created quite a stir by appearing nude and nine months pregnant on the August 1991 cover of the magazine *Vanity Fair* (though she was not really entirely nude), Moore in August 1992 again appeared on the magazine's cover, this time seeming to be clothed but actually wearing nothing but body paint made to look like a pin-striped suit.

She married actor Bruce Willis in 1987; they have three daughters.

FURTHER READING

"Demi wants. . . ." MELINA GEROSA. *Ladies Home Journal,* Oct. 1995.
"Demi-tough." TAD FRIEND and HERB RITTS. *Vogue,* Oct. 1995.
"Why we want more and more. . . ." LEO JANOS. *Cosmopolitan,* Sept. 1995.
"Anywhere but here." HOLLY MILLEA. *Premiere,* Sept. 1995.
"Demi Moore." MIM UDOVITCH. *Rolling Stone,* Feb. 9, 1995.
"He said. . . ." REBECCA ASCHER-WALSH and BENJAMIN SVETKEY. *Entertainment,* Dec. 16, 1994.
"Moore, Demi." *Current Biography,* Sept. 1993.
"The last pinup." MICHAEL ANGELI and STEVEN KLEIN. *Esquire,* May 1993.
"Demi Moore. . . ." TRIP GABRIEL. *Us,* May 1993.
"Why Demi wants more." PETER WILKINSON. *Redbook,* Jan. 1993.
"Demi's body language." JENNET CONANT and ANNIE LEIBOVITZ. *Vanity Fair,* Aug. 1992.
"Demi Moore." JOE RHODES. *Harper's Bazaar,* June 1992.
"What she did. . . ." JEFF ROVIN. *Ladies Home Journal,* June 1992.

Morrison, Sterling (Holmes Sterling Morrison; 1942–95) Long Island–born rock guitarist and bassist Sterling Morrison attended several colleges, one of them Syracuse University, where he met future collaborator Lou Reed. In 1965, he, Reed, John Cale, and Maureen Tucker formed the high-energy, dissonant rock band Velvet Underground. Adopted by pop-art luminary Andy Warhol, the band became one of the most highly visible features of the youth culture of the 1960s, with such albums as *The Velvet Underground and Nico* (1966), *White Light / White Heat* (1968), *The Velvet Underground* (1969), and *Loaded* (1970). After he left the band in 1971, Morrison

went back to school, ultimately earning a Ph.D. in medieval studies at the University of Texas. In the late 1980s, Morrison worked with Tucker's band, touring and recording. In 1993, the Velvet Underground made a European reunion tour and recording. He was survived by his wife, Martha Dargan Morrison, a daughter, a son, his parents, a sister, and a brother. (d. Poughkeepsie, New York; August 29, 1995)

FURTHER READING

"Velvet warrior." LOU REED. *New York Times Magazine,* Dec. 31, 1995.
Obituary. *Rolling Stone,* Oct. 19, 1995.
Obituary. *Billboard,* Sept. 16, 1995.
Obituary. *New York Times,* Sept. 2, 1995.

Mosley, Walter (1952–   ) Easy (Ezekiel) Rawlins came to the screen in the person of Denzel Washington in 1995, in the film version of Walter Mosley's first novel, *Devil in a Blue Dress* (1990); Carl Franklin directed from his own script and Jennifer Beal costarred in the mystery set in post–World War II Los Angeles. Mosley himself laid aside Rawlins—temporarily, his fans hope—to produce a mainstream novel, *RL's Dream.* This work focuses on Atwater "Soupspoon" Wise, who had once played backup to the great blues guitarist Robert Johnson (the RL of the title), and Kiki Waters, a young survivor of violence and incest who helps ease his pain, and her own. It was also released as an audiobook.

Still in the wings were two more Rawlins mysteries, tentatively titled *The Little Yellow Dog* and *Bad Boy Bobby Brown.*

On the personal side, as chairman of the Open Book committee of the international writers and editors organization PEN, Mosley convened a panel to address the causes of the lack of non-White people in publishing—both the industry's inability to attract them and the isolation and discrimination they face within the field.

Born in south-central Los Angeles, Mosley headed east to attend Goddard College, and received his B.A. from Johnson State College. While working as a computer programmer in New York City, he studied writing at City College, submitting his already completed *Devil in a Blue Dress* manuscript to his professor; passed on to an agent, it was quickly sold. (An earlier, nonmystery novel, *Gone Fishing,* had been widely rejected.) Mosley's other published novels are *A Red Death* (1991), *The White Butterfly* (1992), and *Black Betty* (1994). He is married to dancer-choreographer Joy Kellman.

FURTHER READING

"Living easy" talking with. . . ." V. R. PETERSON. *People,* Oct. 30, 1995.

"Easy virtue." ROBERT YATES. *Guardian,* Oct. 10, 1995.

"On LA's mean streets." JIM IMPOCO. *U.S. News & World Report,* Aug. 21, 1995.

"Mosley, Walter." *Current Biography*, Sept. 1994.

"Walter Mosley. . . ." BOB MCCULLOUGH. *Publishers Weekly,* May 23, 1994.

"Double agent. . . ." SARA M. LOMAX. *American Visions,* Apr.–May 1992.

Mubarak, Hosni (Mohammed Hosni Mubarak; 1928–)

Egyptian President Hosni Mubarak narrowly escaped another assassination attempt in 1995, this one in Addis Ababa, Ethiopia, where he had arrived to attend a meeting of the Organization of African Unity. He blamed Islamic fundamentalists and suggested Sudanese involvement. In Egypt, the Islamic fundamentalist guerrilla insurgency continued, but without much success, as government forces continued their all-out shoot-first attacks, and mass arrests and executions continued while worldwide civil rights organizations criticized government actions, which they charged routinely included the torture of prisoners. Mubarak's government participated in international attempts to build a united effort against terrorism.

Mubarak continued to play a considerable role in the still-developing Middle East peace process, in February hosting a Cairo summit that included Yasir Arafat, Yitzhak Rabin, and King Hussein of Jordan. Throughout the year, he played a role in the off-and-on Israeli-Palestinian talks that ultimately resulted in the September Palestinian home rule agreement.

Mubarak was a career air force officer who moved up to direct the Air Academy (1967–69), became air force chief of staff (1969–72), and was commander in chief (1972–75). He became Anwar Sadat's vice president in 1975 and moved into the presidency in 1981 after Sadat's assassination. He won a second term in the 1987 elections. In 1988, the Mubarak government moved against the fundamentalists, beginning a period of widespread arrests under emergency decrees in effect since the Sadat assassination.

Mubarak has been a moderate within the Arab world throughout his presidency, as well as a considerable force in the search for Middle East and Arab-Israeli peace. As president of the Organization of African Unity (1989–90), he tried to help settle such regional conflicts as those in Ethiopia, Chad, and Namibia. After the August 1990 Iraqi attack on Kuwait, he led moderate Arab response, convening an Arab summit meeting and attempting to convince Saddam Hussein to withdraw. When the Iraqis would not do so, Mubarak led in the formation of the multinational Arab army sent to Saudi Arabia. In the wake of the Persian Gulf War, Egypt received massive infusions of foreign aid and forgiveness of $25 billion in foreign debt, greatly strengthening Mubarak's government, at least for a time. His position in the Arab world was greatly improved as well. Egypt, cast out by hard-line, anti-Israeli Arab nations after the 1979 Camp David Accords with Israel, had regained some prestige in the late 1980s, and after the Gulf War resumed a major position at the center of the Arab world. Mubarak's main challenge in the early 1990s came from Egypt's developing Islamic fundamentalist guerrilla insurgency, which featured high-profile terrorist attacks on foreign tourists and historic sites.

Mubarak attended the Egyptian military and air academies. Little is known of his private life, except that he is married to Suzanne Mubarak and has at least two children.

FURTHER READING

Hosni Mubarak. JOHN SOLECKI. Chelsea House, 1991.

Murayama, Tomiichi (1924–) Japanese

premier Tomiichi Murayama continued to rule at the head of a coalition government during 1995, but his always-narrow majority grew even smaller as Japan's growing New Frontier Party gained strength in the July elections to the Diet, while his own small Social Democratic Party lost strength, as did the much larger Liberal Democratic Party, his main coalition partner.

The year saw Japanese government intervention to prop up several major financial institutions, a far-too-strong performance of the yen against the dollar that helped fuel a sharp selloff on the Nikkei stock index, and a continuing properties market crisis at home. It also saw a continuing war of words on adverse American-Japanese foreign trade imbalances, which became very real in June, when the U.S. imposed massive sanctions on Japanese automobile imports after a Clinton-Murayama summit failed to resolve differences. President Clinton canceled the sanctions after Japanese automakers made some modest, nonbinding agreements to purchase more American car parts and to produce more cars in the U.S.

On August 15, in a speech commemorating the 50th anniversary of Japan's unconditional surrender, ending World War II, Murayama broke new ground for a Japanese leader; he expressed "deep remorse" and offered "heartfelt apologies" for Japanese aggressive acts and colonial rule during World War II. His statement was welcomed by some of Japan's former victims, but with reservations, as it was not supported by many in Murayama's Cabinet and was attacked by many Japanese natonalists.

Given Japan's massive and growing economic problems, the political position of Murayama's coalition seemed increasingly fragile throughout the year; he resigned in early January 1996.

Born in Oita, Murayama received his degree in economics from Meija University, joining the Socialist Party after graduation. He worked as a civil servant and then local elected official in Oita for two decades before his 1972 election to the Diet. He became head of the Social Democratic Party in 1993. In 1994, he became coali-tion premier, maintaining power in part by leading his party away from socialism and toward Liberal Democratic positions. In 1994, he for the first time offered payment to some of those who had been brutally treated by Japanese forces during World War II, including the hundreds of thousands of "comfort women" who had been enslaved as sex providers for the Japanese soldiery. Murayama has two daughters.

FURTHER READING

"Japan gets. . . ." ANTHONY HEAD. *New Statesman & Society*, July 8, 1994.

Murdoch, Rupert (Keith Rupert Murdoch;

1931–) Always controversial communications mogul Rupert Murdoch was very much in the news during 1995. In the United States, he surmounted heavy criticism from congressional Democrats, who charged that in late 1994 he had lobbied House Speaker Newt Gingrich, and that Gingrich's $4.5 million two-book advance from Murdoch's HarperCollins publishing conglomerate was ethically questionable. Ultimately, Gingrich canceled the advance, though going ahead with the books. In February, NBC settled its dispute with Murdoch over his allegedly illegal foreign ownership of the Fox network; Murdoch agreed to distribute two NBC cable television channels through his Asian broadcasting network. In July, the Federal Communications Commission dropped its investigation of Fox Television's ownership. Congressional Democrats also got nowhere with their criticism of a special tax break received by Murdoch's News Corporation on the sale of two U.S. television stations; the break was signed into law by Democratic President Bill Clinton in April. Murdoch also financed a new American conservative magazine, the *Weekly Standard*. Murdoch's American political honeymoon, however, seemed to rest squarely on the continuing electoral success of the Republican Party, always a dangerous situation for someone in what could again become a heavily regulated industry, should the American political pendulum shift to the Democrats.

Around the world, Murdoch continued to develop his massive and increasing holdings in all the communications media, in Britain bidding for television's Channel Five, in Italy bidding for

Silvio Berlusconi's television holdings, in Asia expanding his pan-Asian satellite network, and in Australia strongly expanding his broadcasting activities, as in his Australian national pay television network, a coventure with sometime rival Kerry Packer. In Vietnam, his News Corporation made an agreement to operate a "Fox Film of the Week" on Vietnamese national television, and also signed a licensing agreement with Vietnamese pay television for the Star movie channel.

Australian-American publisher Murdoch started with a small Adelaide, Australia family newspaper in 1952 and from it built a large worldwide communications company, controlling such publications and companies as Fox Television, 20th Century Fox Films, *The Times* (of London), HarperCollins Publishers, Sky Television, *The Australian* and many other publications in Australia, *New York* magazine, and Triangle Publications. Murdoch became dangerously overextended financially in 1990, but by 1993, with an easing economic climate, had recovered. He then expanded Sky Television and made new acquisitions, including the online service Delphi and pan-Asian Star Television. Murdoch attended Oxford University. He married Anna Maria Torv in 1967; they have two children.

FURTHER READING

"Magnetic magnates. . . ." MARTIN PEERS and JOE FLINT. *Variety,* Nov. 6, 1995.
"Buying his way. . . ." ROBERT SHERRILL. *Nation,* May 29, 1995.
"The empire strikes back." *Guardian,* May 22, 1995.
"RuperTVision." MICHAEL KNISLEY. *Sporting News,* Jan. 2, 1995.
"How Rupert. . . ." RONALD GROVER. *Business Week,* June 13, 1994.
"Thanks millions." ANTHONY BALDO. *Financial World,* May 10, 1994.
"There are more. . . ." JAMES W. MICHAELS and NANCY ROTENIER. *Forbes,* Mar. 14, 1994.
"Paper lions." EDWARD KLEIN. *Vanity Fair,* Oct. 1993.
Murdoch. WILLIAM SHAWCROSS. Simon & Schuster, 1993.

Murphy, Eddie (1961–) Actor Eddie

Murphy starred in 1995 as Maximilian, the vampire in the film comedy *Vampire in Brooklyn,* directed by Wes Craven, and based on a story by

Murphy, Vernon Lynch, Jr., and Charlie Murphy. Angela Bassett costarred as Rita, a police officer who is genetically a half-vampire, although she has no knowledge of that inheritance. The cast included Allen Payne, Kadeem Hardison, John Witherspoon, and Zakes Mokae. The film was not a critical success, adding another to the lengthening string of less-than-successful Murphy films. Forthcoming were starring film roles in *The Nutty Professor,* directed by Tom Shadyac, and in *Sandblast.*

Brooklyn-born Murphy became one of the leading entertainment celebrities of the 1980s, beginning with his regular featured role on television's "Saturday Night Live" (1980–84). His recording career began with the album *Eddie Murphy* (1982), and included *Eddie Murphy: Comedian* (1983), *So Happy* (1989), and *Love's Alright* (1993). He began a spectacular film career with *48 Hours* (1982), moving on to *Trading Places* (1983), *Beverly Hills Cop* (1983; *II,* 1987), *Coming to America* (1988), *Harlem Nights* (1989), *Another 48 Hours* (1990), *Boomerang* (1992), *The Distinguished Gentlemen* (1992), and *Beverly Hills Cop III* (1994). He married model Nicole Mitchell Murphy in 1993; they have two daughters and a son.

FURTHER READING

"For Murphy. . . ." ANNE THOMPSON. *Entertainment,* Nov. 10, 1995.
"Eddie Murphy. . . ." WALTER LEAVY. *Ebony,* June 1994.

"The Us interview. . . ." JON PARELES. *Us*, Jan. 1993.

Eddie Murphy. DEBRAH WILBOURN. Chelsea House, 1993.

"Eddie Murphy." JOHN CLARK. *Premiere*, Aug. 1992.

"Do you still . . . ?" RICHARD CORLISS. *Time*, July 6, 1992.

"Trading places." PETER RICHMOND. *GQ*, July 1992.

"The taming of Eddie." JILL NELSON. *Essence*, June 1992.

N

Nasrin, Taslima (Taslima Nasreen;
1962–) In June 1995, a court in the Bangladeshi capital of Dhaka ruled that feminist writer and physician Taslima Nasrin could be tried on a charge of insulting religion. In a case reminiscent of that of Salman Rushdie (who has helped mobilize international support for her), Nasrin had in 1994 become the object of death threats from Islamic fundamentalists who accused her of insulting Islam in a novel and calling for revision of the Koran. She denied any intent to insult Islam, and has explained that she had called for revision of the revisable Sharia, toward more equal treatment of women, not for revision of the Koran. After a warrant was issued for her arrest in mid-1994, she went into hiding while fundamentalists mounted widespread demonstrations. She appeared in court in August; was freed on nominal bail, though allowed to keep her passport; and then fled to asylum in Sweden. At the end of 1995, she remained outside her homeland while lawyers sought dismissal of charges against her.

In late 1994, Nasrin was awarded the £15,000 Kurt Tucholsky Award, given to writers in exile to allow them to continue working. In 1995, a book of her writings, *The Game in Reverse: Poems and Essays,* was published in English, translated by Carolyne Wright. Some of the poems had appeared in English in publications such as *The New Yorker,* but this was her first book to be published in English.

Nasrin was born in Mymensingh, in what was then in East Pakistan. After graduating from Mymensingh Medical College, she worked in a family planning clinic there, later moving to Dhaka, where she worked in gynecology in a government hospital (1990–93). A prolific writer, she has published numerous poems, essays, and novels, including *Shame (Lajja)* (1993), her fifteenth novel, banned because of fundamentalist pressure. She has been three times married and twice divorced.

FURTHER READING

"Woman under. . . ." ANNE McELVOY. *Times* (of London), Sept. 7, 1994.

Navratilova, Martina

Navratilova, Martina (1956–) Martina Navratilova, one of the greatest tennis players ever, may have retired from professional singles competition at the end of 1994, but she was still very much on the tennis scene in 1995, playing doubles and mixed doubles in several tournaments, and singles at various exhibitions. At Wimbledon, she and Jonathan Stark won the mixed doubles (her 19th Wimbledon title), though the two had not previously met; it was her 22nd consecutive competitive appearance at Wimbledon, 2 short of Virginia Wade's 24. Navratilova and Steffi Graf had been scheduled to play doubles, but Graf, plagued by injuries, pulled out to "save her body" for singles competition.

While at Wimbledon, Navratilova made her debut as an on-air tennis analyst, covering matches for the HBO television network. At the U.S. Open, she continued her broadcasting career, working as one of CBS's crew of analysts. This new role was especially satisfying, since, despite her tennis eminence, Navratilova has received little of the endorsement income stellar athletes customarily command—largely, she believes, because she long ago openly declared her lesbian sexual orientation.

As the new president of the WTA Tour Players Association (she decided to serve for one year only), she helped arrange the comeback of Monica Seles, who had been out of professional play since being knifed by a Graf-obsessed fan in April 1993. That return came in August, in an exhibition game against Navratilova, who was hampered by a groin pull; Seles won handily. At year's end, at the WTA Tour Championships (formerly the Virginia Slims Tournament), Navratilova and Chris Evert shared cohosting honors for the WTA awards.

Prague-born Navratilova emerged as a leading Czech tennis player while still in her early teens and was Czech national champion (1972–75). Defecting to the West in 1975, she went on to become the top-ranked female tennis player in the world for four years in a row (1982–85), enjoying 271 successive weeks as number one—a record for men *or* women—and 332 weeks overall. She also had a Grand Slam (1983–84) and in 1983 a record annual tally of 86-1. She won a record 167 tournament titles, more than any tennis player ever. Among those titles were the U.S. Open four times (1983–84; 1986–87), with a Triple Crown of singles, doubles, and mixed doubles, in 1987, and an unprecedented nine singles titles at Wimbledon (1978–79; 1982–1987; 1990), with a record six consecutive titles, and 17 Wimbledon titles overall through 1994. As doubles partners, Navratilova and Pam Shriver won three Grand Slams (1983–84; 1984–85; 1986–1987) and a record 109 consecutive matches (April 24, 1983–July 6, 1985). Navratilova and Gigi Fernandez won the U.S. Open doubles championships in 1990, sweeping the main doubles championships in the same year she had both knees surgically rebuilt. Navratilova was named female athlete of the 1980s by *National Sports Review,* UPI, and AP. At her retirement, after 22 years of competitive play, she held a record 167 women's singles championship titles, had won 18 Grand Slam singles titles, and was still ranked 4th in the world. In 1985 she published *Martina: Autobiography,* written with George Vecsey. In 1994, she published *The Total Zone,* the first of a projected series of mysteries, coauthored with Liz Nickles and set in the tennis world. Navratilova became a U.S. citizen in 1981.

FURTHER READING

"The Martina and Steffi. . . ." MARK MARVEL. *Interview*, July 1995.
"Net result." HELEN OLDFIELD. *Guardian*, Jan. 18, 1995.
"The end of an era. . . ." CINDY SHMERLER. *Women's Sports and Fitness*, Nov.–Dec. 1994.
"Martina the opponent." CHRIS EVERT. "Martina the doubles partner." PAM SHRIVER. "Martina the Czech." JOSEF SKVORECKY. "Martina: an appreciation." FRANK DEFORD. *Tennis*, Nov. 1994.
"The last hurrah." S. L. PRICE. *Sports Illustrated*, July 11, 1994.
"Martina remembers. . . ." DONNA DOHERTY. *Tennis*, July 1994.
Martina Navratilova. GILDA ZWERMAN. Chelsea House, 1994.
Martina Navratilova: Tennis Star. DENISE WILLI. Blackbirch, 1994.
Love Match. SANDRA FAULKNER and JUDY NELSON. Birch Lane/Carol, 1993.

Nazarbayev, Nursultan Abishevich

Nazarbayev, Nursultan Abishevich (1940–) President Nursultan Nazarbayev of Kazakhstan moved his country from democracy to dictatorship in 1995. It was quickly and simply done, without any significant opposition. After Kazakhstan's constitutional court had ruled that the March 1994 parliamentary elections were invalid, Nazarbayev on March 11 dissolved the national parliament, then ruling by decree. But on April 29, instead of moving toward new elections, as he had promised, and toward the scheduled 1996 presidential elections, he ran a presidential referendum and the next day announced that an extension of his rule until the year 2000 had been approved by more than 95 percent of those voting, and that more than 90 percent of eligible voters had indeed voted for him.

During 1995, Nazarbayev continued to build links between Kazakhstan and the other countries of the former Soviet Union, favoring closer economic and military ties through the Commonwealth of Independent States (CIS), including a binding mutual security treaty, although military ties were rejected by many of the other former Soviet countries and especially strongly by Ukraine, with those opposed citing the history of Russian imperialism in their countries. Nazarbayev also continued to seek foreign capital investment, notably welcoming agreements to exploit Kazakhstan's natural resources, while simultaneously seeking funds from abroad to lessen the immense environmental damage expected from such projects as oil drilling in the Caspian Sea.

Nazarbayev, who joined the Communist Party in 1962, worked as an economist at the Karaganda Metallurgical Combine (1960–69), and then moved into party work. After holding a series of local posts, he emerged as Kazakh central committee secretary (1979–84), was leader of his party in Kazakhstan from 1984, and was a member of the Soviet Communist Party central committee from 1986. He became president of the Soviet Republic of Kazakhstan in 1990. While he supported the continued existence of the Soviet Union, he opposed the August 1991 attempted coup, resigning all his Communist Party positions and then leading his country to independence. An economist and economic radical, he quickly and effectively moved toward a market economy with the aid of foreign advisers, and made more than 100 development deals with Western companies during the early 1990s. One of these was the 1993 Kazakh–Chevron Corporation agreement to develop the huge Tengiz oilfield in western Kazakhstan, on the northern shore of the Caspian Sea. In 1994, he signed the Nuclear Nonproliferation Treaty, in return receiving over $200 million more in American aid plus $85 million more for the cost of dismantling nuclear weapons. He also negotiated massive new World Bank loans for environmental purposes and joined with other former Soviet nations to try to deal with the Aral Sea environmental disaster.

FURTHER READING

"A 'temporarily nuclear. . . .' " MIKHAIL USTIUGOV. "Bridging east and west." VLADIMIR ARDAEV. *Bulletin of the Atomic Scientists*, Oct. 1993.
"The end of the U.S.S.R." GEORGE J. CHURCH. *Time*, Dec. 23, 1991.
"Warily seeking. . . ." ROBIN KNIGHT. *U.S. News & World Report*, Sept. 23, 1991.
"The khan of Kazakhstan. . . ." CARROLL BOGERT. *Newsweek*, July 8, 1991.

Nearing, Helen K. (1904–95)

New Jersey–born writer, socialist, pacifist, and back-to-the-land advocate Helen Nearing and her lifelong partner and coauthor Scott Nearing (1883–1983) were leading American radical political dissenters for half a century. They were also leading advocates of the rural life, whose writings and personal example were very highly regarded by three generations of those seeking a better life by fleeing the cities and material striving. In 1932, the Nearings headed for Vermont and took up farming, while continuing to write and publicly dissent, and developed a way of life that rejected most machines and stressed their vegetarianism and a frugal overall lifestyle, becoming models for many who followed. They later moved to Maine. Their widely circulated seminal works on the good rural life were the booklets "Living the Good Life" and "Continuing the Good Life," both later published as books. Among Helen Nearing's books were *Wise Words for the Good Life* (1983), *Simple Food for the Good Life* (1983), *Light on Aging and Dying* (1995), and her autobiographical *Loving and Leaving the Good Life* (1992). She was survived by a sister. (d. Harborside, Maine; September 17, 1995)

FURTHER READING

Obituary. *Economist*, Oct. 7, 1995.
Obituary. *Times* (of London), Sept. 21, 1995.
Obituary. *New York Times*, Sept. 19, 1995.
"The view from ninety." TAMI SIMON. *Whole Earth Review*, Winter 1994.

"Helen Nearing." MATTHEW SCANLON. *Mother Earth News*, June-July 1994.

Needham, Joseph (Noël Joseph Terence Montgomery Needham; 1900–95) London-born British historian of science, sinologist, and biochemist Joseph Needham was one of the towering figures of 20th-century science and history. He studied at Caius College, Cambridge, before serving as a very young surgical assistant toward the end of World War I. After the war he returned to Caius, with which he would be associated all his life. During the interwar period, Needham emerged as a leading biochemist and historian of science, also developing his lifelong interest in Chinese science and culture. He published his massive *Chemical Embryology* in 1931, which included his history of embryology. He also emerged as as a leading person of the Left in British science. Needham served as a British scientific counselor in China (1942–46), and from 1946 as science director of the United Nations Educational, Scientific, and Cultural Organization (UNESCO), which he had helped to found.

On returning to Cambridge in 1948, he began his masterwork, the immense, unique exploration of the history of Chinese science and of its place in Chinese civilization, *Science and Civilization in China,* which by the time of his death had grown into 16 massive volumes, with many more volumes still to come from the scientists and historians at Cambridge's Needham Research Institute. Needham became a world figure in the final decades of his life, who lectured and taught in many countries, and was heaped with honors—even though he was not allowed into the United States for some years, after his 1954 charge that the U.S. had practiced germ warfare in Korea. He was Master of Caius College (1966–76), and in 1972 became president of the International Union of the History and Philosophy of Science. He married the biochemist Dorothy Moyle in 1924. After her death, he in 1990 married their lifelong friend and his longtime colleague, Chinese biochemist and historian of science Lu Gwei-Djen, who died in 1991. There were no survivors. (d. Cambridge; March 24, 1995)

FURTHER READING

Obituary. *Times* (of London), Mar. 27, 1995.
Obituary. *Independent*, Mar. 27, 1995.
Obituary. *New York Times*, Mar. 27, 1995.
"The builder. . . ." Marguerite Holloway. *Scientific American*, May 1992.

Liam Neeson (left) and Ben Kingsley.

Neeson, Liam (1953–   ) Irish actor Liam Neeson became a very familiar face on television screens in 1995, as *Schindler's List* (1993) continued its worldwide rollout, and was joined by *Nell* (1994) on home video.

In 1995, Neeson starred in the title role of the costume drama *Rob Roy,* an epic set in Scottish history. Michael Caton-Jones directed; costarring were Jessica Lange as his wife, John Hurt, Tim Roth, and Eric Stoltz. Neeson also starred as one of the voices in the television film *Out of Ireland,* about the lives of eight emigrants from Ireland; Kelly McGillis narrated.

Forthcoming were starring roles opposite Meryl Streep in the film *Before and After,* directed and produced by Barbet Schroeder; and in the title role in *Michael Collins,* a biofilm about the Irish revolutionary, written and directed by Neil Jordan and costarring Julia Roberts, Stephen Rea, and Aidan Quinn.

On the personal side, he and his wife, Natasha Richardson, who had married after their costarring roles in *Nell,* had their first child, Michael Richard Antonio Neeson.

Belfast-born Neeson studied at the Belfast Players' Theatre and at Dublin's Abbey Theatre and began his career in the theater, making his screen debut in *Excalibur* (1981). He moved into substantial screen roles in the late 1980s, in such films as *The Dead Pool* (1988), *The Good Mother* (1988), *Next of Kin* (1989), *Darkman* (1990), *Leap of Faith* (1991), *Schindler's List* (1993), *Deception* (1993), *Ethan Frome* (1993), and *Nell* (1994). His stage roles included a 1993 revival of *Anna Christie,* opposite Natasha Richardson.

FURTHER READING

"What will we pass. . . ." Gail Buchalter. *Parade,* May 7, 1995.
"The lusty charm. . . ." David Gritten. *Cosmopolitan,* Feb. 1995.
"Neeson, Liam." *Current Biography*, Nov. 1994.
"Ladies' man." GIL GIBSON and HUNTON DOWNS. *Ladies Home Journal*, Sept. 1994.
"Oskar winner." TIM APPELO. *Entertainment*, Jan. 21, 1994.
"Liam's leap." GEORGINA HOWELL. *Vogue*, Jan. 1994.
"Liam Neeson. . . ." STEPHANIE MANSFIELD. *GQ*, Dec. 1993.
"A touch of the poet." BARBARA KANTROWITZ. *Newsweek*, Feb. 8, 1993.
"Rugged, romantic. . . ." SUSAN SPILLMAN. *Cosmopolitan*, Dec. 1991.

Neill, Sam (1947–) Actor Sam Neill starred in 1995 as 17th-century British king Charles II in the film *Restoration,* set during the relatively sexually liberated Stuart Restoration. Robert Downey, Jr., starred as the physician Merivel, who becomes a court favorite of Charles, and whom Charles sets up as the titled, landed, in-name-only husband of one his mistresses, played by Polly Walker. When Charles learns that Merivel has fallen in love with her—despite pledges to do no such thing—he banishes Merivel from court and takes away all that has been previously granted. Costarring were Meg Ryan, Hugh Grant, Ian McKellen, and David Thewlis. Michael Hoffman directed; Rupert Walters wrote the screenplay, based on the Rose Tremain novel.

Neill also starred in the horror-fantasy film *In the Mouth of Madness,* directed by John Carpenter, as an insurance investigator who discovers the genesis of spreading worldwide chaos in the New England–based works of an author of horror fiction, and pursues them to their source. In a wholly different vein, Neill, himself a New Zealander, directed the documentary *Cinema of Unease,* a survey of New Zealand films and filmmaking.

Forthcoming was a starring role in the film *Children of the Revolution,* written and directed by Peter Duncan and costarring Judy Davis, Richard Roxburgh, Rachel Griffiths, and F. Murray Abraham.

Born in Northern Ireland, Neill made his film debut in *Land Fall* (1976). His breakthrough role came in *My Brilliant Career* (1980); he went on to such films as *Plenty* (1985), *The Good Wife* (1987), *A Cry in the Dark* (1988), *Dead Calm* (1989), *The Hunt for Red October* (1990), *Until the End of the World* (1991), *Memoirs of an Invisible Man* (1992), *Jurassic Park* (1993), *The Piano* (1993), *Sirens* (1994), and *Country Life* (1994). He has also appeared in many television films, and starred in the television miniseries *Reilly Ace of Spies* (1986). Neill attended New Zealand's University of Canterbury. He is married to Noriko Watanabe and has three children.

FURTHER READING

"Who the heck. . . ." ANNE THOMPSON. *Entertainment,* July 23, 1993.
"Sam Neill's. . . ." GRAHAM FULLER. *Interview*, June 1993.

Nelson, Willie (1933–) Celebrated singer and songwriter Willie Nelson had a very active and prolific 1995, issuing several albums, writing new songs, and continuing to make music on what has become a lifelong tour. On July 4, co-incident with his annual picnic at Luckenbach, Texas, he issued not one, but two new albums, on two different labels: *Just One Love* and the 3-CD *Willie Nelson: A Classic and Unreleased Collection.* The first, a country collection, carried such songs as "Smoke, Smoke, Smoke," "Eight More Miles to Louisville," "Four Walls," and the title cut, which was also issued as a hit country single. The second was a very wide-ranging collection that included his earliest recordings, many of his classics, and some previously unreleased material. He also released the retrospective 3-CD set *Willie Nelson: Revolutions of Time . . . The Journey, 1975–1993.*

Nelson, Johnny Cash, Kris Kristofferson, and Waylon Jennings, as The Highwaymen, issued the country collection album *The Road Goes On Forever,* containing a new song by each of the four stars, along with a selection of standards written by others. They also issued a hit single from the album, the blues song "It Is What It Is." They also released an audiobook dramatization of Louis L'Amour's western novel *Riding for the Brand.*

Nelson and Merle Haggard also issued the Christmas album *Pancho, Lefty and Rudolph,* each singing five previously released songs. He also sang "Bird on a Wire" on the album *Tower of Song: The Songs of Leonard Cohen.*

Nelson also appeared in the television film *Big Dreams and Broken Hearts: The Dottie West Story,* starring Michele Lee as the country singer and costarring several leading country singers, among them Dolly Parton, Kris Kristofferson, Chet Atkins, Loretta Lynn, and Kenny Rogers.

Texas-born Nelson attended Baylor University. While working at various jobs, he began composing and recording in the early 1960s, emerging as a country music star in the mid-1970s, then crossing over to become a major popular music star on records, in concert, and on screen. His first national hit was the song "Blue Eyes Cryin' in the Rain," from his *Redheaded Stranger* album (1975). He went on to become one of the most popular musicians of the 1970s and 1980s with such songs as "Georgia on My Mind," "Stardust," "On the Road Again," "Always on My Mind," and "Blue Skies," and such albums as *Waylon and Willie* (1978), *Stardust* (1978), and *Honeysuckle Rose,* the soundtrack album of his 1980 film of that name. He has also appeared in such films as *Barbarossa* (1982),

Red-Headed Stranger (1986), and *Pair of Aces* (1990).

Nelson ran into severe tax difficulties in 1990, and much of his property was seized and auctioned off by the U.S. Internal Revenue Service, generating his album *Who'll Buy My Memories (The I.R.S. Tapes)* (1991). His recent albums include *Across the Borderline* (1993), *Moonlight Becomes You* (1994), *Healing Hands of Time* (1994), *The Early Years* (1994), *The Legend Begins* (1994), and *The Classic, Unreleased Collection* (1994). In 1988 he published his autobiographical *Willie.* He was given the Country Music Association's Pioneer Award in 1992 and elected to the Country Music Hall of Fame in 1993. He has been married three times and has six children; a seventh, Billy, was a probable suicide late in 1991.

FURTHER READING

"Country punk'ins. . . ." GRANT ALDEN. *Rolling Stone,* Sept. 21, 1995.
"In step with. . . ." JAMES BRADY. *Parade,* Aug. 20, 1995.
"A 'stranger'. . . ." ALANNA NASH. *Entertainment,* July 21, 1995.
"Willie Nelson." JANCEE DUNN. *Rolling Stone,* Mar. 9, 1995.
"20 questions with. . . ." MICHAEL BANE. *Country Music,* Mar.–Apr. 1993.
"The ballad of. . . ." RON ROSENBAUM. *Vanity Fair,* Nov. 1991.

Nichols, Terry Lynn: See McVeigh, Timothy James.

Nicholson, Jack (1937–) Long a worldwide film star, and therefore one of the world's most familiar faces, Jack Nicholson in 1995 appeared on home video screens as the werewolf in his 1994 film *Wolf.*

In quite a different kind of role, Nicholson starred in 1995 in the film *The Crossing Guard,* written and directed by Sean Penn. Nicholson plays Freddy Gale, a man whose life fell apart six years earlier, when a drunken driver named John Booth (played by David Morse) killed his son. Morse has served his prison sentence, and Nicholson sets out to kill him. Anjelica Huston

Jack Nicholson (right) and Ellen Barkin

costarred as Mary, Nicholson's former wife, along with Robin Wright and Piper Laurie.

Forthcoming was a starring role opposite Shirley MacLaine in the film *The Evening Star,* a sequel to their 1983 hit *Terms of Endearment.* Robert Harling wrote and directed; the cast includes Jennifer Grant, Antonia Bogdanovich, and China Kantner. He was also slated to star as a jewel thief in the film *Blood and Wine,* directed by Bob Rafelson and costarring Michael Caine as his partner; Stephen Dorff as Nicholson's stepson, also a thief; Judy Davis as Nicholson's wife; and Jennifer Lopez as the love interest of both Nicholson and Dorff.

New Jersey–born Nicholson played strong supporting roles beginning in the late 1950s, most notably in *Easy Rider* (1969), then moved into the powerful dramatic roles that made him a major figure for the next two decades, in such films as *Five Easy Pieces* (1970), *Chinatown* (1974), *One Flew Over the Cuckoo's Nest* (1975; he won a best actor Oscar), *The Postman Always Rings Twice* (1981), *Reds* (1981), *Terms of Endearment* (1983; he won a best supporting actor Oscar), *Prizzi's Honor* (1985), *Heartburn* (1986), *Ironweed* (1987), *Batman* (1989), *A Few Good Men* (1992), *Hoffa* (1992), *Man Trouble* (1992), and *Wolf* (1994). In 1990, he directed and starred in *The Two Jakes,* a sequel to *Chinatown.*

Nicholson was formerly married to Sandra Knight; they had one daughter. He had a 17-year relationship with actress Anjelica Huston that ended in 1990. He and actress Rebecca Broussard had a daughter and a son; the couple separated in 1992.

FURTHER READING

"Jack's life." PATRICK McGILLIGAN. *Cosmopolitan,* Sept. 1994.
"Gentleman Jack." FRED SCHRUERS. *Us,* July 1994.
"Wolf, man, Jack." NANCY COLLINS. *Vanity Fair,* Apr. 1994.
Jack Nicholson. JACKIE SHIRLEY. Smithmark, 1994.
Jack's Life: A Biography of Jack Nicholson. PATRICK McGILLIGAN. Norton, 1994.
"Jack in the box." TY BURR. "King leer." JAMES KAPLAN. *Entertainment,* Jan. 8, 1993.
Jack Nicholson: An Unauthorized Biography. DONALD SHEPERD. St. Martin's, 1991.
Jack Nicholson: The Unauthorized Biography. BARBARA SIEGEL and SCOTT SIEGEL. Avon, 1991.

Nolte, Nick (1942–) Screen star Nick Nolte appeared in the title role of the 1995 film *Jefferson in Paris,* directed by James Ivory and produced by Ismail Merchant, screenplay by Ruth Prawer Jhabvala, in a large and luminous cast that included Greta Scacchi, Thandie Newton, James Earl Jones, Jean-Pierre Aumont, and Simon Callow. The film, set in the five years that Thomas Jefferson was U.S. ambassador to France (1784–89), focused more on the personal than the political side of Jefferson and his times; it and Nolte's performance received respectful but mixed reviews.

Forthcoming were starring roles in the film *Mulholland Falls,* directed by Lee Tamahori and costarring Melanie Griffith, John Malkovich, and Daniel Baldwin; and in the spy thriller *Mother Night,* directed by Keith Gordon.

Nebraska-born Nolte spent several years in regional theater before emerging as a film star in the mid-1970s in *The Deep* (1977), and went on to star in such films as *Who'll Stop the Rain* (1978), *North Dallas Forty* (1979), *Cannery Row* (1982), *48 Hours* (1982), *Under Fire* (1983), *Down and Out in Beverly Hills* (1986), *Three Fugitives* (1989), *Everybody Wins* (1990), *Another 48 Hours* (1990), *Q&A* (1990), *Cape Fear* (1991), *The Prince of Tides* (1991), *Lorenzo's Oil* (1992), *I'll Do Anything* (1994), *Blue Chips* (1994), and *I Love Trouble* (1994). He has also appeared in television, most notably in *Rich Man, Poor Man* (1976). Nolte attended Pasadena City College. He has been married three times and has one child.

FURTHER READING

"Nick Nolte." TRIP GABRIEL. *Us,* Jan. 1992.
"Off-balance heroes." PETER DE JONGE. *New York Times Magazine,* Oct. 27, 1991.
"Nick Nolte. . . ." STEPHANIE MANSFIELD. *GQ,* Oct. 1991.
"Prince of Hollywood." MEREDITH BRODY. *Connoisseur,* Sept. 1991.
"Nick Nolte." PETER BECKER. *M Inc.,* Sept. 1991.
"The passions of. . . ." ERIC GOODMAN. *McCall's,* Sept. 1991.

Nomo, Hideo (1968–) One of the most striking new faces on the American baseball scene in 1995 was Hideo Nomo. In his rookie season in the major leagues with the Los Angeles Dodgers, the righthanded pitcher led the National League in strikeouts, with 236, over 191 1/3 innings. With a season record of 13-6, he also tied Cy Young award winner Greg Maddux with three shutouts, and posted a season earned-run average of 2.54, second only to Maddux. Dubbed "The Tornado" for his twisting, whirling delivery and perhaps most feared for his forkball, Nomo was the starter for the National League team in the All-Star game (though he might have come off the bench had Maddux not been injured), pitching two flawless innings; he was the first Japanese player in baseball's All-Star game.

At season's end, Nomo was named Rookie of

the Year; it was the first time that a Japanese player had won a major American baseball award, and Nomo said he hoped his win would open doors for others. He is only the second Japanese player ever to play in the American major leagues, the first being Masanori Murakami (1964–65), also a pitcher. Nomo is the second-oldest player to win the award; the oldest was Jackie Robinson, also a Dodger, who was 28 when he broke baseball's color barrier in 1947. In the National League divisional playoffs against the Cincinnati Reds, Nomo pitched in game three of a best-of-five series, with the Dodgers behind 2-0, but was unable to stave off elimination.

During the regular season "Nomomania" swept the country, and attendance soared for games when he was pitching. His games were transmitted live to Japan, though they aired there in the middle of the night; Japanese tourists signed up for "Nomo Tours, " including Dodgers tickets; and in his honor starting lineups were sometimes delivered in both English and Japanese. Nomo himself was accompanied by an interpreter, Michael Okunura. A Hideo Nomo sports card was introduced and traded briskly.

Born in Osaka, Japan, Nomo had previously received Rookie of the Year honors in the Japan's Pacific League (1990), where he was a five-time All-Star (1990–94), playing for the Kintetsu Buffaloes. He also won the Sawamura Award (equivalent to the Cy Young award) in

1990. Even though hampered by tendinitis in his right shoulder in his final season in Japan, he still struck out 126 batters in 114 innings, for an average of 9.9 strikeouts per nine innings. On his retirement from the Pacific League, Nomo had a career record of 78-46, a 3.15 earned-run average, and 1,204 strikeouts. He then signed with the Los Angeles Dodgers as a free agent (1995–). Nomo had been a member of the 1988 silver-medal-winning Japanese team at the Seoul Olympics. Nomo and his wife, Kikuko, have a son, Takahiro.

FURTHER READING

"Tornado watch. . . ." STEVE DOUGHERTY. *People*, July 17, 1995.

Norman, Greg (Gregory John Norman; 1955–)

In 1995, Greg Norman became the top golfer in the world, once again at the top of the Sony World Rankings. Of the 16 PGA tournaments he entered, he won three: the Memorial Tournament and the Greater Hartford Open, both in June, and the World Series of Golf in August. The latter raised his lifetime earnings to $9.49 million, making him the PGA Tour's all-time leading money winner. He also led the 1995 money list with more than $1.6 million, was voted *Golf Digest* player of the year for the second time, and won that magazine's Byron Nelson award for most season victories. And he had the lowest stroke average of the year, at 69.06. What he did *not* have was the Vardon Trophy, awarded to the player with the lowest average score, being barred by a technicality: In April, after injuring his back during warmup for the second round of the MCI Heritage Classic, he hit a practice tee shot to see if he could go on. Only later, he found that this barred him from receiving the Vardon Trophy, since anyone who withdraws in mid-round is ineligible. It would have been his fourth Vardon Trophy (1989; 1990; 1994). Norman also had a heartbreaking loss at the U.S. Open, where he came in second to Corey Pavin; it was the seventh time he had been runner-up in one of golf's four major championships.

Norman's plans for a new, $25 million, eight-tournament World Tour for the top 30 players in the world, announced in 1994, came to nought. The PGA Tour requires its players to get re-leases to play in competing events; the World Tour charged that was restraint of trade, a charge that the Federal Trade Commission investigated, then dropped. Rather than face a major legal battle, Norman and his sponsors dropped the World Tour.

Born in Queensland, Australia, but now based in Florida, Norman turned professional in 1976, winning his first victory that year in Australia's West Lakes Classic, and joining the Professional Golfers Association (PGA) Tour in 1983. Among his notable wins have been the Martini International (1977; 1979; 1981), French Open (1980), Australian Open (1980; 1985; 1987), Dunlop Masters (1981; 1982), Australian Masters (1981; 1983; 1984; 1987; 1989; 1990), Kemper Open (1984; 1986), Canadian Open (1984; 1992), British Open (1986; 1993, with Open records for his final round 64 and four-round total 267), European Open (1986), Australian Tournament Players Championship (1988; 1989), Italian Open (1988), Doral Ryder Open (1990; 1993), and Memorial Tournament (1990).

Norman was the leading PGA money winner in 1986 (when he led all four major tournaments going into the final round, but won only one) and 1990. After a 27-month slump (1990–92) without a win, and with several close losses, Norman made a notable comeback. He was voted World Player of the Year by *Golf Digest* in 1993. Norman has also played on numerous Australian national teams, winning two Dunhill Cups. In 1994, he won the Players Championship by a tournament record 24 strokes, moving him into first place in the rankings and on the PGA Tour money list. He has published *Shark Attack!: Greg Norman's Guide to Aggressive Golf* (1988) and *Greg Norman's Instant Lessons* (1993), both written with George Peper. He is married to Laura Norman and has two children.

FURTHER READING

"Peace of mind." JOHN FEINSTEIN. *Golf*, July 1994.
"Return of the shark." JAMES DEACON. *Maclean's*, Sept. 13, 1993.
"Shark attack." RICK REILLY. *Sports Illustrated*, July 26, 1993.

Nosair, El Sayyid A.: See Abdel Rahman, Omar.

Oates, Joyce Carol (1938–) The prolific
Joyce Carol Oates exhibited several aspects of
her literary personality in 1995. In the novel
Zombie, she explored in pseudojournal form the
psyche of a Jeffrey Dahmer–like serial killer,
Quentin P.; the result was a chilling portrait
from a writer who specializes in illuminating the
dark side of life. On a very different note, she
contributed a volume to the Writers on Art series, *George Bellows: American Artist,* exploring
his artistic vision. A new collection of short
works, *Will You Always Love Me? and Other Stories,* was scheduled for 1996 publication.

In a comic vein, 1995 saw the production of a
new play, *The Truth-Teller,* focusing on the return of a free-spirited wanderer to the bosom of
her uptight family in the Buffalo suburbs, on the
occasion of her parents' 35th anniversary. Opening in New York, the play was directed by Gloria
Muzio and starred Lynn Hawley, Andrew Polk,
John Seitz, Kathleen Widdoes, Barbara Gulan,
Craig Bockhorn, and Richard Seff. Oates also
published a collection of plays, *The Perfectionist
and Other Plays,* which included the title play;
Here She Is, about the Miss America pageant;
and *Homesick,* coming full circle with another
portrait of a serial killer. Oates also experi-
mented with opera, writing a libretto based on
her novel *Black Water,* about the Chappaquiddick incident, and contributed an essay to
Women on Hunting, edited by Pam Houston.

Oates emerged as a major American novelist
in the mid-1960s, with a group of powerful novels that had in common their view of the United
States as an insane place inhabited by people on
or over the edge of madness; these included *With
Shuddering Fall* (1964), *A Garden of Earthly
Delights* (1967), and *them* (1969), which won a
National Book Award. She later wrote such novels as *Childworld* (1976), *Son of the Morning*
(1978), *Bellefleur* (1980), *Solstice* (1985), *Black
Water* (1992), *Foxfire: Confessions of a Girl Gang*
(1993), and *What I Lived For* (1994). She has
also written, by her own estimate, more than
400 short stories, which appeared in various
magazines and collections, including several collections of her own, from *By the North Gate*
(1963) through *Where Is Here?: Stories* (1992),
*Where Are You Going, Where Have You Been?
Selected Early Stories* (1993), and *Haunted:
Tales of the Grotesque* (1994).

Other works include several poetry collections,
beginning with *Women in Love* (1968); several
plays, including *Miracle Play* (1974) and *In
Darkest America* (1990); and several volumes of
essays, including *On Boxing* (1987) and *Woman
Writer: Occasions and Opportunities* (1988). She
has also edited numerous works, most notably
The Oxford Book of American Short Stories
(1992). Oates has taught at the University of
Detroit (1961–67), the University of Windsor at
Ontario (1967–87), and Princeton University
(1987–). Her B.A. was from Syracuse University, and her M.A. from the University of Wisconsin. She is married to Raymond Smith.

FURTHER READING

*Who's Writing This?: Notations on the Authorial I,
with Self-Portraits.* DANIEL HALPERN, ed. Ecco,
1994.

"Oates, Joyce Carol." *Current Biography*, June 1994.

Joyce Carol Oates. GREG JOHNSON. Macmillan, 1994.

"Playboy interview. . . ." LAWRENCE GROBEL. *Playboy*, Nov. 1993.

Broken Silences: Interviews with Black and White Women Writers. SHIRLEY M. JORDAN, ed. Rutgers University Press, 1993.

O'Bannon, Ed

O'Bannon, Ed (Edward Charles O'Bannon, Jr.; 1972–) In 1995, Ed O'Bannon fulfilled every college basketball player's dream. He won the NCAA national championship as part of the UCLA Bruins, a team that also included his younger brother, Charles. Ed himself scored a game-high 31 points, took down 17 rebounds, and was named the most outstanding player of the NCAA Division I tournament. The win was the more remarkable because—less than three minutes into the final game—the team lost their ball-handling guard, Tyus Edney, to a wrist injury; Ed O'Bannon was largely credited with uniting his team to win. After the game, he honored Edney, saying he was the "real MVP." At the end of his college play, O'Bannon also won the coveted Wooden Award, and was named to the *Sporting News* All-America second team.

In the 1995 NBA draft, O'Bannon was selected by the New Jersey Nets in the first round, the ninth pick overall; he probably would have been higher on the list, except that in 1990 he had had a potentially career-ending knee injury, a tear of the anterior cruciate ligament, which had required major reconstructive surgery. Some teams were worried about how O'Bannon would bear up through the 82-game professional season. Nets fans hoped that O'Bannon would bring to the troubled Nets team some of his celebrated team leadership, starting in the 1995–96 season. Whether that would happen was still unclear at year's end. A quick lefthander with long arms and three-point shooting range, the 6′8″ O'Bannon was a forward in college, but is expected to become a swing player in the pros, as both small forward and shooting guard.

Los Angeles–born O'Bannon attended Artesia High School in Lakewood, California, and then went to UCLA in 1990. Sidelined from basketball for the 1990–91 season and most of the 1991–92 season, after his knee injury, he played in the last four of his five years at UCLA (1991–1995), where in his final year he averaged 20.4 points and 8.3 rebounds per game. O'Bannon and his fiancée, Rosa Bravo, have a son, Aaron, born in 1994.

FURTHER READING

"Logical positivism. . . ." *Sports Illustrated*, Oct. 16, 1995.

"O'Bannon sparks. . . ." *Jet*, Apr. 24, 1995.

"O'Bannon brothers. . . ." *Jet*, Mar. 14, 1994.

"It's a family affair." RICHARD HOFFER. *Sports Illustrated*, Jan. 31, 1994.

"Hard lessons." PHIL TAYLOR. *Sports Illustrated*, Nov. 25, 1991.

O'Connor, Sandra Day

O'Connor, Sandra Day (1930–) Although in the previous Supreme Court term often described as part of an emerging centrist "swing" group, Justice Sandra Day O'Connor during 1995 voted consistently with a narrow conservative majority, turning the Court sharply toward the conservative side on several key issues. However, she also made it clear that she continued to be a wholly independent figure, with great reservations as to going very far in either a conservative or liberal direction, and so should still be considered a centrist and possibly still a swing figure.

O'Connor wrote the 5–4 majority opinion in the landmark *Adarand Constructors* v. *Pena* case, ruling that the federal government was required to use the same strict standards as the states in carrying out affirmative action programs, and thereby reversing the Court's long-held position on federal affirmative action programs. The decision was widely viewed as a major conservative victory. She also wrote the 5–4 majority opinion in *Florida Bar* v. *Went For It Inc.*, ruling valid a Florida state law barring lawyers from direct mail solicitation of people injured in accidents and their relatives for 30 days after the accident. She wrote a concurring opinion in the landmark *Miller* v. *Johnson* case, in which the Court voted 5–4 to declare organization of Georgia's Eleventh Congressional District unconstitutional because it was organized primarily to provide racial representation, rather than to respond to specific discrimination. The decision was widely viewed as threatening the legality of scores of recently redrawn congressional districts. She also wrote a concurring opinion in another landmark case decided 5–4: *Rosenberg* v. *Rector and Visitors of the Univer-*

sity of Virginia, in which the Court ruled that the publicly funded University of Virginia was required to finance a Christian magazine run by students, a sharp change of Court direction on a basic constitutional issue.

O'Connor joined the 5–4 majority in *U.S.* v. *Lopez,* declaring unconstitutional the federal Gun-Free School Zones Act of 1990, which made possession of a gun within 1,000 feet of a school illegal, ruling that this was an invalid extension of congressional ability to regulate interstate commerce. The ruling was widely seen as a major conservative reinterpretation of the power of Congress to legislate on a very broad range of issues, reopening formerly long-settled federal-state powers questions. She joined the 5–4 dissent in the landmark *U.S. Term Limits Inc.* v. *Thornton* decision, ruling that to limit congressional terms required a constitutional amendment; 23 state laws imposing terms limits were invalidated and Congress was barred from passing a term limits law.

In *Missouri* v. *Jenkins,* O'Connor was again part of a 5–4 majority, in that decision effectively limiting the level of state spending allowed to carry out a federally managed school desegregation plan in Kansas City. She also joined the majority in *Capital Square Review and Advisory Board* v. *Pinette,* ruling that it was unconstitutional to bar display of a large Ku Klux Klan cross in an Ohio public park; and in *Babbitt* v. *Sweet Home Chapter of Communities for a Greater Oregon,* ruling that the federal government had the right under the Endangered Species Act to sharply restrict logging and other activities harmful to the northern spotted owl.

O'Connor wrote a solo dissenting opinion in *Lebron* v. *National Railroad Passenger Co.,* which ruled that Amtrak was a federal government agency, although Congress had otherwise defined it, and must respect the constitutional right to free speech; Amtrak had refused to display a political billboard at New York's Pennsylvania Station by claiming that it was a private corporation. She also wrote a dissenting opinion in *Veronia School District* v. *Acton,* in which the Court ruled that an Oregon school district's random drug testing program was constitutional.

El Paso–born O'Connor made history in 1981 when she became the first woman Supreme Court justice, the climax of long careers in law and politics. She had moved from private practice to become Arizona assistant attorney general (1965–69), into politics as an Arizona state

senator (1969–75), and then back into a series of Arizona judicial posts, ultimately becoming a state court of appeals judge (1979–81). O'Connor's 1950 B.A. and 1952 LL.B. were from Stanford University. She married John Jay O'Connor in 1952; they have one child.

FURTHER READING

Sandra Day O'Connor: Independent Thinker. D. J. HERDA. Enslow, 1995.
"My mentor, myself." JOSHUA B. ADAMS. *Town & Country,* Aug. 1994.
Sandra Day O'Connor. CHRISTOPHER E. HENRY. Watts, 1994.*Sandra Day O'Connor: Justice for All.* BEVERLY GHERMAN. Puffin, 1993.
Sandra Day O'Connor: American Women of Achievement. PETER HUBER. Chelsea House, 1992.
Sandra Day O'Connor. PAUL DEEGAN. Abdo & Daughters, 1992.*Sandra Day O'Connor.* NORMAN L. MACHT. Chelsea House, 1992.
Sandra Day O'Connor: A New Justice, a New Voice. BEVERLY BERWALD. Fawcett, 1991.
Sandra Day O'Connor. BEVERLY GHERMAN. Viking Penguin, 1991.

Ōe, Kenzaburō (1935–) The awarding of a Nobel Prize for literature always spurs interest in the laureate's early work. So it was that Kenzaburō Ōe's first novel, *Nip the Buds, Shoot the Kids,* written in 1958, received its first English publication in 1995. Several reviewers noted that the mythical World War II–set tale, which in some ways parallels William Golding's

Lord of the Flies, is a fine novel for a writer of any age, much less a first novel by a 23-year-old student. Also drawing on the experiences of World War II was the first American edition of Ōe's *Hiroshima Notes,* a series of essays written between 1963 and 1965, based on numerous visits to the city and interviews with survivors of the atomic bombing. Near the 50th anniversary of the bombings, Ōe visited the United States to promote the books; his appearances included interviews with NBC's Katie Couric and on NPR's "All Things Considered," and a reading from *Hiroshima* on "Good Morning, America." In November 1995, at the International Emmys, *Kenzaburō Ōe's Long Road to Fatherhood,* produced by Japan's NHK-Japan Broadcasting Corporation, won the award for best arts documentary.

The year also saw publication of *Japan, the Ambiguous and Myself: The Nobel Prize Speech and Other Lectures.* Shortly before receiving the Nobel Prize for literature in 1994, Ōe had completed the first draft of a trilogy, "A Green Tree in Flames," named after a poem by William Butler Yeats; he said it would be his last novel. Ōe also refused the Bunka Kunsho, Japan's prestigious Order of Culture award.

Born and raised in a rural setting on the Japanese island of Shikoku, Ōe began publishing short stories even before receiving his 1959 degree in French literature from Tokyo University. In 1958 he published his novella *The Catch,* which won the prestigious Akutagawa Prize, and *Nip the Buds, Shoot the Kids.* His other publications include *Our Age* (1959), *Screams* (1962), *The Perverts* (1963), *Adventures in Daily Life* (1964), *A Personal Matter* (1964; sparked by the 1963 birth of his eldest son with severe brain damage), *Football in the First Year of Mannen* (1967), *The Silent Cry* (1967; probably his best-known work), *Teach Us to Outgrow Our Madness* (1977), and *The Crazy Iris and Other Stories of the Atomic Aftermath* (1984). His nonfiction works include *Youth in the West* (1961), *Hiroshima Notes* (1963), and *Japan's Dual Identity: A Writer's Dilemma* (1988). Ōe married Yukari Itami, daughter of novelist Mansaku Itami, and has two sons and a daughter.

FURTHER READING

"Kenzaburō Ōe. . . ." SAM STAGGS. *Publishers Weekly,* Aug. 7, 1995.
"Hiroshima made me." EDWARD PILKINGTON. *Guardian,* July 31, 1995.
"Reading Japan." DAVID REMNICK. *The New Yorker,* Feb. 6, 1995.
"Bittersweet honors. . . ." *Time,* Oct. 24, 1994.
"Japanese novelist. . . ." *Publishers Weekly,* Oct. 17, 1994.
Escape from the Wasteland: Romanticism and Realism in the Fiction of Mishima Yukio and Ōe Kenzaburō. Susan J. Napier. Harvard University Press, 1991.

O'Grady, Scott F. (1965–) On June 2, 1995, U.S. Air Force captain Scott F. O'Grady was shot down by a Serbian antiaircraft missile while flying an American F-16 fighter plane on a North Atlantic Treaty Organization (NATO) patrol near the Serbian-held town of Banya Luka. O'Grady ejected and landed safely in hill country, then successfully hid from Serbian search parties for six days, living on his small store of rations, supplemented by grass and insects, while waiting for a possible rescue. Ultimately, his radio signals were picked up by American naval forces on station offshore in the Adriatic Sea. On the morning of June 8, a helicopter-borne Marine rescue team from the U.S.S. *Kearsarge,* guided by the beacon that was part of O'Grady's standard-issue survival equipment, landed and took him out. The rescue operation took only a few minutes, and no casualties were suffered, although some Serbian fire was directed at the aircraft involved.

Coming as it did at a time of great Allied discouragement over Bosnia, O'Grady's rescue was hailed as a major success by the American and NATO military and by President Bill Clinton, who welcomed him home in a televised June 12 White House ceremony. In July, O'Grady announced that he would be leaving active service. Late in the year, O'Grady published *Return with Honor,* written with Jeff Coplon, describing his experiences, and was widely seen promoting the book, which became a best-seller; an audio version was also released.

Brooklyn-born O'Grady grew up in Spokane, Washington. He is a 1989 graduate of the Embry-Riddle Aeronautical University at Prescott, Arizona. He was enrolled in the ROTC, and received his air force commission on graduation. He had flown F-16 missions in western Europe and northern Iraq before serving in Bosnia.

FURTHER READING

"Good soldier. . . ." *People,* Dec. 25, 1995.
"Hero's welcome. . . ." RICHARD JEROME. *People,* June 26, 1995.
"All for one." KEVIN FEDARKO and MARK THOMPSON. *Time,* June 19, 1995.
" 'One amazing kid.' " BRUCE B. AUSTER. *U.S. News & World Report,* June 19, 1995.

Okada, Eiji (1920–95)

Japanese stage and screen star Eiji Okada was best known to worldwide audiences for three films. In the French film *Hiroshima Mon Amour,* directed by Alain Resnais and written by Marguerite Duras, he played a Japanese architect in post–atomic holocaust Hiroshima. In the Hollywood film *The Ugly American* (1963), starring Marlon Brando, Okada costarred as the leader of an unnamed Southeast Asian country. In director Hiroshi Teshigahara's highly symbolic and allegorical Japanese film *Woman in the Dunes* (1964), he starred as the entomologist trapped and enslaved in a sandpit. Among his other films were *Until the Day We Meet Again* (1950), *She and He* (1962), *The Scent of Incense* (1964), *Tunnel to the Sun* (1968), *Antarctica* (1983), and *The Death of a Tea Master* (1989). He was also a highly regarded figure on the Japanese stage. No information as to survivors was available. (d. Japan; September 14, 1995)

FURTHER READING

Obituary. *Independent,* Oct. 9, 1995.
Obituary. *New York Times,* Oct. 5, 1995.

Olajuwon, Hakeem Abdul (1963–)

To the surprise of virtually everyone, the Houston Rockets won the NBA championship for the second consecutive time in 1995. Their success was due in no small part to the man in the center: Hakeem Olajuwon. It had not been a good regular season. The team had lost several key players to injuries, some during the playoffs; Olajuwon himself missed eight games in late March and early April with iron-deficiency anemia. However, in February a key trade added to the team one of Olajuwon's old teammates from the University of Houston: Clyde Drexler. Together these two veterans led a much younger team on the difficult path to a repeat championship. They had two grueling series with a five-game win over the Utah Jazz and a seven-game win over the Phoenix Suns, had a slightly easier time defeating the San Antonio Spurs in six games for the Western Conference championship, and then surprisingly swept the Orlando Magic in the NBA Finals. Olajuwon himself was named Most Valuable Player of the finals for the second time in a row.

During the regular season Olajuwon was second in the league in scoring (with 29.3 points a game), second in blocked shots (3.36), and seventh in rebounds (tied with David Robinson at 10.8). In the 1995–96 season, Olajuwon and the Rockets started out strong, with a division-leading record at year's end of 22-8, third in the league. Olajuwon himself was fifth in scoring, with 24.4 points a game; fourth in blocked shots, averaging 3.03 a game; and sixth in rebounding, with 11.2 a game. Having finally gotten the respect of basketball aficionados, the Rockets were seen by many as favorites for another appearance in the finals, and possibly a "three-peat" as champions.

In September, Olajuwon and Shaquille O'Neal, star of the Orlando Magic, were scheduled to have a one-on-one pay-per-view televised contest in Atlantic City; that was canceled because of a back injury Olajuwon suffered in the McDonald's championship, in which the NBA champions play European and Australian championship teams. Olajuwon was one of several NBA stars featured in the 1995 video *NBA Jams: The Music Videos.* Olajuwon's *Living the Dream: My Life and Basketball,* written with Peter Knobler, was scheduled for February 1996 publication.

Born in Lagos, Nigeria, where he attended Muslim Teachers College, Olajuwon came late to basketball, in 1978, having started as a soccer and handball player. Even so, he quickly became a dominant force on the basketball court, first as a student at the University of Houston (1980–84), leading the Cougars (dubbed Phi Slamma Jamma) to three straight NCAA Final Fours (1982–84), himself being named MVP of the Final Four in 1983, though his team lost. He then joined the Houston Rockets (1984–   ) as the top pick overall in the NBA college draft. He was named to the NBA All-Star Team nine times (1985–90; 1992–95), the All-NBA first team six times (1987–89; 1993–95), and the NBA All-Defensive first team six times (1987–88; 1990; 1992; 1994–95). He led his team to two consecutive NBA titles (1994–95), being named Most Valuable Player of the finals both times. In 1994, he was also named NBA defensive player of the year, only the second person (after Michael Jordan) to win both titles in the same season. Olajuwon was also the first NBA player ever to have 200 blocked shots and 200 steals in a single season (1989). Earlier called Akeem Olajuwon, he added the *H* to his first name in 1991. He became a United States citizen in 1993.

FURTHER READING

"Dream fulfilled. . . ." BARRY M. BLOOM. *Sport*, Nov. 1995.
"Double time. . . ." PAUL ATTNER. *Sporting News*, June 12, 1995.
Hakeem Olajuwon: Superstar Center. BILL GUTMAN. Millbrook, 1995.
"Hakeem Olajuwon. . . ." ROBERT DRAPER. *Texas*, Sept. 1994.
"Quest for the ring." RICK WEINBERG. *Sport*, May 1994.
"Slam dunk." SPIKE LEE. *Interview*, Feb. 1994.
"Hakeem Olajuwon." FRAN BLINEBURY. *Sport*, Jan. 1994.
Hakeem Olajuwon: The Dream. MILES HARVEY. Childrens, 1994.
"Olajuwon, Hakeem." *Current Biography*, Nov. 1993.
Hakeem Olajuwon: Tower of Power. GEORGE R. REKELA. Lerner, 1993.
Sports Great Hakeem Olajuwon. RON KNAPP. Enslow, 1992.

Oldman, Gary (1958–   ) British actor Gary Oldman starred as Reverend Arthur Dimmesdale opposite Demi Moore as his lover, Hester Prynne, who gives birth to their adulterously conceived child and is branded with an *A* for

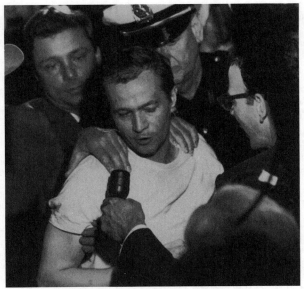
Gary Oldman (center) as Lee Harvey Oswald.

adulteress, in a 1995 film version of *The Scarlet Letter,* very loosely adapted by Douglas Day Stewart from the Nathaniel Hawthorne novel. Roland Joffrey directed; the cast included Robert Duvall as her long-lost husband, Roger Prynne, Robert Prosky, Edward Hardwicke, and Joan Plowright. The film, far more erotic in style and substance than Hawthorne's novel of Puritan New England, was not very well received by critics or at the box office.

Oldman also starred as the prison warden, opposite Christian Slater and Kevin Bacon, in the film *Murder in the First,* the story of Henry Young, who spent more than three years in solitary confinement in Alcatraz, killed a man in prison after his release from solitary, and went on trial for the killing, defended by young lawyer James Stamphill, played by Bacon.

London-born Oldman spent several years in the British theater before making his film debut as Sid Vicious in *Sid and Nancy* (1986), which he followed with a starring role as playwright Joe Orton in *Prick Up Your Ears* (1987). He continued to emerge as a star in *Track 29* (1988), *We Think the World of You* (1988), *Criminal Law* (1988), *Paris by Night* (1989), *Chattahoochee* (1990), *State of Grace* (1990), *Rosencrantz and Guildenstern Are Dead* (1991), *JFK* (1991), *Bram Stoker's Dracula* (1992), *Romeo Is Bleeding* (1993), *True Romance* (1993), *The Professional* (1994), and *Immortal Beloved* (1994). He has also appeared in several television films.

Oldman attended Rose Buford Dramatic College. He has been married twice and has one child.

FURTHER READING

"Immortal bedeviled." REBECCA ASCHER-WALSH. *Entertainment*, Feb. 10, 1995.
"Neck romance." RACHEL ABRAMOWITZ. *Premiere*, Dec. 1992.
"A vicious undertaking. . . ." SUSAN DWORKIN. *New York Times Magazine*, Nov. 8, 1992.
"Gary Oldman." DENNIS HOPPER. *Interview*, Jan. 1992.

O'Leary, Hazel Rollins (1947–) Secretary of Energy Hazel O'Leary found herself attacked by friends and foes in early November, when it was revealed that the Energy Department had in 1994 hired a consulting firm, Carma International, to evaluate how the department was viewed by others, and that the evaluations, which cost a total of $43,500, had included rankings of reporters covering the department. Republicans, who had been trying very hard to abolish the department altogether, called for her resignation. The White House lukewarmly stated that she could keep her job, as a practical matter not offering any support at all. O'Leary apologized publicly several times and tried to ride out the storm, which some observers viewed as a highly political tempest in a teapot and others viewed as a real freedom-of-the-press issue.

During 1995, while awaiting the possible dismemberment of her department, O'Leary developed no major new initiatives, though in February she led a U.S. trade delegation to India and China, and signed previously negotiated agreements in both countries, totaling several billion dollars. Her department also issued its final report on the two-year-long investigation of the U.S. government Cold War radiation experiments on humans, likened by many to inhumane World War II Nazi medical experiments, though defended by others as contributing to scientific advances. The department had previously indicated that there had been approximately 9,000 victims, but the final count indicated that 16,000 had been used and, in some instances, killed in this way.

Virginia-born O'Leary was a New Jersey assistant attorney general, an assistant Essex County, New Jersey prosecutor, and a partner in the Coopers and Lybrand accounting firm, before entering the arena of federal energy regulation with the U.S. Department of Energy during the Ford administration. She also worked in the Department of Energy during the Carter administration. In 1981, she joined O'Leary Associates, a consulting firm in the energy field operated by her husband, John O'Leary, now deceased, who was a deputy energy secretary in the Carter administration. She became executive vice president of the Minneapolis-based Northern States Power Company in 1989. She became secretary of energy in 1993, the first woman and the first African-American to hold the post. O'Leary's 1959 B.A. was from Fisk University, and her 1966 J.D. from Rutgers University. She has one son.

FURTHER READING

"An indefatigable. . . ." LISA LEITER and JAMIE DETTMER. *Insight on the News*, June 12, 1995.
"High energy. . . . ." WILL NIXON. *E*, June 1995.
"As O'Leary. . . ." ANDREW LAWLER. *Science*, May 19, 1995.
"Hazel O'Leary." LINDA TURBYVILLE. *Omni*, Apr. 1995.
"Hazel O'Leary. . . ." DANIEL GLICK. *Working Woman*, Nov. 1994.
"Curbing a sick practice." *Emerge*, Oct. 1994.
"Department of horrors." DOUGLAS PASTERNAK and PETER CARY. *U.S. News & World Report*, Jan. 24, 1994.
"O'Leary, Hazel R." *Current Biography*, Jan. 1994.

O'Neal, Shaquille Rashaun (1972–) Through 1994, Shaquille O'Neal and the Orlando Magic had yet to win a playoff game. That changed in the 1994–95 National Basketball Association season, when the team posted a strong 57-25 record to lead the Eastern Conference with a home record of 39-2, second-best in NBA history. In the 1995 playoffs, O'Neal and the Magic started off strong, defeating the Boston Celtics in four games; withstood a tough challenge from the Chicago Bulls, with Michael Jordan back from retirement; and then won a grueling seven-game series against the Indianapolis Pacers. But in the NBA finals, the experience of the defending champion Houston Rockets was too much for them, and the Magic were swept in four games.

During the regular season, O'Neal himself topped the league in scoring (with 29.3 points), was second in field-goal percentage (.583), third in rebounding (11.4), and sixth in blocks (2.43); it was the third year in a row that he was in the top ten in four categories. He was runner-up to David Robinson for Most Valuable Player honors, was named to the NBA all-league second team, and was selected as a starter in the All-Star game for the third year in a row. During All-Star Weekend, he performed a new song, "Nobody," at an MTV celebration, and during the game itself, he led the Eastern Conference team with 22 points and 7 rebounds, a contrast to the "freeze-out" he had experienced in 1994.

Just before the start of the 1995–96 season, O'Neal broke a bone in his right thumb and missed the first 22 games of the regular season, until mid-December. However, his team continued strong, at year's end posting a 23-6 record; with O'Neal's return they were poised to make another run for the championship.

An "army brat," New Jersey–born O'Neal and his family lived in various places, including Germany twice, where Louisiana State University coach Dale Brown spotted him in a basketball clinic. He attended Cole High School in San Antonio, Texas, then moved on to Louisiana State, where he was named national player of the year by AP, UPI, and *Sports Illustrated* after his sophomore season, during which he broke his leg, and was a two-time consensus first-team All-American. Leaving college after his junior season in 1992, O'Neal was the top pick in the NBA college draft, going to the Orlando Magic, with a seven-year, $40 million contract. He was named Rookie of the Year after the 1992–93 season. He

has also published *Shaq Attaq! My Rookie Year* (1993), written with Jack McCallum; released two rap albums, *Shaq Diesel* (1993) and *Shaq-Fu: Da Return* (1994); and opened in his first movie, *Blue Chips* (1994).

FURTHER READING

"He's back." PHIL TAYLOR. *Sports Illustrated*, Dec. 25, 1995.

"It may be Magic." GARY SHELTON. *Sporting News*, Dec. 25, 1995.

"Double time. . . ." PAUL ATTNER. *Sporting News*, June 12, 1995.

"NBA gazelle. . . ." TOM BROKAW. *Interview*, May 1995.

"The new NBA strategy. . . ." TERRY FREI. *Sporting News*, Mar. 27, 1995.

"At home with. . . ." LISA C. JONES. *Ebony*, Mar. 1995.

Shaquille O'Neal. RICHARD RAMBECK. Childs World, 1995.

Sports Great Shaquille O'Neal. MICHAEL J. SULLIVAN. Enslow, 1995.

"Observing Shaq." RICK BARRY and DAN DIEFFENBACH. "The rivalries no one expected." DONALD HUNT. "An eye for talent. . . ." DONALD HUNT. "Power play. . . ." STEVE GORDON. " 'The world is mine.' " DARRYL HOWERTON. *Sport*, Dec. 1994.

"Shaquille O'Neal." *Playboy*, Jan.1994.

Shaquille O'Neal. MICHAEL E. GOODMAN. Creative Ed, 1994.

Shaquille O'Neal. EDWARD TALLMAN. Macmillan, 1994.

Shaquille O'Neal. BOB WOODS. Troll, 1994.

Shaquille O'Neal: Basketball Sensation. BILL GUTMAN. Millbrook, 1994.

Sport Shots: Shaquille O'Neal. MARILYN SOUDERS. Scholastic, 1994.

Shaquille O'Neal. KEN RAPPOPORT. Walker, 1994.

Shaquille O'Neal, Center of Attention. BRAD TOWNSEND. Lerner, 1994.

Shaquille O'Neal. ELLEN E. WHITE. Scholastic, 1994.

Ongania, Juan Carlos (1914–95) Former Argentine president Juan Ongania spent his entire career in the military. A graduate of Argentina's National Military College, he became a cavalry officer, achieved the rank of brigadier general in 1959, and became head of the cavalry corps. He was until very late in his career a nonpolitical officer, little involved in the series of coups and countercoups that dominated his country's political life. In 1962, however, after being removed from his command, he led the military forces that took power, restored democracy, and allowed the election of liberal Arturo Illia. Ongania was commander in chief of the armed forces (1962–65), and then retired. Only a year later, armed forces leaders deposed Illia and installed Ongania as president. Ongania then functioned as a military dictator (1966–70); his government arrested dissenters, dissolved Congress, sent troops to attack students and faculty at the University of Buenos Aires, destroyed the judiciary, and installed a pervasive censorship system. In 1980, Ongania was himself deposed in a military coup. No information as to survivors was available. (d. Buenos Aires; June 8, 1995)

FURTHER READING

Obituary. *Current Biography*, Aug. 1995.
Obituary. *Independent*, June 10, 1995.
Obituary. *Times* (of London), June 10, 1995.
Obituary. *New York Times*, June 10, 1995.

Oppenheimer, Philip (1911–95) British

diamond magnate Philip Oppenheimer was long a major figure in the world's diamond industry. A graduate of Harrow and of Jesus College, Cambridge (1933), he went to work at DeBeers, controlled by the Oppenheimer family, in 1934, and continued in a variety of jobs for the worldwide firm until World War II. After active military service, he returned to the family business, and in 1948 took over management of the London office of the Central Selling Organization, a worldwide diamond marketing cartel led by De-Beers, which came to control the lion's share of world diamond sales. He became chairman of the Central Selling Organization and a member of the DeBeers board of directors in 1956. In that year, he was instrumental in bringing the Soviet Union into the cartel. Oppenheimer was also a major figure in British horse racing, as a leading breeder and as sponsor, through DeBeers, of the annual King George VI and Queen Elizabeth Stakes at Ascot. He was survived by his wife, Pamela Fenn Stirling, and their daughter and son. (d. London; October 8, 1995)

FURTHER READING

Obituary. *New York Times*, Oct. 20, 1995.
Obituary. *Times* (of London), Oct. 11, 1995.
Obituary. *Independent*, Oct. 10, 1995.

O'Rourke, P. J. (Patrick Jake O'Rourke;

1947–) Political humorist par excellence, P. J. O'Rourke in 1995 drew on writings ranging from his hippie days to his current stance as a con-

servative, to produce a new collection: *Age and Guile Beat Youth, Innocence, and a Bad Haircut: Twenty-five Years of P. J. O'Rourke*. The quirky and often hilarious results run from a notable 1970s hoax piece about Nixon in China and a review of *Emily Post's Etiquette* for (of all things) *House and Garden* to a Capote-esque gossip piece, "La Rent Est Due," and "100 Reasons Why Jimmy Carter Was a Better President Than Bill Clinton." O'Rourke went on a promotional book tour, a practice also deftly dissected in the book. Meanwhile, his *All the Trouble in the World: The Lighter Side of Overpopulation, Famine, Ecological Disaster, Ethnic Hatred, Plague, and Poverty* (1994) was published in paperback. The year also saw publication of *Very Seventies: A Cultural History of the 1970s from the Pages of Crawdaddy,* which included some of his earlier work, and which O'Rourke coedited with two others.

Ohio-born O'Rourke was an "underground press" writer, editor, and poet (1968–71), and a features editor for the *New York Herald* (1971–72). He joined New York's *National Lampoon* in 1973, as executive and managing editor, and became editor in chief of the magazine (1978–81). He then worked as a freelance writer, publishing articles in a wide range of magazines, among them *Rolling Stone,* for which he became foreign affairs desk chief. O'Rourke's early books include *Modern Manners: Etiquette for Very Rude People* (1983), *Republican Party Reptile* (1987), and *Holidays in Hell* (1988), but he broke through as a best-selling author with *Parliament of Whores: A Lone Humorist Attempts to Explain the U.S. Government* (1991) and *Give War a Chance: Eyewitness Accounts of Mankind's Struggle Against Tyranny, Injustice, and Alcohol-Free Beer* (1992). O'Rourke's 1969 B.A. was from Miami University of Ohio, and his 1970 M.A. from Johns Hopkins University. He is married to Amy Lumet, daughter of film director Sidney Lumet.

FURTHER READING

"White mischief." BOB ICKES. *New York*, Dec. 21, 1992.

"P. J. O'Rourke. . . ." CHRIS GOODRICH. *Publishers Weekly*, Mar. 16, 1992.

"Of cows, scuds and scotch. . . ." MICHAEL RILEY. *Time*, Apr. 15, 1991.

Othmer, Donald Frederick (1904–95)

Omaha-born chemical engineer Donald Othmer received his 1924 B.S. from the University of Nebraska, and his 1925 M.S. and 1927 Ph.D. from the University of Michigan. After graduation, he went to work for the Eastman Kodak Company, and there began his long career an an inventor; his first and very notable work was the invention of the "Othmer still" to distill acetic acid. That very lucrative invention and two score that followed became the property of his employers. After he went on his own as an inventor and consultant in 1931, he became the holder of more than 150 patents, for a very wide range of industrial products and processes. He also published more than 350 scientific and technical articles. Othmer and his colleague Raymond Kirk also conceived and Othmer carried through the development of the *Kirk-Othmer Encyclopedia of Chemical Technology,* the standard work in its field. Othmer taught chemical engineering at Brooklyn Polytechnical University (1933–95). He was also a very successful investor and well-known philanthropist. He was survived by his wife, Mildred Topp Othmer, and a sister. (d. New York City; November 1, 1995)

FURTHER READING

Obituary. *New York Times*, Nov. 3, 1995.

P

Pacino, Al (Alfredo Pacino; 1940–) Celebrated actor Al Pacino in 1995 starred as topnotch, personally troubled Los Angeles Police Department detective Vincent Hanna opposite Robert De Niro as soon-to-retire master criminal Neil McCaulay and Val Kilmer as De Niro's second in command, in the very well-received crime film *Heat,* written and directed by Michael Mann. While a highly violent cops-and-robbers genre work, the film also focuses on the personal lives of many in its large cast of characters, and reflects Mann's deeply pessimistic view of modern American urban life. Costarring are

Jon Voight, Diane Venora, Tom Sizemore, Amy Brenneman, and Ashley Judd.

Pacino also starred as Grandpa, the wise, dying old man in the film *Two Bits,* directed by James Foley, written by Joseph Stefano, and costarring Jerry Barone as his 12-year-old grandson and Mary Elizabeth Mastrantonio as the boy's mother, with narration by Alec Baldwin, as the grandson telling the story many years later.

Forthcoming were starring roles in the films *Donnie Brasco,* costarring Johnny Depp, and *City Hall,* directed by Harry Becker and costarring Martin Landau, John Cusack, Bridget Fonda, Danny Aiello, and David Paymer.

New York–born Pacino is one of the leading alumni of the Actors Studio, beginning his long association with the group in 1966 and becoming one of its artistic directors (1982–84). He worked in the theater through the 1960s, and in the early 1970s emerged as a major film star, breaking through as Michael Corleone in *The Godfather* (1972). He went on to star in such films as *Serpico* (1973), *The Godfather, Part II* (1974), *Dog Day Afternoon* (1975), *Cruising* (1980), *Scarface* (1983), *Sea of Love* (1989), *Dick Tracy* (1990), *The Godfather, Part III* (1990), *Frankie and Johnny in the Clair De Lune* (1991), *Scent of a Woman* (1992; he won a best actor Academy Award), *Glengarry Glen Ross* (1992), and *Carlito's Way* (1993). He also continued to work in the theater, in such plays as *Camino Real* (1973), *Richard III* (1973), *American Buffalo* (1981), *Salome* (1992), and *Chinese Coffee* (1992).

FURTHER READING

"Pacino's edgy genius." JOHN POWERS. *Vogue*, Jan. 1996.

The Films of Al Pacino. WILLIAM SCHOELL. Citadel/Carol, 1995.

". . . And justice for all." BRONWEN HRUSKA. *Entertainment Weekly*, Nov. 12, 1993.

"Conquest of space." DAVID DENBY. *New York*, Dec. 21, 1992.

"Al alone." MAUREEN DOWD. *GQ* Sept. 1992.

Bomb: Interviews. BETSY SUSSLER, ed. City Lights, 1992.

"Al Pacino." JULIAN SCHNABEL. *Interview*, Feb. 1991.

"Pacino powers. . . ." JOHN PODHORETZ. *Insight*, Jan. 14, 1991.

Life on the Wire: The Life and Art of Al Pacino. ANDREW YULE. Fine, 1991.

Packwood, Bob (1932–)

On September 7, 1995, Oregon Senator Bob Packwood resigned from the U.S. Senate. The day before, September 6, the Senate Ethics Committee had concluded an almost three-year-long investigation of sexual harassment charges against Packwood, and recommended 6–0 that he be expelled from the Senate. The committee, composed of three Republicans and three Democrats, had long been split on party lines, but ultimately the weight—perhaps even the sheer quantity—of the evidence against Packwood seemed overwhelming. The committee's 179-page report, accompanied by thousands of pages of evidence, found that the nature of Packwood's sexual advances to at least 17 women had demonstrated a "pattern of sexual abuse" of women subordinate to him or who might be put at a financial disadvantage if they complained. The committee also accused Packwood of evidence-tampering in regard to his diaries and raised questions of possible financial misconduct. Packwood on September 6 had responded by saying that he would not resign; but by the next day had faced the inevitable and did so, leaving the Senate a month later. In December, he announced that he was starting a Washington-based political consulting business.

Portland-born Packwood served in the Oregon House of Representatives (1963–69), and in 1968 scored a major upset victory over longtime Democratic Senator Wayne Morse, becoming at 36 the youngest senator of his day. A thoroughly independent Republican liberal, he often voted in opposition to his party's positions, although equally often he voted with his party. He was chairperson of the powerful Senate Finance Committee (1985–86) and was a key figure in the passage of the 1986 tax law revision. Ironically, he was for many years one of the Senate's most vocal and effective women's rights advocates, and was one of only two Republicans to vote against the confirmation of Clarence Thomas to be Supreme Court justice, after the Thomas–Anita Faye Hill confrontation over sexual harassment charges. In 1992, Packwood won another Senate term. After the Republican victory in the 1994 congressional elections, Packwood again became chairperson of the Senate Finance Committee.

Packwood's B.A. was from Willamette University, and his LL.B. from New York University. Formerly married, he has two children.

FURTHER READING

Packwood: The Public and Private Life from Acclaim to Outrage. MARK KIRCHMEIER. HarperCollins, 1995.

"The trials of. . . ." TRIP GABRIEL. *New York Times Magazine*, Aug. 29, 1993.

Panetta, Leon Edward (1938–)

In his first full year as White House chief of staff, Leon Panetta continued to serve a president who was searching for ways to withstand the onslaught of a Republican Congress and at the same time build a "comeback" public image that could take him to victory in the 1996 presidential elections. Bill Clinton was also a president who characteristically liked to do things himself, and in the process tended to make hash of the always-uncertain lines of authority within his White House. Panetta encountered job-threatening difficulties in the spring of 1995, when President Clinton brought in former Republican political consultant Dick Morris to advise him on his current image and 1996 campaign strategies; but these seemed to be reasonably well resolved by year's end—at least for the present.

As the budget crisis deepened throughout the year, Panetta emerged as President Clinton's chief budget negotiator and spokesperson, playing whatever role seemed indicated by events, whether hard-line or conciliatory—but always without making sharply abrasive attacks on the Republican side of the long argument. At year's end, and well into January, his contribution to the resolution of the problem was as yet unclear.

California-born Panetta began his political career as a congressional assistant after his navy service (1964–66). He was director of the U.S. Office of Civil Rights in the Department of Health, Education, and Welfare (1969–70), but was fired by the Nixon administration for his strong civil rights advocacy. He then served as executive assistant to New York Mayor John Lindsay (1970–71). After practicing law (1971–76), he successfully ran for Congress, and was an eight-term California Democratic representative (1977–93), only leaving to become Clinton administration director of the Office of Management and Budget (OMB). While in Congress, he was on the House of Representatives Budget Committee for 12 years, four of them as committee chairperson. During the Reagan and Bush administrations, he was a key critic of the often-distorted budgets submitted to Congress, and a leading liberal who was especially concerned about the environmental threats posed by offshore oil drilling in his California coastal district. He sponsored the establishment of a national marine sanctuary at Monterey Bay. He become White House chief of staff on July 14, 1993, replacing Mack McLarty.

Panetta's 1960 B.A. was from the University of Santa Clara, and his 1963 J.D. from the University of Santa Clara Law School. He is married to Sylvia Marie Varni; they have three sons.

FURTHER READING

"Panetta's moment." MATTHEW COOPER. *New Republic*, Nov. 6, 1995.
"Leon lays it. . . ." KEN KELLEY. *Mother Jones*, Sept.–Oct. 1993.
"Panetta, Leon E." *Current Biography*, June 1993.

Pargeter, Edith Mary (1913–95)
Shropshire-born Edith Pargeter began writing novels while still in her early teens. After graduating from high school, she worked in a drugstore while beginning her writing career; her debut novel was *Friend of Nero* (1936). She served in a military communications unit during World War II. After the war, she earned her living as a writer with such highly regarded works as the World War II–set trilogy "The Eighth Champion of Christendom" and the "Heaven Tree" trilogy, set in the early Middle Ages, a period that she later very fully explored as a mystery author. Her debut mystery novel, still as Pargeter, was *Fallen into the Pit* (1951). As Ellis Peters, she became a highly regarded and very prolific mystery novelist, first with a set of modern police dramas (the George Felse series) and then with the long and extraordinarily successful 12th century–set "Brother Caedfel" series, starting with *A Morbid Taste for Bones* (1977), its central character a medieval monk who is a skilled criminal investigator. Several of the Brother Caedfel books became the bases of television films. She also published *Shropshire* (1993), with photographs by Roy Morgan. There were no survivors. (d. Shropshire, England; October 14, 1995)

FURTHER READING

Obituary. *Times* (of London), Oct. 16, 1995.
Obituary. *New York Times*, Oct. 16, 1995.
"Scheherazade. . . ." JOHN W. DONOHUE. *America*, Apr. 16, 1994.

Parks, Rosa (1913–) The quality of a life often shows in little things. In Rosa Parks's case, a small, seemingly simple action sparked a revolution. In Montgomery, Alabama, on December 1, 1955, after a long day's work, Parks refused to give up her seat on a bus to a White man and move to the back of the bus, as was common practice for Blacks to do in the South at that time. In response to the furor that resulted, min-

isters Martin Luther King, Jr., and Ralph D. Abernathy organized the historic 381-day Montgomery bus boycott, beginning the modern American civil rights movement and its attack on American racism. Many people were arrested during the boycott, including Parks herself. In 1995, 40 years after that event, Rosa Parks told the story of that experience and the religion that has sustained her throughout her life in *Quiet Strength: The Faith, the Hope and the Heart of a Woman Who Changed a Nation,* written with her attorney, Gregory J. Reed. December also saw release of a new record honoring her, *Something Inside So Strong,* performed by numerous gospel and rhythm and blues stars calling themselves the Rosa Parks Tribute Singers, including Vanessa Bell Armstrong, Howard Hewetyt, Sounds of Blackness, and Tramaine Hawkins.

Alabama-born Parks was working as a seamstress and was active in the local chapter of the National Association for the Advancement of Colored People (NAACP) at the start of the boycott. After it ended, she could no longer find work in Montgomery and moved to Detroit in 1957. She worked as an aide to Michigan Representative John Conyers (1965–88); often dubbed the "mother of the civil rights movement," she also spoke widely. In 1986, she founded the Rosa and Raymond Parks Institute for Self-Development in Los Angeles. She had earlier published the children's book *Rosa Parks: Mother to a Movement* (1992) and *Rosa Parks: My Story* (1994). In 1994, Parks was robbed and beaten in her Detroit home by a robber who knew her, but failed to recognize his personal debt to this extraordinary woman. Parks is a widow.

FURTHER READING

"Quiet crusader. . . ." JANICE MIN. *People,* Dec. 18, 1995.

"Taking a seat. . . ." VINCENT F. A. GOLPHIN. *Christianity Today,* Apr. 24, 1995.

"The sixth Essence awards." AUDREY EDWARDS. *Essence,* May 1993.

Young Rosa Parks: A Civil Rights Heroine. ANNE BENJAMIN. Troll, 1995.

Rosa Parks: Civil Rights Leader. MARY HULL. Chelsea House, 1994.

Rosa Parks: Fight for Freedom. KEITH BRANDT. Troll, 1993.

Picture Book of Rosa Parks. DAVID A. ADLER. Holiday, 1993.

The Year They Walked: Rosa Parks and the Montgomery Bus Boycott. BEATRICE SIEGEL. Simon & Schuster, 1992.

Rosa Parks: Hero of Our Time. GARNET N. JACKSON. Modern Curriculum, 1992.

Rosa Parks. Did You Know, 1992.

Rosa Parks and the Montgomery Bus Boycott. TERESA CELSI. Millbrook, 1991.

Parrish, Robert (1916–95)

Georgia-born film director, editor, and actor Robert Parrish began his more than five-decades-long film career as a child actor. His debut film was *Mother Machree* (1928); among his many other films were *All Quiet on the Western Front* (1930), *City Lights* (1931), and John Ford's *The Informer* (1935). He continued to work with Ford as an adult, but as a film editor, assisting on several Ford 1930s classics, and editing Ford's Oscar-winning wartime documentaries *Battle of Midway* (1942) and *December 7* (1943). After the war, he shared his own first Oscar for coediting *Body and Soul* (1947) and won a second Oscar for coediting *All the King's Men* (1948). He made his directorial debut with *Cry Danger* (1951); among his later films as director were *The Purple Plain* (1954), *The Wonderful Country* (1959), and *Journey to the Dark Side of the Sun* (1969). His memoirs were *Growing Up in Hollywood* (1976) and *Hollywood Doesn't Live Here Any More* (1988). He was survived by his wife, Kathleen Thompson, a daughter, and a son. (d. Southampton, New York; December 4, 1995)

FURTHER READING

Obituary. *Independent,* Dec. 11, 1995.

Obituary. *Variety,* Dec. 7, 1995.

Obituary. *New York Times,* Dec. 6, 1995.

Pataki, George Elmer (1945–)

During his first year in office, New York Republican governor George Pataki encountered the same massive problems that had beset his predecessor, three-time Democratic governor Mario Cuomo, including a continuing state fiscal crisis, job loss due to the flight of industry, and the growing cost of the social service network, with more and more costs dumped by the federal government onto the states. In fact, Pataki ran into a far-from-cooperative legislature, finding powerful opposition in both parties to the large spending cuts he had promised. The 1995 fiscal budget, finally passed in early June, provided for total spending of only 1 percent less than the 1994 budget. His education budget freeze proposal was rejected, and the education budget was increased. There were very modest face-saving tax cuts; even these would mean a loss of revenue that would worsen the state's already very shaky credit ratings. Pataki had a hard time getting the compromise budget through, pressuring legislators by withholding his own salary and those of the legislators from April 1, the original deadline for passage. Such preelection issues as the flight of industry and deficit reduction were not seriously addressed.

Pataki did make good on one major campaign promise. On March 7, 1995, he signed a law reinstating the state's death penalty; New York then became the 38th state to legalize capital punishment. Governor Cuomo had vetoed the death penalty every year in office, as had Governor Hugh Carey before him.

Born in Peekskill, New York, Pataki is a graduate of Yale University and Columbia Law School. He was an associate with Dewey, Ballantine, Palmer, Busby, and Wood (1970–74), and practiced in Peekskill with the White Plains–based firm of Plunket & Jaffe (1974–84) before going on his own in partnership with his brother, Louis (1984–89). He served as mayor of Peekskill (1981–84), in the New York State Assembly (1985–92), and in the New York State Senate (1992–93). He defeated incumbent governor Mario Cuomo in 1994. He is married to Elizabeth Rowland; they have four children.

FURTHER READING

" 'Spread the pain'. . . ." ROBERT FITCH. *Nation*, May 8, 1995.
"Pataki for governor." *National Review*, Nov. 21, 1994.

Patrick, John (John Patrick Goggan; 1905–95) Louisville-born playwright and screenwriter John Patrick began his long career in the early 1930s, as a radio scriptwriter, and began writing for the New York stage in the mid-1930s. His first Broadway success was the play *The Hasty Heart* (1945), the story of a dying soldier, which was adapted into the 1949 film, starring Ronald Reagan, Patricia Neal, and Richard Todd. His second success was the Pulitzer Prize–winning comedy *The Teahouse of the August Moon*

(1953); he adapted the play into the 1956 film, starring Marlon Brando and Glenn Ford. Among Patrick's other screenplays were *Educating Father* (1936), *International Settlement* (1938), *The President's Lady* (1953), *Three Coins in the Fountain* (1954), *Love Is a Many Splendored Thing* (1955), *High Society* (1956), *Les Girls* (1957), *Some Came Running* (1968), *The World of Suzie Wong* (1961), *Gigot* (1962), and *The Shoes of the Fisherman* (1968). No information as to survivors was available. (d. Delray Beach, Florida; November 7, 1995)

FURTHER READING

Obituary. *New York Times*, Nov. 9, 1995.

Patterson, Clair Cameron (1922–95) Iowa-born Clair Patterson was one of the world's leading geochemists. He received his 1943 B.A. in chemistry from Grinnell College, his 1944 M.S. from the University of Iowa, and his 1951 Ph.D. from the University of Chicago. He spent his entire career at the California Institute of Technology, starting as a teaching fellow in 1952 and ultimately becoming an emeritus full professor in 1992. Patterson's major interest was in the geochemistry and history of the metals found in such substances as rock, water, and air, whether originating on or off Earth. In 1953, very soon after beginning his career at Caltech, he became a major figure, publishing a seminal study of the lead isotopes found in meteorites, establishing the age of Earth at 4.6 billion years, far older than previously thought. Using the same techniques, and studying samples taken from such widely separated sources as polar ice caps and ocean bottom sediments, he established the presence of increasingly large amounts of deadly lead in the world's environment, then making a massive contribution to the campaign to eliminate lead from gasoline, the main source of lead in the environment, and from other sources as well. In addition to specialist works, Patterson published *Rome's Ruin by Lead Poison* (1990). He was survived by his wife, Lorna, two daughters, two sons, a sister, and a brother. (d. Sea Ranch, California; December 5, 1995)

FURTHER READING

Obituary. *New York Times*, Dec. 8, 1995.

Pavarotti, Luciano (1935–) Celebrated

tenor Luciano Pavarotti in 1995 continued to build on the major commercial success that began with the "three tenors" (Pavarotti, José Carreras, and Placido Domingo) 1990 Rome World Cup concert, watched by 800 million people, followed by their Grammy-winning album *Carreras-Domingo-Pavarotti: The Three Tenors in Concert,* the best-selling classical album of all time, with more than 10 million record and video sales worldwide. Their 1994 Los Angeles World Cup concert, watched by 1.3 billion people, had generated the best-selling album *Encore! The Three Tenors*, which received a 1995 best album of the year Grammy nomination, and created the opportunity for the 1995 video *The Making of the Three Tenors*. The trio also announced plans for a "three tenors" 1996–97 five-country tour, with scheduled appearances in Tokyo June 29, 1996; London July 6; New York July 20; Munich August 3; and Melbourne March 1, 1997.

Pavarotti continued to develop the popular music side of his career in 1995, releasing the album *Pavarotti & Friends 2,* a followup on the 1993 *Pavarotti and His Friends*. In the new album, Pavarotti and pop star Bryan Adams sing duets of Adams's "All for Love" and "O Sole Mio." On Frank Sinatra's album *Sinatra 80th: Live In Concert,* he joined in a duet version of "My Way," also issued as a single.

On the classical side, Pavararotti continued to appear in concert and opera. He undertook a no-table challenge in November, the role of Tonio in Donizetti's *Daughter of the Regiment,* at the Metropolitan Opera. His 1972 performance in the role had been one of the highlights of his early career, earning him the informal title "king of the high C's"—but it was an extraordinarily difficult role for the deepened voice of a 60-year-old. He did encounter difficulties, once being forced to leave the stage and abort a performance, but in later performances completed it in his customary high style.

Pavarotti in 1995 published the autographical *My World,* written with William Wright, also appearing in a public television biographical film of that name.

Born in Modena, Italy, Pavarotti received his diploma from Istituto Magistrale Carlo Sigo in 1955, and was an elementary schoolteacher and insurance salesman before turning to a musical career. He made his opera debut at Reggio Emilia, Italy, in 1961. As his reputation grew, he debuted at the Staatsoper Vienna and London's Royal Opera House in 1963, at the Metropolitan Opera in 1968, and the Paris Opera in 1973, also participating in a La Scala European tour (1963–64). Pavarotti has carried on an active solo recital and concert schedule since 1973, including notable concerts in London's Hyde Park (1991) and New York's Central Park (1993). He has also made numerous albums, among the most recent being *Pavarotti in the Park* (1991) and *Pavarotti and Friends* (1993). Pavarotti's many honors include winning the Concorso International at Reggio Emilia in 1961, and four Grammys for best classical vocal soloist performance (1978; 1979; 1981, with others; 1988). With the Opera Company of Philadelphia, he founded the Luciano Pavarotti Vocal Competition (1980). With William Wright, he wrote *Pavarotti: My Own Story* (1982). He is also a sometime painter. Pavarotti married Adua Veroni in 1961; they have three daughters.

FURTHER READING

"Tale of two tenors." WALTER PRICE. *Opera News,* Sept. 1993.
"Nights at the opera. . . ." DAVID REMNICK. *New Yorker,* June 21, 1993.
The Tenor's Son: My Days with Pavarotti. CANDIDO BONVICINI. St. Martin's, 1993.
"Lunch with. . . ." LIDIA BASTIANICH. *New York Times Magazine,* Oct. 11, 1992.

Pavarotti: Life with Luciano. ADUA PAVAROTTI and MIRELLA RICCIARDI. Rizzoli, 1992.

Penn, Sean (1960–) Actor, writer, director, and producer Sean Penn wrote and directed the 1995 film *The Crossing Guard,* starring Jack Nicholson as Freddy Gale, a man whose life fell apart six years earlier, when a drunken driver—David Morse, as John Booth—killed his son. Morse has served his prison sentence, and Nicholson sets out to kill him. Anjelica Huston is Mary, Nicholson's former wife; Robin Wright and Piper Laurie costar. The film's soundtrack includes songs by Bruce Springsteen.

Penn starred in the acclaimed film *Dead Man Walking,* written and directed by Tim Robbins, and starring Susan Sarandon as nun Helen Prejean opposite Penn as convicted rapist and murderer Matthew Poncelot, awaiting execution on the death row of of New Orleans' Angola Prison. Sister Prejean has responded as a matter of conscience to Poncelot's letter, asking her to visit him in prison, and then to his plea that she become his religious adviser during his final days. The film, based on Sister Prejean's best-selling book, costarred Robert Prosky, Raymond J. Barry, R. Lee Ermey, Celia Weston, Lois Smith, Scott Wilson, and Roberta Maxwell. Penn was nominated for a Golden Globe award as best actor in a drama for the role.

California-born Penn, son of director Leo Penn, emerged as one of the leading young film stars of the 1980s in such films as *Taps* (1981), *Fast Times at Ridgemont High* (1982), *Bad Boys* (1983), *Racing with the Moon* (1984), *The Falcon and the Snowman* (1985), *At Close Range* (1986; with his brother Christopher Penn), *Colors* (1988), *Judgment in Berlin* (1988), *Casualties of War* (1989), *We're No Angels* (1989), and *State of Grace* (1990). On stage, he has appeared in such plays as *Heartland* (1981) and *Hurlyburly* (1988). He wrote and directed the film *The Indian Runner* (1990) and appeared in *Carlito's Way* (1993). He was formerly married to Madonna (1985–89). Penn and actress Robin Wright have a daughter and a son.

FURTHER READING

"Sean Penn." GRAHAM FULLER. *Interview,* Oct. 1995.

"Penn, Sean." *Current Biography,* June 1993.
"Playboy interview. . . ." DAVID RENSIN. *Playboy,* Nov. 1991.
"Sean Penn. . . ." GAVIN SMITH. *Film Comment,* Sept.–Oct. 1991.

Peres, Shimon (Shimon Persky; 1923–) On November 4, right-wing Israeli terrorist Yigal Amir assassinated Israeli prime minister Yitzhak Rabin, who had just addressed a peace rally in Tel Aviv. Rabin was succeeded as prime minister by his longtime Labour Party associate, Foreign Minister Shimon Peres, who quickly moved to stabilize the badly shaken Israeli government and nation, investigate the inadequate security measures that had let the murderer get to Rabin so easily, and continue the Mideast peace process that he and Rabin had been so successfully developing. Peres became head of the Labour Party and immediately formed a new government, unopposed by the severely damaged right-wing Likud Party, which denounced the assassination but was widely accused of having greatly contributed to the climate in which it occurred.

Although his right-wing critics claimed that he had inaugurated a witchhunt in the wake of the Rabin assassination, Peres in fact stressed reconciliation between the far more isolated political and religious right and the majority of Israelis, who now strongly supported the government and the peace process. At the same time, he sought to even further isolate the extremely violent fringe groups that had generated the assassination and many other terrorist acts since the peace process began.

Peres also quickly demonstrated that he was determined to move the peace process forward, continuing to observe the previously agreed upon timetable for the withdrawal of Israeli forces from all major West Bank cities but Hebron by year's end, and scoring a possible breakthrough when long-stalled Syrian-Israeli peace negotiations restarted near Washington late in December. By the turn of the year, Peres firmly led Israel, continuity had been established, and the peace process was going forward.

Born in Vishneva (Wisniewa), Poland (now Belarus), Peres emigrated to Palestine with his family in 1934. He went into politics while still in his teens, becoming secretary of the Labor Youth movement in his early 20s. He fought with the Haganah during the Israeli War of Independence, then pursued a military career that included several senior naval and defense ministry posts. He headed a military mission to the United States in the late 1940s and early 1950s, and in that period studied at Harvard University and New York University. He was director-general of the Ministry of Defense (1953–59), then going directly into politics and winning election to the Knesset in 1959. He was deputy minister of defense (1959–65), and then held several senior government and Labour Party posts. He was acting prime minister briefly in 1977, became Labour Party head, and was coalition prime minister (1984–86), thereafter serving in a series of senior coalition government posts. He became foreign minister in 1992, then quickly emerged as a major figure in the developing Mideast peace process. Along with Rabin and Yasir Arafat, he was awarded the Nobel Peace Prize in 1994. His books include *The Next Step* (1965), *David's Sling* (1970), *Tomorrow Is Now* (1978), *From These Men* (1979), *The New Middle East* (1993), and the autobiography *Battling for Peace: A Memoir* (1994). Peres is married to Sonia Gelman; they had two sons, one now deceased.

FURTHER READING

" 'You can't live in fear.' " LILLY WEYMOUTH. *Newsweek*, Dec. 4, 1995.
"Rabinical. . . ." GERSHOM GORENBERG. *New Republic*, Dec. 4, 1995.
" 'We will pick up. . . .' " DAVID MAKOVSKY. *U.S. News & World Report*, Dec. 4, 1995.
"Shimon Peres's. . . ." JACOB HEILBRUNN. *New Republic*, July 10, 1995.
"Shimon Peres." MARK MARVEL. *Interview*, July 1995.

Perot, H. Ross (Henry Ross Perot; 1930–)

As the run-up to the 1996 presidential campaign began, Texas billionaire and failed 1992 independent presidential candidate H. Ross Perot stepped up his political activity. He began in a big way, hosting a Dallas conference of his United We Stand organization (Aug. 8–11, 1995) to discuss a possible third party and to hear many Republican presidential candidates, among them Bob Dole, Phil Gramm, Lamar Alexander, and Pat Buchanan, and such other politicians as Newt Gingrich and Democrats Richard Gephardt and Jesse Jackson. Perot addressed the meeting, but did not reveal his own plans.

In late September, during an appearance on the Larry King interview show, Perot announced the formation of the Independence Party, which would run a presidential candidate. Although he did not announce his own candidacy, the inference was strong, and became even stronger on October 24, when he claimed that the new party had met its first major deadline, and had filed the 900,000 signatures necessary to get on the ballot in California. If he ran, Perot was expected to spend tens of millions of dollars of his own money to press much the same issues as those taken up in his 1992 candidacy, including government economies, balancing the budget, congressional reforms, and electoral reforms. Many Republican politicians viewed his possible candidacy with dismay, believing that he had taken most of his votes in 1992 from George Bush, making it possible for Bill Clinton to win.

Born in Texarkana, Perot graduated from the U.S. Naval Academy in 1953, afterward serving four years in the navy. He worked as an IBM salesperson (1957–62), then founded Electronic Data Systems in 1962, and in the decades that followed built it into a major company, selling it to General Motors for $2.5 billion in 1984, and in doing so becoming GM's major stockholder. He resigned from the GM board of directors in 1986, and in 1988 founded Perot Systems. He has long been associated with attempts to secure more information about and possible release of

U.S. prisoners of war thought to be held in Vietnam.

In 1992, Perot used substantial sums of his own money to build what seemed in the spring to be a promising run for the presidency, making the campaign a three-way race. But his campaign faded in June and July, and he withdrew from the race on July 17, shocking and dismaying thousands of active campaigners and millions of supporters. On October 1, Perot reversed course again, announcing that he was once again a presidential candidate. He then proceeded to actively campaign, spending tens of millions of dollars on television advertising, and becoming a full participant in the Clinton-Bush-Perot televised presidential debates. But his candidacy had been fatally compromised by his earlier withdrawal, and although he won 19 percent of the popular vote on November 3, he won no electoral votes.

Perot and Margot Birmingham married in 1956; they have five children.

FURTHER READING

"Thunder in the center. . . ." KENNETH T. WALSH and JENNIFER SETER. *U.S. News & World Report*, Aug. 14, 1995.

" 'Stealth' candidates. . . ." CHI CHI SILEO. *Insight on the News*, Apr. 3, 1995.

"Party of spoilers." LAURENCE I. BARRETT. *Time*, Mar. 13, 1995.

Ross Perot: Billionaire Politician. CARMEN BREDESON. Enslow, 1995.

Ross Perot: Businessman Politician. AARON BOYD and MICHAEL CAUSEY. M. Reynolds, 1994.

Ross Perot: An American Maverick Speaks Out. BILL ADLER, ed. Carol, 1994.

"Does the Sphinx. . . ." WICK ALLISON. *National Review*, Sept. 20, 1993.

"Loving too much. . . ." FRED BARNES. *New Republic*, Aug. 9, 1993.

"Perot and con." CHRISTOPHER GEORGES. *Washington*, June 1993.

"Perot keeps. . . ." GLORIA BORGER and JERRY BUCKLEY. "Not thinking big enough." PAUL GLASTRIS. "The magnificent obsession." KENNETH T. WALSH and STEVEN V. ROBERTS. "A diversionary 'little war.' " DAVID R. GERGEN and GLORIA BORGER. *U.S. News & World Report*, May 17, 1993.

H. Ross Perot: The Man Who Woke Up America. BOB ITALIA. Abdo & Daughters, 1993.

H. Ross Perot. GENE BROWN. Rourke, 1993.

The Big Bio of Ross Perot. CAROLE MARSH. Gallopade, 1992.

Ross Perot: the Candidate: A Portrait of the Man and His Views. CECIL JOHNSON. Summit, 1992.

Ross Perot: In His Own Words. TONY CHIU. Warner, 1992.

Ross Perot Speaks Out: In His Own Words. JAMES W. ROBINSON. Prima, 1992.

Ross Perot: The Man Behind the Myth. KEN GROSS. Random House, 1992.

Perry, Anne (Juliet Hulme; 1938–) The exposure of murder mystery writer Anne Perry as herself a convicted murderer received a great deal of media attention in 1994 and 1995. The celebrated 1954 New Zealand case involved two girls, 16-year-old Pauline Yvonne Parker and 15-year-old Juliet Marion Hulme, who killed Parker's mother by beating her on the head with a brick inside a stocking. The two were convicted (Pauline's diary had outlined plans for the murder) and served five and a half years in prison; on release, they were given new identities on the proviso that they never see each other again. Peter Jackson's 1994 film, *Heavenly Creatures*, revived interest in the case, and journalist Lin Ferguson of New Zealand's *Sunday News* discovered that Hulme was now Perry. Perry did not deny the identification, saying she had not kept her past secret from close friends. She strongly denied the lesbian overtones of the film. She suggested that her judgment at the time of the murder may have been affected by a medication she was taking.

After opening in the United States in 1994, the film went into wide release in early 1995. At the same time, Perry was on a 23-city book promotion tour for *Traitors' Gate,* the 15th novel in her series featuring the late Victorian detectives Thomas and Charlotte Pitt. The tour included interviews on the "Today" show and in *People* magazine, though she declined appearances on "The Oprah Winfrey Show" and "60 Minutes." Later in the year she published another book, *Cain His Brother,* the sixth in the series featuring mid-Victorian detective William Monk; an audio version was read by Simon Jones.

London-born Hulme was frequently hospitalized with respiratory illnesses, was sent at age eight to the Bahamas for her health, and moved with her family to New Zealand a year later. When Hulme was again hospitalized, Parker was the only schoolmate to write to her consistently. Later, on the dissolution of her parents' marriage, Hulme was to be sent away from New Zealand; when Parker's mother refused to let her daughter go along, the two girls killed her.

On her release from prison, Perry worked in northern England for several years, then moved to the United States, mostly living in California, where she became a Mormon and worked at various jobs, including sales clerk, limousine dispatcher, and flight attendant. She returned to Britain in the early 1970s. Her first published mystery was *The Cater Street Hangman* (1978), introducing the Pitts. Her Monk series began with *Face of a Stranger* (1990). In 1992, she signed a $1 million contract for her next eight mysteries.

FURTHER READING

"Anne Perry. . . ." DULCY BRAINARD. *Publishers Weekly,* Mar. 27, 1995.
"Slaughter by." LOUISE CHUNN and SARAH GRISTWOOD. *Guardian,* Jan. 30, 1995.

Perry, Frank (1930–95) New York City–born Frank Perry began his career on the production side of the New York theater, moving into television as coproducer and host of the the documentary series "Playwright at Work." In 1961, he and his wife, playwright and screenwriter Eleanor Perry, collaborated on their debut and by far their most highly regarded film, the very low budget *David and Lisa,* winning directing and screenwriting Oscar nominations. They also collaborated as producers, directors,

and writers on *The Swimmer* (1968), *Last Summer* (1969), *Trilogy* (1969), and *Diary of a Mad Housewife* (1970). Frank Perry also directed and produced several other films, among them *Play It as It Lays* (1972), *Mommie Dearest* (1981), *Compromising Positions* (1985), *Hello Again* (1987), and his celebrated documentary about cancer, *On the Bridge* (1992), made after he had been diagnosed as having terminal cancer. Perry attended the University of Miami. He was survived by his third wife, Virginia, and two brothers. (d. New York City; August 29, 1995)

FURTHER READING

Obituary. *Current Biography,* Nov. 1995.
Obituary. *Times* (of London), Sept. 4, 1995.
Obituary. *Independent,* Sept. 2, 1995.
Obituary. *New York Times,* Aug. 29, 1995.

Perry, William James (1927–) Secretary of Defense William Perry continued to steadily pursue his middle-of-the-road military and political course in 1995, while overseeing the complex, worldwide American military establishment. Although facing far less budgetary pressure than most of his Clinton administration colleagues, he gave full public support to administration military base closing plans, at home and abroad. However, when congressional Republicans took steps to reduce American peace-keeping expenditures abroad, Perry came down on the other side, urging the president to use his veto power.

During 1995, the Bosnian War took much of Perry's time and attention. While urging caution, he supported American and NATO air strikes, full American logistical support to UN peace-keeping forces, and ultimately the use of American troops as peace-keepers.

Born in Vandergrift, Pennsylvania, Perry saw military service after World War II. He graduated from Stanford University in 1949, and holds a Ph.D. in mathematics from Pennsylvania State University. He has taught mathematics at Penn State and engineering at Stanford. He began his work as a military contractor in 1954, with GTE Sylvania, and founded his own highly successful military electronics firm, ESL Inc., in 1964. He was undersecretary of defense for research and engineering during the Carter administration (1976–1981), in that period developing the "stealth program," which would build the enormously expensive and quite effective radar-evading "stealth" aircraft that were later prominently displayed during the Persian Gulf War. He became secretary of defense early in 1994, succeeding Les Aspin and after the withdrawal of Bobby Ray Inman, who had first been nominated for the post. Perry has coauthored numerous reports, among them *A New Concept of Cooperative Security* (1992), *New Thinking and American Defense Technology* (1993), and *Science, Technology, and Government for a Changing World* (1993). Perry is married to Lee (Leonilla) Mary Green; they have three sons and two daughters.

FURTHER READING

"Perry, William J." *Current Biography*, Jan. 1995.
"The old boy. . . ." NICK GILBERT and JENNIFER REINGOLD. *Financial World*, Aug. 16, 1994.
"Perry's parry. . . ." CHARLES LANE. *New Republic*, June 27, 1994.
"Perry forges. . . ." ANTHONY L. VELOCCI. *Aviation Week & Space Technology*, Nov. 15, 1993.

Peters, Ellis: See Pargeter, Edith.

Peterson, Melvin Norman (1929–95)

Illinois-born Melvin Peterson was one of the world's leading marine geologists. He received his 1951 B.S. and 1956 M.S. from Northwestern University, and his 1960 Ph.D. from Harvard University, then joining the faculty of La Jolla's Scripps Institute of Oceanography of the University of California (1960–87). Peterson, whose major field was the study of ocean sediments, was chief scientist of the landmark Scripps Deep Sea Drilling Project (1967–72), and later director of the project (1973–87). In its more than 15 years of worldwide cruising and core sampling, the project's drilling ship, the *Glomar Challenger*, made a major contribution to understanding of the structures and workings of Earth's crustal plates and to marine geology, also providing irrefutable support for the tectonic plate theory. Peterson was chief scientist of the National Oceanic and Atmospheric Administration (1987–89), and then director of Honolulu's Ocean Policy Institute (1989–95). He was survived by his wife, Margaret, two daughters, and two sons. (d. Mexico; September 20, 1995)

FURTHER READING

Obituary. *New York Times*, Sept. 23, 1995.

Pfeiffer, Michelle (1959–)

Film star Michelle Pfeiffer remained a very familiar face on American television screens during 1995, with *Love Field* and *The Age of Innocence* in wide release, and her 1994 *Wolf* a home video rental hit.

She starred in the 1995 film *Dangerous Minds*, as LouAnne Johnson, a former Marine who becomes an innovative, successful English teacher in a tough, depressed urban area high school. John N. Smith directed; Ronald Bass wrote the screenplay, adapted from Johnson's autobiographical book *My Posse Don't Do No Homework*. The cast included George Dzundza, Courtney B. Vance, Robin Bartlett, Bruklin Harris, Renoly Santiago, and Wade Dominguez.

Forthcoming were starring roles opposite Robert Redford in the film *Up Close and Personal*, directed by Jon Avnet and costarring Stockard Channing, Joe Mantegna, Dedee Pfeiffer, Glenn Plummer, and Kate Nelligan; and in the film *To Gillian, on Her 37th Birthday*, directed by Michael Pressman and costarring Kathy Bates, Clair Danes, and Peter Gallagher. Pfeiffer will also produce and star in the forthcoming film *Vanished*. Still forthcoming was a starring role opposite Richard Gere in the film *Higgins and Beach*, directed by Jon Amiel.

315

California-born Pfeiffer very quickly emerged as one of the leading film players of the 1980s, starring in such films as *Grease 2* (1982), *Scarface* (1983), *Into the Night* (1984), *Ladyhawke* (1985), *Sweet Liberty* (1986), *The Witches of Eastwick* (1987), *Married to the Mob* (1988), *Tequila Sunrise* (1988), *Dangerous Liaisons* (1989), *The Fabulous Baker Boys* (1989; she was nominated for an Oscar), *The Russia House* (1990), *Frankie and Johnny* (1991), *Batman Returns* (1992), *Love Field* (1992), *The Age of Innocence* (1993), and *Wolf* (1994). In the summer of 1989, she appeared as Olivia in *Twelfth Night* at the New York Shakespeare Festival. Pfeiffer attended Whitley College. Formerly married to actor Peter Horton, she is married to David Kelley. She has a daughter and two sons.

FURTHER READING

"Michelle Pfeiffer. . . ." ROB TANNENBAUM. *Us*, Aug. 1995.
"Michelle Pfeiffer." GRAHAM FULLER. *Interview*, July 1994.
"Belle Michelle." LESLIE BENNETTS. *Vanity Fair*, Sept. 1993.
"Blond ambivalence." JAMES KAPLAN and TY BURR. *Entertainment*, Jan. 29, 1993.
"The bat's meow. . . ." GERRI HIRSHEY. *Rolling Stone*, Sept. 3, 1992.
"What she did. . . ." JEFF ROVIN. *Ladies Home Journal*, June 1992.
"Tough guise." JONATHAN VAN METER. *Vogue*, Oct. 1991.
"Queen for a decade." MARC ELIOT. *California*, Sept. 1991.
"The fabulous. . . ." ROBERT SEIDENBERG. *American Film*, Jan. 1991.

Pleasence, Donald (1919–95) English actor Donald Pleasence made his stage debut in 1939, in a regional production of *Wuthering Heights*. After World War II military service, he built his theater career, appearing on both sides of the Atlantic; he made his Broadway debut in *Caesar and Cleopatra* (1951), and made a major breakthrough as Davies in Harold Pinter's *The Caretaker* (1960). From the early 1970s, he focused on theatrical films and television, in a wide range of starring and strong supporting roles. His most notable television roles were as Septimus Harding in *The Barchester Chronicles* (1982) and as the old spy, opposite Tom Conti in Dennis Potter's *Blade on the Feather*. He played

in scores of horror films, often as the central villain of the piece, and also in a wide range of other films, among them *Look Back in Anger* (1959), *Sons and Lovers* (1960), *The Caretaker* (1963), *You Only Live Twice* (as Blofeld), *The Madwoman of Chaillot* (1969), *The Eagle Has Landed* (1976), and *Shadows and Fog* (1992). He was survived by his fourth wife, Linda, and five daughters. (d. St. Paul de Vence, France; Feb. 2, 1995)

FURTHER READING

Obituary. *Times* (of London), Feb. 3, 1995.
Obituary. *Independent*, Feb. 3, 1995.
Obituary. *New York Times*, Feb. 3, 1995.
Obituary. *Variety*, Feb. 3, 1995.

Porter, Eric Richard (1928–95) London-born Eric Porter began his half-century in the British theater in 1945, as a bit player in repertory, and continued to play in repertory companies, among them the Birmingham Rep and the Old Vic, during the late 1940s and early 1950s, in increasingly strong supporting roles. Multiple breakthroughs into starring roles came in 1954, when he starred in his first *King Lear,* and in *Uncle Vanya* and *Volpone*. In 1957, he created the Romanoff role in Peter Ustinov's *Romanoff and Juliet,* and in 1959 won the *Evening Standard* best actor of the year award for his Rosmer in *Rosmersholm*. He was to star in a wide range of classic and modern stage roles well into the 1990s, and in 1988 won another *Evening Standard* best actor award for his Big Daddy in Tennessee Williams's *Cat on a Hot Tin Roof*. Porter was best known to worldwide audiences for his role as Soames Forsyte in television's *The Forsyte Saga* (1967). Among his other major television roles were the title role in *Cyrano de Bergerac* (1966), and his Polonius to Derek Jacobi's Hamlet in 1980. He also appeared in several theatrical films, among them *The Heroes of Telemark* (1965), *Nicholas and Alexandra* (1971), *The Day of the Jackal* (1973), and *The 39 Steps* (1978). There were no survivors. (d. London; May 15, 1995)

FURTHER READING

Obituary. *Variety*, May 22, 1995.
Obituary. *Times* (of London), May 17, 1995.
Obituary. *New York Times*, May 17, 1995.
Obituary. *Independent*, May 17, 1995.

Powell, Colin Luther (1937–) Former

Joint Chiefs of Staff chairman General Colin Powell emerged as a major American political figure in 1995. With very large numbers of Americans disenchanted with the leadership of both major political parties, and although he had not announced his candidacy, he clearly became the presidential choice of millions of American voters, for months running far ahead of President Bill Clinton and Senator Bob Dole in most presidential polls. What made his status even more extraordinary was that he was the first African-American who might have become a major-party presidential candidate. Some observers thought that he even might have won as a third-party candidate.

Powell published his autobiography, *My American Journey,* written with Joseph E. Persico, in September; it was a runaway best-seller, and his triumphal author's tour in support of the book made it very clear that a great many Americans were ready to press his candidacy. But it was not to be. On November 8, Powell announced that he would not run, and would not consider a vice-presidential candidacy. For the first time, he also announced a political affiliation, stating that he was a Republican. He did not reveal any other future plans.

New York–born Powell began his long military career in 1958. He held a series of line and staff posts in Europe and the United States, including command posts in the 101st Airborne and 4th Infantry divisions. He was national security affairs assistant to President Reagan (1987–89). He was then appointed chairman of the Joint Chiefs of Staff by President George Bush on August 10, 1989; it was a historic "first," as he was the first African-American to hold the post. One of his earliest major tasks was the organization of the December 1989 Panama invasion. He also sent American forces into El Salvador, Liberia, and the Philippines, and played a major role in the Persian Gulf War. He retired in September 1993. In 1994, he, former president Jimmy Carter, and Senator Sam Nunn negotiated a peaceful surrender and agreement by Haiti's military rulers to step down, averting an American invasion of Haiti.

Powell's 1958 B.S. was from the City University of New York, and his 1971 M.B.A. from George Washington University. Most unusual for one who went so far in the U.S. Army, he is not a West Point graduate, instead having become an officer through the Reserve Officer Training Corps (ROTC). He married Alma Johnson in 1962; they have three children.

FURTHER READING

"The culture of caution." ORLANDO PATTERSON. "Family or country?" *New Republic*, Nov. 27, 1995.
"America's son." *National Review*, Nov. 27, 1995.
"Why he got out." EVAN THOMAS. *Newsweek*, Nov. 20, 1995.
"Rivals or partners?" *Economist*, Nov. 4, 1995.
"Why almost everybody. . . ." LAURA B. RANDOLPH. *Ebony*, Nov. 1995.
"General on parade." MARK LAWSON. *Guardian*, Oct. 11, 1995.
"Politics by the book." DANIEL SCHORR. *The New Leader*, Oct. 9, 1995.
"Tour de force. . . ." THOMAS FIELDS-MEYER and LINDA KRAMER. *People*, Oct. 2, 1995.
"The great black hope." MARJORIE WILLIAMS. *Vanity Fair*, Oct. 1995.
"Why Powell's race. . . ." JONATHAN ALTER. "A Powell scenario. . . ." HOWARD FINEMAN. *Newsweek*, Sept. 25, 1995.
"Can he stay on. . . ." JEFFREY H. BIRNBAUM. *Time*, Sept. 25, 1995.
" 'I've got to make. . . .' " JOHN F. STACKS and MICHAEL KRAMER. "My American journey." COLIN L. POWELL and JOSEPH E. PERSICO. "Powell on Powell." JAMES KELLY. *Time*, Sept. 18, 1995.
"There is something . . . ." DAVID HALBERSTAM. *Parade*, Sept. 17, 1995.
"Looking for a hero." STEPHEN E. AMBROSE. "The very model. . . ." JOHN BARRY. "Powell on the March." EVAN THOMAS et al. *Newsweek*, Sept. 11, 1995.
"Beltway warrior." MICHAEL R. GORDON and BERNARD E. TRAINOR. *New York Times Magazine*, Aug. 27, 1995.
"The man to watch." JOHN WALCOTT. *U.S. News & World Report*, Aug. 21, 1995.
"The Powell factor." JOHN T. STACKS. *Time*, July 10, 1995.
"The legend of . . . ." *New Republic*, Apr. 17, 1995.
" 'Stealth' candidates. . . ." CHI CHI SILEO. *Insight on the News*, Apr. 3, 1995.
"The candidate of dreams." J. F. O. MCALLISTER. *Time*, Mar. 13, 1995.
Colin Powell: Military Leader. MELISSA BANTA. Chelsea House, 1994.
Sacred Honor: Colin Powell: The Inside Account of His Life and Triumphs. DAVID ROTH. Zondervan, 1993.
Colin Powell. DAVID ROTH and LINDA L. MAIFAIR. Zondervan, 1993.
Colin Powell: A Biography. HOWARD MEANS. Ballantine, 1993.
Colin Powell: Soldier-Statesman-Statesman-Soldier. HOWARD MEANS. Fine, 1992.

Colin Powell: A Man of War and Peace. CARL SENNA. Walker, 1992.

Colin Powell. CATHERINE REEF. 21st Century Books, 1992.

Colin Powell: A Biography. JAMES HASKINS. Scholastic, 1992.

Colin Powell. WARREN BROWN. Chelsea House, 1992.

Story of Colin Powell and Benjamin Davis. KATHERINE APPLEGATE. Dell, 1992.

Preston, Lewis Thompson (1926–95)

New York City–born Lewis Preston was one of the world's leading bankers. After his 1951 graduation from Harvard University, he began his long career at J. P. Morgan and Co. and its successors, and completed his long climb to the top of the bank in the late 1970s, becoming president of J. P. Morgan and the Morgan Guaranty Trust Co. in 1978, and board chairman of both organizations in 1980. He retired from Morgan in February 1991, and that September became chairman of the World Bank. In that position, he exerted a good deal of influence on the course of economic and political events in many developing countries, during his period as chairman deemphasizing such matters as payback guarantees and austerity programs in borrowing countries, and emphasizing the beneficial impact of the World Bank's loans. Preston especially encouraged loans for environmental improvement purposes, adding many environmental loan officers in a period in which he was sharply cutting the bank's bureaucracy. He was survived by his wife, Gladys (Patsy) Pulitzer Preston, and five daughters. (d. Washington, D.C.; May 4, 1995)

FURTHER READING

Obituary. *Independent,* June 2, 1995.
Obituary. *New York Times,* May 6, 1995.

Price, Reynolds (1933–)

In 1995, American writer Reynolds Price published the third (and presumably final) novel about the Mayfield family, *The Promise of Rest,* a saga that had begun twenty years earlier with *The Surface of Earth* (1975) and continued with *The Source of Light* (1981). Its central character is Hutch Mayfield, a North Carolina university teacher, estranged from his wife, who, on learning that his only child, Wade, is dying of AIDS, brings him home to die. Though some critics regarded the work as flawed, suggesting that its characters were "assemblages of attitudes" rather than fully realized characters, others called this Price's best novel so far and lauded the book's richness and beauty.

Born in Macon, North Carolina, Price received his 1955 A.B. summa cum laude from Duke University, and his 1958 B.Litt. after study as a Rhodes scholar at Merton College, Oxford University. A novelist, poet, essayist, playwright, and short story writer, he returned to Duke to teach English and remained there, except for occasional periods as writer-in-residence or visiting professor elsewhere. *A Long and Happy Life* (1962), probably still his best-known work, won the William Faulkner award for most notable first novel. His other works include *The Names and Faces of Heroes* (1963), *A Generous Man* (1966), *Love and Work* (1968), *Permanent Errors* (1970), *Things Themselves* (1972), *The Surface of Earth* (1975), *Early Dark* (1977), *A Palpable God* (1978), *The Source of Light* (1981), *Vital Provisions* (1982), *Private Contentment* (1984), *Kate Vaiden* (1986; it won the National Book Critics Circle Award), *The Laws of Ice* (1986), *A Common Room* (1987), *Good Hearts* (1988), *Clear Pictures* (1989), *The Tongues of Angels* (1990), *The Use of Fire* (1990), *New Music* (1990), *The Foreseeable Future* (1991), *Conversations with Reynolds Price* (1991), *Blue Calhoun* (1992), *Full Moon* (1993), and *The Collected Stories* (1993). In 1994, Price published *A Whole New Life: An Illness and a Healing,* about his experience with and treatment of spinal cancer, diagnosed in 1984.

FURTHER READING

"Outlaw Christian. . . ." SARAH J. FODOR. *The Christian Century,* Nov. 22, 1995.
Parting the Curtains: Interviews with Southern Writers. DANNYE R. POWELL. Blair, 1994.
"Reynolds Price. . . ." WENDY SMITH. *Publishers Weekly,* May 9, 1994.
"Not so awfully. . . ." RICHARD E. NICHOLLS. *New York Times Book Review,* July 4, 1993.
"A conversation with. . . ." JAMES T. BLACK. *Southern Living,* Sept. 1992.
"Reynolds Price. . . ." BARBARA HOFFERT. *Library Journal,* Apr. 15, 1992.
Conversations with Reynolds Price. JEFFERSON HUMPHRIES, ed. University Press of Mississippi, 1991.

Prince (Prince Rogers Nelson; 1958–)

Though still called Prince by his fans the world over, "the artist formerly known as Prince" has since 1993 been legally named an unpronounceable, nonstandard male-female "love" symbol. Whatever his name, the artist received a 1995 American Music Awards Award of Merit for his entire body of work, rather than for a specific current work or works. He also received a best pop vocal performance Grammy nomination for "The Most Beautiful Girl in the World."

Prince's 1995 album was the well-received *The Gold Experience,* most of the songs stressing the sexual side of life, as in his earlier work. Among the songs were his hit single "I Hate You," "The Most Beautiful Girl in the World," "Now," and "Endorphinmachine."

On the personal side, Prince put his Beverly Hills home on the market in October; he has other homes in his native Minneapolis and in France.

Minneapolis-born Prince emerged as a recording star in the late 1970s and early 1980s, and starred in the film *Purple Rain* (1984), winning a 1985 Oscar for best original score. He also won three Grammys in 1985. His albums include *For You* (1978), *Dirty Mind* (1979), *Controversy* (1981), *Purple Rain* (1984), *Around the World in a Day* (1985), *Parade* (1986), *Sign O' the Times* (1987), *Lovesexy* (1988), *Batman* (1989), *Diamonds and Pearls* (1991), his album titled with the Prince-symbol (1992), the three-CD collection *The Hits* (1993), *The Black Album* (1994; made in 1987, but withheld by Prince), and *Come* (1994). He also released the video film *3 Chains O' Gold* (1994) and the multimedia CD-ROM *Interactive* (1994). Prince has also appeared in the films *Under the Cherry Moon* (1986), *Sign O' the Times* (1987), and *Graffiti Bridge* (1990). The enormously prolific Prince also writes songs for other artists, and composed the music for the ballet *Billboards* (1993).

FURTHER READING

"Audience with...." DAN GLAISTER. *Guardian,* Mar. 3, 1995.
"Prince's purple reign." BOB CANNON. *Entertainment,* July 22, 1994.

Pryce, Jonathan (1947–) British actor Jonathan Pryce starred in 1995 as noted biographer Lytton Strachey opposite Emma Thompson as Dora Carrington in the title role of the film *Carrington;* both were members of the group of loosely associated, very talented friends who lived and worked in and around London's Bloomsbury area, and so became known as the Bloomsbury Group. Christopher Hampton directed and wrote the screenplay, adapted from Michael Holroyd's biography *Lytton Strachey;* the cast included Steve Waddington, Samuel West, Rufus Sewell, Penelope Wilton, and Janet McNeer. Pryce won the Cannes Film Festival best actor award.

Pryce also starred on the London stage as Fagin in a revival of the musical *Oliver,* Lionel Bart's adaptation of the Charles Dickens novel *Oliver Twist.*

Forthcoming was a starring role as Argentine dictator Juan Perón in the film *Evita,* adapted from the Andrew Lloyd Webber/Andrew Rice hit stage musical, directed by Alan Parker and co-starring Madonna in the title role as Evita Perón and Antonio Banderas as Che Guevara.

A leading British actor, Pryce has played in a series of major stage roles from the mid-1970s. He won a Tony for *The Comedians* (1976), a production originating in England that transferred to New York. His 1980 *Hamlet* won Britain's Olivier Award. His plays include *The Caretaker* (1981), *Accidental Death of an Anarchist* (1984), *The Seagull* (1985), *Macbeth* (1986; he played the title role), and *Uncle Vanya* (1988). Pryce was widely acclaimed for his portrayal of the Eurasian pimp in the musical *Miss Saigon* (1989), with which he moved from London to Broadway, where he won a 1991 Tony as leading actor in a musical. He has also appeared in such films as *The Ploughman's Lunch* (1983), *Brazil* (1985), *The Doctor and the Devils* (1986), *Consuming Passions* (1988), *The Adventures of Baron Munchausen* (1988), *The Rachel Papers* (1989), *The Man from the Pru* (1991), *Glengarry Glen Ross* (1992), *The Age of Innocence* (1993), *A Business Affair* (1993), and *Thicker Than Water* (1994); in several television films, including *Barbarians at the Gate* (1993); and in television series, notably "Roger Doesn't Live Here Any More" (1981). Pryce attended the Royal Academy of Dramatic Art. He is married to actress Kate Fahy; they have three children.

FURTHER READING

"In step with...." JAMES BRADY. *Parade,* Dec. 10, 1995.
"What Pryce glory...." JEFF GORDINIER. *Entertainment,* Nov. 17, 1995.
"Mr. Saigon." MICHAEL BILLINGTON. *Interview,* Apr. 1991.
"Mr. Saigon...." CHRIS SMITH. *New York,* Mar. 11, 1991.

R

Rabin, Yitzhak (1922–95) Israeli Prime Minister Yitzhak Rabin was assassinated on November 4 in Tel Aviv after addressing a peace rally. His assassin was 25-year-old Yigal Amir, who was seized on the scene, confessed to the murder, and later reenacted it for the police. Amir, who claimed to have acted alone, was associated with right-wing terrorist groups opposing the Middle East peace process. Israeli police, charging conspiracy, arrested several of his associates shortly after the murder, as a wide-ranging investigation of the murder—and of why Israeli security measures failed—proceeded.

Yigal Amir (1970–) was an Israeli seminary and law student, a right-wing, ultrareligious zealot who opposed the Middle East peace process and thought Rabin a traitor who deserved to die. At year's end, the trials of Amir and any alleged coconspirators had not yet been scheduled, and Israeli public opinion had swung decisively toward the peace process, now being led for Israel by Prime Minister Shimon Peres. Whether Amir acted alone or with others was a matter of intense debate, and probably would be for decades.

Rabin's November 6 state funeral was attended by many Arab leaders and included a eulogy by King Hussein of Jordan. President Bill Clinton and Hillary Rodham Clinton led an American delegation that included former presidents Carter and Bush, with the leaders of many other nations also in attendance.

Many Israelis and others, including members of Rabin's family, charged that the murder had been greatly encouraged by the hard-line Israeli

opposition to the peace process, led by the Likud Party, which had repeatedly charged Rabin and other Israeli leaders with being traitors; there had certainly been many death threats from the far right fringe of the antipeace movement. Likud leaders and others in opposition publicly condemned Rabin's murder and denied all responsibility. But the Israeli public, formerly split almost evenly, was shaken by the murder, and moved decisively toward Rabin's party and the peace movement, so much so that the Likud Party quickly announced that it would not oppose formation of a new Labour-led government, led by former foreign minister Shimon Peres, who had become acting prime minister after Rabin's death. In power, Peres continued to implement the Middle East peace process.

During 1995, before his assassination, Prime Minister Rabin had continued to develop the peace process. On September 28, in a White House ceremony, he and Palestine National Authority (PNA) leader Yasir Arafat had signed a detailed agreement providing for greatly increased Palestinian home rule on the West Bank and in the Gaza Strip, areas occupied by Israel in 1967, after the Six-Day War (Third Arab-Israeli War). After more than a year of hard negotiation, the agreement had been initialed by Arafat and Shimon Peres on September 24; Rabin had then pushed it through the Israeli parliament, despite bitter opposition from hardliners. Opposition had continued afterward, with mounting rioting by hard-line Israeli settlers and intensified terrorism by Hamas Islamic fundamentalists. Many issues also remained unsettled, most notably the future of Jerusalem, apparently regarded as nonnegotiable by both sides. During 1995, Rabin had also been engaged in the as-yet unproductive peace talks with Syria and negotiations with Iran and other neighboring countries.

Jerusalem-born Rabin spent all of his adult life involved in war and politics. He was an officer in the Israeli frontline fighting force, the Palmach (1943–48), through the Israeli War of Independence (First Arab-Israeli War), and remained a soldier, rising to become commander in chief of the Northern Command (1956–59), deputy chief of staff (1960–64), and chief of staff (1964–68), achieving the rank of major-general. He was later Israeli ambassador to the United States (1968–73). Rabin entered the Knesset (Parliament) in 1974, in that year briefly serving as minister of labor, then became head of the Labour Party and prime minister, holding both posts until 1977.

Rabin became defense minister in the 1984 coalition government, taking personal responsibility for the repression of the Palestinian Intifada (Uprising) that began in 1988. He became leader of the Labour Party in February 1992 and prime minister after Labour's victory in June 1992. On September 13, 1993, after long, complex negotiations that often seemed on the point of collapse, Rabin and PLO Chairman Yasir Arafat shook hands on the White House lawn, approving the historic declaration of principles that established the basis for Palestinian

self-rule. On May 4, 1994, Rabin and Arafat concluded the equally historic agreement on Palestinian self-rule in the Gaza Strip and Jericho, which was followed by Arafat's return to Palestine and the founding of the Palestine National Authority. Rabin, Arafat, and Peres were awarded the 1994 Nobel Peace Prize for their roles in developing the Middle East peace process.

Rabin published *The Rabin Memoirs* (1979) and, with Uri Lubrani, *Israel's Lebanon Policy: Where To?* (1984). He was educated at the Kadoorie Agricultural School and at military colleges. He was survived by his wife, Leah Schlossberg, and two children. (d. Tel Aviv; November 4, 1995)

FURTHER READING

Obituary. *National Review*, Dec. 11, 1995.
"Rabinical. . . ." GERSHOM GORENBERG. *New Republic*, Dec. 4, 1995.
"Swamp man." MOSHE HALBERTAL. *New Republic*, Nov. 27, 1995. [on Amir]
"Death of a soldier." PETER W. RODMAN. *National Review*, Nov. 27, 1995.
"Israel divided." MILTON VIORST. "Rabin's legacy." *Nation*, Nov. 27, 1995.
"Determined to bury. . . ." FRED COLEMAN. "Yigal Amir. . . ." LARRY DERFNER and JONATHAN SAPERS. "The struggle for. . . ." RICHARD Z. CHESNOFF and DAVID MAKOVSKY. "The tears of autumn. . . ." FOUAD AJAMI. *U.S. News & World Report*, Nov. 20, 1995.
" 'We became more. . . .' " SCOTT MACLEOD. *Time*, Nov. 20, 1995.
"Made in Israel." THOMAS FIELDS-MEYER. *People*, Nov. 20, 1995.
"Yitzhak Rabin. . . ." DANIEL T. WACKERMAN. *America*, Nov. 18, 1995.
"An indispensable man. . . ." PETER McGRATH. "Israel vs. Israel." TOM MASLAND. "Can peace survive?" EVAN THOMAS. *Newsweek*, Nov. 13, 1995.
"A martyr to peace. . . ." NOMI MORRIS. *Maclean's*, Nov. 13, 1995.
"Man of Israel." KEVIN FEDARKO. "Thou shalt not kill." STEVE WULF. " 'A majority of one.' " *Time*, Nov. 13, 1995.
Obituary. *Economist*, Nov. 11, 1995.
"The gun's argument." *Economist*, Nov. 11, 1995. [on Amir]
Obituary. *Times* (of London), Nov. 6, 1995.
Obituary. *Independent*, Nov. 6, 1995.
Obituary. *New York Times*, Nov. 5, 1995.
" 'What we ask. . . .' " DAVID MAKOVSKY. *U.S. News & World Report*, Apr. 24, 1995.
"Rabin, Yitzhak." *Current Biography*, Jan. 1995.
" 'I understand. . . .' " LALLY WEYMOUTH. *Newsweek*, Mar. 14, 1994.

"Yitzhak Rabin. . . ." NANCY GIBBS. "To conquer the past." LANCE MORROW. *Time*, Jan. 3, 1994. (Men of the Year: The Peacemakers)
Rabin of Israel. ROBERT SLATER. St. Martin's, 1993.

Rafsanjani, Ali Akbar Hashemi

(1934–) Although his domestic opponents continued to gain strength in 1995, Iranian President Ali Akbar Rafsanjani made some gains in his effort to break Iran out of its economic isolation. Despite United Nations sanctions, still in effect, Iran was largely able to sell its oil abroad—though President Bill Clinton did block a proposed Conoco-Iran oil deal in March and reaffirmed U.S. prohibitions on all such deals by U.S. oil companies with Iran. Rafsanjani also concluded a major agreement to supply Turkey with natural gas, made major arms purchases from Russia, and extended Iranian trade with the countries of the former Soviet Union and east throughout Asia. Citing Iran's continuing support of international terrorism, and responding to domestic pressures, the U.S. and its closest Western allies had some success in forcing Russia to at least delay fulfilling its agreement to sell nuclear plants to Iran. President Clinton in May formally strengthened its embargo on trade with Iran; but most other industrial nations continued to expand their trade with Iran, even while expressing mild support for the embargo. Yet although Rafsanjani's position strengthened somewhat abroad during 1995, his domestic opposition also strengthened, raising renewed questions about his future.

Rafsanjani was long associated with Ayatollah Ruholla Khomeini. He became a key figure in Iranian politics as speaker of the national assembly during the 1980s. As speaker, he sometimes played the role of hard-line Iranian politician, as in 1989 when he called for the assassination of the author Salman Rushdie for writing *The Satanic Verses,* but sometimes functioned as a relative moderate who made very tentative overtures to the West in a bid to reestablish broken relationships.

He became president of Iran in August 1989, during the period of maneuvering that followed Khomeini's death. Facing a mounting economic crisis at home and growing American power in the Middle East, he took a markedly conciliatory attitude after the Persian Gulf War defeat of Iraq, calling for economic ties with the West and other Gulf nations. This conciliatory attitude also extended to the American and European hostages held in Lebanon by the Iranian-controlled Hezbollah (Party of God). In autumn 1991, following a September 10–13 Tehran meeting between UN Secretary-General Javier Pérez de Cuéllar and Rafsanjani, nine of the eleven remaining Western hostages held in Lebanon were released. In June 1993, Rafsanjani was elected to a second four-year presidential term, gaining a reported 63 percent of the vote, in an election in which three opposing candidates were not allowed to campaign. As Iran's economic problems deepened during 1993 and 1994, Rafsanjani encountered increasing domestic opposition, including low-level antigovernment guerrilla actions and a continuing Kurdish insurgency.

Rafsanjani's personal life has been kept very private, but it is known that he is married and has several children.

FURTHER READING

"Rafsanjani's advice. . . ." JAMES R. GAINES and KARSTEN PRAGER. *Time*, May 31, 1993.

Raitt, Bonnie Lynn (1949–) Singer and songwriter Bonnie Raitt won a 1995 Grammy Award for best pop album for her hit 1994 album *Longing in Their Hearts,* as well as a best pop vocal performance Grammy nomination for her rendition of the title song from the album. She also received Grammy nominations for best female rock vocal performance and best record for "Love Sneakin' Up on You," a hit single from the album.

In 1995, Raitt issued yet another hit album, the very well-received two-CD *Road Tested,* recorded during her 1995 summer tour, which included six new songs in its 22 tracks. The album contained a duet with Bryan Adams, "Rock Steady," which became a hit single; and another version of "Love Sneakin' Up on You," plus such other songs as "Feeling of Falling" and "I Can't Make You Love Me."

Raitt sang Roy Orbison's "You Got It" in the soundtrack album of Whoopi Goldberg's 1994 film *Boys on the Side;* her song, which begins and ends the album, became a hit single. She also sang three duets with her father, John Raitt, in his 1995 album *John Raitt—Broadway*

Legend. She also joined Whoopi Goldberg again, with Goldberg appearing as her interviewer in the ABC After-School Special *Bonnie Raitt Has Something to Talk About.*

California-born Raitt attended Radcliffe College, dropping out to pursue a musical career and becoming a popular folk and blues figure in the early 1970s with such albums as *Bonnie Raitt* (1971), *Give It Up* (1972), *Streetlights* (1974), and *Sweet Forgiveness* (1977). Far less popular in the 1980s, she made a major comeback with *Nick of Time* (1989), sweeping the 1990 Grammy Awards for best album, best female pop vocal, and best female rock vocal for the album and its title song, as well as best traditional blues recording for "I'm in the Mood," a duet with John Lee Hooker on his album *The Healer.* She followed this with *Luck of the Draw* (1991), *Something to Talk About* (1992), and *Longing in Their Hearts* (1994). She married actor Michael O'Keefe in 1991.

FURTHER READING

"Prime Raitt...." CHRIS GILL. *Guitar Player* Aug. 1994.
"Bonnie and the blues." RICHARD CORLISS. *Time*, Apr. 4, 1994.
"Bonnie Raitt." JAS OBRECHT. *Guitar Player*, Feb. 1994.

Rao, P. V. Narasimha (Pamulaparti Venkate Narasimha Rao; 1921–) During 1995 Indian Prime Minister P. V. Rao continued his effort to redirect India's massive economy, largely through privatization of previously state-operated functions; price deregulation, even of long-regulated basic commodities and energy sources; and cuts in India's large social service network expenditures. His efforts met with little success, at least in the short term, instead generating social unrest and continuing massive electoral losses for his Congress Party. Late in the year, with mid-1996 all-India elections approaching, many Congress Party leaders were discussing new leadership candidates. He did, however, seem to have survived the Cabinet-level corruption scandals that late in 1994 had seemed an immediate threat to his career, although he was in no way involved.

Rao was also plagued by continuing guerrilla war in Kashmir and other areas of northern India, where Pakistani-assisted Muslim insurgent movements continued their now 48-year-long war of secession, while pressure grew on Rao and Pakistani Prime Minister Benazir Bhutto to escalate the long confrontation into a third India-Pakistan war. Both resisted escalation, and both at great personal and political risk. On August 31, civil war again intensified in Punjab, as Sikh separatists detonated a car bomb outside the government center at Chandigarh, the state capital, killing 13 people, including Chief Minister Beant Singh.

Born in Uttar Pradesh, Rao is a longtime Congress Party leader, who supported Indira Gandhi during her rise to power and went with her faction when the party split in 1969. He was chief minister of the state of Andra Pradesh (1971–73) and held several Cabinet positions thereafter, including four years as Indian foreign minister (1980–84). Rao was named prime minister on June 20, 1991, after the assassination of Indian Prime Minister Rajiv Gandhi.

Initially expected to serve as a caretaker, Rao held on to power once he had it, introducing major economic changes that shifted India's socialist, central-planning commitment to focus on the development of a market economy, including the privatization of many state-run enterprises. This impacted adversely on the great masses of India's poor, who lost some of what was already a very slim social services support network, worsening the effects of India's massive economic problems. During the early 1990s, Rao's government was also forced to cope with India's deep and long-standing ethnic and religious problems, with massive Hindu-Muslim clashes throughout India after the December 1992 Hindu fundamentalist destruction of the historic Ayodhya mosque, a wave of 1993 bombings, and continuing guerrilla wars in Kashmir, Jammu, and several other states throughout his period in office.

Rao is also a well-known translator and writer. He attended the universities of Bombay and Nagpur. He has eight children.

FURTHER READING

"Moon-faced matador...." DONALD TRELFORD. *Observer*, Feb. 7, 1993.
"The accidental...." SUBRATA CHAKRAVARTY. *Forbes*, July 20, 1992.
"Rao, P. V. Narasimha." *Current Biography*, Jan. 1992.
Prime Minister P. V. Narasimha Rao: The Scholar and the Statesman. South Asia Books, 1991.

Rather, Dan

Rather, Dan (1931–) Veteran broadcaster Dan Rather was a survivor in 1995. The "CBS Evening News," which he coanchored with Connie Chung, had dropped to third place, slightly behind the "NBC Nightly News," with both far behind ABC's "World News Tonight." Even worse, all the major network news programs suffered losses in audience shares because other channels carried live coverage of the O. J. Simpson trial. The CBS news division had its budgets slashed, and with CBS's later merger with Westinghouse, more cuts seemed likely in the future. There was even talk that Rather might be ousted as anchor, but in May it was Chung who was removed from the evening news. Rather remained as the show's single anchor, under a contract that runs to the year 2000.

Apart from low ratings, the Rather-Chung partnership apparently foundered over her desire to have more hard news reporting and his resistance to that, field reporting being his traditional area of expertise. Though he continued to express support for Chung personally and professionally, Rather was reportedly unhappy that Chung alone was sent to cover the Oklahoma City bombing, and that he was not recalled from vacation to join her. In November, Rather went to Jerusalem to cover the funeral of Israeli Prime Minister Yitzhak Rabin. In December, he traveled to Bosnia to cover deployment of U.S. peacekeeping forces.

Rather's prime-time newsmagazine program, "48 Hours," was also renewed in 1995. In January, Rather joined Mike Wallace and Ed Bradley in a special "CBS Reports: In the Killing Fields of America," on violence in American cities. Near the anniversary of the end of World War II in the Pacific, Rather also hosted the special "CBS Reports: Victory in the Pacific."

In a change of pace, Rather also turned editor in 1995, taking Mark Sullivan's classic six-volume study of the United States in the first quarter of the 20th century (published 1926–36) and condensing it into a single large volume: *Our Times: America at the Birth of the Twentieth Century*. Rather also added a preface, conclusion, and some section notes, along with numerous illustrations. In June, Rather also appeared as a guest on the "Late Show with David Letterman."

Texas-born Rather became CBS news anchor in 1981, climaxing a long career that began in Houston in the early 1950s. His breakthrough came when, as a young CBS correspondent in Dallas, he reported live to the nation the November 22, 1963 assassination of President John F. Kennedy. He became CBS White House correspondent in 1964, and after going abroad for two years, returned to that position (1966–74), playing a substantial role as an investigative reporter during the unfolding Watergate affair and the resignation of Richard Nixon. He then succeeded Walter Cronkite as one of the three chief American reporters and interpreters of the news. Rather's "CBS Evening News" dominated the ratings in the 1980s, and was number one for 211 weeks in a row (1982–86), until ABC took the lead in 1989. In 1993, he was joined by Chung; he also signed a new contract through the year 2000. Rather's other written works include *The Palace Guard* (1974), with Gary Gates; *The Camera Never Blinks* (1977) and the sequel *The Camera Never Blinks Twice: The Further Adventures of a Television Journalist* (1994), both with Mickey Herskowitz; and his personal memoirs *I Remember: Fifty Years Ago in America* (1991), with Peter Wyden. Rather's B.A. was from Sam Houston State College, in 1951. He is married to Jean Goebel; they have two children.

FURTHER READING

"The survivor. . . ." CLAUDIA DREIFUS. *New York Times Magazine*, Sept. 10, 1995.
"Over to you, Dan. . . ." JON KATZ. *Rolling Stone*, Oct. 14, 1993.
"Dan Rather is. . . ." ROBERT DRAPER. *Texas*, Nov. 1991.

Ravidat, Marcel

Ravidat, Marcel (1923–95) French mechanic Marcel Ravidat made an extraordinary discovery in September 1940. In the woods near his home at Montignac, in France's Dordogne region, he and three friends found a hole in the ground. Some accounts have it that they found the hole while they were searching for his dog, and yet other accounts say that Ravidat found the hole himself and brought his friends with him a few days later to explore it. In any event, he and his friends widened the hole, Ravidat went down to investigate—and found the Lascaux Cave, full of magnificent, completely preserved, prehistoric Aurignacian cave paintings, 20,000 years old or more, all of them in their original full colors, as the cave had been sealed for many thousands of years. Ravidat's magnificent find was kept a secret during the rest of World War II, so secret that the Résistance used the cave to store weapons. After the war, Lascaux's art works drew archeologists and art historians the world over. The cave was opened to the public in 1948, with Ravidat as a guide and protector of its treasures, but had to be closed again in 1963, as climate and traffic began to damage the artwork. Ravidat then went back to his career as a mechanic. He was survived by his wife and daughter. (d. Montignac, France; March 29, 1995)

FURTHER READING

Obituary. *New York Times*, Mar. 31, 1995.

Redgrave, Vanessa (1937–) Stage,

screen, and television star Vanessa Redgrave returned to the classics and to her roots in the theater in 1995, directing and starring opposite Paul Butler in the title roles of Shakespeare's *Antony and Cleopatra.* Her contemporary and highly political reading of the work drew mixed reviews. Redgrave and costar Eileen Atkins won Obie Awards for their roles in the American production of *Vita and Virginia.*

Redgrave starred opposite Edward Fox as her lover in the film *A Month by the Lake,* directed by John Irvin, about a holiday romance between two mature people, set in northern Italy, near Lake Como, in 1937. Redgrave received a Golden Globe nomination as best actor in a musical or comedy for the role. She also starred opposite Laura Dern, Raul Julia, and Jay O. Sanders in the television film *Down Came a Blackbird,* as a Holocaust survivor and therapist who counsels and treats more recent survivors of political torture. She received a CableAce nomination as best actress in a movie or miniseries for the role.

Vanessa Redgrave is one of the most celebrated stage and screen actresses of her time, emerging in the early 1960s in the classics and then in her very notable starring role in the stage version of Muriel Spark's *The Prime of Miss Jean Brodie* (1966). She reached world audiences on screen in such films as *Isadora* (1968), *Julia* (1977), *Agatha* (1978), and in television's *Playing for Time* (1979), *The Bostonians* (1983), and *Comrades* (1986). Her recent work includes Peter Hall's acclaimed revival of Tennessee Williams's *Orpheus Descending* (1989 on

Broadway; 1990 on television); a London stage version of *The Three Sisters* (1990–91); and the films *Howards End* (1992), *Di Ceria dell'Unore* (*The Plague Sower*) (1992), *Stalin's Funeral* (1992), *The House of the Spirits* (1994), *Little Odessa* (1994), and *Mother's Boys* (1994). Active in far-left politics for many years, and notably as a supporter of the Palestine Liberation Organization, she also produced and narrated *The Palestinians* (1977). Her autobiography is *Vanessa Redgrave: An Autobiography* (1994).

Vanessa Redgrave attended the Central School of Speech and Drama (1955–57). She is the daughter of actor Michael Redgrave and actress Rachel Kempson, and the sister of Lynn Redgrave and actor-director Corin Redgrave, who is the father of actress Jemma Redgrave. Formerly married to the late director Tony Richardson, she has a son and two daughters, the actresses Natasha Richardson and Joely Richardson.

FURTHER READING

"A woman. . . ." NICHOLAS WROE. *New Statesman and Society,* Oct. 4, 1991.
"Who's afraid of. . . ." STEPHEN SCHIFF. *Vanity Fair,* July 1991.
"The Redgrave sisters." RODDY MCDOWALL. *Interview,* Feb. 1991.

Reeve, Christopher (1952–) On May

31, 1995, actor Christopher Reeve was severely injured when thrown from his horse during a show-jumping competition. He suffered fractures in his first and second cervical vertebrae, high in his spinal column at the base of his neck, and was at first completely paralyzed from the neck down. After surgery and months of intensive rehabilitation, he was reportedly able to move his neck and some shoulder muscles. He was still paralyzed and needed the help of a ventilator for breathing when he made his first public appearance, on October 16, at the Creative Coalition's anual Spotlight Awards dinner, at New York's Pierre Hotel. However, he had made substantial progress in the four months since his injury and was clearly determined to resume his productive life and career. In late September, he was widely seen in a television interview with Barbara Walters.

Two television films that he made before the accident aired during 1995. In *Black Fox,* set in

Texas in 1861, Reeve starred opposite Tony Todd as his friend and former slave, whom he had freed before both fled with their families from the Carolinas to Texas after the outbreak of the Civil War. Reeve also starred opposite Kirstie Alley in a remake of the 1960 British science fiction thriller *Village of the Damned*.

New York City–born Reeve is best known by far for his title-role performances in the four "Superman" films (1978; 1980; 1983; 1987), although much of his other work has been in the theater. He has appeared on Broadway in *A Matter of Gravity* (1978) and *Fifth of July* (1980), and has played a wide range of roles in regional theater, also working in London opposite Vanessa Redgrave and Wendy Hiller in *The Aspern Papers* (1984). His recent work in the theater includes a New York Shakespeare Festival production of Shakespeare's *Winter's Tale* (1989) and a London stage production of Chekhov's *The Three Sisters* (1990–91), with Lynn and Vanessa Redgrave. He has also appeared in such films as *Somewhere in Time* (1980), *Deathtrap* (1982), *Monsignor* (1982), *The Bostonians* (1984), *Switching Channels* (1988), *Noises Off* (1992), *Morning Glory* (1995), and *The Remains of the Day* (1995). His television films include *The Great Escape* (1988), *Bump in the Night* (1991), *Death Dreams* (1991), *The Last Ferry Home* (1992), and *The Sea Wolf* (1995), and he hosted the travel series *Earth Journey with Christopher Reeve*. Reeve attended the Juilliard School; his B.A. was from Cornell University. He is married to singer-actress Dana Morosini and has three children.

FURTHER READING

"Christopher Reeve." *People*, Dec. 25, 1995.
"A tragic fall. . . ." KENDALL HAMILTON and ALDEN COHEN. *Newsweek*, June 12, 1995.
"The will to live. . . ." *People*, June 26, 1995.
"Fallen rider." GREGORY CERIO. *People*, June 12, 1995.
The Magic of Theater. DAVID BLACK. Macmillan, 1993.

Rehnquist, William Hubbs (1924–)

Chief Justice William Rehnquist, the Supreme Court's leading conservative, was no longer in a minority in 1995, instead seeing the Court swing sharply toward his views, although on several major cases only by the narrowest of margins.

Rehnquist wrote the majority opinion in *U.S. v. Lopez*, in which a sharply divided Court voted 5–4 to declare unconstitutional the federal Gun-Free School Zones Act of 1990, which made possession of a gun within 1,000 feet of a school illegal, ruling that this was an invalid extension of the congressional ability to regulate interstate commerce. The ruling was widely seen as a major conservative reinterpretation of the power of Congress to legislate on a very broad range of issues, reopening formerly long-settled federal-state powers questions. Rehnquist also wrote the majority opinion in *Missouri v. Jenkins*, in which the Court voted 5–4 to effectively limit the level of state spending allowable to carry out a federally managed school desegregation plan in Kansas City.

Rehnquist joined a conservative 5–4 majority in several other key cases, among them *Miller v. Johnson*, ruling that Georgia's Eleventh Congressional District was unconstitutional because it was organized primarily to provide racial representation, rather than to respond to specific discrimination; *Rosenberg v. Rector and Visitors of the University of Virginia*, which found that the publicly funded University of Virginia was required to finance a Christian magazine run by students, apparently a sharp change of Court direction on a basic constitutional issue; and *Adarand Constructors v. Pena*, holding that the federal government was required to use the same strict standards as the states in carrying out affirmative action programs, and so reversing the Court's long-held position on federal affirmative action programs.

Rehnquist joined the dissent in the landmark *U.S. Term Limits Inc. v. Thornton*, which held that to limit congressional terms required a constitutional amendment; 23 state laws imposing terms limits were invalidated and Congress was barred from passing a term limits law. He wrote a dissenting opinion in *U.S. v. National Treasury Employees Union*, ruling that federal employees, other than members of Congress, policymakers, and those in the judiciary, had the right to accept payments for their speeches and writings, as long as these were not related to their work. He also dissented in *Babbitt v. Sweet Home Chapter of Communities for a Greater Oregon*, ruling that the federal government had the right under the Endangered Species Act to sharply restrict logging and other activities harmful to the northern spotted owl.

Rehnquist joined the majority in *Capital

Square Review and Advisory Board v. *Pinette,* ruling that it was unconstitutional to bar display of a large Ku Klux Klan cross in an Ohio public park; and in *Veronia School District* v. *Acton,* ruling that an Oregon school district's random drug testing program was constitutional.

Milwaukee-born Rehnquist clerked with Supreme Court Justice Robert Jackson (1952–53), and then practiced law in Phoenix until 1969. He was a Washington-based assistant attorney general (1969–71), then was named to the Supreme Court by President Richard Nixon in 1971, being confirmed only after a sharp Senate battle over his allegedly extreme conservative views. President Ronald Reagan appointed him Chief Justice in 1986; he was confirmed after another Senate battle.

Rehnquist received his 1948 B.A. from Stanford University, his 1949 M.A. from Harvard University, and his 1952 LL.B. from Stanford. His written works include *The Supreme Court: The Way It Was—the Way It Is* (1987) and *Grand Inquests: The Historic Impeachments of Justice Samuel Chase and President Andrew Johnson* (1992). He married Natalie Cornell in 1953; they have two children.

FURTHER READING

Brennan vs. Rehnquist: The Battle for the Constitution. PETER H. IRONS. Knopf, 1994.
Turning Right: The Making of the Rehnquist Supreme Court. DAVID G. SAVAGE. Wiley, 1993.
"Dead end. . . ." JOHN TUCKER. *New Republic,* May 4, 1992.
Chief Justice William Rehnquist. BOB ITALIA. Abdo & Daughters, 1992.

Reiner, Rob (1945–) Director, producer, writer, and actor Rob Reiner directed and produced the 1995 film comedy *The American President,* starring Michael Douglas as President Michael Shepherd, a liberal, exceedingly decent human being and a widower, who, while about to run for reelection, falls in love with environmental lobbyist Sydney Wade, played by Annette Bening. Their rather innocent love affair, set in the White House, cannot be kept secret, although the White House staff tries very hard, and instead becomes a major scandal, fanned by villainous opposition Senator Bob Rumson, played by Richard Dreyfuss. Martin Sheen co-

starred as the president's chief of staff, with Michael J. Fox as an adviser who very much resembles the real-life George Stephanopolous, and Anna Deavere Smith as the president's press secretary, in a cast that also included David Paymer and Samantha Mathis. Scripted by Aaron Sorkin, the film received generally favorable reviews, though some reviewers felt that the gentle comedy could have gone considerably deeper. Reiner received a best director Golden Globe nomination for the film.

Reiner also played a supporting role as a long-winded talk-show doctor in the film comedy *Bye Bye, Love,* directed by Sam Weisman and starring Matthew Modine, Randy Quaid, Paul Reiser, Janeane Garofalo, and Amy Brenneman.

New York City–born Reiner became a television scriptwriter in the late 1960s. He became a television star as Meathead in the series "All in the Family" (1974–78), a role for which he won two Emmys (1974; 1978). He moved into film direction in the mid-1980s with the pseudodocumentary *This Is Spinal Tap* (1984), and then directed several well-received feature films, including *The Sure Thing* (1985), *Stand By Me* (1986), and *The Princess Bride* (1987). His breakthrough film was *When Harry Met Sally* (1989), which he directed and coproduced; the film starred Billy Crystal, Meg Ryan, and Carrie Fisher. He also directed *Misery* (1990), *A Few Good Men* (1992), *North* (1994), and the television series "Morton and Hayes" (1991). Son of actor-writer-director Carl Reiner, he attended the University of California at Los Angeles. Previously married to actress-director Penny Marshall, he married photographer Michele Singer in 1989; he has two children.

FURTHER READING

"Rob Reiner's . . ." JEFF SILVERMAN. *New York Times,* July 21, 1991.

Reiser, Paul (1957–) Actor and comedian Paul Reiser seemed to be everywhere in 1995. Most prominently, he was seen costarring with Helen Hunt as Paul and Jamie, the young marrieds in the romantic comedy television series "Mad About You," which began its fourth season in late 1995. Reiser is cocreator and coproducer of the show; his own dog, Frankie, is even a model for the neurotic on-screen Murray. For his

talk shows. He emerged as a major star in the television comedy series "Mad About You" (1992–). Reiser received his 1977 B.F.A. in music from the State University of New York at Binghamton. He is married to Paula Reiser.

FURTHER READING

"It's a mad, mad. . . ." DAVID WILD. *Rolling Stone*, Apr. 20, 1995.
"What Paul Reiser. . . ." PAUL NELSON. *Redbook*, Mar. 1995.

work on the popular series, Reiser was for the second consecutive year nominated for an Emmy for best lead actor in a comedy series and for a Screen Actors Guild award for best actor in a comedy series, telefilm, or miniseries; at year's end he also was nominated for a Golden Globe award as best actor in a musical or comedy series. Reiser served as host for the 1995 Grammy Awards, and was a presenter at the Emmy Awards.

Reiser's 1994 book *Couplehood,* a collection of humorous essays and sketches, had reached the top of the hardcover best-seller lists, selling well over 1.2 million copies. In 1995, it was published in paperback and in an audio version, read by Reiser himself. During 1995, Reiser also opened in a new feature film, *Bye Bye, Love,* directed by Sam Weisman, in which he, Matthew Modine, and Randy Quaid play a trio of divorced fathers dealing with child custody and rediscovering romance.

New York City–born actor and comedian Reiser began his career as a stand-up comic in and around New York City in the late 1970s. He made his feature film debut in *Diner* (1982); among his other films are *Aliens* (1986), *Beverly Hills Cop II* (1987), *Cross My Heart* (1987), *Crazy People* (1990), and *Mr. Write* (1994). On television, he has also appeared in the series "My Two Dads" (1987–91), the special *Paul Reiser: Out on a Whim* (1987), and in several pilots and films, such as *The Tower* (1993), and been a highly visible perennial guest on several leading

Reno, Janet (1938–) While continuing to deal with the whole range of U.S. law enforcement concerns, Attorney General Janet Reno focused very strongly on terrorism after the April 19, 1995 Oklahoma City federal building car bombing, which killed 169 people, the worst such terrorist attack in American history. She mobilized the entire federal law enforcement apparatus to investigate the crime, promised that she would seek the death penalty for those responsible, instituted new safety precautions at federal buildings at home and abroad, and helped draft new antiterrorism legislation, though reportedly with some reservations about the sweeping nature of some aspects of the legislation—reservations clearly shared by many in both political parties, as the bill stalled in Congress.

In August 1 testimony before a congressional investigating committee, Reno stood fast in her defense of government actions in the 1993 Waco, Texas Branch Davidian siege and fire, in which 4 federal agents and 86 Branch Davidians were killed, 17 of them children. She continued to take full responsibility for the action, a position that at the time of the siege and later won her considerable respect.

On the personal side, on November 16 Reno disclosed that she had Parkinson's disease, with mild symptoms that were being fully controlled by medication, and that her ability to do her job was in no way impaired.

Miami-born Reno received her 1960 B.A. from Cornell University, and her 1963 LL.B. from Harvard Law School. She practiced law in Miami (1963–71), then became staff director for the Florida House of Representatives Judiciary Committee (1971–72) and worked in the Dade County (including Miami) state attorney's office

(1973–76), before going back into private practice for two years (1976–78). She was appointed Dade County state prosecutor in 1978, becoming the first woman in that position, and stayed in office through five reelections (1978–93). She was confirmed as U.S. attorney general by a unanimous Senate on March 11, 1993, becoming the first woman to hold that position. Her popular appointment was something of a triumph for President Bill Clinton, after his damaging withdrawals of Zoë Baird and Judge Kimba Wood from consideration for the position.

FURTHER READING

"Death and Reno." *New Republic*, May 15, 1995.
"Children of Waco." PETER J. BOYER. *New Yorker*, May 15, 1995.
Janet Reno: United States Attorney General. VIRGINIA MEACHUM. Enslow, 1995.
"Janet Reno's choice." LINCOLN CAPLAN. *New York Times Magazine*, May 15, 1994.
"The big time!. . . ." *Cosmopolitan*, May 1994.
"The trials of Janet Reno." JEFFREY ROSEN. *Vanity Fair*, Apr. 1994.
"Can Reno be. . . ." DIANA R. GORDON. *Nation*, Mar. 21, 1994.
"Miami nice. . . ." JEFF LEEN. *New Republic*, Mar. 21, 1994.
Janet Reno: Doing the Right Thing. PAUL ANDERSON. Wiley, 1994.
Janet Reno: First Woman Attorney General. CHARNAN SIMON. Childrens, 1994.
"Gambling on Reno." RICH LOWRY. *National Review*, Nov. 15, 1993.
"Reno, Janet." *Current Biography*, Sept. 1993.
"Truth, justice. . . ." NANCY GIBBS and ELAINE SHANNON. *Time*, July 12, 1993.
"Rough rider." TED GEST. *U.S. News & World Report*, June 7, 1993.
"The reluctant star." MELINDA LIU and BOB COHN. *Newsweek*, May 17, 1993.

Reston, James Barrett (1909–95)

Scottish-born journalist James Reston grew up in Dayton, Ohio, and received his 1932 B.A. from the University of Illinois. He began his long career as a sportswriter at the *Springfield Daily News,* moved to New York and the Associated Press (AP) in 1934, and went to London for the AP in 1937. In 1939, he joined the *New York Times* London staff and there went through the Blitz, then going on assignment to Washington, before going back to London as head of the U.S.

information office (1942–45). After the war, he became a *Times* national correspondent in Washington, and in the years that followed published a widely read thrice-weekly column and became a major figure in American journalism. He was head of the *Times* Washington bureau (1953–64) and later headed the *Times* news department (1968–69), but from then until his retirement focused on his column. Among his many honors were 1945 and 1957 Pulitzer Prizes. He published several books, including *Artillery of the Press* (1967) and *Deadline: A Memoir* (1991). He was survived by his wife, Sally Fulton Reston, and their three sons, including the writer James Reston, Jr. (d. Washington, D.C.; December 6, 1995)

FURTHER READING

"The man in the middle. . . ." JONATHAN ALTER. *Newsweek*, Dec. 18, 1995.
"The best ones. . . ." ALLAN FOTHERINGHAM. *Maclean's*, Dec. 18, 1995.
Obituary. *Times* (of London), Dec. 8, 1995.
Obituary. *Independent*, Dec. 8, 1995.
Obituary. *New York Times*, Dec. 6, 1995.
"A perspective. . . ." ALVIN P. SANOFF. *U.S. News & World Report*, Oct. 28, 1991.

Rice, Anne (Howard Allen O'Brien; 1941–)

The publication of Anne Rice's new novel *Memnoch the Devil,* the fifth in her "Vampire Chronicles" series, was the occasion for a massive four-month publicity campaign. It began in New Orleans where Rice, dressed in a vintage wedding gown, was carried in a closed coffin in a mock jazz funeral to a bookstore signing. This was followed by interviews and signings in 30 cities, before winding up back in New Orleans with a Memnoch Ball in late October. Response was satisfactory: The hardcover book debuted at the top spot on the best-seller lists. The audiobook version of *Memnoch,* read by Roger Rees, was also a best-seller, as were the paperback versions of *Lasher* and *Taltos.* A new version of *Interview with the Vampire,* read by F. Murray Abraham, was published on 3 CDs. Rice has contracted to write two more "Vampire Chronicles" books. She was also working on a new series, "The Ghost Trilogy"; the first novel, *The Servant of the Bones,* was scheduled for 1996 publication.

New Orleans–born Rice attended Texas Wom-

RICE, JERRY LEE

en's University, later receiving her 1964 B.A. and 1971 M.A. from San Francisco State College. Her novels include *Interview with the Vampire* (1976), *The Feast of All Saints* (1980), *Cry to Heaven* (1982), *The Vampire Lestat* (1985), *The Queen of the Damned* (1988), *The Mummy or Ramses the Damned* (1989), *The Witching Hour* (1990), *Tale of the Body Thief* (1992), and the trilogy *The Witching Hour* (1990), *Lasher* (1993), and *Taltos: Lives of the Mayfair Witches* (1994). Several other novels were published pseudonymously: as A. N. Roquelaure, *The Claiming of Sleeping Beauty* (1983), *Beauty's Punishment* (1984), *Beauty's Release: The Continued Erotic Adventures of Sleeping Beauty* (1985), and *Beauty's Release* (1991); and as Anne Rampling, *Exit to Eden* (1985) and *Belinda* (1986). She married Stan Rice in 1961; she has one son; she also had a daughter, who died. Novelist Alice Borchardt is her older sister.

FURTHER READING

"Mistress of the macabre." Jane Salodof. *First for Women*, Feb. 14, 1994.
Anne Rice. Bette B. Roberts. Macmillan, 1994.
The Anne Rice Trivia Book. Katherine Ramsland. Ballantine, 1994.
"Anne Rice." *Playboy*, Mar. 1993.
"Rice, Anne." *Current Biography*, July 1991.
Prism of the Night: A Biography of Anne Rice. Katherine Ramsland. NAL-Dutton, 1991.

Rice, Jerry Lee (1962–) In his eleventh season with the San Francisco 49ers, receiver Jerry Rice continued to smash records. In February 1995, in his fourth Super Bowl win, Rice caught three touchdown passes, which tied a Super Bowl record he had set in 1990—even though he was recovering from the flu and in the second quarter suffered a shoulder separation, returning to play with extra padding. Beyond that, he continued to build up his Super Bowl career records to 7 touchdowns, 7 touchdown receptions, 42 points, 28 receptions, 512 yards receiving, and 527 combined yards. He also holds or shares many other postseason and Super Bowl records. Shortly before the Super Bowl, Rice had mused about whether that would be his last game in the NFL, but retirement talk was later shelved. Rice's current contract runs through the 1997 season.

In the 1995 regular season, Rice gained 1,884 total yards from scrimmage, including an NFL season record of 1,848 receiving yards, with an average of 15.1 yards over 122 receptions. Overall, he scored 17 touchdowns, 15 receiving, 1 rushing, and 1 returning. These were added to his previously established records for most total career touchdowns and most receiving touchdowns, which at year's end stood at 156 and 146, respectively. He also became the NFL's all-time career leader in receiving yardage, breaking James Lofton's record of 14,004 yards. Rice also led single-game rankings for the season with 289 total receiving yards, with three touchdowns, in a December 18 game against Minnesota. In the final game of the year, he also threw his first career touchdown pass.

Despite injuries to many other key players, Rice remained healthy and was a key factor in the 49ers building a division-leading regular-season record of 12–5. To no one's surprise, Rice was again named to the Pro Bowl. At year's end, he and the 49ers were looking at another run at the Super Bowl, but in early January they were knocked out by the Green Bay Packers, whose defense virtually shut down Rice.

Mississippi-born Rice was a football, basketball, and track star at Crawford Moor High School before moving on to Mississippi Valley State, where he was a consensus All-American, with over 100 receptions in both his junior and senior years and over 1,000 yards in three consecutive years; he set numerous National Collegiate Athletic Association (NCAA) records. A first-round draft pick in 1985, Rice exploded in

1986 to lead the league with 86 receptions, 15 receiving touchdowns, and 1,570 receiving yards; he was named *Sports Illustrated*'s NFL Player of the Year. In 1987, he was named the NFL's Most Valuable Player, gathering 138 points and setting records by catching a total of 22 receiving touchdowns, and also by catching receiving touchdowns in 13 consecutive games. He again led the league in number of receptions in 1989 and 1990, and in receiving yardage in 1990, when he was once more named *Sports Illustrated*'s NFL Player of the Year. He has helped win four Super Bowls (1985; 1989; 1990; 1994), in 1989 being named Super Bowl MVP. With ten consecutive years of over 1,000 reception yards, Rice has been named to eleven consecutive Pro Bowls (1985–95); he did not play in 1988 and 1994 due to injury. Rice and his wife, Jackie, have a son and a daughter.

FURTHER READING

"Mississippi yearning." TERRY FREI. *Sporting News*, July 31, 1995.
"Man to man. . . ." DAVE KINDRED. *Sporting News*, Feb. 6, 1995.
"Jerry Rice. . . ." RON KROICHICK. *Sport*, Jan. 1995.
Jerry Rice. RICHARD RAMBECK. Childs World, 1995.
Jerry Rice. G. S. PRENTZAS. Chelsea House, 1994.
Jerry Rice. JOHN ROLFE. Bantam, 1993.
Jerry Rice: Touchdown Talent. J. EDWARD EVANS. Lerner, 1993.
Sports Great Jerry Rice. GLENN DICKEY. Enslow, 1993.

Jerry Rice: Touchdown Talent. NATHAN AASENG. Lerner, 1993.

Rich, Charlie (1932–95) Country singer, songwriter, and pianist Charlie Rich, known as the "Silver Fox" for his prematurely white hair, formed his first group, the Velvetones, in the early 1950s, while he was in the air force. He began his professional career in the late 1950s, and scored his first recording hit in 1960, with the single "Lonely Weekends." But it was more than a decade before his real breakthrough came, with his hit "I Take It On Home" (1972), followed by his 1973 smash number one country hits "Behind Closed Doors" and "The Most Beautiful Girl"; each sold more than 2 million copies, and together they established him as one of the leading country singers of his time. His period of great popularity was brief, however, and his ratings slide was hastened by his highly publicized alcohol problem; after 1981, he released only one more album, in 1992. Rich attended the University of Arkansas. He was survived by his wife, Margaret, two daughters, and two sons. (d. Hammond, Louisiana; July 25, 1995)

FURTHER READING

Obituary. *Rolling Stone*, Sept. 7, 1995.
Obituary. *Billboard*, Aug. 5, 1995.
Obituary. *Times* (of London), July 27, 1995.
Obituary. *Independent*, July 27, 1995.
Obituary. *New York Times*, July 26, 1995.
Obituary. *Variety*, July 26, 1995.

Rifkind, Simon Hirsch (1901–95) Born in Meretz, Russia, leading lawyer Simon Rifkind emigrated to the United States in 1910 with his family and grew up on New York City's Lower East Side. He received his 1922 B.A. from City College and his 1925 LL.B. from Columbia Law School. Early in his career, he was liberal Democratic Senator Robert Wagner's legislative assistant (1927–33), in that position from 1933 working near the center of Franklin Delano Roosevelt's Depression-era New Deal. Rifkind was a partner in Wagner's law firm (1930–41) and then was a federal district court judge (1941–50). In 1950, he became a partner in the powerful New York law firm Paul, Weiss, Rifkind, Wharton & Garrison, which had by the time of his death grown into a huge firm of almost 400 lawyers, with a client list that included many major corporate and individual clients. Rifkind was also active in philanthropy and in Jewish organizations as the board chairman of the Jewish Theological Seminary and on the executive board of the American Jewish Committee. He was survived by two sons. (d. New York City; November 14, 1995)

FURTHER READING

Obituary. *New York Times*, Nov. 15, 1995.

Riggs, Bobby (Robert Larimore Riggs; 1918–95)

Los Angeles–born tennis great Bobby Riggs began playing competitive tennis while in his early teens, and at 16 became national junior singles champion. He moved into adult competition in 1935, was singles champion at Wimbledon in 1939, and was U.S. amateur singles champion (1939–41). Riggs turned professional in 1941, and became a dominant figure in world tennis in the late 1940s, as U.S. and world singles champion (1945; 1946; 1947; 1949). He continued to play competitive tennis into the 1970s, while at the same time becoming executive vice president of the American Photograph Corporation (1954–72). Riggs also became a promoter of tennis events: In 1973, he challenged and defeated women's champion Margaret Court in an exhibition match, and later that year was defeated by Billie Jean King in a second widely publicized challenge exhibition match, in which he took advantage of the publicity being generated by the women's movement of the day to create a very lucrative promotion opportunity. He was survived by a daughter, four sons, a sister, and two brothers. (d. Leucadia, California; October 25, 1995)

FURTHER READING

"My favorite chauvinist." BILLIE JEAN KING. *Sports Illustrated*, Nov. 6, 1995.
"Bobby Riggs. . . ." *Economist*, Nov. 4, 1995.
Obituary. *New York Times*, Oct. 27, 1995.

Riley, Pat (Patrick James Riley; 1945–)

Pat Riley's reign in New York came to an end in 1995. His New York Knicks basketball team had lost in the National Basketball Association fi-

nals in 1994, but had hoped to do better in 1995. Instead, they fell in the second round of the 1995 Eastern Conference playoffs, losing a heartbreaking seven-game series to the Indianapolis Pacers. In his end-of-season address to his team, Riley charged that internal dissension and self-destructive behavior had cost the team a championship. Riley had a year to go on his current coaching contract, and had been offered a five-year, $15 million extension. But in mid-June, he stunned the basketball world by resigning, reportedly because the Knicks would not grant him complete autonomy in team management, as well as part ownership. At his resignation, Riley's career won-loss record was 756-299, for a winning percentage of .717, the highest in league history.

Several disputatious months followed, as the Miami Heat wooed Riley, the Knicks filed tampering charges, and both faced a league hearing. In the end, Miami gave New York $1 million and a 1996 first-round draft choice to win Riley's contract release, and then signed him to a five-year contract reportedly worth $40 million (more than some of the game's stars), which includes part ownership: 10 percent on signing and another 10 percent later. In early November, Riley pulled off a notable coup when Miami acquired center Alonzo Mourning from the Charlotte Hornets. Unfortunately Mourning was later injured, and the team that started 11-3 had, by late in the year, slipped considerably in the standings.

It remained to be seen how Miami would fare in the long run under Riley.

Born in Schenectady, New York, Riley has spent his whole career in and around basketball. During his eight-year career as a professional basketball player, he was a guard with the San Diego Rockets (1967–70), the Los Angeles Lakers (1970–75), and the Phoenix Suns (1975–76). He was an assistant coach of the Lakers (1979–81), and then began his extraordinarily successful nine-year run as Laker head coach (1981–90). Under Riley, the Lakers had a won-lost record of 533-194, and won four NBA championships (1982; 1985; 1987; 1988). In June 1990, after a winning season but an early elimination in the playoffs, Riley resigned from the Lakers. He is only the fifth coach ever to be named coach of the year twice (1990; 1993).

Having earlier broadcast Laker games (1977–79), Riley joined NBC television for the 1990–91 season. He then returned to coaching with the New York Knicks (1991–95), taking them to the top of their division and into three successive Eastern Conference finals (1992–94). He published *Show Time: Inside the Lakers' Breakthrough Season* (1988) and *The Winner Within: A Life Plan for Team Players* (1993), and hosted HBO's special *The History of the NBA* (1992). Riley is also a much-in-demand motivational speaker for major corporations, also producing video games and motivational videos. He is married to Chris Riley; they have two children.

FURTHER READING

"Escape from New York." MARK KRIEGEL. *Esquire*, Dec. 1995.
"Satin steel. . . ." DAN DIEFFENBACH. *Sport*, June 1995.
"The fire from within. . . ." MARK HEISLER. *Sporting News*, Jan. 9, 1995.
"Character study." DAVID HALBERSTAM. *New York*, Dec. 21, 1992.
"The life of Riley." KEN AULETTA. *Vanity Fair*, Apr. 1992.

Ripken, Cal (Calvin Edwin Ripken, Jr.; 1960–) One of 1995's most heartening sports stories revolved around Cal Ripken, Jr. In a year largely dominated by strikes, lockouts, and big-money talk in major sports, Baltimore Orioles shortstop Ripken kept on playing the game he loves, and doing it so consistently that on September 6, with his 2,131st game in a row, he broke the 56-year-old record of Lou Gehrig for most consecutive games played, a stretch that covered more than 13 years, from March 30, 1982. The event won national attention, and was attended by such luminaries as President Bill Clinton and Joe DiMaggio. Gehrig had played 2,130 games before being forced to retire by amyotrophic lateral sclerosis (ALS, or Lou Gehrig's disease); in his honor, Ripken's team set aside many seats for the record-breaking game, to earn $1 million to establish a foundation to research muscular diseases such as ALS.

Ripken has not just played, but played *well*. He is the only major league player ever to start in 12 consecutive All-Star games (1983–95); no one else had started more than 10 in a row. He was named Sportsman of the Year for 1995 by both *Sporting News* and *Sports Illustrated*.

Early in 1995, Ripken's record had seemed in jeopardy because of the baseball strike; many owners wanted to start the season with replacement players, a move strongly resisted by Orioles owner Peter Angelos; fortunately the strike was settled before the question arose. Ripken himself had made it clear that he would not play if the strike were in effect at the season's opening.

Also in 1995, Ripken published the autobiographical children's book *Count Me In* and, with Harry Connolly and Stephen King, Jr., *Heading Home: Growing Up in Baseball*, an illustrated book about the Little Leagues.

Born in Havre de Grace, Maryland, Ripken graduated from Aberdeen High School. Selected by the Baltimore Orioles in the 1978 free-agent draft, he played for various minor league teams (1978–81), in Bluefield, Miami, Charlotte, and Rochester, where he played all 33 innings of the longest game in professional baseball history (1981). He came to the Baltimore Orioles in 1981 and was named American League Rookie of the Year in 1982, his first full season. In the following year (1983), he was named the league's Most Valuable Player, the only player ever to go directly from the one award to the other. He was also named *Sporting News* major league player of the year (1983) and American League MVP again in 1991. He also holds the record for highest single-season fielding percentage (.996), set in 1990. He played in all 8,243 innings between June 5, 1982, and September 14, 1987, believed to be the longest string of consecutive innings.

Ripken and his wife, Kelly, have a son, Ryan, and a daughter, Rachel. His father, Cal Ripken,

Sr., spent 29 years with the Orioles as a minor league ball player, manager, and coach; his brother, Bill Ripken, played second base and shortstop for the Orioles and the Texas Rangers (1987–94).

FURTHER READING

"Iron clan." STEVE MARANTZ. Sporting News, Dec. 18, 1995. Sportsman of the Year Issue.

"Hand it to Cal." RICHARD HOFFER. Sports Illustrated, Dec. 18, 1995. (Sportsman of the Year Issue.)

"Man at work. . . ." WILLIAM PLUMMER. People, Sept. 18, 1995.

" 'You have to. . . .' " MICHAEL KNISLEY. Sporting News, Sept. 11, 1995.

"Man of iron." TIM KURKJIAN. Sports Illustrated, Aug. 7, 1995.

Sport Shots: Cal Ripken, Jr. BILL MORGAN. Scholastic, 1994.

Cal Ripken, Jr.: Star Shortstop. JEFF SAVAGE. Enslow, 1994.

"Local hero." PETER RICHMOND. GQ, May 1993.

Sports Great Cal Ripken, Jr. GLEN MACNOW. Enslow, 1993.

Cal Ripken Jr.: The Authorized Political History. Summit, 1993.

Cal Ripken, Jr.: Quiet Hero. LOIS NICHOLSON. Cornell Maritime, 1993.

Cal Ripken, Jr.: Oriole Ironman. STEW THORNLEY. Lerner, 1992.

Cal Ripken. RICHARD RAMBECK. Childs World, 1992.

Robards, Jason, Jr. (Jason Nelson Robards, Jr.; 1922–   ) Veteran theater, film, and television star Jason Robards, Jr., in 1995 appeared as Andy opposite Blythe Danner as Bel in a New York production of Harold Pinter's play Moonlight, with Melissa Chalsma, Barry McEvoy, Liev Schreiber, Kathleen Widdoes, and Paul Hecht; Karel Reisz directed. He also starred as the grandfather in the very well-received television film version of Willa Cather's novel My Antonia, directed by Joseph Sargent. Costarring were Eva Marie Saint as the grandmother, Neil Patrick Harris as young Jim Burden, and Elina Lowensohn as the young Bohemian-American girl with whom Jim falls in love.

Robards played a second grandfather's role, in the television film Journey, opposite Max Pomerance as his grandson, 11-year-old Journey; their difficult, ultimately successful relationship is at the heart of the film. Brenda Fricker as the grandmother and Meg Tilly as the boy's mother costarred; Tom McLaughlin directed the work, based on Patricia MacLachlan's book Journey.

Forthcoming was a starring role in the New York production of Brian Friel's new play Molly Sweeney.

Chicago-born Robards became a leading player on the American stage in 1956 as Hickey in Eugene O'Neill's The Iceman Cometh, a role he repeated in 1976 and 1988. His other O'Neill performances include Long Day's Journey into Night (1956; 1976; 1986), A Moon for the Misbegotten (1973), and A Touch of the Poet (1977). He won a Tony in The Disenchanted (1958), and also starred in such plays as A Thousand Clowns (1962; and the 1965 film), After the Fall (1964), The Country Girl (1972), Park Your Car in Harvard Yard (1991), and No Man's Land (1994). On screen, he has appeared in many films, largely in strong supporting roles. His most notable films include The Loves of Isadora (1969), All the President's Men (1976; he won a best supporting actor Oscar), Julia (1977; for which he won a second best supporting actor Oscar), Melvin and Howard (1979), Parenthood (1989), Black Rainbow (1990), Reunion (1990), Storyville (1992), Philadelphia (1993), The Trial (1993), and The Paper (1994). He has also appeared in many television films, most notably The Iceman Cometh (1961), One Day in the Life of Ivan Denisovitch (1963), Haywire (1980), The Day After (1983), Sakharov (1984), Inherit the Wind (1988), Chernobyl: The Final Warning (1991), The Perfect Tribute (1991), and Mark Twain and Me (1991).

Robards attended the American Academy of Dramatic Arts. Son of actor Jason Robards, he has been married four times and has seven children.

FURTHER READING

"The players." ANDREW CORSELLO and AMY DONOHUE. Philadelphia, Dec. 1993.

Robbins, Tim (1958–   ) Actor, writer, and director Tim Robbins remained a high-quality presence on American television screens in 1995; home video rentals were strong for his 1994 films, the prison drama The Shawshank Redemption and the comedy I.Q. For his Shaw-

shank role, he received a Screen Actors Guild nomination as best leading actor in a motion picture.

Robbins wrote, directed, and coproduced the searing 1995 film *Dead Man Walking,* starring Susan Sarandon as nun Helen Prejean opposite Sean Penn as convicted rapist and murderer Matthew Poncelot, awaiting execution on the death row of New Orleans' Angola Prison. The tough, realistic film is set during the week just before Poncelot's execution; Sister Prejean has responded as a matter of conscience to Poncelot's letter, asking her to visit him in prison, and then to his plea that she become his religious adviser during his final days. The film, based on Sister Prejean's best-selling book, co-starred Robert Prosky, Raymond J. Barry, R. Lee Ermey, Celia Weston, Lois Smith, Scott Wilson, and Roberta Maxwell. Robbins was nominated for a Golden Globe award for best screenplay for the film.

California-born Robbins grew up in New York's Greenwich Village, the child of a theater family (his father, Gil Robbins, was a folksinger and cabaret manager). He made his stage debut in his early teens, studied theater at the Plattsburgh campus of the State University of New York and the University of California at Los Angeles, and while still in school was a founder of the Actors' Gang; he is still artistic director of the group. He has written several experimental plays. He made his film debut in *No Small Affair* (1984) and went on to roles in such films as *The Sure Thing* (1985) and *Five Corners* (1987), his breakthrough role coming in *Bull Durham* (1988). This was followed by such films as *Eric the Viking* (1989), *Cadillac Man* (1990), *Jacob's Ladder* (1990), *The Player* (1992), and *Bob Roberts* (1992; he wrote script and songs, directed, and starred), *Short Cuts* (1993), *The Hudsucker Proxy* (1994), *The Shawshank Redemption* (1994), *I.Q.* (1994), and *Ready to Wear* (*Prêt-à-Porter*) (1994). Robbins and Susan Sarandon have two children.

FURTHER READING

"Playboy interview. . . ." MARSHALL FINE. *Playboy,* Feb. 1995.
"Rendezvous with. . . ." *Interview,* Jan. 1995.
"The Tim man." MEREDITH BERKMAN. *Mademoiselle,* Jan. 1995.
"Robbins, Tim." *Current Biography,* July 1994.
"A dangerous man." STEPHANIE MANSFIELD. *GQ,* Oct. 1992.

"Renaissance radical." JONATHAN ALTER. *Vogue,* Sept. 1992.

Robinson, Cleveland Lowellyn

(1915–95) Jamaica-born Cleveland Robinson was a leading African-American figure in the U.S. labor movement. He grew up in Jamaica and emigrated to the U.S. in 1944. In 1946, he organized his first retail establishment, the Manhattan store in which he was employed, and a year later began his long career as a professional labor organizer for District 65, then a catch-all independent industrial union that organized many kinds of New York area establishments. He became a vice president of the union in 1950 and its secretary-treasurer in 1952, holding that position for 40 years, until his retirement in 1992. Robinson was also a leading political figure who worked with Martin Luther King, Jr., and the Southern Christian Leadership Conference during the civil rights era, and was a key organizer of the 1963 March on Washington, the occasion of King's "I Have a Dream" speech. Robinson was survived by his wife, Doreen McPherson Robinson, a daughter, two sons, and a sister. (d. New York City; August 23, 1995)

FURTHER READING

"Rites held. . . ." *Jet,* Sept. 18, 1995.
Obituary. *New York Times,* Aug. 25, 1995.

Robinson, David Maurice (1965–)

The man called "The Admiral" was honored as the Most Valuable Player of the National Basketball Association for the 1994–95 season, winning 61 first-place votes and 286 points overall. Center David Robinson had led his San Antonio Spurs team to a regular season record of 62-20, the best in the league (and in team history). Individually, he was third in the league in scoring (27.6 a game), fourth in blocks (3.23), and seventh in rebounding (10.8); he holds the all-time NBA career record for highest average number of blocked shots per game, with 3.65. In the All-Star game, where he was backup center, Robinson had a respectable 10 points.

Unfortunately, this did not translate into the desired trip to the NBA finals. The Spurs swept the Denver Nuggets 3–0 in the first round of the Western Conference playoffs and won a tighter seven-game series against the Los Angeles Lakers in the semifinals. But in the conference championship, the Spurs met the defending champion Houston Rockets and were defeated in a bizarre six-game series in which neither team won on its home court.

By the start of the 1995–96 season, the Spurs had lost strong rebounder Dennis Rodman, so Robinson needed to play closer to the basket. At year's end, the Spurs were 19-8, placing them fifth in the league, and Robinson himself was second in the league in scoring, with an average of 26.5 points a game, and in blocked shots, with 3.67 a game, and third in rebounding, with 12.0 a game.

Florida-born Robinson attended Osbourn Park High School in Manassas, Virginia. He graduated from the U.S. Naval Academy in 1987, where he averaged 21.0 points and 10.3 rebounds; in 1987, he was named *Sporting News* college player of the year and won the Naismith and Wooden awards. He was the top pick overall in the 1987 NBA college draft, selected by the San Antonio Spurs, but instead of turning professional immediately served as a commissioned ensign in the U.S. Navy (1987–89). In 1989, he joined the San Antonio Spurs, and was named NBA Rookie of the Year (1990). He has also been named an All-Star six times (1990–95) and defensive player of the year (1992). He was also named to the All-NBA first team three times (1991; 1992; 1995), to the second team once (1994), and third team twice (1990; 1993). He was also a member of the 1988 and 1992 U.S. Olympic basketball teams, the latter the gold medal–winning "Dream Team" in Barcelona. Robinson married Valerie Hoggatt in 1991; they have a son.

FURTHER READING

"David Robinson. . . ." DARRYL HOWERTON and GLENN ROGERS. *Sport*, Jan. 1996.

"David Robinson. . . ." DAN DIEFFENBACH. *Sport*, Nov. 1994.

"Spur of the moment." PHIL TAYLOR. *Sports Illustrated*, Mar. 7, 1994.

David Robinson: The Admiral. R. CONRAD STEIN. Childrens, 1994.

David Robinson. BILL GUTMAN. Troll, 1994.

David Robinson: Star Center. GLEN MACNOW. Enslow, 1994.

David Robinson. CARL R. GREEN and M. ROXANNE FORD. Silver Burdett, 1994.

"Robinson, David." *Current Biography*, July 1993.

David Robinson, NBA Super Center. BILL GUTMAN. Millbrook, 1993.

Sports Great David Robinson. NATHAN AASENG. Enslow, 1992.

David Robinson Sports Shots. Scholastic, 1992.

This Is David Robinson. BILL GUTMAN. Scholastic, 1992.

The Force: The NBA's Newest Sky-High Sensation, David Robinson. JIM SAVAGE. Dell, 1992.

David Robinson. JAMES R. ROTHAUS. Childs World, 1991.

David Robinson. JOHN ROLFE. Little, Brown, 1991.

David Robinson: Backboard Admiral. DAWN MILLER. Lerner, 1991.

Rogers, Ginger (Virginia Katherine McMath; 1911–95)

Film star Ginger Rogers began her long career as a dancer in vaudeville in the 1920s, moving into theater roles in the late 1920s. Her breakthrough roles came in the Broadway musical *Top Speed* (1929), and in George Gershwin's musical *Girl Crazy* (1930). Her film debut came in *Young Man of Manhattan* (1930). Her breakthrough film year was 1933, with roles in *42nd Street, Gold Diggers of 1933,* and her role opposite Fred Astaire, *Flying Down to Rio,* the first of their ten classic film musicals together. She and Astaire went on to star in *The Gay Divorcée* (1934), *Roberta* (1935), *Top Hat* (1935), *Follow the Fleet* (1937), *Swing Time* (1937), *Shall We Dance* (1937), *Carefree* (1938), *The Story of Vernon and Irene Castle* (1939), and *The Barkleys of Broadway* (1949). A versatile actress, Rogers also starred in a wide range of dramatic roles, winning a best actress Academy Award for her title role in *Kitty Foyle* (1941), and also starring in *Roxie Hart* (1942) and *Lady in the Dark* (1944). Her autobiography was *Ginger: My Story* (1991). Rogers married and divorced five times, to variety performer Edward Culpepper (Jack Pepper), actor Lew Ayres, actor Jack Briggs, actor Jacques Bergerac, and director William Marshall. Her career was fostered by her mother, Lela Rogers, who remained her manager until her death in 1977. There were no survivors. (d. Rancho Mirage, California; April 25, 1995)

FURTHER READING

Obituary. *National Review*, May 29, 1995.

"Ginger Rogers." ARLENE CROCE. *New Yorker*, May 8, 1995.

"Sophisticated lady." TOM GLIATTO. *People*, May 8, 1995.

"A woman's movement." LISA SCHWARZBAUM. *Entertainment*, May 5, 1995.

Obituary. *Independent*, Apr. 26, 1995.

Obituary. *Times* (of London), Apr. 26, 1995.

Obituary. *New York Times*, Apr. 26, 1995.

Obituary. *Variety*, Apr. 26, 1995.

"Ginger Rogers. . . ." MICHAEL FRANK. *Architectural Digest*, Apr. 1994.

Ginger Rogers: A Bio-Bibliography. JOCELYN FARIS. Greenwood, 1994.

Roker, Roxie (1929–95)

Miami-born stage and screen actress Roxie Roker began her career in small roles on the New York stage, while workng in NBC's New York offices. In the late 1960s she was able to leave NBC to fully pursue her acting career, beginning in 1969 with several Negro Ensemble Company plays. Her stage breakthrough came in her Obie-winning and Tony-nominated role as Mattie Williams in *The River Niger* (1974). The breakthrough that was to make her a very familiar face on American and world television screens came a year later, in her role as Helen Willis in Norman Lear's hit prime-time television comedy series "The Jeffersons," his spin-off from "All in the Family." For ten years (1975–85), Black actress Roker played the wife of White actor Franklin Cover, as the ever-present neighbors of George and Louise Jefferson. The Willises were television's trailblazing first interracial couple, whose interracial daughter ultimately married the Jeffersons' son. Roker also appeared in several other works made for television, and continued her stage career. She was survived by a son, the singer and rock guitarist Lenny Kravitz, and by her father. (d. Los Angeles; December 2, 1995)

FURTHER READING

Obituary. *New York Times*, Dec. 6, 1995.

Romney, George Wilcken (1907–95)

Politician and industrialist George Romney was born in a Mormon colony in Chihuahua, Mexico, and was a Mormon missionary in Britain (1927–28) before turning to secular pursuits. He was a Washington speechwriter (1929–30) and lobbyist (1932–38), and in 1939 joined the Automobile Manufacturers Association, becoming its general manager (1942–48). Romney became a Nash-Kelvinator company executive in 1948, became the company's executive vice president, and emerged from its 1954 merger with ailing American Motors as president of American Motors (1954–62). He then left industry for politics, winnng election as Republican governor of Michigan (1963–69). In 1968, he made an unsuccessful run for the Republican presidential candidacy, dropping out just before the New Hampshire primary. President Richard M. Nixon appointed Romney secretary of the Department of Housing and Urban Development (HUD) (1969–72). He was survived by his wife, Lenore, two daughters, and two sons. (d. Bloomfield Hills, Michigan; July 26, 1995)

FURTHER READING

Obituary. *Current Biography*, Oct. 1995.

Obituary. *Times* (of London), July 28, 1995.

Obituary. *Independent*, July 27, 1995.

Obituary. *New York Times*, July 27, 1995.

Ronstadt, Linda Marie (1946–)

Popular, country, and Latin singer Linda Ronstadt returned in 1995 to the kind of music that had brought her early acclaim in the mid-1970s, with issuance of her very well received country rock album *Feels Like Home*. Among the hit songs on the album were "After the Goldrush," a trio sung with Valerie Carter and Emmylou Harris; her 1970s hit "Walk On," sung as a duet with Alison Krauss; the ballad "Lover's Return"; "The Waiting"; and the title track, composed by Randy Newman.

"Walk On" was also issued as a hit single. Another 1995 hit single was "High Sierra," while a third was "A Dream Is a Wish," a popular Christmas-season offering from the Disney album *The Music of Cinderella,* in which Ronstadt appeared, along with several other artists. Ronstadt's Grammy-winning Latin albums *Frenesí* and *Más Canciones* (*More Songs*) also continued to do well in their special markets.

Tucson-born Ronstadt began her recording and touring career in the late 1960s, and emerged in the mid-1970s as a very versatile popular and country star. Her first hit album was *Heart Like a Wheel* (1974), containing two of her most popular songs: "You're No Good" and "I

Can't Help It If I'm Still in Love with You." She went on to record such albums as *Different Drum* (1974), *Prisoner in Disguise* (1975), *Hasten Down the Wind* (1976), *Blue Bayou* (1977), *Living in the U.S.A.* (1978), *Mad Love* (1980), *Lush Life* (1984), the Grammy-winning *Trio* (1986; with Dolly Parton and Emmylou Harris), *'Round Midnight* (1987), *Canciones de Mi Padre* (1987), *Cry Like a Rainstorm—Howl Like the Wind* (1989), *Warm Your Heart* (1991), *Frenesí* (1992), *Más Canciones (More Songs)* (1992), and *Winter Light* (1993). On stage, she starred in *Pirates of Penzance* (1981; on film, 1983), and off-Broadway in *La Bohème* (1984).

FURTHER READING

"Linda Ronstadt." CHRIS MUNDY. *Rolling Stone*, July 13, 1995.
"Linda Ronstadt. . . ." LISA LIEBMAN. *New Woman*, Apr. 1994.
Linda Ronstadt: Mexican-American Singer. RICHARD AMDUR. Chelsea House, 1994.

Rose, Jack

Rose, Jack (1911–95) Born in Warsaw, Poland, Jack Rose emigrated to the United States with his family as a child and grew up in Brooklyn. After attending Ohio State University, he went into show business as a comedy writer, and became one of Bob Hope's radio show gag writers. He made his screenwriting debut with Hope's film *Road to Rio* (1947), and went on to write or cowrite many other films, among them *My Favorite Brunette* (1947), *Sorrowful Jones* (1949), *Riding High* (1950), *I'll See You in My Dreams* (1952), *April in Paris* (1953), and *Living It Up* (1954). He also moved into fim production, writing and producing *The Seven Little Foys* (1955), *Beau James* (1957), *Houseboat* (1958), *The Five Pennies* (1959), *It Started in Naples* (1960), and several other films. He and Melvin Frank shared an Academy Award nomination for *A Touch of Class* (1973). He was survived by two daughters, a son, and a brother. (d. Los Angeles; October 20, 1995)

FURTHER READING

Obituary. *Independent*, Nov. 4, 1995.
Obituary. *New York Times*, Oct. 27, 1995.

Roseanne

Roseanne (Roseanne Barr Arnold; 1952–) Surviving broadcast time changes and the inevitable slow decline of "Roseanne," her long-running series, Roseanne continued to be a major figure in television and a highly visible celebrity in 1995. She won Emmy and Screen Actors Guild nominations as best actress in a comedy for her role. She also appeared at the end of the 1994–95 season on Garry Shandling's "The Larry Sanders Show," as a brief, but stormy love interest.

Roseanne also costarred in the film comedy *Blue in the Face,* directed by Wayne Wang and Paul Auster. The film, a quickly made sequel to Wang's film *Smoke,* starred Harvey Keitel as Brooklyn cigar store owner Augie, in a cast that also included Lily Tomlin, Madonna, Lou Reed, Michael J. Fox, and Jim Jarmusch.

On the personal side, Roseanne married her third husband, her former bodyguard, Ben Thomas. She had become pregnant through in-vitro fertilization with Thomas in 1994 and in August gave birth to their son, Buck Thomas.

Salt Lake City–born Roseanne began her career as a stand-up comedian in variety in the late 1970s. A decade later, as Roseanne Barr, she emerged as the star of the very popular television series "Roseanne" (1988–), which was generally at or near the top of the ratings from 1989 onward. Propelled by her personal style, she also emerged as a major celebrity. Her theatrical films include *She-Devil* (1989) and *Even Cowgirls Get the Blues* (1994); her television films have included *Backfield in Motion* (1991) and *The Woman Who Loved Elvis* (1993). An animated series, "Little Rosey," based on the Roseanne character, aired during the 1990–91 television season.

She has published *Roseanne: My Life as a Woman* (1989), *Stand Up!* (1989), and *My Lives* (1994). In 1991, speaking to an incest survivors group, Arnold went public with charges that she had been sexually abused as a child, a charge her parents denied. She has been married twice, during her 1991–94 marriage to Tom Arnold performing as Roseanne Arnold. She has five children, one of whom she bore as a teenager and gave up for adoption.

FURTHER READING

"Dealing with. . . ." JOHN LAHR. *New Yorker*, July 17, 1995.
"All the rage." LISA SCHWARZBAUM. *Entertainment*, Apr. 21, 1995.
"Her life as a woman." PETER GALVIN. *Advocate*, Jan. 24, 1995.
"Really Roseanne." KEVIN SESSUMS. *Vanity Fair*, Feb. 1994.

"Clash of the titans." MICHAEL A. LIPTON. *People*, May 2, 1994.

"Strange bedfellows." FRANK SWERTLOW. *Redbook*, June 1993.

"Roseanne and Tom Arnold." *Playboy*, June 1993.

"Roseanne Arnold. . . . " LEO JANOS. *Cosmopolitan*, Feb. 1993.

Roseanne Arnold: Comedy's Queen Bee. KATHERINE E. KROHN. Lerner, 1993.

"Roseanne!" LESLIE VAN BUSKIRK. *Us*, May 1992.

Roseanne Barr. ROBERT ITALIA. Abdo & Daughters, 1991.

Roth, Henry (1906–95)

Born in Galicia, Austria-Hungary, Henry Roth emigrated to the United States with his family in 1912, and grew up on New York City's Lower East Side and in Harlem. His first—and until 1993 his only—novel was *Call It Sleep* (1934), the semiautobiographical story of an American Jewish boy growing up in New York. It was acclaimed for its realism and imagination, and sold a few thousand copies, while the literary world waited for Roth's further works. And waited; although he wrote a few short pieces of fiction, no further novels came, for he apparently had developed a "writer's block" of epic proportions. In 1964, *Call It Sleep* was reissued in paperback—and Irving Howe "rediscovered" the work and its author in a full-page *New York Times* review, haling Roth as a great American author. Roth's life became easier with the royalties generated by the now-best-selling book—but he issued no new novel. Finally, in the late 1970s, he began to write seriously again, conceiving and writing thousands of manuscript pages of what was intended to be a six-volume work, "Mercy of a Rude Stream," about the adolescence and further life of a New York Jewish boy. He published two very well received volumes of the work before his death: *A Star Shines over Mt. Morris Park* (1993) and *A Diving Rock on the Hudson* (1994). He was survived by two sons and a sister. (d. Albuquerque, New Mexico; October 13, 1995)

FURTHER READING

Obituary. *Independent*, Oct. 18, 1995.

Obituary. *Times* (of London), Oct. 17, 1995.

Obituary. *New York Times*, Oct. 15, 1995.

Roth, Philip (1933–)

Mickey Sabbath is an awful person, all the reviewers agree, but it is a measure of Roth's skill as a novelist that, in *Sabbath's Theater,* he makes this acerbic, sar-

donic, outrageously irreverent man, with all the sexual fascinations of a Portnoy 30 years on, someone readers are drawn to follow as he attempts to deal with the enormities of life, love, and death. *Sabbath's Theater* won the National Book Award, announced in November 1995. Roth had been nominated four times before and won once, with his first novel, which brought him to prominence, *Goodbye, Columbus* (1959). An interview with Roth was also included in the 1995 book *An Unsentimental Education: Writers and Chicago,* edited by Molly McQuade, recalling his time in Chicago.

Newark-born Roth received his 1954 B.A. from Bucknell University and his 1955 M.A. from the University of Chicago. After service in the U.S. Army, he returned to teach at the University of Chicago (1956–58), before moving to New York. It was in his army and Chicago years that he began to write *Goodbye, Columbus* (1959), basis of the 1969 film, which won the National Book Award. The book was rooted in Jewish-American life, like much of his later work, which includes the novels *Letting Go* (1962), *Portnoy's Complaint* (1969), *The Breast* (1972), *The Great American Novel* (1973), *The Professor of Desire* (1977), *The Ghost Writer* (1979), *Zuckerman Unbound* (1981), *The Anatomy Lesson* (1983), *Zuckerman Bound* (1985), *The Prague Orgy* (1985), *The Counterlife* (1987; it won the National Book Critics Circle award), *Deception* (1990), and *Operation Shylock: A Confession* (1993). Roth is also a prolific short story writer.

His other works include *Reading Myself and Others* (1975), *The Facts: A Novelist's Autobiography* (1988), and *Patrimony* (1991), about his father, which won the National Book Critics Circle award for biography or autobiography. Roth has taught at several colleges and universities and received numerous honors. Previously married to Margaret Martinson (1959–68), he married actress Claire Bloom in 1990; they later separated.

FURTHER READING

Philip Roth and the Jews. Alan Cooper. State University of New York Press, 1996.
Beyond Despair: Three Lectures and a Talk with Philip Roth. AHARON APPELFELD. Fromm International, 1994.
Philip Roth Revisited. JAY L. HALIO. Twayne, 1992.
Conversations with Philip Roth. GEORGE J. SEARLES, ed. University Press of Mississippi, 1992.
"Roth, Philip Milton." *Current Biography*, May 1991.
" 'All new to me. . . .' " BARTH HEALEY. *New York Times Book Review*, Jan.6, 1991.

Rozsa, Miklos (1907–95) Budapest-born Miklos Rozsa, one of the leading composers of Hollywood's golden age, began his film career by scoring several British films, among them *Knight Without Armor* (1937), *The Four Feathers* (1939), and *The Thief of Bagdad* (1940). In Hollywood from 1941, he created the scores of dozens of films, winning three Academy Awards, for *Spellbound* (1945), *A Double Life* (1947), and *Ben-Hur* (1959). Among his other films were *Five Graves to Cairo* (1943), *Double Indemnity* (1944), *The Lost Weekend* (1945), *The Strange Love of Martha Ivers* (1946), *The Naked City* (1948), *Quo Vadis* (1951), *Ivanhoe* (1952), *Julius Caesar* (1953), *El Cid* (1961), *The Green Berets* (1968), *Fedora* (1978), and *Time After Time* (1979). Rozsa also wrote a considerable body of classical music. His autobiography was *A Double Life* (1982). He attended the University of Budapest, and studied music in Leipzig and Paris. He was survived by his wife, Margaret, a daughter, a son, and a sister. (d. Los Angeles, July 27, 1995)

FURTHER READING

"Music man." ROBERT HORTON. *Film Comment*, Nov.–Dec. 1995.
Obituary. *Current Biography*, Oct. 1995.
Obituary. *Independent*, July 31, 1995.
Obituary. *Times* (of London), July 31, 1995.
Obituary. *New York Times*, July 29, 1995.
Obituary. *Variety*, July 28, 1995.
"Rozsa, Miklos." *Current Biography*, Feb. 1992.

Rubin, Robert Edward (1938–) Treasury Secretary Robert Rubin continued to function at the center of Clinton administration economic and fiscal policy during 1995, as he had during the first two Clinton years, while head of the White House–based National Economic Council. One of his earliest challenges was the Mexican financial crisis; he played a major role in designing the expensive bailout that helped the Mexican government survive the crisis. He was also a chief designer and proponent of the comprehensive banking law changes before Congress for much of the year; if passed, these would have freed banks to engage in several kinds of financial businesses that had been prohibited since passage of the Depression-era Glass-Steagall Act in 1933. Rubin was also involved in the year-long effort to support the value of the dollar, and in developing Clinton administration budget policies.

Rubin began his career as a lawyer at the New York City firm of Cleary, Gottlieb, Steen, and Hamilton (1964–66). In 1966, he began his long career at the Wall Street investment banking firm of Goldman, Sachs & Co. He became a partner in 1971 and a member of the firm's management committee in 1980, then becoming vice chairman and co–chief operating officer (1987–90), and co–senior partner and cochairman (1990–92). He also advised New York City and New York State on financial matters, serving on a wide range of other government advisory boards and for-profit and nonprofit organization boards of directors. He was also a key Democratic Party fundraiser throughout the 1980s and early 1990s, and was chairperson of the New York committee that hosted the 1992 Democratic National Convention. He succeeded retiring treasury secretary Lloyd Bentsen in 1994.

New York City–born Rubin received his 1960 A.B. from Harvard University and did postgraduate work at the London School of Economics (1960–61). His 1964 LL.B. came from Yale Law School. He is married to Judith Leah Oxenberg; they have two children.

FURTHER READING

"Guy next door. . . ." KEVIN RAFFERTY. *The Observer*, Oct. 22, 1995.

"How's he doing?" EVAN THOMAS. *Newsweek*, Mar. 20, 1995.

"Robert Rubin's. . . ." OWEN ULLMANN and PAUL MAGNUSSON. *Business Week*, Mar. 28, 1994.

"Old master. . . ." JOHN B. JUDIS. *New Republic*, Dec. 13, 1993.

"Unholy trinity. . . ." JOHN B. JUDIS. *Mother Jones*, Mar.–Apr. 1993.

Ruiz Massieu, Mario: See Salinas de Gortari, Carlos.

Rushdie, Salman (Ahmed Salman Rushdie; 1947–   ) Salman Rushdie moved cautiously out of seclusion in 1995. In September, he made his first scheduled public appearance in six years, at a public debate on "Writers and the State" in London, in what he called his "coming out." The appearance was announced in the newspapers with the permission of Scotland Yard, which has provided bodyguards for Rushdie since Iranian Muslim fundamentalists (led by the late Ayatollah Ruhollah Khomeini) pronounced a death sentence (*fatwa*) on him on February 14, 1989, and offered $1 million for his murder. This took place after rioting and protests greeted publication of his best-selling 1988 novel *The Satanic Verses*, which some fundamentalist Muslims regarded as blasphemous, though Rushdie denied any intent to insult those of Muslim faith.

In 1995, unlike previous years, the Iranian government did not formally renew the death threat on its anniversary. The International Rushdie Defense Committee regarded as hopeful a statement asked for by the Danish government and signed by Iran's ambassador to Denmark, saying that Iran "never had sent, was not sending and would not in the future send anyone to kill Salman Rushdie." However, the statement was not affirmed, and was somewhat contradicted, by the Iranian government. The European Union also asked for and received from Iran a disavowal of any assassination attempt.

The danger has been real, for Rushdie and others. In 1993 a mob set fire to an Istanbul hotel, killing 35 people, though their target, Aziz Nesin, Rushdie's translator, escaped. Later that year, William Nygaard, publisher of the Norwegian translation, was shot three times and seriously wounded. In 1991, in separate attacks, Rushdie's Japanese translator, Hitoshi Igarashi, was murdered, and his Italian translator, Ettore Caprioli, was badly wounded.

Meanwhile, work completed in seclusion was being published. Rushdie's new novel *The Moor's Last Sigh*, his first since *Satanic Verses*, was published in Britain to wide critical acclaim. Following its publication, the normally gregarious Rushdie was increasingly seen in London and elsewhere in Britain and was a frequent guest on talk shows. His public appearances were marked by some protests, but were well attended. In India, the book initially sold well, but was later banned in that country, reportedly because of its unflattering parody of the leader of a Bombay-based Hindu nationalist group; its publisher was appealing the ban. The novel's American publication was set for January 1996. Earlier in 1995, Rushdie had also published his first collection of short stories, *East, West: Stories*, many of which had previous been published in periodicals.

Bombay-born but long resident in Britain, Rushdie is a leading novelist, whose works also include *Midnight's Children* (1981), which won the 1981 Booker Prize and the 1993 "Booker of Bookers" as the best winner in the award's 25-year history, and *Shame* (1983). His *Haroun and the Sea of Stories* (1990) was named best children's novel of the year by the Writers' Guild of Great Britain. He has also published *Imaginary Homelands: Essays and Criticisms 1981–1991* (1991). Rushdie attended King's College, Cambridge. His second marriage, to American novelist Marianne Wiggins, ended in divorce in 1993, after two years of separation. He has one son, Zafar, with whom in his years of seclusion he was able to communicate only by telephone.

FURTHER READING

"The last laugh." MAYA JAGGI. *New Statesman & Society*, Sept. 8, 1995.

"A talk with. . . ." SYBIL STEINBERG. *Publishers Weekly*, Jan. 30, 1995.

"Guarding Salman. . . ." TOBY YOUNG. *Vanity Fair*, Aug. 1994.

"The fundamental. . . ." FRED HALLIDAY. *New Statesman & Society*, Feb. 12, 1993.

"The martyr." PHILIP WEISS. *Esquire*, Jan. 1993.

"Salman Rushdie. . . ." GERALDINE BROOKS. *New Republic*, July 27, 1992.

Bomb: Interviews. BETSY SUSSLER, ed. City Lights, 1992.

" 'Free speech is life itself.' " KARSTEN PRAGER. *Time*, Dec. 23, 1991.

"The fugitive. . . ." MARK ABLEY. *Saturday Night*, May 1991.

"Keeping up with. . . . " JAMES FENTON. *New York Review of Books*, Mar. 28, 1991.

Salman Rushdie. JAMES HARRISON. Macmillan, 1991.

Ryan, Meg (Margaret Mary Emily Hyra; 1961–) Film star Meg Ryan was a familiar face on home video screens in 1995, as her 1994 hit film *When a Man Loves a Woman* also became a hit in video rentals. She won a People's Choice favorite actress award and a Screen Actors Guild best leading actress nomination, and was also honored by receiving a Women in Film annual Crystal Award.

In 1995, Ryan starred opposite Robert Downey, Jr., in the film *Restoration,* set in 17th-century England. Directed by Michael Hoffman, the film costarred Sam Neill as Charles II, Hugh Grant, Ian McKellen, and David Thewlis. Ryan played an insane asylum inmate who has a child by Merivel (Downey), a disgraced court physician. Ryan also starred opposite Kevin Kline and Timothy Hutton in the comedy *French Kiss,* directed by Lawrence Kasdan. The film's convoluted story line involved two cross-cutting romances, stolen and then lost jewels, a trip to France, and a long chase.

Forthcoming were starring roles opposite Denzel Washington in *Courage Under Fire,* directed by Ed Zwick and costarring Matt Daman, Lou Diamond Phillips, Scott Glenn, and Michael Moriarty; and opposite Julia Roberts in the film *The Women,* written and directed by Diane English and based on the Clare Boothe Luce play. Ryan was also to be one of the voices for the animated film *Anastasia.*

Ryan was born in Fairfield, Connecticut, and attended New York University. She made her film debut in *Rich and Famous* (1980); among her 1980s films were *Top Gun* (1986), *Innerspace* (1987), *Promised Land* (1987), and *The Presidio* (1988). Her breakthrough starring role came in *When Harry Met Sally* (1989). Her later films included *The Doors* (1991), *Prelude to a Kiss* (1992), *Sleepless in Seattle* (1993), *Flesh and Bone* (1993), and *When a Man Loves a Woman* (1994). She is married to actor Dennis Quaid; they have a son.

FURTHER READING

"Losing Meg." SUSAN JORDAN. *Good Housekeeping*, Aug. 1995.

"Star lite. . . ." RICHARD CORLISS. *Time*, May 22, 1995.

"Maximum Meg." KEVIN SESSUMS. *Vanity Fair*, May 1995.

"The Meg Ryan mystique." BETH LANDMAN et al. *Redbook*, Apr. 1995.

"True romance." JULIANN GAREY. *Us*, Dec. 1994.

"Loving Meg." BRIGID O'SHAUGHNESSY. *Redbook*, June 1994.

"Educating Meg." KAREN S. SCHNEIDER. *People*, Aug. 2, 1993.

"Tough love." CHARLES SALZBERG. *Redbook*, July 1993.

"When Dennis met Meg." GEORGE KALOGERAKIS. *Vogue*, Nov. 1993.

Ryder, Winona (Winona Laura Horowitz; 1971–) For her role in the 1994 film *Little Women,* actress Winona Ryder received a best actress Academy Award nomination. She also remained a very familiar face on home video screens, as *Little Women* became a hit in video.

In 1995, Ryder starred as Finn Dodd in the film *How to Make an American Quilt,* directed by Jocelyn Moorhouse, adapted for film by Jane Anderson from the Whitney Otto novel, and costarring Maya Angelou, Anne Bancroft, Ellen

Burstyn, Samantha Mathis, Kate Nelligan, and Jean Simmons. Ryder is at the center of the film, as a woman who temporarily flees a complicated life, returning to her hometown and to a quilting circle, a vehicle for seven women's personal stories.

Forthcoming was a starring role in the film version of Arthur Miller's play *The Crucible,* directed by Nicholas Hyner from Miller's screenplay, and costarring Daniel Day-Lewis, Paul Scofield, Joan Allen, and Bruce Davison. Still forthcoming was a starring role opposite Lukas Haas in *Boys,* directed by Stacy Cochran.

Born in Winona, Minnesota, Ryder became a teenage film star in the late 1980s, making her debut in *Lucas* (1986). She appeared in *Beetlejuice* (1988), played a breakthrough role as Veronica in *Heathers* (1989), and went on to star in such films as *Great Balls of Fire* (1989), *Welcome Home Roxy Carmichael* (1990), *Mermaids* (1991), *Edward Scissorhands* (1991), *Bram Stoker's Dracula* (1992), *The Age of Innocence* (1993), *Little Women* (1994), *Reality Bites* (1994), and *The House of the Spirits* (1994). She studied at the American Conservatory Theater.

FURTHER READING

"Take a bow. . . ." RICHARD CORLISS. *Time,* Jan. 9, 1995.
"Little woman. . . ." JENNY ALLEN. *Life,* Dec. 1994.
"The bigger they get. . . ." CHARLA KRUPP. *Glamour,* Nov. 1994.
"Ryder, Winona." *Current Biography,* June 1994.
"Kindred spirits. . . ." LISA LIEBMAN. *New Woman,* Apr. 1994.
"Women who run. . . ." DANA KENNEDY. *Entertainment,* Feb. 11, 1994.
"Riding high." DAVID HANDELMAN. *Vogue,* Oct. 1993.
"Winona among. . . ." MICHAEL HIRSCHORN. *Esquire,* Nov. 1992.
Winona Ryder. EVAN KEITH. Dell, 1992.

S

Sacks, Oliver Wolf (1933–) Unlike many other writing doctors, Oliver Sacks has become known not as a novelist, playwright, or poet, but as a keen observer of the art and science of medicine, and of the people he has met in its practice. That these people prove fascinating stems partly from Sacks's literary skills but also from the nature of his specialty, for Sacks is a neurologist focusing on the elusive, enigmatic human brain. Sacks is best known to wide audiences from the 1990 film *Awakenings* (based on his 1973 book), in which he was played by Robin Williams; this told of his discovery that many people who, after encephalitis, had effectively been "asleep" for decades could, at least temporarily, be brought back to consciousness with some new medications. Sacks's 1995 work, *An Anthropologist on Mars: Seven Paradoxical Tales,* focuses on some individuals who have experienced unusual neurological conditions and what their experiences mean to our understanding of the brain and its workings. These include an artist who became color-blind after an accident; a blind man who regained his sight after decades; a woman with autism who has difficulty relating to people but became an expert in animal behavior; and a surgeon with Tourette's syndrome, whose symptoms (spasmodic tics) disappear while he is performing operations on patients.

London-born Sacks received his 1954 B.A. from Oxford University and received his medical training at London's Middlesex Hospital, interning there (1958–60) before coming to the United States and interning at San Francisco's Mt. Zion

Hospital (1961–62). He was a resident in neurology at the University of California at Los Angeles (1962–65) and then joined New York's Albert Einstein College of Medicine in 1965, becoming a fellow (1965–66), instructor in neurology (1966–75), assistant professor (1975–78), associate professor (1978–85), and clinical professor of neurology (1985–). He was concurrently associated with Beth Abraham Hospital (1965–), Bronx State Hospital (1965–91), and several other institutions. His books include *Migraine* (1970; rev. ed. 1992), *Awakenings* (1973), *A Leg to Stand On* (1984), the best-seller *The Man Who Mistook His Wife for a Hat: And Other*

Clinical Tales (1986), and *Seeing Voices: A Journey into the World of the Deaf* (1989).

FURTHER READING

"Oliver Sacks. . . ." TOM MCINTYRE. *Whole Earth Review*, Summer 1995.
"The man who mistook. . . ." *Psychology Today*, May–June 1995.
"The case of the quirky. . . ." JOE CHIDLEY. *Maclean's*, Mar. 13, 1995.
"Where biology meets. . . ." MARGALIT FOX. *New York Times Book Review*, Feb. 19, 1995.
"Scribe of the spirit. . . ." ERICA E. GOODE. *U.S. News & World Report*, Jan. 21, 1991.

Saleh, Mohammed: See Abdel Rahman, Omar.

Salinas de Gortari, Carlos (1948–)

After being succeeded by Ernesto Zedillo Ponce de León on December 1, 1994, former Mexican president Carlos Salinas began 1995 as a much-honored statesman and a leading candidate for the post of head of the World Trade Organization—but then suffered an extraordinary reversal of fortune. On February 28, his older brother, **Raúl Salinas de Gortari** (ca. 1946–), was arrested by the Mexican government and charged with playing a central role in the September 1994 assassination of ruling Institutional Revolutionary Party (PRI) Secretary General José Francisco Ruiz Massieu. Ruiz's brother, **Mario Ruiz Massieu** (1950–), had served in the interior ministry and then been deputy attorney general in Salinas's government (1988–94), but had resigned after charging that the government had blocked his assigned investigation of the murder of his brother; Mario Ruiz Massieu was arrested on February 3 by the U.S. authorities at Newark airport on apparently unrelated charges, although press reports alleged links to several earlier Mexican murders and corruption scandals.

Carlos Salinas was not charged with complicity in any of these events, but was inevitably drawn into a year-long web of accusations and counteraccusations, and a barrage of media speculation. At the same time, he was being widely accused of having withheld information on the seriousness of Mexico's developing economic crisis during his last months in office. He responded to all of this by going on a two-day hunger strike, reached an agreement with President Zedillo that salvaged some of his former reputation, and went into U.S. exile on March 11, reportedly for at least the balance of Zedillo's term of office. He also withdrew his World Trade Organization candidacy.

In late November, the Mexican government charged that Raúl Salinas had approximately $105 million hidden in secret European bank accounts. Carlos Salinas expressed amazement, denied all knowledge or complicity, and publicly attacked former president Luis Echeverría as the power behind attacks on him; the growing set of disputes and scandals continued to rack Mexico's leading elites and political party. In mid-November, Raúl Salinas's wife, Paulina Castanon, and her brother Antonio were arrested after attempting to withdraw millions of dollars from a secret Swiss bank account, using a photograph of her husband under a false name.

Carlos Salinas spent his whole career in a series of increasingly responsible Mexican federal government financial planning posts, beginning with his term as assistant director of public finance in the finance ministry (1971–74). Before his 1987 presidential nomination, he was minister of planning and the federal budget (1982–87). He scored a major victory in 1993, his final full year in office, with U.S. ratification of the Mexican-U.S.-Canadian North American Free Trade Agreement (NAFTA), which provided for elimination of a wide range of tariff barriers, some immediately and others over a fifteen-year period, and which contained many other provisions aimed at essentially merging the economies of the three countries. Carlos Salinas attended the National University of Mexico and Harvard University. He has published various works, including *Political Participation, Public Investment, and Support for the System: A Comparative Study of Rural Communities in Mexico* (1982). He is married to Yolanda Cecilia Occelli González; they have three children.

Raúl Salinas de Gortari, a prominent businessman, was an official in Mexico's staple food agency during his brother's administration. He published *Rural Reform in Mexico: The View from the Comarca Lagunera* (1994), written with José L. Solis-González.

FURTHER READING

" 'Salinas' is fast. . . ." GERI SMITH. *Business Week*, Dec. 25, 1995.
"A family's value. . . ." SALLIE HUGHES. *Maclean's*, Dec. 11, 1995.

"Sibling embarrassment." *Economist*, Dec. 2, 1995.

"Tracking two amigos." TIM PADGETT. *Newsweek*, June 12, 1995.

"The fall of Carlos. . . ." GERI SMITH and STEPHEN BAKER. *Business Week*, Mar. 27, 1995.

"Real-life soap opera. . . ." MICHAEL S. SERRILL. *Time*, Mar. 20, 1995.

"Scandal in high places. . . ." SCOTT MORRISON. *Maclean's*, Mar. 13, 1995.

"Blood relations." RUSSELL WATSON. *Newsweek*, Mar. 13, 1995.

"Carlos Salinas de Gortari." *Newsweek*, Dec. 26, 1994.

"A talk with. . . ." GERI SMITH. Dec. 6, 1993.

"Salinas. . . ." GERI SMITH and FRANK J. COMES. Feb. 1, 1993. *Business Week*.

"The real revolutionary." "The world's other newsmakers." JAMES WALSH. *Time*, Jan. 4, 1993.

"Salinas's Mexican standoff." DEIRDRE MCMURDY. *Maclean's*, Sept. 7, 1992.

"Interview with. . . ." ALFREDO J. ESTRADA. "A man for all seasons." MICHELE HELLER. *Hispanic*, Sept. 1992.

Salinas de Gortari, Raúl: See Salinas de Gortari, Carlos.

Salk, Jonas Edward (1914–95) New York City–born Jonas Salk, the medical researcher who developed the first successful polio vacccine, received his 1939 M.D. from New York University medical school, and began his work on viruses at the University of Michigan in 1942, there and later at the University of Pittsburgh working on the development of flu vaccines. In the early 1950s, he developed his successful killed-virus vaccine against polio (infantile paralysis); the virus was first grown in monkeys, then killed before use as a vaccine. In 1955, the National Foundation for Infantile Paralysis funded an overwhelmingly successful field test of one million people, which was followed by worldwide vaccination of more than 200 million children (1955–60), with new polio cases dropping dramatically among those vaccinated. Some early vaccine contamination cast doubt on the results, but these were soon resolved in favor of the vaccine, which Salk declined to patent. With the introduction in 1961 of the live-virus vaccine developed by Dr. Albert Sabin, the Salk vaccine fell into disuse in the United States, though it continued to be used in many other countries. In 1963, Salk, now a world figure, opened San Diego's Salk Institute, dedicated to anticancer research. In the early 1980s, he expanded the Institute's work to include AIDS research. Among Salk's publications were *The Survival of the Wisest* (1973), *How Like an Angel* (1974), *World Population and Human Value: A New Reality* (1982; written with Jonathan Salk), and *Anatomy of Reality: Merging of Intuition and Reason* (1983). He was survived by his second wife, Françoise Gilot, and three sons. (d. La Jolla, California; June 23, 1995)

FURTHER READING

Obituary. *JAMA, The Journal of the American Medical Association*, Dec. 13, 1995.

Obituary. *Current Biography*, Aug. 1995.

"Hero in a white lab coat." MICHAEL NEILL. *People*, July 10, 1995.

"The savior of summer. . . ." SHARON BEGLEY. *Newsweek*, July 3, 1995.

"The good doctor. . . ." RICHARD LACAYO. *Time*, July 3, 1995.

Obituary. *Economist*, July 1, 1995.

Obituary. *Independent*, June 28, 1995.

Obituary. *Times* (of London), June 26, 1995.

Obituary. *New York Times*, June 25, 1995.

Jonas Salk. MICHAEL TOMLINSON. Rourke, 1993.

Jonas Salk: Discoverer of the Polio Vaccine. CARMEN BREDESON. Enslow, 1993.

Jonas Salk: Research for a Healthier World. VICTORIA SHERROW. Facts on File, 1993.

"Dr. Salk speaks out." *Architectural Record*, Jan. 1992.

Salvi, John C., III (1972–) On Friday, December 30, 1994, abortion foe John Salvi allegedly walked into a Planned Parenthood abortion clinic on Beacon Street, in Brookline, Massachusetts, and opened fire with a rifle, killing receptionist Shannon Lowney and wounding three others. Approximately ten minutes later, he walked into the Preterm Health Service clinic, also on Beacon, a little more than a mile away, and again opened fire, killing receptionist Leanne Nichols and wounding two more; he then exchanged fire with security guards, leaving a duffel bag at the scene. Police traced him through the contents of the bag, and later that night raided his Hampton Beach, New Hampshire home; but he had fled. Twenty-five hours later, on Saturday, December 31, he allegedly opened fire on the Hillcrest abortion clinic, in Norfolk, Virginia, without injury to anyone, and then fled; he was picked up by Norfolk police a few blocks away. Extradited to Brookline, he pleaded not guilty to murder and attempted murder charges in early January, and in August was ruled mentally competent to stand trial, despite defense pleas of mental incompetence. His trial was expected in early 1996.

A devout Roman Catholic who was studying hairdressing, Salvi was reportedly not an active member of any antiabortion action group. However, the murders were viewed by many as greatly influenced by the fanatic fringe of the antiabortion movement, coming as they did after a wave of killings, physical attacks, and the mass harassment of doctors and clinics.

FURTHER READING

"An armed fanatic. . . ." MICHAEL D. LEMONICK. *Time*, Jan. 9, 1995.

Sampras, Pete (1971–) It was a highly

emotional year for Pete Sampras. He began and ended 1995 ranked number one, but rode a roller coaster all the way. At the Australian Open, after his coach Tim Gullikson was forced to return home for treatment of a brain tumor, Sampras won a nearly four-hour quarterfinal match over Jim Courier, breaking into tears at the end; he later lost in the finals to Andre Agassi. In the next few months, Sampras faltered and Agassi came on to take the top ranking in April. Sampras later rallied to win two Grand Slam titles: Wimbledon, where he defeated Boris Becker, and the U.S. Open, over Agassi. In November, with Agassi out for two months with a chest muscle injury, Sampras regained the number one ranking. He then led the United States to victory at the Davis Cup tournament, where the U.S. team was captained by Tom Gullikson, twin brother of Sampras's coach, and ended the year with a total of five tournament wins. Sampras and Agassi had a strong but friendly rivalry over the top ranking, used lightheartedly in a television commercial that showed them setting up the net and playing on a Manhattan street.

Maryland-born Sampras grew up in Palos Verdes, California, where he was groomed for tennis stardom from the second grade. He dropped out of Palos Verdes High School after his junior year to turn professional, at 19 becoming the youngest male ever to win the U.S. Open, in 1990, when he

was ranked 81st in the world. Two uncertain years followed, but by early 1993 Sampras had reached the number one ranking, trading it back and forth with Jim Courier through the year, but then taking it firmly with two consecutive Grand Slam wins, at Wimbledon and the U.S. Open. At that point, still only 22, he had won 19 tournament titles. He was ranked first throughout 1994, a year when he won the Australian Open and Wimbledon, for his third and fourth consecutive Grand Slam titles, as well as the Japan Open; during that year he had the biggest lead in points over the other competitors in the history of the ATP world rankings.

FURTHER READING

"In step with. . . ." JAMES BRADY. *Parade*, Aug. 27, 1995.
"Sampras or. . . ." PETER DE JONGE. *New York Times Magazine*, Aug. 27, 1995.
"Crossfire! . . ." DAVID HIGDON. *Tennis*, May 1995.
"Courier and. . . ." DAVID HIGDON. July 1994. "The Pete Sampras serve." TIM GULLIKSON and TONY TRABERT. Feb. 1994, *Tennis*.
"Sampras, Pete." *Current Biography*, May 1994.
" 'Sweet Pete'. . . ." CURRY KIRKPATRICK. *Newsweek*, Sept. 6, 1993.
"Sampras. . . ." HAL HIGDON. *Boys' Life*, Sept. 1991.
"The Sampras stakes." PETER M. COAN. *World Tennis*, July 1991.

Sanders, Deion Luwynn (1967–) In

January 1995, Deion Sanders got what he had come to San Francisco for: a Super Bowl ring. In Super Bowl XXIX, the San Francisco 49ers decisively defeated the San Diego Chargers 49-26. Sanders contributed an interception, but also distorted San Diego's offense—as he usually does—by causing them to throw *away* from the receiver he was covering, so freeing his own team's safeties to concentrate their attentions elsewhere. Win or lose, he would still have been the only athlete ever to play in both the World Series (1992) and the Super Bowl. In February, Sanders played in his fourth straight Pro Bowl.

With football season over, Sanders turned to baseball and the Cincinnati Reds, to whom he had been traded in 1994. In July he was traded to the San Francisco Giants; when they were eliminated from the playoffs, in late September, Sanders skipped the team's last seven games to have arthroscopic surgery on his left ankle. He ended his baseball season with a .268 batting average, 6 homers, 28 runs batted in, and 24 stolen bases, over 85 games.

Free agent Sanders also sought a new football contract in 1995. Though San Francisco wanted him back, they were not willing to pay the amount of money he asked; eventually he signed a seven-year contract with the Dallas Cowboys, for $35 million. From his October 29 Dallas debut, he played primarily on defense, but also occasionally on offense as well, as a receiver. Though the team had mid-season troubles over injuries, the Cowboys ended the season with a record of 12-4, and by mid-January were set to meet the Pittsburgh Steelers in Super Bowl XXX.

Sanders had strongly suggested that he was giving up baseball. In December, the Giants declined to offer him a new contract, making him a free agent. It remained to be seen what he would do in the 1996 baseball season.

On the personal side, in May a jury found Sanders not guilty of three charges relating to a dispute with a security guard at Cincinnati's Riverfront Stadium; a fourth charge had been dismissed by the judge.

Florida-born Sanders graduated from North Fort Myers High School and attended Florida State University, where he was named to the *Sporting News* Collegiate All-American football team (1986–88). He joined the New York Yankees baseball team (1989–90), then moved to the Atlanta Braves (1991–94), and the Cincinnati Reds (1995); meanwhile he also played football with the Atlanta Falcons (1989–93), the San Francisco 49ers (1994), and the Dallas Cowboys (1995–). Nicknamed "Neon Deion" or "Prime Time," Sanders has been named to the National Football League (NFL) Pro Bowl four times (1991–94). In 1992, he was NFL kickoff return leader, while also leading baseball's National League in triples. He was also named NFL defensive player of the 1994 season, an honor rarely given to a cornerback, who covers the other team's wide receivers. He has also released a rap video, "Must Be the Money" (1994). Deion and his wife, Carolyn, have a son, Deion Jr., and a daughter, Deiondra.

FURTHER READING

"Deion for a day." DAN DIEFFENBACH. *Sport,* Dec. 1995.

"How they make. . . ." BRUCE SCHOENFELD. *New York Times Magazine,* Nov. 19, 1995.

"All that glitters. . . ." PAUL ATTNER. *Sporting News,* Nov. 13, 1995.

"Lord of the realm." JOHN ED BRADLEY. *Sports Illustrated,* Oct. 9, 1995.

"Deion Sanders. . . ." WILLIAM LADSON. *Sport,* Feb. 1995.

"Sanders, Deion." *Current Biography,* Jan. 1995.

Deion Sanders. AARON KLEIN. Walker, 1995.

"Deion Sanders." KEVIN COOK. *Playboy,* Aug. 1994.

Deion Sanders. CARL R. GREEN and M. ROXANNE FORD. Macmillan, 1994.

Deion Sanders: Prime Time Player. STEW THORNLEY. Lerner, 1993.

"The neon nineties." MIKE LUPICA. *Esquire,* June 1992.

Sarandon, Susan (Susan Abigail Tomalin; 1946–)

Actress Susan Sarandon was again honored by her colleagues in 1995. For her 1994 role in *The Client,* she was named best actress of the year by the British Academy of Film & Television Arts (BAFTA). She also received a best actress Academy Award nomination and a best actress in a motion picture Screen Actors Guild nomination for the role. The film was also a hit in home video distribution, as was her 1994 film *Little Women.*

In 1995, Sarandon starred in the acclaimed film *Dead Man Walking,* written, directed, and coproduced by Tim Robbins. Sarandon played Sister Helen Prejean opposite Sean Penn as convicted rapist and murderer Matthew Poncelot, awaiting execution on the death row of New Orleans' Angola Prison. The tough, realistic film is set during the week just before Poncelot's execution; Sister Prejean has responded as a matter of conscience to Poncelot's letter, asking her to visit him in prison, and then to his plea that she become his religious adviser during his final days. The film, based on Sister Prejean's bestselling book, costarred Robert Prosky, Raymond J. Barry, R. Lee Ermey, Celia Weston, Lois Smith, Scott Wilson, and Roberta Maxwell. Sarandon received a Golden Globe nomination as best actress in a drama for the role.

Sarandon also appeared in the documentary *The Celluloid Closet,* which reviews the treatment of homosexuality in Hollywood films, from their beginnings until the present. On television, Sarandon narrated the *One Woman, One Vote* segment of the documentary series "The American Experience," about the long, successful fight for woman's suffrage.

New York City–born Sarandon began her film career with *Joe* (1970), and went on to play a wide variety of roles in the next two decades, in such films as *The Rocky Horror Picture Show* (1974), *Pretty Baby* (1978), *Loving Couples* (1980), *Atlantic City* (1981), *The Hunger* (1983), *Compromising Positions* (1985), *The Witches of Eastwick* (1987), *Bull Durham* (1988), *A Dry White Season* (1989), *White Palace* (1990), *Thelma and Louise* (1991), *Bob Roberts* (1992), *Light Sleeper* (1992), *Lorenzo's Oil* (1992), *The Client* (1994), *Little Women* (1994), and *Safe Passage* (1994). She has also appeared in several plays and on television.

Sarandon's B.A. was from Catholic University of America. She and actor-director Tim Robbins have two children; she also has a third child. She was formerly married to actor Chris Sarandon.

FURTHER READING

"Saint on a schedule." LAWRENCE O'TOOLE. *New Woman*, Jan. 1995.
"Susan Sarandon. . . ." GRAHAM FULLER. *Interview*, Oct. 1994.
"Susan Sarandon. . . ." JIM JEROME. *Ladies Home Journal*, Aug. 1994.
"Laying down the law." JESS CAGLE. *Entertainment*, July 29, 1994.
"Susan Sarandon. . . ." GAVIN SMITH. *Film Comment*, Mar.–Apr. 1993.
"Rebel, rebel." NUALA BOYLAN. *Harper's Bazaar*, Jan. 1993.
"The prime of. . . ." BEN YAGODA. *American Film*, May 1991.

Saro-Wiwa, Ken (Kenule Beeson Saro-Wiwa; 1941–95) On November 10, 1995—after a worldwide campaign for clemency had been ignored by the military government of General Sani Abacha—Nigerian author and democratic movement leader Ken Saro-Wiwa was hanged, along with eight codefendants. Their trial, on murder charges, had been condemned as a travesty of justice by many governments, human rights organizations, and world leaders, and their lawyers, themselves leading Nigerian jurists, had resigned in protest earlier in the year. After the executions, Nigeria's membership in the British Commonwealth was suspended, many other nations condemned the act and withdrew their representatives, and the

United Nations condemned the killings. The United States also condemned the executions, but did not apply sanctions to Nigerian oil imports. Shell Oil, accused of massive environmental damage in the Ogoni region by the Movement for the Survival of the Ogoni Peoples, headed by Saro-Wiwa, announced formal regret but took no public action aimed at discouraging the executions.

Born in the Ogoni region, in southern Nigeria, Saro-Wiwa was a graduate of the University of Ibadan. He was a high school teacher and university teacher before entering government service as an administrator (1968–73). In the decades that followed, he emerged as one of Nigeria's leading writers, whose poetry, novels, television plays, and essays won wide Nigerian and international audiences; he also became a leader of Nigeria's democratic protest movement. He was imprisoned by the Babandiga government in 1993, and again by the Abacha government after protesting attacks by the Nigerian military in the Ogoni region. A book of his prison writings, *A Month and a Day: A Detention Diary,* was published posthumously. He was survived by his wife and children. (d. Port Harcourt, Nigeria; November 10, 1995)

FURTHER READING

"Death of a writer." WILLIAM BOYD. *New Yorker*, Nov. 27, 1995.
"There's only one. . . ." JOHN VIDAL. *Guardian*, Nov. 17, 1995. (Interview with Ken Saro-Wiwa, Jr.)
"The evil at. . . ." *Independent*, Nov. 14, 1995. (Saro-Wiwa's final interview)
Obituary. *Times* (of London), Nov. 11, 1995.
Obituary. *Independent*, Nov. 11, 1995.

Sarton, May (Eleanor May Sarton; 1912–95) A multifaceted writer, Belgium-born May Sarton was best known by far as a feminist poet, whose work was highly esteemed by many in the new feminist movements that began in the 1960s. She began her working life in the late 1920s, as an actress with Eva Le Gallienne's Civic Repertory Theater, and in the early 1930s organized her own theater, at New York's New School for Social Research. Sarton left the theater to move fully into her writing career in the mid-1930s; her first book was the poetry collection *Encounter in April* (1937). Among her other

poetry collections were *Inner Landscape* (1939), *The Lion and the Rose* (1948), *The Land of Silence* (1953), *In Time Like Air* (1957), *Sun, Vine* (1961), *A Private Mythology* (1965), *Collected Poems* (1974), *Collected Poems: 1930–1993* (1993), and *Coming into Eighty: Poems* (1994). Among her novels were *The Single Hound* (1938), *Faithful Are the Wounds* (1955), *The Small Room* (1961), *Mrs Stevens Hears the Mermaids Singing* (1965), *As We Are Now* (1973), and *Anger* (1982). She also wrote several volumes of nonfiction, including *After the Stroke* (1988) and several journals, among them *Journal of a Solitude* (1973), *Endgame: Journal of the Seventy-Ninth Year* (1992), *Encore: A Journal of the Eightieth Year* (1993), and the posthumously published *At Eighty-Two: A Journal* (1995). There were no survivors. (d. York, Maine; July 16, 1995)

FURTHER READING

Obituary. *Current Biography*, Sept. 1995.
Obituary. *Independent*, July 25, 1995.
Obituary. *New York Times*, July 18, 1995.
"May to December." CLAIRE MESSUD. *Guardian*, Jan. 11, 1995.
A House of Gathering: Poets on May Sarton's Poetry. MARILYN KALLET, ed. University of Tennessee Press, 1993.
That Great Sanity: Critical Essays on May Sarton. SUSAN SWARTZLANDER and MARILYN R. MUMFORD, eds. University of Michigan Press, 1992.
Conversations with May Sarton. EARL G. INGERSOLL, ed. University Press of Mississippi, 1991.

Scali, John Alfred (1918–95) Ohio-born journalist and diplomat John Scali received his 1942 B.A. in journalism from Boston College. He began his career as a reporter for the *Boston Herald* (1942) and then moved to the United Press (1942–43). He was a war correspondent with the Associated Press (1943–44), staying with them after the war as a Washington-based diplomatic correspondent (1945–61). He then moved into broadcast journalism, with ABC News in Washington (1961–71). In 1962, Scali played a substantial role in the Cuban Missile Crisis, as an intermediary between the American and Soviet governments.

Scali moved from broadcast journalism into government when appointed a White House special consultant on foreign affairs by President Richard M. Nixon (1971–73). His career took a quantum leap when Nixon appointed him United States representative to the United Nations (1973–75). He then returned to ABC, where he worked on special assignments until his retirement in 1993. He was survived by his wife, Denise St. Germain Scali, and three daughters. (d. Washington, D.C.; October 9, 1995)

FURTHER READING

Obituary. *New York Times*, Oct. 10, 1995.

Scalia, Antonin (1936–) Justice Antonin Scalia continued during 1995 to be one of the Court's leading conservatives; but now he was no longer in the minority, but rather part of a very narrow conservative majority. Scalia wrote a concurring opinion in the landmark *Adarand Constructors* v. *Pena,* ruling that the federal government was required to use the same strict standards as the states in carrying out affirmative action programs, reversing the Court's long-held position on federal affirmative action programs. The decision was widely viewed as a major conservative victory. He also joined the majority in several other key cases, among them *U.S.* v. *Lopez,* declaring unconstitutional the federal Gun-Free School Zones Act of 1990, which made possession of a gun within 1,000 feet of a school illegal, ruling that this was an invalid extension of congressional ability to regulate interstate commerce, and thereby reopening formerly long-settled federal-state powers questions; *Miller* v. *Johnson,* which held that Georgia's

Eleventh Congressional District was unconstitutional because it was organized primarily to provide racial representation, rather than to respond to specific discrimination; *Rosenberg* v. *Rector and Visitors of the University of Virginia,* which held that the publicly funded University of Virginia was required to finance a Christian magazine run by students, a sharp change of Court direction on a basic constitutional issue; and *Missouri* v. *Jenkins,* effectively limiting the level of state spending to carry out a federally managed school desegregation plan in Kansas City. He dissented in the landmark *U.S. Term Limits Inc.* v. *Thornton,* which held that to limit congressional terms required a constitutional amendment; 23 state laws imposing terms limits were invalidated, and Congress was barred from passing a term limits law.

Scalia wrote the majority opinion in *Lebron* v. *National Railroad Passenger Co.,* ruling that Amtrak was a federal government agency, although Congress had otherwise defined it, must therefore respect the constitutional right to free speech, and could not therefore refuse to display a political billboard at New York's Pennsylvania Station by claiming that it was a private corporation. He also wrote the majority opinion in *Veronia School District* v. *Acton,* ruling that an Oregon school district's random drug testing program was constitutional; and in *Capital Square Review and Advisory Board* v. *Pinette,* ruling that it was unconstitutional to bar display of a large Ku Klux Klan cross in an Ohio public park. He wrote dissenting opinions in *McIntyre* v. *Ohio Election Commission,* voiding an Ohio law banning anonymous political literature as a violation of First Amendment–guaranteed free speech rights; and in *Babbitt* v. *Sweet Home Chapter of Communities for a Greater Oregon,* which held that the federal government had the right under the Endangered Species Act to sharply restrict logging and other activities harmful to the northern spotted owl.

New Jersey–born Scalia taught law at the University of Virginia (1967–74), was an assistant attorney general (1974–82), and taught law again at the University of Chicago (1977–82). He was appointed to the District of Columbia U.S. Court of Appeals by President Ronald Reagan in 1982, and to the Supreme Court by Reagan in 1986. Scalia received his 1957 B.A. from Georgetown University, and his 1960 LL.B. from Harvard Law School. He married Maureen McCarthy in 1960; they have nine children.

FURTHER READING

"Scalia the terrible." JOE MORGENSTERN. *Playboy,* July 1993.
"The leader of. . . ." JEFFREY ROSEN. *New Republic,* Jan. 18, 1993.
Justice Antonin Scalia and the Supreme Court's Conservative Moment. CHRISTOPHER E. SMITH. Greenwood, 1993.
Antonin Scalia. BOB ITALIA. Abdo & Daughters, 1992.

Schmidt, Mike

Schmidt, Mike (Michael Jack Schmidt; 1949–) Five years retired and in his first year of eligibility for baseball's Hall of Fame, Mike Schmidt set a new record in 1995 when he was named on 444 of the 460 ballots cast, the only player elected in 1995. That was the highest number of votes ever cast for a single player, breaking the record of 436 set in 1994 by pitcher Steve Carlton, Schmidt's former teammate on the Philadelphia Phillies; it was the fourth highest election percentage (96.52), following Tom Seaver, Ty Cobb, and Hank Aaron. Schmidt was the 220th inductee, and only the 26th elected in his first year of eligibility.

Schmidt was that rare player noted not only for his power hitting but also for his preeminent defensive skills, perhaps the greatest all-around third baseman ever. In his emotional induction at Cooperstown, on July 30, Schmidt warned both players and owners about their responsibility to the game (in the wake of the baseball strike and World Series–less 1994 season). He also made an emotional appeal for the induction of Pete Rose, the great player and his former Phillies teammate, who had been an inspiration for Schmidt, as for many others, before he ran into gambling and tax trouble in the 1980s, and was banned from the game in 1989, and so made ineligible for the Hall of Fame. (Rose himself has not applied for reinstatement.)

Born and raised in Dayton, Ohio, Schmidt attended Fairview High School and received his 1971 B.A. in business administration from Ohio University in Athens. He spent his entire major league career with the Philadelphia Phillies (1972–89). During that period he was named the National League's Most Valuable Player three times (1980; 1981; 1986) and Most Valuable Player of the World Series (1980), the Phillies' first and only Series win, when he had a Series average of .381, with two home runs and seven runs batted in. He was also named an All-Star

12 times (1974; 1976–77; 1979–84; 1986–87; 1989; he did not play in 1980 or 1989). *Sporting News* named him major league player of the year twice (1980; 1986) and also player of the 1980s. Schmidt is seventh on the list for career home runs, with 548, and led the National League in home runs a record eight times (1974–76; 1980–81; 1983–84; 1986). He also posted 174 stolen bases, 1,595 runs batted in, and 5,045 assists, and shares various single-season and third-base records.

In retirement, Schmidt plays in tournaments sponsored by the Celebrity Golf Association; he also owns a sandwich shop chain, is involved in a boat dealership, and serves as assistant baseball coach at his son's Benjamin School in North Palm Beach, Florida. He has published *Always on the Offense* (1982), written with Barbara Walder, and *The Mike Schmidt Study: Hitting Theory, Skills, and Technique* (1993), with a youth version subtitled *Building a Foundation* (1993). Schmidt is married to Donna Wightman and has a son and a daughter.

FURTHER READING

Mike Schmidt. Lois P. Nicholson. Chelsea House, 1995.
Home-Run Hitters. John A. Torres. Simon & Schuster, 1995.

Scorsese, Martin (1942–) Celebrated

film director Martin Scorsese directed the Las Vegas–set 1995 film *Casino*, based on the book by Nicholas Pileggi, screenplay by Scorsese and Pileggi. Robert De Niro starred as 1970s mob syndicate–connected gambler and casino operator Sam "Ace" Rothstein, opposite Sharon Stone as his wife, Las Vegas gambler Ginger McKenna; their violent life together and ultimate breakup supplies much of the drama of the film, although Las Vegas and the illegal world are the sea in which they swim. Joe Pesci costarred as Nicky Santoro, Rothstein's mad-dog killer friend, and James Woods as Ginger's small-time con-man lover, before and during her marriage; the cast also included Don Rickles, Alan King, Kevin Pollak, L. Q. Jones, and Dick Smothers, with several other show business celebrities appearing as themselves. Scorsese was nominated for a Golden Globe award as best director for the film.

Scorsese also appeared in a cameo acting role in David Salle's comedy-thriller *Search and Destroy*. Forthcoming was the film *Kundun*, script by Melissa Mathison, a biographical picture about the 14th Dalai Lama.

Scorsese received the Board of Governors award of the American Society of Cinematographers for his work in film preservation; for that work and his fight against undisclosed alteration of films, Scorsese was also awarded the third annual John Huston Award for Artists Rights, presented by the Artists Rights Foundation. He also became the 11th annual honoree of New York's American Museum of the Living Image, and was awarded a Golden Lion for career achievement at the Venice Film Festival. With Peter Cowie, Scorsese also published *World Cinema: Diary of a Day,* including diary excerpts from some hundreds of film people (including Scorsese himself) for the day June 10, 1993, in honor of the 100th anniversary of cinema's centenary, marked from the 1895 showing of a Lumière film.

New York–born Scorsese scored his first major success with *Mean Streets* (1973), set on the underside of New York life. He went on to become one of the major directors of the modern period, with such films as *Alice Doesn't Live Here Anymore* (1974), *Taxi Driver* (1976), *New York, New York* (1977), the classic *Raging Bull* (1980), *The Color of Money* (1986), the highly controversial *The Last Temptation of Christ* (1988), *GoodFellas* (1990), *Cape Fear* (1991), and *The Age of Innocence* (1993). He also appeared as an actor in a small but key role as Van Gogh in *Akira Kurosawa's Dreams* (1990). Scorsese's 1964 B.S. and 1966 M.A. in film communications were from New York University. He has been married four times and has two children.

FURTHER READING

"The rules of the game." Howard Feinstein. *Guardian*, Nov. 15, 1995.
"Scorsese tips his hand. . . ." Steve Daly. *Entertainment*, Nov. 3, 1995.
"Martin Scorsese interviewed." Gavin Smith. "Artist of the beautiful." Kathleen Murphy. *Film Comment*, Nov.–Dec. 1993.
"Martin Scorsese's mortal sins." Marcelle Clements. *Esquire*, Nov. 1993.
"A beautiful present from the past. . . ." Graham Fuller. *Interview*, Oct. 1993.
Martin Scorsese: An Analysis of His Feature Films, with a Filmography of His Entire Directorial Career. Marie K. Connelly. McFarland, 1993.
The Scorsese Picture: The Art and Life of Martin

Scorsese. DAVID EHRENSTEIN. Birch Lane/Carol, 1992.

Martin Scorsese. LESTER KEYSER. Twayne, 1992.

"Martin Scorsese." GRAHAM FULLER. *Interview*, Nov. 1991.

"Slouching toward Hollywood. . . ." PETER BISKIND. *Premiere*, Nov. 1991.

"Playboy interview. . . ." DAVID RENSIN. *Playboy*, Apr. 1991.

Martin Scorsese: A Journey. MARY P. KELLY. Thunder's Mouth, 1991.

The Future of the Movies: Interviews with Martin Scorsese, George Lucas, and Steven Spielberg. ROGER EBERT and GENE SISKEL. Andrews & McMeel, 1991.

Scribner, Charles, Jr. (1921–95) Publisher Charles Scribner, Jr., was the inheritor of the great American book publishing house of Charles Scribner's Sons. Scribner graduated from Princeton University in 1943, and then saw navy service in World War II as a cryptanalyst, a function he performed again during the Korean War. He joined Scribner's after the war and became president of the firm (1952–77). He was later chairman of the Scribner Book Companies (1978–86), which had become part of the Macmillan publishing empire. He also remained active in Princeton matters, as a trustee of the Princeton University Press (1949–81), president of the Press (1969–79), and a university trustee (1969–79). Scribner was president of the American Book Publishers Council (1966–68). Scribner was also a writer, whose published works include his memoir *In the Company of Writers: A Life in Publishing* (1991). He also published the essay collection *In the Web of Ideas: The Education of a Publisher* (1993). He was survived by his wife, Joan Sunderland Scribner, and their three sons. (d. New York City; November 11, 1995)

FURTHER READING

Obituary. *New York Times*, Nov. 13, 1995.

Seal (Sealhenry Olumide Samuel; 1962–) London-born of Nigerian parents, the singer Seal trained as an architect and worked at a wide range of jobs before focusing on a musical career, writing songs from 1987. He worked with touring bands in Japan and Thailand before making his 1990 recording debut with the top-of-the-British-charts single "Killer," written in collaboration with Adamski (Adam Tinley). Seal's 1991 debut album *Seal* was also a hit, and its chart-topping single "Crazy" made Seal an award-winning international star.

Seal's second album, also named *Seal*, was issued in June 1994; it, too, became a hit, its success enhanced by issuance of the hit singles "Kiss from a Rose" and "Prayer for the Dying." In 1995, "Kiss from a Rose" was issued as part of the soundtrack album of the film *Batman Forever*. The previously issued second *Seal* album and "Kiss from a Rose" single then became even greater hits, with the album topping 4 million in sales and winning nominations for Grammy album of the year and best pop album. In 1995, Seal also issued two more hit singles from the album, "I'm Alive" and "Don't Cry."

FURTHER READING

"Seal. . . ." BILL MURPHY. *Guitar Player*, Oct. 1994.

"Seal, delivered. . . ." DAVID THIGPEN. *Rolling Stone*, Aug. 25, 1994.

"Seal is set. . . ." DAVID SINCLAIR. *Times* (of London), Feb. 8, 1992.

"His name is Seal. . . ." CHRISTIAN LOGAN WRIGHT. *Vogue*, Nov. 1991.

"Signed, Seal delivers." STEVE DOUGHERTY and LAURA SANDERSON HEALY. *People*, Oct. 28, 1991.

Seifert, George Gerald (1940–) Others get the attention, with their flamboyant personal styles and sidelines antics. George Seifert, with his always-calm professional demeanor, is often overlooked. But football aficionados are well aware that in his seven years as coach he has taken the San Francisco 49ers to five National Football Conference championships (1989–90; 1992–94) and two Super Bowls (1989 and 1994 seasons), winning both. In late January 1995, in Super Bowl XXIX, the 49ers beat the San Diego Chargers, but it was their crushing victory over the two-time defending champion Dallas Cowboys in the mid-January NFC championship that showed their dominance.

Though Seifert's predecessor, Bill Walsh, created San Francisco's winning system, he was now seven years gone. Finally people were beginning to get the message: if key players are injured, and if most of the coaching staff has changed, then much of the credit for a team's winning record must be given to the current head coach, Seifert. Indeed, when in November 1994 Seifert reached his 100th game as coach of the 49ers, his winning percentage was .770, a career NFL record, ahead of (in this order) Paul Brown, George Halas, Vince Lombardi, and Don Shula.

In the 1995 regular season, San Francisco had a rocky start, with injuries to several key players, including quarterback Steve Young, dropping them at one point to a 5-4 won-lost record. But another crushing win over the Cowboys—with the 49ers under backup quarterback Elvis Grbac—turned their season around. Their final regular season record of 11-5 set an NFL record of 13 consecutive seasons with 10 or more victories. At year's end, the 49ers seemed poised to defend their Super Bowl title, but in the playoffs they were knocked off by the rising Green Bay Packers.

San Francisco–born Seifert graduated from that city's Polytechnic High School and received his 1963 bachelor's degree in zoology and 1966 master's degree in physical education from the University of Utah. In between, he served as assistant football coach at Utah (1964) and head coach at Utah's Westminster College (1965), then served six months in the U.S. Army (1966). Briefly assistant coach at the University of Iowa (1966), he became defensive backs coach at the University of Oregon (1967–71) and Stanford

University (1972–74; 1977–79), with a brief head-coaching stint at Cornell University (1975–76). He joined the San Francisco 49ers as defensive backs coach (1980–82), then defensive coordinator (1983–88), and finally head coach (1989–). Seifert was named *Sporting News* NFL coach of the year twice (1990; 1994 seasons). He is married to Linda Seifert; they have a son and a daughter.

FURTHER READING

"TSN's NFL awards." IRA MILLER and TERRY HUTCHENS. *Sporting News*, Jan. 30, 1995.
"George who?" PETER KING. *Sports Illustrated*, Dec. 20, 1993.
"NFL Coach. . . ." ANN KILLION. *Sporting News*, Mar. 18, 1991.

Seldes, George (1890–1995) New Jersey-born George Seldes was a leading journalist and social critic, whose career stretched from his first reporting job, with the *Pittsburgh Leader* (1909–10), through publication of his memoirs, *Witness to a Century* (1987). He was an editor with *The Pittsburgh Post* (1910–16) and New York's *Pulitzer's Weekly* (1916) before becoming a war correspondent (1917–18). He remained in Europe after the war, working for the *Chicago Tribune* as a bureau head (Berlin, 1920–25; Rome, 1926) and war correspondent (Syria, 1926–27). The first of his many books followed: *You Can't Print That* (1928). Then he was back in Europe, covering the Spanish Civil War for the *New York Post* (1936–37), although his main work of the 1930s was as the author of two major books, both highly critical of the American press and of the pressures brought to bear on the press by advertisers: *Lords of the Press* (1935) and *Freedom of the Press* (1938). He published the highly regarded newsletter *In Fact* (1940–50), which carried a great many muckraking stories that were not otherwise to be found, and continued to sharply criticize the large-scale commercial press. Among his other books were *Facts and Fascism* (1943), *The People Don't Know* (1949), *Tell the Truth and Run* (1953), *Never Tire of Protesting* (1968), *Even the Gods Cannot Change History* (1976), *The Great Thoughts* (1985), and his autobiography *Witness to a Century: Encounters with the Noted, the Notorious, and the Three SOB's* (1987). He was predeceased by his wife, Helen Larkin Weisman, and his brother, Gilbert

Seldes. He was survived by a niece and a nephew. (d. Windsor, Vermont; July 2, 1995)

FURTHER READING

Obituary. *Current Biography*, Sept. 1995.
Obituary. *Nation*, July 31, 1995.
Obituary. *Independent*, July 14, 1995.
Obituary. *New York Times*, July 2, 1995.

Selena (Selena Quantanilla Perez; 1971–95) On March 31, 1995, in a motel at Corpus Christi, Texas, Mexican-American popular music star Selena was shot and killed by Yolande Salvidar, the chief organizer of Selena's fan club. Salvidar had managed a clothing store owned by Selena's family, and a dispute over financial matters apparently generated the shooting. For ten hours after the shooting, Salvidar sat outside the motel in her pickup truck, threatening to shoot herself; after surrendering, she signed a confession. She was convicted of the murder by a Houston jury on October 23.

During her brief career, Selena had become a Grammy-winning major Tejano performer, whose Spanish-language recordings, led by *Amor Prohibido,* had repeatedly gone to the top of the Latino music charts. At the time of her death, she was poised for "crossover" entry into the English-language entertainment world as well, with a film role in *Don Juan DeMarco* and a forthcoming bilingual album. That album, *Dreaming of You,* was released posthumously, making its debut at the top of the *Billboard* 200 chart, the first album by any Latino artist to do so. She was survived by her husband, Chris Perez, her parents, a brother, and a sister. (d. Corpus Christi, Texas; March 31, 1995)

FURTHER READING

"A star for. . . ." MANDALIT DEL BARCO. *Scholastic Update*, Nov. 17, 1995.
"Selena born again." JOHN MORTHLAND. *Entertainment*, Aug. 18, 1995.
"As fans pay. . . ." "After Selena." CYNTHIA SANZ and BETTY CORTINA. *People*, July 10, 1995.
"Selena aside." ANA CASTILLO. *Nation*, May 29, 1995.
"The queen is dead." JOE NICK PATOSKI. *Texas Monthly*, May 1995.
"Requiem for." ROBERT SEIDENBERG. *Entertainment*, Apr. 14, 1995.
"Hasta la bye-bye." *Economist*, Apr. 8, 1995.
Obituary. *Variety*, Apr. 10, 1995.
Obituary. *New York Times*, Apr. 1, 1995.
Selena! The Phenomenal Life and Tragic Death of the Tejano Music Queen. Pocket Books, 1995.

Seles, Monica (1974–) For tennis star Monica Seles, 1995 was the year of the return. She had not played professionally since April 30, 1993, when she was stabbed in the back on the sidelines during a tournament by a fan obsessed with her chief rival, Steffi Graf. Seles had begun to practice intensively by early 1994, but did not actually return until mid-1995. Her comeback took place at an exhibition game on July 29, with a decisive win against Martina Navratilova, now retired from professional singles competition. President of the WTA players' association, Navratilova had waged a strong campaign for Seles to be coranked number one (with Graf) on her return, since she had held the top rank when injured. In August, Seles returned to professional play at the du Maurier Ltd. Canadian Open, where she quickly won her 33rd title. She and Graf did not meet until the finals of the U.S. Open, where Graf emerged the victor. Tendinitis in her left knee and a later ankle sprain forced Seles to withdraw from later 1995 tournaments. Even so, at the WTA Tour Championships in November, Seles was named comeback player of the year and, by vote of the fans, most exciting player. She was scheduled to return again in January 1996 at Sydney, warming up for the Australian Open, where her record is 21-0.

The man who attacked Seles, Gunther Parche, had spent five months in prison between his arrest and his sentencing, but then was freed, after receiving only a two-year suspended sentence. That decision sparked international protest, but was upheld in German courts in April 1995. Still pending is a $10 million suit Seles filed in 1994 against the German Tennis Federation for failing to provide reasonable security, as was a suit against Seles herself by Fila, a sports apparel firm, charging that she had reneged on a contract to promote their clothing line, costing them more than $6 million.

Of Hungarian ancestry, Seles was born in a Serb-dominated region of the former Yugoslavia, becoming a leading amateur tennis player there and throughout Europe, before emigrating to America with her family at age 11 to train with Nick Bollettieri in Florida. She was also coached by her father, cartoonist and documentary filmmaker Xarolj Seles. She turned professional in 1989, and the following year emerged as a dominating presence on the women's tennis scene, winning the Italian and German opens, and defeating then-top-ranked Graf at the French Open, becoming the youngest player since 1887 to win a Grand Slam event. She later won the French Open twice again (1991; 1992); her other Grand Slam titles include the U.S. Open (1991; 1992) and the Australian Open (1991; 1992; 1993). She reached the finals of all 16 events she entered in 1991 and all but 1 of 15 in 1992, including a string of 22 consecutive finals, second only to Navratilova's earlier 23. In that same period, she won 10 tournaments, including six Grand Slams, setting two successive single-year earnings records, with over $2.4 million in 1991 and over $2.6 million in 1992, broken by Graf in 1993. She became a U.S. citizen in 1994.

FURTHER READING

"Smashing return. . . ." WILLIAM PLUMMER. *People*, Sept. 4, 1995.
"The return." S. L. PRICE. *Sports Illustrated*, July 17, 1995.
"The second life. . . ." PETER BODO. *Tennis*, Mar. 1994.
Monica Seles. MICHAEL E. GOODMAN. Creative Ed, 1994.
"Bloody obsessions. . . ." DAVID ELLIS. *People*, May 17, 1993.
"Savage assault." SALLY JENKINS. *Sports Illustrated*, May 10, 1993.

Selig, Bud (Allan H. Selig; 1934–) On September 6, 1995, the day that Baltimore Orioles shortstop Cal Ripken, Jr., broke Lou Gehrig's record for most consecutive games played (with 2,131), Bud Selig broke a record of his own: He served his 1,092nd day as baseball's "acting commissioner," surpassing the tenure of his predecessor, Commissioner Fay Vincent, who had been forced out of the job by the team owners. Despite criticisms, within baseball and also in Congress, that the commissioner should not also be an owner, Selig has retained the support of other owners. The question may become moot, since Selig's Milwaukee Brewers are in serious financial difficulty. If the team is forced to move, Selig may give up ownership and the "acting" part of his title; the acting commissioner's job reportedly pays him $1.25 million annually.

Meanwhile the labor strife that had forced cancellation of the 1994 World Series continued. The owners originally planned to start the 1995 season with "replacement players," but on April 2, on the eve of the opening, Selig announced that players should report to spring training camps; the shortened 144-game season began on April 25. At year's end, a new agreement between owners and players had still not been reached and prospects for baseball in 1996 were uncertain. Also unclear was the status of baseball's special antitrust exemption, under review in Congress, but shelved by more pressing business; legislators have been concerned that Vincent's forced resignation had weakened the office of commissioner, originally intended to be an independent guarantor of fairness and incorruptibility of the sport. Among the changes approved for the coming baseball season were several that would speed up the game, which in the past two decades has increased its average length from 2 1/2 hours to 3 hours.

Milwaukee-born Selig graduated from the University of Wisconsin at Madison in 1956. After service in the U.S. Army (1956–58), he worked in automobile leasing and sales (1959–90). He was part-owner of the Milwaukee Braves (1963–65) until their move to Atlanta, and co-owner and president of the Milwaukee Brewers (1970–), becoming acting commissioner of baseball (1991–). He has also served on the board of the Green Bay Packers football team, was cofounder of the Child Abuse Prevention Fund (1988), and has received numerous awards. Selig married Suzanne Lappin Steinman in 1977 and has two daughters.

FURTHER READING

"What would . . . ?" RONALD BLUM. Sales & Marketing Management, Oct. 1995.
"A healthy game. . . ." JOHN RAWLINGS. Sporting News, Oct. 25, 1993.

Shabazz, Betty (Qubilah Bahiyah Shabazz; 1960–)

On January 12, 1995, Betty Shabazz was arrested by federal agents in Minneapolis, having been charged by a grand jury with attempting to hire an assassin to murder Louis Farrakhan, leader of the Nation of Islam. Shabazz is the daughter of Black Muslim leader Malcolm X, murdered in 1965; she and her family have long accused Farrakhan of complicity in her father's death. Michael Fitzpatrick, her friend since high school, claimed that Shabazz had moved to Minneapolis in an attempt to hire him to kill Farrakhan. She denied the accusation, claiming that she had moved there because she wanted to marry Fitzpatrick. As the case developed, it became clear that Fitzpatrick had been a government informer since 1977, when he had pleaded guilty of complicity in a Jewish Defense League bombing. He had subsequently entered a federal witness protection program, and faced trial on a 1993 arrest for cocaine possession; he reentered a federal witness protection program after the Shabazz indictment.

Farrakhan, the alleged object of the attack, stated that he refused to believe that Shabazz had tried to hire his murderer; he and Shabazz later appeared together publicly in a gesture of reconciliation. Farrakhan did not admit complicity in Malcolm X's murder, but did state that Nation of Islam members were involved, and apologized to Shabazz. On April 30, the government essentially withdrew its case against Shabazz, canceling her scheduled May 1 trial in return for a statement linking her to the murder plan, and a two-year period of probation.

Shabazz grew up in Mt. Vernon, New York, and attended Princeton University. She later worked in Paris and New York. She has one son.

FURTHER READING

"Malcolm X. . . ." GORDON PARKS. MPLS–St. Paul Magazine, Apr. 1995.

John Shalikashvili (center), Gordon R. Sullivan (left), and William A. Owens.

Shalikashvili, John Malchase David

(1936–) As head of the Joint Chiefs of Staff, General John Shalikashvili in 1995 concerned himself wth a worldwide range of military and related matters, with focus on Bosnia, the multiple convulsions shaking the Muslim world, Iraq, the NATO military alliance, China and Taiwan, and Russia, unstable and still in possession of its massive, potentially humanity-destroying nuclear arsenal. There were scores of other matters as well, among them the end of the American occupation of Haiti; the threat of resumed hostilities in Korea; normalization of relations with Vietnam; damaged relations with Japan, after the rape of a schoolgirl on Okinawa by American servicemen; and at home such matters as military funding, base closings, and the treatment of gays in the military.

The Bosnian War drew Shalikashvili's greatest attention by far, and the success or failure of the very risky American peace-keeping intervention will probably provide much of the basis on which future generations judge his contribution—whether or not he agreed with all or even most of American policy at the time. Right up to the summer 1995 change of American position on the commitment of ground forces, Shalikashvili reportedly favored effective American and NATO bombing of the Bosnian Serbs, and deplored the United Nations' inadequate military moves in Bosnia—but continued to steadfastly oppose troop commitment. He was consistent in this; ever since the beginning of the war, he and the overwhelming majority of other Western military professionals had pointed out that most of Bosnia, including Sarajevo, was mountain country, and that a determined local force could wage a very effective war from those mountains for years without being defeated. In this, Bosnia was thought to be more like Afghanistan than Vietnam—but carrying the same enormous military and political risks. However, when American policy changed, the head of the Joint Chiefs of Staff loyally supported his commander in chief and set about the task of pouring 20,000 heavily armed peace-keeping troops into Bosnia in midwinter, supported by tens of thousands more in neighboring countries and on station at sea.

Warsaw-born Shalikashvili, who had emigrated to the United States with his family after World War II, received his B.S.M.E. from Bradley University in 1958. He began his military career as a draftee, attended Officers Candidate School, and emerged a second lieutenant in 1959. He served in Vietnam (1968–69), and began moving up in earnest after earning an M.A. in international affairs from George Washington University in 1970. He was later a divisional commander, commanded Allied forces in Kurdish-held northern Iraq after the Persian Gulf War, and became supreme Allied commander in Europe (1992–93). On August 11, 1993, President Bill Clinton selected General Shalikashvili to head the Joint Chiefs of Staff, to

succeed retiring general Colin Powell. That his father, Dimitri Shalikashvili, had fought with Nazi-organized Georgian units during World War II did not impede his acceptance as Joint Chiefs head.

Shalikashvili married Gunhild Bartsch in 1963; she died two years later. In 1966 he married Joan E. Zimpleman; they have one son.

FURTHER READING

"Shalikashvili, John." *Current Biography*, Nov. 1995.
"What we need to do." TAD SZULC. *Parade*, May 1, 1994.
"Globo-cops. . . ." TOM MORGANTHAU and JOHN BARRY. *Newsweek*, Aug. 23, 1993.
"The rules of. . . ." BRIAN DUFFY. *U.S. News & World Report*, Aug. 23, 1993.

Shandling, Garry (1949–) Comedian-actor Garry Shandling was occasional guest host on the "Tonight Show" in the 1980s, and was thought likely to take over the show on Johnny Carson's retirement. He lost out to Jay Leno, but not to worry: Shandling has his own talk show, "The Larry Sanders Show," on HBO, and it has won a strong following. As his earlier series "It's Garry Shandling's Show"—about a comedian starring in his own television show—lampooned situation comedies, so "Larry Sanders" satirizes talk shows. Shandling as Sanders is joined by several key regulars, most notably Jeffrey Tambor as his on-air sidekick Hank Kingsley, and Rip Torn, as hair-tearing producer Artie, as well as often ad-libbed interviews with real-life guests, such as Billy Crystal, Robin Williams, Chevy Chase, and Roseanne, who played a brief and stormy love interest on the show at the end of the 1994–95 season. In 1995, Sanders won the CableAce award for best actor in a comedy series and (with his coauthors, and for the second year in a row) for best writing of a comedy series, while the show's Todd Holland won for best direction of a comedy series. Shandling himself also won a CableAce award as best entertainment host for *HBO Comedy Hour: The 1995 Young Comedians Special Hosted by Garry Shandling*. To complete the picture, Shandling published a book, *The Autobiography of Larry Sanders*, written with David Rensin. He also served as a presenter at the 47th Annual Emmy Awards; he was nominated as best lead actor in a comedy series, but lost to Kelsey Grammer. At year's end, Shandling was nominated for a Golden Globe award as best actor in a musical or comedy series.

Chicago-born Shandling was largely raised in Arizona and graduated from the University of Arizona with a marketing degree. He began his show business career after moving to Los Angeles in 1973, quickly catching on as a highly regarded supplier of material to the situation comedies "Sanford and Son," "Welcome Back Kotter," and "Three's Company." He began appearing as a stand-up comic in the late 1970s, scoring a breakthrough as a 1981 guest on the "Tonight Show." It was the first of many guest appearances on the show; he also became a frequent substitute for Johnny Carson on the show (1983–88). He became a major television star with his own "It's Garry Shandling's Show" (1986–90). He followed that with his long-running television hit, the satirical "The Larry Sanders Show" (1992–). Shandling has also hosted various specials, such as *Garry Shandling: Alone in Las Vegas* (1984), *It's Garry Shandling's Show 25th Anniversary Special* (1986), and *Garry Shandling: Stand-Up* (1991). He also appeared in the film *Love Affair* (1994).

FURTHER READING

"Playboy interview. . . ." DAVID RENSIN. *Playboy*, Dec. 1994.

"Hey Now!" R. DANIEL FOSTER. *Los Angeles Magazine*, Aug. 1994.

"True lies. . . ." JAY MARTEL. *Rolling Stone*, Sept. 8, 1994.

"Garry Shandling's. . . ." TAD FRIEND. *Esquire*, July 1993.

"Garry does Larry. . . ." JOE RHODES. *Entertainment*, Aug. 28, 1992.

Shapiro, Robert Leslie (1942–) On June 12, 1994, Nicole Brown Simpson and Ronald Goldman were murdered outside her Los Angeles home. Her former husband, O. J. Simpson, quickly became the prime suspect in the case. Three days later, on June 15, Simpson hired prominent Los Angeles criminal lawyer Robert Shapiro as his chief lawyer. Simpson was arrested on June 17 and later charged with both murders; Shapiro continued to be his chief lawyer throughout the long, highly publicized murder trial that ended with Simpson's acquittal on October 3, 1995. It was Shapiro who put together the defense team that won the case, and it was also Shapiro who broke sharply and publicly with Simpson chief courtroom spokesperson Johnnie Cochran, charging that Cochran had appealed to African-American jurors by breaking his agreement to Shapiro and playing "the race card," and dealing from the "bottom of the deck." Shapiro also publicly broke with lawyer F. Lee Bailey, whom he had brought into the case. Shapiro's postvictory role was unclear, as Simpson prepared to defend several civil suits brought by the families of Nicole Brown and Ronald Goldman. Forthcoming in the spring of 1996 was Shapiro's book *The Search for Justice: A Defense Attorney's Brief on the O. J. Simpson Case.*

New Jersey–born Shapiro is a graduate of the University of California at Los Angeles (1965) and Loyola University (1968). He was a deputy district attorney in Los Angeles (1969–72), and since then has practiced as an increasingly well-known criminal lawyer in Los Angeles. Among his most notable cases was the 1990 murder case of Christian Brando, son of actor Marlon Brando; Shapiro pleaded his client guilty to manslaughter, which carried a relatively light ten-year prison sentence. He is married to Linell Thomas; they have two children.

FURTHER READING

"Bitter harvest. . . ." LUCINDA FRANKS. *People*, Oct. 16, 1995.

"Not exactly. . . ." MARK MILLER and ANDREW MURR. *Newsweek*, Jan. 23, 1995.

"An incendiary defense." JEFFREY TOOBIN. *New Yorker*, July 25, 1994.

"Three for the defense." DAVID A. KAPLAN. *Newsweek*, July 11, 1994.

"Master of disaster." MICHELLE GREEN. *People*, July 11, 1994.

Shatner, William (1931–) The man best known as Captain James Tiberius Kirk continued to develop his writing career in 1995. Inextricably linked with that role, he published his first Star Trek novel, *The Ashes of Eden,* for which he did wide publicity, including online appearances. Also published in audiobook form, the work is planned as the first of a trilogy, written with Judith and Garfield Reeves-Stevens.

Voyage Home (1986), *The Final Frontier* (1989), which he also directed, *The Undiscovered Country* (1991), and *Star Trek Generations,* the seventh featuring the original cast, in which his character died. He also appeared in *National Lampoon's Loaded Weapon* (1992). Shatner's other science fiction detective series novels include *TekWar* (1989), *TekLords* (1991), *TekLab* (1991), *Tek Vengeance* (1992), *Tek Secret* (1993), and *Tek Power* (1994). He also published the best-selling *Star Trek Memories* (1993). Shatner is twice divorced and has three daughters.

FURTHER READING

"Captain of enterprise." JOE CHIDLEY. *Maclean's*, Nov. 28, 1994.
"Star Trek. . . ." *Entertainment*, Aug. 26, 1994.
William Shatner: A Bio-Bibliography. DENNIS WILLIAM HAUCK. Greenwood, 1994.

Shatner also published the seventh novel in his "Tek" series: *Tek Money,* featuring 2040s detective Jake Cardigan. However, his 1994 *Star Trek Movie Memories,* written with Chris Kreski, proved to be a commercial disappointment, perhaps because of a glut of Star Trek titles that year. On the personal side, he was seen as National Safety Council spokesman and also organized his fifth annual Hollywood Charity Horse Show.

Montreal-born Shatner graduated from McGill University in 1952, the same year he made his stage debut at the Montreal Playhouse. He performed at Ottawa's Canadian Repertory Theatre (1952–54), primarily in juvenile roles, and the Stratford Shakespeare Festival in Ontario (1954–56), receiving the Tyrone Guthrie award in 1956, before appearing on Broadway in *Tamburlaine the Great* (1956), *The World of Suzie Wong* (1958), and *A Shot in the Dark* (1961). Early film appearances include *The Brothers Karamazov* (1958), *The Explosive Generation* (1961), *Judgment at Nuremburg* (1961), *The Intruder* (1962), and *The Outrage* (1964), but it was "Star Trek" (1966–69) that brought him lasting fame. Much other television work followed, including the animated "Star Trek" series (1973–75), "Barbary Coast" (1975–76), "T. J. Hooker" (1982–86), and as host, "Rescue 911" (1989–   ). His movie career became dominant with the enormous success of the film *Star Trek* (1979), and its successors: *The Wrath of Khan* (1982), *The Search for Spock* (1984), *The*

Sheehy, Gail Henion (1937–   )

Gail Sheehy's skill in charting and guiding her generation through the stages of their lives is undiminished. That was the critical consensus on the 1995 publication of her latest book *New Passages: Mapping Your Life Across Time.* She first came to wide public attention with her hugely popular *Passages: Predictable Crises of Adult Life* (1976), which outlined what her generation could expect as they approached middle age. Oddly, it soon became clear that what characterized her generation most was that the old predictable order of life was breaking down. That understanding is a basic part of her *New Passages,* which explores the what she calls the "Second Adulthood" of people over 45. To no one's surprise, the book became another best-seller, debuting on national best-seller lists. Sheehy herself did a 12-city promotional tour and was widely seen on shows such as "Dateline," "Today," "Larry King Live," "Charlie Rose," and "The Late, Late Show with Tom Snyder." She also read the audiobook version of the book.

On another front, Sheehy contributed a notably critical profile of House Speaker Newt Gingrich in *Vanity Fair.* Long an East Coast resident, she recently moved to California, where her husband, longtime magazine editor Clay Felker, in 1995 established the Felker Center for Magazine Journalism at the University of California at Berkeley.

Born in Mamaroneck, New York, Sheehy received her 1958 B.S. from the University of Vermont. Her early career was spent largely as a journalist, with the *Rochester Democrat and Chronicle* (1961–63) and the *New York Herald Tribune* (1963–66). She was a contributing editor to *New York* magazine (1968–77), *Vanity Fair* (1988–), and several other magazines in the years that followed. Her early books include the novel *Lovesounds* (1970), *Panthermania: The Clash of Black Against Black in One American City* (1971), and *Hustling: Prostitution in Our Wide-Open Society* (1973). Following her best-selling *Passages,* her later works included *Pathfinders* (1981), *Character: America's Search for Leadership* (1988), *Gorbachev: The Man Who Changed the World* (1990), and *The Silent Passage: Menopause* (1992), and the play *Maggie and Misha* (1991). She married her second husband, Clay Felker, in 1984; they have an adopted daughter, Mohm, a Cambodian refugee whose story was told in Sheehy's *Spirit of Survival* (1986). She also has a daughter from her first marriage.

FURTHER READING

"The late show. . . ." NANCY MATSUMOTO. *People,* July 31, 1995.
"Advancing age. . . ." JOHN F. BAKER. *Publishers Weekly,* Mar. 27, 1995.
"Sheehy, Gail." *Current Biography,* June 1993.

Shevardnadze, Eduard Amvroslyevich (1928–)

Georgian leader Eduard Shevardnadze to a large extent completed the reorganization and pacification of his small country in 1995. On August 24, the Georgian Parliament approved a new constitution, establishing a new governmental framework. On August 29, while on his way to sign the constitution in Tbilisi, the Georgian capital, Shevardnadze and others in his party were wounded when a car bomb was detonated near his motorcade. He survived the assassination attempt and went on to sign the document. In the months that followed, his government successfully disarmed the main local guerrilla leaders who had grown to power during the Georgian civil war, the Georgia-Abkhazia war, and the underlying undeclared Georgia-Russia war, which had ended with Russian victory in 1993.

On November 5, Shevardnadze won the Georgian presidential election by a landslide, with a reported 70 percent of the vote. What lay ahead was a major effort to restore the Georgian economy, helped somewhat by expected revenues from the projected international oil pipeline across Georgia on its way from the Caspian Sea to the West. Shevardnadze also attempted to use his immense international prestige to bring Western investment directly into Georgia, coupled with a continuing attempt to steer a course as independent of Russia as possible.

Until his return to Georgia in 1992, Shevardnadze had spent his whole life in Communist Party and Soviet government work, beginning in the late 1940s, and rising through a series of Communist Party positions in his native Georgia through the early 1970s. His first major move came in 1972, when he led an anticorruption campaign in Georgia and replaced the Republic's party leader. He was first secretary of the Georgian Communist Party (1972–85), becoming a Soviet Central Committee member in 1976.

Long associated with Mikhail Gorbachev, Shevardnadze replaced Andrei Gromyko as Soviet foreign minister in 1985 and remained in that position throughout most of the extraordinary Gorbachev era. He broke with Gorbachev and resigned as foreign minister on December 20, 1990, because of the too-slow pace of reform and Gorbachev's appointment of hard-line conservative Communists to key positions; at the time, he warned against a restoration of right-wing Communist dictatorship, raising the prospect of a disastrous civil war should that happen. He then founded the Soviet Foreign Policy Association and the Democratic Reform Movement. In December 1991, he served briefly as the last Soviet foreign minister. He joined Boris Yeltsin in resisting the August 1991 coup he had predicted and feared, but did not rejoin the government.

Shevardnadze was chosen to head Georgia's State Council in March 1992, and then tried to unify his fragmented country, with armed secession movements in South Ossetia and Abkhazia, and the armed forces of deposed Georgia president Zviad K. Gamsakhurdia in western Georgia. On October 11, 1992, Shevardnadze was elected parliamentary speaker, and as such effectively president of Georgia. He immediately moved to deal with the civil war in Abkhazia. He and Russian President Boris Yeltsin had arranged a cease-fire in that war on September 3, 1992, followed by major Georgian force reductions in the area. But Abkhazian rebel forces, helped by Russian "volunteers" and armed with Russian weapons and supplies, then quickly moved in to take much of Abkhazia, while Yeltsin ordered Russian forces in Abkhazia to protect Russians there; in early 1993 the conflict became an undeclared Georgian-Russian war. In September 1993, Georgian forces withdrawing during a cease-fire were smashed by attacking Abkhazian forces, which then took Abkhazia, while insurrection also grew in western Georgia, led by former president Gamsakhurdia. On October 22, 1993, Shevardnadze reluctantly took Georgia into the Commonwealth of Independent States (CIS), secured Russian armed intervention against Gamsakhurdia's forces, and then quickly defeated Gamsakhurdia. In 1994, Georgia and Abkhazia agreed on a cease-fire, followed by the dispatch of Russian peacekeeping forces to Abkhazia, both Georgia and Abkhazia becoming de facto Russian protectorates.

Shevardnadze attended the Kutaisi Pedagogical Institute. He has published *The Future Belongs to Freedom: World Peace and Democracy in the U.S.S.R.* (1991).

FURTHER READING

"Struggling with. . . ." *Time,* July 25, 1994.
"Curious Georgia." SIMON SEBAG MONTEFIORE. *New Republic,* June 29, 1992.
" 'Mikhail Gorbachev has. . . .' " *U.S. News & World Report,* Sept. 2, 1991.
"A growing momentum. . . ." PIERRE BOCEV. *World Press Review,* Sept. 1991.
"Shevardnadze. . . ." *Fortune,* May 20, 1991.

Shields, Carol Ann (1935–) Writer and teacher Carol Shields was showered with honors in 1995. *The Stone Diaries,* her novel disguised as a biography following a seemingly ordinary woman through her 20th-century life, won the Pulitzer Prize and the National Book Critics Circle Award for fiction. In Shields's adopted land of Canada, it also won the Governor General's Literary Award, and in Britain was short-listed for the prestigious Booker Prize. Shields herself toured widely in 1995, doing publicity for the newly published paperback version of the 1994 novel. Reading group guides were made available, as was an audiobook version. Meanwhile a film version of her 1987 novel *Swann* was being

shot in Toronto, starring Miranda Richardson and Brenda Fricker. In 1995, Toronto also saw a production of her 1993 play *Thirteen Hands,* about three generations of bridge players.

Born in Oak Park, Illinois, Shields received her 1957 B.A. from Hanover College, emigrating to Canada later that year. She became a Canadian citizen in 1974 and received her 1975 M.A. from the University of Ottawa. Her first published book was the poetry collection *Others* (1972); other poetry collections were *Intersect* (1974) and *Coming to Canada* (1991). Her other novels include *Small Ceremonies* (1976), *The Box Garden* (1977), *Happenstance* (1980), *A Fairly Conventional Woman* (1982), *Swann: A Mystery* (1987; U.S., 1989), and *The Republic of Love* (1992). She has also written short story collections such as *Various Miracles* (1985) and *The Orange Fish* (1989), and several plays, including *Women Waiting* (1973), *Departures and Arrivals* (1974), and *Thirteen Hands* (1993). She has taught English at the University of Ottawa (1976–77), University of British Columbia (1978–80), and University of Manitoba (1980–). She is married to Donald Hugh Shields, a professor of engineering; they have four daughters and a son.

FURTHER READING

"A prairie Pulitzer." DIANE TURBIDE. *Maclean's,* May 1, 1995.
"Carol Shields. . . ." ELGY GILLESPIE. *Publishers Weekly,* Feb. 28, 1994.

Shula, Don (Donald Francis Shula;1930–)
The unthinkable happened in 1995: many Miami
Dolphins football fans began calling for the resignation or firing of Dolphins coach Don Shula. It
was unthinkable because for 25 years Shula had
been practically a deity in Miami. He was, after
all, the winningest coach in National Football
League history, having broken the records for career lifetime wins in 1993 and regular-season
wins in 1994. He had taken Miami to the Super
Bowl five times (after the 1971, 1972, 1973, 1982,
and 1984 seasons), and Baltimore once, after the
1968 season; he had also won back-to-back Super
Bowls (1972 and 1973 seasons), taken the Dolphins to the NFL's only undefeated season
(1972), and won the American Football Conference East Division 15 times.

For Shula, as for his record-breaking quarterback Dan Marino, the problem was that, since
1985, the Dolphins had not even reached the Super Bowl, and in seven seasons had failed to
make the playoffs. At the end of the 1994 season,
they reached the AFC championship game, only
to lose—literally at the last minute—to the San
Diego Chargers. Many people expected Miami to
be strong contenders for a championship in the
1995 season. Instead, after a promising 4-0 start,
the Dolphins stumbled, losing games to seemingly weaker teams, and coming to the end of the
regular season with a record of only 9-7. They
just squeaked into the playoffs, but then were
eliminated by the Buffalo Bills. Days later, with
one season to go on his contract, Shula decided

to step down, though he remained part-owner of
the team; he was replaced by Jimmy Johnson. At
his retirement, Shula had built his lifetime
record to 347-173-6, and his regular-season
record was 328-156-6.

On the personal side, Shula published a new
book in 1995: *Everyone's a Coach: You Can In-
spire Anyone to Be a Winner,* written with Ken
Blanchard. In September, Shula had successful
arthroscopic surgery on his right knee; in 1994,
he had had surgery to repair a ruptured Achilles
tendon.

Ohio-born Shula attended Harvey High School
in Painesville, Ohio, and received his 1951 B.S.
in sociology from Cleveland's John Carroll University and his 1953 M.A. from Case Western
Reserve University. He began his professional
career as a defensive back with the Cleveland
Browns (1951–52), moved to the Baltimore Colts
(1953–56), and the Washington Redskins
(1957), then became defensive backs coach at
the University of Virginia (1958) and running
backs coach at the University of Kentucky
(1959). He moved back into professional ranks
as defensive coordinator of the Detroit Lions
(1960–62), then became head coach of the Baltimore Colts (1963–69), the youngest NFL head
coach ever, and finally head coach of the Miami
Dolphins (1970–95). He was named Coach of the
Year five times (1964; 1966; 1970; 1971; 1972);
Coach of the Decade (1980) by the Pro Football
Hall of Fame; and Sportsman of the Year (1993)
by *Sports Illustrated.* He published *The Winning
Edge* (1972). Shula's first wife, Dorothy, died of
cancer in 1991; they had five children, including
David, head coach of the Cincinnati Bengals, and
Mike, tight ends coach of the Chicago Bears. In
1994, Don and David Shula became the first
father-and-son NFL head coaches to play
against each other. Shula married his second
wife, Mary Anne, in 1993.

FURTHER READING

"The waning of a legend." MICHAEL SILVER. *Sports
  Illustrated,* Dec. 11, 1995.
"Secrets of. . . ." WILLY STERN and ELIAS LEVENSON.
  Business Week, Oct. 9, 1995.
"Jaw to jaw." MICHAEL KNISLEY. *Sporting News,* Oct.
  3, 1994.
Don Shula: Football's Winningest Coach. R. CONRAD
  STEIN. Childrens, 1994.
"Don Shula." PAUL ZIMMERMAN. *Sports Illustrated,*
  Dec. 20, 1993. (Sportsman of the Year issue.)

Shulman, Irving (1913–95) Brooklyn-born writer and teacher Irving Shulman received his 1937 B.A. from Ohio State University, his 1938 M.A. from Columbia, and his 1972 Ph.D. from the University of California at Los Angeles. His first novel was the very well-received story of slum life *The Amboy Dukes* (1947); it was the basis of the 1949 film *City Across the River*. Among his other novels were *Cry Tough* (1949), *The Big Brokers* (1951), *The Square Trap* (1953), *Children of the Dark* (1956), *Good Deeds Must Be Punished* (1956), and *The Velvet Knife* (1959). He also collaborated on many screenplays, for a time as a Warner Bros. screenwriter, and wrote several biographies. Shulman taught at George Washington University (1943–47) and California State College (1964–65). He was survived by his wife, Julia, and by two daughters and a brother. (d. Sherman Oaks, California; March 23, 1995)

FURTHER READING

Obituary. *New York Times*, Mar. 29, 1995.

Siad Barre, Mohammed (ca. 1910–95) Born in Ganane, Somalia, Mohammed Siad Barre became a police officer in 1941, during the period of British occupation (1941–50). He rose to a chief inspector's rank during the succeeding Italian occupation (1950–60), and then transferred into the new nation's military, becoming national army commander in 1965. He seized power in the bloodless army coup of 1969, and proceeded to build a one-party "scientific socialist" state, complete with an all-pervasive cult of personality, on the Stalin-Mao model. He also became a major Soviet client in East Africa, building a powerful national army, and nurturing strong regional territorial ambitions.

Siad Barre took his country to war against Ethiopia over the disputed Ogaden region in 1977, scored early successes, and besieged Harar. But the Soviets took the side of Ethiopia, also their ally and major client, helping the Ethiopians to hold Harar and demanding that Siad Barre end the war. He responded by changing sides in the Cold War, expelling Soviet forces and closing Soviet bases, and accepting American military support—which proved insufficient. In February 1978, Soviet-backed Cuban and Ethiopian forces relieved Harar, and in March

smashed the Somali military at Diredawa-Jijiga, forcing Siad Barre to withdraw and sue for peace. Although his rule was fatally damaged, he held on to power until the Somali Civil War began in 1988. He fled Mogadishu in January 1991, as the civil war continued, and from havens in Kenya and Nigeria continued to try to regain power. No information was available as to survivors, though he reportedly had more than a score of children. (d. Lagos, Nigeria; January 1, 1995)

FURTHER READING

Obituary. *Times* (of London), Jan. 3, 1995.
Obituary. *New York Times*, Jan. 3, 1995.

Simpson, Nicole Brown: See **Simpson, O. J.**

Simpson, O. J. (Orenthal James Simpson; 1947–   ) On October 3, 1995, a Los Angeles jury ended the very highly publicized murder trial of O. J. Simpson by declaring him not guilty of the June 12, 1994 murders of his former wife, Nicole Brown Simpson, and her friend, Ronald L. Goldman, both of whom had been killed outside her Los Angeles home. The trial had taken 16 months, and had been the focus of unremitting worldwide media attention throughout the entire period, while prosecution and defense developed huge bodies of evidence and argument, much of it the result of conflicting expert testimony. To the great surprise of everyone involved, the jury, composed of nine African Americans, two White Americans, and one Hispanic-American, took only about three hours to reach its verdict, adding fuel to what was already an intense argument and deepening chasm between African Americans and White Americans over the case. During the trial and afterward, the overwhelming majority of African Americans in the country thought Simpson innocent, and the overwhelming majority of Whites thought him guilty, with the outcome of the case seeming to have no real impact on most views. Jury members, on the other hand, stated that they had reached their conclusions because they had reasonable doubts about Simpson's guilt—and especially so after the racist remarks of Los Angeles detective Mark Fuhrman—but few on either side seemed ready to rationally discuss the verdict. Adding even further fuel to the controversy, Simpson lawyer Robert Shapiro publicly broke with co-counsel Johnnie L. Cochran, charging that Cochran had broken their agreement and played "the race card" during the trial, and dealt from "the bottom of the deck," in order to stir African-American jurors' sympathies and get Simpson acquitted.

At year's end, the dispute was still very much alive, and many books and film projects were being prepared, to be added to the many already in existence, one of them Simpson's own book *I Want to Tell You: My Response to Your Letters, Your Messages, Your Questions,* a best-seller while the trial was going on. The Simpson case also continued in the courts, as Simpson prepared to defend several civil suits brought by the families of the deceased.

Nicole Brown Simpson (ca. 1959–94) had been homecoming queen at Dana Hills High School in southern California in 1977. That year, just 18 years old, she began dating football star Simpson. They married in 1985 and had two children before their divorce, in 1992. In 1989, O. J. Simpson had pleaded no contest to a charge of spousal abuse, and was fined, sentenced to community service, and placed on probation for two years. Denise Brown, Nicole's sister, founded the Nicole Brown Simpson Charitable Foundation to work against domestic violence.

Ronald L. Goldman (ca. 1969–94), a friend of Nicole Brown Simpson, was a part-time waiter and model, and an aspiring actor.

Simpson grew up in San Francisco, emerging as a star high school football player at Galileo High School. He went on to star at San Francisco City College and then at the University of Southern California, where he quickly became a national celebrity, leading the country in rushing in his two years there. He won the Heisman Trophy (1968) as a senior, was the first player selected in the 1969 college draft, and played as a professional with the Buffalo Bills (1969–79), setting many professional records, among them the 2,003 yards gained rushing during the 1973 season, and becoming a major celebrity. He retired after the 1979 season, but remained a leading celebrity, appearing in many Hollywood films, in such television films as *Roots,* and as a sportscaster and sports talk show host, as well as in many highly visible and lucrative commercials. He carried the torch in the 1984 Los Angeles Olympics and was inducted into football's Hall of Fame in 1985. With Pete Axthelm he published *O. J.: The Education of a Rich Rookie* (1970).

Simpson and his first wife, Marguerite Whitley, had three children, one of whom drowned in a swimming accident in 1979, the year of their divorce. He and Nicole Brown Simpson had two children.

FURTHER READING

"O. J.'s life sentence. . . ." Dec. 1995. "The 'n' word. . . ." Nov. 1995. "The two faces of O. J." Sept. 1995. "If the gloves fit." Aug. 1995. DOMINICK DUNNE. *Vanity Fair.*

"Notes on the trial. . . ." DIANA TRILLING. *New Republic,* Oct. 30, 1995.

"Sport TV. . . ." LINCOLN CAPLAN. "The Simpsons." JIM SLEEPER. "My race, my gender." JONETTA ROSE BARRAS. "After the cheers. . . ." RANDALL KENNEDY. "From King to Cochran." ROBERT L. WOODSON, SR. "Quit worrying." MATTHEW COOPER. "Jury dismissed. . . ." MICHAEL LIND. "Unreasonable doubt." *New Republic,* Oct. 23, 1995.

"Why O. J. Simpson. . . ." ALDORE COLLIER. *Jet,* Oct. 23, 1995.

"Is all discrimination. . . ." RANDALL KENNEDY. "Scared speechless." MICHAEL KRAMER. "Riding the backlash. . . ." RICHARD STENGEL. "The trials to come. . . ." CHRISTOPHER JOHN FARLEY. "Heat on the beat. . . ." ERIC POOLEY. "Preventable murders." MARGARET CARLSON. "The lessons of the trial." JAMES WALSH. "Making the case." HOWARD CHUA-EOAN and ELIZABETH GLEICK. "A nation of pained hearts." ROGER ROSENBLATT. *Time,* Oct. 16, 1995.

"Bitter harvest. . . ." LUCINDA FRANKS. "The jurors. . . ." PATRICK ROGERS. "Now that it's over." RICHARD JEROME and CYNTHIA SANZ. *People,* Oct. 16, 1995.

"Black & white. . . ." JERELYN EDDINGS. *U.S. News & World Report,* Oct. 16, 1995.

"Black and white justice." *New York,* Oct. 16, 1995.

"Drawing lines and lessons." ANDREA SACHS. "An ugly end to it all." RICHARD LACAYO. "A trial for our times." LANCE MORROW. *Time,* Oct. 9, 1995.

"Judgment day." LARRY REIBSTEIN. *Newsweek,* Oct. 9, 1995.

"The real story. . . ." DAVID GELERNTER. *National Review,* Oct. 9, 1995.

" 'We tried to save. . . .' " TANYA BROWN and SHEILA WELLER. *Redbook,* July 1995. [on Nicole Brown Simpson]

"O. J. Simpson case. . . ." *Jet,* June 26, 1995.

"Live, from L.A. . . ." BOB LEVIN. "North versus south. . . ." RAE CORELLI. *Maclean's,* May 29, 1995.

"Will race taint. . . ." ELLIS COSE. "Disorder in the court." LARRY REINSTEIN. *Newsweek,* Apr. 17, 1995.

SINATRA, FRANK

"'She's with me. . . .'" MELINA GEROSA. *Ladies Home Journal*, Apr. 1995. [on Nicole Brown Simpson]
"America and the Simpson trial." PATRICIA J. WILLIAMS. *Nation*, Mar. 13, 1995.
"Making sense of Simpson." BETSY ISRAEL. *People*, Mar. 13, 1995.
"Facing the rage. . . ." SHELLEY LEVITT. *People*, Feb. 20, 1995. [on Nicole Brown Simpson] "Getting a word. . . ." GREGORY JAYNES. "Did he or didn't he?. . . ." ELIZABETH GLEICK. *Time*, Feb. 6, 1995.
Raging Heart: The Intimate Story of the Tragic Marriage of O. J. and Nicole Brown Simpson. SHEILA WELLER. Pocket Books, 1995.
"Who's who in court. . . ." "The people vs. Simpson." "The clues." "Tangles in. . . ." "If the genes fit. . . ." "The only witness." *People*, Oct. 10, 1994.
"To live and die. . . ." SUSAN SCHINDEHETTE. [on Nicole Brown Simpson] "California dreamer. . . ." WILLIAM PLUMMER. [on Ronald Goldman] *People*, Aug. 1, 1994.
Juice: The O. J. Simpson Story. JACK WILLIAMS. Princeton, 1994.
Nicole Brown Simpson. FAYE D. RESNICK. Dove Audio, 1994.
O. J. Simpson. MARC CERASINI. Windsor, 1994.

Sinatra, Frank (Francis Albert Sinatra; 1915–) Legendary singer Frank Sinatra, his friends, his business associates, and a good many other people very publicly celebrated his 80th birthday on December 12, 1995. One major celebration was the three-concert late-July Carnegie Hall series celebrating his life and work, which he did not attend. Another, in which he fully participated, was the November 17 Los Angeles Shrine Auditorium concert in his honor, which raised a reported $1 million for the AIDS Project Los Angeles and for the Eisenhower Medical Center's Barbara Sinatra Children's Center. The concert, which included performances by a wide range of stars, including Bruce Springsteen, Tony Bennett, Bob Dylan, and Natalie Cole, was taped and televised as the special *Sinatra: 80 Years My Way,* aired by ABC on December 14. His birthday was also celebrated by publication of the biography *Frank Sinatra: An American Legend,* by his daughter, Nancy Sinatra, who also read the audiobook version.

Sinatra himself issued the 1995 album *Sinatra 80th: Live in Concert,* which included his "My Way" duet with Luciano Pavarotti, also issued as a single. Consisting mainly of reissues, it also included several recent performance recordings. Also reissued was the 20-CD retrospective set *Frank Sinatra: the Complete Reprise Studio Recordings.* Sinatra had received a 1995 best traditional pop vocal performance Grammy nomination for his *Duets II.*

Sinatra began his singing career in cabaret in 1935. He became a popular singer and recording artist in 1940, while appearing with Tommy Dorsey's orchestra. In January 1943, at a four-week engagement at New York's Paramount Theater, he became the first of the modern teenage idols, whose fans "swooned" and rioted over him. He also became a radio and film star on "Your Hit Parade," and in such musicals as *Anchors Aweigh* (1945) and *On the Town* (1949), and won a special Oscar for his role in *The House I Live In* (1945).

But he ran into serious throat problems in 1952, and his career all but vanished. He then made an extraordinary comeback as a dramatic actor, winning a best supporting actor Oscar as Maggio in *From Here to Eternity* (1953), and went on to such films as *Guys and Dolls* (1955), *The Joker Is Wild* (1957), *The Manchurian Candidate* (1962), and *The Detective* (1968). His vocal problems eased as well; he reemerged as one of the leading song stylists of his time, continuing to tour through the mid-1990s. His records in recent years have included *Duets* (1993), *Duets II* (1994), *The Sinatra Christmas Album* (1994), and many reissues of earlier work. He has also written a book about his other vocation: *A Man and his Art* (1990), in 1991 retitled *Paintings: A Man and his Art.* Sinatra has been married four times, and has three children, including singers Nancy Sinatra and Frank Sinatra, Jr.

FURTHER READING

"Frank analysis. . . ." GREGORY CERIO. *People*, Dec. 18, 1995.
"A very good 80 years. . . ." FRANK MCCONNELL. *Commonweal*, Dec. 15, 1995.
"Voice of the century." RICHARD WILLIAMS. *Guardian*, Dec. 8, 1995.
"Sinatra. . . ." NANCY SINATRA. *Life*, Oct. 1995.
Frank Sinatra: Portrait of the Artist. RAY COLEMAN. Turner, 1995.
Frank Sinatra: An American Legend. NANCY SINATRA. General Publishing Group, 1995.
The Frank Sinatra Reader. STEVEN PETKOV and LEONARD MUSTAZZA. Oxford University Press, 1995.
"Stranger in the night." PETER PLAGENS. *Newsweek*, Mar. 21, 1994.
"Frank n' style." DAVID BROWNE. "Sinatrapalooza." DAVID HAJDU and DAVID BROWNE. *Entertainment*, Feb. 18, 1994.

366

"Frank Sinatra. . . ." NAT HENTOFF. *Down Beat*, Feb. 1994.

"The man who. . . ." JOSEPH SOBRAN. *National Review*, Feb. 17, 1992.

Frank Sinatra. JESSICA HODGE. Outlet, 1992.

"Frank Sinatra. . . ." WALTER THOMAS. *Interview*, July 1991.

Sinclair, Donald: See Herriot, James.

Slovo, Joe (Joseph Slovo; 1926–95)

Lithuanian-born Joe Slovo emigrated to South Africa with his family at the age of eight. He served in the South African military during World War II, joining the Communist Party in 1942. After the war, he became a lawyer, a period in which he and Nelson Mandela became friends and began what would become a lifelong political association, although Mandela was not a Communist. In sharp conflict with the South African government from the late 1940s, Slovo was charged with treason in 1956, acquitted in 1958, spent some years underground in South Africa, and fled into what became a 27-year-long exile in 1963. He became a member of the African National Congress (ANC) in 1985, and in 1986 became head of the South African Communist Party. He remained a Communist who strongly defended every aspect of Soviet policy well into the 1980s, when he began to moderate his public stance, and to say that he had had reservations about Soviet policies since the 1960s. Slovo was appointed housing minister in the Mandela government, in that position attempting to develop a national housing policy that actively engaged a wide range of South African political groups and commercial interests. He was survived by his second wife, Helena, and by three daughters from his marriage to writer and activist Ruth First, who was killed by a letter bomb in 1982. (d. South Africa; January 6, 1995)

FURTHER READING

"Bazooka Joe." RICHARD STENGEL. *New Republic*, Jan. 30, 1995.

Obituary. *Jet*, Jan. 23, 1995.

Obituary. *Times* (of London), Jan. 7, 1995.

Obituary. *New York Times*, Jan. 7, 1995.

Obituary. *Independent*, Jan. 7, 1995.

Smiley, Jane Graves (1949–) After her rather grim, *Lear*-like, Pulitzer Prize–winning *A Thousand Acres*, novelist Jane Smiley produced a complete change of pace with *Moo: A Novel*. This light satirical tale focuses on shady doings at a midwestern agricultural university dubbed "Moo U." The farcical sendup of academic life has dozens of characters in wild profusion, though the most notable is certainly the 700-pound hog named Earl Butz, a key figure in a secret study of porcine behavior and, as some reviewers have pointed out, a comic version of Moby Dick. *Moo* leapt onto the best-seller lists even before its official publication date, April Fool's Day, with Smiley making a 20-city publicity tour, including an interview on NPR's "All Things Considered." Smiley also was coeditor, with Katrina Kenison, of *The Best American Short Stories 1995;* a contributing editor to the new Library of Congress–sponsored periodical *Civilization;* and one of four national judges for a campaign to choose the best American fiction writers under age 40, sponsored by the British literary magazine *Granta;* winners were scheduled to be announced in 1996.

Los Angeles–born Smiley received her 1971 B.A. from Vassar College, and her 1976 M.F.A., 1978 M.A., and 1978 Ph.D. from the University of Iowa. She was a Fulbright Scholar (1976–77). She became an assistant professor at Iowa State University in 1981, moving up to associate professor in 1984 and full professor in 1989. At the same time, she began to produce the works for which she is by far best known, including *Barn Blind* (1980), *At Paradise Gate* (1981), *Duplicate Keys* (1984), *The Age of Grief* (1987), *The Greenlanders* (1988), *Ordinary Love and Goodwill* (1989), and the best-selling *A Thousand Acres* (1992), which won the Pulitzer Prize and the National Book Critics Circle Award. She and her second husband, Stephen Mark Mortensen, have a son. She also has two daughters from her first marriage.

FURTHER READING

"Sharper than. . . ." RUPERT CHRISTIANSEN. *Observer*, Oct. 25, 1992.
"Of serpents' teeth. . . ." MICHELLE GREEN and BARBARA KLEBAN MILLS. *People*, Jan. 13, 1992.

Smith, Emmitt J., III (1969–) Some

say, "As Smith goes, so go the Cowboys." Certainly in 1993, their second consecutive Super Bowl year and his own MVP year, he missed three games—and the Dallas Cowboys lost all three. Looking closer, to mid-January 1995, some suggest that if Smith had not been hobbled by a hamstring injury in the National Football Conference championships, the Cowboys would not have been blown out by the San Francisco 49ers and missed the chance to three-peat at the Super Bowl.

In the 1995 season, Smith won his fourth NFL rushing title, leading the league with 1,773 yards. His 25 regular-season touchdowns set a new NFL record and put him on pace to reach 100 rushing touchdowns faster than any running back in NFL history. Though the Cowboys stumbled at times during the season, they finished strong, and by mid-January had won the NFC championship and were set to meet the Pittsburgh Steelers in Super Bowl XXX. Smith was selected as an NFC starter in the Pro Bowl, scheduled for February 1996.

While still in high school, in Escambia, Florida, Smith was outstanding: he was a consensus All-America running back and was named Player of the Year by *Parade* and *USA Today*. During his three seasons at the University of Florida, he reached 1,000 rushing yards in only his seventh game, faster than anyone in college football history. He left college after his junior year and joined the Cowboys (1990–), in his first season being named the Associate Press's Offensive Rookie of the Year. Smith helped win

the Cowboys' two consecutive Super Bowl championships (1992 and 1993 seasons); for the latter, he was named Most Valuable Player of both the National Football League and the Super Bowl, also tying a Super Bowl record for most rushing touchdowns (2). He also won three straight NFL rushing titles (1991–93), only the fourth player ever to do so, despite missing three 1993 games, and was only 14 yards short of being the first person ever to have three consecutive 1,500-yard seasons. Smith has been named to the Pro Bowl six times (1990–95 seasons), but was unable to play twice because of injury (1993 and 1994 seasons). In 1994, he published *The Emmitt Zone,* written with Steve Delsohn. Smith is studying therapeutic recreation at the University of Florida, and works with various charitable organizations. His cousin Willie Harris is a wide receiver with the Jacksonville Jaguars.

FURTHER READING

"Emmit Smith." MICKEY SPAGNOLA. *Sport,* Aug. 1995.
"Smith, Emmitt." *Current Biography*, Nov. 1994.
"Star power." PAUL ATTNER. Dec. 19, 1994. "Running mates." TERRI FREI. Sept. 5, 1994. *Sporting News.*
"Guide 'em Cowboys. . . ." BRUCE SCHOENFELD. *Sport,* July 1994.
"Dare to be great." PETER KING. *Sports Illustrated,* Jan. 31, 1994.
Emmitt Smith: Finding Daylight. TED COX. Childrens, 1994.

Smith, Margaret Chase (1897–1995)

Born in Skowhegan, Maine, Margaret Chase did not attend college, but held a series of jobs after her high school graduation. She married Clyde R. Smith in 1930; the Smiths went to Washington when he was elected to the House of Representatives as a Republican in 1937. He died while in office in 1940; she won election to his unexpired term and then won election to the seat on her own. She served four full terms in the House, and in 1948 won election to the Senate, where she served four more terms, becoming the first woman to win election to both houses of Congress. Smith was a remarkably independent figure, a moderate Republican who voted her conscience far more than her party's position. She did not hesitate to vote with the Democrats on a substantial number of issues of social conscience, including women's rights matters and a wide range of civil rights issues, though she certainly voted far more often with her party than against it. In 1952, she was one of seven Republican senators who signed a "declaration of conscience," opposing the witchhunting tactics of Senator Joseph McCarthy. She was a candidate for the Republican presidential nomination in 1964. She was survived by a sister. (d. Skowhegan, Maine; May 29, 1995)

FURTHER READING

"Straight shooter. . . ." KEVIN GRAY. *People*, June 12, 1995.
Obituary. *Times* (of London), May 31, 1995.
Obituary. *New York Times*, May 30, 1995.
Politics of Conscience: A Biography of Margaret Chase Smith. PATRICIA W. WALLACE. Greenwood, 1995.
Woman of Conscience: Margaret Chase Smith of Maine. DENNIS MORRISON. Brandywine, 1994.
Is There a Woman in the House—or Senate? BRYNA J. FIRESIDE. A. Whitman, 1993.

Snipes, Wesley (1962–) Actor Wesley

Snipes starred in 1995 in the comedy-thriller film *Money Train,* directed by Joseph Ruben, as African-American police officer John, opposite Woody Harrelson as his White foster brother Charlie, who is also his police officer partner and a compulsive gambler, always in money trouble. They work together, arresting muggers in the New York subways. The brothers both fall in love with a policewoman, played by Jennifer Lopez, supplying some of the film's momentum. Ultimately, the story line has Charlie hijacking the subway's "money train," which transports the day's fare revenue. A major controversy about violence in films erupted when, soon after the film opened in New York, two men attacked a subway toll booth and fatally burned the toll changer trapped inside, using exactly the techniques shown in the film, in what seemed to many a "copycat" crime.

Snipes also starred opposite Patrick Swayze and John Leguizamo, all three playing drag queens, in the antic comedy *To Wong Foo, Thanks for Everything! Julie Newmar*, directed by Beeban Kidron, and costarring Stockard Channing , Blythe Danner, Arliss Howard, and Robin Williams in a cameo role.

Forthcoming were starring roles in the film *The Fan,* directed by Tony Scott and costarring Robert De Niro, Ellen Barkin, John Leguizamo, and Renicio Del Toro; and in the action film *Sandblast,* directed by David Carson and set in Kuwait in the aftermath of the Persian Gulf War.

Florida-born Snipes appeared in several New York plays in the late 1980s, including *The Boys of Winter, Death and the King's Horsemen,* and *Execution of Justice.* His film debut came in *Streets of Gold* (1986), which was followed by a CableAce Award–winning appearance in the television film *Vietnam Story* (1987). In 1987, he also appeared in Michael Jackson's music video "Bad." After playing in several small supporting film roles, he emerged as a rising young film star as jazz saxophonist Shadow Henderson in Spike Lee's *Mo' Better Blues* (1989), followed by major roles in *New Jack City* (1991), *Jungle Fever* (1991), *White Men Can't Jump* (1992), *Passenger 57* (1992), *Rising Sun* (1993), *Demolition Man* (1993), *Boiling Point* (1993), *Sugar Hill* (1993), and *Drop Zone* (1994). Snipes was formerly married.

FURTHER READING

"20 questions. . . ." *Playboy*, Oct. 1993.
"Snipes, Wesley." *Current Biography*, Sept. 1993.
Who's Hot: Wesley Snipes. RAY ZWOCKER. Dell, 1993.
"Hot shots." JERRY LAZAR. *Us*, Apr. 1992.
"Wesley Snipes. . . ." LAURA RANDOLPH. *Ebony*, Sept. 1991.
"Wesley fever. . . ." RALPH RUGOFF. *Premiere*, July 1991.

Solzhenitsyn, Alexander Isayevich

(1918–) Prophet and scourge, Alexander Solzhenitsyn was most visible in 1995 as a talk-show host on the state-controlled public television station in Russia, to which he had returned with enormous fanfare in 1994, after 20 years in exile, mostly in the United States. Called "A Meeting with Solzhenitsyn," the 15-minute biweekly show originally had him talking with a wide variety of people, from ambassadors to eye surgeons, but he then dispensed with guests, instead delivering monologues criticizing current Russian government and society. This seems to have driven many viewers away; in September 1995, after only a year, the show was abruptly canceled, reportedly because of low ratings. Certainly many of his criticisms, and his support of the Chechen rebels, made him unpopular with the government.

After 1974 treason charges against Solzhenitsyn had been dropped in 1991, his wife, Natalya, went ahead to Russia to prepare a home for his return, a new dacha overlooking the Moscow River. On his 1994 arrival, Solzhenitsyn made a 55-day, 5,700-mile cross-country tour of his homeland; the BBC-"Frontline" documentary of that journey, *The Homecoming,* aired in 1995. The year also saw the English-language publication of *Invisible Allies.*

Solzhenitsyn had survived imprisonment and exile to create powerful works that strongly affected Soviet and world thinking, and helped pave the way for the reforms of the Gorbachev era and the dissolution of the Soviet Union. He was imprisoned in a labor camp (1948–53), and then internally exiled to Siberia (1953–57), using these experiences to create his novel *One Day in the Life of Ivan Denisovich* (1962), a trailblazing exposé of the Soviet penal system. Denied publication in the Soviet Union, he published his major works abroad, including *The First Circle* (1968), *The Cancer Ward* (1968), *August 1914* (1971; expanded 1989), and *The Gulag Archipelago* (in three parts; 1973–79). His nonfiction works include *The Oak and the Calf: A Memoir* (1980), *Rebuilding Russia: Toward Some Formulations* (1991), *"The Russian Question" at the End of the 20th Century* (1994), and *August 1914: The Red Wheel—I* (1989), the first volume of a history of the Russian Revolution. Solzhenitsyn won the 1970 Nobel Prize for literature.

Solzhenitsyn attended Rostov University. After his 1974 expulsion from the Soviet Union, he spent two years in Geneva before moving to the United States. He and his second wife, mathematician Natalia Svetlova Solzhenitsyn, have three sons.

FURTHER READING

The Solzhenitsyn Files: Secret Soviet Documents Reveal One Man's Fight Against the Monolith. MICHAEL SCAMMELL, ed. Edition Q, 1995.
"A call to repentance. . . ." PEGGY JACKSON. *Christianity Today,* Aug. 15, 1994.
"A conscience returns home." *Economist,* May 28, 1994.
" 'Zhirinovsky is. . . .' " PAUL KLEBNIKOV. *Forbes,* May 9, 1994.
Solzhenitsyn and the Modern World. EDWARD E. ERICSON, JR. Regnery, 1993.
"The grand inquisitor. . . ." TATYANA TOLSTAYA and JAMEY GAMBRELL. *New Republic,* June 29, 1992.

Souphanouvong

Souphanouvong (1912–95) Born in Luang Prabang, Laos, Prince Souphanouvong was the son of Prince Boun Khong and the half-brother of Prince Souvanna Phouma. A French-trained civil engineer, Souphanouvong returned home in 1938, served in the French Indo-China government until 1945, and in the late 1940s and early 1950s led the Lao Patriotic Front and was a founder of the Pathet Lao, fighting in alliance with Vietminh forces during the war against French colonial forces in Indochina. He twice participated on behalf of the Pathet Lao in coalition governments organized by Souvanna Phouma (1957–58; 1962–63), but all attempts at reconciliation between the Western-oriented Souvanna Phouma government and the Communist Pathet Lao failed. The civil war resumed side by side with the Vietnam War, and Souphanouvong ultimately resumed his position as a leader of the Pathet Lao. After Communist victory in 1975, Souphanouvong became president of Laos, serving until his death in the largely ceremonial post. No information was available as to survivors. (d. Laos; January 9, 1995)

FURTHER READING

Obituary. *Independent,* Jan. 17, 1995.
Obituary. *Times* (of London), Jan. 11, 1995.
Obituary. *New York Times,* Jan 11, 1995.

Souter, David Hackett

Souter, David Hackett (1939–) No longer part of the centrist "swing" group that had briefly emerged in the previous Supreme Court term, Justice David Souter instead became a leading Court dissenter during 1995.

Souter wrote a sharply dissenting opinion in the landmark *U.S.* v. *Lopez,* in which the Court invalidated as unconstitutional the federal Gun-Free School Zones Act of 1990, which made possession of a gun within 1,000 feet of a school illegal, ruling that this was an invalid extension of the congressional ability to regulate interstate commerce. His dissent called the decision far too broad, and criticized it as damagingly reopening long-settled federal-state powers questions. He also very sharply dissented in the landmark *Rosenberg* v. *Rector and Visitors of the University of Virginia,* which held that the publicly funded University of Virginia was required to finance a Christian magazine run by students, calling the decision a breach of the constitutional separation of church and state. A third major dissenting opinion came in *Adarand Constructors* v. *Pena,* which held that the federal government was required to use the same strict standards as the states in carrying out affirmative action programs, reversing the Court's long-held position on federal affirmative action programs.

Souter also joined the dissent in other key cases, among them *Miller* v. *Johnson,* which held that Georgia's Eleventh Congressional District was unconstitutional because it was organized primarily to provide racial representation, rather than to respond to specific discrimination; *Missouri* v. *Jenkins,* which effectively limited the level of state spending allowable to carry out a federally managed school desegregation plan in Kansas City; and *Veronia School District* v. *Acton,* which ruled that an Oregon school district's random drug testing program was constitutional.

Souter joined the majority in the landmark *U.S. Term Limits Inc.* v. *Thornton,* which held that to limit congressional terms required a constitutional amendment; 23 state laws imposing terms limits were invalidated and Congress was barred from passing a term limits law. He also joined the majority in *Capital Square Review and Advisory Board* v. *Pinette,* which ruled that it was unconstitutional to bar display of a large Ku Klux Klan cross in an Ohio public park; and in *Babbitt* v. *Sweet Home Chapter of Communities for a Greater Oregon,* ruling that the federal government had the right under the Endangered Species Act to sharply restrict logging and other activities harmful to the northern spotted owl. He wrote the unanimous opinion in *Hurley* v. *Irish-American Gay, Lesbian and Bisexual Group of Boston,* ruling that the Boston St. Patrick's Day parade was private, rather than

public, and that the organizers of the parade had a free speech right to bar banner-carrying participation by the gay rights group.

Massachusetts-born Souter received his 1961 B.A. and 1966 LL.B. from Harvard University; he was also a Rhodes Scholar. He moved up in the New Hampshire attorney general's office (1968–76) and became state attorney general (1976–78). He was a state court judge (1978–83) and a state supreme court justice (1983–89) until his appointment by President George Bush to the U.S. Supreme Court.

FURTHER READING

"Poetic justice. . . ." JEFFREY ROSEN. *New Republic,* Mar. 8, 1993.
David Souter. BOB ITALIA. Abdo & Daughters, 1992.
"Souter, David Hackett." *Current Biography,* Jan. 1991.

Southern, Terry (1921–95) Texas-born novelist and screenwriter Terry Southern received his 1948 B.A. from Northwestern University and attended the Sorbonne (1948–50). He became a figure in the then-developing counterculture of the late 1950s with his sexually explict novel *Candy* (1958), written with Mason Hoffenberg. In the same period he also published the satirical novel *The Magic Christian* (1959), basis of the 1969 film. He became a major countercultural figure in the 1960s, with collaborations on the screenplays of the classic anti–nuclear war film *Dr. Strangelove or: How I Learned to Stop Worrying and Love the Bomb* (1964), and the equally classic *Easy Rider* (1969). Among his other screenplays were *The Cincinnati Kid* (1965) and *Barbarella* (1968). A recent novel was *Texas Summer* (1992). Late in his career, Southern taught screenwriting at New York University and Columbia. He was survived by his companion, Gail Gerber, and a son. (d. New York City; October 29, 1995)

FURTHER READING

Obituary. *Independent,* Nov. 10, 1995.
Obituary. *Times* (of London), Nov. 1, 1995.
Obituary. *New York Times,* Oct. 31, 1995.

Spacek, Sissy (Mary Elizabeth Spacek; 1949–) Film and television star Sissy Spacek in 1995 starred as West Texas schoolteacher Spring Renfrom opposite Tommy Lee Jones as

modern cowboy Hewey Calloway in the television film *The Good Old Boys,* written and directed by Jones and costarring Terry Kinney, Frances McDormand, Wilford Brimley, and Sam Shepard. The story revolves around Jones's attempt to help his brother save his home from foreclosure. Spacek received a best supporting actress in a miniseries or special Emmy nomination for the role. She also received a Screen Actors Guild best actress in telefilm or miniseries award for her 1994 role in *A Place for Annie.*

Spacek also starred as a schoolteacher who was formerly a prostitute, opposite James Garner in the very well-received five-hour television miniseries *Larry McMurtry's "Streets of Laredo,"* a sequel to McMurtry's acclaimed 1989 miniseries *Lonesome Dove.* She also costarred in the film *The Grass Harp,* based on Truman Capote's autobiographical novel; the cast also included Walter Matthau, Piper Laurie, Jack Lemmon, Mary Steenburgen, and Charles Durning, and was directed by Matthau's son, Charles Matthau.

Texas-born Spacek emerged as a star in the mid-1970s in such films as *Prime Cut* (1972), *Badlands* (1974), and in her breakthrough role in *Carrie* (1976), for which she won an Oscar nomination for best actress. She went on to star in such films as *Three Women* (1977), *Coal Miner's Daughter* (1980), for which she won a best actress Oscar, *Raggedy Man* (1981), *Missing* (1982), *The River* (1984), *'Night Mother* (1986), *Crimes of the Heart* (1986), *The Long Walk Home* (1989), *JFK* (1991), *A Private Matter* (1992), *Hard Promises* (1993), *Trading Mom* (1994), and *A Place for Annie* (1994). Spacek attended the Lee Strasberg Theatrical Institute. She is married to art director Jack Fisk and has two children.

FURTHER READING

"Mettle of the belle." PAT DOWELL. *American Film,* Mar. 1991.
" 'I've kinda found. . . .' " MICHAEL J. BANDLER. *McCall's,* Feb. 1991.

Specter, Arlen (1930–   ) On March 30, 1995, Pennsylvania Republican Senator Arlen Specter declared his candidacy for the 1996 Republican presidential nomination. By far the most politically liberal of the Republican hopefuls, Specter openly attacked the religious Right,

disputing its position on several key issues and contending that by adopting ultraconservative positions the Republican Party was in danger of isolating itself from the mainstream of American politics. Specter declared himself prochoice as to abortion and opposed the school prayer amendment. On many other key matters, Specter ran as a conservative, stressing his anticrime credentials as a former prosecutor, favoring the balanced-budget amendment, and calling for major tax law changes, notably in capital gains taxes and investment credits. In the early running, his candidacy received only modest support, which quickly faded, as did his ability to raise money. He withdrew from the campaign on November 21. Specter was the first Jew to seek the Republican presidential nomination.

Specter was born in Wichita, Kansas. He studied at the University of Oklahoma and received his 1951 B.A. from the University of Pennsylvania, and his 1956 LL.B. from Yale University. He then practiced law in Philadelphia, becoming a partner at Dechert, Price, and Rhoads (1956–66). Specter entered public life as a Philadelphia assistant district attorney (1959–63) and was an assistant counsel with the Warren Commission in 1964. He was Philadelphia district attorney (1966–74), then returned to his law firm. In 1980, he won election to the U.S. Senate and has served in the Senate since 1981. A member of the Senate Judiciary Committee, he drew massive television coverage before worldwide audiences during the 1991 Anita Faye Hill–Clarence

Thomas confrontation for his very sharp attacks on Hill, even directly accusing Hill of perjury, a charge that was never pursued. Specter married Joan L. Levy in 1953; they have two children.

FURTHER READING

"A frightful Specter." RICHARD BROOKHISER. *National Review*, July 10, 1995.
"The looming Specter. . . ." MICHAEL RUST. *Insight on the News*, Apr. 3, 1995.
"A man of choice. . . ." JOHN F. DICKERSON. *Time*, Mar. 13, 1995.
"Darlin' Arlen. . . ." RUTH SHALIT. *New Republic*, Mar. 13, 1995.
"The transmogrification of. . . ." ALICIA MUNDY. *Philadelphia Magazine*, Mar. 1992.

Spender, Stephen Harold (1909–95)

Poet, critic, novelist, and translator Stephen Spender was one of the leading literary figures of the English-speaking world. He was, however, primarily a poet, the contemporary of W. H. Auden, Christopher Isherwood, Cecil Day-Lewis, and those other young, then-radical Oxford-trained poets who made an enormous impact on English letters in the 1930s. His first published collection was *Poems* (1933). His *Collected Poems* was published in 1955, and his *Collected Poems 1930–1985* in 1985. In 1985 he also published his *Journals 1939–1982*. He also published the novel *The Temple* (1988), a new translation of the *Oedipus* trilogy (1983), autobiographical works such as *Memoirs: The Thirties and After; Poetry, Politics, People* (1978) and *China Diary* (1982; with David Hockney); and several collections of poems and criticism as writer and editor. His most recent book was the poetry collection *Dolphins* (1994).

Spender served as coeditor of *Oxford Poetry* (1929–30); cofounded and coedited the journal *Horizon* (1939–41), and later coedited the journal *Encounter* (1953–66). He was a visiting professor at several American institutions in the late 1960s and 1970s, and was professor of English at London's University College (1970–77), then professor emeritus. In 1994, Spender charged that *While England Sleeps*, a new novel by David Leavitt, plagiarized Spender's 1951 memoir *World Within World*. Though Leavitt said his use of the material was in line with general literary standards, the lawsuit was settled in Spender's favor, with Leavitt's novel be-

ing withdrawn from publication, while Spender issued a new edition of his memoir. He was survived by his wife, pianist Natasha Litvin, a daughter, and a son. (d. London; July 16, 1995)

FURTHER READING

"English lessons from. . . ." JOSEPH BRODSKY. *New Yorker*, Jan. 8, 1996.
Obituary. *Current Biography*, Sept. 1995.
Obituary. *Economist*, July 22, 1995.
Obituary. *Independent*, July 18, 1995.
Obituary. *Times* (of London), July 18, 1995.
Obituary. *New York Times*, July 18, 1995.

Springsteen, Bruce (1949–   )

Celebrated rock singer and songwriter Bruce Springsteen was greatly honored by his peers in 1995. His song "Streets of Philadelphia," from the soundtrack of the 1993 film *Philadelphia*, had won many awards in 1994, including an Academy Award as best original song, the first rock song to be honored with an Oscar. In 1995, it won a good many more honors, including four Grammys: best male rock performance, best rock song, best song written specifically for a motion picture or for television, and song of the year.

Springsteen issued the acclaimed 1995 album *The Ghost of Tom Joad*, a spare, deeply emotional work that spoke of working people and poor people, some of them on the underside of American life in difficult times, in such songs as the title cut, "Straight Time," "Highway 29," and

"Youngstown." He also issued a smash *Greatest Hits* album, which included several new songs, some of them recorded with his reunited E Street Band. Two hit singles released from the album were "Murder Incorporated" and "Secret Garden." The album quickly went to the top range of the charts, topping 2 million sales by year's end, while his early album *Born to Run* topped 15 million sales.

In a very busy year, Springsteen also found the time to appear in the television miniseries *The History of Rock 'n' Roll,* narrated by Gary Busey. Also on the film side, he wrote songs for the soundtrack of the film *The Crossing Guard,* written and directed by Sean Penn, and starring Jack Nicholson, David Morse, and Anjelica Huston. He also wrote and sang the title song for the Tim Robbins film *Dead Man Walking.*

New Jersey–born Springsteen was discovered by legendary record producer John Hammond in 1972. After two early albums, *Greetings from Asbury Park, New Jersey* (1973) and *The Wild, the Innocent and the E-Street Shuffle* (1974), Springsteen had enormous success with *Born to Run* (1975), emerging as a rock superstar. He went on to record *Darkness on the Edge of Town* (1978), *The River* (1980), the personal *Nebraska* (1982), the classic *Born in the U.S.A.* (1984), *Bruce Springsteen and the E Street Band Live/ 1975–1985* (1986), *Tunnel of Love* (1987), and *Chimes of Freedom* (1988), as well as politically aware pieces such as *No Nukes* (1979) and *We Are the World* (1985). Later albums included *Human Touch* and *Lucky Town* (both 1992). Previously divorced, he married singer Patti Scialfa in 1991; they have two sons and one daughter.

FURTHER READING

"A chip off the old Boss." ADAM SWEETING. *Guardian,* Nov. 10, 1995.
"The birth of the Boss." BETH JOHNSON. *Entertainment,* May 19, 1995.
Bruce Springsteen. Andrews & McMeel, 1994.
Bruce Springsteen. RON FRANKL. Chelsea House, 1994.
Wild and Innocent: The Recordings of Bruce Springsteen, 1972–1985. BRAD ELLIOTT. Popular Culture, 1994.
"Springsteen, Bruce." *Current Biography,* Aug. 1992.
"Springsteen. . . ." JAMES HENKE. *Rolling Stone,* Aug. 6, 1992.
Down Thunder Road: The Making of Bruce Springsteen. MARC ELIOT. Knightsbridge, 1991.

Stallone, Sylvester Enzio (1946–)

Film star Sylvester Stallone appeared in two high-profile, high-cost films in 1995. He played the title role in the high-tech, massively violent special-effects science-fiction thriller *Judge Dredd,* as a future police officer confronted by a master criminal, played by Armand Assante. Danny Cannon directed; the cast included Diane Lane, Rob Schneider, Joan Chen, Jurgen Prochnow, Joanna Miles, and Max Von Sydow. The film was very badly received by the critics and was also a box office disaster.

Stallone's second film was the thriller *Assassins,* directed and coproduced by Richard Donner. Stallone starred as a seasoned professional "hit man" opposite Antonio Banderas as his young rival, who has been hired to assassinate him. The film, an expensive, high-tech series of murders, was also not very well received, either by critics or at the box office, though it was not as universally panned as *Judge Dredd.*

Forthcoming was a starring role in the high-cost special-effects disaster film *Daylight,* in a cast that includes Amy Brenneman, Claire Bloom, Jay O. Sanders, Stan Shaw, Viggo Mortensen, and Karen Young.

On the business side, Stallone signed a three-picture contract with MCA, reportedly for $60 million or more.

On the personal side, he and actress Angie Everhardt announced their engagement.

In 1976, New York City–born Stallone starred in *Rocky;* he also wrote the screenplay. The movie won a best film Oscar and was a world-wide hit; Stallone immediately became an international star. He did four sequels: *Rocky II* (1979; he wrote the screenplay and directed); *Rocky III* (1982); *Rocky IV* (1985; he directed); and *Rocky V* (1990). He also starred as Rambo in *First Blood* (1982), *Rambo: First Blood Part II* (1985), and *Rambo III* (1988), and in such other films as *F.I.S.T.* (1978), *Paradise Alley* (1978), *Nighthawks* (1981), *Rhinestone* (1984), *Cobra* (1986), *Over the Top* (1987), *Lock Up* (1989), *Tango and Cash* (1989), *Oscar* (1991), *Stop! Or My Mom Will Shoot* (1992), *Cliffhanger* (1993), *Demolition Man* (1993), and *The Specialist* (1994). Stallone attended the American College of Switzerland and Miami University. He has been married twice and has two children.

FURTHER READING

"Sly hits. . . ." LAURA C. SMITH. *Entertainment*, Nov. 17, 1995.
"Sly." JOEL SILVER. *Interview*, July 1995.
"Rocky ending." KAREN S. SCHNEIDER and JOHNNY DODD. *People*, May 2, 1994.
"Stallone, Sylvester." *Current Biography*, Feb. 1994.
"Sly's body electric." ZOE HELLER. *Vanity Fair*, Nov. 1993.

Starr, Ringo (Richard Starkey; 1940–)

Former Beatle Ringo Starr joined two other living legends, former Beatles Paul McCartney and George Harrison, in a three-segment, six-hour television biography of the group, *The Beatles Anthology*, broadcast on ABC November 19, 20, and 22, 1995. The show, which included the world premiere of the John Lennon song "Free as a Bird," drew enormous audiences. It was followed by release of their two-disc set *The Beatles Anthology, Volume. 1;* volumes 2 and 3 were to be released in 1996. Volume I contained more than 40 selections drawn from the years 1958–1964, including some from the period when they were still called the Quarrymen and others before Starr replaced Pete Best as drummer. Included were the unreleased Lennon–McCartney songs "Hello Little Girl" and "Like Dreamers Do," as well as the 1977 John Lennon song "Free as a Bird." Two other Lennon songs, "Real Love" and "Grow Old with Me," were scheduled to be released in the 1996 volumes. A *Beatles Anthology* book was also to be released in 1996, as was a ten-hour home video version of the anthology.

The anthology albums and a "Free as a Bird" single were released in early December; both immediately became record-breaking chart toppers.

During the spring and summer of 1995, Starr also toured with his All-Starr Band Mark III.

Liverpool-born Starr played with The Hurricanes (1959–62), and joined the Beatles in 1962. He became a worldwide celebrity in the 1960s, as he, Paul McCartney, John Lennon, and George Harrison created a revolution in popular music, in concert and with such records as *Please, Please Me* (1963), *She Loves You* (1963), *I Want to Hold Your Hand* (1963), *Yesterday* (1965), *Revolver* (1966), and *Sergeant Pepper's Lonely Hearts Club Band* (1967), and in such films as *A Hard Day's Night* (1964), *Magical Mystery Tour* (1967), and *The Yellow Submarine* (1968). After the group broke up in 1970, Starr recorded several albums and appeared in such films as *200 Motels* (1969), *Stardust* (1975), *Son of Dracula* (1975), *Caveman* (1981), and *Give My Regards to Broad Street* (1984). His first solo tour came in 1989. He issued the comeback album *Time Takes Time* in 1992. He has been married twice, most recently to Barbara Bach, and has three children.

FURTHER READING

"Get back. . . ." RICHARD CORLISS. *Time*, Nov. 20, 1995.
"Ringo." DAVID WILD. *Rolling Stone*, July 9, 1992.
"Ringo Starr. . . ." TOM PETTY. *Interview*, June 1992.
"In search of. . . ." GILES SMITH. *Independent*, Apr. 16, 1992.
Ringo Starr: Straight Man or Joker? ALAN CLAYSON. Paragon House, 1992.
Strange Days: The Music of John, Paul, George and Ringo Twenty Years On. WALTER PODRAZIK. Popular Culture, 1991.

Steenburgen, Mary (1953–)

Actress Mary Steenburgen in 1995 costarred in three quite diverse films. In *The Grass Harp*, set in a small midwestern town in the 1930s, she played Sister Ida, a traveling revivalist, in a cast that included Walter Matthau, Piper Laurie, Sissy Spacek, Jack Lemmon, and Charles Durning. Based on Truman Capote's autobiographical novel, the film was directed by Matthau's son, Charles Matthau. In the film *Powder*, written and directed by Victor Salva, Steenburgen starred as teacher Jessie Caldwell, opposite

Sean Patrick in the title role as a mutant teenage genius and saint; Lance Henriksen and Jeff Goldblum costarred.

Third, and far from least, Steenburgen appeared in the highly controversial film biography *Nixon*, directed, cowritten, and coproduced by Oliver Stone, as the mother of former president Richard M. Nixon, opposite Anthony Hopkins as the disgraced, very nearly impeached, resigned president.

On the personal side, Steenburgen married screen star Ted Danson, her costar in the 1994 film *Pontiac Moon*.

Arkansan Steenburgen made her film debut in *Goin' South* (1978), and went on to such films as *Ragtime* (1981), *Time After Time* (1979), *Melvin and Howard* (1980; she won a best supporting actress Oscar), *Cross Creek* (1983), *Dead of Winter* (1987), *End of the Line* (1987), *Parenthood* (1989), *Back to the Future Part III* (1990), *The Butcher's Wife* (1991), *Philadelphia* (1993), *What's Eating Gilbert Grape* (1993), *Pontiac Moon* (1994), and *Clifford* (1994). She also produced and played a bit role in *The Whales of August* (1987). In addition, she appeared in such telefilms as *Tender Is the Night* (1985) and *The Attic: The Hiding of Anne Frank* (1988). In 1993, she starred on the New York stage in a revival of George Bernard Shaw's *Candida*. Steenburgen attended Hendricks College and studied at New York's Neighborhood Playhouse. She has two children from her previous marriage to actor Malcolm McDowell.

FURTHER READING

"Mary, Mary uncontrary." JESS CAGLE. *Ladies Home Journal*, Nov. 1994.

Stennis, John Cornelius (1901–95)

Mississippi-born John Stennis was a 1923 graduate of Mississippi State University and earned his 1928 law degree from the University of Virginia. He won election to the Mississippi House of Representatives in 1929, and then became a prosecutor and judge. In 1947, he began his long career in the U.S. Senate, winning the seat formerly held by leading segregationist Democrat Theodore Bilbo. Stennis was to serve uninterrupted for more than 41 years in the Senate, for most of that time as a leader of the southern conservative wing of the Democratic Party; although less virulently racist than Bilbo, he was at one with Bilbo on civil rights and other social issues, joining other southern senators to filibuster against civil rights legislation and urging southern resistance to federal enforcement of desegregation in education, as mandated by the Supreme Court in 1954.

Stennis became chairman of the powerful Senate Armed Services Committee, and in that position supported the American military and the CIA on a wide range of issues during the Cold War, among them virtually unlimited funding and the conduct of the Vietnam War—although he early opposed American involvement in that war. Highly respected by many of his colleagues, he was the chairman of the Senate committee that unanimously voted to censure Senator Joseph McCarthy—even though Stennis was as strongly anti-Communist as anyone in public life. He published *Role of Congress in Foreign Policy* (1971). Stennis was survived by a daughter and a son. (d. Jackson, Mississippi; April 23, 1995)

FURTHER READING

Obituary. *Times* (of London), Apr. 25, 1995.
Obituary. *New York Times*, Apr. 24, 1995.

Stephens, Robert (1931–95)

Bristol-born stage and screen actor Robert Stephens worked in provincial repertory until his mid-20s. In 1956, he joined the new English Stage Company at London's Royal Court Theater, where he understudied Laurence Olivier in *The Entertainer*. He joined Olivier's National Theater Company in the 1960s, playing many roles, among them Horatio to Olivier's *Hamlet*, also becoming associate director of the company. He left the company in 1970, and played opposite his third wife, Maggie Smith, in a notable 1972 revival of *Private Lives*, but during the balance of the 1970s and the 1980s was not able to move into many of the major roles he had seemed destined to play. His career revived greatly with Royal Shakespeare Company roles as Falstaff in *Henry IV* (1991) and an acclaimed *King Lear* (1993). He also appeared in many films, largely in supporting roles, with the notable exception of the title role in *The Private Life of Sherlock Holmes* (1970). He was survived by his wife, actress Patricia Quinn, and four children. (d. London; November 12, 1995)

FURTHER READING

Obituary. *Independent*, Nov. 14, 1995.
Obituary. *Times* (of London), Nov. 14, 1995.
Obituary. *New York Times*, Nov. 12, 1995.
Obituary. *Variety*, Nov. 12, 1995.

Stern, David Joel (1942–   ) National Basketball Association Commissioner David Stern needed all his negotiating skills in 1995. The previous agreement between the league and the players' association had expired on June 24, 1994, but the two sides (unlike baseball and hockey) had agreed to continue playing through the regular season and on through the playoffs. When no agreement was reached, a lockout began on July 1, 1995; it was the off-season, so no games were affected, but contract negotiations were frozen, as were payments due for the 1995–96 season, while summer camps and tournaments were put into limbo.

When the league and the players' association finally *did* agree on a proposal, in early August, a group of players—led by stars such as Michael Jordan and Patrick Ewing—strongly objected to it, attempted to decertify the union, and filed lawsuits against the league, throwing the whole process into turmoil. In mid-September, the players overwhelmingly rejected that approach and accepted the agreement. Training camps opened October 6, later than usual, but in time for the new season, which began on November 3, leaving basketball still the only major team sport not to have lost part of a season to a work stoppage. The new agreement increased the players' share of revenue and the payroll cap; will reduce the NBA draft from two rounds to one in 1998; and modified handling of rookie salary caps, payroll cap exceptions, free agency, and contracts. The lack of personal animosity in basketball negotiations continues to be a credit to Stern's style and influence.

But Stern faced another challenge, this one from the NBA officials. With them he was less successful, and the 1995–96 season began with replacements officiating in games. Not only were they less experienced, but only two replacements worked each game, rather than the usual three referees. Not until December was this labor dispute settled.

In 1995 Stern announced that each year's NBA championship team, starting with the 1994–95 champion Houston Rockets, would play in the McDonald's Championships, an exhibition tournament held in Europe each October (in non-Olympic years), involving 15 other teams from Europe and Australia. Previously the league had appointed a team to play in the McDonald's tournament.

New York–born Stern received his B.A. from Rutgers University in 1963 and his LL.B. from Columbia University. He was associated with the NBA's law firm, Proskauer Rose Goetz & Mendelsohn (1966–78), before being named NBA general counsel in 1978. He became the NBA's executive vice president for business and legal affairs (1980), then NBA commissioner (1984–   ). He has also served as adjunct professor of law at New York's Cardozo Law School (1983–   ). He published *NBA Jam Session: A Photo Salute to the NBA Dunk* (1993). Stern married Dianne Bock in 1963; they have two sons.

FURTHER READING

"Air Stern." MIKE LUPICA. *Esquire*, Dec. 1995.
"Stern, David Joel." *Current Biography*, Apr. 1991.

Howard Stern in drag.

Stern, Howard (1954–   ) In November 1995, shock maven Howard Stern published his second book, the autobiographical *Miss America*, featuring Stern himself on the cover in drag, wearing a bra, high heels, and fishnet stockings, and starting off with a 1-million-copy first printing, a company record. The book immediately began to break sales records, becoming the fastest-selling book ever—indeed, selling more in its first week than had those by Colin Powell and O. J. Simpson *combined.* Stern toured widely promoting his book; among his appearances was one with Jay Leno on "The Tonight Show."

Clearly, his taboo-breaking humor appeals to many people, despite (or because of) its cruelty. That brought him into fresh trouble in 1995, when he made fun of the murdered Tejano singer Selena on the day of her funeral by playing her music to the accompaniment of gunfire tapes, and also mocked her mourners and Mexican-Americans in general. A South Texas judge issued a warrant charging Stern with disorderly conduct; faced with widespread protests, Stern explained that he was a satirist, but did not mean to cause pain, and that he was incensed at the mindless murder.

Stern's employer, Infinity Broadcasting, ended a three-year-old dispute with the Federal Communications Commission over more than 100 claims of indecency in Stern's broadcasts, with a settlement of more than $1.7 million (the largest of its kind) to be paid to the U.S. Treasury. Late in the year, Stern was in negotiations with Infinity on a new contract, the old one having lapsed. Late in 1995, Stern indicated that the long-delayed film version of his 1993 best-selling book, *Private Parts,* for which he had rejected numerous scripts, was scheduled to go into production shortly.

Long Island–born Stern began his radio career as a disc jockey at WRNW, Briarcliff Manor, New York (1976–78), then working at WCCC, Hartford, Connecticut (1978–79), and WWWW, Detroit (1979–80). He emerged as a rather popular and highly controversial figure at WWDC, Washington, D.C. (1980–82). After being fired from that job, he went to work at WNBC, New York City (1982–85), broadcasting along the same lines and again building a following. Fired from that job as well, he moved to WXRK with his "Howard Stern Show" (1986–), there building a national following by pursuing the same tactics, despite FCC fines and widespread condemnation. He also hosted weekly cable television interview shows on WWOR-TV (1990–92) and E! Entertainment Television (1992–), which carries televised versions of his radio shows. Stern received his B.S. from Boston University, where he met his wife, Alison Berns; they have three daughters.

FURTHER READING

"Poor little rich boy." MAER ROSHAN. *New York*, Nov. 20, 1995.
"Playboy interview:...." MARSHALL FINE. *Playboy*, Apr. 1994.
The Howard Stern Book: An Unauthorized, Unabashed, Uncensored Fan's Guide. JIM CEGIELSKI. Carol, 1994.
Sternmania: The Unofficial Guide to the Howard Stern Show. RAY D. OFAN. Dell, 1994.
"Big mouths." KURT ANDERSEN. *Time*, Nov. 1, 1993.
"Blow Hard." BRUCE FRETTS. *Entertainment*, Oct. 15, 1993.
Howard Stern: Big Mouth. JEFF MENELL. Windsor, 1993.
"Bad mouth...." JEANIE KASINDORF. *New York*, Nov. 23, 1992.
"I love myself...." BARBARA KRUGER and REBECCA JOHNSON. *Esquire*, May 1992.

Stevens, John Paul (1920–)

Once again part of a liberal minority, Supreme Court Justice John Paul Stevens found himself in dissent on several key decisions during 1995. He did, however, write the majority opinion in the landmark *U.S. Term Limits Inc.* v. *Thornton,* ruling that to limit congressional terms required a constitutional amendment; 23 state laws imposing term limits were invalidated and Congress was barred from passing a term limits law.

Stevens wrote a sharply dissenting opinion in the landmark *U.S.* v. *Lopez,* which found unconstitutional the federal Gun-Free School Zones Act of 1990, making possession of a gun within 1,000 feet of a school illegal, ruling that this was an invalid extension of congressional ability to regulate interstate commerce. The ruling, sharply criticized by Stevens as far too sweeping and regressive, was widely seen as a major conservative victory, reopening long-settled federal-state powers questions. Stevens also wrote a dissenting opinion in the landmark *Adarand Constructors* v. *Pena,* which held that the federal government was required to use the same strict standards as the states in carrying out affirmative action programs, criticizing this reversal of the Court's long-held position on federal affirmative action programs. Stevens also dissented in other key cases, among them *Miller* v.

Johnson, which found that Georgia's Eleventh Congressional District was unconstitutional because it was organized primarily to provide racial representation, rather than to respond to specific discrimination; and *Rosenberg* v. *Rector and Visitors of the University of Virginia,* which held that the publicly funded University of Virginia was required to finance a Christian magazine run by students, another sharp change of Court directon on a basic constitutional issue.

Stevens wrote the majority opinion in *Schlup* v. *Delo,* ruling that a death row inmate had the right to present new evidence so compelling as to cause jurors to feel that his execution might well be unwarranted; *U.S.* v. *National Treasury Employees Union,* ruling that federal employees, other than members of Congress, policy-makers, and those in the judiciary, had the right to accept payments for their speeches and writings, as long as these were not related to their work; *Babbitt* v. *Sweet Home Chapter of Communities for a Greater Oregon,* ruling that the federal government had the right under the Endangered Species Act to sharply restrict logging and other activities harmful to the northern spotted owl; and *McIntyre* v. *Ohio Election Commission,* voiding an Ohio law banning anonymous political literature as a violation of First Amendment–guaranteed free speech rights. He wrote a concurring opinion in *American Airlines* v. *Wolens,* ruling that airlines were not protected by federal law from class action lawsuits, and that American Airlines could therefore be sued for making changes in frequent flyer contracts.

He wrote a dissenting opinion in *Capital Square Review and Advisory Board* v. *Pinette,* which held that it was unconstitutional to bar display of a large Ku Klux Klan cross in an Ohio public park, and also dissented in *Veronia School District* v. *Acton,* which held that an Oregon school district's random drug testing program was constitutional; and in *Missouri* v. *Jenkins,* which effectively limited the level of state spending allowable to carry out a federally managed school desegregation plan in Kansas City.

Chicago-born Stevens received his 1941 B.A. from the University of Chicago, and his 1947 LL.B. from Northwestern. He practiced law for two decades before being appointed to the Seventh Circuit U.S. Court of Appeals in 1970. President Gerald Ford appointed him to the Supreme Court in 1975. Stevens was thought to be a moderate conservative at the time of his appoint-

ment, as was Ford; the estimate was right, for Stevens often functioned as a middle force between the conservative and liberal wings of the Court in the years that followed. But in later years, as the Court turned sharply to the right, he was more often seen as a moderate liberal, in most instances agreeing with Justices Blackmun, Marshall, and Brennan, all three since retired. Stevens has been married twice, last to Maryann Mulholland Simon in 1979, and has four children.

FURTHER READING

John Paul Stevens. BOB ITALIA and PAUL DEEGAN. Abdo & Daughters, 1992.

Stewart, Rod (1945–) Popular music icon Rod Stewart, a star recording artist in the 1970s and again in the 1990s, issued yet another hit album in 1995: *A Spanner in the Works.* The very well received album featured a wide range of old and new songs, including Tom Petty's new hit "Leave Virginia Alone," Bob Dylan's classic "Sweetheart Like You," "This," "So Far Away," "Maggie May," and "Muddy Sam and Otis." Issued as a single, "Leave Virginia Alone" headed for the top range of the charts. The heavily orchestrated ballad "This" was also a hit single. By late summer, the album had sold more than half a million copies, and at year's end was headed for its first million.

Stewart was also one of the many artists who appeared in the long-form video *Tapestry Revisited: A Tribute to Carole King.* He sang King's song "So Far Away," also issued as a hit single.

Sting, Stewart, and Bryan Adams received a best pop vocal Grammy nomination for their performance of the song "All for Love," written for the film *The Three Musketeers* by Adams, Robert Lange, and Michael Kamen. The work also won an ASCAP award as one of the most performed works from motion pictures.

London-born Stewart sang with the Jeff Beck Group (1968–69) and Faces (1969–75). He began his solo recording career with the album *An Old Raincoat Won't Let You Down* (1969), and in the 1970s became one of the most popular recording artists of the era. Among his best-known albums are *Every Picture Tells a Story* (1971), *Never a Dull Moment* (1972), *Smiles* (1974), *Atlantic Crossing* (1975), and *A Night on the Town*

(1976). He continued to compose and tour throughout his career, into the mid-1990s. In 1993, he reemerged as a major current figure in popular music, with the hit album *Unplugged . . . and Seated*. Stewart is married to model Rachel Hunter.

FURTHER READING

Rod Stewart: The Biography. RAY COLEMAN. Trafalgar, 1995.
Rod Stewart: Vagabond Heart. GEOFFREY GIULIANO. Carroll and Graf, 1994.
Rod Stewart: A Biography. TIM EWBANK and STAFFORD HILDRED. Trafalgar, 1992.
Rod Stewart: The Visual Documentary. STEVE HOLMES and JOHN GRAY. Omnibus (NY), 1992.
"Some guys. . . ." BILL ZEHME. *Rolling Stone*, July 11, 1991.

Stockton, John Houston (1962–) He

is the quiet man on the basketball court. Others may be celebrities with million-dollar faces; John Stockton often goes unrecognized. But his work speaks for him. In February 1995, with a pass to longtime Utah Jazz teammate Karl Malone, Stockton passed the great Earvin (Magic) Johnson to set a new all-time National Basketball Association career record for assists, with 9,922. He also holds single-season records for most assists, with 1,164 (1990–91 season), and highest average number of assists per game, with 14.5 (1989–90 season). He has led the league in assists for seven consecutive seasons, one short of Bob Cousy's record, which—if he keeps his health—Stockton could tie in the 1995-96 season and break in the next. In 1995, Stockton was also named to the All-NBA first team, for the second consecutive time, and the NBA All-Defensive team. Stockton is also astonishingly durable, missing only four games in his ten seasons, in one case even being sent home by the coach.

Still missing is a championship ring. Though Stockton's Utah Jazz have been a strong team for years, and have made it to the Western Conference finals the last two years, they have not so far been able to break through to the NBA finals. At year's end, his team was once more pointed toward the goal, and Stockton was again leading the league in assists, with an average of 10.9 per game. He was also fifth in the league in three-point percentage, with .487.

Stockton was born in Spokane, Washington, where he attended Gonzaga Prep School and then Gonzaga University, from which he graduated in 1984. Turning professional, he joined the Utah Jazz (1984–). A seven-time All-Star (1989–95), Stockton shared Most Valuable Player honors at the 1993 All-Star game with teammate Karl Malone. He was named to the All-NBA first team twice (1994; 1995), the second team five times (1988; 1989; 1990; 1992; 1993), and the third team once (1991). He also led the league in steals in 1989, with 3.21 per game, and 1992, with 2.98, and was four times named to the NBA All-Defensive team (1989; 1991; 1992; 1995). Stockton was also a member of the celebrated "Dream Team," the U.S. team that won the gold medal in basketball at the Barcelona Olympics. He married Nada Stepovich in 1986; they have three sons and a daughter.

FURTHER READING

"Stockton, John." *Current Biography*, June 1995.
"One man's passion." KEVIN SIMPSON. *Sporting News*, Feb. 20, 1995.
Sports Great John Stockton. NATHAN AASENG. Enslow, 1995.
"Flash and trash." PHIL TAYLOR. *Sports Illustrated*, May 30, 1994.

Stone, Oliver (1946–) Four years after

his highly controversial film *JFK*, on the assassination of President John F. Kennedy, director, writer, and producer Oliver Stone released a second major political film, this one the biographical film *Nixon*, starring Anthony Hopkins as disgraced president Richard M. Nixon, Joan Allen as Pat Nixon, James Woods as H. R. Haldeman, Bob Hoskins as J. Edgar Hoover, Powers Boothe as Alexander Haig, Ed Harris as E. Howard Hunt, E. G. Marshall as John Mitchell, Paul Sorvino as Henry Kissinger, and Mary Steenburgen as Hannah Nixon, in a large cast that also included David Paymer, David Hyde Pierce, J. T. Walsh, Brian Bedford, Kevin Dunn, Larry Hagman, Tony Goldwyn, Ed Herrman, and Madeleine Kahn as Martha Mitchell. The work, liberally using flashbacks, ultimately presented Stone's view of Nixon's life history, motivations, and development from early days in California through Watergate and his forced resignation to avoid impeachment and dismissal. The film was

Oliver Stone (left) and Anthony Hopkins.

attacked by Nixon supporters for many months before its release; after seeing it, many still attacked it as a vicious libel. Others saw it as far too sympathetic to Nixon and to his associates, while still others saw it as merely an inconsistent and considerably flawed work of the filmmaker's art. Whatever their reactions to the work, Stone and his film seemed capable of generating highly emotional reactions from most of those who had lived through the time.

A companion book was published in December, when the film opened: *Nixon: An Oliver Stone Film,* edited by Eric Hamburg. It contained an interview with Stone, an annotated original screenplay, and related materials.

Forthcoming was the film *The Fountainhead,* directed by Stone and based on the Ayn Rand novel. Also forthcoming was the film *Freeway,* written and directed by Matthew Bright, produced by Stone, and starring Kiefer Sutherland and Reese Witherspoon.

New York–born Stone fought in Vietnam (1965–66), an experience that has deeply affected some of his most notable work. He has won three Oscars. His first was for his *Midnight Express* (1978) screenplay. His second was for his direction of *Platoon* (1986), a film that he also wrote and that won an Oscar for best picture. His third was as best director for *Born on the Fourth of July* (1989), filmed from the Oscar-nominated screenplay by Stone and Ron Kovic, based on Kovic's autobiography; Stone himself

appeared in a small role in the film, which also won several other awards. Stone also cowrote and directed such films as *Scarface* (1983), *Wall Street* (1987), *Talk Radio* (1988), *The Doors* (1991), *JFK* (1991), *Heaven and Earth* (1993), and *Natural Born Killers* (1994).

Stone attended Yale University; his 1971 B.F.A. was from the New York University Film School. He has been married twice, first to Najwa Sarkis, with whom he had a son. In 1981 he married nurse Elizabeth Cox, who filed for divorce in 1994. Their son, Sean, at age six, played the young Jim Morrison in *The Doors.*

FURTHER READING

"Whose obsession. . . ." EVAN THOMAS. "Hollywood's most controversial. . . ." STRYKER McGUIRE and DAVID ANSEN. *Newsweek,* Dec. 11, 1995.

"The David Letterman disease." NATHAN GARDELS. *New Perspectives Quarterly,* Spring 1995.

Cinema of Oliver Stone. NORMAN KAGAN. Continuum, 1995.

Stone: The Controversies, Excesses, and Exploits of a Radical Filmmaker. JAMES RIORDAN. Hyperion, 1995.

"Oliver Stone's. . . ." GRAHAM FULLER. *Interview,* Sept. 1994.

"The last wild man." STEPHEN SCHIFF. *New Yorker,* Aug. 8, 1994.

" 'The camera. . . .' " GAVIN SMITH. *Film Comment,* Jan.–Feb. 1994.

"Oliver Stoned." GREGG KILDAY. *Entertainment,* Jan. 14, 1994.

Oliver Stone: Maverick Filmmaker. FRANK BEAVER. Macmillan, 1994.

"What does. . . ." DAVID ANSEN. *Newsweek,* Dec. 23, 1991.

"60s something. . . ." STEPHEN TALBOT. *Mother Jones,* Mar.–Apr. 1991.

"Oliver Stone. . . . " DAVID BRESKIN. *Rolling Stone,* Apr. 4, 1991.

"Stone unturned." MARK ROWLAND. *American Film,* Mar. 1991.

Stone, Sharon

Stone, Sharon (1958–) In Martin Scorsese's very notable 1995 film *Casino,* actress Sharon Stone created a "signature" role in what may very well become a classic film. Set in 1970s Las Vegas and the illegal world, the film starred Stone as Las Vegas gambler Ginger McKenna, opposite Robert De Niro as her husband, mob syndicate–connected gambler and casino operator Sam "Ace" Rothstein; their violent life together and ultimate breakup supplies much of the drama of the film. Joe Pesci costarred as Nicky Santoro, Rothstein's mad-dog killer friend, and James Woods as Ginger's small-time con-man lover, before and during her marriage. Scorsese directed and with Nicholas Pileggi cowrote the screenplay, based on Pileggi's book. Stone received a Golden Globe nomination as best actress in a drama for the role. She also received a Crystal Award from Women in Film.

Stone also starred as gunfighter Ellen, who ultimately finds the revenge she seeks, opposite Gene Hackman as gunfighter and evil town boss Herod in the offbeat, violent, sometimes surreal western *The Quick and the Dead,* directed by Sam Raimi.

Forthcoming were starring roles in the films *Diabolique,* directed by Jeremiah Chechick and costarring Kathy Bates, Chazz Palminteri, and Isabelle Adjani; and *Last Dance,* costarring Rob Morrow, Randy Quaid, and Charles Dutton.

A former model, Pennsylvania-born Stone made her film debut in *Stardust Memories* (1980), and went on to play mainly in supporting roles for more than a decade, in such films as *Bolero* (1982), *Irreconcilable Differences* (1984), *King Solomon's Mines* (1985), *Allan Quartermaine and the Lost City of Gold* (1987), *Personal Choice* (1989), *Total Recall* (1990), and *Year of the Gun* (1991). Her breakthrough film came with her steamily sexual role in the thriller *Ba-*

sic Instinct (1992), which was followed by *Sliver* (1993), *Intersection* (1994), and *The Specialist* (1994). She attended Edinboro College.

FURTHER READING

"The diva." GERRI HIRSHEY. *GQ*, Nov. 1995.
"The truly shocking. . . ." STEPHEN REBELLO. *Cosmopolitan*, Oct. 1995.
"Is Sharon Stone. . . ." BILL ZEHME. *Esquire*, Mar. 1995.
"She's got it covered." JESS CAGLE. *Entertainment*, Oct. 14, 1994.
"Basic superstar." SIMON BANNER. *Ladies Home Journal*, Sept. 1994.
"Star turn." CHARLES GANDEE. *Vogue*, Dec. 1993.
"Sharon Stone." MARGY ROCHLIN. *Us*, June 1993.
"Stone free." FRED SCHRUERS. *Premiere*, May 1993.
"Stone goddess." KEVIN SESSUMS and ANNIE LIEBOVITZ. *Vanity Fair*, Apr. 1993.
"Sharon Stone." *Playboy*, Dec. 1992.
"Hot cover." BILL ZEHME. *Rolling Stone*, May 14, 1992.
"A role no. . . ." BRIAN D. JOHNSON. *Maclean's*, Mar. 30, 1992.

Streep, Meryl (Mary Louise Streep; 1949–) Celebrated actress Meryl Streep was highly visible on television screens in 1995, as her 1994 change-of-pace action film *The River Wild* became a hit in home video. For her role in the film, she received a Screen Actors Guild nomination as best leading actress in a motion picture.

In 1995, Streep starred in the film version of Robert James Waller's best-selling novel *The Bridges of Madison County,* adapted for film by Richard LaGravenese. Streep played Iowa farm housewife Francesca Johnson opposite Clint Eastwood, who directed and starred as roving photographer Robert Kincaid, in a cast that included Annie Corley, Victor Slezak, and Jim Haynie. Set in Madison County, Iowa farm country in 1965, the film straightforwardly tells the story of the brief, passionate love affair between Johnson, whose husband and children are away, and Kincaid, an affair portrayed as central to their lives, although they never met again. The film was very well received by the critics and at the box office. She received a Golden Globe nomination as best actress in a drama for the role.

Forthcoming were starring roles in the films *Before and After,* produced and directed by Barbet Schroeder and costarring Liam Neeson, and *Marvin's Room,* directed by Jerry Zaks and co-

starring Diane Keaton, Leonardo Dicaprio, Robert De Niro, Hume Cronyn, Gwen Verdon, and Hal Scardino.

New Jersey–born Streep's 1971 B.A. was from Vassar, and her 1975 M.F.A. from Yale. She was quickly recognized as a major dramatic star in the late 1970s; her work includes such films as *The Deer Hunter* (1978), *Manhattan* (1979), *Kramer vs. Kramer* (1980; she won a best supporting actress Oscar), *Sophie's Choice* (1982; she won a best actress Oscar), *Silkwood* (1983), *Out of Africa* (1985), *Ironweed* (1987), *She-Devil* (1989), *Postcards from the Edge* (1990), *Defending Your Life* (1991), *The River Wild* (1994), and *The House of the Spirits* (1994). She married sculptor Donald J. Gummer in 1978; they have four children.

FURTHER READING

"Meryl in. . . ." Jim Jerome and Brooke Comer. *Ladies Home Journal*, Aug. 1995.

"Heart land." Shelley Levitt. *People*, June 26, 1995.

"Meryl Streep." Julian Garey. *Us*, Oct. 1994.

"Meryl Streep. . . ." Charla Krupp and Jane Galbraith. *Glamour*, Oct. 1994.

"The perils of Meryl." James Greenberg. Oct. 7, 1994.

"Women who run. . . ." Dana Kennedy. Feb. 11, 1994. *Entertainment*.

"Kindred spirits . . . ." Lisa Liebman. *New Woman*, Apr. 1994.

"Hope I die. . . ." Teresa Carpenter. *Premiere*, Sept. 1992.

"Winning Streep." David Handelman. *Vogue*, Apr. 1992.

Streisand, Barbra (Barbara Joan Streisand; 1942–   ) For celebrated singer, actress, director, and producer Barbra Streisand, 1995 was a year of acclaim from her peers, which included eight Emmy awards. Her television special, *Barbra Streisand: The Concert,* won five Emmys, including best music variety or comedy special and best individual performance in a variety or music program. Her drama, *Serving in Silence: The Margarethe Cammermeyer Story,* won three Emmys: for best actress Glenn Close, best supporting actress Judy Davis, and best writer Alison Cross. Streisand had conceived and been executive producer of the project, the story of Colonel Margarethe Cammermeyer, a Bronze Star–winning soldier discharged from the U.S. Army in 1992 after openly declaring herself a lesbian.

Forthcoming were the film *The Mirror Has Two Faces,* directed and produced by Streisand, who stars opposite Jeff Bridges and Lauren Bacall; and a starring role in the film *The Normal Heart,* adapted from the Larry Kramer play, about the early days of the AIDS epidemic.

On the political side of her life, Streisand continued to be a highly articulate liberal. In early February, she spoke at Harvard University's John F. Kennedy School of Government on "The Artist as Citizen."

Brooklyn-born Streisand is one of the great popular music stars of the modern period, whose work also includes several very notable film,

stage, and television credits. Her breakthrough roles came on stage in musical theater, in *I Can Get It for You Wholesale* (1962) and as Fanny Brice in *Funny Girl* (1964), a role for which she won a best actress Oscar in the 1968 film version. She became a worldwide recording star in the mid-1960s for such Grammy-winning songs as "People" (1964) and "Evergreen" (1977; also an Oscar winner), and such Grammy-winning albums as *The Barbra Streisand Album* (1963) and *My Name Is Barbra* (1965). A six-time best vocalist Grammy winner, she issued many old, but many new, songs in the four-CD *Just for the Record* (1991), followed by *Back to Broadway* (1993). In 1994, she made a major, highly successful tour, for the first time in 27 years, resulting in the television special and video *Barbra Streisand: The Concert.*

Streisand also starred in such films as *Hello Dolly* (1969), *On a Clear Day You Can See Forever* (1970), *The Owl and the Pussycat* (1971), *The Way We Were* (1973), *Funny Lady* (1975), and *Nuts* (1987). She produced and starred in *A Star is Born* (1976); directed, produced, and starred in *Yentl* (1983); and directed and starred in *The Prince of Tides* (1991). Her 1965 television special, *My Name is Barbra,* won five Emmys. A leading liberal, she was a key supporter of President Bill Clinton during his election campaign, and thereafter. She was formerly married to the actor Elliott Gould, and has one son.

FURTHER READING

"A star is reborn." MICHAEL SHNAYERSON. *Vanity Fair*, Nov. 1994.
"Barbra's fight against fear." SUSAN PRICE. *Ladies Home Journal*, July 1994.
"Vox popular." JESS CAGLE. *Entertainment*, Apr. 15, 1994.
"Her name is Barbra." RANDALL RIESE. *Cosmopolitan*, Feb. 1994.
Barbra Streisand: Untold Story. NELLIE BLY. Windsor, 1994.
The Barbra Streisand Scrapbook. ALLISON J. WALDMAN. Carol, 1994.
"The unguarded Barbra." JULIA REED. *Vogue*, Aug. 1993.
"President Streisand." JAMIE MALANOWSKI. *Us*, Aug. 1993.
Her Name Is Barbra: An Intimate Portrait of the Real Barbra Streisand. RANDALL RIESE. Birch Lane/Carol, 1993.
Barbra Streisand: A Biography. PETER CARRICK. Ulverscroft, 1993.
"Streisand, Barbra." *Current Biography*, Sept. 1992.

Barbra—An Actress Who Sings, The Unauthorized Biography of Barbra Streisand. JAMES KIMBRELL. Branden, Vol. I, 1989; Vol. II, 1992.

Strode, Woody (Woodrow Wilson Woolwine Strode; 1914–94)

Los Angeles–born Woody Strode was a professional football player and professional wrestler before turning to his more than half-century-long acting career. He made his film debut in *Sundown* (1941), and emerged during the 1960s as one of Hollywood's leading African-American actors. He played in small supporting roles in several 1950s films, including *The Ten Commandments* (1956) and *Pork Chop Hill* (1959). His major breakthrough came in 1960, when he played the title role in John Ford's film *Sergeant Rutledge* (1960), as the African-American army officer unjustly accused and tried for murder and rape. He spent the next three decades in a series of strong supporting roles, also playing in several leads; among his films were *Spartacus* (1960), *The Man Who Shot Liberty Valance* (1962), *The Professionals* (1966), *Black Jesus* (1968; in title role), *Once Upon a Time in the West* (1968), *The Italian Connection* (1972), *The Cotton Club* (1984), and *Posse* (1993). With Sam Young, he wrote *Goal Dust: An Autobiography* (1990). He was survived by his wife, Tina, a son, and a daughter. (d. Glendora, California; December 31, 1994)

FURTHER READING

Obituary. *Jet*, Jan. 23, 1995.
Obituary. *Independent*, Jan. 5, 1995.
Obituary. *New York Times*, Jan. 4, 1995.

Sutherland, Donald McNichol
(1934–) In the television film *Citizen X*, written and directed by Chris Gerolmo and based on Robert Cullen's book *The Killer Department*, stage and screen star Donald Sutherland played a real-life Russian colonel (Fetisov), who ultimately fought through the Soviet bureaucracy to help unmask mass murderer Andrei Chikatilo, the "Rostov Ripper" who murdered at least 53 people (1978–90) in what was then the Soviet Union. Stephen Rea played Viktor Burakov (Citizen X), opposite Jeffrey DeMunn as Chikatilo, in a cast that included Max von Sydow, Joss Ackland, and Imelda Staunton. Sutherland received

an Emmy nomination as best supporting actor for the role, as well as a Golden Globe nomination as best supporting actor in a series, miniseries, or telefilm.

Sutherland also played a strong supporting role in the popular biological disaster film *Outbreak,* directed by Wolfgang Petersen, starring Dustin Hoffman and costarring Rene Russo, Morgan Freeman, and Kevin Spacey.

Forthcoming were starring roles in the films *A Time To Kill,* directed by Joel Schumacher and costarring Sandra Bullock, Samuel L. Jackson, Matthew McConaughey, Kevin Spacey, and Charles S. Dutton; and *The Shadow Conspiracy,* directed by George P. Cosmatos and costarring Charlie Sheen, Linda Hamilton, Sam Waterston, Stephen Lang, Ben Gazzara, and Gore Vidal. Sutherland was also slated to star in the forthcoming film *Natural Enemy,* directed by Doug Jackson and costarring William McNamara, Lesley Ann Warren, Joe Pantoliano, and Tia Carrere.

Sutherland attended the University of Toronto. He began his film career in the mid-1960s, and emerged as a star playing Korean War surgeon Benjamin Franklin "Hawkeye" Pierce in the original film *M*A*S*H* (1970). He went on to a wide variety of dramatic roles, many of them chosen primarily for their quality, in such films as *Klute* (1971), *The Day of the Locust* (1975), *1900* (1976), *Casanova* (1976), *Ordinary People* (1980), *Eye of the Needle* (1981), *Gauguin* (1986), *A Dry White Season* (1989), *Lock Up* (1989), *Eminent Domain* (1991), *Backdraft* (1991), *JFK* (1992), *The Railway Station Man* (1992), *Buffy the Vampire Slayer* (1992), *Six Degrees of Separation* (1993), *Shadow of the Wolf* (1993), *Benefit of the Doubt* (1993), *The Puppet Masters* (1994), and *Disclosure* (1994). His television films include the Canadian miniseries *Bethune: The Making of a Hero.* Sutherland has been married three times, and has five children, including actor Kiefer Sutherland.

FURTHER READING

"Donald Sutherland. . . ." GERMANO CELAND and BRIGITTE LACOMBE. *Interview*, Sept. 1990.

Swayze, John Cameron (1906–95) Born in Wichita, Kansas, radio and television broadcast journalist John Cameron Swayze attended the University of Kansas (1925–27) and studied

drama in New York City (1928–29). He worked briefly as a newspaper reporter and then as a newscaster in radio (1930–47). In 1947, then working for NBC in Hollywood, he became one of the first veteran radio broadcast journalists to move into television, though in the early period also continuing to work in radio. In 1949, with at least some apparent reservations, he made the decisive move into television, at the same time becoming a historic figure in broadcasting as the host of NBC's "Camel News Caravan" (1947–56), a prototypical television news show, its brief picture stories, national and international location pickups, and human interest features still national news-show staples. Swayze's show was light, focusing on features, rather than on hard news; in this, it was far more like the sound bite–laden, feature-filled news shows of the 1990s than the news shows of his own day. He was survived by his wife, Beulah Mae, a daughter, and a son. (d. Sarasota, Florida; August 15, 1995)

FURTHER READING

Obituary. *Independent*, Aug. 18, 1995.
Obituary. *New York Times*, Aug. 15, 1995.

Swayze, Patrick (1954–) Actor Patrick Swayze starred in 1995 as the saintly 1950s hippie Jack McCloud in the film *Three Wishes,* directed by Martha Coolidge and costarring Mary Elizabeth Mastrantonio, Joseph Mazzella, Jay O. Sanders, Seth Muny, and Michael O'Keefe. The story revolves around vagrant McCloud's impact on the family of Jeanne Holman (Mastrantonio), who runs him down in her car and then takes him in, and on her very conventional small town. Triumph finally comes when he coaches the town's Little League team to a championship; Holman and McCloud make love, and he hits the road again.

In a very different kind of role and film, Swayze, Wesley Snipes, and John Leguizamo starred as drag queens in the antic comedy *To Wong Foo, Thanks for Everything! Julie Newmar,* directed by Beeban Kidron; the cast included Stockard Channing, Blythe Danner, and Arliss Howard, with Robin Williams in a cameo role. Swayze received a best actor in a musical or comedy Golden Globe nomination for the role.

Trained for ballet, Swayze began his career as

a dancer, and danced and acted a lead in *Grease* for two years on Broadway before emerging as a leading film player late in the 1980s. His breakthrough role was as Johnny Castle in *Dirty Dancing* (1987). It was followed by a starring role in the fantasy-action film *Steel Dawn* (1987); and by starring roles in *Road House* (1989), *Next of Kin* (1989), *Ghost* (1990), *Point Break* (1991), *City of Joy* (1992), and *Father Hood* (1993). Swayze also appeared in the television miniseries *North and South* (1990), and in several other television films. Swayze married actress-dancer Lisa Niemi in 1975.

FURTHER READING

"Swayze goes crazy." HILARY DE VRIES. *Ladies Home Journal*, Oct. 1995.
"Risky business." CHARLES BUSCH. *Advocate*, Sept. 5, 1995.
"Patrick Swayze." TOM O'NEILL. *Us*, Sept. 1995.
"Patrick Swayze." *Playboy*, June 1992.
"Patrick Swayze. . . ." STEPHANIE MANSFIELD. *GQ*, Feb. 1992.
"Body and soul." JEANNIE PARK. *People*, Aug. 26, 1991.
"From here to. . . ." *Seventeen*, July 1991.

Sweeney, John Joseph (1934–) On October 24, 1995, the American Federation of Labor–Congress of Industrial Organizations (A.F.L.-C.I.O) elected John Joseph Sweeney as its president, to succeed retiring Lane Kirkland. Sweeney defeated former A.F.L.-C.I.O secretary-treasurer Thomas R. Donahue, long associated with Kirkland. President of the strong and growing 1.1 million–member Service Employees International Union, Sweeney pledged a rebirth of American labor militancy and a drive to bring millions more into the labor movement, long in disarray, which had lost more than half of its membership in 40 years. His running mates, Linda Chavez-Thompson of the American Federation of State, County and Municipal Employees, and Richard L. Trumka of the United Mine Workers, expressed similar views. Sweeney's program stressed organizing the unorganized, taking a much harder line in negotiations with employers, paying more attention to the needs of low-paid workers, and initiating mass action if necessary to the point of civil disobedience. As a substantial token of new intent, Sweeney, Chavez-Thompson, and Trumka went to Ever-

ett, Washington, in mid-November to lead a mass rally of thousands of workers from many unions in support of the Boeing International Association of Machinists strike, which was soon settled. Whether Sweeney and his colleagues would be able to take American labor on a new, more successful course was, at the end of 1995, a matter of conjecture.

New York City–born Sweeney, the child of Irish immigrants, is a graduate of the College of New Rochelle. He worked in the research department of the International Ladies Garment Workers Union (ILGWU) before joining New York's Local 32B of the Service Employees Union, and became president of the local in 1976. He became the Washington-based president of the union in 1980, during the next 15 years building its membership while most other unions were losing strength. He is married to Maureen Power; they have two children.

FURTHER READING

"What have you. . . ." WARREN COHEN. *U.S. News & World Report*, Nov. 6, 1995.
"Sweeney agonistes. . . ." JOHN B. JUDIS. *New Republic*, Aug. 21, 1995.

Switzer, Barry (1937–) The hot seat got hotter in the 1995 professional football season. In 1994, Barry Switzer took over as coach of the Dallas Cowboys, a team his predecesssor, Jimmy Johnson, had just led to two consecutive Super Bowl championships. He was expected to "three-peat"—and failed. The team was on course throughout the 1994 season, but in mid-January 1995, the Cowboys met the San Francisco 49ers in the National Football Conference championship and were demolished; with an interception and two fumbles on the first three plays of the game, the Cowboys fell behind 21-0 and never recovered, though they struggled back to 38-28.

From then on, the Cowboys focused on the 49ers, whom they would likely have to beat for another chance at the Super Bowl. In the first part of the 1995 regular season, the Cowboys looked liked the team to beat—with Dallas at one point having the league's leading quarterback, running back, and receiver—while the 49ers were hobbled by injuries. But in a crucial mid-November meeting between the two teams, the 49ers again trounced the Cowboys, as quickly and devastatingly as in that January championship. From that point on, the Cowboys were a team in turmoil, losing to seemingly weaker teams. Though Dallas itself now had injuries to several key players, many sports analysts and fans blamed Switzer directly for the team's failure and predicted or called for his firing. Even some team members, including quarterback Troy Aikman, were publicly questioning Switzer's coaching ability (indirectly, if not directly), and in mid-December an against-the-odds decision to try for short yardage on a fourth down—a drive that failed and cost the Cowboys a key game against the Philadelphia Eagles—became a sports cause célèbre.

Despite these troubles, the team ended the regular season with a record of 12-4, securing home-field advantage throughout the playoffs. In the end, the 49ers were knocked off in the playoffs by the Green Bay Packers, who then fell to the Cowboys. By mid-January 1996, the Cowboys were set to meet the Pittsburgh Steelers in Super Bowl XXX.

Born in Crossett, Arkansas, Switzer played football at the University of Arkansas (1955–59) and was captain of the 1959 team that won the Gator Bowl. After army service, he received his 1960 B.A. in business administration, remaining at Arkansas as assistant football coach (1960–65), notably for the 1964 undefeated national championship team on which both Cowboys owner Jerry Jones and former Cowboys coach Jimmy Johnson played. Then Switzer went to the University of Oklahoma, as assistant football coach (1966–72), then head coach (1972–89), winning three national championships (1974; 1975; 1985), with an overall record of 157-29-4. But Switzer was forced to leave and his program placed on probation in 1989, for what was described as his failure to "exercise supervisory control," after several players were charged with rape, another with selling cocaine, and another with a shooting.

With Bud Shrake, Switzer wrote his autobiography, *Bootlegger's Boy* (1990). His 1963 marriage to Kay Switzer ended in divorce in 1983; he has two sons and a daughter.

FURTHER READING

"Barry Switzer. . . ." BUD SHRAKE. *Texas Monthly*, Jan. 1995.

"Welcome to Switzerland." PAUL ATTNER. *Sporting News*, Sept. 12, 1994.

"New 'boy in town . . . ." WILLIAM PLUMMER. *People*, Sept. 5, 1994.

"Barry Switzer." MIKE FREEMAN. *New York Times Magazine*, Aug. 7, 1994.

"In charge." RICK TELANDER. *Sports Illustrated*, Aug. 1, 1994.

"Doomsday in Dallas? . . . ." BRUCE SCHOENFELD. *Sport*, July 1994.

T

Tagliabue, Paul John (1940–) In 1995, as he began his second term as commissioner, Paul Tagliabue was facing a National Football League in revolt. Before the beginning of the 1995 regular season, over league objections, both of Los Angeles's professional football teams left for other cities, the Rams to St. Louis and the Raiders back to Oakland. Tagliabue had worked hard to keep one or both in the city; his failure meant that Los Angeles, the country's second-largest television market, was without an NFL team. Then during the season two more teams announced that they would be moving, the Cleveland Browns to Baltimore—sparking enormous protest, Cleveland having been a long-established franchise with loyal fans—and the Houston Oilers possibly to Nashville. Other rumored moves included the Chicago Bears to a new Gary, Indiana stadium; the Tampa Bay Buccaneers to Orlando; and the Seattle Seahawks possibly to Los Angeles. At year's end, Tagliabue was attempting to halt the unauthorized movement of teams, especially the Browns, and the consequent erosion of fan support.

Tagliabue was faced with other violations of league policy. Early in 1995, he fined the Carolina Panthers $150,000 and their second- and sixth-round draft picks for attempting to hire Dom Capers (which they eventually did), while he was still under contract to the Pittsburgh Steelers. When Dallas Cowboys' owner Jerry Jones signed sponsorship deals with Nike, Pepsi, and Dr. Pepper, in direct competition with the league owners' NFL Properties, which makes cooperative marketing and licensing deals using team names, logos, and trademarks with sponsors such as Reebok and Coca-Cola, Tagliabue as commissioner filed a suit for $300 million in damages. Jones filed a countersuit for $750 million, saying that his deals were with the Texas Stadium (which he owns), not the Cowboys. The NFL Properties operates under an agreement with the owners that runs into the year 2003.

With NFL officiating coming under frequent criticism, Tagliabue has asked teams to send him videos of their most controversial plays, and did not rule out the return of instant replay in a future season, possibly using the league's own cameras for replay reviews. Two new teams were added for the 1995 season, the Carolina Panthers and the Jacksonville Jaguars; Tagliabue said the next expansion, unlikely before the year 2000, might include either Mexico or Canada.

One bright light was that the NFL collective bargaining agreement, negotiated by Tagliabue in 1993 and running through 1998, made football the only professional sports league not to experience some kind of labor trouble in 1995. NFL football was also operating under a lucrative television contract, negotiated in 1993 and running through 1997.

Tagliabue's 1962 B.A. was from Georgetown University, where he played basketball. After receiving his 1965 J.D. from New York University, Tagliabue worked at the Defense Department in Washington (1965–69), and then for 20 years as a lawyer at Covington and Burling, becoming a partner in 1974. He became commissioner of the National Football League in 1989. He is married and has two children.

FURTHER READING

"The face of. . . ." RICK TELANDER. *Sports Illustrated*, Sept. 10, 1990.
"Tagliabue. . . ." PAUL ATTNER. *Sporting News*, Feb. 12, 1990.

Tan, Amy Ruth (1952–) Continuing to mine themes of cultural dislocation among Chinese-American women, Amy Tan published her third novel in 1995. *The Hundred Secret Senses* focuses on the difficult relationship between two half-sisters: Olivia Bishop, American-born daughter of a Chinese father and American mother, and Kwan, older by 12 years, child of her father's first marriage, in China. Particularly troubling is Kwan's insistence on the importance of the spiritual world, which Olivia initially finds embarrassing but eventually comes to embrace. Like her previous work, this is drawn from Tan's own life experience; she did not meet her Chinese half-sisters until she was in her 30s. The novel was also published in two audiobook forms, one abridged, the other unabridged, both read by Tan herself. She also contributed a piece to the collection *Under Western Eyes: Personal Essays from Asian America.* Tan and others have cowritten the script for a possible film version of her second novel, *The Kitchen God's Wife.*

Born in Oakland, California, of Chinese immigrant parents, Tan received a B.A. and M.A. in linguistics and English from California's San Jose State University in 1974 and 1976. She worked as a specialist in language development for the Alameda County Association for the Mentally Retarded, in Oakland (1976–80), and as project director for M.O.R.E. in San Francisco (1980–81), then becoming a freelance writer. In addition to numerous short stories and essays, her book-length works include the novels *The Joy Luck Club* (1989), basis for the 1993 film, on which Tan was coscreenwriter and coproducer, and *The Kitchen God's Wife* (1991), and the children's books *The Moon Lady* (1992), based on a chapter in *Joy Luck,* and *The Chinese Siamese Cat* (1994). Tan married Louis M. DeMattei in 1974.

FURTHER READING

"The spirits are with her." ERICA K. CARDOZO. *Entertainment*, Oct. 27, 1995.

"Fresh voices. . . ." JOHN F. BAKER and CALVIN REID. *Publishers Weekly*, Aug. 9, 1993.
Writers Dreaming—Dreamers Writing: 25 Writers Discuss Dreams and the Creative Process. NAOMI EPEL. Crown, 1993.
Writers and Company. ELEANOR WACHTEL. Knopf, 1993.
"Amy Tan." *Bon Appetit*, Oct. 1992.
"Tan, Amy." *Current Biography*, Feb. 1992.

Tarantino, Quentin (1963–) Quentin Tarantino was highly honored by his peers in 1995, for his 1994 film *Pulp Fiction,* which he wrote, directed, and appeared in. He and Roger Avery shared the best original screenplay Academy Award for the work; Tarantino had also received a best director Oscar nomination. From the National Society of Film Critics, he received awards for best film, director, and screenplay. He also won a best screenplay Golden Globe award and received a Directors Guild of America best director nomination. *Pulp Fiction* also won Italy's Donatello Award for best foreign film and received a best film nomination from the British Academy of Film & Television Arts (BAFTA). It had previously won the Palme D'Or at the 1994 Cannes Film Festival and had scored a resounding critical and commercial success.

In 1995, Tarantino wrote, directed, and starred opposite Bruce Willis in the film *The Man from Hollywood,* one of the group of four short films presented as the anthology *Four Rooms,* all set in a hotel on New Year's Eve, coproduced by Alexandre Rockwell and Tarantino. He also appeared as an actor in Jack Baran's film *Destiny Turns On the Radio.*

Forthcoming were three acting roles, in the films *From Dusk Till Dawn,* directed by Robert Rodriguez; *Girl 6,* directed, produced by, and starring Spike Lee; and *Hands Up,* written and directed by Virginie Thevenet.

Writer, director, and actor Tarantino was born in Knoxville, Tennessee, and grew up in Torrance, California. His first major work was the screenplay for *True Romance,* which he wrote in 1987; the film was released in 1993. He also wrote the screenplay for Oliver Stone's *Natural Born Killers* (1994). His directorial debut came with the film *Reservoir Dogs* (1992), which he directed, wrote, and appeared in.

FURTHER READING

"Quentin Tarantino." J. HOBERMAN. *Us*, Jan. 1996.
"Tarantino, Quentin." *Current Biography*, Oct. 1995.

"Four x four." PETER BISKIND. *Premiere*, Nov. 1995.

"My heroes. . . ." ADRIAN WOOTTON. *Guardian*, Feb. 4, 1995.

Quentin Tarantino. JEFF DAWSON. Applause Theatre Book, 1995.

"Quentin Tarantino." TIM APPELO. *Entertainment*, Dec. 30, 1994.

"Quentin Tarantino." MARGY ROCHLIN. *Playboy*, Nov. 1994.

"Hollywood's new hit men." GODFREY CHESHIRE. *Interview*, Sept. 1994.

"A conversation with. . . ." *Newsweek*, Dec. 26, 1994.

"Quentin Tarantino." DAVID WILD. *Rolling Stone*, Nov. 3, 1994.

"The movie junkie." ANDREW PULVER. *Guardian*, Sept. 19, 1994.

"Tarantino bravo." LYNN HIRSCHBERG. *Vanity Fair*, July 1994.

"Colours of the charnel house." MICHAEL CHURCH. *Observer*, Jan. 3, 1993.

"All's well. . . ." PETER MCALEVEY. *New York Times Magazine*, Dec. 6, 1992.

"Adding kick to the chic." RICHARD CORLISS. *Time*, Nov. 16, 1992.

Teng, Teresa (Deng Lijun; 1953–95)

Taiwan-born Teresa Teng, one of the most popular of East Asian singers, began her career as a child, and released her debut recording at the age of 16. She began recording with Polygram in 1973, and quickly became an enormous hit throughout East and Southeast Asia, her soft, gentle voice becoming part of the lives of hundreds of millions of people of all ages, classes, and ethnicity. Among her most popular recordings were the songs "Story of a Small Town," "Thousands of Words," and "When Will You Return." Music industry sources report that her 22 albums sold a total of 22 million copies for which royalties were paid, and that pirated copy sales amounted to at least 50 million more. She was extraordinarily popular in the People's Republic of China, where sales of her records reportedly mirrored the changing political winds: in periods of loosened conservative control, her sales soared, while in periods of repression, they were sharply discouraged. In the 1980s, Teng became very critical of the Chinese government, refusing to perform in China, and was especially critical of the 1989 Tienanmen Square student massacre. She moved to France in 1989, citing the repression of women in Chinese culture as her reason for leaving East Asia. No information was available on survivors. (d. Chang Mai, Thailand; May 8, 1995)

FURTHER READING

Obituary. *Billboard*, May 20, 1995.

Obituary. *New York Times*, May 10, 1995.

Tesh, John (1953–)

John Tesh is a two-career man. He is best known as cohost, with Mary Hart, of "Entertainment Tonight," Paramount television's five-night-a-week entertainment news program. But Tesh has another life, as a musician-composer, which brought him wide attention in 1995. His televised concert *John Tesh: Live at Red Rocks*—with flamboyant pianist Tesh backed by the Colorado Symphony Orchestra—was broadcast in March, and proved to be the leading draw in PBS's fundraising drive. The album drawn from the concert won Tesh a gold record, signifying more than 500,000 copies sold, and topped *Billboard*'s New Age albums chart; the video version was also a bestseller. Like his previous albums, the record was released by his own GTS Records; in October 1995, Tesh sold 51 percent of GTS to PolyGram Records for a reported $8–10 million, with PolyGram assuming marketing and distribution, while GTS retains creative control. Scheduled for spring release is *Virtuosos: The Undiscovered Artists,* in which unknown artists will perform Tesh compositions and well-known songs; a new album by Tesh himself is scheduled for fall 1996.

While working on his daily "ET" show, Tesh still performs more than 50 concerts a year, mostly on weekends, and often with his eight-piece John Tesh Project. In mid-1995, Tesh sought a three-month leave of absence to tour in support of his *Red Rocks* album; that was refused, and Paramount sought a temporary restraining order to stop him from leaving. Tesh eventually rescheduled some concert dates and took the equivalent of two months in bits and pieces, while Paramount arranged to tape some segments of "ET" on the road, during Tesh's tour. Late in 1995, rumors suggested that he would leave "ET" in June 1996.

Born in Garden City, New York, Tesh was educated at North Carolina State University. After early experience as an anchor and reporter in Durham (NC), Orlando, and Nashville, Tesh came to WCBS-TV in New York (1976–81), and then joined CBS Sports (1981–86), before moving on to "Entertainment Tonight" (1986–). During this period, he was also writing, arranging, and performing music, much of it for numerous sports broadcasts, including the 1992 Barcelona Olympics, the 1991 World Track and Field Championships, the 1983 Pan American Games, and the 1987 Tour de France bicycle race. His scores for the music of the latter two brought him two of his four Emmy Awards (the others were for reporting). His albums include *Tour de France* (1988), *Garden City* (1988); *The Early Years* (1990), *Ironman* (1992), *The Games* (1992; music from the Barcelona Olympics score), *Monterey Nights* (1993), and *A Romantic Christmas* (1993). He has also composed theme music for various television series, such as "Bobby's World" and "NFL Live," and has made occasional film appearances, as in *Shocker* (1989) and *Soapdish* (1991). Previously divorced, Tesh married actress Connie Sellecca in 1992; they have a daughter; she also has a son from a previous marriage.

FURTHER READING

"King of the keyboards." DAN JEWEL. *People*, Dec. 4, 1995.

"Connie & John. . . ." BOB THOMAS. *Good Housekeeping*, Mar. 1994.

"Love is better. . . ." JEAN LIBMAN BLOCK. *Good Housekeeping*, June 1992.

"Oh, what a night!" JEANNIE PARK. *People*, Apr. 20, 1992.

Thagard, Norman Earl (1943–) Astronaut Norman Thagard had a unique experience in 1995: he was the first American to visit the Russian space station *Mir,* where he spent

nearly four months. In the first flight under a U.S.-Russian space agreement, Thagard and two Russian colleagues, Vladimir Dezhurov and Gennady Strekalov, were lifted into space from the Baikonur Cosmodrome in Kazakhstan aboard a Russian Soyuz rocket on March 14, linking up with the *Mir* on the 16th. On their arrival aboard, the current *Mir* crew, which soon returned to Russia, offered the newcomers bread and salt, a traditional Russian custom showing hospitality. Thagard and his colleagues installed new solar panels and carried out other technical upgrades designed to extend the life of the nine-year-old *Mir,* originally intended to last only for three to five years. Thagard also carried out medical experiments on the effects of weightlessness on the body and established the first radio link between orbiting American and Russian spaceships, talking with the seven American astronauts who were orbiting in the space shuttle *Endeavor.*

On June 27, after several delays, the U.S. space shuttle *Atlantis* blasted off from Florida's Kennedy Space Center carrying five American astronauts and two Russian cosmonauts, replacement crew for the *Mir.* Thagard, Dezhurov, and Strekalov underwent a grueling battery of medical tests aboard the *Atlantis,* after its historic U.S.-Russian space docking on June 29. (The last time U.S. and Russian spacecraft docked in orbit was in July 1975.) The three then returned to Earth with the five other American astronauts on July 7; the two new Russian astronauts stayed aboard the *Mir.* Though some Russian cosmonauts have spent far longer in space, Thagard's 115-day mission set an American space endurance record.

Thagard is fluent in Russian and so was able to communicate with both his fellow cosmonauts and ground staff, but said he found it hard not to be able to talk to anyone in English. He also complained about the nature of the food, especially canned perch. He had been in Russia since February 1994, preparing for the space mission.

Florida-born Thagard received his 1965 B.S. and 1966 M.S. from Florida State University, then joined the U.S. Marine Corps (1966–70), becoming a fighter pilot in Vietnam, and winning 11 air medals as well as the Navy Commendation Medal. Returning to the U.S., he briefly served as weapons officer with the Marines, then continued his education, receiving his 1977 M.D. from the University of Texas Southwest Medical School and interning at the Medical University of South Carolina. He then joined NASA (1978–), flying on four space shuttle missions (1983; 1985; 1989; 1992). He has also contributed articles to numerous journals. Thagard and his wife, teacher Rex Kirby Johnson, have three sons.

FURTHER READING

"An American in Russia's orbit." BETH DICKEY. *Russian Life,* Aug. 1995.
"Right stuff, wrong food." BELINDA LUSCOMBE. *Time,* July 17, 1995.
"Thagard wrestles. . . ." JAMES T. McKENNA. *Aviation Week & Space Technology,* Apr. 17, 1995.

Thomas, Clarence (1948–) Justice Clarence Thomas became part of a narrow conservative Supreme Court majority during 1995. He joined the majority and wrote a concurring opinion in the landmark *Adarand Constructors* v. *Pena,* which held that the federal government was required to use the same strict standards as the states in carrying out affirmative action programs, reversing the Court's long-held position on federal affirmative action programs. He also joined the majority in other key cases, among them *U.S.* v. *Lopez,* invalidating as unconstitutional the federal Gun-Free School Zones Act of 1990, which made possession of a gun within 1,000 feet of a school illegal, ruling that this was an invalid extension of the congressional ability to regulate interstate commerce; *Miller* v.

Johnson, which held that Georgia's Eleventh Congressional District was unconstitutional because it was organized primarily to provide racial representation, rather than to respond to specific discrimination; *Rosenberg* v. *Rector and Visitors of the University of Virginia,* which held that the publicly funded University of Virginia was required to finance a Christian magazine run by students, a sharp change of Court direction on a basic constitutional issue. He wrote a concurring opinion in *Missouri* v. *Jenkins,* which effectively limited the level of state spending allowable to carry out a federally managed school desegregation plan in Kansas City. He also joined the majority in *Capital Square Review and Advisory Board* v. *Pinette,* which held that it was unconstitutional to bar display of a large Ku Klux Klan cross in an Ohio public park; and *Veronia School District* v. *Acton,* which held that an Oregon school district's random drug testing program was constitutional.

Thomas wrote a dissenting opinion in the landmark *U.S. Term Limits Inc.* v. *Thornton,* which held that to limit congressional terms required a constitutional amendment; 23 state laws imposing terms limits were invalidated and Congress was barred from passing a term limits law. He also wrote dissenting opinions in *City of Edmonds* v. *Oxford House,* which held that residential zoning laws in the city of Edmonds, Washington, could not be used to discriminate against the establishment of group homes for people with disabilities; and in *O'Neal* v. *McAninch,* which held that prisoners could obtain habeas corpus federal reviews of their state convictions when federal judges had grave doubts as to possible state court errors. He also dissented in *Babbitt* v. *Sweet Home Chapter of Communities for a Greater Oregon,* which held that the federal government had the right under the Endangered Species Act to sharply restrict logging and other activities harmful to the northern spotted owl. Thomas also wrote the unanimous opinion in *Wilson* v. *Arkansas,* ruling that the Fourth Amendment required police officers with search warrants to announce their presence to those within before entering a home, and therefore struck down a drug-trafficking conviction.

Savannah-born Thomas received his 1971 B.A. from Holy Cross, and his 1974 J.D. from Yale Law School. He was, from early in his career, a protégé of John Danforth, then U.S. senator from Missouri. Thomas was Missouri assistant attorney general (1974–77) when Danforth was state attorney general. Thomas was a corporate lawyer for the Monsanto Company (1977–79), a legislative assistant to Senator Danforth (1979–81), assistant secretary for civil rights in the federal Education Department (1981–82), and chairperson of the U.S. Equal Opportunity Employment Commission (1982–89), before being named by President Ronald Reagan to the U.S. Court of Appeals for the District of Columbia in 1989. Thomas was named to the Supreme Court by President George Bush in 1991, and confirmed after his historic confrontation on the issue of sexual harassment with law professor and former aide Anita Faye Hill, before the Senate Judiciary Committee and a worldwide television audience.

Thomas's second wife, Virginia Lamp Thomas, is a lawyer at the U.S. Labor Department, and formerly at the U.S. Chamber of Commerce. Thomas has one son, from a previous marriage.

FURTHER READING

"Courting change. . . ." CHI CHI SILEO. *Insight on the News*, Sept. 4, 1995.
"Strange lies." DAVID BROCK. *The American Spectator*, Jan. 1995.
Clarence Thomas. NORMAN L. MACHT. Chelsea House, 1995.
African American Women Speak Out on Anita Hill–Clarence Thomas. GENEVA SMITHERMAN, ed. Wayne State University Press, 1995.
"Confirmations. . . ." JEFFREY ROSEN. *New Republic*, Dec. 19, 1994.
Resurrection: The Confirmation of Clarence Thomas. JOHN C. DANFORTH. Viking Penguin, 1994.
Strange Justice: The Selling of Clarence Thomas. JUNE MAYER and JILL ABRAMSON. Houghton Mifflin, 1994.
The Clarence Thomas–Anita Hill Hearings. NINA TOTENBERG, ed. Academy Chicago, 1994.
Nomination of Judge Clarence Thomas and the Testimony of Anita Hill, 10 vols. Gordon Press, 1994.
Clarence Thomas and the Tough Love Crowd: Counterfeit Heroes and Unhappy Truths. RONALD S. ROBERTS. New York University Press, 1994.
"Her word against his." DAVID BROCK. *National Review*, May 10, 1993.
Clarence Thomas: Supreme Court Justice. WARREN J. HALLIBURTON. Enslow, 1993.
The Real Anita Hill: The Untold Story. DAVID BROCK. Free Press, 1993.
Clarence Thomas. PAUL DEEGAN. Abdo & Daughters, 1992.
Clarence Thomas: Confronting the Future. L. GORDON CROVITZ, ed. Regnery Gateway, 1992.
Capitol Games: Clarence Thomas, Anita Hill, and the Behind-the-Scenes Story of a Supreme Court Nomination. TIMOTHY M. PHELPS and HELEN WINTERNITZ. Disney, 1992.

Thomas, Rachel (1905–95)

Born in Glamorgan, the child of a mining family, Rachel Thomas was a leading Welsh film actress for more than half a century, who played a long series of notable character roles, many of them as an indomitable Welsh mother. Her first major role came opposite Paul Robeson in the film *Proud Valley* (1939), set in a Welsh mining village. The film, a hit in Britain, made her a star in Wales and brought her more strong character roles in British films. Among her many films were *The Captive Heart* (1946), a war story; *Tiger Bay* (1959), set in Cardiff and starring John Mills and Hayley Mills; and *Under Milk Wood* (1973), starring Richard Burton and Elizabeth Taylor. Thomas was very active in Welsh radio and television, as in her starring role in *How Green Was My Valley* (1968) and her continuing role in the daytime soap "People of the Valley." She was survived by a daughter. (d. Cardiff, Wales; February 8, 1995)

FURTHER READING

Obituary. *Variety*, Feb. 13, 1995.
Obituary. *Times* (of London), Feb. 11, 1995.
Obituary. *Independent*, Feb. 10, 1995.

Thomas, Ross Elmore (1926–95)

Oklahoma City–born Ross Thomas began his writing career while still in college, as a reporter for the *Daily Oklahoman*. After receiving his 1949 B.A. from the University of Oklahoma, he joined the public relations staff of the National Farmers Union, becoming the union's national public relations director (1952–56) and then briefly running his own political consulting firm. He worked in several Washington-based public relations jobs until the mid-1960s, making his debut as a mystery writer with the novel *The Cold War Swap* (1965). Among his further novels were *The Seersucker Whipsaw* (1967), *Cast a Yellow Shadow* (1967), *The Singapore Wink* (1969; as Oliver Bleeck), *The Brass Go-Between*

(1969), *The Fools in Town Are on Our Side* (1971), *The Back-Up Men* (1971), *The Procane Chronicle* (1972), *The Highbinders* (1974), *Chinaman's Chance* (1978), *Briarpatch* (1984), and *Ah, Treachery!* (1994). He also wrote or cowrote several screenplays. He was survived by his wife, Rosalie. (d. Santa Monica, California; December 18, 1995)

FURTHER READING

Obituary. *New York Times*, Dec. 18, 1995.
A *Checklist of Ross Thomas.* C. P. STEPHENS. Ultramarine, 1992.

Emma Thompson (left) and Kate Winslet.

Thompson, Emma (1959–) Actress and

writer Emma Thompson wrote the screenplay and starred as Elinor, the oldest of the three Dashwood sisters, in the very well-received 1995 film *Sense and Sensibility,* a period comedy she adapted from the classic Jane Austen novel; Ang Lee directed. The cast included Kate Winslet and Emilie Francois as the two younger sisters, Gemma Thompson as their mother, Alan Rickman and Hugh Grant as sometime suitors, Robert Hardy, Elizabeth Spriggs, Harriet Walter, James Fleet, Greg Wise, and Imogen Stubbs. Thompson was named best screenwriter of the year by the New York Film Critics Circle and the Los Angeles Film Critics Association for the work, and received Golden Globe nominations as best actor in a drama and for best screenplay.

Thompson also starred as early 20th-century British artist Dora Carrington in the title role of the film *Carrington.* Jonathan Pryce costarred as her bisexual lover, noted biographer Lytton Strachey; both were members of the group of loosely associated, very talented friends who lived and worked in and around London's Bloomsbury area, and so became known as the Bloomsbury Group. Christopher Hampton directed and wrote the screenplay, adapted from Michael Holroyd's biography *Lytton Strachey*; the cast included Steve Waddington, Samuel West, Rufus Sewell, Penelope Wilton, and Janet McNeer.

On the personal side, Thompson and actor/director Kenneth Branagh stated that they intended to divorce; they had been married since 1989.

After playing small roles in British theater and television in the early 1980s, Thompson's breakthrough came with a starring role in the musical *Me and My Girl* (1985). After playing in the television comedy series "Tutti Frutti," she had another starring role, in the television miniseries "The Fortunes of War," opposite Kenneth Branagh, winning a British Academy of Film and Television Arts (BAFTA) best television actress award for the role. Her films include *Henry V* (1989), *Impromptu* (1991), *Dead Again* (1991), *Howards End* (1992; she won a best actress Oscar); *The Remains of the Day* (1993), *In the Name of the Father* (1993), *Much Ado About Nothing* (1993), *Junior* (1994), and the television film *The Blue Boy* (1994). She attended Newnham College, Cambridge.

FURTHER READING

"Emma Thompson." JUDY WIEDER. *Advocate*, Sept. 19, 1995.
"Thompson's turn." GEORGINA HOWELL. *Vogue*, June 1993.
"Emma Thompson's. . . ." RUSSELL MILLER. *New York Times Magazine*, Mar. 28, 1993.
"Much ado about Emma." CHRIS HEATH. *Us*, Mar. 1993.
"Classy sassy. . . ." DAVID GRITTEN. *Cosmopolitan*, Jan. 1993.

Townsend, Peter Wooldridge

(1914–95) British aviator Peter Townsend was one of the heroes of the Battle of Britain (Aug.–Oct. 1940), when the vastly outnumbered pilots of the Royal Air Force (RAF) fought Hitler's

Luftwaffe to a standstill, forcing the Germans to abort their planned invasion of Britain. In 1940, he was credited with shooting down the first German bomber on British soil during World War II. A fighter squadron commander, he became a group captain, the title he was to carry for the rest of his life. Twice shot down, the much-decorated Townsend shot down 11 German planes during his 20 months of combat duty.

After the war, Townsend became an aide to Britain's royal family. In the early 1950s, he and Princess Margaret, then 22, fell in love and wanted to marry. But Townsend had by then divorced his first wife, and the marriage of a member of the royal family to a divorced person was prohibited by the Anglican Church. Queen Elizabeth, newly crowned, disapproved of their marriage and essentially banished Townsend to a minor diplomatic post in Belgium. When Margaret reached the age of 25, and no longer needed Elizabeth's approval to marry, she ultimately decided against marriage to Townsend, rather than give up her royal status. Townsend never went home, living in Belgium and then in France for the rest of his life. He undertook a variety of occupations, ultimately becoming a successful author, whose books included *Duel of Eagles* (1970), about the Battle of Britain, and *The Postman of Nagasaki* (1984). His autobiography was *Time and Chance* (1978). He was survived by his second wife, Marie Luce Jamagne, and by two daughters and two sons. (d. Paris; June 19, 1995)

FURTHER READING

Obituary. *Times* (of London), June 21, 1995.
Obituary. *Independent*, June 21, 1995.
Obituary. *New York Times*, June 21, 1995.

Travolta, John (1954–   ) For his 1994 film *Pulp Fiction*, actor John Travolta received a best actor Oscar nomination, as well as best actor nominations from the British Academy of Film and Television Arts (BAFTA) and Screen Actors Guild.

In 1995, Travolta starred as gangster-turned–movie producer Chili Palmer in the well-received, Hollywood-set film comedy *Get Shorty*, opposite Gene Hackman as bottom-of-the-barrel producer Harry Zimm and costarring Rene Russo and Danny DeVito, who also coproduced, with director Barry Sonnenfield; Scott Franklin

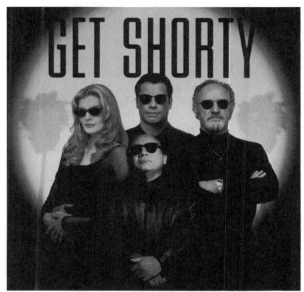

John Travolta (rear center), Gene Hackman (right), Danny DeVito (front center), and Rene Russo.

adapted the Elmore Leonard novel. The cast included Dennis Farina and Delroy Lindo, with Bette Midler, Harvey Keitel, and Penny Marshall in cameo roles. Travolta received a Golden Globe nomination as best actor in a musical or comedy for the role.

Travolta also starred opposite Harry Belafonte and Kelly Lynch in the film *White Man's Burden*, written and directed by Desmond Nakano. The work is a fantasy about a United States in which racial roles are reversed; Travolta is an oppressed White factory worker and Belafonte a Black factory owner, ultimately kidnapped by Travolta. Their developing, though ultimately aborted, friendship during a single day provides the film's story line.

Forthcoming was a starring dual role in the film comedy *The Double*, directed by Roman Polanski. Also forthcoming were starring film roles in *Michael*, directed by Nora Ephron and costarring Andie MacDowell; the science fiction tale *Broken Arrow*, directed by John Woo and costarring Christian Slater and Samantha Mathis; and *Phenomenon*, directed by George Bamber and costarring Kyra Sedgwick, Forest Whitaker, and Robert Duvall.

New Jersey–born Travolta became a well-known actor on television in "Welcome Back Kotter" (1975–79). On screen, he played minor roles until emerging as a star in the hit *Saturday Night Fever* (1977), followed by other popular starring roles in *Grease* (1978), *Urban Cowboy*

(1980), and *Staying Alive* (1983). After some lean years, Travolta came back as a star of the comedy hit *Look Who's Talking* (1989), opposite Kirstie Alley and the voice of Bruce Willis as Mikey, the baby in the film. Travolta and Alley also paired in the sequels *Look Who's Talking Too* (1990) and *Look Who's Talking Now* (1993). Travolta also starred in the films *Run* and *Shout* (both 1991) and *Pulp Fiction* (1994), and has made several records. He and actress Kelly Preston (his costar in *Run*) were married in 1991; it was his first and her second marriage. They have one son.

FURTHER READING

"A star is reborn...." MICHAEL SEGELLI. *Cosmopolitan*, Jan. 1996.
"Harry Belafonte and...." *Jet*, Dec. 4, 1995.
"Travolta." LESLIE VAN BUSKIRK. *Us*, Dec. 1995.
"'You have to....'" DOTSON RADER. *Parade*, Oct. 22, 1995.
"John Travolta...." TOM JUNOD. *GQ*, Oct. 1995.
"Stayin' alive." TY BURR. "The man in...." JEFF GORDINIER. *Entertainment*, Oct. 21, 1994.
"Rebound for glory." NICK COHN. *Vogue*, Oct. 1994.
"Look who's talking." ROSANNA ARQUETTE. *Interview*, Aug. 1994.
"Saturday night feeding." CHARLES SALZBERG. *Redbook*, Feb. 1993.

vision series "American Cinema," hosted by John Lithgow. She also starred opposite Colm Feore in the television movie *Friends at Last,* about a divorced couple finally becoming friends.

Missouri-born Turner attended Southwest Missouri State University and received her M.F.A. from the University of Maryland. After working in the theater and on the NBC soap opera "The Doctors" in the 1970s, she moved into films in the early 1980s, and quickly emerged as a leading movie star in such films as *Body Heat* (1981), *Romancing the Stone* (1984), *Prizzi's Honor* (1985), *The Jewel of the Nile* (1985), *Peggy Sue Got Married* (1986), *Switching Channels* (1988), *The Accidental Tourist* (1988), *The War of the Roses* (1989), *V. I. Warshawski* (1991), *House of Cards* (1993), *Undercover Blues* (1993), *Serial Mom* (1994), and *Naked in New York* (1994). She also starred in a 1989 New York revival of Tennessee Williams's *Cat on a Hot Tin Roof,* and was the voice of the sexy cartoon figure, Jessica, in *Who Framed Roger Rabbit* (1988). Turner married Jay Weiss in 1984; they have one child.

FURTHER READING

"Kathleen Turner." GRAHAM FULLER. *Interview*, Aug. 1995.
"The ups and downs...." CHRIS CHASE. *Cosmopolitan*, July 1993.

Turner, Kathleen (1954–) Stage and screen star Kathleen Turner returned to the theater in 1995, starring as the mother in the hit American production of *Indiscretions,* a translation from the French of Jean Cocteau's comedy *Les Parents Terribles,* set in Paris in the late 1930s. Sean Mathias directed, as he had the 1994 British production. Costarring were Jude Law as her son, Eileen Atkins, Roger Rees, and Cynthia Nixon.

Turner also appeared as a mother on screen—in this instance the stepmother of two young women in a four-person women's support group in the film *Moonlight and Valentino,* directed by David Anspaugh and adapted by Ellen Simon from her own play, in a cast that included Whoopi Goldberg, Elizabeth Perkins, Gwyneth Paltrow, Peter Coyote, and Jon Bon Jovi in his film debut.

On television, Turner appeared as narrator of the segment *The Star,* in the ten-part public tele-

Turner, Lana (Julia Jean Mildred Frances Turner; 1920–95) Idaho-born Lana Turner began her film career with small parts in *A Star Is Born* (1937) and *They Won't Forget* (1937), and moved into larger roles in the early 1940s, while being successfully publicized as the "Sweater Girl." Among her early films were *Dr. Jekyll and Mr. Hyde* (1941), *Johnny Eager* (1942), and *Somewhere I'll Find You* (1942). She emerged as a dramatic star in *The Postman Always Rings Twice* (1946), *Green Dolphin Street* (1947), and *Cass Timberlane* (1947). Among her later films were *The Three Musketeers* (1948), *A Life of Her Own* (1950), *The Bad and the Beautiful* (1952), *Peyton Place* (1957; she received an Academy Award best actress nomination), *Imitation of Life* (1959), and *By Love Posessed* (1961), as well as many smaller roles later in her career. Turner also appeared in the television series "The Survivors" (1969–70) and "Falcon Crest" (1982–83), and in several theater roles.

Her personal life drew a great deal of media attention, most notably in 1958, when Turner's teenage daughter, Cheryl Crane, stabbed and killed her mother's lover, reputed mob figure John Stompanato. Crane was acquitted, on a finding of justifiable homicide committed because of her fear for her mother's life. Turner was married eight times. Her autobiography was *Lana: The Legend, the Lady, the Truth* (1982). She was survived by her daughter. (d. Los Angeles; June 29, 1995)

FURTHER READING

Obituary. *Current Biography*, Sept. 1995.
"The bad and. . . ." Susan Schindehette. *People*, July 17, 1995.
"Imitation and life." Ty Burr. *Entertainment*, July 14, 1995.
Obituary. *Times* (of London), July 1, 1995.
Obituary. *New York Times*, July 1, 1995.
Obituary. *Variety*, June 30, 1995.
Lana's Men: The Life and Loves of Lana Turner. Jane E. Wayne. St. Martin's, 1995.
"Lana Turner." Michael Frank. *Architectural Digest*, Apr. 1992.

Turner, Ted (Robert Edward Turner, III; 1938–) With the September sale of the Turner Broadcasting System (TBS) to Time Warner Inc. for $7.5 billion in stock, TBS founder Ted Turner became vice chairman of the joined companies, together the world's largest media conglomerate. Turner held 10 percent of the joined companies, was to keep his independence of action as the head of TBS, and was to remain in Atlanta. Whether he would long be happy as anything less than the freewheeling entrepreneur he had been for three decades remained to be seen.

Turner scored a major triumph in 1995, when his Atlanta Braves defeated the Cleveland Indians in baseball's World Series, in six games. It was the Braves' first world championship, and the first championship brought home to Atlanta by any professional sports team.

Turner began building what ultimately became a set of major enterprises in the 1960s, and emerged as a leading American industrial and sports figure during the 1970s. He founded the "superstation" Turner Broadcasting System (TBS) in 1976 and, after encountering serious financial problems, in the late 1980s emerged as a world communications industry leader, his em-

pire including the Cable News Network (CNN) and Turner Network Television (TNT), launched in 1988. From 1989, CNN grew into a worldwide broadcast news network, with hundreds of millions of viewers, through its 24-hour coverage of such massive events as the Tiananmen Square demonstrations and massacre, the tearing down of the Berlin Wall, and the Persian Gulf War. Largely because of such important coverage, Turner was named *Time* magazine's man of the year for 1991.

As owner of the Atlanta Braves baseball team, the Atlanta Hawks basketball team, and World Championship Wrestling, Turner is also a major figure in American sports. A leading yachtsman, he won the America's Cup in 1977. He sponsored the Goodwill Games at Moscow in 1986 and at Atlanta in 1990. Turner attended Brown University. Before marrying actress Jane Fonda in 1991, he had been married twice previously, and has five children.

FURTHER READING

"Citizen Turner." Robert Goldberg and Gerald Jay Goldberg. *Cosmopolitan*, Sept. 1995.
"Citizen Turner." Robert Goldberg and Gerald Jay Goldberg. *Playboy*, June 1995.
"King Ted's. . . ." Daniel Jeffries. *Independent*, May 30, 1995.
Citizen Turner: The Wild Rise of an American Tycoon. Robert Goldberg and Gerald J. Goldberg. Harcourt Brace, 1995.
"The Sporting News. . . ." Michael Knisley and John Rawlings. *Sporting News*, Jan. 3, 1994.
It Ain't as Easy as It Looks: The Story of Ted Turner and CNN. Porter Bibb. Crown, 1993.
Ted Turner. David M. Fischer. Rourke, 1993.
"Prince of the global village." "The taming of Ted Turner." Priscilla Painton. "History as it happens." William A. Henry, III. "Inside the world of CNN." Richard Zoglin. *Time*, Jan. 6, 1992. (Man of the Year issue)
Ted Turner: Television's Triumphant Tiger. Rebecca Stefoff. Garrett, 1992.

Turturro, John (1957–) Versatile, still-emerging film star John Turturro in 1995 starred as a homicide detective in the film *Clockers*, Spike Lee's study of violence within African-American communities, often accompanying the drug trade and often inspired by the macho, moneyed images conveyed to young people by drug dealers. The cast included Harvey Keitel as

Turturro's partner, Delroy Lindo as a drug dealer, Mikti Phifer in the killer's role, and Isaiah Washington as Phifer's brother, who tries to make a false confession to save him.

Turturro also starred as the inventor-father in the very well-received comedy-drama *Unstrung Heroes,* directed by Diane Keaton and costarring Andie MacDowell, in a cast that included Nathan Watt, Michael Richards, Maury Chaykin, and Kendra Krull. He also played a strong supporting role in the film comedy *Search and Destroy,* directed by David Salle and costarring Griffin Dunne, Rosanna Arquette, Dennis Hopper, Christopher Walken, Illeana Douglas, and Martin Scorsese.

On television, Turturro starred as mob figure Sam Giancana opposite Mary-Louise Parker as singer Phyllis McGuire in the film *Sugartime.*

Forthcoming were starring roles in the film *Box of Moonlight,* written and directed by Tom DeCillo, and in Spike Lee's film *Girl 6.*

New York City–born Turturro first came to public notice in John Patrick Shanley's Off-Broadway play *Danny and the Deep Blue Sea* (1984), winning an Obie. His films include *To Live and Die in L.A.* (1985), *Five Corners* (1987), *The Sicilian* (1987), *Do the Right Thing* (1989), *Miller's Crossing* (1990), *Mo' Better Blues* (1990), *Jungle Fever* (1991), *Barton Fink* (1991; he won a best actor Golden Palm for the role at the Cannes Film Festival), *Mac* (1992; he starred and directed), *Brain Donors* (1992), *Fearless* (1993), *Quiz Show* (1994), and *Being Human* (1994). Turturro graduated from the State University of New York College at New Paltz in 1978 and later attended Yale University's School of Drama. He and Katherine Borowitz have one son. His younger brother, Nicholas Turturro, is also an actor.

FURTHER READING

"What it's like. . . ." MARTHA FRANKEL. *Cosmopolitan,* Oct. 1995.
"John Turturro. . . ." VERONICA CHAMBERS. *Premiere,* Feb. 1993.
"Homebody." JOSEPH A. CINCOTTI. *GQ,* Oct. 1991.
"Honest John. . . ." PHOEBE HOBAN. *New York,* Aug. 12, 1991.

Tyler, Anne (1941–   ) What would happen if I just walked away into a new life? That is the question asked by the main character in Anne Tyler's 1995 novel *Ladder of Years,* in which De-

lia Grinstead on impulse leaves a family tangle involving her obtuse physician-husband, three grown children, a sister, and assorted other relatives. Departing from the family's vacation in just her beach clothes, and with the family's weekly grocery money, she hitches a ride to a new town, where she establishes herself as a spinster and finds a job, seeking to find her identity independent of her family. But she finds herself drawn into another family situation, as housekeeper to a father and son whose wife-mother has left them, and comes full circle when she returns home for a daughter's wedding, and eventually must choose how—and with whom—she will live her life. As always in Tyler novels, readers found closely observed explorations of individuals and relationships, especially marriage, presented with humor, compassion, and a clear eye.

Minneapolis-born Tyler received her 1961 B.A. from Duke University, and also studied at Columbia University (1962). She began building a devoted following with her first novel, *If Morning Ever Comes* (1964); it was followed by numerous others, including *The Tin Can Tree* (1965), *A Slipping-Down Life* (1970), *The Clock Winder* (1972), *Celestial Navigation* (1974), *Searching for Caleb* (1976), *Earthly Possessions* (1977), *Morgan's Passing* (1980), *Dinner at the Homesick Restaurant* (1982), *The Accidental Tourist* (1985; basis for the 1988 movie), *Breathing Lessons* (1988; it won the 1989 Pulitzer Prize for fiction and was the basis for the 1994 television miniseries), *Saint Maybe* (1991), and the children's book *Tumble Tower* (1993), illustrated by Mitra Modarressi, her daughter. Tyler has also published numerous short stories. She married Taghi M. Modarressi in 1963; they have two children.

FURTHER READING

Anne Tyler: A Bio-Bibliography. ROBERT W. CROFT. Greenwood, 1995.
Anne Tyler as Novelist. DALE SALWAK, ed. University of Iowa Press, 1994.
"My mother. . . ." DIANE ROBACK. *Entertainment*, May 7, 1993.
Anne Tyler. ELIZABETH EVANS. Twayne/Macmillan, 1993.
Critical Essays on Anne Tyler. ALICE H. PETRY. G. K. Hall, 1992.
Modern American Women Writers. ELAINE SHOWALTER et al. Simon & Schuster, 1991.

Tyson, Mike (Michael G. Tyson; 1966–)

Former heavyweight champion Mike Tyson returned to the boxing world in 1995. Convicted in 1992 on a charge of raping Miss Black America contestant Desiree Washington in his hotel room in Indianapolis in July 1991 (Tyson has maintained that they had consensual sex), he was released from prison on March 25, having received time off his six-year sentence for good behavior. On his return to Harlem in June, Tyson was given a public celebratory welcome, scaled down after many people criticized a lavish welcome as inappropriate for a man just returned from prison. Many were also concerned that he had signed with controversial boxing promoter Don King.

Even though he had not fought for half a decade, Tyson was still a prime focus of attention in a boxing world bereft of a clear heavyweight champion. The much-ballyhooed August 19 pay-per-view nontitle fight against Peter McNeeley that marked Tyson's return to boxing lasted only 1:29, being controversially stopped when McNeeley's manager entered the ring. A second pay-per-view fight, against Buster Mathis, Jr., was postponed after Tyson fractured his right thumb. When finally held, on December 16 on free television, it also resulted in a Tyson victory—though doubts about the caliber of his opponent left lingering questions about Tyson's current boxing prowess. At year's end, Tyson's record stood at 43-1, with 37 knockouts. His next fight was scheduled to be a title event on March 16, 1996, against Britain's Frank Bruno, the World Boxing Council heavyweight champion. The two previously met in 1989, when Tyson stopped Bruno in five rounds with a technical knockout.

On the personal side, Tyson said he had converted to the Muslim religion while in prison. In May he attended ceremonies at which his fiancée, Monica Turner, received her medical degree from Georgetown University Medical School; the two had met in the late 1980s.

Brooklyn-born Tyson turned professional in 1985, and quickly became a leading heavyweight title contender. From 1986 to 1988, he successively defeated several boxers, the last of them Michael Spinks in June 1988, in the process uniting the three boxing titles to become sole world heavyweight champion, the youngest ever. He held the title until his unexpected defeat, his first as a professional, by James "Buster" Douglas in February 1990. Tyson was formerly married, to actress Robin Givens. He also has a daughter.

FURTHER READING

"Why Mike Tyson. . . ." ROBERT E. JOHNSON. *Jet*, Sept. 11, 1995.
"Ebony interview. . . ." ROBERT E. JOHNSON. *Ebony*, Sept. 1995.
"He's back." JOHN SEDGWICK and ALLISON SAMUELS. *Newsweek*, Aug. 21, 1995.
"The love doctor. . . ." PATRICK ROGERS. *People*, Aug. 21, 1995.
"Mike Tyson says. . . ." ROBERT E. JOHNSON. *Jet*, July 17, 1995.
"Second chance. . . ." STEVE RUSHIN and SONJA STEPTOE. *Sports Illustrated*, July 3, 1995.
"Two champs are back." STEVE WULF. *Time*, Apr. 3, 1995.
Bad Intentions: The Mike Tyson Story, rev. ed. PETER HELLER. Da Capo, 1995.
The Inner Ring: The Set-up of Mike Tyson and the Uncrowning of Don King. RUDY GONZALEZ et al. Oliver, 1995.
Heavy Justice: The State of Indiana vs. Michael G. Tyson. J. GREGORY GARRISON and RANDY ROBERTS. Addison-Wesley, 1994.
Down for the Count: The Shocking Truth Behind the Mike Tyson Rape Trial. MARK SHAW. Sagamore, 1993.
Mike Tyson: Money Myth Betrayal. MONTEIL ILLINGWORTH. Carol, 1991.

U

U Nu (1907–95) Born in Burma (now Myanmar), politician, writer, and educator U Nu became a high school headmaster after his 1929 graduation from Rangoon University. While a law student at Rangoon (now Yangon) in the mid-1930s, he joined and became a leader of the Burmese independence movement, and was arrested by the British several times, last in 1940. Freed by the Japanese, he became a minister in the Japanese-dominated wartime Burmese puppet government, then became a minister in the postwar British colonial government. After the 1947 assassination of prime minister–designate Aung San, U Nu became the first prime minister of independent Burma. He also became a world figure, as a key organizer of the 1955 Bandung (Indonesia) conference, who called for an end to the Cold War and became a leader of the non-aligned movement. With two interruptions, he was the prime minister of Burma until the 1962 Ne Win–led military coup that deposed his democratically elected government; he was then imprisoned by Ne Win until 1967. He led prodemocracy insurgent forces from exile until 1972, then retiring to central India. He was allowed to return home by the military in 1980, on his promise to stay out of politics. In 1988, he came out of retirement briefly, to serve as titular head of the short-lived democratic government that was deposed by the September 1988 military takeover, and was then under house arrest until 1992. To the end, he campaigned for the release of Aung San Suu Kyi, daughter of Aung San, and for the restoration of democracy. He published *U Nu: Saturday's Son* (1972). He was survived by five children. (d. Yangon [Rangoon]; February 14, 1995)

FURTHER READING

Obituary. *Independent*, Feb. 20, 1995.
Obituary. *Times* (of London), Feb. 15, 1995.
Obituary. *New York Times*, Feb. 15, 1995.

Unabomber (Unabomb serial bomber; ?–   ) The unknown serial bomber known in the media as the "Unabomber" was very much in the news during 1995. On April 24, a package bomb killed Gilbert B. Murray, a lobbyist for the California Forestry Association, in that organization's Sacramento offices. It was the 16th such bombing since the first bomb exploded at Northwestern University in 1978; and the third killing, with 22 injuries. Once again, the bomb proved untraceable, and the bomber or bombers remained uncaught. No one has ever even known whether the bomber was male or female, or acted alone or in a group, although the bomber is referred to as "he" because law enforcement officials have thought the bombings done by a White male acting alone.

In this instance, much more than the bombing developed. Before the bombing, the bomber had written letters to *The New York Times* and other newspapers, claiming credit for the bombings, calling himself an "anarchist," describing himself as the terrorist group "FC" (an unknown organization), and offering to stop the bombings in return for publication of a long article detailing his views. The long, so-far-fruitless investigation of the bombings continued. On June 27, in a letter to the *San Francisco Chronicle,* the bomber threatened to blow up an air flight out of Los Angeles International Airport within six days; massive tie-ups resulted as rigid security precautions were instituted throughout the state and neighboring areas. The bomber then delivered a 35,000-word manuscript to *The New York Times* and *The Washington Post,* calling for its publication and labeling the California bombing message a "prank." Ultimately, after much soul-searching and with the approval of the federal government and the *Times,* the *Post* did on September 19 publish the entire Unabomb document. Whether the bombing would then entirely stop remained to be seen.

FURTHER READING

"Publish or perish." PAUL GRAY. *Time,* Aug. 14, 1995.
"Give the Unabomber. . . ." JOHN LEO. *U.S. News & World Report,* Aug. 14, 1995.
"Toward a portrait. . . ." KIRKPATRICK SALE. *New York Times.* Aug. 6, 1995.
"Mail bomber. . . ." ROBERT D. MCFADDEN. *New York Times,* June 30, 1995.
"A man 'intoxicated. . . .'" PAUL TAYLOR. *Washington Post,* June 30, 1995.

Updike, John Hoyer (1932–) Though

his "Rabbit" series has ended, it continued to reverberate in John Updike's life during 1995. He received the William Dean Howells Medal of the American Academy of Arts and Letters for the best novel of the past five years, for his *Rabbit at Rest* (1990). He also contributed an introductory essay to a new single-volume edition of the four novels, published under the title *Rabbit Angstrom.* His *The Afterlife and Other Stories* topped the list of best works of fiction in 1994, selected by *Booklist,* the journal of the American Library Association.

Updike's new work for 1995 was a complete change of pace: *A Helpful Alphabet of Friendly Objects,* a children's book, illustrated by his son, David Updike. A new novel, *In the Beauty of the Lilies,* a tale of movies and loss of faith, focusing on a 20th-century New Jersey family, was scheduled for January 1996 publication.

Pennsylvania-born Updike is best known for his "Rabbit" quartet: *Rabbit Run* (1960), *Rabbit*

Redux (1977), *Rabbit Is Rich* (1981), and *Rabbit at Rest* (1990), which won the Pulitzer Prize and the National Book Award. Among his other novels are the National Book Award–winning *The Centaur* (1963), *Couples* (1968), *Bech: A Book* (1970), *Bech is Back* (1982), *The Witches of Eastwick* (1984), *Memories of the Ford Administration* (1992), and *Brazil* (1994). He has also written short stories, many of them first published in *The New Yorker,* most recently his 11th collection *The Afterlife: And Other Stories* (1994), as well as essays, a play, and poetry, gathered in *Collected Poems 1953–1993* (1993). His recent work also includes the autobiography *Self-Consciousness: Memoirs* (1990) and the collection *Odd Jobs: Essays and Criticism* (1990) and *Hugging the Shore: Essays and Criticism* (1994). Updike's 1954 B.A. was from Harvard University. Formerly married to Mary Pennington, he married Martha Bernhard in 1977, and has four children.

FURTHER READING

"Self-consciousness." ANTHONY QUINN. *Guardian,* July 21, 1995.
"John Updike. . . ." TOM ROBERTS. *National Catholic Reporter,* May 26, 1995.
Conversations with John Updike. JAMES PLATH, ed. University Press of Mississippi, 1994.
John Updike: A Bio-Bibliography, 1967–1993. JACK DE BELLIS, ed. Greenwood, 1994.
"Personally speaking." *Vogue,* Sept. 1992.

V

Vaughn, Mo (Maurice Samuel Vaughn; 1967–   ) First baseman Mo Vaughn was named Most Valuable Player of the American League for the 1995 baseball season, just barely edging out competitor Albert Belle of the Cleveland Indians. Vaughn and Belle were tied in leading the league in runs batted in, with 126. A righthander who bats lefthanded because he learned batting from his lefthanded mother, Vaughn was also fourth in the league in home runs, with 39; fifth in total bases, with 316; and tied for tenth in runs scored, with 98. But more than that, voters looked at his importance to the team, especially in keeping them ahead early in the season, when the Red Sox were hobbled by injuries to several key players. In the end, Boston won the Eastern Division by seven games, though in the divisional playoffs they lost 3-0 to the Cleveland Indians.

In 1995, Vaughn also played in his first All-Star game. He missed two games in mid-July after a fight with a man who was harassing Vaughn's girlfriend; Vaughn held a news conference to apologize to his team and his fans, especially the kids.

Born in Norwalk, Connecticut, Vaughn graduated from Trinity Pawling Preparatory School, in New York, then attended Seton Hall University (1987–89). Selected by the Boston Red Sox in the 1989 free-agent draft, he played in the minor leagues (1989–91) with New Britain and Pawtucket, before coming into the major leagues with the Boston Red Sox (1991–92). After a poor 1992 season start as regular first baseman, he returned to Pawtucket (1991–92), finally making it back to Boston (1993–   ). In 1994, he es-

tablished the Mo Vaughn Youth Development Program for inner-city Boston children.

FURTHER READING

"Sox appeal." GERRY CALLAHAN. *Sports Illustrated*, Oct. 2, 1995.
"Mo." CHARLES P. PIERCE. *Boston Magazine*, July 1994.

Victor, Paul-Emile (1907–95) Geneva-born French explorer, ethnologist, and engineer Paul-Emile Victor began his long career as an explorer of the planet's polar regions in the mid-1930s, joining Paul Charcot's Greenland expedition (1934–35). His own first Greenland expedition came in 1936; it was followed by expeditions in the Alps and Lapland, and then by World War II service as a polar rescue adviser to the Allies. After the war, he emerged as a major explorer of both poles, organizing French polar expeditions and leading several Antarctic expeditions. He also became a major force in the campaign to preserve the delicate ecosystem of the Antarctic region, advising the French government during the development of the worldwide effort that created the nuclear-free, demilitarized, multinational laboratory that is Antarctica.

In 1977, he moved to Bora-Bora, adopting a wholly different lifestyle close to the natural world while continuing his polar work. A much-honored member of the international community, Victor was also a prolific writer of scientific papers and popular books. Among his books were *Boréal* (1938), *Adventure Esquimaux* (1948), *La grand faim* (1958), *Pôle Nord–Pôle Sud* (1968), *La vie des Eskimos* (1975), *Les Pôles et leurs secrets* (1982), and *La Planète Antarctique* (1992). He was survived by his second wife, Colette, and four children. (d. Bora-Bora, French Polynesia; March 8, 1995)

FURTHER READING

Obituary. *Independent*, Mar. 10, 1995.
Obituary. *Times* (of London), Mar. 9, 1995.
Obituary. *New York Times*, Mar. 9, 1995.

Vidal, Gore (1925–) Gore Vidal's newest book, *Palimpsest: A Memoir,* is less about his life than about his opinions of other people as they impinged on his life. Though he writes movingly about his only true love, his "other half," Jimmie Trimble, who died at Iwo Jima in 1945, Vidal spends much of the book delightedly skewering others, from E. M. Forster and Anaïs Nin to various Kennedys to Charlton Heston and the powers at *The New York Times,* though most of all his mother, Nina Kay Gore. The book's title refers to a piece of manuscript that has been written over more than once, so as to somewhat obscure the original writing. Vidal's early semi-autobiographical novel *The City and the Pillar* (1948) was reissued in a 1995 edition, along with seven stories.

Vidal appeared in the 1995 documentary *The Celluloid Closet,* directed by Rob Epstein and Jeffrey Friedman, which reviews the treatment of homosexuality in Hollywood films. In a film tentatively titled *The Shadow Conspiracy,* shot in 1995 and scheduled for 1996 release, he played a corrupt southern congressman, alongside Charlie Sheen, Linda Hamilton, Donald Sutherland, Sam Waterston, Stephen Lang, and Ben Gazzara. He was scheduled to write a screenplay based on Edith Wharton's *The Buccaneers* and another on the Alger Hiss–Whittaker Chambers case. An earlier screenplay, *Theodora,* about the actress who married Eastern Roman Emperor Justinian, was scheduled for production by Martin Scorsese.

Born at West Point, New York, Vidal is one of the most prolific novelists, satirists, and social critics of the last four decades. His celebrated series of novels on American historical themes includes *Burr* (1972), *Lincoln* (1984), *Empire* (1987), and *Hollywood: A Novel of America in the 1920s* (1989). He has also written several novels set in the Greco-Roman world, including *Julian* (1964), *Myron* (1974), and *Creation* (1981). His many other works include novels such as *Myra Breckenridge* (1968), and the satirical time-traveling *Live from Golgotha* (1992); the plays *Visit to a Small Planet* (1957) and *The Best Man* (1960); several screenplays; occasional nonfiction works, such as *Vidal in Venice* (1987); and a wide range of essays, reviews, and letters, including *Screening History* (1992), *The Decline and Fall of the American Empire* (1992), and the National Book Award–winning *United States: Essays 1952–1992* (1993). Under the pseudonym Edgar Box, the young Vidal wrote several mysteries, including *Death in the Fifth Position* (1952), *Death Before Bedtime* (1953), and *Death Likes It Hot* (1954). As an actor, he appeared as Senator Brickley Paiste in Tim Robbins's satirical film *Bob Roberts* (1992) and as the cynical, conservative professor in Alek Keshishian's film *With Honors* (1994). A liberal, he was twice an unsuccessful candidate for public office, and was head of the short-lived New Party (1971–72). He graduated from Philips Exeter Academy in 1943.

FURTHER READING

"Pursuit of the whole." *Psychology Today*, Jan–Feb. 1996.
"La dolce Vidal." CHRISTOPHER HITCHENS. *Vanity Fair*, Nov. 1995.
"Vidal on Vidal." JUDY WIEDER. *Advocate*, Oct. 31, 1995.
"Heston and Vidal. . . ." CHRIS PETRIKIN. *Variety*, Oct. 16, 1995.
"Gore Vidal. . . ." ANDREW SOLOMON. *New York Times Magazine*, Oct. 15, 1995.
Gore Vidal. DIPAOLO. Macmillan, 1995.
"Gore Vidal." *Vanity Fair*, Oct. 1994.
"Gore Vidal. . . ." MICHAEL MEWSHAW. *Architectural Digest*, Jan.1994.
"The importance. . . ." ANDREW KOPKIND. *Nation*, July 5, 1993.
"Rebel, rebel." NUALA BOYLAN. *Harper's Bazaar*, Jan. 1993.
Gore Vidal: Writer Against the Grain. JAY PARINI, ed. Columbia University Press, 1993.
"A gadfly . . . ." MARTHA DUFFY. *Time*, Sept. 28, 1992.

W

Walesa, Lech (1943–) Polish President Lech Walesa's popularity dropped steadily throughout the early part of 1995, as Poland's major problems remained unsolved, unemployment remained high, sharp conflicts arose on a number of social issues, deep cuts in social services continued, foreign debts and foreign trade deficits continued to rise, and public dissatisfaction grew. His opposition to abortion, though welcomed by the Roman Catholic Church, was a distinctly minority view in his country, costing him a great deal of his support, especially among women. In June, he made a very late and very general condemnation of anti-Semitism, but did not condemn the virulently anti-Jewish comb-

ments of Polish Catholic priest Henryk Jankowski, made while Walesa was in his church. This brought widespread charges that Walesa was ready to play the anti-Semitism card in his coming election campaign. His campaign, stressing his anti-Communist record and sharply attacking his chief opponent, former Communist Aleksander Kwasniewski, spoke little to current Polish concerns; all over Eastern Europe, former Communists were coming to power, and anti-communism without economic and social accomplishments was no longer enough to win many elections.

In the weeks before the November 5 presidential election, Walesa did make a significant comeback, coming in a close second to Kwasniewski and forcing a November 19 runoff election. But in the runoff, Kwasniewski won a five-year presidential term by a narrow margin, with 52 percent of the vote. For the Polish Catholic Church hierarchy, which had campaigned more and more openly for Walesa as the election developed, the vote was a major defeat. For Walesa, the first leader of post-Soviet Poland, who was still only in his early 50s, many years of public life remained, if he still wanted to pursue his political career.

After graduating from vocational school, Walesa worked as an auto mechanic (1962–65), served in the army for two years, and then became an electrician at the Lenin Shipyard in Gdansk in 1967, becoming a leader of the 1970 strike. He continued to organize Poland's developing labor movement, even after he was fired in 1976. In 1980, he led the successful Lenin Shipyard strike, which sparked a nationwide series of largely successful strikes, and was a founder and first president of the Polish trade union confederation, Solidarity. He was imprisoned for a year after Solidarity was outlawed in 1981, but continued to serve as underground leader of the union and movement, returning to the Gdansk Shipyard in 1983.

As the Gorbachev era developed, Walesa and Solidarity emerged openly once again, and Solidarity was legalized under his leadership in 1989. He led in the negotiations that resulted in the Polish turn toward democracy, and to the free elections of June 1989, won by Solidarity. Walesa refused the Polish presidency at that point, but ran and was elected in 1990, winning a five-year term.

Walesa was awarded the 1983 Nobel Peace Prize. His books include the autobiographies *A Way of Hope: An Autobiography* (1987) and *The Struggle and the Triumph* (1994). He married Danuta Walesa in 1969; they have four daughters and four sons.

FURTHER READING

"Walesa may. . . ." KAREN LOWRY MILLER. *Business Week*, Oct. 30, 1995.
Lech Walesa. CAROLINE E. LAZO. Macmillan, 1993.
Lech Walesa: Democrat or Dictator? JAROSLAW KURSKI. Westview, 1993.
"L'état, c'est Lech. . . ." *Economist*, May 2, 1992.
Lech Walesa. ANN ANGEL. Gareth Stevens, 1992.
Lech Walesa: The Road to Democracy. REBECCA STEFOFF. Fawcett, 1992.

Walken, Christopher (1943–) Actor and writer Christopher Walken appeared in several films that opened in 1995, most of them in the horror and crime genres. In the horror film *The Addiction*, directed by Abel Ferrara, he starred as a vampire opposite Annabella Sciorra as another vampire and Kathleen Conklin as Sciorra's intended victim. In the fantasy-horror film *Prophecy*, written and directed by Gregory Widen, he starred as a killer angel named Gabriel, who with other killer angels was attacking the planet Earth.

On the crime genre side, Walken appeared as a villainous kidnapper in the film *Nick of Time*, produced and directed by John Badham, opposite Johnny Depp as a man whose child has been kidnapped; the price of her release is that he assassinate the governor of California, played by Marsha Mason. In *Search and Destroy*, directed by David Salle, Walken played a comic role, as a crooked moneyman. In *Things to Do in Denver When You're Dead*, directed by Gary Feder, he played a former mob boss who needs a favor from a retired mob figure, played by Andy Garcia.

On stage, Walken wrote and starred as a mythical Elvis Presley in the absurdist fantasy *Him*, directed by Jim Simpton, which was not very well received by the New York critics.

Forthcoming was a starring role opposite Bruce Willis in the film *Welcome to Jericho*, written and directed by Walter Hill and costarring Bruce Dern, William Sanderson, and David Patrick Kelly.

New York City–born Walken attended Hofstra University. He gained his early experience in a wide range of regional theater and New York stage roles, making his 1959 Broadway debut in *J.B.* His early stage work also included a notable appearance in *The Lion in Winter* (1966), and his later work a New York Shakespeare Festival appearance in *Coriolanus* (1988). He made his film debut in *The Anderson Tapes* (1972), played substantial roles in *Next Stop Greenwich Village* (1976), *Roseland* (1977), and *Annie Hall* (1977), and had a breakthrough role in *The Deer Hunter* (1978), winning a best supporting actor Oscar. He went on to major roles in such films as *The Dogs of War* (1980), *Heaven's Gate* (1980), *Pennies from Heaven* (1981), *The Milagro Beanfield War* (1988), *Biloxi Blues* (1988), *Communion* (1989), *McBain* (1991), *The Comfort of Strangers* (1991), *Batman Returns* (1992), *Day of Atonement* (1992), *Wayne's World 2* (1993), *True Romance* (1993), *A Business Affair* (1994), and *Pulp Fiction* (1994). He is married to casting director Georgianne Walken.

FURTHER READING

"Out there on a visit." GAVIN SMITH. *Film Comment*, July–Aug. 1992.

Walker, Junior (Autry DeWalt, Jr.; 1942–95) Arkansas-born Junior Walker, a saxophonist and bandleader, began his career while still in his teens, playing in cabaret. In the early 1960s, then living in Battle Creek, Michigan, he formed Junior Walker and His All Stars band. Walker became a Motown recording star in the mid-1960s, his first hit the smash rhythm and

blues single "Shotgun" (1965). This was followed by such hits as "Road Runner" (1966), "How Sweet It Is" (1966), "What Does It Take to Win Your Love" (1969), and "These Eyes" (1969), and later by such albums as *Back Street Boogie* (1979), *Blow the House Down* (1983), and *Nothing But Soul* (1994). Walker continued to tour and record until shortly before his death; in the later years, his band included his son, drummer Autry DeWalt III. No other information on survivors was available. (d. Battle Creek, Michigan; November 23, 1995)

FURTHER READING

Obituary. *Jet*, Dec. 11, 1995.
Obituary. *Billboard*, Dec. 9, 1995.
Obituary. *New York Times*, Nov. 24, 1995.

Wallach, Ira (1913–95) New York City–born novelist, screenwriter, playwright, and songwriter Ira Wallach attended Cornell University. His debut book was *The Horn and the Rose* (1947), which he followed with several very well-received satirical and comedic works, among them *How to Be Deliriously Happy* (1950), *Hopalong-Freud* (1951), *Hopalong-Freud Rides Again* (1952), and *Absence of a Cello* (1960), basis of the 1964 Broadway play. *Muscle Beach* (1959), perhaps his best-known novel, was the basis of the 1967 film *Don't Make Waves,* which starred Tony Curtis and Claudia Cardinale. His screenplays included *Boys' Night Out* (1962), *The Wheeler Dealers* (1964), and *Hot Millions* (1968; he received an Oscar nomination). Among his plays were *Drink to Me Only* (1958; with Abram S. Ginnes) and *Smiling the Boy Fell Dead* (1961). He was survived by his wife, Lillian, a daughter, a son, and a brother. (d. New York City; December 2, 1995)

FURTHER READING

Obituary. *New York Times*, Dec. 5, 1995.
Obituary. *Variety*, Dec. 15, 1995.

Waller, Robert James (1939–   ) In mid-September 1995, Robert James Waller made news when his 1992 novel *The Bridges of Madison County* dropped *off* the best-seller lists. The fastest-selling work of hardcover fiction ever, according to *Publishers Weekly,* with 9.5 million copies sold through mid-1995, it had spent an unprecedented 162 weeks (from August 1992) on *The New York Times* best-seller list, much of that in the top spot. In that period, Waller had published other books, which themselves arrived on the best-seller list, then dropped off, while *Bridges* still rode high. Not until four months after the May 1995 release of the film version, starring Meryl Streep and Clint Eastwood, who also directed; until virtually everyone in the country had learned about the romance between farm housewife Francesca Johnson and photographer Robert Kincaid; until the real Madison County had become a tourist attraction (prompting Waller to relocate to Texas); until the book had also spawned other books, CDs, and even perfumes, did the book finally drop out of the top echelons among best-sellers.

Meanwhile, Waller continued writing. Early 1995 saw publication of *Border Music,* on the romance between a former topless dancer and a part-time cowboy. October saw the arrival of *Puerto Vallarta Squeeze,* focusing on down-at-the-heels writer Danny Pastor and his involvement with an assassin on a chase through Mexico. Despite mixed reviews, both also became best-sellers. Waller himself read the audio version of *Puerto Vallarta.*

Waller has spent most of his career teaching business management. He studied at the University of Iowa and the University of Northern

Iowa (1957–58) and received his 1968 Ph.D. from Indiana University. He then went back to the University of Northern Iowa at Cedar Falls as a professor of management (1968–91), and also dean of the university business school (1979–95), going on leave to write in 1991. His early works include *Just Beyond the Firelight: Stories & Essays* (1988), and *One Good Road Is Enough: Essays* (1990). His runaway best-selling novel *The Bridges of Madison County* (1992) was inspired by his own 1990 tour photographing old covered bridges. It was followed by *Slow Waltz in Cedar Bend* (1993) and *Old Songs in a New Cafe: Selected Essays* (1994). He also recorded the album *The Ballads of Madison County* (1993). Waller married sculptor Georgia Ann Wiedemeier in 1961; they have one daughter.

FURTHER READING

"Working for a cowboy outfit.. . . ." CATHERINE BENNETT. *Guardian*, June 8, 1995.
"Lonesome cowboy." MIMI SWARTZ. *Texas Monthly*, Apr. 1995.
"Slow waltz in Big Bend." SARA BOURBON. *Texas Monthly*, May 1994.
"Waller, Robert James." *Current Biography*, May 1994.

Walton, Ernest Thomas Sinton

(1903–95) Irish nuclear physicist Ernest Walton received his 1922 bachelor's degree from Methodist College, Belfast, and his advanced degrees from Dublin's Trinity College. In 1931, he became a research fellow at Cambridge University's Cavendish Laboratory, working with celebrated British physicist Ernest Rutherford. At Cavendish in 1932, Walton and British physicist John Douglas Cockcroft made an epochal advance in nuclear physics: they created the first human-made nuclear reaction, using a particle accelerator (atom smasher) they had designed and built to bombard lithium nuclei with speeded-up protons to produce two helium nuclei. The historical Cockcroft-Walton device was still in limited use in the 1990s. Walton and Cockcroft shared the 1951 Nobel Prize in physics. Walton did not later pursue nuclear research, instead spending the rest of his career as a much-honored professor and administrator at Trinity College, retiring in 1974. Like many other scientists involved in the development of nuclear physics, he was deeply concerned about the threat of nuclear weapons, and headed the Irish section of the antiwar Pugwash movement. He was survived by two daughters and two sons. (d. Belfast; June 25, 1995)

FURTHER READING

Obituary. *Current Biography*, Sept. 1995.
Obituary. *Times* (of London), June 29, 1995.
Obituary. *Independent*, June 29, 1995.
Obituary. *New York Times*, June 28, 1995.

Washington, Denzel (1954–) Actor

Denzel Washington in 1995 starred in the post–Cold War thriller *Crimson Tide,* as the new executive officer of the American nuclear submarine *Alabama,* opposite Gene Hackman as his captain. With civil war under way in Russia, dissident nationalists have seized a Russian nuclear installation and are threatening to begin World War III by attacking the U.S. Hackman moves toward a preemptive strike against the Russians; Washington organizes a mutiny to prevent a humanity-destroying war.

Washington also starred as detective Easy Rawlins opposite Jennifer Beals in the mystery thriller *Devil in a Blue Dress,* written and directed by Carl Franklin, and based on the Walter Mosley book. The cast included Tom Sizemore, Don Cheadle, and Maury Chaykin. A third starring role was in the film *Virtuosity,* directed by Brett Leonard, and costarring Kelly Lynch, a high-tech thriller featuring Washington's encounters with computer-generated virtual reality.

Forthcoming was a starring role opposite Meg Ryan in the film *Courage Under Fire,* directed by Ed Zwick, and costarring Matt Daman, Lou Diamond Phillips, Scott Glenn, and Michael Moriarty. Washington was also slated to star in the title role of the biofilm *Jackie Robinson,* directed by Spike Lee, and opposite Whitney Houston in *The Preacher's Wife,* directed by Penny Marshall.

Washington attended Fordham University and studied at San Francisco's American Conservatory Theater. He emerged as a strong stage player from the mid-1970s at the New York Shakespeare Festival and in several Off-Broadway plays, one of them the Negro Ensemble Company's *A Soldier's Play,* re-creating his role in the 1984 film *A Soldier's Story.* He starred in the title role of *Richard III* (1990) at the New York Shakespeare Festival in Central Park. He became a television star in the 1980s as Dr. Otis Chandler in "St. Elsewhere" (1982–88). His films include *Cry Freedom* (1987), as South African Black leader Steve Biko, *For Queen and Country* (1989), *The Mighty Quinn* (1989), *Heart Condition* (1989), *Glory* (1989; he won the 1990 best supporting actor Oscar), *Mo' Better Blues* (1990), *Ricochet* (1991), *Mississippi Masala* (1991), *Malcolm X* (1992), *The Pelican Brief* (1993), *Philadelphia* (1993), and *Much Ado about Nothing* (1993). Washington is married to singer Paulette Pearson; they have two children.

FURTHER READING

"Pride of place. . . ." CHRISTOPHER J. FARLEY. *Time*, Oct. 2, 1995.
"Denzel Washington. . . ." LYNN NORMENT. *Ebony*, Oct. 1995.
"A league of his own." LLOYD GROVE. *Vanity Fair*, Oct. 1995.
"Denzel Washington. . . ." *Jet*, Aug. 21, 1995.
"Denzel Washington. . . ." *Jet*, May 15, 1995.
"The players." ANDREW CORSELLO and AMY DONOHUE. *Philadelphia Magazine*, Dec. 1993.
Who's Hot!: Denzel Washington. EVAN KEITH. Dell, 1993.
"Denzel Washington." *People*, Dec. 28, 1992.
"Denzel Washington. . . ." LAURA B. RANDOLPH. *Ebony*, Dec. 1992.
"Denzel Washington." CLAUDE REED. *Us*, Dec. 1992.
"Denzel on Malcolm." JOE WOOD. *Rolling Stone*, Nov. 26, 1992.
"Denzel Washington." JOHN CLARK. *Premiere*, Nov. 1992.
"Playing with fire. . . ." LENA WILLIAMS. *New York Times Magazine*, Oct. 25, 1992.
"Washington, Denzel." *Current Biography*, July 1992.

Watanabe, Michio (1923–95) Born in Tochigi, Japan, politician Michio Watanabe attended the Tokyo University of Commerce and practiced accounting before beginning his political career. A member of the then-ruling Liberal Democratic Party, he won election to the national parliament in 1963, ultimately winning nine terms. Aggressive and ambitious—and often embarrassingly outspoken—he moved up to Cabinet level in the late 1970s, becoming a highly visible minister of finance (1980–82), minister of international trade and industry (1985–86), foreign minister (1991–93), and deputy prime minister (also 1991–93). He also rose within his party, ultimately making two failed attempts to gain its presidency, which would also have meant the post of prime minister. Watanabe created several major problems during his later period in public life, as when his derogatory comments about African-Americans caused an international outcry, forcing him to publicly apologize. He was survived by his wife, Sumiko, a daughter, and two sons. (d. Tokyo; September 15, 1995)

FURTHER READING

Obituary. *Times* (of London), Sept. 16, 1995.
Obituary. *Independent*, Sept. 16, 1995.
Obituary. *New York Times*, Sept. 16, 1995.

Wayne, David (Wayne James McKeekan; 1914–95) Michigan-born David Wayne began his long stage career in 1936, joining Cleveland's Shakespeare Repertory Company. He made his New York stage debut in 1939, in *The American Way,* saw World War II military service, and resumed his career after the war. His breakthrough stage role came in 1947, as the leprechaun in *Finian's Rainbow,* for which he won a Tony Award. In 1948, he created the Ensign Pulver role opposite Henry Fonda in *Mister Roberts,* and in 1953 won his second Tony, as Sakini in *The Teahouse of the August Moon.* Other notable roles were in *The Ponder Heart* (1956), *Say Darling* (1964), *The Happy Time* (1968), and Lincoln Center Company appearances in *After the Fall, Marco's Millions, But for Whom Charlie,* and *Incident at Vichy.* He also appeared in many films, among them *Portrait of Jennie* (1949), *The Tender Trap* (1955), *The Three Faces of Eve* (1957), and *The Front Page* (1974). He also starred in the television series "Norby" (1955), and had continuing roles in the series "The Good Life" (1971–72), "The Adventures of Ellery Queen" (1975–76), "Dallas" (1976), and "House Calls" (1979–82), as well as appearing in many television films and miniseries. His wife, actress Jane Gordon, predeceased him. He was survived by two daughters. (d. Santa Monica, California; February 9, 1995)

FURTHER READING

Obituary. *New York Times*, Feb. 13, 1995.
Obituary. *Variety*, Feb. 13, 1995.

Weaver, Sigourney (Susan Weaver; 1949–)

Actress Sigourney Weaver starred in 1995 as psychologist Helen Hudson, whose specialty is serial killers, in the crime thriller *Copycat,* directed by Jon Amiel and costarring Holly Hunter and Dermot Mulroney as homicide detectives, Harry Connick, Jr., as a serial killer, and William McNamara. The film's story line followed a familiar course; Weaver helps the police to find a serial killer, who in turn is stalking a terrified but ultimately victorious Weaver. The film was well received by the critics, with Weaver's portrayal praised for its intelligence and the film seen as one of the best in its genre.

Weaver also played a supporting role in the film version of Paul Rudnick's Off-Broadway comedy *Jeffrey,* set in New York's AIDS-afflicted gay and lesbian community and starring Steven Weber in the title role, as a gay man who ultimately gives up sex.

New York City–born Weaver was on stage from the mid-1970s, most notably in *Hurlyburly* (1984), *The Merchant of Venice* (1987), and in the 1991 London stage run of Chekhov's *The Three Sisters.* She is best known by far for the "Aliens" films, and for such films as *Eyewitness* (1981), *Deal of the Century* (1983), *The Year of Living Dangerously* (1983), *Ghostbusters* (1984; and its 1989 sequel), *Gorillas in the Mist* (1988; in the Oscar-nominated role of Dian Fossey), *Working Girl* (1988), *Ghostbusters II* (1989), *Alien 3* (1992), *1492: Conquest of Paradise* (1992), *Dave* (1993), and *Death and the Maiden*

(1994). Weaver attended Stanford and the Yale Drama School. She married James Simpson in 1984; they have one child.

FURTHER READING

"Sigourney Weaver." RYAN MURPHY. *Us,* Mar. 1995.
"Sigourney Weaver." ROBERT HOFLER. *Us,* June 1992.

West, Dorothy (1907–)

In an astonishing literary rebirth, Dorothy West—described as the last surviving member of the Harlem Renaissance—published not one, but two books in 1995. January saw publication of her second novel *The Wedding* (47 years after her first), focusing on the tangled relationships within an upper-middle-class Black family, especially the family's wayward daughters, who—to the dismay of their parents and neighbors—wish to marry men with skin of the wrong shade. The book was offered by the Book-of-the-Month Club and the Quality Paperback Book Club, and Oprah Winfrey bought the film rights to it. July saw publication of *The Richer, the Poorer: Stories, Sketches and Reminiscences,* containing 30 pieces, only 19 of which had been published before.

Daughter of a self-made man freed from slavery, West was raised in an upper-middle-class Black family in Boston. From age 10 she attended Boston's prestigious Girls' Latin School, and at 14 published her first short stories, in the Boston *Post.* Three years later, she moved to New York, after her story "The Typewriter" shared second prize (with Zora Neale Hurston) in a short story contest. While attending the Columbia School of Journalism she met many of the Black artists who would create the cultural flowering dubbed the Harlem Renaissance. After touring in the play *Porgy* at home and abroad, she returned to a job in the New York Ciy welfare department, publishing numerous short stories, many in the *New York Daily News* fiction section. She founded and edited the literary quarterly *Challenge* (1934–37) and, with Richard Wright, the short-lived left-political *New Challenge* (1937). In 1943, she moved permanently into her family's longtime vacation cottage on Martha's Vineyard. In 1948 she published her first novel, *The Living Is Easy,* reprinted in 1982. While continuing to write, she worked at the local newspaper as a billing clerk and later writer, and, summers, as a restaurant cashier.

FURTHER READING

"Mild West." CLAIRE MESSUD. *Guardian*, Sept. 28, 1995.
"Dorothy West's. . . ." VALARIE SMITH. *Emerge*, July 17, 1995.
"Dorothy West. . . ." SYBIL STEINBERG. *Publishers Weekly*, July 3, 1995.
"The last leaf." LYNN KARPEN. *New York Times Book Review*, Feb. 12, 1995.
"Rediscovering. . . ." DOROTHY A. CLARK. *American Visions*, Apr.–May 1993.
"A slave's daughter." EDIE CLARK. *Yankee*, Mar. 1991.

Whipple, Dorothy (1901–95)

Pediatrician Dorothy Whipple received her bachelor's and master's degrees from the University of Wisconsin, and then became the first married woman to enter Johns Hopkins Medical School. During the New Deal era, she became a considerable federal government figure, helping to develop the new Social Security Administration and serving as Commissioner of Labor Statistics. Her widely circulated and highly regarded book *Our American Babies* (1944), coupled with her revision of the federal "Infant Care" publication and her newspaper column, placed her at the center of the child-care movement of her day. From the early 1940s, she practiced in Arlington, Virginia, while continuing to publish a considerable body of articles on child-care questions. She was survived by a daughter and two sons. (d. Washington, D.C.; May 5, 1995)

FURTHER READING

Obituary. *JAMA, The Journal of the American Medical Association*, Dec. 13, 1995.
Obituary. *New York Times*, May 8, 1995.

Wickes, Mary (Mary Isabelle Wickenhauser; 1910–95)

For six decades, St. Louis–born Mary Wickes was a highly regarded character actress, largely in comic roles. After graduating from St. Louis's Washington University, she made her 1935 debut in repertory, and her Broadway debut in *Spring Dance* (1936). Her breakthrough role was that of Nurse Preen in George S. Kaufman's *The Man Who Came to Dinner,* a role she reprised in the 1941 film version, the first of her more than 50 films of the following five decades. Wickes also played in hundreds of television episodes and films, appearing in eight series, among them "The Halls of Ivy" (1954–55), "Dennis the Menace" (1959–61), "The Gertrude Berg Show" (1961–62), "Julia" (1968–71), and "Doc" (1975–76). She created the role of Mary Poppins in a 1949 "Studio One" telefilm, and received a 1962 best supporting actress Emmy nomination for her role in "The Gertrude Berg Show." In the early 1990s, she made a considerable comeback as Sister Mary Lazarus in the "Sister Act" films (1992; 1993). There were no survivors. (d. Los Angeles; October 22, 1995)

FURTHER READING

Obituary. *Variety*, Oct. 26, 1995.
Obituary. *New York Times*, Oct, 25, 1995.

Wigner, Eugene (1902–95)

Budapest-born Eugene Wigner, one of the leading physicists of the century, studied chemical engineering at the Berlin Institute of Technology in the early 1920s, and after earning his 1925 Ph.D. taught in Berlin. Working with such Hungarian colleagues as John von Neumann, Leo Szilard, and Edward Teller, he quickly emerged as a major figure in modern physics, with his work in group theory and quantum mechanics. A notable early book was *Group Theory and Its Application to Atomic Spectra* (1931). Wigner emigrated to the United States in 1930, and taught at Princeton University (1930–71). During the 1930s, his work on the constituent parts of atomic nuclei was part of the development of nuclear fission and the atom bomb. In 1939, he was one of those who urged Albert Einstein to write to President Franklin D. Roosevelt, advocating development of the atom bomb, and worked during the war on the Manhattan Project and on nuclear fuel reactor development. Although a political conservative and anti-Communist who urged the building of backyard bomb shelters in the 1950s, he later called the World War II use of the atomic bomb unnecessary. Wigner won the 1963 Nobel Prize in physics for his work in quantum mechanics. In addition to specialist works, he wrote *Symmetries and Reflections* (1970). He was survived by his wife, Eileen Hamilton Wigner, three children, and two sisters. (d. Princeton, New Jersey; January 1, 1995)

FURTHER READING

Obituary. *Independent*, Jan. 13, 1995.
Obituary. *New York Times*, Jan. 9, 1995.
Obituary. *Times* (of London), Jan. 4, 1995.
The Recollections of Eugene P. Wigner as Told to Andrew Szanton. ANDREW SZANTON. Plenum, 1992.

Williams, Robin (1952–) Actor Robin Williams in 1995 starred in the Christmas-season children's special effects spectacular *Jumanji*, about a supernatural board game named Jumanji, which conjures up real-life, heart-stopping jungle adventures for those who play. The film, directed by Joe Johnston, was based on the Chris Van Allsburg children's book and co-starred Bonnie Hunt, Kirsten Dunst, Bradley Pierce, and Bebe Neuwirth.

Williams also appeared as an incompetent doctor in the film comedy *Nine Months*, written and directed by Chris Columbus and costarring Hugh Grant, Julianne Moore, Tom Arnold, Joan Cusack, and Jeff Goldblum; and played a cameo role in the antic comedy *To Wong Foo, Thanks for Everything! Julie Newmar*. In November, Williams, Billy Crystal, and Whoopi Goldberg hosted *Comic Relief VII*, their fund-raising marathon to benefit the homeless.

Forthcoming were starring roles in the film *Jack*, directed by Francis Coppola and costarring Bill Cosby, Diane Lane, Brian Kerwin, and Jennifer Lopez; and as the Genie in the film *Aladdin and the King of Thieves*, the third in the "Aladdin" series. He was also slated to star in the film *The Birdcage*, directed by Mike Nichols and costarring Nathan Lane, Gene Hackman, and Dianne Wiest; and in a change of pace was scheduled to play Osric in Kenneth Branagh's film adaptation of Shakespeare's *Hamlet*, with Branagh starring and directing a celebrity cast.

Chicago-born Williams attended Claremont College, Marin College, and the Juilliard School. He began his career as a comic in cabaret, playing many West Coast clubs, and then moved into television, in variety, and then as a star in "Mork and Mindy" (1978–82). He became a leading film star of the 1980s, in such movies as *The World According to Garp* (1982), *Moscow on the Hudson* (1984), *Good Morning, Vietnam* (1987), *The Adventures of Baron Munchausen* (1989), *Dead Poets Society* (1989; he received a best actor Oscar nomination), *Cadillac Man* (1989), *Awakenings* (1990), *Dead Again* (1991), *Hook* (1991), *The Fisher King* (1991), *Aladdin* (1992), *Toys* (1992), *Mrs. Doubtfire* (1993), and *Being Human* (1994). In 1989, he published *To Be Somebody*. Formerly married to Valerie Velardi, Williams married Marsha Garces in 1989 and has three children.

FURTHER READING

"Robin Williams's. . . ." JESSE KORNBLUTH. *New York*, Nov. 22, 1993.
"Mr. and Mrs. Williams." LILLIAN ROSS. *New Yorker*, Sept. 20, 1993.
"Playboy interview. . . ." *Playboy*, Jan. 1992.
"A Peter Pan for yuppies." KURT ANDERSEN. *Time*, Dec. 16, 1991.
"Peter pandemonium." FRED SCHRUERS. *Premiere*, Dec. 1991.
"Robin Williams. . . ." JEFF GILES and MARK SELIGER. *Rolling Stone*, Feb. 21, 1991.
"Awake and sing." FRED SCHRUERS. *Premiere*, Jan. 1991.
"Talking with. . . ." CARSON JONES. *Redbook*, Jan. 1991.

Williams, Vanessa (1963–)

Up-and-coming singer and actress Vanessa Williams continued to build her career in 1995. Her hit single "The Sweetest Days," the title song of her 1994 album, was in the top 25 on the charts, while the album itself topped 1 million sales. Early in the year, untll she left the role, she also continued to be a headliner on Broadway in *Kiss of the Spider Woman*. She also generated another hit single from *The Sweetest Days* album, "The Way That You Love Me." Williams had yet another 1995 hit single, "Colors of the Wind," from the soundtrack album of the film *Pocahontas*.

On the acting side, she also made a very well-received appearance as Rosie, in a television film version of the theater musical *Bye Bye Birdie*, opposite Jason Alexander and Chynna Phillips. She also starred opposite Brooke Shields in the television hospital film *Nothing Lasts Forever,* and appeared in the theatrical film *Restoration*. Forthcoming was a starring role opposite Arnold Schwarzenegger and James Caan in the action film *Eraser,* directed by Chuck Russell.

As a Syracuse University student, in 1983, Williams first came to public attention as the first African-American Miss America, then received unwanted notoriety when *Penthouse* magazine found and printed nude photographs of her; in the succeeding uproar, she was forced to resign as Miss America. Instead of folding up, she went on with her planned career, which included a role in the Off-Broadway musical *One Man Band* (1985) and roles in such films as *Pickup Artist* (1986), *Harley Davidson and the Marlboro Man* (1991), *Another You* (1991), and *The Candyman* (1992). She also began her recording career, making her breakthrough with the hit album *The Right Stuff* (1988), which won three Grammy nominations. Her second album was *The Comfort Zone* (1991), containing the single "Save the Best for Last," which topped *Billboard*'s pop chart for five weeks; *Billboard* named it 1992's top adult contemporary hit and Williams top female rhythm and blues artist. She and Brian McKnight also had a number one hit duet in 1993 with "Love Is," from the soundtrack album of *Beverly Hills 90210*. Williams also hosted a weekly rhythm and blues show for the VH-1 cable network and had various television acting roles, including *Stompin' at the Savoy, Perry Mason: The Case of the Silenced Singer,* and *The Jacksons—An American Dream* (all 1992).

A native of Millwood, New York, Williams married Ramon Hervey II, formerly her publicist and now her manager, in 1987; they have two daughters and one son.

FURTHER READING

"Vanessa Williams. . . ." *Jet*, Jan. 16, 1995.
"Rock-a-bye. . . ." CHRISTINA KELLY. *Entertainment*, Dec. 16, 1994.
"Success is. . . ." JACK KROLL. *Newsweek*, Aug. 15, 1994.
"Vanessa Williams. . . ." JOAN MORGAN and AUDREY EDWARDS. *Essence*, Aug. 1994.
Who's Hot!: Vanessa Williams. G. DINERO. Dell, 1993.
"Vanessa Williams." BETSY BORNS. *Harper's Bazaar*, June 1992.
"Too legit to quit." ROB TANNENBAUM. *Us*, Apr. 1992.
"Vanessa Williams' . . . ." DEBORAH NORVILLE. *McCall's*, Apr. 1992.

Willingham, Calder (Calder Baynard, Willingham, Jr.; 1922–95)

Atlanta-born Calder Willingham attended a South Carolina military school, The Citadel, and the University of Virginia. His experiences at The Citadel were the basis of his acclaimed first novel, *End as a Man* (1947), a probing, satirical study of student sadism. He adapted the novel into the 1953 play and the 1975 film *The Strange One*. His works also included the novels *Geraldine Bradshaw* (1950), *Reach to the Stars* (1951), *Natural Child* (1952), *To Eat a Peach* (1955), *Eternal Fire* (1963), *Providence Island* (1969), *Rambling Rose* (1972), and *The Big Nickel* (1975), and the short story collection *The Gates of Hell* (1951). He adapted *Rambling Rose* into the 1991 Martha Coolidge film. Willingham was also a highly regarded screenwriter, who won a best screenplay Academy Award nomination for *The Graduate* (1967). His other screenplays included *Paths of Glory* (1957), *One-Eyed Jacks* (1961), *Little Big Man* (1971), and *Thieves Like Us* (1974). He was survived by his wife, Jane, two daughters, four sons, a sister, and a brother. (d. Laconia, New Hampshire; February 10, 1995)

FURTHER READING

Obituary. *Independent*, Feb. 25, 1995.
Obituary. *Variety*, Feb. 23, 1995.
Obituary. *Times* (of London), Feb. 22, 1995.
Obituary. *New York Times*, Feb. 21, 1995.

Willis, Bruce (1955–) Movie star Bruce Willis in 1995 once again appeared as heroic police officer John McClane in the big-budget action film *Die Hard with a Vengeance,* the third in his worldwide hit "Die Hard" series. John Mc-Tiernan directed and coproduced; the cast included Jeremy Irons in a change-of-pace role as a terrorist, Samuel L. Jackson as a Harlem shopkeeper drawn into the whirl of violence, Graham Greene, Colleen Camp, Larry Bryggman, Anthony Peck, Nick Wyman, and Sam Phillips. The film was another massive commercial hit and critical disaster.

Willis also starred in the post- and preapocalypse big-budget special-effects science fiction film *Twelve Monkeys,* directed by Terry Gilliam, screenplay by David Peoples and Janet Peoples, and costarring Madeleine Stowe, Brad Pitt, and Christopher Plummer. Willis is a time traveler to the early 1990s from post–worldwide plague 2035 A.D., a world in which the remaining 1 percent of humanity lives underground. Back in 1990, he winds up in a mental institution, thinking himself mad; Stowe is his psychiatrist and later lover, Pitt a disaster-predicting fellow inmate, Plummer Pitt's scientist father. The film is based on the brief 1962 film *La Jetée,* directed by Chris Marker.

Willis also appeared in the film *The Man from Hollywood,* written, directed, and coproduced by Quentin Tarantino, who also costarred; it was one of the group of four short films presented as the anthology film *Four Rooms,* all set in a hotel on New Year's Eve.

Forthcoming was a starring role in the film *Welcome to Jericho,* written and directed by Walter Hill and costarring Bruce Dern, William Sanderson, and David Patrick Kelly.

German-born Willis worked in the New York theater from the late 1970s, and appeared in several small film roles in the early 1980s. He emerged as a television star in the long-running series "Moonlighting" (1985–89). With *Blind Date* (1987), he moved into starring roles in films, including *Sunset* (1988), *Die Hard* (1988; and its 1989 sequel), *In Country* (1989), *The Bonfire of the Vanities* (1990), *Hudson Hawk* (1991), *Mortal Thoughts* (1991), *The Last Boy Scout* (1991), *Death Becomes Her* (1992), *Striking Distance* (1993), *Pulp Fiction* (1994), *North* (1994), and *Nobody's Fool* (1994). He was also the featured voice of baby Mikey in *Look Who's Talking* (1989) and *Look Who's Talking Too* (1990). Willis attended Montclair State College. He and Demi Moore married in 1987; they have three daughters.

FURTHER READING

"Samuel L. Jackson and. . . ." *Jet,* June 12, 1995.
"Bruce Willis. . . ." GARRY JENKINS. *Cosmopolitan,* June 1995.
"Bruce Willis. . . ." JAY McINERNEY. *Esquire,* May 1995.
"Brass bald. . . ." JEFF GORDINIER. *Entertainment,* May 19, 1995.
"Bruce on the loose." ANTHONY HADEN-GUEST. *Vanity Fair,* Jan. 1991.

Wilson, Harold (James Harold Wilson; 1916–95) British Labour Party leader and twice prime minister Harold Wilson, an economist and teacher, was born in Huddersfield and attended schools there and in Cheshire. He won a scholarship to Oxford University, graduating with high honors in 1937, taught at New College, Oxford, and then worked with economist William Beveridge at University College, Oxford. He continued to work with Beveridge and in government during World War II, then in 1945 won election as a Labour Member of Parliament. Wilson rose very swiftly in Clement Attlee's postwar Labour government, entering the Cabinet as president of the Board of Trade in 1947. He resigned from the Cabinet in 1951, but remained an increasingly powerful figure in the Labour Party, and in 1963 won election to the leadership of his party.

With the Labour victory in the 1964 elections, Wilson became prime minister. He won reelection in 1966, but a worsening economic situation and conflict within his party brought a surprise Tory electoral victory in 1970, and he was replaced as prime minister by Edward Heath. Wilson and Labour, in coalition with the Liberal Party, defeated the Tories in 1970, and Wilson again became prime minister. Labour won again in 1974, and he retained his office. His surprise resignation, on March 16, 1976, was a major event in British 20th-century political life.

For decades, allegations persisted about right-wing political plotting against him that forced his resignation, though the Tory government of Margaret Thatcher denied all charges and refused to appoint a commission of enquiry into the matter. In 1981, Wilson himself charged that there had been elements of a conspiracy against him. In 1988, former British intelligence officer Peter Wright, in his best-seller *Spycatcher*, alleged that Wilson had indeed been the victim of a faction within his own intelligence services. Thatcher government efforts to suppress the book were ultimately unsuccessful.

Wilson's books included *The Labour Government, 1964-70* (1971), *The Governance of Britain* (1976), *A Prime Minister on Prime Ministers* (1977), and two autobiographical works (1979; 1986). He was survived by his wife, Gladys Mary Baldwin Wilson, and their two sons. (d. London; May 24, 1995)

FURTHER READING

Obituary. *Times* (of London), May 25, 1995.
Obituary. *Independent*, May 25, 1995.
Obituary. *New York Times*, May 25, 1995.
"Epoch-making. . . ." VICTOR KEEGAN et al. *Guardian*, May 25, 1995.
Harold Wilson: A Life. AUSTEN MORGAN. Westview, 1992.

Wilson, Pete (Peter Barton Wilson; 1933–)

On June 22, 1995, California Republican governor Pete Wilson declared his candidacy for the 1996 Republican presidential nomination. He had in reality been in the race for several months by then, building a campaign fund and national campaign organization, although his campaign had been set back by his April throat surgery. A leading advocate of strict curbs on immigration and punitive action against illegal aliens, Wilson had also been seriously hurt when it was revealed that he had in 1978 hired a Mexican illegal alien as a housemaid, and had not paid legally required Social Security taxes for her. His 1995 late payment of the taxes and penalties in no way softened the damage to his public image. Beyond taking action against immigrants, Wilson's campaign focused on actions to dismantle affirmative action programs, cut social service spending, take strong anticrime action, and lower taxes. He at first opposed the Republican antiabortion platform plank, then seemed to soften his opposition, and then reaffirmed it. Wilson's once-popular candidacy faded in the summer and fall of 1995, his national campaign never really getting off the ground. He withdrew from the race on September 29.

Wilson was born in Lake Forest, Illinois. His 1955 B.A. was from Yale University, and his 1962 J.D. from the University of California at Berkeley. He saw military service in the Marine Corps (1955–58). He was a member of the California State Legislature (1966–71), mayor of San Diego (1971–83), and a two-term U.S. senator from California (1983–91) before becoming governor of California in 1991. With Lloyd Bentsen, he wrote *The Congress and Mexico: Bordering on Change* (1989). Wilson's second wife is Gayle Edlund.

FURTHER READING

"California schemer." DALE MAHARIDGE and ROMESH RATNESAR. *Mother Jones*, Nov.–Dec. 1995.
"Making waves. . . ." MARC COOPER. *Nation*, Sept. 18, 1995.
"Pete Wilson. . . ." WALTER SHAPIRO. *Esquire*, June 1995.
"Blowing in the wind." HAROLD JOHNSON. *National Review*, May 15, 1995.
"Riding the wave." HOWARD FINEMAN. *Newsweek*, May 22, 1995.
"Race and rage." HOWARD FINEMAN. *Newsweek*, Apr. 3, 1995.
"A Californian. . . ." GAYLE M. B. HANSON. *Insight on the News*, Apr. 3, 1995.
"California dreams. . . ." JIM IMPOCO. *U.S. News & World Report*, Mar. 20, 1995.
"Suburban everyman. . . ." JORDAN BONFANTE. *Time*, Mar. 13, 1995.
"The curse of the statehouse." ROBERT REINHOLD. *New York Times Magazine*, May 3, 1992.
"Five who fit the bill." *Time*, May 20, 1991.
"Sweet Pete. . . ." FRED BARNES, *New Republic*, Apr. 15, 1991.
"Wilson, Peter Barton." *Current Biography*, Apr. 1991.

Winfrey, Oprah (1954–)

Oprah Winfrey continues to be the queen of afternoon television talk-show hosts. Like other regular scheduled programming of all types, her show lost viewers in 1995, especially to live coverage of the O. J. Simpson trial, but at year's end, it was still firmly in the top spot, with ratings still sometimes nearly double those of her nearest competitor, usually "The Ricki Lake Show." Winfrey was particularly pleased at this because, since 1994, she has chosen to focus on more positive, constructive issues, rather than on victims and people in abnormal, dysfunctional relationships. For the second year in a row, she also won two Emmys, one for outstanding talk show host (for the fifth consecutive time) and one for best talk show (her second consecutive). She also appeared at the Academy Awards in March as a presenter.

She decided in October to extend her contract at least through the 1997–98 season. Meanwhile, through her Harpo Productions (that's Oprah, spelled backward), she made a four-year agreement with Capital Cities/ABC to produce six television movies as "Oprah Winfrey Presents," and a five-year agreement with the Walt Disney studios to develop and produce feature films, in some of which she may star. The first scheduled Disney film is *Beloved,* based on Toni Morrison's postslavery novel about a woman haunted by the baby daughter she murdered; Winfrey will star. Harpo purchased the film rights to several works, including Dorothy West's *The Wedding,* about plans for an interracial marriage; *Katherine,* by Chinese writer Anchee Min; *Third and Indiana,* a Steve Lopez novel set in South Philadelphia; and Karl Ackerman's first novel *The Patron Saint of Unmarried Women.* Also partnered with Capital Cities/ABC, she launched "Oprah Online," on America Online, in October. Forthcoming was a one-hour news special on the state of television news, to be hosted by Winfrey. On *Forbes*'s annual money list, she was listed as the second-highest-paid entertainer (after Steven Spielberg), with 1994 earnings of $72 million and estimated 1995 earnings of $74 million.

On a personal note, on a January show she admitted that she had used cocaine earlier in her life, with her then-boyfriend. She had never discussed it publicly, though she had written about it in her autobiography, originally scheduled for 1993, but later shelved. Winfrey's longtime companion Stedman Graham, a sports and entertainment marketing consultant, coauthored the 1995 book *The Ultimate Guide to Sporting Event Management and Marketing.*

Mississippi-born Winfrey attended Tennessee State University. She began her broadcasting career in 1972, as a reporter for WVOL radio while still in school and then for WTVF-TV (both in Nashville), before moving to Baltimore's WJZ-TV as coanchor in 1976. Becoming cohost of the station's morning show, she entered a new career, scoring a major success as the host of "AM Chicago" for Chicago's WLS-TV; it was renamed "The Oprah Winfrey Show" in 1984, and became a nationally syndicated hit show. She also starred in the 1989 television mini-series *The Women of Brewster Place* and the subsequent short-lived television prime-time series, "Brewster Place." She has appeared in several films, including *The Color Purple* (1985) and *Native Son* (1986); narrated *Scared Silent* (1992); and starred in the television film *There Are No Children Here* (1993). She was inducted into the Television Academy Hall of Fame in 1994.

FURTHER READING

"Oprah exhales." LIZ SMITH. *Good Housekeeping,* Oct. 1995.

"The Oprah. . . ." JOE DZIEMIANOWICZ and ZIBA KASHEF. *McCall's,* Aug. 1995.

"What Oprah really wants. . . ." KATHARINE KEST. *Redbook,* Aug. 1995.

"Oprah!" LAURA B. RANDOLPH. *Ebony,* July 1995.

"Inside story." AMBY BURFOOT. *Runner's World,* Jan. 1995.

"Seven who. . . ." GEOFFREY JOHNSON et al. *Chicago,* Jan. 1995.

"In full stride." LUCHINA FISHER et al. *People,* Sept. 12, 1994.

"Oprah: act two." DANA KENNEDY. *Entertainment,* Sept. 9, 1994.

"The big time!. . . ." *Cosmopolitan,* May 1994.

"Oprah at 40. . . ." MIRIAM KANNER. *Ladies Home Journal,* Feb. 1994.

Oprah Winfrey: Entertainer. NATHAN I. HUGGINS. Chelsea House, 1994.

Oprah Winfrey: The Real Story. GEORGE MAIR. Carol, 1994.

Meet Oprah Winfrey. AUDREEN BUFFALO. Random, 1993.

Oprah Winfrey: Media Success Story. ANNE SAIDMAN. Lerner, 1993.

Oprah Winfrey: Television Star. STEVE OTFINOSKI. Blackbirch, 1993.

Wolfman Jack (Robert Smith; 1938–95) Brooklyn-born Wolfman Jack began his long radio career in the late 1950s. He emerged as a leading disk jockey and host as Daddy Jules on WYOU in Newport News, Virginia (1960–61). He became a continent-wide radio personality as Wolfman Jack in the early 1960s, as a figure in "border radio," broadcasting from just across the Mexican border from stations with far more power than permitted by United States regulations. He broadcast rock and roll and rhythm and blues from XERF-AM, Via Cuña Cohuilla, Mexico (1963–66), then moving to XERB, Rosario, Mexico, a station powered at 250,000 watts, which reached most of North America. He played himself in the film *American Graffiti* (1973). Moving to New York, he worked at WNBC Radio, then moved to Los Angeles in 1974, there hosting a syndicated radio show and also moving into television as the host of NBC's "Midnight Special" (1973–81). In recent years, he had developed a syndicated radio show, broadcast from a Planet Hollywood restaurant in Washington, D.C. His autobiography was *Have Mercy!: Confessions of the Original Rock-and-Roll Animal* (1995), written with Byron Laursen. He was survived by his wife, Lou Lamb Smith, and by a daughter and a son. (d. Belvidere, North Carolina; July 1, 1995)

FURTHER READING

Obituary. *Billboard*, July 15, 1995.
Obituary. *Variety*, July 3, 1995.
Obituary. *Independent*, July 3, 1995.
Obituary. *New York Times*, July 2, 1995.

Wonder, Stevie (Steveland Judkins Morris; 1950–   ) In an extraordinary burst of creativity, after four years without a new album, Stevie Wonder issued *three* albums in 1995, all acclaimed, and any one of them enough to make it a very good and productive year for an ordinary mortal. He also embarked on a world tour, sang on the albums of other artists, and continued his lifelong commitment to a wide variety of social causes.

The first of his albums was *Conversation Peace,* which had been in development for several years. The work became a showpiece for a wide and varied range of groups and individual artists, among them Anita Baker, Sounds of Blackness, Branford Marsalis, and Ladysmith Black Mambazo, and contained such Wonder works as the title song, "Edge of Eternity," "Sensuous Whisper," "For Your Love," "Tomorrow Robins Will Sing," "Take the Time Out," "I'm New," and "My Love Is with You." "For Your Love" was also issued as a hit single. His second album was the "great hits" collection *Stevie Wonder's Original Musicquarium,* containing many of the hits that had made him a leading figure in popular music during the 1970s, including "You Are the Sunshine of My Life." His third album, issued in early December, was *Natural Wonder,* a two-CD set recorded live on tour in Osaka, Japan, and Tel Aviv, Israel; it included many of his standards and several new pieces as well.

Wonder also appeared in Quincy Jones's equally wide-ranging album, *Q's Jook Joint,* singing "Let the Good Times Roll" with Ray Charles and Bono. He also participated in the multi-artist single "Come By Here (Kum Ba Ya)," from the album *Motown Come Home,* and on the album *Inner City Blues—the Music of Marvin Gaye.*

Saginaw, Michigan–born singer, composer, and instrumentalist Stevie Wonder is one of the leading popular musicians of the past four decades, his extraordinary accomplishments made even more so because of his lifelong blindness. Wonder was a child prodigy, a multitalented musician who sang and played harmonica, piano, organ, and drums, and later composed much of his work for the synthesizer. His first record, for Motown, was *Little Stevie Wonder, the 12 Year*

Old Genius (1967). He went on to become one of the most popular musicians of the next three decades. Many of his songs have become American and worldwide standards, such as "My Cherie Amour" (1969), the Grammy-winning "You Are the Sunshine of My Life" (1972), "Superstition" (1973), "Living for the City" (1975), and the Oscar-winning "I Just Called to Say I Love You" (1984). His many records include such works as the Grammy-winning *Innervisions* (1973), the Grammy-winning *Songs in the Key of Life* (1976), *Journey Through the Secret Life of Plants* (1979), *In Square Circle* (1986), *Characters* (1987), and *Music from the Movie "Jungle Fever"* (1991).

FURTHER READING

"In a gangsta-rap world. . . ." DAVID RITZ. *Rolling Stone*, July 13, 1995.
"Stevie Wonder returns. . . ." ROBERT E. JOHNSON. *Jet*, May 8, 1995.
"Stevie Wonder." AMY LINDEN. *Us*, May 1995.
"The Wonder stuff." CHRIS WELLS. *Guardian*, Feb. 24, 1995.
Stevie Wonder: Musician. NATHAN I. HUGGINS, ed. Chelsea House, 1995.
"Stevie's jungle adventure." JAMES T. JONES, IV. *Down Beat*, Sept. 1991.

Wood, Evelyn (1909–95) Utah-born reading teacher Evelyn Wood received her degree from the University of Utah in 1929, and embarked on a career as a high school English teacher. She developed a keen interest in developing remedial reading programs; in 1958, she coauthored the book *Reading Skills*. In 1959, she and her husband, Doug Wood, founded the Evelyn Wood Reading Dynamics Institute, and with it a speed-reading technique and movement that swept the country. Her technique involved reading down the page, use of the hand on the page as a pacer, and the reading of connected groups of words, rather than one word at a time, and often did result in dramatic reading speed gains. Short-term retention was also often good, although the questions of long-term retention and the use of the technique as an aid to learning were always matters of debate. Her career came to a premature end after she suffered a stroke in 1976. She was survived by a daughter. (d. Tucson, Arizona; August 26, 1995)

FURTHER READING

Obituary. *New York Times*, Aug. 30, 1995.

Woods, Eldrick: See **Woods, Tiger.**

Woods, James (1947–) Veteran actor James Woods costarred in three quite notable films in 1995. In the highly controversial biographical film *Nixon,* directed, cowritten, and coproduced by Oliver Stone, he played once-powerful White House Chief of Staff H. R. Haldeman, thought by many at the time to wield power second only to that of his president, Richard M. Nixon; Anthony Hopkins played the disgraced, very nearly impeached president. Haldeman resigned in 1973, later to be convicted on Watergate-connected charges and jailed for 18 months.

Woods also costarred in Martin Scorsese's film *Casino,* set in Las Vegas and the illegal world in the 1970s, opposite Robert De Niro as mob-connected gambler and casino operator Sam "Ace" Rothstein, Sharon Stone as Las Vegas gambler Ginger McKenna Rothstein, and Joe Pesci as mad-dog killer Nicky Santoro. Woods plays McKenna's small-time con-man lover, before and during her marriage to Rothstein.

On television, Woods played a leading role as defense lawyer Danny Davis, opposite Mercedes Ruehl as prosecutor Leah Rubin, in the film *Indictment: The McMartin Trial,* about the six-year-long Los Angeles McMartin preschool child sexual abuse trial, which ended with a hung jury and dismissal of all charges by the court. Sada Thompson, Henry Thomas, Lolita Davidovich, and Shirley Knight costarred. For his role, Woods received a best lead actor in a miniseries or special Emmy nomination, a best actor in a miniseries or telefilm Golden Globe nomination, and a best actor in a movie or miniseries CableAce award nomination.

Still forthcoming were starring roles in the films *Stranger Things,* directed by Jason Alexander and costarring Lolita Davidovich and Joe Mantegna; and *Killer,* written and directed by Tim Metcalfe.

Utah-born Woods appeared on the New York stage and in films in the early 1970s, and emerged as a star in such films as *The Onion*

Field (1979), *Fast Walking* (1982), *Split Image* (1982), *Videodrome* (1983), *Once Upon a Time in America* (1984), *Against All Odds* (1984), *Joshua Then and Now* (1985), *Best Seller* (1987), *Cop* (1987), *True Believer* (1989), *Immediate Family* (1989), *The Hard Way* (1991), *The Boys* (1991), *Diggstown* (1992), *Straight Talk* (1992), *The Specialist* (1994), and *The Getaway* (1994). He has also appeared in many telefilms, winning an Emmy for *Promise* (1986), and a second Emmy as Bill Wilson, a cofounder of Alcoholics Anonymous, in *My Name is Bill W* (1989), and starring as Roy Cohn in *Citizen Cohn* (1992). Woods attended the University of California and the Massachusetts Institute of Technology. He has been married twice.

FURTHER READING

"A trip through. . . ." BERNARD WEINRAUB. *Cosmopolitan*, Oct. 1994.

Woods, Tiger (Eldrick Woods; 1975–   ) In August 1995, history repeated itself when Tiger Woods won his second consecutive U.S. Amateur Golf Championship. In August 1994, he had been the youngest person and the first Black (actually African-Asian-American) golfer ever to win the title, as he had been with his first U.S. Junior Amateur title in 1991. Woods was only the ninth amateur, and the first in 12 years, to successfully defend the title. He is also the only person ever to win three consecutive U.S. Junior Amateur Championships (1991–93), and to win both the junior amateur and amateur titles, and the first male golfer since the great Bobby Jones to win a USGA association title in five consecutive years.

Woods gained enormous media and spectator attention as he made his debuts at the Masters and the U.S. and British opens, the youngest person ever to play on the PGA Tour. However he was hampered by injuries, including a mid-year shoulder separation, back spasms at the Masters, and a wrist sprain that forced him to withdraw from the U.S. Open. In December 1994, he had arthroscopic surgery on his left knee.

Playing for the Stanford University golf team, he won several college tournaments, was named Pac-10 player of the year, and was named to the All-America team, with a 71.37 scoring average, while maintaining a B average. As an amateur, Woods still plays under stringent NCAA rules; he was briefly suspended from the Stanford team in November because Arnold Palmer took him to dinner and paid the bill; Woods was reinstated after he reimbursed Palmer.

Californian Woods was swinging a golf club from his high chair at ten months, according to his father, and played nine holes in under 50 strokes by age three. In his 1994 title win, Woods made the greatest comeback in U.S. Amateur history, coming from six strokes down to take a one-stroke victory, playing four under par for the match's last 12 holes. Woods graduated from high school in 1994 and entered Stanford University, studying business and economics. Other notable wins include the Western Amateur, Southern California Amateur, and Pacific Northwest Amateur, all in 1994.

FURTHER READING

"Encore! Encore!" TIM ROSAFORTE. *Sports Illustrated*, Sept. 4, 1995.
"Goodness gracious. . . ." RICK REILLY. *Sports Illustrated*, Mar. 27, 1995.
"The comeback kid." TIM ROSAFORTE. *Sports Illustrated,* Sept. 5, 1994.
"Tiger on the tee." ROBERT E. HOOD. *Boys' Life*, Sept. 1992.

Wright, Eric: See **Eazy-E.**

Wright, Peter Maurice (1916–95)

Chesterfield-born British electronic surveillance specialist, intelligence officer, and author Peter Wright, a largely self-taught physicist, worked in naval research during World War II, and after the war worked in military electronics research. In 1950, he joined MI5, the British intelligence service, as a part-time scientific adviser, and in 1955 became a full-time employee, rising through that service to become a deputy chief of science (1962), and head of counterespionage research (1967–76), until his retirement.

Wright became the center of a storm of controversy on publication of his 1987 book *Spycatcher,* written with Paul Greengrass, which Margaret Thatcher's Conservative government unsuccessfully tried to suppress—in the process creating tremendous publicity for the book, which became an international best-seller. In his book, Wright made a number of sensational charges, among them that former MI5 head Roger Hollis had been a Soviet spy, and that a faction within MI5 had conspired to force the surprise resignation of Labour Party Prime Minister Harold Wilson in 1976. Claiming violation of the British Official Secrets Act, and simultaneously claiming that the book was full of falsehoods, the Thatcher government suppressed publication in Britain, and brought suit to suppress publication in Australia. But it could do nothing about American publication of the book, and in 1988 the Australian courts found for Wright and publication. Later in 1988, the British House of Lords unanimously refused to enjoin publication in Britain.

Wright was survived by his wife, Lois, two daughters, and a son. (d. Tasmania; April 27, 1995)

FURTHER READING

Obituary. *Independent,* Apr. 28, 1995.
Obituary. *Times* (of London), Apr. 28, 1995.
Obituary. *New York Times,* Apr. 28, 1995.

Wu, Harry (1937–)

On July 8, 1995, Chinese-American human rights activist Harry Wu was arrested by Chinese border guards as he attempted to enter western China from Kazakhstan, seeking further evidence that would expose the abuses of the Chinese prison and labor camp system. Wu had been imprisoned by the Chinese government before; he had been held in labor camps for 19 years (1960–79), and well knew that capture might mean lifelong imprisonment or execution. His arrest generated worldwide protest, made far more effective by the threat that Hillary Rodham Clinton might not attend the September United Nations International Women's Conference in Beijing. Pressure swiftly mounted, and despite hard-line Chinese government statements and a televised "confession," in which he actually admitted very little, he was released on August 25. His release came in the form of an "expulsion" from China, the day after a government court convicted him of spying and sentenced him to a 15-year prison term—although in fact it specified that Wu be expelled, not imprisoned. Hillary Rodham Clinton did attend the Beijing UN International Women's Conference.

Also in 1995, Wu published two books: his autobiography, *Bitter Winds: A Memoir of My Years in China's Gulag,* written with Carolyn Wakeman; and *Rural Enterprises in China,* coedited with Christopher Findlay and Andrew Watson.

Shanghai-born Wu was a college student in Beijing in the late 1950s; encouraged by Mao Zedong's invitation to criticize the Communist regime—the Hundred Flowers Campaign (1957–58)—Wu did so, and like so many others was in return imprisoned as an antistate dissenter. He was "rehabilitated" in 1979, and was able to leave China in 1984, gaining asylum in the United States. In exile, he had become a leading critic of China's gulag, or penal system, returning to China many times for additional proofs of the inhumanity of the system, such as the film shown on television's "60 Minutes" in 1991.

Wu became a U.S. citizen in 1992. Previously married in China, Wu is now married to Ching Lee Wu; they work together in the Laogai Legal Foundation; *laogai* means "reform through labor," the Chinese government's slogan and name for its prison system. He is also a resident scholar at the Hoover Institution at Stanford University.

FURTHER READING

"Talking again. . . ." Lincoln Kaye. *World Press Review,* Oct. 1995.
"The trials of. . . ." Mike Tharp. *U.S. News & World Report,* Sept. 11, 1995.
"Harry the hero. . . ." Ruaridh Nicoll. *The Observer,* Sept. 3, 1995.

Yeltsin, Boris Nikolayevich (1931–)

Russian President Boris Yeltsin continued to face basic, largely unresolved problems during 1995, although he did not face the kind of armed insurrection that had nearly brought full-scale civil war in 1993. Although Russia's new market economy had brought some jobs and distribution of goods and services, it still worked very badly, had spawned a new class of rapacious rich, brought runaway crime, triggered massive inflation, taken the remaining savings of millions of Russians, destroyed the pensions of millions more, and done nothing to solve the country's health-care crisis. The skyrocketing Russian death rate, far higher than it had been under communism, was like that of some of the world's poorest countries.

The war in breakaway Chechnya, which had begun in December 1993, raged until midsummer 1995. Several divisions of Russian troops, with armor and aircraft, finally took the Chechen capital, Grozny, but could not defeat the poorly armed Chechens, who never surrendered, instead continuing to fight from mountain positions. The July 30 peace treaty, though seeming to end the war, did not; by year's end, Chechen guerrillas had set bombs in Moscow and Grozny and attacked Russian forces throughout Chechnya, demanding full autonomy, while the Russian military set itself to fight a long, extremely unpopular war.

In these overall circumstances, Yeltsin's prestige and popularity hit new lows in Russia. Seeking the appearance of strength, as resurgent Communists and nationalists gained popularity, Yeltsin appeared to oppose the spread of NATO into Eastern Europe and the Western intervention in Bosnia, but later gave way on both issues after his late-October minisummit meeting with President Bill Clinton.

Yeltsin's political position was also greatly damaged by the state of his personal health, which cast doubt on his ability to continue to lead his country during 1996. He was hospitalized for a heart condition on July 11, returned to work August 7, was again hospitalized for a heart condition on October 26, and had not fully returned to work at year's end.

In the December 17 Russian parliamentary elections, Yeltsin's disunited reformist allies suffered significant losses, while the resurgent Communist Party more than doubled its seats in parliament, winning almost one third of the vote. On the other hand, right-wing nationalist parties lost a good deal of ground. Yeltsin's—and Russia's—political future remained a matter of conjecture.

Yeltsin worked as an engineer (1955–68), then went into Communist Party work in his home city of Sverdlovsk. During the early 1980s, he strongly supported and was close to Mikhail Gorbachev; Yeltsin moved into far higher party positions in 1985, when Gorbachev came to power. He was mayor of Moscow (1985–87) and secretary of the Communist Party central committee (1985–86). He moved into opposition in 1987, becoming a leader of those who felt that reform was not proceeding quickly enough; he was for some years a "maverick" in Soviet politics who was not taken very seriously, and whose relations with Gorbachev were often abrasive.

In 1989, Yeltsin won the Moscow elections to the Congress of People's Deputies by an overwhelming majority, and became an opposition leader in the Soviet parliament. In March 1990, he refocused, winning election as a delegate to the Russian Federation's Supreme Soviet. On May 29, 1990, he was elected president of the Russian Federation and began a campaign to secure greater Russian autonomy from the central government. In July 1990, he resigned from the Communist Party.

On August 19, 1991, Gorbachev was placed under house arrest while vacationing in the Crimea, and a right-wing Communist coup began. Yeltsin became the center of opposition to the coup, gathering huge unarmed crowds and key capital military units around him at the White House, the Russian parliament building in Moscow. On August 21, the aborted coup collapsed, Yeltsin was a national hero, and a second, democratic Russian Revolution quickly swept away the remnants of Soviet communism and the Soviet state. Gorbachev on his return to Moscow was unable to hold the Soviet state together, or in the following period to resist the rise of Yeltsin to effective power in the Russian Republic.

During the balance of 1991 and throughout 1992, Yeltsin gambled much on crash market economy reforms, without much success and encountering growing conservative opposition, which was able to blame him for the continuing economic disaster, while itself greatly contributing to it by blocking major elements of the reform program. After a series of parliamentary and electoral confrontations, some conservatives, led by Vice President Alexandr Rutskoi and parliamentary speaker Ruslan Khasbulatov, went over to armed insurrection. On October 3, 1993, an estimated 5,000 marchers broke through riot police lines to gather before the Russian White House, going over to armed action en route, with small military formations in the line of march opening automatic weapons fire on the police during the breakthrough. Rutskoi, addressing the crowd, urged them to form military units and seize the Moscow broadcasting center, the mayor's office, and the Kremlin. Previously prepared formations, swelled by new recruits, stormed and took the mayor's office and attacked the broadcasting center. On October 4, the armed forces responded on behalf of the government; armored infantry and airborne units surrounded, shelled, and forced the surrender of rebel forces at the Russian White House, in an action that took 12 hours.

Yeltsin has published an autobiography, *Against the Grain* (1990), and *The Struggle for Russia* (1994). He attended the Urals Polytechnic Institute. He is married to Naina Iosifovna Girinia, a Urals Polytechnic–trained civil engineer, and has two daughters.

FURTHER READING

"No laughing matter. . . ." SANDER THOENES and BRUCE B. AUSTER. *U.S. News & World Report*, Nov. 6, 1995.
"Heading for the summit." JAMES R. GAINES. *Time*, May 8, 1995.
"The wrong man. . . ." *Economist*, Jan. 7, 1995.
Boris Yeltsin: First President of Russia. CALVIN C. MILLER. M. Reynolds, 1995.
"Shooting down. . . ." ALAN COOPERMAN. *U.S. News & World Report*, Dec. 26, 1994.
"A presidential portrait." OLGA KUCHKINA. *Russian Life*, Summer 1994.
"The man in charge." MAYNARD PARKER. " 'I never wavered. . . .' " *Newsweek*, May 2, 1994.
" 'The president. . . .' " JOHN KOHAN and YURI ZARAKHOVICH. *Time*, Apr. 26, 1993.
"The softest coup. . . ." MARTIN MALIA. *New Republic*, Apr. 19, 1993.
World Leaders—Boris Yeltsin. SHLOMO LAMBROZA. Rourke, 1993.
Boris Yeltsin. KATE S. SCHECTER. Chelsea House, 1993.
Boris Yeltsin: A Political Biography. VLADIMIR SOLOVYOV and ELENA KLEPIKOVA. Putnam, 1992.
Gorbachev–Yeltsin: The Fall of Communism. STUART A. KALLEN. Abdo & Daughters, 1992.
Gorbachev, Yeltsin and the Last Days of the Soviet Empire. NEIL FELSHMAN. Thomas Dunne/St. Martin's, 1992.
Boris Yeltsin: Man of the People. ELEANOR H. AYER. Dillon/Macmillan, 1992.
Boris Yeltsin: Russia's First President. JOHN MORRISON. NAL-Dutton, 1991.

Yglesias, José

Yglesias, José (1919–95) Tampa-born novelist and essayist José Yglesias studied at Black Mountain College (1946–47) and was a film critic for *The Daily Worker* before embarking upon his career as a novelist and social commentator, whose main focus was on Hispanic-American life, in his native United States and in

Spanish-speaking countries. His first book was the novel *A Wake in Ybor City* (1963), set in the Cuban-American section of Tampa. Among his other novels were *An Orderly Life* (1968), *The Truth About Them* (1971), *Double Double* (1974), *The Kill Price* (1976), *Home Again* (1987), and *Tristan and the Hispanics* (1989). He also published several nonfiction works, including *The Goodbye Land* (1967), about his father's home province of Galicia, Spain; *The Fist of the Revolution* (1968), about Cuba during the early days of the Castro government; *Down There* (1970), set in contemporary Latin America, and *The Franco Years,* set in Spain. Yglesias was also a prolific short story and magazine article writer. He was survived by a daughter, two sons (one of them the writer Rafael Yglesias), and a sister. His former wife was author Helen Bassine Yglesias. (d. New York City; November 7, 1995)

FURTHER READING

Obituary. *New York Times*, Nov. 8, 1995.

Young, Neil (1945–) Veteran rock star Neil Young, always as attractive to the younger generation as to his own, found himself equally attracted to the new generation in rock music in 1995. One major result was the album *Mirror Ball,* a collaboration between Young and the up-and-coming rock group Pearl Jam, the result being widely viewed as opening huge new "Gen-

eration X" audiences to Young and his music. Among the songs featured were "Song X," "Act of Love," "Throw Your Hatred Down," and "Downtown," which became a hit single, while the album headed for its first million sales.

Young was named top singer of the year at Canada's Juno Awards ceremony. He received a best male rock vocal Grammy nomination for "Philadelphia," from the soundtrack of the film *Philadelphia,* and a best rock album Grammy nomination for *Sleeps with Angels,* by Young and Crazy Horse. His 1983 video *Human Highway* was also rereleased.

On the social service side of his life, Young continued to be associated with Farm Aid and with the Bridge School for children with disabilities. On the business side, he and his manager, Elliot Roberts, launched Vapor Records. They announced that the label's first project would be the music to the soundtrack of the forthcoming film *Dead Men,* which includes performances by Young.

Born in Toronto, Ontario, singer-songwriter-instrumentalist Young played in various bands before he and Stephen Stills formed the group Buffalo Springfield (1966–68). He began his solo recording career with the albums *Neil Young* (1969) and *After the Goldrush* (1970), then broke through to wide solo popularity with *Harvest* (1972), both the album and the single "Heart of Gold" becoming number one hits. Other solo albums included *Time Fades Away* (1973), *On the Beach* (1974), *American Stars 'n' Bars* (1977), *Decade* (1977), *Comes a Time* (1978), *Hawks and Doves* (1980), *Trans* (1983), *Neil and The Shocking Pink: Everybody's Rocking* (1983), *Old Ways* (1985), *Freedom* (1989), *Ragged Glory* (1990), *Harvest Moon* (1992), *Unplugged* (1993), and *Sleeps with Angels* (1994).

Young is also well known for his association with various groups. Crosby, Stills, Nash, & Young albums included *Deja Vu* (1970), *Four-Way Street* (1971), *So Far* (1974), and *American Dream* (1988); Young and Stills also recorded *Long May You Run* (1976). His association with Crazy Horse began even earlier, and produced *Everybody Knows This Is Nowhere* (1969), *Tonight's the Night* (1975), *Rust Never Sleeps* (1979), *Live Rust* (1987), *Ragged Glory* (1990), and *Weld, Arc,* and *Arc Weld* (all 1991). He also composed soundtracks for the films *Journey Through the Past* (1973; album 1972), *Where the Buffalo Roam* (1980), and *Human Highway* (1982).

Young and his wife, Pegi, have a son and a daughter; he also has a son from a relationship with Carrie Snodgress.

FURTHER READING

Neil Young: His Life and Music. MICHAEL HEATLEY. Trafalgar, 1995.
A Dreamer of Pictures: Neil Young: The Man and His Music. DAVID DOWNING. Da Capo, 1995.
Neil Young, the "Rolling Stone" Files. . . . ROLLING STONE EDITORS, eds. Hyperion, 1994.
Neil Young: A Visual Documentary. Omnibus, 1994.
"Forever Young." ALAN LIGHT. *Rolling Stone*, Jan. 21, 1993.
Neil Young: Don't Be Denied. JOHN EINARSON. InBook, 1993.
"Neil Young. . . ." JAS OBRECHT. *Guitar Player*, Mar. 1992.

Young, Steve (Jon Steven Young; 1961–   )
Steve Young started 1995 on a high. In mid-January, in the National Football Conference championships, Young and his San Francisco 49ers handed the two-time defending Super Bowl champion Dallas Cowboys a devastating defeat. Then, in Super Bowl XXIX, they defeated the San Diego Chargers in equally convincing fashion. Young himself completed 24 out of 36 passes, for a total of 325 yards and six touchdowns (which broke the Super Bowl record previously set by Joe Montana, his illustrious predecessor as 49ers quarterback). The first of

these, a 44-yard touchdown pass to Jerry Rice on the game's third play, was the fastest touchdown in Super Bowl history, 84 seconds into the first quarter. Young's four touchdown passes in the first half also tied a Super Bowl record; he even led the game in rushing, with 49 yards. Not surprisingly, he was unanimously named the Super Bowl's Most Valuable Player. With this performance, which had capped a 1994 MVP season, many observers felt Young had finally stepped out from Montana's shadow. Young was also starting NFC quarterback in the February 1995 Pro Bowl.

In the 1995 season, however, an injury to Young's left shoulder (his throwing arm), which eventually required arthroscopic surgery, left Young out of the MVP running. With his and other injuries, the 49ers at one point fell to a record of 5-4, but then—with Young coaching from the sidelines—the team rallied behind backup quarterback Elvis Grbac to deal the Cowboys another crushing defeat. From then on, the 49ers' record began to improve, and Young returned to lead the team to a division-leading final regular-season record of 11-5. In the playoffs, however, they were badly beaten by the rising Green Bay Packers and were unable to defend their championship title.

Overall, Young had a quarterback rating of 92.3, which was fifth in the league. However, his completion percentage still led the league, at 66.9, with 299 completions on 447 attempts, for a total of 3,838 yards and an average of 7.16 yards per pass, with 11 interceptions. In the December 18 game against Minnesota, Young set the season record for most passing yards, with 425 yards, and three passing touchdowns. Young was again selected to the Pro Bowl, but this time to play behind Green Bay's Brett Favre, who also succeeded Young as the league MVP.

Also in 1995, Young published *Football: The Perfect Pass: To Parents and Kids,* written with Tom Newell, part of the Backyard Coach series.

A great-great-great-grandson of the Mormon leader Brigham Young, Steve Young was born in Salt Lake City and attended high school in Greenwich, Connecticut. At Brigham Young University, he was a consensus All-American and runner-up for the Heisman Trophy; in an extraordinary senior year, he completed 306 of 429 passes, for 3,902 yards and 33 touchdowns, setting a then-record pass percentage of .713, and winning 11 of 12 games, passing for over 300 yards in all but two. In 1991, Young led the list in *Sports Illustrated*'s statistical analysis of college quarterback records, their personal statistics and team winning percentages. He began his professional career with the L.A. Express of the U.S. Football League (1984–85), becoming the first professional football player ever to rush for 100 yards and pass for 300 yards in the same game. Released by the Express, Young signed with the Tampa Bay Buccaneers (1985–86), then was traded to the San Francisco 49ers (1987–   ). Young saw only sporadic playing time until 1991, when starting quarterback Joe Montana was injured. Taking over that role, Young became the highest-rated quarterback in the National Football League four seasons running (1991–94), all four times with over a 100-point rating, and was twice named the league's Most Valuable Player (1992; 1994). His rating of 112.8 for the 1994 season broke Montana's record of 112.4, set in 1989. He has been named to the Pro Bowl four times (1992–95). Young completed law school at BYU in the off-season in 1992.

FURTHER READING

"The arm with. . . ." Peter Richmond. *GQ*, Sept. 1995.

"Steve Young.. . . ." Dan Dieffenbach. *Sport*, July 1995.

"Simply captivating." Paul Attner. *Sporting News*, Feb. 6, 1995.

"Second to one." Michael Knisley et al. *Sporting News*, Sept. 19, 1994.

"Young, Steve." *Current Biography*, Oct. 1993.

"Steve Young." Mark Fainaru. *Sport*, Aug. 1993.

"Quarterbacks quantified." Douglas S. Looney. Fall 1991. "The Young 49ers." Rick Reilly. Sept. 30, 1991. "Young and rich." Peter King. Sept. 16, 1991. *Sports Illustrated*.

Z

Zedillo Ponce de León, Ernesto

(1951–   ) Incoming Mexican president Ernesto Zedillo Ponce de León took office on December 1, 1994, succeeding President Carlos Salinas de Gortari, and was immediately plunged into a massive financial crisis that grew into a scandal-punctuated set of major political and economic crises. Faced with a worldwide speculative attack on the value of the peso, accompanied by a catastrophic stock market crash, Zedillo's government on December 20, 1994, sharply devalued the peso and left it unsupported—that is, floating free—in international money markets. In early January, with peso and stock market both down by a third of their former value, Zedillo announced a new austerity program, bolstered by promised emergency economic bailout loans from the United States and other countries. On February 21, Zedillo concluded the specific bailout agreement and announced even harsher austerity measures that guaranteed the loss of at least a million jobs in Mexico, and sharply reversed the course of the formerly growing Mexican economy, while promising more than $50 billion in bailout funds from abroad, including $20 billion from the United States, half of what was orginally promised and then rejected by the Republican-dominated U.S. Congress. On October 10, Zedillo visited Washington and met with President Bill Clinton for the first time since Zedillo's inauguration, bringing with him a token payment on the principal of the U.S. loan, achieved by borrowing money through a bond issue.

On the internal political side, Zedillo was plagued by the still-unsettled Chiapas insurgency, and even more by a series of assassination and financial scandals reaching into the highest levels of his own party and government. All were as yet unresolved late in the year, although by then Raúl Salinas de Gortari, brother of former present Carlos Salinas de Gortari, had been arrested and charged with playing a central role in the September 1994 assassination of ruling Institutional Revolutionary Party (PRI) secretary general José Francisco Ruiz Massieu. Former Mexican deputy attorney general Mario Ruiz Massieu had been arrested by the U.S. authorities at Newark airport, reportedly in connection with several other Mexican murder and corruption scandals. Former president Carlos Salinas de Gortari, though not charged with complicity in any illegal acts, had left Mexico, going into exile in the United States.

Born in Mexico City, Zedillo studied economics at National Polytechnic Institute, and went to the United States to pursue graduate studies in economics, earning his Ph.D. at Yale University in 1981. Returning home, he worked as an economist with Mexico's national bank (1982–87), joined the budget and planning ministry in 1987, and was appointed budget and planning minister by incoming president Carlos Salinas de Gortari in 1988. He moved to the education ministry in 1992. He became his party's presidential candidate in 1994, after the assassination of PRI candidate Luis Colosio Murrieta, whose campaign Zedillo was managing. Zedillo was elected president on August 21, 1994, winning more than 50 percent of the vote.

FURTHER READING

"Does Mexico's. . . ." LINDA ROBINSON. *U.S. News & World Report*, Dec. 25, 1995.
" 'I want justice.' " JAMES R. GAINES et al. *Time*, June 19, 1995.
"Under the volcano.. . . ." ARTHUR JOHNSON. *Canadian Business*, June 1995.
" 'I have great. . . .' " MICHAEL ELLIOTT and TIM PADGETT. *Newsweek*, Apr. 10, 1995.
"Zedillo hits. . . ." GERI SMITH and ELISABETH MALKIN. *Business Week*, Apr. 3, 1995.
" 'We have to. . . .' " WARREN CARAGATA. *Maclean's*, Dec. 5, 1994.
"The politics of fear." JEFF SALLOT and DAMIAN FRASER. *World Press Review*, June 1994.

Zhirinovsky, Vladimir Volfovich

(1946–) Russian fascist and ultranationalist Vladimir Zhirinovsky, head of the Liberal Democratic Party, lost strength in 1995, despite his continuing attempt to fan right-wing fears and hates. In the December 1995 Russian parliamentary elections, his party won less than half the votes it had won two years earlier, with 11 percent instead of 23 percent. Underscoring the fragility of Zhirinovsky's support, most of his lost voters seemed to have gone over to the Communist Party, which more than doubled its showing. Zhirinovsky could still be counted on to seek headlines at home and abroad during 1996, but for the present at least he seemed a diminished threat to Russian democracy and world peace.

Kazakhstan-born Zhirinovsky reportedly saw some military service before working as a lawyer for Mir Publications (1983–89). He was a founder of the Liberal Party of the Soviet Union in 1990. In the December 1993 Russian elections, a chilling development was the emergence of Zhirinovsky's fascist and ultranationalist Liberal Democratic Party, which won the single largest proportion of the popular vote, variously reported as in the 18–25 percent range. However, the party won too few parliamentary seats to form a government.

Though he denied it after the election, the ultranationalist Zhirinovsky clearly ran as a fascist. During the election campaign, he among other things threatened to use nuclear weapons against Japan; demanded the return of Alaska, with compensation, from the United States; made thinly veiled anti-Jewish threats; attacked and threatened the U.S. and Germany for interfering in Russian internal affairs; and threatened reprisals against the countries of the former Soviet Union for alleged discrimination against Russians. He and his views were condemned by President Bill Clinton and a wide range of other world leaders, deeply concerned about the possibility that the Russian nuclear arsenal might fall into his or other undesirable hands.

Zhirinovsky has published the autobiography *The Last Play for the South* (1993). He attended Moscow State University. He has been married to Galina Zhirinovsky since 1971, and has two children.

FURTHER READING

"Zhirinovsky, Vladimir." *Current Biography*, Nov. 1995.
"Playboy interview. . . ." JENNIFER GOULD. *Playboy*, Mar. 1995.
Zhirinovsky! VLADIMIR KARTSEV. Columbia University Press, 1995.
Zhirinovsky: Russian Fascism and the Making of a Dictator. VLADIMIR SOLOVYOV et al. Addison-Wesley, 1995.
"Plots, plots. . . ." JOHN KOHAN. Nov. 21, 1994. "Rising czar. . . ." KEVIN FEDARKO. July 11, 1994. *Time*.
"Nightmare on. . . ." MAUREEN ORTH. *Vanity Fair*, Sept. 1994.
" 'The great Russia. . . .' " MICHAEL SPECTER. *New York Times Magazine*, June 19, 1994.
"The Zhirinovsky threat." JACOB W. KIPP. *Foreign Affairs*, May–June 1994.
"Pantie-hero." PAUL QUINN-JUDGE. *New Republic*, Feb. 14, 1994.
"Russia's surprise. . . ." *World Press Review*, Feb. 1994.
"A Russian Hitler?" WENDY SLOANE. *New Statesman & Society*, Jan. 14, 1994.
Absolute Zhirinovsky: A Transparent View of the Distinguished Russian Statesman. GRAHAM FRAZER and GEORGE LANCELLE. Viking-Penguin, 1994.
"The laughing fascist." CARROLL BOGERT and DORINDA ELLIOTT. *Newsweek*, Dec. 27, 1993.
"The coup next time." VLADIMIR KLIMENKO. *Mother Jones*, Nov.–Dec. 1991.

PHOTO CREDITS

Abdul, Paula. Virgin Records (Photo: Alberto Tolot 0991)

Abu-Jamal, Mumia. Addison-Wesley (Photo: Jennifer Beach)

Allen, Tim. Hyperion (Photo: Deborah Feingold)

Allende, Isabel. HarperCollins (Photo: Jerry Bauer)

Anaya, Rudolfo. Warner Books (Photo: Marion Ettlinger)

Armey, Dick. U.S. House of Representatives

Atwood, Margaret. Houghton Mifflin (Photo: © Isolde Ohlbaum)

Babyface. Epic/Hervey & Co. © 1993 Sony Music (Photo: Randee St. Nicholas)

Bacon, Kevin. Copyright © 1992 Castle Rock Entertainment. All rights reserved (Photo: Sidney Baldwin)

Baldwin, Alec. Copyright © 1994 Universal City Studios (Photo: Ralph Nelson)

Ballantine, Ian. Bantam Books (Photo: © David Ballentine)

Barkley, Charles. Phoenix Suns

Barry, Marion. Mayor's Office, Washington, DC

Barrymore, Drew. Copyright © 1994 Twentieth Century Fox (Photo: Lance Staedler)

Bates, Kathy. Copyright © 1995 Castle Rock Entertainment (Photo: John Clifford)

Belle, Albert. Cleveland Indians

Bening, Annette. Castle Rock Entertainment (Photo: Francois Duhamel)

Bennett, Tony. Columbia. Copyright © 1994 Sony Music (Photo: Jesse Frohman)

Berenger, Tom. Warner Bros. Copyright © 1994 Morgan Creek Productions. All rights reserved (Photo: Van Redin)

Bolton, Michael. Columbia, Copyright © 1993 Sony Music (Photo: Timothy White)

Boutros Ghali, Boutros. United Nations Photo 178980 (Photo: M. Grant)

Bowie, David. Virgin Records (Photo: Enrique Badulescu 8/95)

Bradley, Bill. U.S. Senate

Branagh, Kenneth. Castle Rock Entertainment (Photo: Rolf Konow)

Bridges, Jeff. Copyright © 1993 Twentieth Century Fox (Photo: Ralph Nelson)

Brinkley, David. Knopf (Photo: Ed Swiatkowski)

Bristow, Lonnie. American Medical Association

Broderick, Matthew. Copyright © 1994 Fine Line Features (Photo: Joyce Rudolph)

Burroughs, William S. Viking (Photo: Alastair Thain)

Byrne, Gabriel. Roberts Rinehart

Cage, Nicolas. © 1993 Castle Rock Entertainment. All rights reserved (Photo: Jim Bridges)

Cardoso, Fernando. Brazilian Embassy

Carey, Mariah. Horizon Entertainment Management Group/Columbia © 1994 Sony Music (Photo: Daniela Federici)

Chandrasekhar, Subrahmanyan. University of Chicago Press

Chopra, Deepak. Harmony Books (Photo: Dana Fienman, 1993)

Chrétien, Jean. Canadian Embassy

Çiller, Tansu. Turkish Embassy

Conroy, Pat. Nan A. Talese/Doubleday (Photo: Joyce Ravid)

Costner, Kevin. Copyright © 1994 Universal City Studios (Photo: Richard Felber)

Crichton, Michael. Knopf (Photo: Jonathan Exley)

Crow, Sheryl. A & M Records (Photo: Naomi Kaltman 10/94)

D'Amato, Alfonse. Hyperion (Photo: Deborah Feingold)

Daschle, Tom. U.S. Senate

Davies, Robertson. Viking (Photo: Copyright © Jill Krementz)

Davis, Geena. © 1994 Metro-Goldwyn-Mayer. All rights reserved (Photo: David James)

De Niro, Robert. Copyright © 1992 Twentieth Century Fox (Photo: Louis Goldman)

Depardieu, Gérard. Sony Pictures Classics © 1995 Sony Pictures Entertainment

Desai, Anita. Knopf (Photo: Jerry Bauer)

Deutch, John M. Central Intelligence Agency, Department of Defense

DeVito, Danny. Copyright © 1993 Twentieth Century Fox (Photo: Melinda Sue Gordon)

Dillon, Matt. Copyright © 1993 Warner Bros. All rights reserved (Photo: John Clifford)

Dornan, Robert. U.S. Senate

Douglas, Michael. Castle Rock Entertainment (Photo: Francois Duhamel)

Downey, Robert, Jr. © 1993 Fine Line Features. All rights reserved (Photo: Joyce Rudolph)

Dreyfuss, Richard. Castle Rock Entertainment (Photo: Francois Duhamel)

Dylan, Bob. Columbia. © 1993 Sony Music (Photo: Randee St. Nicholas)

Eastwood, Clint. Copyright © 1993 Castle Rock Entertainment. All rights reserved

Elkin, Stanley. Hyperion (Photo: Miriam Berkley)

Estefan, Gloria. Epic © 1995 Sony Music (Photo: Alberto Tolot)

Etheridge, Melissa. W. F. Leopold Management/Island (Photo: Frank Ockenfels)

Ewing, Patrick. New York Knickerbockers

Favre, Brett. Green Bay Packers

Fishburne, Laurence. Castle Rock Entertainment (Photo: Rolf Konow)

Ford, Harrison. Copyright © 1992 Paramount Pictures (Photo: Merrick Morton)

Foreman, George. Villard Books (Photo: Howard Berman/Villard Books)

Foster, Jodie. Copyright © 1994 Warner Bros. (Photo: Andrew Cooper)

Fox, Michael J. Castle Rock Entertainment (Photo: Francois Duhamel)

Fuentes, Carlos. Farrar, Straus and Giroux (Photo: Carlos Fuentes, Jr., Copyright © 1990)

Garcia, Jerry. Arista (Photo: Ken Friedman)

García Márquez, Gabriel. Knopf (Photo: Palomares)

Gibson, Mel. Copyright © 1995 B. H. Finance C. V. (Photo: Andrew Cooper)

Gingrich, Newt. U.S. House of Representatives

Glavine, Tom. Atlanta Braves

Glover, Danny. Copyright © 1992, Warner Bros. Inc.

Goldblum, Jeff. Copyright © Hollywood Pictures Company. All Rights Reserved (Photo: Dean Williams)

Goodman, John. Copyright © 1992 Universal City Studios Inc. All rights reserved (Photo: Dean Williams)

Graham, Billy. Word

Gramm, Phil. U.S. Senate

Grant, Hugh. Copyright © 1995 Columbia Pictures Industries, Inc. All rights reserved. (Photo: Clive Coote)

Gray, John. HarperCollins (Photo: Twain Newhart)

Griffith, Melanie. Copyright © 1994 Twentieth Century Fox (Photo: Jon Farmer)

Grisham, John. Doubleday. (Photo: Jane Rule Burdine)

Groom, Winston. Pocket Books (Photo: © Tom Corcoran)

427

Hackman, Gene. Copyright © TriStar Pictures, Inc. (Photo: Murray Close)

Hatch, Orrin. U.S. Senate

Heaney, Seamus. Farrar, Straus and Giroux (Photo: © Nancy Crampton)

Hijuelos, Oscar. HarperCollins (Photo: Klaus Moser)

Hockenberry, John. Hyperion © Capital Cities/ABC, Inc.

Hoffman, Dustin. Copyright © 1992 Columbia Pictures Industries

hooks, bell. Henry Holt (Photo: Carl Posey)

Hopkins, Anthony. Copyright © Cinergi Pictures Entertainment Inc. and Cinergi Productions N.V. Inc. All Rights Reserved (Photo: Sidney Baldwin)

Horgan, Paul. Farrar, Straus and Giroux (Photo: © Jerry Bauer)

Hunter, Holly. Copyright © 1995 Monarchy Enterprises. All Rights Reserved (Photo: Melissa Moseley)

Huston, Anjelica. Copyright © 1995 The Samuel Goldwyn Company

Ice Cube. Copyright © 1992 Universal City Studios (Photo: Sam Emerson)

Irons, Jeremy. Copyright © 1993 Geffen Pictures. All rights reserved (Photo: Takashi Seida)

Jackson, Alan. Arista (Photo: Randee St. Nicholas)

Jackson, Michael. Epic © 1995 Sony Music

Jackson, Samuel L. Copyright © 1992 Paramount Pictures Corp. All rights reserved (Photo: Merrick Morton)

Jagger, Mick. Virgin Records (Photo: Mark Seliger 6/94)

Jhabvala, Ruth Prawer. Doubleday (Photo: James Ivory)

John Paul II. Vatican Embassy

Johnson, Randy. Seattle Mariners

Jones, James Earl. Miramax Films Copyright © 1995

Jones, Tommy Lee. Copyright © 1994 Metro-Goldwyn-Mayer (Photo: Bruce Birmelin)

Jordan, Michael. Chicago Bulls

Keneally, Thomas. Nan A. Talese/Doubleday. (Photo: Kerry Klayman)

King, Stephen. Viking (Photo: Tabitha King)

Kingsolver, Barbara. HarperCollins (Photo: Steven L. Hopp)

Kohl, Helmut. © Inter Nationes / dpa—Abdruck honorarfrei

Kuhn, Maggie. Gray Panthers (Photo: Julia Jensen/Photography)

Kunitz, Stanley. Norton (Photo: Renate Ponsold)

Kunstler, William. Birch Lane Press (Photo: Ricardo Betancourt)

Kuralt, Charles. Putnam (Photo: © 1995 Curt Norman)

Lange, Jessica. Copyright © 1992 Twentieth Century Fox (Photo: Louis Goldman)

Leakey, Richard. Doubleday (Photo: Royce Carlton, Inc.)

le Carré, John. Knopf (Photo: The Douglas Brothers)

Lee, Spike. Copyright © 1991 Universal City Studios, Inc. All rights reserved (Photo: David Lee)

Leigh, Janet. Harmony Books (Photo: © Harry Langdon)

Leigh, Jennifer Jason. © 1994 Fine Line Features. All rights reserved (Photo: Joyce Rudolph)

Lemmon, Jack. Copyright © 1993 Warner Bros. All rights reserved. (Photo: Ron Phillips)

Lovell, James. Pocket Books

MacDowell, Andie. Copyright © 1994 Twentieth Century Fox (Photo: Lance Staedler)

McEntire, Reba. MCA Nashville (Photo: Peter Nash 0493A)

MacLaine, Shirley. Bantam Books (Photo: © 1994 Annie Leibovitz)

MacNeil, Robert. Nan A. Talese/Doubleday (Photo: Don Perdue)

Mailer, Norman. Atlantic Monthly Press (Photo: Copyright © 1995 Nancy Crampton)

Mandela, Nelson. Miramax Films Copyright © 1995

Marino, Dan. Miami Dolphins

Marsalis, Wynton. Norton/Sony Classical Film & Video/Texaco/ Thirteen-WNET © 1995 Sony Music (Photo: Frank Stewart)

Martin, Steve. Copyright © 1992 Universal City Studios

Matthau, Walter. Copyright © 1993 Warner Bros. All rights reserved (Photo: Marsha Blackburn)

Maxwell, William. Knopf (Photo: Dorothy Alexander)

Mayle, Peter. Knopf (Photo: Jennifer Mayle)

Merrill, James. Knopf (Photo: © 1988 Dorothy Alexander)

Mfume, Kweisi. U.S. House of Representatives

Mirren, Helen. Boneau/Bryan-Brown (Photo: Carol Rosegg)

Mitchell, Joni. © 1994 Reprise Records (Photo: Gregory Heisler)

Modine, Matthew. Copyright © 1994 Paramount Pictures (Photo: Clive Coote)

Moore, Demi. Copyright © 1992 Castle Rock Entertainment (Photo: Sidney Baldwin)

Mosley, Walter. Norton (Photo: © Peter Serling)

Murphy, Eddie. Copyright © 1994 Paramount Pictures (Photo: Bruce W. Talamon)

Nasrin, Taslima. George Braziller (Photo: Ulla Monta)

Neeson, Liam. Copyright © 1993 Universal City Studios (Photo: David James)

Nelson, Willie. Liberty/SBK Records (Photo: E.J. Camp 9/94A)

Nicholson, Jack. Copyright © 1992 PentAmerica Communications (Photo: Herb Ritts)

Nolte, Nick. Copyright © 1994 Paramount Pictures (Photo: Bob Greene)

Nomo, Hideo. Los Angeles Dodgers © Copyright 1995

Ōe, Kenzaburō. Marion Boyars

O'Grady, Scott. Doubleday (Photo: © Wide World)

Oldman, Gary. Copyright © 1991 Warner Bros. Inc. Regency Enterprises V.O.F. and Le Studio Canal. All rights reserved.

O'Neal, Shaquille. Copyright © 1994 Paramount Pictures (Photo: Bob Greene)

O'Rourke, P.J. Atlantic Monthly Press (Photo: Bob Wagner)

Pacino, Al. Miramax Films Copyright © 1995 (Photo: John Clifford)

Parks, Rosa. Zondervan (Photo: Monica Morgan Photography; 313-963-9402)

Pavarotti, Luciano. Crown (Photo: Robert Cahen)

Peres, Shimon. Embassy of Israel

Perry, Anne. Ballantine (Photo: Peter R. Simpkin)

Perry, William. U.S. Army

Rabin, Yitzhak. Embassy of Israel

Reiser, Paul. Bantam Books (Photo: © 1994 Firooz Zahedi)

Rice, Anne. Knopf (Photo: © Joyce Ravid)

Rice, Jerry. San Francisco 49ers

Riley, Pat. New York Knickerbockers

Roth, Philip. Houghton Mifflin (Photo: Copyright © 1995 Nancy Crampton)

Ryan, Meg. Copyright © 1992 Twentieth Century Fox (Photo: Herb Ritts)

Sacks, Oliver. Knopf (Photo: Joyce Ravid)

Sarton, May. Norton (Photo: © Gabriel Amadeus Cooney, Whately, MA 01093)

Seifert, George. San Francisco 49ers

Selena. EMI Records © 1995 (Photo: Maurice Rinaldi)

Seles, Monica. WTA Tour (Photo: Fred Mullane)

Shalikashvili, John. U.S. Department of Defense

Shatner, William. Pocket Books (Photo © Joel Lipton)

Shields, Carol. Penguin (Photo: Gerry Kopelow)

Shula, Don. Miami Dolphins

Smiley, Jane. Knopf (Photo: Stephen Mortensen)

Snipes, Wesley. Copyright © 1995 Columbia Pictures Industries, Inc. All rights reserved. (Photo: Bruce Mc-Broom)

Specter, Arlen. U.S. Senate

Springsteen, Bruce. Columbia © 1995 Sony Music

Stallone, Sylvester. Copyright © 1994 Warner Bros. (Photo: Ron Phillips)

Stern, Howard. HarperCollins

Stone, Oliver. Copyright © 1995 Cinergi Pictures Entertainment Inc. and Cinergi Productions N.V. Inc. All Rights Reserved (Photo: Sidney Baldwin)

Stone, Sharon. Copyright © 1995 TriStar Pictures (Photo: Murray Close)

Streep, Meryl. Copyright © 1994 Universal City Studios (Photo: Melissa Moseley)

Streisand, Barbra. Columbia (Photo: Kevin Mazur)

Tesh, John. Entertainment Tonight Copyright © 1995 Paramount Pictures

Thagard, Norman E. National Aeronautics and Space Administration (NASA)

Thompson, Emma. Copyright © 1995 Columbia Pictures Industries, Inc. All rights reserved. (Photo: Clive Coote)

Travolta, John. © 1995 Metro-Goldwyn-Mayer, Inc. All rights reserved. (Photo: Firooz Zahedi)

Tyler, Anne. Knopf (Photo: © Diana Walker)

Updike, John. Knopf (Photo: Martha Updike)

Walesa, Lech. Embassy of Poland

Waller, Robert James. Warner Books (Photo: Taisuke Yokoyama)

Weaver, Sigourney. Copyright © 1995 Monarchy Enterprises (All Rights Reserved) (Photo: Melissa Moseley)

West, Dorothy. Doubleday (Photo: Alison Shaw)

Williams, Robin. Copyright © 1993 Twentieth Century Fox (Photo: Phil Bray)

Willis, Bruce. Copyright © 1995 Twentieth Century Fox, Cinergi Pictures Entertainment Inc. and Cinergi Productions N. V. Inc. All rights reserved (Photo: Barry Wetcher)

Wolfman Jack. Warner Books

Woods, Tiger. Stanford University

Young, Neil. Reprise Records © 1995 (Photo: Leslie Hirsch)

Young, Steve. San Francisco 49ers

Cumulative Alphabetical Index

For ease of access, we have here provided a cumulative alphabetical index of all those people who have appeared in any edition of **People in the News.** The index gives the year of any edition in which a person appears, and (after the colon) the page number where the entry begins. In addition, where any edition includes a photo of the person, an asterisk will appear following the appropriate edition and page number. For example, basketball star Shaquille O'Neal appeared in four of the first six editions, and had a photo in three, so his index entry reads:

O'Neal, Shaquille **'96:301* / '95:271* / '94:285 / '93:299***

Note that this 1996 edition of **People in the News** also includes a cumulative index by occupation, beginning on page 448.

Altman, Robert **'95:9*** / **'94:10*** /
  '93:8 / **'92:7** / **'91:7**
Altman, Roger C. **'95:10** / **'94:10** /
  '93:9*
Alvarez, Victor (under Abdel Rah-
  man, Omar) **'96:1**
Alzado, Lyle **'93:9** / **'92:8**
Ameche, Don **'94:11**
Ames, Aldrich (Rick) **'95:10**
Ames, Leon **'94:12**
Ames, Rosario (under Ames, Al-
  drich) **'95:10**
Amir, Yigal (under Rabin,
  Yitzhak) **'96:320**
Amis, Kingsley **'96:13**
Amis, Martin **'96:13** / **'91:7**
Anaya, Rudolfo **'96:14***
Anderson, Judith **'93:10**
Anderson, Lindsay Gordon
  '95:11
Anderson, Marian **'94:12**
Anderson, Terry **'94:12***; (under
  Lebanon hostages) **'92:210***
Andreotti, Giulio **'93:10** / **'92:8*** /
  '91:8
Andrew, Duke of York **'93:11*** /
  '92:9* / **'91:8**
Andrews, Bert **'94:13**
Andrews, Dana **'93:12**
Andrews, Julie **'96:14**
Andrews, Maxene **'96:15**
Andronikos, Manolis **'93:12**
Anfinsen, Christian Boehmer
  '96:15
Angelo, Richard **'91:9**
Angelou, Maya **'95:11** / **'94:14*** /
  '91:9
Annenberg, Walter H. **'94:15** /
  '92:10 / **'91:9**
Antall, Jószef **'94:15** / **'93:12** /
  '92:11 / **'91:10***
Anthony, Joseph **'94:16**
Antoon, A. J. **'93:13**
Aoun, Hacib **'93:13**
Appiah, Joe **'91:11**
Aquino, Corazon **'93:13** /
  '92:11* / **'91:11***
Arafat, Yasir **'96:16** / **'95:12** /
  '94:16 / **'93:14** / **'92:12** / **'91:12***
Aramony, William **'96:17**
Archer, Bill **'95:13***
Arden, Eve **'91:13**
Ardolino, Emile **'94:16**
Arévalo Bermejo, Juan José
  '91:13
Arias Sánchez, Oscar **'91:13**
Arias, Roberto **'91:13**
Aristide, Jean-Bertrand **'96:17** /
  '95:13 / **94:17** / **'92:13***
Arletty **'93:15**
Armey, Dick (Richard) **'96:18*** /
  '95:14*
Arnall, Ellis **'93:15**
Arnett, Peter **'92:14***
Arnold, Roseanne. *See* Roseanne.

Arnold, Tom **'96:19**
Arrau, Claudio **'92:15**
Arrupe, Pedro **'92:16**
Arthur, Jean **'92:16**
Asahara, Shoko **'96:19**
Ashcroft, Peggy **'92:16**
Ashe, Arthur **'94:18** / **'93:16***
Ashman, Howard **'92:17**
Asimov, Isaac **'93:17**
Aspin, Les **'96:20** / **'94:19** /
  '93:18 / **'92:17** / **'91:14***
Assad, Hafez al- **'96:21** / **'95:15** /
  '94:20 / **'93:18** / **'92:17** /
  '91:14*
Atanasoff, John Vincent **'96:21**
Attenborough, Richard **'95:15** /
  '94:20
Atwater, Lee **'92:18***
Atwood, Margaret **'96:21*** /
  '94:21* / **'92:18*** / **'91:15**
Aubuisson Arrieta, Robert d'. *See*
  D'Aubuisson Arrieta, Robert.
Auger, Arleen **'94:21**
Aung San Suu Kyi **'96:22** /
  '95:16 / **'94:22** / **'93:19** / **'92:19**
Ayckbourn, Alan **'92:20** / **'91:15**
Aykroyd, Dan **'95:17** / **'94:23** /
  '93:19 / **'92:20** / **'91:16**
Aylwin Azócar, Patricio **'94:23*** /
  '93:20* / **'92:21*** / **'91:16***
Azinger, Paul **'95:17** / **'94:24***
Aziz, Tariq **'93:21** / **'92:22** /
  '91:17*
Babbitt, Bruce **'94:25** / **'93:23**
Babyface (Kenneth Edmonds)
  '96:24*
Bacon, Francis **'93:23**
Bacon, Kevin **'96:25***
Bailey, Pearl **'91:18**
Baird, Zoë **'94:26***
Baiul, Oksana **'95:18**
Baker, James **'93:24** / **'92:23*** /
  '91:18*
Bakhtiar, Shapour **'92:24**
Baldwin, Alec **'96:25*** / **'95:18*** /
  '94:26* / **'93:24*** / **'92:24**
Baldwin, Hanson **'92:25**
Ball, George Wildman **'95:19**
Ball, William **'92:25**
Ballantine, Ian **'96:26***
Baltimore, David **'92:25**
Barber, Red **'93:25**
Barbie, Klaus **'92:26**
Barco Vargas, Virgilio **'91:19**
Bardeen, John **'92:26**
Bardot, Brigitte **'91:19**
Barkley, Charles **'96:27*** /
  '95:19* / **'94:27*** / **'93:25***
Barnet, Charlie **'92:27**
Barnett, Marguerite Ross **'93:27**
Baron, Salo W. **'91:20**
Barr, Roseanne. *See* Roseanne.
Barrault, Jean-Louis **'95:21**
Barry, Dave **'96:28*** / **'95:21** /
  '94:28*

Barry, Marion **'96:28*** / **'95:21** /
  '93:27 / **'92:27*** / **'91:21***
Barrymore, Drew **'96:29***
Bartholomew, Freddie **'93:27**
Baryshnikov, Mikhail **'93:28** /
  '92:28 / **'91:21***
Basinger, Kim **'95:22*** / **'94:29** /
  '93:28 / **'92:28** / **'91:22**
Bastian, Gerd (under Kelly,
  Petra) **'93:217**
Bates, Alan **'93:29** / **'92:29** /
  '91:22
Bates, Kathy **'96:30*** / **'95:23** /
  '94:29* / **'93:29*** / **'92:29***
Baudouin I of Belgium **'94:30**
Baulieu, Etienne-Emile **'92:30** /
  '91:23
Bauza, Mario **'94:30**
Bazargan, Mehdi **'96:31**
Bazelon, David Lionel **'94:31**
Bean-Bayog, Margaret **'93:30**
Beatty, Warren **'95:23** / **'93:31** /
  '92:30* / **'91:23**
Beck, Dave **'94:31**
Beckett, Samuel **'91:24**
Beckwith, Byron De La **'95:24**
Beers, Katie (Katharine) **'94:31**
Beery, Noah, Jr. **'95:24**
Begelman, David **'96:31**
Begin, Menachem **'93:31**
Belfrage, Cedric **'91:24**
Belfrage, Sally **'95:24**
Bell, James "Cool Papa" **'92:31**
Bellamy, Madge **'91:25**
Bellamy, Ralph **'92:31**
Belle, Albert **'96:31***
Benedek, Laszlo **'93:32**
Bening, Annette **'96:32*** / **'95:25** /
  '92:32*
Bennett, Alan **'96:33**
Bennett, Charles **'96:34**
Bennett, Joan **'91:25**
Bennett, John Coleman **'96:34**
Bennett, Tony **'96:34*** / **'95:25***
Bennett, William J. **'96:35** /
  '91:25
Benson, Ezra Taft **'95:26**
Bentsen, Lloyd **'95:27*** / **'94:32*** /
  '93:32*
Bérégovoy, Pierre **'94:32**
Berenger, Tom **'96:36*** / **'95:27*** /
  '94:33*
Berg, Jack "Kid" **'92:32**
Bergen, Candice **'93:32** / **'92:32** /
  '91:25*
Berger, Samuel R. "Sandy"
  '93:33
Berghof, Herbert **'91:26**
Bergman, Ingmar **'96:37** /
  '95:28 / **'94:33*** / **'93:33** / **'92:33** /
  '91:26
Berlusconi, Silvio **'96:37** / **'95:29***
Bermudez Varela, Enrique
  '92:34
Bernays, Edward **'96:38**

Rappaport, David **'91:261**
Rashid bin Said al Maktoum
 '91:262
Rather, Dan **'96:324 / '95:296 /
 '94:305 / '93:322 / '92:288* /
 '91:262***
Rauh, Joseph Louis **'93:323**
Ravidat, Marcel **'96:324**
Ray, Aldo **'92:289**
Ray, Dixy Lee **'95:296**
Ray, Johnnie **'91:263**
Ray, Satyajit **'93:323**
Raye, Martha **'95:297**
Reagan, Ronald **'95:297 /
 '94:306 / '93:323 / '92:289* /
 '91:263**
Reasoner, Harry **'92:290**
Redford, Robert **'95:298 /
 '94:307* / '93:324* / '92:290 /
 '91:264**
Redgrave, Lynn **'94:308 /
 '93:325* / '92:291* / '91:264***
Redgrave, Vanessa **'96:325 /
 '95:299 / '94:308 / '93:326* /
 '92:292 / '91:265***
Redmond, Liam **'91:266**
Reed, Robert **'93:326**
Reeve, Christopher **'96:325 /
 '94:309 / '93:327 / '92:292 /
 '91:266**
Rehnquist William **'96:326 /
 '95:299 / '94:309 / '93:327 /
 '92:293* / '91:266***
Reich, Robert **'95:300* /
 '94:310* / '93:328***
Reichenbach, François **'94:311**
Reid, Kate **'94:311**
Reilly, William K. **'93:329 /
 '92:294* / '91:267***
Reiner, Rob **'96:327 / '95:301 /
 '94:312* / '93:330* / '92:295 /
 '91:268**
Reischauer, Edwin O. **'91:268**
Reiser, Paul **'96:327***
Remick, Lee **'92:295**
Renaud, Madeleine **'95:301**
Reno, Janet **'96:328 / '95:302* /
 '94:312***
Renoir, Claude **'94:313**
Reshevsky, Samuel **'93:330**
Reso, Sidney J. (under Seale,
 Arthur) **'93:353**
Reston, James **'96:329**
Revelle, Roger **'92:295**
Revere, Anne **'91:268**
Rey, Fernando **'95:302**
Reyes, Mario Moreno. *See* Cantin-
 flas.
Reynolds, Burt **'94:313* /
 '93:331 / '92:296 / '91:269**
Rice, Anne **'96:329* / '95:303* /
 '94:314**
Rice, Jerry **'96:330* / '95:304* /
 '94:315 / '93:331***
Rich, Charlie **'96:331**

Richards, Ann **'92:296* /
 '91:269***
Richardson, Natasha **'95:304* /
 '94:315**
Richardson, Tony **'92:297**
Ridgway, Matthew Bunker
 '94:316
Riding, Laura **'92:298**
Ridley, Nicholas **'94:316**
Riegle, Donald W., Jr. **'92:298 /
 '91:270***
Rifkin, Joel **'94:316**
Rifkind, Simon Hirsch **'96:331**
Riggs, Bobby **'96:332**
Riley, Pat **'96:332* / '95:305* /
 '94:317* / '93:332* / '92:298* /
 '91:270**
Riley, Richard W. **'93:333***
Ripken, Jr., Cal **'96:333**
Ritt, Martin **'91:271**
Ritter, Bruce **'91:271***
Rivers, Larry **'94:318***
Rivlin, Alice Mitchell **'93:333***
Rizzo, Frank **'92:299**
Rizzuto, Phil **'95:306**
Roach, Hal **'93:334**
Robards, Jason, Jr. **'96:334 /
 '95:307* / '94:318 / '93:334* /
 '92:299* / '91:272**
Robbins, Tim **'96:334 / '95:307* /
 '94:319* / '93:335**
Robbins, Tom **'95:308***
Roberts, Julia **'95:309* /
 '94:320* / '93:336 / '92:300***
Robinson, Cleveland **'96:335**
Robinson, David **'96:335**
Robinson, Earl Hawley **'92:301**
Robinson, Mary **'93:336 /
 '92:301***
Robinson, Roscoe **'94:320**
Rodale, Robert **'91:272**
Roddenberry, Gene **'92:302**
Rodney, Red (Robert) **'95:310**
Rogers, David E. **'95:310**
Rogers, Ginger **'96:336**
Rogers, Shorty (Milton) **'95:310**
Rogers, Will, Jr. **'94:321**
Roh Tae Woo **'93:337 / '92:302* /
 '91:273***
Roker, Roxie **'96:337**
Roland, Gilbert **'95:311**
Romanov, Vladimir Kirillovich
 '93:337
Rome, Harold **'94:321**
Romero, Cesar **'95:311**
Romney, George W. **'96:337**
Ronson, Mick **'94:321**
Ronstadt, Linda **'96:337 /
 '94:322 / '93:338 / '92:303 /
 '91:273**
Rooney, Andy **'91:274**
Roosevelt, Elliott **'91:274**
Roosevelt, James **'92:304**
Rose, David **'91:274**
Rose, Jack **'96:338**

Rose, Pete **'92:304 / '91:275**
Roseanne **'96:338 / '95:311; (un-
 der Arnold, Roseanne) '94:18 /
 '93:15 / '92:14*; (under Barr,
 Roseanne) '91:20***
Ross, Diana **'94:322 / '92:305* /
 '91:275**
Ross, Steven Jay **'93:338**
Rossi, Bruno **'94:322**
Rostenkowski, Dan **'95:312 /
 '94:323***
Rostov Ripper (under Chikatilo,
 Andrei) **'93:76**
Rostropovich, Mstislav **'93:339 /
 '92:305 / '91:276***
Roth, Henry **'96:339 / '95:312***
Roth, Philip **'96:339* / '94:323***
Rothstein, Nathaniel M. V.
 '91:276
Rowan, Chad (under Akebono)
 '94:4
Rozsa, Miklos **'96:340**
Rubin, Jerry **'95:313**
Rubin, Robert E. **'96:340 /
 '95:313 / '93:339***
Rudé, George **'94:324**
Rudolph, Wilma **'95:314**
Ruehl, Mercedes **'94:324***
Ruffin, David **'92:306**
Ruiz Massieu, Mario (under Sali-
 nas de Gortari, Carlos)
 '96:345
Rushdie, Salman **'96:341 /
 '95:314 / '94:325* / '93:340 /
 '92:306* / '91:277**
Rusk, Dean **'95:315**
Rusk, Howard **'91:277**
Russell, Paul **'92:307**
Rutskoi, Alexandr **'94:327**
Ryan, Meg **'96:342***
Ryan, Nolan **'94:327 / '92:307 /
 '91:278***
Ryder, Winona **'96:342 / '95:315 /
 '94:328 / '93:341 / '92:308**
Rypien, Mark **'93:341***
Sabah, Jaber al-Ahmed al-Jabir
 al- **'93:343 / '92:309 / '91:279***
Sabin, Albert **'94:329**
Sachar, Abram Leon **'94:329**
Sacks, Oliver **'96:344***
St. Jacques, Raymond **'91:280**
Sakharov, Andrei **'91:280**
Salant, Richard S. **'94:329**
Saleh, Mohammed (under Abdel
 Rahman, Omar) **'96:1**
Salerno, Anthony "Fat Tony"
 '93:343
Salinas de Gortari, Carlos
 **'96:345 / '95:317 / '94:330 /
 '93:344 / '92:309* / '91:280***
Salinas de Gortari, Raúl (under
 Salinas de Gortari, Car-
 los) **'96:345**
Salisbury, Harrison **'94:330**
Salk, Jonas **'96:346**

Smith, Maggie '94:353 / '93:365 /
'92:330 / '91:299
Smith, Margaret Chase '96:368
Smith, Oliver '95:339
Smith, Susan '95:339
Smith, William French '91:299
Smith, William Kennedy
'92:331*
Smoktunovsky, Innokenti
'95:339
Smoot, George F. '93:366*
Snelling, Richard Arkwright
'92:331
Snipes, Wesley '96:369* /
'95:340* / '94:354*
Snoop Doggy Dogg. See Dogg,
Snoop Doggy.
Snyder, Mitch '91:299*
Solomon, Gerald '95:340*
Solzhenitsyn, Alexander
'96:369 / '95:341 / '93:366 /
'92:332 / '91:300
Somes, Michael '95:341
Sondheim, Stephen '95:342 /
'94:354 / '93:367 / '92:332 /
'91:301
Sontag, Susan '94:355 /
'93:367*
Soupault, Philippe '91:301
Souphanouvong '96:370
Soustelle, Jacques '91:302
Souter, David '96:370 / '95:342 /
'94:355 / '93:368 / '92:333* /
'91:302*
Southern, Terry '96:371
Spacek, Sissy '96:371 / '95:343 /
'93:369* / '92:334*
Spader, James '95:344* /
'94:356 / '93:370 / '92:334
Spadolini, Giovanni '95:344
Speck, Richard '92:335
Specter, Arlen '96:372*
Spender, Stephen '96:373 /
'95:344*
Sperry, Roger '95:345
Spessivtseva, Olga '92:335
Spewack, Bella Cohen '91:302
Spielberg, Steven '95:345* /
'94:356* / '93:370 / '92:335 /
'91:303
Spivak, Lawrence '95:346
Spock, Benjamin '95:347
Springsteen, Bruce '96:373* /
'95:347* / '93:371 / '91:303
Stallone, Sylvester '96:374* /
'95:348 / '94:357 / '93:372 /
'92:336 / '91:304
Stander, Lionel '95:349
Stanwyck, Barbara '91:304
Stark, Freya '94:358
Starr, Ringo '96:375 / '93:372 /
'91:305
Starzl, Thomas '93:373* /
'91:305
Steber, Eleanor '91:306

Steegmuller, Francis '95:349
Steen, Alann (under Lebanon
hostages) '92:210
Steenburgen, Mary '96:375 /
'95:350 / '94:358* / '93:374 /
'92:337 / '91:306
Stegner, Wallace '94:359
Steinbrenner, George '95:350* /
'94:360 / '93:374* / '92:337 /
'91:307*
Sten, Anna '94:360
Stennis, John '96:376
Stephanopolous, George
'94:360* / '93:375*
Stephens, Robert '96:376
Stern, David '96:377 /
'95:351* / '94:361 / '93:375 /
'92:337*
Stern, Howard '96:377* /
'95:352 / '94:362
Stern, Philip '93:376
Stevens, John Paul '96:378 /
'95:352 / '94:362 / '93:376 /
'92:338* / '91:307
Stewart, J. I. M. '95:353
Stewart, Rod '96:379 / '94:363*
Stigler, George '92:339
Sting '94:364* / '93:377 /
'92:340 / '91:308
Stirling, James Frazer '93:378
Stockton, John '96:380
Stone, Ezra '95:354
Stone, Oliver '96:380* /
'95:354* / '94:364* / '93:378* /
'92:340* / '91:308
Stone, Sharon '96:381* /
'95:355*
Strand, Mark '91:309
Stratton, Julius A. '95:355
Streep, Meryl '96:382* /
'95:356* / '94:365* / '93:379* /
'92:341 / '91:309
Streisand, Barbra '96:383* /
'95:356* / '94:366 / '93:380 /
'92:341
Strode, Woody (Woodrow)
'96:384
Strout, Richard Lee '91:310
Struebig, Heinrich (under Leba-
non hostages) '92:210
Stuart, Carol DiMaiti (under Stu-
art, Charles) '91:310*
Stuart, Charles '91:310*
Sturges, John '93:381
Styne, Jule '95:358
Styron, William '94:367* /
'91:311*
Subber, (Arnold) Saint '95:358
Sullivan, Barry '95:358
Sullivan, Louis Wade '93:381 /
'92:342* / '91:311*
Sulzberger, C. L. (Cyrus Leo)
'94:368
Sununu, John '93:381 /
'92:343* / '91:312

Sutherland, Donald '96:384 /
'95:359* / '93:382* / '92:344* /
'91:313
Sutherland, Kiefer '94:369*
Sutherland, Thomas (under Leba-
non hostages) '92:210
Sutton, Denys Miller '92:344
Swanberg, William A. '93:382
Swann, Donald '95:359
Swayze, John Cameron '96:385
Swayze, Patrick '96:385 /
'94:369 / '93:383 / '92:345 /
'91:313
Sweeney, John '96:386
Swenson, May '91:314
Switzer, Barry '96:386 /
'95:360
Sydow, Max von '94:370 /
'93:383 / '92:345 / '91:314
Symons, Julian '95:361
Syms, Sylvia '93:384
Synge, Richard Millington
'95:361
Tagliabue, Paul '96:388 /
'95:362* / '94:371 / '93:385 /
'92:347* / '91:315*
Tal, Mikhail '93:386
Tamayo, Rufino '92:348
Tambo, Oliver '94:372 / '91:316
Tan, Amy '96:389 / '94:372
Tanaka, Kakuei '94:373
Tandy, Jessica '95:363 / '94:373 /
'93:386* / '92:348* / '91:316
Tanenbaum, Marc Herbert
'93:387
Tannen, Deborah '95:363
Tarantino, Quentin '96:389
Tayback, Vic '91:317
Taylor, A. J. P. '91:317
Taylor, Elizabeth '95:364 /
'94:374 / '93:387 / '92:349 /
'91:317
Taylor, Harold '94:374
Taylor, Lawrence '92:350 /
'91:318*
Taylor, Peter '95:364
Tchelistcheff, André '95:365
Teillac, Jean '95:365
Temin, Howard '95:365
Teng, Teresa '96:390
Terkel, Studs '93:388*
Terris, Norma '91:318
Terry-Thomas '91:319
Tesh, John '96:390*
Thagard, Norman '96:391*
Tharp, Twyla '93:389 / '92:350 /
'91:319
Thatcher, Margaret '94:375* /
'93:389 / '92:350* / '91:319*
Theremin, Leon '94:376
Tho, Le Duc '91:320
Thomas, Clarence '96:392 /
'95:366 / '94:376 / '93:390* /
'92:351*
Thomas, Danny '92:353

Cumulative Index by Occupation

For ease of access, we have here indexed by occupation or other area of news interest those individuals profiled in **People in the News**. Under the appropriate headings, such as "Law and Court Cases" or "Stage and Screen," readers will find volume and page references for all who have appeared in any of the first six editions of **People in the News**.

For each person, the index gives the year of any editions in which he or she appears, and (after the colon) the page number where the entry begins. In addition, if a photo of the person is included in an edition, an asterisk will appear following the appropriate page number. For example, the basketball star Shaquille O'Neal appears in four of the first six editions, and has a photo in three editions, so his index entry under the heading "Sports and Games" reads:

O'Neal, Shaquille **'96:301*/'95:271*/'94:285/'93:299***

Note that some people are listed under more than one heading. Since O'Neal has also released some records, he is one of those people, so his index entry can also be found under "Music."

The index headings are:

Business and Finance	Politics
Dance	Religion
Education	Science, Technology, and Medicine
Journalism and Publishing	Social Activism
Law and Court Cases	Social Sciences
Literature	Sports and Games
Military	Stage and Screen
Miscellaneous	Visual Arts
Music	

The main body of each edition of **People in the News** is, of course, self-indexed, with individuals listed alphabetically. However, the second and succeeding volumes also contain a cumulative alphabetical index (see page 430).

CUMULATIVE INDEX BY OCCUPATION

Law and Court Cases

Abdelgani, Amir (under Abdel Rahman, Omar) **'96:1**

Abdelghani, Fadil (under Abdel Rahman, Omar) **'96:1**

Abdel Rahman, Omar **'96:1**; (under Rahman, Omar Abdel) **'94:304**

Abu-Jamal, Mumia **'96:4***

Accardo, Anthony **'93:2**

Alvarez, Victor (under Abdel Rahman, Omar) **'96:1**

Ames, Aldrich (Rick) **'95:10**

Ames, Rosario (under Ames, Aldrich) **'95:10**

Amir, Yigal (under Rabin, Yitzhak) **'96:320**

Angelo, Richard **'91:9**

Aramony, William **'96:17**

Arnall, Ellis **'93:15**

Asahara, Shoko **'96:19**

Baird, Zoë **'94:26***

Barbie, Klaus **'92:26**

Barry, Marion **'96:28*** / **'95:21** / **'93:27** / **'92:27*** / **'91:21***

Bazelon, David Lionel **'94:31**

Bean-Bayog, Margaret **'93:30**

Beck, Dave **'94:31**

Beckwith, Byron De La **'95:24**

Beers, Katie (Katharine) **'94:31**

Begelman, David **'96:31**

Berger, Samuel R. "Sandy" **'93:33**

Biden, Joseph **'94:35** / **'93:35** / **'92:36*** / **'91:29***

Billington, James H. **'94:36***

Blackmun, Harry **'95:31** / **'94:38** / **'93:36** / **'92:37*** / **'91:31**

Bobbitt, John Wayne **'95:34**

Bobbitt, Lorena **'95:34**

Borsellino, Paolo **'93:38**

Bosze, Jean-Pierre **'91:33**

Boudin, Leonard **'91:34**

Bowman, Patricia J. **'92:41**

Brandley, Clarence Lee **'91:36**

Brennan, William J., Jr. **'91:37**

Breyer, Stephen **'96:49** / **'95:40***

Briseno, Theodore J. (under King, Rodney) **'94:210** / **'93:228**

Brown, John R. **'94:50**

Buckey, Raymond **'91:42**

Buettner-Janusch, John **'93:56**

Burch, Dean **'92:49**

Burger, Warren Earl **'96:57**

Carlos (Ilich Ramirez Sanchez) **'95:57**

Carswell, George Harrold **'93:69**

Central Park Jogger **'91:52**

Chikatilo, Andrei (Rostov Ripper) **'93:76**

Christopher, Warren **'96:75** / **'95:67*** / **'94:71** / **'93:77**

Clark, Marcia **'96:79** / **'95:70**

Clausen, Cara (under DeBoer, Jessica) **'94:95**

Clifford, Clark **'93:78** / **'92:67**

Clinton, Hillary Rodham **'96:82** / **'95:73*** / **'94:76*** / **'93:80***

Coleman, Roger Keith **'93:83**

Collins, LeRoy **'92:69**

Connally, John, Jr. **'94:80**

Cooper, John Sherman **'92:73**

Cornfeld, Bernard **'96:86**

Costa Mendez, Nicanor **'93:88**

Coughlin, Paula **'95:81**

Cruzan, Nancy Beth **'91:70**

Dahmer, Jeffrey L. **'95:89** / **'92:82**

DeBoer, Jessica **'94:95**

Dershowitz, Alan M. **'95:97***

Devlin, Patrick Arthur **'93:111**

Dogg, Snoop Doggy **'95:100***

Duran, Francisco **'96:112**

Emerson, Thomas Irwin **'92:109**

Escobar Gaviria, Pablo **'94:117**

Esposito, John (under Beers, Katie) **'94:31**

Esposito, Meade **'94:117**

Faubus, Orval **'95:115**

Faulk, John Henry **'91:100**

Faulkner, Shannon **'96:128** / **'95:116**

Ferguson, Colin **'96:129**

Finley, Karen **'93:135** / **'92:115** / **'91:101***

Fisher, Amy **'93:137**

Fisher, Bernard **'95:119**

Fiske, Robert **'95:120**

Foretich, Eric (under Morgan, Elizabeth) **'91:219***

Foretich, Hilary (under Morgan, Elizabeth) **'91:219**

Fortier, Michael (under McVeigh, Timothy) **'96:255**

Foster, Vincent W. **'94:127**

Freeh, Louis J. **'94:128***

Frondizi, Arturo **'96:138**

Garcia Robles, Alfonso **'92:130**

Gardiner, Gerald Austin **'91:115**

Garrison, Jim **'93:147**

Garrison, Lloyd **'92:131**

Garry, Charles R. **'92:131**

Gates, Daryl **'93:149*** / **'92:131**

Gellhorn, Walter **'96:145**

Gesell, Gerhard **'94:138**

Gilmore, Mikal **'95:134***

Ginsburg, Ruth Bader **'96:151** / **'95:137*** / **'94:142***

Goldberg, Arthur J. **'91:123**

Goldman, Ronald L. (under Simpson, O. J.) **'96:364** / **'95:336**

Gotti, John **'93:162**

Griffin, Michael F. **'95:149**

Grisham, John **'96:167*** / **'95:150** / **'94:156** / **'93:164***

Griswold, Erwin **'95:150**

Guinier, Lani **'94:157**

Hallinan, Vincent **'93:172**

Harding, Tonya **'95:155**

Harris, Robert Alton **'93:175**

Havers, Roger M. O. **'93:177**

Helmsley, Leona **'91:146***

Hennard, George **'92:161**

Hill, Anita **'95:161** / **'94:168** / **'93:181** / **'92:163***

Hill, Paul Jennings **'95:162**

Jordan, Vernon **'93:209**

Jouret, Luc **'95:188**

Kantor, Mickey **'96:210** / **'95:190** / **'94:200** / **'93:213**

Kaufman, Irving R. **'93:214**

Keating, Charles, Jr. **'94:201** / **'93:214** / **'92:189** / **'91:172***

Kelso, Louis Orth **'92:192**

Kennedy, Anthony **'96:214** / **'95:193** / **'94:205** / **'93:220** / **'92:193*** / **'91:174***

Kennedy, John F., Jr. **'91:175***

Kerrigan, Nancy **'95:195***

Kessler, David **'96:216** / **'95:196*** / **'94:207** / **'93:224** / **'92:197***

Kevorkian, Jack **'96:216** / **'95:197** / **'94:207** / **'93:225** / **'92:197***

Khallafalla, Fares (under Abdel Rahman, Omar) **'96:1**

King, Rodney **'94:210** / **'93:228**

Kingsley, Gregory **'93:229**

Koon, Stacey C. (under King, Rodney) **'94:210** / **'93:228**

Koresh, David **'94:215**

Kray, Ron **'96:223**

Krim, Arthur **'95:202**

Kuchel, Thomas H. **'95:203**

Kunstler, William **'96:227***

Kutner, Luis **'94:217**

List, John E. **'91:189***

London, Ephraim **'91:191**

Lozano, Paul (under Bean-Bayog, Margaret) **'93:30**

MacDonald, Peter, Sr. **'91:196***

McHaney, James M. **'96:250**

McKissick, Floyd **'92:223**

McMartin, Virginia **'96:252** (*See* also Buckey, Raymond **'91:42**)

McVeigh, Timothy **'96:255**

Mahfouz, Naguib **'95:230**

Mandela, Winnie **'96:263** / **'93:264** / **'92:230** / **'91:201***

Marcos, Imelda **'92:231** / **'91:203**

Marshall, Thurgood **'94:246** / **'92:233*** / **'91:204***

Mays, Kimberly **'94:250**

Menendez, Erik **'95:239**

Menendez, Lyle **'95:239**

Milken, Michael **'94:252** / **'93:273** / **'92:242** / **'91:213***

Mitnick, Kevin **'96:276**

Morgan, Elizabeth **'91:219***

Nasrin, Taslima **'96:286*** / **'95:253**

Nichols, Terry Lynn (under McVeigh, Timothy) **'96:255**

Literature